THE FAR EAST

PAUL HIBBERT CLYDE

Professor of History
Duke University

THE FAR EAST

A History of the Impact of the West on Eastern Asia

THIRD EDITION

Englewood Cliffs, N.J.
PRENTICE-HALL, INC.

LIBRARY OF CONGRESS
CATALOG CARD NO.: 58-6867

First printing .... February, 1958
Second printing .... November, 1958
Third printing .... June, 1960
Fourth printing .... January, 1962

PRINTED IN THE UNITED STATES OF AMERICA

30299–C

To

Mary Kestler Clyde

We are by nature observers,
and thereby learners.
—EMERSON

Preface to the Third Edition

The story of the Far East is an exciting one, and its importance in our day looms larger as each year passes, but most Americans either neglect it entirely or, at best, view it with a cursory interest. Although we have lived through the second World War, the occupation of Japan, the communist conquest of China, and the birth of independent nations in South and Southeast Asia, the history of the Far East is still largely the affair of the scholar, the specialist, and, for most of us, remains in the periphery of our interests.

Our intellectual perspectives are Western rather than cosmopolitan. The histories of the West have always assumed a vitality for us—our roots are there, those events have shaped our lives. The Far East, on the other hand, has, until a few decades ago, been slow to exercise any perceptible effect upon us, and our interests have been correspondingly unresponsive. Yet, now that East is truly meeting West, every day and in many crucial ways, the study of Eastern civilization takes on an urgency that cannot be ignored. Efforts to bring Asia's culture to the position it deserves in American thought have been made, particularly since World War II, but progress has not been equal to the need. As a part of these efforts, *The Far East,* with its emphasis on the collision of Eastern and Western ideas, attempts to present to Americans the historical elements that have fashioned contemporary Eastern Asia.

The present edition is more than a revision, for, although the structure and organization remain substantially as they were, the book has been for the most part rewritten to give far more attention to Asia's response to the Western impact, to embody many findings of recent research, and to modify interpretations where new evidence has required it. The institutional background of Old China and Old Japan has been treated in greater detail. The subject of international relations, although compressed into smaller space, continues to receive the attention it merits in any discussion of the meeting of East and West. Greater emphasis has also been given to the clash between dominant ideas and ideals, Eastern and Western.

As in the former editions, this history is addressed chiefly to Americans seeking their first organized approach to an Asian world which is now close at hand and with which they will have to live in peace or war. For those who would go further, there is a general reference bibliography, various authorities are cited throughout the book, and selected lists for further reading appear at the end of each chapter. These references suggest many, but by no means all, of the scholars, colleagues, and friends whose knowledge has contributed to this survey.

In an area so broad in space and time as the modern Far East, the historian who ventures a narrative and an interpretation such as this, will, of course, be guilty of errors in fact or in shading. It is my hope that they are few, and for them I am responsible, not those who have made it possible for me to pursue this interest through more than thirty years of university teaching.

PAUL H. CLYDE

Preface to the First Edition

THE Japanese attack at Pearl Harbor, December 7, 1941, was one expression of powerful and complex revolutionary forces which have been stirring in the Orient for more than half a century. Japanese militarism was only one manifestation, though admittedly an important one, of a restless Asia seeking new orders for old. Considered historically, Asia's contemporary revolution is a child of westernization and modernization. Its character has been shaped by the impact of European and American thought and action upon the traditional cultures of the East. The societies which will emerge from the present chaos of change have not yet taken shape. They are being fashioned by patterns of thought and action which arise out of Asia's own long and rich past, and also by patterns which are new and in large measure still foreign, namely the confused and often mutually hostile philosophies of the West. To those who seek an historical introduction to this eastern Asia, to a revolution that we in part have created and with which we are now inextricably involved, the following pages are addressed.

The story is modern. It concerns principally growing contacts between the Western world and the Far East in the nineteenth and twentieth centuries. In consequence, this book contains no extended account of the early history of the Chinese, the Japanese, or of other East Asiatic peoples. Rather, the stress so far as Asia's history is concerned is on the modern institutional life of the Far East, where such knowledge is essential to an understanding of modern contacts. The approach to the subject is derived from more than twenty years of classroom discussion with American university students seeking their first intellectual contacts with Asia. To them, the natural approach to the field of things Asiatic lies through our own contacts with the modern Far East.

Even this limited approach is too vast to be treated in detail in a single volume. I have therefore limited or subordinated many phases of the subject and have emphasized those events or movements most closely concerned with the central story of Western contacts and resulting modernization. Phases of the subject which have been subordinated may be followed adequately in the references listed. Since history does not take place in a vacuum, I have introduced a considerable measure of interpretation. Moreover, in a book designed primarily for Americans, I have felt justified in devoting larger space to the activities of Americans and to critical appraisal of American policies than is given to the treatment of other countries. In the final chapters, which deal with events that are immediately contemporaneous, interpretation must be regarded of course as tentative and subject to revision.

The limitations set by the theme of these pages still leave a subject so large and a liability of error so great that I have called upon the time and generosity of many of my colleagues in the field of far eastern studies. Their response has been most cordial and helpful. Without in any sense minimizing my debt to others, I mention especially those who have worked through most of the semi-final draft of the manuscript: Meribeth Cameron, of Milwaukee-Downer College; Homer H. Dubs, of University College, Oxford; Lennox A. Mills, of the University of Minnesota; and John Gilbert Reid, of the Department of State. Criticism and constructive suggestions on single chapters or groups of chapters were given by: Thomas A. Bailey, of Stanford University; Knight Biggerstaff, of Cornell University; Claude A. Buss, of Stanford University; George B. Cressey, of Syracuse University; Allan B. Cole, of Claremont College; Rupert Emerson, of Harvard University; John K. Fairbank, of Harvard University; Bruno Lasker, of the Southeast Asia Institute; Kenneth S. Latourette, of Yale University; Owen Lattimore, of The Johns Hopkins University; the late Harley F. MacNair, of the University of Chicago; Earl H. Pritchard, of Wayne University; Lawrence K. Rosinger, of the Foreign Policy Association; G. Nye Steiger, of Simmons College; Laurence E. Salisbury, editor of the *Far Eastern Survey;* Maxwell S. Stewart, of the Public Affairs Committee; Amry Vandenbosch, of the University of Kentucky; and Richard L. Watson, Jr., of Duke University. These scholars are not responsible, of course, for errors in fact or judgment I may have made. Their assistance, however, is gratefully acknowledged. If in any case I have failed either here or by letter to express this debt, I trust that my failure will be understood as an oversight. Special editorial assistance was given by George Kao, of the Chinese News Service; suggestions on Chinese politics were given by P. M. A. Linebarger. Among those who cannot be mentioned here individually are the many authors whose works I have quoted or from which I have drawn parts of the story and the interpretation. Members of the staff of the Duke University libraries who have given freely of their time in aiding my research include: Miss Evelyn Harrison, Mrs. Spears Hicks, Miss Gertrude Merritt, Miss Helen Oyler, and Miss Allene Ramage. I am also indebted to Mrs. Marjorie F. Scarlett, who typed the entire manuscript, and to Mrs. Betty Miller Unterberger and Mr. John Chalmers Vinson, who assisted in making the index.

PAUL H. CLYDE

Acknowledgments

In addition to the credits given throughout the text, grateful acknowledgment is made to the following publishers and individuals, who have given permission for material to be used from the items listed:

American Council, Institute of Pacific Relations, Inc., New York
E. Herbert Norman, *Japan's Emergence as a Modern State* (1940)

D. Appleton-Century Company, Inc., New York and London
G. B. Sansom, *Japan: A Short Cultural History* (New York, 1931)
Reginald F. Johnston, *Twilight in the Forbidden City* (London, 1934)

William Blackwood & Sons Ltd., Edinburgh and London
Alexander Michie, *The Englishman in China* (2 vols., New York, 1900)

The Cambridge University Press, London
The Cambridge Modern History

The Contemporary Review, London
Hugh Byas, "The Communist Movement in Japan," CXLI (1932)

Doubleday & Company, Inc., New York
Tyler Dennett, *Roosevelt and the Russo-Japanese War* (1925)

Far Eastern Survey, American Council, Institute of Pacific Relations, New York
Andrew J. Grajdanzev, "Korea Divided," XIV (1945)

Foreign Affairs, New York
Henry L. Stimson, "The Nuremberg Trial: Landmark in Law," XXV (1947)

Harcourt, Brace and Company, Inc., New York
A. Whitney Griswold, *The Far Eastern Policy of the United States* (1938)

Harper & Brothers, New York
Henry L. Stimson, *The Far Eastern Crisis* (1936)

Harvard University Press, Cambridge, Mass.
Merle Fainsod and others, *Japan's Prospect* (1946)

Institute of Pacific Relations, New York
Irving S. Friedman, *British Relations with China: 1931-1939* (1940)

The Johns Hopkins Press, Baltimore, Maryland
E. B. Price, *The Russo-Japanese Treaties of 1907-1916 Concerning Manchuria and Mongolia* (1933)

W. W. Willoughby, *Japan's Case Examined* (1940)
Kelly & Walsh, Ltd., Shanghai
H. A. Giles, *Gems of Chinese Literature* (Verse) (2nd rev. ed., 1923)
H. B. Morse, *The Gilds of China* (2nd ed., 1932)
Longmans, Green & Co., Inc., New York
M. [E. R.] Huc, *A Journey Through the Chinese Empire* (2 vols., 1859)
H. B. Morse, *The International Relations of the Chinese Empire* (London, 1910-1918)
L. B. Lippincott Company, Philadelphia
J. O. P. Bland and E. Backhouse, *China Under the Empress Dowager* (1912)
Louisiana State University Press, Baton Rouge
M. Frederick Nelson, *Korea and the Old Orders in Eastern Asia* (1945)
The Macmillan Company, New York
The Cambridge Modern History
Engelbert Kaempfer, *The History of Japan* (1906)
McGraw-Hill Book Company, Inc., New York
P. M. A. Linebarger, *Government in Republican China* (1938)
Minnesota Law Review, University of Minnesota
Nathan April, "An Inquiry into the Juridical Basis for the Nuernberg War Crimes Trial," XXX (1946)
Publishers' Weekly, New York, and Frank E. Taylor
Frank E. Taylor, "Censorship of Writers and Publishers in China," CL (1946)
G. P. Putnam's Sons, New York
Bayard Taylor, *India, China, and Japan* (1855)
F. W. Williams, *The Life and Letters of Samuel Wells Williams* (1899)
Princeton University Press, Princeton, New Jersey
Harold M. Vinacke, *Modern Constitutional Development in China* (1920)
Charles Scribner's Sons, New York
Sir Henry Yule, ed., *The Book of Ser Marco Polo* (3d rev. ed., 1926)
Smithsonian Institution, Washington, D. C.
John F. Embree, *The Japanese* (1943)
Stanford University Press
M. E. Cameron, *The Reform Movement in China* (1931)
Yamato Ichihashi, *The Washington Conference and After* (1928)
Thomas E. LaFargue, *China and the World War* (1937)
The University of Chicago Press
Tatsuji Takeuchi, *War and Diplomacy in the Japanese Empire* (1936)
The University of Illinois Press, Urbana
Earl H. Pritchard, *Anglo-Chinese Relations during the Seventeenth and Eighteenth Centuries* (1929)

Contents

List of Maps

1

Introduction

HISTORY—the record of what man has thought and done—is a subject so all-inclusive that there is good reason to begin a particular history such as this one with some remarks on its scope and treatment, on the major theme that gives it unity, on its limitations, and on the audience to which it is addressed. The theme of the following story—the meeting of West and East in the nineteenth and twentieth centuries—is in itself so vast a record that it cannot be compressed readily into a single volume. What follows then in these pages is a selection from and an introduction to the larger and richer storehouse of history. The study has been written primarily for an audience of American students, old and young, who will certainly shape in part at least the future history of relations between Asia and the West. It is offered to them in order to provide them with some experience of the past. The subject and purpose cannot be dismissed as merely academic, for Eastern and South Asia in the mid-twentieth century are as much a part of American politics as was Cuba in 1898 or the Mississippi Valley in 1800.

This fact is the more striking since, for most Americans during the greater part of this country's history, the world as a field of realistic interest has tended to reach only from the Atlantic seaboard to the Pacific Coast, and from the 49th parallel to the Gulf of Mexico and the Rio Grande. When in 1898 President McKinley acknowledged that he was somewhat uncertain just where the Philippine Islands might be, his confession was one to which most of his fellow countrymen could also subscribe. The political geography of Asia, when it was thought of at all, was considered a subject that might well be left to academicians with a fancy for strange and outlandish regions of the world. To be sure, there were Americans—traders, businessmen, sea captains, missionaries, and historians—who were not strangers to Asia's lands and peoples. But, apart from these special groups, very few Americans were possessed of any systematic politico-geographical knowledge of China, Japan, India, or the lesser countries of the East.

For a time in the 1940's, when many American school boys were as familiar with Buna, Biak, and Bataan as they were with Buffalo, Butte, and Baltimore, this capacity of the nineteenth-century American mind to ignore half the world's physical surface and more than half of its peoples seemed hardly credible. Yet, as a typical example, a popular school history, published in 1863 in New York, advised its readers that "China, a vast country of eastern Asia, may be almost said to have no history of any interest to the general reader, it has so few revolutions or political changes to record."[1]

There are of course many historical factors that explain the willingness of Americans to neglect the world beyond their own borders. Here it is sufficient to suggest that as the American built his new society in the United States he found satisfaction in certain negative rather than positive realities of geography, because these realities (the Atlantic Ocean, for example) enabled him to achieve that separation from Europe which he so ardently desired. Geography was not a means by which cultural, political, or economic influence could be furthered. Later, when this American had acquired a coastline on the Pacific, he saw, to be sure, visions of a great commerce with Asia; he even pictured the Pacific as an American lake; yet he was more than ever dominated by a philosophy of political isolation, and it was thus very satisfying for him to note that the Pacific Ocean was wide and the "teeming millions" of Asia were far away. If, as many American forefathers saw it, there was little reason to be concerned about the political affairs of Europe (since they were largely a matter of the sinister rivalries of kings), there was even less to recommend the civilization of Asia, inhabited as that continent was by Oriental despots and a heathen, "uncivilized" society.

"The march of events," however, often has scant respect for man's deep-rooted and hallowed habits and traditions. The military and naval campaigns of World War II gave to thousands of Americans an undreamed of familiarity with those same distant lands which their fathers and grandfathers had called strange and outlandish. The old and convenient American-made stereotypes of Asia and the

[1] Marcius Willson, *Outlines of History* (New York, 1863), 286-287.

Asiatic became less convincing. The Chinese, or the "Chinaman," as most Americans called him in the late nineteenth century, was a coolie, a species of unskilled cheap laborer. He was poverty-stricken, dirty, illiterate, and heathen, though sometimes endowed, it was said, with a fine simple honesty. Some Americans knew the Chinese villain of American fiction, personalized by the dark ways of Dr. Fu Manchu, and there was the popular conception of the Chinese as a philosopher who was oblivious to the passage of time. Even more than the Chinese, the Japanese were mentally stereotyped as "a quaint little people devoted to cherry blossoms and Mount Fuji." It is quite true that the people were little, that they liked both cherry blossoms and Mount Fuji, but they were not thereby quaint by any means. Now, as a result of the broadened horizons that have come out of World War II, there are fewer Americans who can be satisfied with this kind of capsule human geography.

The Continent of Asia

The Far East, though an immense area in itself, is but a part of the world's largest continent, Eurasia. It was in this Asian continent, probably in the hinterland of the Arabian Sea, that the race-home of man was located, somewhere in the area that is the traditional site of the Garden of Eden. Asia is pre-eminent among all the continents in both size and altitude. Covering one-third of the land-surface of the world, Asia comprises some 17 million square miles. It is larger than the combined area of North and South America, and more than four times the size of Europe, which in reality is but a peninsula on the western rim of Asia. If considered in terms of linear distance, Asia extends for some 6,000 miles from east to west and for more than 5,000 miles from its most northerly to its most southerly point. However, the most compelling characteristic of Asia's physical formation is neither its unique size nor its towering altitudes, but rather "the gigantic development of plateau" extending for some 9,000 miles in a great arc from the eastern Mediterranean to the Bering Strait, widening in some areas to nearly 2,000 miles in the heart of the Tibetan tableland. As geographers measure this plateau, it covers nearly two-fifths of Asia's land mass, but it supports only a limited and mostly pastoral population.

Here it is pertinent to note that Asia's physical diversity is matched by an even greater social diversity including three major civilizations, the Chinese, the Hindu, and the Islamic. Asia is therefore a geographical term, since Asia as a social unit has no existence at all. The conventional concepts of East and West, Asia and Europe, are apt to be meaningless for purposes of comparison until they are defined in specific terms.[2]

Of the estimated two and one-half billion inhabitants of the world, more than half live in Asia. Most of this multitude is in the southern and eastern fringes of the continent: in India, China, Japan, Korea, and the East Indies. Important, too, is the fact that the overwhelming proportion of this vast population are tillers of the soil. Just prior to World War II, Japan was the only Asiatic country with a highly developed industry, and even in Japan some 50 per cent of the population still lived by the soil.

The climates of Asia are sufficiently varied to satisfy the most extreme tastes, yet there are certain broad features that may be said to affect the continent as a whole. Of these the best known, and, to the early European navigators, the most useful, was the monsoon (from the Arabic "season"), seasonal winds blowing south and westerly from the heart of the continent in the winter or dry season, and north and easterly from the Indian Ocean in the summer or wet season. From the sixteenth to the mid-nineteenth century, it was on the spring or summer monsoon that the European navigators sailed to Canton, and it was on the winter monsoon that they turned their course homeward. But of greater importance to the population of Asia was the fact that the wet monsoon brought the seasonal rains that in southern Asia made it possible for so many to live on the land. Farther inland, where the moisture did not reach, were the arid and semi-arid regions of the Mongolian plateau where the land maintained only a sparse population.

Relief and climate in Asia are reflected not only in the distribution of Asia's population but also in its racial and cultural traits. In Asia, immense size, virtually impassable barriers of mountain and desert, and extreme variations of climate precluded, in the main, communication over the continent as a whole. Furthermore, it should be observed that geography not only separated the great civilizations of Asia one from another, but it also maintained their remoteness until very recent times from other centers of civilization such as western Europe. Indeed it may be said that this isolation re-

---

[2] John M. Steadman, "The Myth of Asia," *The American Scholar,* 25 (1956), 163-175.

mained for practical purposes unbroken until so recently as the late nineteenth century. When the barriers of separation were broken by the expansion of an aggressive Western World, it meant that the Far East was at first overwhelmed. There had been no preparation in Asia to meet the modern West enriched and empowered by all that Europe had achieved since the Renaissance in government, trade, invention, science, industry, and literature.

The Far East

The eastern half of Asia may be labelled conveniently *The Far East.* More specifically, it comprises those lands of the Asiatic continent and adjacent islands that lie east of longitude 90° east of Greenwich. These include, on the mainland: eastern Siberia, Korea or Chōsen, China and its borderland territories—Manchuria, Mongolia, Sinkiang or Chinese Turkestan, and Tibet; and to the south, Burma, Siam (Thailand), Indochina, and Malaya; and the insular areas: Japan, the Philippines, and the East Indies or Indonesia. To Americans of the eighteenth and nineteenth centuries as well as to Europeans, the term Far East was more descriptively suggestive than it is to Americans today, since, in those days, mariners sailing to China skirted Africa and sailed eastward. Thus in a very real sense China and the lands immediately surrounding it were the Far East, the ultimate destination of these early mariners. For Americans of the mid-twentieth century the region is neither east nor far, yet for the vast majority of them it remains a remote and often a mysterious world, intellectually and culturally.

The Theme of This History

Throughout the past 150 years the Far East has been the stage for a revolution that is perhaps unequalled in all history in the breadth and depth of its penetration. It has involved two great movements. The first was the expansion of Western civilization in all its aspects and power against and eventually into the old and traditional societies of Middle and Eastern Asia. This movement, which began in the early nineteenth century and is usually called the impact of the West, had all but conquered Asia in terms of political power by the beginning of the twentieth century. By that time, however, the second aspect of this revolution was well under way. The response of Asia to the Western impact was at first faltering, uneven, and unchartered, but by the end of World War II it had gathered an irresistible momentum. The result in mid-twentieth century was a new Eastern Asia—chaotic, often irresponsible, jealous of its "rights" and its new-found political freedom, torn between the fiercely-opposed Western ideologies of democracy and communism (both of which few Asians understood), and overwhelmed by poverty in the resources and skills that could raise their world to new standards but suspicious that bounty from the West would substitute an economic for the older political "enslavement."

It is this story of the Western impact and of Eastern Asia's response to it that is the central theme of the following pages. There are, of course, many avenues of approach to this subject. The one that will be found here is the avenue of history. Asia's revolution is a product of historical growth. The successes and the failures in the meeting of East and West today can be understood only in the light of that disciplined background knowledge that history must provide. Within broad topics, therefore, this is a chronological story, since time and history are inseparable. It will be noted, too, that the study begins with a descriptive survey of some principal ideas and institutions of Old China and Old Japan. These, the major countries of the Far East, had developed rich and enduring civilizations very unlike the cultural background of the modern Western World. A study of the Western impact must therefore provide some foundations in Asiatic values.

The most conspicuous aspects of the meeting of West and East have been in the areas of war and diplomacy, often termed the field of international relations. These matters will be given some prominence because they were and are important. The institutions of diplomacy and war were often the principal meeting ground of Orient and Occident. Yet these agencies alone were not the sole means of contact, nor were they necessarily the most significant. Accordingly, a continuing emphasis will be given to the West-East traffic in ideas and values, and to the institutions through which man gives expression to them. Asia's contemporary revolutions were born in the migration of ideas from West to East that spans the past century. Here, too, attention will be given to the reception accorded to Western thought by Asians. It is remarkable that the West gave surprisingly little attention to this key subject until so recently as World War II. The result was a shocking failure to understand Asia's aspirations, the sources from which they arose, or the means she might use to achieve them.

Perhaps, too, it is well to be reminded at the start that the narrative that is to follow is in itself only an introduction to Eastern Asia's recent experience with the West. The vastness and the variety, the age and the wealth of Eastern Asia's civilizations as they have entered upon the modern age cannot be disposed of within the covers of a single book. The purpose here, less ambitious, is to provide foundations on which those who would know the Far East tomorrow may first learn how it came to be as it is today.

The Sources of This History

A list of all the sources, primary and secondary, that deal with the impact of the West on Eastern Asia would fill many books the size of this one. It is the business of the historian, among other things, to know these sources as well as he may and to suggest to his readers the literature that is likely to be most useful in their further pursuit of the subject. Since the history that follows is an introductory narrative, the suggestions for further reading are selective. Many studies of value are necessarily excluded. Books that have been included are designed to assist the reader in specific ways. Throughout the text footnote citations are given to some of the major sources on which the story is based. At the end of each chapter are suggestions and notes on further reading of both a general and specialized nature. Finally, this survey of the modernization of the Far East would not have been possible were it not for the special studies made by many scholars covering particular subjects or periods. The research of hundreds of authors, whose works are cited in footnotes or listed in the reading suggestions following each chapter, has been utilized in this study.

For Further Reading

The student who is unfamiliar with the political, economic, and cultural geography of the Far East will find it useful, if not imperative, at the outset to pursue a disciplined course of reading in the following geographic sources.

ASIA AND THE FAR EAST

Bergsmark, Daniel Rockman, *Economic Geography of Asia* (New York, 1935).

Cressey, George B., *Asia's Lands and Peoples* (2nd ed., New York, 1951). The physical and social geography of Asia and the Soviet Union.

East, William, and O. H. K. Spate, eds., *The Changing Map of Asia* (New York, 1950). A political geography.

Oliver, Douglas L., *The Pacific Islands* (Cambridge, Mass., 1951). A general history, economic and social.

Spencer, Joseph Earle, *Asia, East by South: A Cultural Geography* (New York, 1954). Covers the area from India to Japan.

Thompson, Warren S., *Population and Peace in the Pacific* (Chicago, 1946). Discusses population pressures and political instability.

Wickizer, V. D., and M. K. Bennett, *The Rice Economy of Monsoon Asia* (Stanford University, 1941). A detailed, basic analysis.

CHINA: GENERAL

Cressey, George B., *China's Geographic Foundations: A Survey of the Land and Its People* (New York, 1934).

———, *Land of the 500 Million: A Geography of China* (New York, 1955). The best general geography of China.

Richard, Louis, *A Comprehensive Geography of the Chinese Empire,* trans. by M. Kennelly (Shanghai, 1908). A classic in the field.

Shabad, Theodore, *China's Changing Map: A Political and Economic Geography of the Chinese People's Republic* (New York, 1956). A recent geographical survey giving special attention to economic factors.

Winfield, Gerald F., *China: The Land and the People* (rev. ed., New York, 1950). The interrelations among deeply rooted mores, economic conditions, and problems of political change.

CHINA: SOILS AND MINERALS

Bain, Harry Foster, *Ores and Industry in the Far East: The influence of key mineral resources on the development of Oriental civilization* (rev. and enl. ed., New York, 1933). A standard work.

Buck, J. Lossing, *Land Utilization in China* (Chicago, 1937). A principal source on the agrarian economy.

Fei Hsiao-t'ung, *Peasant Life in China* (London, 1939). Based on a detailed study of a Chinese village.

———, and Chih-i Chang, *Earthbound China* (Chicago, 1945). Based principally on intensive studies of three Chinese villages.

Lamb, J. D. H., *Development of the Agrarian Movement and Agrarian Legislation in China, 1912-1930* (Peiping, 1931). Treats of policies and laws relating to agriculture during the early republic.

Shên Tsung-han, *Agricultural Resources of China* (Ithaca, 1951). An excellent study.

CHINA: POPULATION

Tawney, Richard H., *Land and Labour in China* (New York, 1932). A well-balanced and comprehensive survey.

CHINA: INDUSTRIALIZATION

Arnold, Julean, *China: A Commercial and Industrial Handbook* (Washington, 1926). Useful statistics.

Hubbard, G. E., *Eastern Industrialization and Its Effect on the West* (2nd ed., Oxford, 1938). Includes Japan and India.

Lieu, D. K., *China's Industry and Finance* (Peking, 1927). Sources of capital and patterns of investment.

Remer, C. F., *The Foreign Trade of China* (Shanghai, 1926).

MANCHURIA

Lattimore, Owen, *Manchuria: Cradle of Conflict* (rev. ed., New York, 1935).

MONGOLIA AND SINKIANG

Cammann, Schuyler, *The Land of the Camel: Tents and Temples of Inner Mongolia* (New York, 1951).

Lattimore, Owen, *The Mongols of Manchuria* (New York, 1934).

———, *Inner Asian Frontiers of China* (2nd ed., New York, 1951). A basic source of materials for the study of Chinese relations with frontier areas.

TIBET

Bell, Charles, *The People of Tibet* (Oxford, 1928).

———, *Tibet, Past and Present* (Oxford, 1924).

Schram, Louis M. J., *The Monguors of the Kansu-Tibetan Frontier: Their Origin, History and Social Organization* (Philadelphia, 1954). A study offering the first description of the social organization of a Mongol tribe.

Shên Tsung-lien, and Liu Shên-chi, *Tibet and the Tibetans* (Stanford, 1953). A short but very informative book.

SIBERIA

Kolarz, Walter, *The Peoples of the Soviet Far East* (New York, 1954). Deals with Soviet colonization policies in the areas east of Lake Baikal.

Shabad, Theodore, *Geography of the USSR: a Regional Survey* (New York, 1951). The most systematic geography of the Soviet Union available in English.

JAPAN: GENERAL

Borton, Hugh, ed., *Japan* (Ithaca, 1950).

Smith, Guy Harold, and Dorothy Good, with the collaboration of Shannon McCune, *Japan: a Geographical View* (New York, 1943). A factual view of Japan at the start of World War II.

Trewartha, Glenn T., *Japan: A Physical, Cultural, and Regional Geography* (Madison, 1945). A splendid study by an authority.

JAPAN: POPULATION

Ishii Ryoichi, *Population Pressure and Economic Life in Japan* (Chicago, 1937). A satisfactory survey.

Penrose, E. F., *Population Theories and Their Application with Special Reference to Japan* (Stanford, 1934). The best work on the subject.

JAPAN: AGRICULTURE AND THE RURAL COMMUNITY

Embree, John F., *Suye Mura: A Japanese Village* (Chicago, 1939). An excellent study.

Nasu Shiroshi, *Aspects of Japanese Agriculture: A Preliminary Survey* (New York, 1941). A helpful addition to his earlier studies.

JAPAN: INDUSTRIAL GEOGRAPHY

Allen, G. C., *Japanese Industry: Its Recent Development and Present Condition* (New York, 1940). The best work covering the entire subject.

Nasu Shiroshi, *Land Utilization in Japan* (Tokyo, 1929). A competent study.

Schumpeter, E. B., ed., *The Industrialization of Japan and Manchukuo, 1930-1940* (New York, 1940). Valuable essays.

Uyehara, S., *The Industry and Trade of Japan* (2nd rev. ed., London, 1936). A basic study.

LIN-CH'IU ISLANDS

Glacken, Clarence, *The Great Loochoo: A Study in Okinawan Village Life* (Berkeley, 1955).

KOREA

McCune, George M., *Korea Today* (Cambridge, Mass., 1950). A comprehensive survey of that nation since World War II.

McCune, Shannon, *Korea's Heritage: A Regional and Social Geography* (Rutland, 1956).

Osgood, Cornelius, *The Koreans and Their Culture* (New York, 1951). An anthropological study, showing the influence of history and environment on the individual.

BURMA

Christian, John L., *Modern Burma* (Berkeley, 1942). The best introductory study covering the modern period. See Ch. 2 on "The Land and the People."

Harvey, G. E., *British Rule in Burma, 1824-1942* (London, 1946). The most critical, definitive work.

THAILAND (SIAM)

Landon, K. P., *Siam in Transition* (Chicago, 1939). Principally a cultural study.

MALAYA

Emerson, Rupert, *Malaysia: A Study in Direct and Indirect Rule* (New York, 1937). A well-documented study, which advocated self-government.

Mills, L. A., *British Rule in Eastern Asia* (London, 1942). An excellent study of Hongkong, the Straits settlements, and the Malay states.

Winstedt, Sir Richard, *Malaya and Its History* (London, 1948). A brief and readable account.

———, *The Malays: A Cultural History* (rev. ed., London, 1950). An excellent interpretation of the people prior to Western influence.

INDONESIA

Furnivall, J. S., *Progress and Welfare in Southeast Asia* (New York, 1941). A competent study by a British scholar.

Reed, Stephen W., *The Making of Modern New Guinea* (Philadelphia, 1943). The outstanding work on the subject.

Thompson, Virginia, *French Indo China* (New York, 1937). An extensive work covering both cultural aspects of the nation and French administration.

Vandenbosch, Amry, *The Dutch East Indies: Its Government, Problems, and Politics* (3rd ed., Berkeley, 1942). Very good on pre-war political structure of the Indies.

THE PHILIPPINES

Forbes, W. Cameron, *The Philippine Islands* (Boston, 1928). By the governor-general of the islands from 1909-1913.

LeRoy, James A., *Philippine Life in Town and Country* (New York, 1905). A picture of the Filipino people at the end of the Spanish regime.

2

Ways of Life in Old China

THE civilization of China is one of the oldest and one of the richest known to man. Yet in the United States, until very recent years, surprisingly little attention has been paid to it. This is the more curious because for more than a century the American people thought of itself as the friend of China, and because, during that same period, the government of the United States held rather firmly to friendly principles in its relations with China. Indeed, the United States was often considered the defender of China's political integrity. Nevertheless, the richness of China's thought and culture has occupied an extraordinarily small corner in the scheme of American education or in the recesses of American thought. Europe, in contrast to America, has often been more conscious of the intellectual gifts that China could offer, but even in the case of Europe enthusiasm for things Chinese has been sporadic. The result is that although there is a long history of intercourse between China and the Western world, in the main the two civilizations have had little mutual understanding. In general, this state of affairs prevailed until very recent times. Thus, before entering on the story of the growth of contacts between China and the West, it will be worthwhile to review briefly some of the highlights of China's history and her philosophy; for without some knowledge of these there can be no understanding of contacts with China in the nineteenth and the twentieth centuries.

The traditional accounts of early Chinese history begin before the time of Hsia, a dynasty supposed to have held sway in northern China from 1994 to 1523 B.C. and to have included such mythical or legendary figures as Huang Ti, Yao, Shun, and Yü, the last being the alleged founder of the Hsia. But all this is mostly a matter of myth.[1]

What may now be called the beginnings of China's history as opposed to legend lie in the five centuries of the Shang or Yin dynasty, *ca.* 1523 to 1027 B.C., the capital of which was at Anyang in the north-central valley of the Yellow River. Even at this early date, the men of Shang had developed a remarkable system of writing that employed most of the important principles involved in modern Chinese written characters. Government, particularly in the cities, appears to have been rather highly developed. Time was calculated by a calendar frequently adjusted to keep it in tune with the seasons. This was important. In an agricultural country and among a credulous people, a king might easily lose favor if the seasons went astray. Shang was also a period of warfare which finally resulted in the defeat and destruction of the dynasty.

The Chou (Jou) Dynasty, 1027-256 B.C.

The long and justly famous Chou dynasty cannot be treated here in detail. Though the origin of the people of Chou is uncertain, they appear to have come from the regions of the modern Shensi and Kansu. The early Chou state covered most of the lower Huang Ho Valley. The Late Chou, 473-256 B.C., was again a period of interstate warfare from which was to emerge the power of Ch'in. Yet, despite its feudal warfare, Chou was a classical age. It was the period of Confucius, perhaps also of that vague figure, Lao-tzŭ, and of other great philosophers who have left their stamp on every succeeding generation in China's long history. In addition it was a period when the Chinese appear to have absorbed ideas from beyond their own borders.[2]

China Becomes an Empire

From 221 to 207 B.C., China passed under the control of Ch'in (Tsin), one of the extreme western states of the late Chou period. By advancing eastward, this people came to control the richest agricultural areas, overcame the rival states, and made their king the

---

[1] The basic study is H. G. Creel, *The Birth of China* (New York, 1937). See also K. S. Latourette, *The Chinese: Their History and Culture* (3rd ed., New York, 1946).

[2] An extremely brief survey, convenient as an introduction, is L. Carrington Goodrich, *A Short History of the Chinese People* (New York, 1943, rev. ed. 1951).

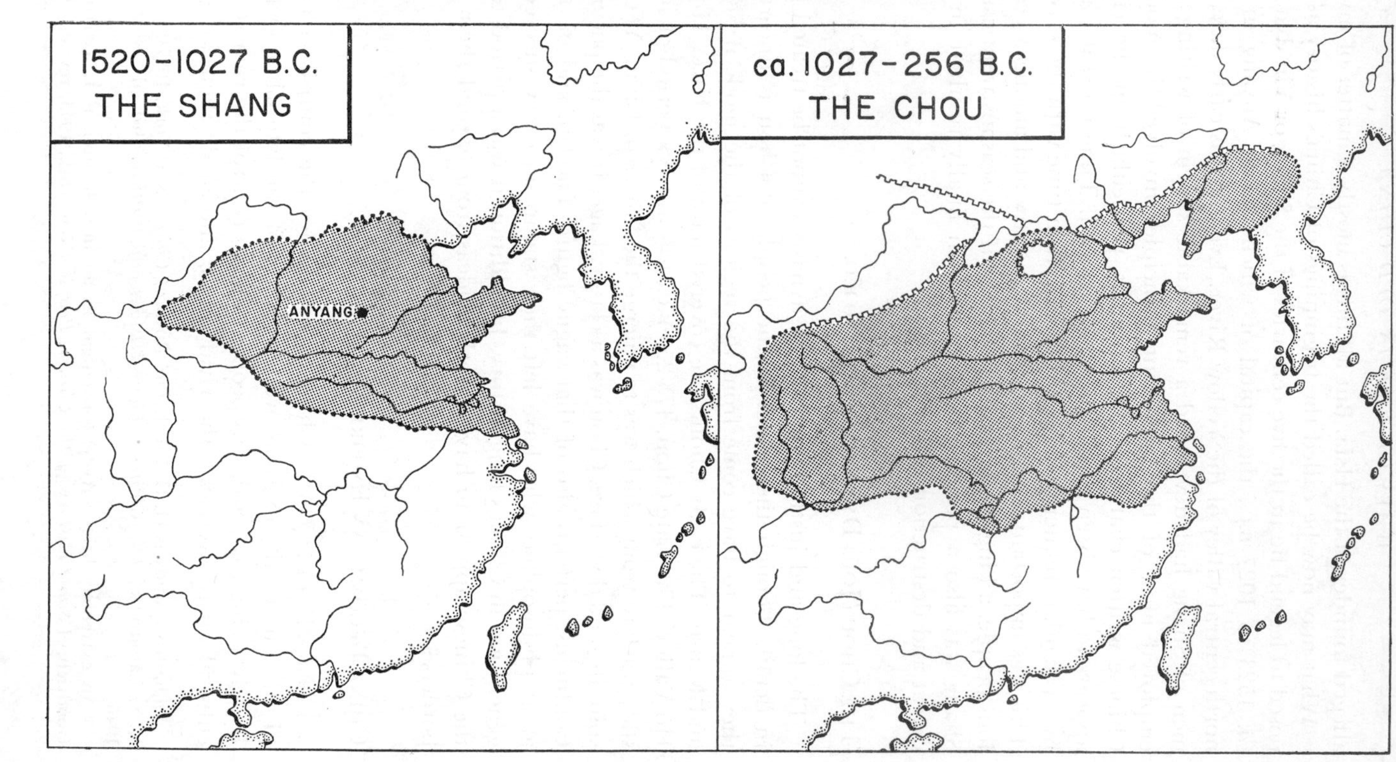
CHINA: GREAT PERIODS IN HISTORY
1520-1027 B.C.
THE SHANG
ANYANG
ca. 1027-256 B.C.
THE CHOU

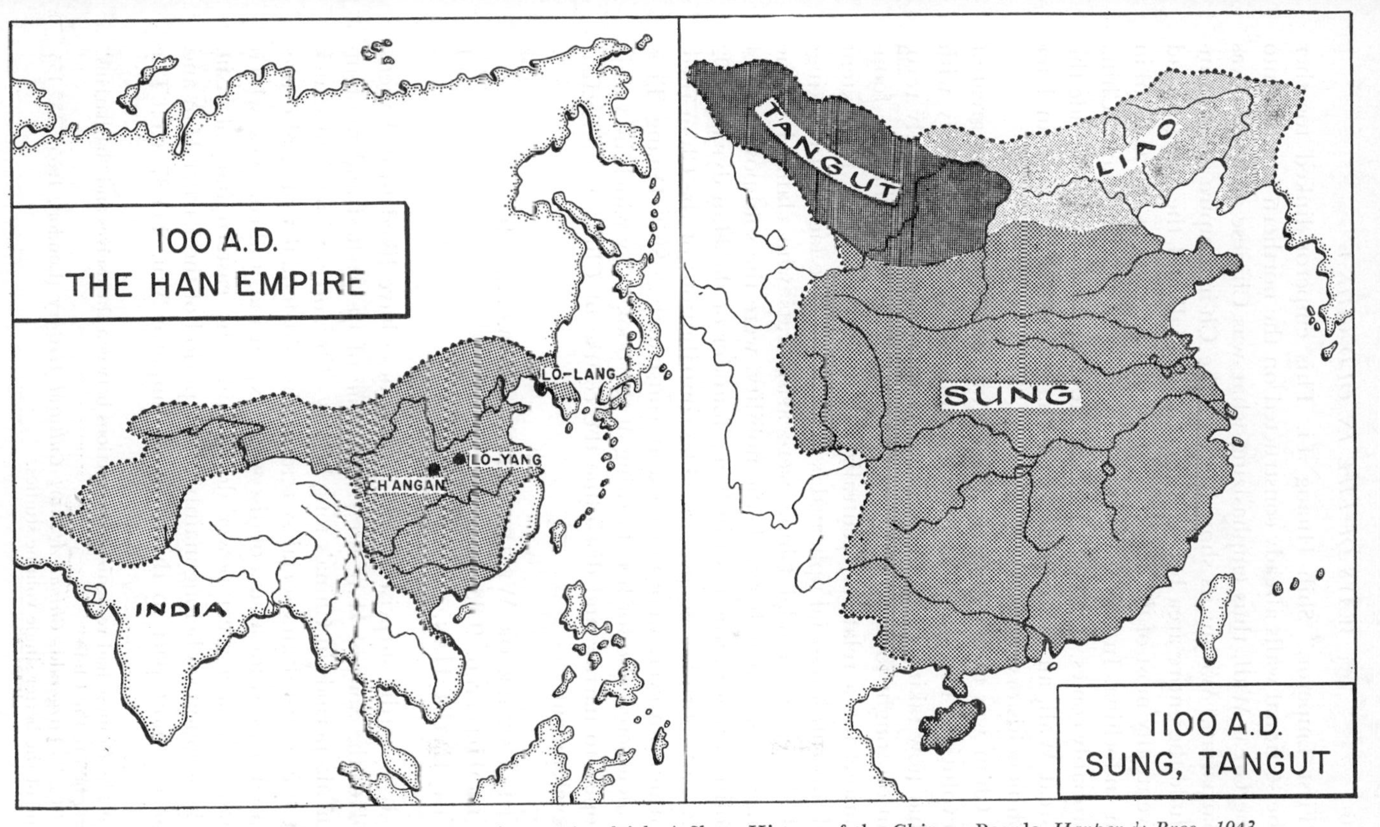

Adapted with permission from L. Carrington Goodrich, A Short History of the Chinese People, *Harper & Bros., 1943.*

"First Emperor," Shih Huang Ti. This emperor linked together the sectional walls already constructed on the northern frontier into the Great Wall, thus emphasizing what was Chinese and what was barbarian.[3] Within its short lifetime, the Ch'in Empire grew to include the entire area between the Great Wall and the Yangtze and eventually most of the territory south of that river as far as Tonkin in Indochina. In this manner, Ch'in, from which the name China probably comes, created the idea of an all-embracing state inside the Great Wall, an idea which was to have great significance in later Chinese history.

Ch'in was thus witness to the beginnings of one of the greatest revolutions in China's history, a revolution comparable only with that now taking place in twentieth-century China. This early revolution sought to destroy the ancient feudal system, laying the foundations for a relatively centralized bureaucratic state. The extent of this ruthless social upheaval is suggested by the fact that the kings of the earlier feudal China were aristocrats who claimed divine ancestry and, together with the nobility, were the sole possessors of political power, whereas Liu Pang, founder of the Han dynasty, 202 B.C., was born a poor peasant. The contributions of the Ch'in revolution, however, were not entirely constructive. Shih Huang Ti is remembered also for his "burning of the books," by which he vainly hoped to narrow and discipline the course of Chinese intellectual development.[4]

The Earlier or Western Han, 202 B.C.-A.D. 9
The Hsin, A.D. 9-23
The Later Han, A.D. 25-220

It is hardly surprising that the Chinese have liked to call themselves the Sons of Han, for Han is one of the richest and most inspiring periods in China's long history. The forces which had struck at the political and social system of the old feudal China also prepared the way for an era of discovery, expansion, and conquest which made China a great power dominating the eastern half of Asia. These conquests belong mainly to the period of the Earlier Han and for the most part to the reign of Emperor Wu, 141-87 B.C. The

[3] The Chinese had recognized the frictions between themselves and "barbarians" long before the Ch'in.

[4] C. P. Fitzgerald, *China: A Short Cultural History* (London, 1935), 133-155. One of the better single volume studies.

energy of Han leaders extended the empire to the east to include South Manchuria, the southern fringe of Outer Mongolia, and the vast central Asian basin of Sinkiang, or modern Chinese Turkestan.

The brief interregnum of the Hsin dynasty, A.D. 9-23, notable principally for the rule of Wang Mang and his efforts to imitate ancient Confucian models, was followed by the resumption of Han rule and the conquest of new lands.

Han culture enriched China's life in numberless ways: in literature and the arts, in government, science, and industry. Here was begun the painstaking search and research to rediscover the proscribed classics. Here was laid the foundation for the Confucian conquest of the Chinese mind. In some ways, however, it was a new Confucianism, not concerned solely with finding a principle of moral authority. An authoritative and stable state already existed in Han, and so Confucianism, tinged by the atmosphere in which it was reborn, acquired an authoritative and religious tone, becoming in time the state cult.[5]

The creative qualities of Han revealed themselves in many ways. A lunar calendar was developed with great mathematical accuracy. A seismograph detected earthquakes that were so slight that people did not notice them. Glazed pottery was being made at the close of the Han period. Elaborately embroidered silks were woven for both the domestic and the foreign trade. Han ladies improved on nature with face powder and rouge. Literature became richer in expression. Manuscripts were collected in an Imperial library. The first standard histories were written. Paper appears to have been made from rags.

Political Division: The "Dark Ages," A.D. 220-590

The four centuries that followed the collapse of the later Han empire may be likened in some degree to Europe's "Dark Ages." The fall of Han, prefaced by that inveterate evil, the inordinate power of irresponsible elements near the throne, was accompanied, like the fall of Rome, by barbarian invasions, though in the case of China the cultural and intellectual collapse was less devastating. In the end, the Chinese did much to absorb their conquerors and to preserve the native language and literature.

[5] Fitzgerald, *China,* 213-222; Richard Wilhelm, *A Short History of Chinese Civilization* (New York, 1929), 171-175; John K. Shryock, *The Origin and Development of the State Cult of Confucius* (New York, 1932).

In this age of invasion, political confusion, and rival kingdoms, Buddhism became an integral part of Chinese thought and all but conquered the Chinese mind. Reaching China first in the first century A.D., Buddhism was able to capitalize on the political downfall of the Confucian Han. If Buddhism did not conquer China, it at least became the most important influence of foreign origin introduced in historic times. It modified Chinese life profoundly, but in the end was itself transformed by China.

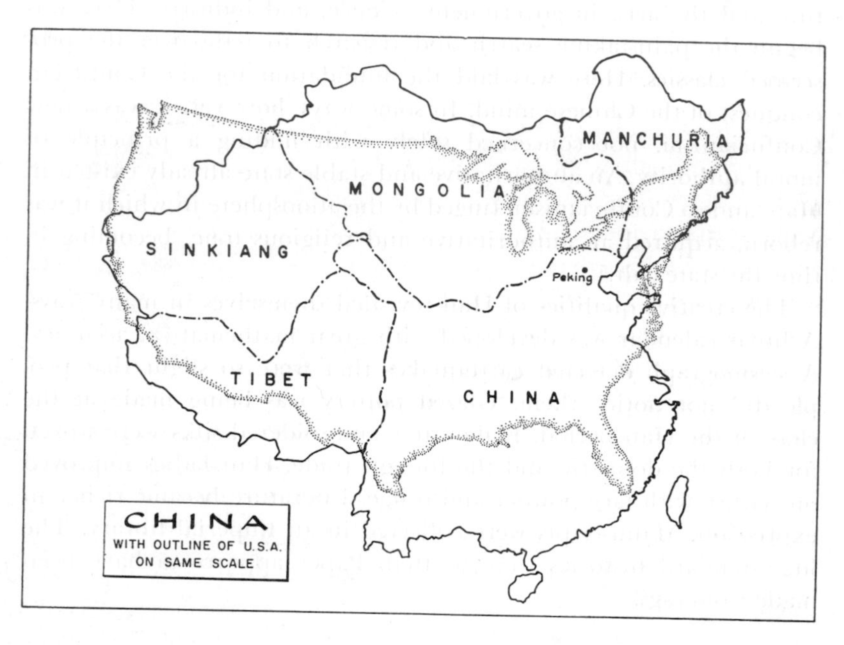

CHINA
WITH OUTLINE OF U.S.A.
ON SAME SCALE

The age of confusion helped along a movement that was at least as old as the Han period—the transformation of the early philosophy of Taoism into a religion. Confucian neglect of the mystical world opened the way to both Buddhism and Taoism. Previously the latter had possessed no doctrine of an after-life. It now became the keeper of the spirit world, with promises of immortality, of making old men young, and of creating gold by chemical processes.

The Sui Dynasty, 590-618

After these long centuries of political disunion, China was again united under the short-lived Sui dynasty. Conquests were renewed in central Asia; Formosa was invaded; and missions sailed south to the East Indies, presumably in the hope of developing commerce. At home, better communications were created by the building of a great canal through the heart of north-central China. This was the work of several million forced laborers. Though its military power was great, and its contributions to China's economy considerable, Sui could not long survive the popular resentment created by its extravagance and its intolerance.

THE T'ANG DYNASTY, 618-906

The new sovereigns of T'ang China were destined to lead the country through what is usually called the most brilliant period of its history. For purposes of administration the country was divided into provinces. Education was officially encouraged. Civil service examinations, an idea adapted from the previous Sui dynasty, were stressed. Though the state cult of Confucius was later favored, religious tolerance in general prevailed. Laws were codified, and commerce was encouraged by further extension of the canal system. In the middle of the eighth century the T'ang Empire covered not only the greater part of what in the nineteenth century was known as China Proper, but also south and central Manchuria and the vast area of Turkestan far to the west. It was T'ang China that challenged the growing political power of Buddhism and other alien religions, subjecting them to the State or suppressing them. Architecture and sculpture reached new peaks of excellence. Ch'ang-an, the capital of T'ang China, with a population of nearly two million in 742, was one of the world's finest cities architecturally. This city formed the model for Japan's first permanent captial, Nara. T'ang was also the great age of Chinese poets: Po Chu-i, Li Po, Tu Fu, Wang Wei, and Wei Ying-wu. Two great encyclopedias were compiled. The short story, which formerly dealt only with the world of spirits, entered the more human and mundane field of life and love. Block printing was invented. A list of the brilliant cultural inventions and attainments of T'ang China could be further enlarged. Yet for all the cultural greatness that filled the land, later T'ang emperors did not learn how to avoid the corruption of a wealthy court.

The Sung Empire, 960-1279

With the fall of the T'ang Empire, China again fell into political confusion. The Khitans, a Mongol people, occupied Mongolia and Manchuria, while in other parts of the empire there were successful secessionist movements. Between 907 and 960 a succession of the so-called "Five dynasties" maintained a precarious hold on what was left of the T'ang Empire. These dynasties were: the Later Liang, the Later T'ang, the Later Tsin, the Later Han, and the Later Chou. In general it was a period of rule by "licentious tyrants," of such sensual refinements as the binding of women's feet (an imposition which seems first to have been imposed upon dancing girls), and of a general breakdown in the entire economic and political structure of society. Out of this chaos, however, rose the Sung dynasty, which, with the exception of the years 1127-1135, ruled China from 960 to 1279. The Sung Empire at its height (about 1100) covered virtually all of China south of the Wall, but not north Hopei and Shansi. In the north, however, it was bordered by the two powerful states of Hsi-hsia and Liao, the latter including southwestern Manchuria, part of northeastern China, and Inner Mongolia. It was the failure of the Sung to check the power of the border states that eventually forced the dynasty to retreat south of the Yangtze River. Nevertheless, Sung China was a period of general advancement in the livelihood of the people. Even the common folk now began to sit on chairs instead of the floor. Sung was also a period of renaissance in the arts and in education. Unlike the period under T'ang, when the poets excelled, under Sung the writers of prose took the lead. There was also advance in the science of algebra, probably introduced through the Arab trade. In religion and philosophy, the influence of Buddhism continued to decline, giving place to a school of thought called Neo-Confucianism, which took what it wanted from both Taoism and Buddhism, discarding the rest. All in all, the civilization of Sung China probably outstripped any of its contemporary rivals so that Shao Yung might well have said: "I am happy because I am a human and not an animal; a male, and not a female; a Chinese, and not a barbarian; and because I live in Loyang, the most wonderful city in all the world."[6]

---

[6] Quoted by Goodrich, *History of the Chinese People,* 159.

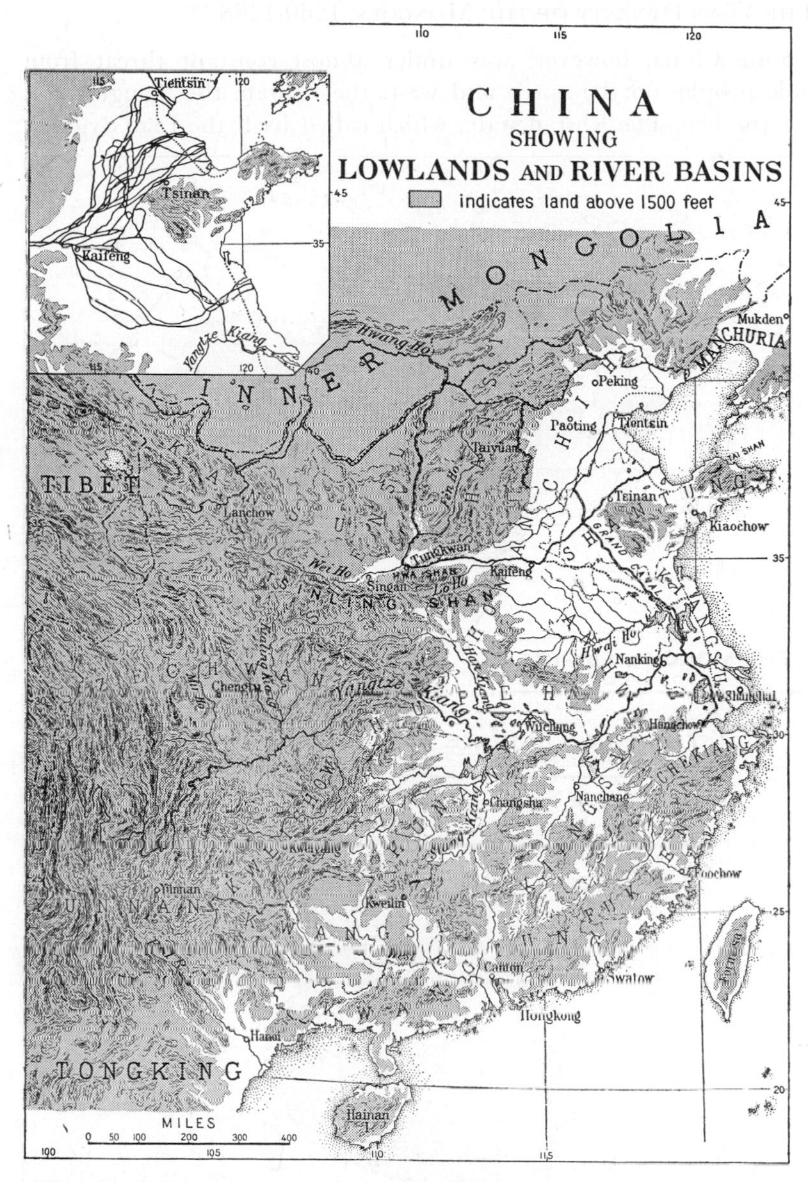

The essentially mountainous character of western and southern China is illustrated. Scale 1:20,000,000. The inset shows changes in the lower course of the Huang Ho and the seaward extension of the shoreline. *Courtesy of the* Geographical Review, *published by the American Geographical Society of New York.*

The Yüan Dynasty of the Mongols, 1260-1368

Sung China, however, was under almost constant threat from rude peoples on the north and west: the Khitan, the Tangut, and the Jurchen. The Khitan state, which called itself the Liao dynasty,

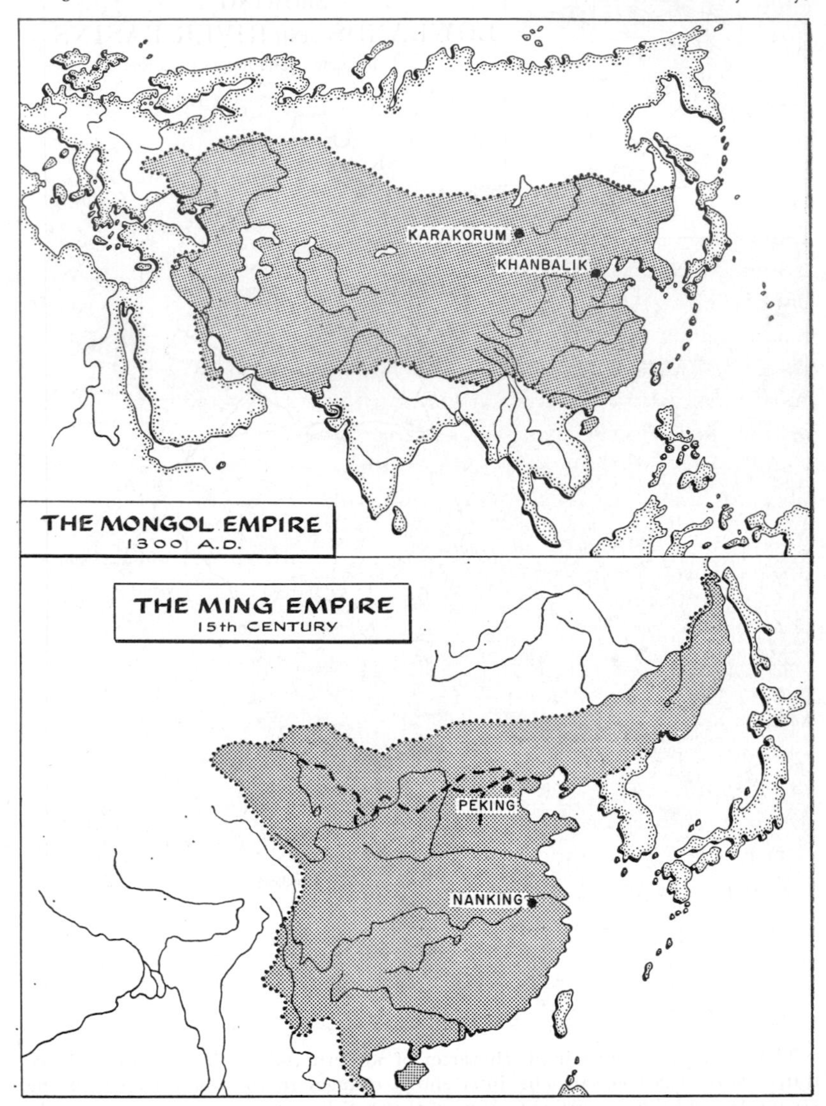

Adapted with permission from L. Carrington Goodrich, A Short History of the Chinese People, *New York, Harper & Bros., 1943.*

stretching across southwestern Manchuria and into China, was able to exact tribute from the Sung court. A second power, which eventually overcame the Khitans, was the Jurchen, which occupied the Amur country. Much later, in 1644, the Jurchens were to conquer China. A third threat to China came from a Tibetan people, the Tangut, who ruled a state in Kansu called Hsia, which had its capital at Ning-hsia. However, in the thirteenth century it was before Mongol power that Sung China was to fall. By the end of that century, the greater Mongol Empire extended from the eastern seaboard of China and as far north as the Amur in a continuous broad belt across the heart of Asia to the borders of Arabia and far into European Russia. The Mongols, in their advance upon China, controlled Mongolia by 1204, overran Korea in 1231, and made Khanbaliq (Peking) their eastern winter capital in 1260. Under Kublai Khan's generals, Yünnan was conquered in 1254, Annam was reduced to vassalage in 1258, and two unsuccessful expeditions were dispatched against Japan. China, indeed, had become merely a part of the world empire. It was the period when, as will be seen in later chapters, the world was shrinking: ideas as well as goods travelled the caravan routes from Peking to the Danube.

The Ming, 1368-1644, and the Ch'ing (Tsing), 1644-1912

With the fall of the Mongol power after a century of rule, China passed under the control of its last native Chinese dynasty, the Ming, which in mid-seventeenth century was overcome by another alien conquerer, the Manchus, who ruled until the establishment of the Republic in 1912. These last dynasties will be treated in greater detail in subsequent pages. Here it remains to set forth in limited detail some Chinese ideas on philosophy, religion, government, and life in general as they have developed out of China's long past.

The Ideas by Which Old China Lived

China's long history from the beginnings to the end of the Manchu dynasty in 1912 may be labelled conveniently as the age of Old China to distinguish it from Republican China, 1912-1949, or the later Communist China after 1949. These latter periods are as yet mere dots on the long course of Chinese history. To say therefore in any basic historical sense that an idea or philosophy or institution is "Chinese" means that it was born and nurtured as a part of Old China. Since this Old China, for all its seeming turbulence, was in the long view a remarkably stable and enduring society, some suggestion must be given as to why this was so. The answer lies mainly in the fact that the prevailing ideas by which the Chinese lived and regulated their conduct were exceedingly old and remained exceedingly constant in their appeal. What then were some of these ideas forming the common denominator, as it were, of China's political and social thought?

1. *The Meaning of Life*

The Chinese, in the first instance, have always been more concerned with the world of nature and of man than with realms of the supernatural. The church and the priesthood played a lesser role in China than in most great civilizations. This is not to say that there were no religious motivations in China. They were present, but they were expressed principally through ancestor worship. The pertinent point to note is that ancestor worship belonged to the single family group. It could not become an institutionalized national or international church. The idea of divinity was, of course, not absent. Sacred mountains and other forms of nature were worshipped, as was the supreme Chinese divinity, T'ien, or Heaven, but these forces remained abstract and were rarely personified. An important consequence was that the Chinese were remarkably free from religious intolerance or bigotry. When persecution occurred it was occasioned not by religious ideas as such, but by religious movements that sought to control the State. Finally, the Chinese were not enticed by proffered rewards in heaven or tormented by threats of everlasting punishment in hell. Such notions did not appear in China until introduced by Buddhism and other alien faiths. In a comparative sense, then, the Chinese were not a religious people.[7]

2. *The Social Philosophy*

If the Chinese were not greatly concerned about other-worldliness, they were very much preoccupied with this world; namely, with nature and with man, which they considered to be one great unity. As a part of this unity man was important, but he was not the su-

[7] A very adequate discussion of the subject is Derk Bodde, "Dominant Ideas," *China,* ed. by H. F. MacNair (Berkeley, 1946), 18-28.

preme triumph of creation which Western religious thought has often attempted to make of him. The idea was that if man was to be in harmony with the universal unity, he would adjust himself to the universe, that is, to nature. In contrast, the modern West has sought what it calls happiness in bending nature to the will of man.

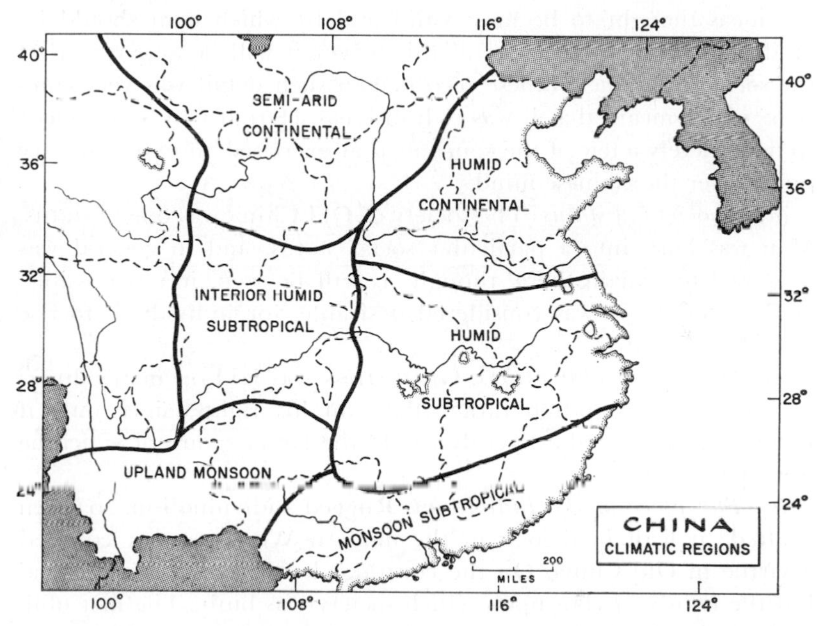

U. S. Department of State, Division of Map Intelligence and Cartography

Traditional Chinese ideas could not have approved an A-bomb, much less an H-bomb. Furthermore, within the universal unity of man and nature, man's problem was also to find and practice the means of getting along with his fellow men. Long before the Christian era began, Chinese thinkers were well aware that progress and growth of material power merely increased the tribulations of men unless they had first solved the riddle of human relations. This concern of the Chinese with the immediate troubles and pleasures of human existence to the relative exclusion of metaphysical speculation on the one hand, or of the development of logic on the other, is what is usually meant when the Chinese are described as a very "practical" people.

3. *Harmony and Stability*

Concerned, as they tended to be, with human problems here and now, the Chinese developed a temporal mindedness that laid great stress on man's experience. They thus became great compilers of history, from which it was believed man could learn how to behave here in the present. Naturally, these historical writings perpetrated the ideas thought to be most valid and by which man should be guided. In subsequent pages of this survey it will be apparent that the society that the Chinese recorded in such detail was very complex, which means that it was rich in ideas. Here it will be sufficient to note merely a few of the concepts that exercised an extraordinary power over the Chinese mind.

(*a*) *A society of status.* The society of Old China was one of status. Man was born into a particular social status, and in general was supposed to remain there, though, as will be seen, it was possible, and in some cases was considered desirable, for individuals to rise to higher stations.

(*b*) *Duties and obligations.* Great stress was laid on man's duties in his particular station rather than on his rights, since only if these were performed diligently would the larger group of which he was a part benefit.

(*c*) *The place of the individual.* Rugged individualism, so often exalted, at least in theory, in the modern West, was not counted a virtue in Old China. On the contrary, it was not the individual but the family or clan upon which society was built. The first obligations of an individual were not directed to himself or to his nation or to his government, but to his family or clan. He expressed these obligations by the worship of his ancestors, by caring for and obeying the family elders, and by breeding and rearing sons to perpetuate the family and its name. The family in turn was the individual's social security, protecting him from a world that was often hard and cold. It was this closely knit family or clan, perhaps more than any other institution, which preserved Chinese civilization in and through periods of political chaos. The primacy of the family in Chinese thought meant also that ideas such as nationalism and patriotism, so inseparable from modern Western thought, exercised little influence in Old China save in a non-political, cultural sense.

(*d*) *The nature of government.* In Old China there were clear and pronounced ideas on government and the emperor, but these ideas were quite different from the political philosophies of the modern West. The state in Old China was, in theory, one large family. The Chinese word for nation, *kuo chia,* means nation-family. The emperor was "the parent of the people." Government was therefore paternalistic. At the same time it was recognized that if the emperor were to exert the proper influence he must live himself by the highest moral standards and select ministers and officials of like character. Moreover, if inferiors were expected to obey, superiors were expected to rule with high moral regard for the rights of lesser men. Americans take great pride in their government *by law,* but Old China held that the best government was achieved through moral persuasion and example rather than through legal compulsion. Laws there were, but they were regarded as a secondary rather than a primary instrument of government. In other words, in Old China, it was believed that government should be *by men* rather than *by law.*

(*e*) *Moral foundations.* In the West, Christianity has emphasized man's depravity. One had to be born again. Old China, in contrast, proceeded from the happier assumption that man was by nature fundamentally good. In Chinese thought, sin never achieved the exalted status it has often enjoyed in some other civilizations. Old China held that the positive force was man's goodness, which could be cultivated by learning. As a result, stress was laid upon education. The good man, through learning, achieved wisdom and thus became a superior being.

The General Character of Old China

The foregoing sketch of some ideas that shaped the body and spirit of Old China make it quite clear that this traditional society was very unlike that of nineteenth-century Western Europe and America. These differences are hardly susceptible to easy generalization, but the following suggestions are to be noted. First, China, like most ancient empires, operated under a government that was centralized politically and decentralized economically. Second, in this empire most large-scale activity, whether political, economic, military, or religious, was controlled by a great and numerous official bureaucracy. Third, this bureaucratic state was dominantly agrarian, deriving its income from the agricultural production of an illiterate but often intelligent peasantry which, in addition to growing the food, provided the conscript labor for public works such as the Great Wall or Grand Canal, or the conscript armies for defence or conquest. Fourth, the bureaucracy of government officials who presided over the construction of public works, who administered the revenue, or who decided on war or peace came from the small literate element of the population who could conduct public affairs in the beautiful but difficult system of ideographic writing of the Chinese language. Since it required many years of education to master the written language and the great literature of the classics, it followed that only the sons of men of means could afford a classical education. So it was that the landed gentry reared educated sons (scholars), scholars became officials, officials ran the empire and invested their wealth, ill- or well-gotten as the case might be, in land. As a result, the ideal man of leadership in Old China was not a merchant, a trader, a general, or a priest, but rather a landlord-scholar-official. Fifth, the family or clan controlled the individual. The individual was subservient to the family, and society governed its conduct by ethics rather than by legal codes. The supremacy of law and the freedom of the individual under law never acquired the position they have enjoyed in the West.

SINITICISM: THE NATIVE RELIGION OF CHINA

The native religion of the Chinese people, which Hu Shih has called Siniticism, probably dates from pre-historic times and includes all such later phases of its development as Taoism, Confucianism as a state religion, and Moism. It was a product of the combined cultures of the Shang and the Chou periods. Among other things, it contributed to the Chinese mind a profound belief in ancestor worship, in divination, in the concept of *Shang-ti* (the Lord on High), or *Hao-t'ien* (August Heaven), and in the idea of retribution for good and evil. These ideas, which had satisfied the Chinese of the early Chou period, failed, however, to meet the needs of men when, in the later years of the dynasty, political disorder and human distress were widespread. Popular discontent was given eloquent expression in the famous *Book of Poetry,* the most widely read of all books in the sixth century B.C. The poets of ancient China were thus paving the way for the appearance in the next century (570 to 420 B.C.) of the founders of Chinese philosophy: Lao-tzŭ,[8] Confucius, and Mo Ti. These

[8] Contemporary scholarship, in particular the researches of Professor Homer H. Dubs, is inclined to consider Lao-tzŭ not as an older contemporary of Confucius, but as living in a much later period—that is, in the third or fourth century B.C.

men must therefore be studied in their relation to the decaying Sinitic religion and to the critical, skeptical atmosphere of their age. All three were revolutionary in their thinking. Applying the language of modern politics to ancient religion, Lao-tzŭ represented the extreme Left; Confucius, the Center, though leaning toward the Left; Mo Ti, the Right. Lao-tzŭ was a thorough heretic in religion and a revolutionary in philosophy. Confucius was a humanist and an agnostic. Mo Ti, devoutly religious, sought to preserve Siniticism by purifying it and infusing it with new life.

Taoist Philosophy and Religion

Taoism, one of the world's greatest pre-systematic bodies of thought, had its beginnings as a magnificent mystical philosophy which continued to influence the Chinese mind far into the twentieth century. In the course of time, Taoism also assumed a secondary form as a popular religion garbed in the trappings of superstition. As a philosophy, Taoism has appealed strongly to China's intellectuals; as a religion, rapidly losing its appeal in the twentieth century, it has played an immense role in the lives of the credulous masses.

Of the traditional founder of these two great systems, the sage Lao-tzŭ (venerable viscount), nothing is known with any certainty. Indeed, his very existence is doubted by some scholars. But the teachings ascribed to him have affected China profoundly. His philosophy resented the notion that God is a personal being, and sought to replace it by the idea of *Tao* (the Way or Road or Process). To Lao-tzŭ the *Tao* was a natural process, something "being so of itself"; thus, there was no need to construct any divine plan or purpose: "the *Tao* always does nothing; and yet it achieves everything." This was a quietistic philosophy, which, if applied, would affect every phase of society. In politics, the best government was the least government. Literature, knowledge, civilization were undesirable, for "when the world knows beauty to be beauty, there is ugliness; when it knows goodness to be good, there is evil."

Taoism by its very nature was the antithesis of and the great opponent of Confucianism (see below). The attack of Taoism was directed against moral idealism and political realism. "Heaven and Earth [the great gods of Old China] are not humane," said Lao-tzŭ. The universe was neither kindly nor righteous, but went its way, ignoring human desires or human standards of conduct. Thus, efforts to reform morals or to right wrongs were a waste of time, since these efforts were an attempt to control the universe. Since the universe was not moral, there was no point to man's cultivation of virtue. Moral ideals were a mistake, since the notion of goodness promptly aroused a corresponding notion of evil. The way to avoid

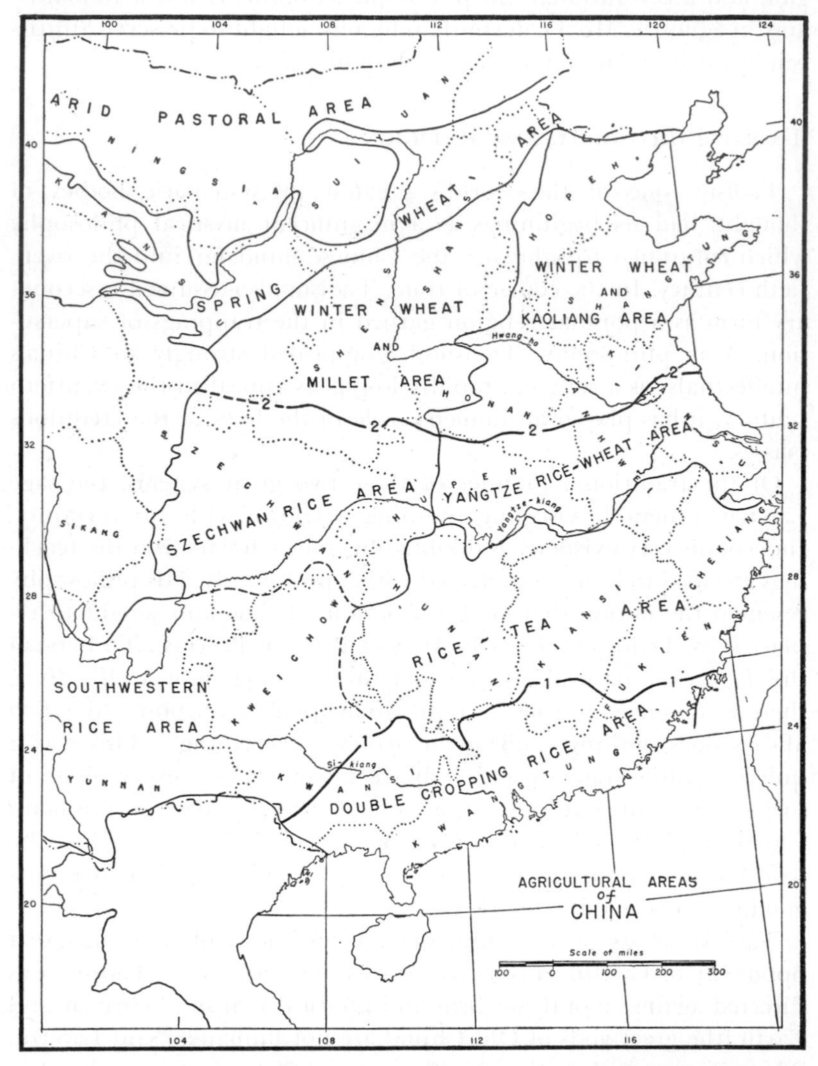

U. S. Department of State, Division of Map Intelligence and Cartography

evil was not to stress good, but to reach beyond both good and evil to the pure essence of the universe, the Way or Tao. The answer then was to be found in effortlessness, in non-action. "The sage," said Lao-tzŭ, "relies on actionless activity and carries on wordless teaching."[9]

Posterity has dealt with Lao-tzŭ much as it has dealt with other great teachers. Although he probably did not consider himself a religious leader, he was credited by later generations with founding a religion. Early chroniclers affirmed that he was born of a virgin. The wisdom ascribed to him and preserved by his followers was published, probably with much padding, in the second century B.C., in a work called the *Tao-Te-Ching*. Many of the virtues which Lao-tzŭ extolled, such as patience, humility, calmness, and deliberation, appealed to thoughtful men, but his quietistic doctrines, reminiscent of some forms of Hindu philosophy, were beyond the understanding of the masses. Hence, out of Lao-tzŭ's "natural way," succeeding generations of priests built the religion of Taoism, a thing miraculous and supernatural. In time Taoism became "the most elaborate and complicated system of magic, myths, spells, charms, incantations, demonology, and all similar forms of superstitious practice that any society has developed."[10] Taoism's control of the world of spirits gave it a foremost place in the scheme of ancestor worship. Man's every act was affected by spirits, either friendly or hostile. Herein lay the power of the Taoist priest to determine the appropriate time for building a house, for celebrating a wedding, or for burying a corpse. Here, too, the practical, matter-of-fact Chinese mind found relief in a world of the unreal: the world of nature, of romance, and of spirits —a world of mysteries. The secret healing power of herbs, the reviving virtues of aphrodisiacs, the wonders of astrology and alchemy— all these and many more were the stock in trade of the Taoist priest. Taoism was superstition, but it was also poetry.

Confucianism: The Traditional Philosophy

The history of China without Confucius would be like the history of America without Washington and Jefferson. China, of course, has not always been dominated by the lives of those who professed to be Confucians. Yet Confucianism has affected China more profoundly

[9] See Homer H. Dubs, "Taoism," in *China*, ed. by H. F. MacNair (Berkeley, 1946), 266-289.

[10] Paul Monroe, *China: A Nation in Evolution* (New York, 1928), 102.

and continuously than any other philosophy. It gave to China a remarkable humanistic philosophy, a recognition that the true bases of society are social and mundane as well as divine.

Confucius (K'ung-fu-tzu, 551-479 B.C.) was not merely an academic theorist. He was also a practical statesman, who, however, spent most of his life moving about the country engaged in teaching. Most of his students were young men of the upper classes for whom politics was the only honorable profession. Confucius presented to them a code of high moral ideas of such force that it became the dominant philosophy of official China and, until 1911, remained as authoritative as the Bible was, until a century ago, in Western thought. In fact, Confucianism was so much a part of the Chinese character that it was in a sense taken for granted. "The Chinese," to quote the American Sinologue, Homer H. Dubs, "said little about it, just as Burke rarely quotes the Bible. Yet this [Confucian] tradition was in the background of every educated person's mind, since every candidate for official position concentrated on it for years, memorized longer accounts of the Confucian classics than our ancestors memorized from the Bible, and, what is more important, became expert in applying it."

The Bible of Confucianism, the Confucian classics, consists of the Four Books and the Five Canons. The Four Books include: (1) the *Analects,* or dialogues of Confucius with his disciples; (2) the *Book of Mencius,* containing the sayings of this sage; (3) the *Great Learning,* an outline of Confucian ethics; and (4) the *Doctrine of the Mean,* a similar treatise. The Five Canons contain: (1) the *Book of Changes,* an elaborate book of divination with a philosophical interpretation of the sixty-four hexagrams; (2) the *Book of History,* a fragmentary history covering the period 2400-619 B.C.; (3) the *Book of Poetry,* a collection of more than three hundred poems of the Chou period; (4) the *Book of Rites,* dealing with ceremonial procedure; and (5) the *Spring and Autumn Annals,* a history of the state of Lu. To these basic works must be added the voluminous commentaries, comprising thousands of volumes, produced through the tireless industry of Confucian scholars both ancient and modern.

The classics and the commentaries provided a minutely detailed plan for human conduct. It was not sufficient to describe how Confucius spoke or acted. Details were provided as to his posture when in bed and the length of his night shirt. All life, in a word, was measured by the Confucian code. Thus it was possible for a wise man to be master of himself at all times and in all circumstances. No detail was considered too small to merit regulation.

Since Confucius was a humanist, his philosophy, broadly considered, was a code of conduct by which man might govern himself in his relations with his fellow men. These relations included five that were considered of prime importance: the relation of prince and minister, of parent and child, of husband and wife, of elder and younger brother, and of friend and friend. Five constant virtues were stressed: benevolence, righteousness, propriety, wisdom, and fidelity. The application of these virtues to human relations would, in the Confucian view of things, achieve the true end of life. Life would be simple, the family happy; and social relations harmonious. Confucianism expressed the practical, matter-of-fact, mundane tendencies in the Chinese character. Thus Confucianism was not a supernatural religion. To the Confucianist, the idea that men "live in order to die, as taught by Christianity, is incomprehensible." When his disciples asked concerning the gods, Confucius replied that he knew little about them. He appears to have been mildly skeptical of the supernatural, on the theory that if man could not understand life, it was unreasonable to suppose that he could understand death. Yet Confucianism included and inculcated the state religion and the sacrifices to the gods, although in Hsün-tzu it denied the existence of all gods. Confucius attended these and taught them. But the common accompaniments of supernatural religion were left to the state and the people, whereas Confucianism attended to mundane matters. There was a state priestcraft, but no Confucian priestcraft. The concept of a future life was vague; it was not non-existent. Matters such as apostolic succession, miracles, sacraments, and the future life were left for other cults to manage as they would. Without the promise of rewards or punishment from the unknown spiritual world, Confucianism directed man in his duty both to his family and to society as a whole.

Buddhism

Buddhism was introduced to China about the beginning of the Christian Era.[11] Gautama, the traditional founder, is said to have been born in northern India on the border of Nepal about 563 B.C.

[11] The term "Buddha" is not a proper name but a title meaning "The Enlightened One."

Despite his noble birth he became dissatisfied with the transient character of worldly things, renounced the world, and began his wanderings in search of truth. His problem was the perplexing one of achieving release from the burden of constant trouble that beset human life, and of achieving the spiritual training necessary to that end. Whether Gautama regarded himself as the founder of a religion or merely as a teacher of ethics need not be argued here. The fact of importance is that from his central theme, the moral life with its virtues of love, wisdom, and the suppression of desire, his followers did erect a religion whose influence has been of the greatest significance. Centuries after Gautama's death his followers divided, and it was the northern as distinct from the southern Buddhist movement that spread its influence to Nepal, Tibet, Mongolia, Cochin China, China, Korea, and Japan. The most influential sect in this northern school of Buddhism developed the idea of the Western Paradise (Heaven), a concept that was lacking in Gautama's original teaching. Buddhism thus concerns itself deeply with man's after-life, whereas Confucianism is interested primarily in the earthly life. One would look in vain in Confucian writings for any mention of, or emphasis upon, this life as a probation for winning heavenly rewards.

China in many ways might have appeared an unpromising field for Buddhism. The emphasis on introspection and the inner life did not seem to harmonize with the practical philosophy of the Confucian mind. Buddhism in its exhortations to the celibate life could, it would seem, have little appeal in a land of ancestor worship.[12] Yet Buddhism was widely accepted in China and for some eight centuries was dominant in Chinese thought. This is explained by the fact that during the years of its introduction the leading intellectuals of China were already deeply immersed in the closely related speculations of Lao-tzŭ, while among the common people popular Taoism was widely practiced. Buddhism appealed therefore both to the learned and to the illiterate. Its elaborate ritual made a natural appeal to the masses. As a religion it was more dignified and comprehensive than Taoism, while as a philosophy it possessed the spiritual warmth so lacking in the Confucian ethical code of conduct. Here lay the explanation of a China "dazzled, baffled, and conquered" by an alien faith. Indeed both Buddhism and Taoism became popular because Confucianism seemed to have failed, in that it did not pre-

[12] Buddhism adjusted itself to ancestor veneration. Who could tell better than the Buddhist priest what became of the spirits of deceased ancestors?

vent the downfall of the deeply Confucian Han dynasty. Hence Chinese leaders experimented for a period of centuries with various philosophies.

Buddhism, however, brought more to China than the spiritual satisfactions of religion. Indian science and art came too. Chinese astronomy was enriched; the written language became less rigid through the adoption of foreign terms; Chinese sculpture and painting took on new and deeper forms; block printing was used in the making of Buddhist and other books. These were permanent contributions to China's culture. In time, Buddhism as a religion tended to give place to the rising influence of Neo-Confucianism; yet much of the nobility of Buddhist thought and spirit remained.

The Gentry and the People

The foregoing dominant ideas marking some principal lines of thought in Old or traditional China were not shared with equal consciousness by all Chinese. The society in which these ideas held sway was composed of two major groups: (1) the gentry, and (2) the people in general. There were major distinctions of great importance between these two groups.

The gentry were the dominant or ruling class of Old China. Members of this group were distinguished from their fellows by many factors. They derived their income from land which they themselves did not cultivate, or from government office, or from academic, intellectual pursuits, and in more recent times from banking, industry, and commerce. Within the gentry class were the intellectuals, since in the main only the sons of gentry could afford an education and thus pass the civil service examinations which provided the principal avenue to government office. Through their control of land the gentry controlled the economy, and through their monopoly of learning they shaped the patterns of intellectual life.

Among the non-gentry, the largest and most significant group, forming indeed the great mass of the people, was the peasantry. In an overwhelmingly agricultural society, they were the cultivators of the land, some as farmers who owned and cultivated their land, others as tenants, and still others as non-landowning laborers. Even as late as the mid-twentieth century something like 80 per cent of China's population belonged to the peasantry. The remainder of the non-gentry elements of the population included handicraftsmen, small merchants, servants, soldiers, priests, actors, and, in more recent times, factory workers.

It is rather important to note here that the traditional China that Western students of history come to know first, the China of the great philosophers such as Confucius, of the great dynasties and systems of government, the China of literature and art, was in a major degree the China of the gentry. Historical writing has often left the impression that the picture of China's gentry was also a picture of the Chinese as a whole, an implication open to some question. This seeming misrepresentation can be understood, however, when it is recognized that the institutionalized patterns of gentry thought and behavior were regarded by all Chinese society as the ideal patterns even if for the most part they were unattainable save by the favored few. Dynasties might rise or fall and conquerors come and go, yet from the third century B.C. until the nineteenth century the indigenous and maturing gentry patterns remained the ideal patterns for all Chinese. In this sense the history of China's gentry, so inseparable from the political, economic, intellectual, and artistic growth of culture, was the history of China.[13]

Non-Development of Science in Traditional China

Finally, it should be noted that one of the striking contrasts between modern Western civilization and the civilization of traditional China was that the former produced what is called modern science while the latter did not. Chinese discoveries in empirical science were of course very extensive. These included findings in astronomy,

[13] Marion J. Levy, Jr., *The Family Revolution in Modern China* (Cambridge, 1949), 42-48. The basic study of the gentry is Chang Chung-li, *The Chinese Gentry* (Seattle, 1955). In contrast to earlier and narrower definitions, the gentry should be described as a privileged group which dominated Chinese society. Its functions covered a wide range of social control, from ideological leadership to the practical management of political, social, and economic affairs. Whether considered as members of a social group or serving as officials of the State, the gentry derived their authority from their educational qualifications as shown in the degrees held. The power of the gentry was not wholly dependent on landowning. The gentry and landlord classes overlapped but did not coincide. A member of the gentry was not necessarily a landlord, nor was a landlord necessarily a member of the gentry. The use of the term gentry as applied to China should not be colored by the meaning of the term as applied to the English gentry. In contrast to the English, the Chinese gentry was not hereditary, nor was the Chinese gentry linked functionally to its land in the manner of the English squires. See the Introduction by Franz Michael, xiii-xxi.

biology, geology, archeology, mathematics, and geography to mention only a few of the major areas. More specifically, the Chinese knew how to compute celestial distances. They had classified more than one hundred plant species before 500 A.D. Cast iron was produced in Western Chou 1500 years in advance of the West. The Chinese knew of the magnetic north in Shang times and had a magnetized needle to indicate direction as early as Chou. A Chinese map of the third century A.D. was almost as accurate as Ptolemy's. The Chinese were probably the inventors of glass (Chou period). They also invented gunpowder (T'ang), made the first bomb (1161), and probably the first cannon about 1250. They were the first to produce paper (50 A.D.), porcelain, and printing (600 A.D.). They produced moveable type in the twelfth century.

Many other items could be added to this impressive list. The notable fact is that these findings were in a sense accidental. Lacking is any suggestion of a body of scientific law, any organized investigation of the physical universe, any over-all interpretation of mass observation, any applied techniques. "Experience and reflection were accumulated without any apparent attempt to tie them all up together, except with a preconceived and semi-mystical cosmology. China had no science because her pragmatic humanism prevented the development of the theoretical analysis essential to an understanding of the physical universe."[14]

For Further Reading

With some exceptions, books and documents cited in the footnotes of the respective chapters are not included in these lists for further reading.

CHINESE HISTORY AND CULTURE—GENERAL

Carter, Thomas, *The Invention of Printing in China and Its Spread Westward* (rev. ed., New York, 1955).

Creel, H. G., *Chinese Thought from Confucius to Mao Tsê-tung* (Chicago, 1953). A good popularization.

Eberhard, Wolfram, *A History of China,* trans. by E. W. Dickes (Berkeley, 1950). Stresses social institutions.

Grousset, René, *The Rise and Splendour of the Chinese Empire* (London, 1952). A concise cultural history.

[14] Rhoads Murphey, "The Non-Development of Science in Traditional China," *Papers on China,* Regional Studies Seminar, Harvard University, 1947, mimeographed.

Hummel, Arthur W., ed., *Eminent Chinese of the Ch'ing Period (1644-1912)* (2 vols., Washington, 1943, 1944). A history of the Ch'ing period as revealed in biographies of its leading men.

Reischauer, Edwin O., *Ennin's Travels in T'ang China* (New York, 1955). A picture of early China as seen through the eyes of a ninth century traveller.

Williams, S. Wells, *The Middle Kingdom* (rev. ed., 2 vols., New York, 1899). If an American fifty years ago had read anything on China, it was probably this book.

CHINESE PHILOSOPHY AND RELIGION

Bell, (Sir) Charles A., *The Religion of Tibet* (Oxford, 1931). Based on Tibetan as well as English sources.

Chan Wing-tsit, "The Story of Chinese Philosophy," in *Philosophy: East and West,* ed. by Charles A. Moore (Princeton, 1944).

Conze, Edward, *Buddhism: Its Essence and Development* (New York, 1951). An interpretative survey of the entire range of Buddhist thought intended for the general student.

Fêng Yu-lan, *A History of Chinese Philosophy,* trans. by Derk Bodde (2 vols., Princeton, 1952, 1953).

Hughes, E. R., and K. Hughes, *Religion in China* (New York, 1950).

Needham, Joseph, *Science and Civilization in China* (Cambridge, Eng., vol. I, 1954; vol. II, 1956).

Weber, Max, *The Religion of China,* trans. by Hans H. Gerth (Glencoe, Illinois, 1951). Essay on Confucianism and Taoism.

Wright, Arthur F., ed., *Studies in Chinese Thought* (Chicago, 1953). A symposium.

ECONOMIC AND SOCIAL ORGANIZATION

Ayscough, Florence, *Chinese Women, Yesterday and Today* (Boston, 1937).

Chang Chung-li, *The Chinese Gentry: Studies on Their Role in Nineteenth-Century Chinese Society* (Seattle, 1955).

Fêng Han-chi, *The Chinese Kinship System* (Cambridge, 1948).

Fried, Morton H., *Fabric of Chinese Society: A Study of the Social Life of a Chinese County Seat* (New York, 1953). A detailed description of Chinese community life.

Gamble, Sidney D., *Ting Hsien, A North China Rural Community* (New York, 1954).

Kirby, E. Stuart, *Introduction to the Economic History of China* (London, 1954).

Lang, Olga, *Chinese Family and Society* (New Haven, 1946).

Lee Chou-ying, *The System of Chinese Public Finance* (London, 1936).

Lin Wei-ying, *The New Monetary System of China* (Chicago, 1936).

Lin Yu-t'ang, *My Country and My People* (rev. ed., New York, 1939). Popular, readable, and sometimes misleading.

Morse, H. B., *The Gilds of China* (2nd ed., Shanghai, 1932). A scholarly study.

Sung Lien, *Economic Structure of the Yüan Dynasty; trans. of chapters 93 and 94 of the Yüan shih, by Herbert Franz Schurmann.* (Cambridge, 1956).

Tamagna, Frank M., *Banking and Finance in China* (New York, 1942).

Yang Lien-shêng, *Money and Credit in China* (Cambridge, 1952).

Yang, Martin C., *A Chinese Village: Taitou, Shantung Province* (New York, 1945).

LITERATURE

Giles, H. A., *A History of Chinese Literature* (New York, 1901).

Hightower, James Robert, *Topics in Chinese Literature* (Cambridge, 1950). An excellent survey with an annotated bibliography of all important translations in Western languages.

Kao, George, ed., *Chinese Wit and Humor* (New York, 1946).

Yohannan, John D., ed., A *Treasury of Asian Literature* (New York, 1957).

ART AND ARCHITECTURE

Fenollosa, Ernest Francisco, *Epochs of Chinese and Japanese Art, an Outline History of East Asiatic Design* (new and rev. ed., 2 vols., New York, 1921). Important for interpretation of art as related to social conditions.

3

Ideas on Government in Old China

THROUGHOUT their long history the Chinese have given a great deal of thought to the subject of government. They have had much to say about what government should be, what it should do, what ideas and ideals should guide it, and so forth. The Chinese were not always in agreement on these matters but they developed nevertheless a pattern of political principles and conduct which may be described in broad general terms. It is important that this be done at the outset, since there can be no grasping of the impact of the West upon China in the nineteenth and twentieth centuries without some basic knowledge of what kind of political society the West was called upon to meet in China.

The principal body of political thought that guided both the rulers and the ruled in China for some two thousand years prior to the beginning of the twentieth century was Confucian. Two thousand years is a long time for any system to survive. What gave the Confucian political habit and tradition this power of survival? How shall its collapse in the twentieth century be explained? These are large questions and the historical answers to them are exceedingly complex. What will be said about Chinese political thought and practice in this chapter should be considered as the foundation on which the answers rest.

As a point of departure, it is well to note that from the earliest times Chinese philosophy was concerned with ethics and politics. Confucius, the most famous of all Chinese political scientists, was a statesman as well as a teacher. In addition, politics in Old China was regarded as the most desirable profession for a young man of "good" family. Moreover, the ruling class—that is, the politicians—was the educated class. Education, in turn, meant mastery not only of the Confucian classics but also of the voluminous commentaries on them made by later scholars. Political problems were discussed, debated, and solved in terms of these classics and commentaries. An apt quotation from the classics could clinch a political argument. Scholarship was thus the key to passing the civil service examinations; these latter were the principal avenue to government office; and government office meant honor and perhaps wealth.

Early Schools of Political Thought

Although, as indicated, Confucianism as a body of political thought has had far greater influence in China than any other political philosophy or system, it has not been without rivals. It had its beginning far back in the pre-Christian era along with other schools of thought.[1] Fortunately perhaps for the Confucians, it was largely their philosophical works alone that survived the burning of the books by Ch'in Shih Huang Ti (246-211 B.C.). The relationship among the early schools of thought is not clear, save that no one of them was able to dominate the others. There were, for example, the *Yin-Yang* (Negative-Positive) School and the School of Names (the Logicians) whose followers, though not averse to politics, have left little evidence of a well-considered theory of political action. Other schools have been more generous in appraising posterity of their political views. The *Tao* School, or Taoists, followers of Lao-tzŭ and of the teaching of Chuang Chou (fourth century B.C.), remain among the great living monuments of Chinese thought. Lao-tzŭ denied the necessity or the wisdom of a society built on elaborate laws and institutions. He would neither approve of nor be happy in society of the twentieth century, either in its democratic or its totalitarian forms. He would doubtless attribute the world's troubles to its departure from his *tao* (way), which, in the philosophical sense, is the effortless union of man and nature.[2]

---

1 Ch'ien Tuan-shêng, *The Government and Politics of China* (Cambridge, Mass., 1950). The most recent and satisfactory study of Confucius is H. G. Creel, *Confucius: the Man and the Myth* (New York, 1949). A popular, brief survey of Chinese thought is Wang Gung-hsing, *The Chinese Mind* (New York, 1946).

2 The recommended translation of Lao-tzŭ's *Tao-te ching* is Arthur Waley, trans., *The Way and Its Power* (London, 1934).

Chuang Chou went even further on the path of negativism. The best government was the least government and thus the essence of simplicity. Men should avoid distinctions between good and bad, high and low, the beautiful and the ugly, since these in turn lead to moralizing and therefore put an end to simplicity.[3]

A contrasting body of thought was advocated by the School of Law or the Legalists, represented by men of action such as Li Li (fifth century B.C.), Shang Yang (fourth century B.C.), and especially Han Fei (third century B.C.). These men were code-makers, insistent upon a uniform body of laws and upon the theory of reward and punishment as the controller of human action.[4]

Again, there was in early China the Mo School, followers of Mo Ti (fifth century B.C.), who sought the interest of the people, opposed war as injurious to all, and wished the sovereign, aided by the ablest men, to reflect the will of the people and in turn to be obeyed by them. Mo Ti extolled a doctrine of mutual love and something of the democratic spirit, though not the democratic theory or the political machinery, of the democratic state.[5]

The Philosophers, or Confucians

Existing alongside these various schools that prescribed what government ought or ought not to be was the *Ju* School (the Philosophers), the followers of Confucius. So it may be said that Confucianism was not formed in a political vacuum but rather in close relationship with other competing ideas. It is not wholly surprising, then, to discover that Confucian teachings are exceedingly rich in that they have drawn upon practically all other teachings of early times. Confucius himself was a person who was widely travelled and had almost unlimited contacts with men in all conditions. In conse-

[3] The ablest brief exposition of the Taoists is by Homer H. Dubs, "Taoism," in H. F. MacNair, ed., *China* (Berkeley, 1946), 266-289. Translations from the work of Chuang-Tzu called the *Chuang Tzu* are found in H. A. Giles, *Chuang Tzu, Mystic, Moralist, and Social Reformer* (2nd ed., London, 1926), and in Fung Yu-lan, trans., *Chuang-Tzu* (Shanghai, 1932).

[4] See J. J. L. Duyvendak, trans., *The Book of Lord Shang: A Classic of the Chinese School of Law* (London, 1928), which is a translation of Shang Yang's work, the *Shang-tzu*. Han Fei, the *Han Fei-Tzu* is found in Liao Wen Kuei, trans., *The Complete Works of Han Fei Tzu: A Classic of Chinese Legalism* (London, 1939).

[5] See Mei Yi-pao, trans., *The Ethical and Political Works of Motse* (London, 1929), and Mei Yi-pao, *Motse, The Neglected Rival of Confucius* (London, 1934).

quence, what emerged on the death of Confucius was not one but some eight schools of Confucianism, among which could be found doctrines almost as unlike as those of the Taoists on the one hand and the Legalists on the other. Yet through all the eight divergent Confucian schools there was a common factor of humanism—"Man lives with and for other Men."

All the principles and values of Confucianism may be attributed to this theory of the position of man among men. These Confucian ideas are concerned with what the Confucians called *Rites, Virtue, Names,* and the *Five Relationships.* Rites were the standards of sane, social living. To live by them was to practice *jen,* the greatest Virtue. Moreover, life was a matter of status (political, social, economic, or intellectual), which was indicated by a name, since things must be known by what they are if there is not to be confusion. Only when persons are designated properly may responsibility be located, honors and punishments bestowed with confidence. From this marking of status come also the Five Relationships with their obligations and privileges already referred to in Chapter 2. Nevertheless, important as status and the Five Relationships were, it is to be noted that there was very little permanent stratification of social groups in Chinese society. A man could rise from humble birth to the Confucian "aristocracy of virtue" and find an illustrious place among scholars. On the other hand, he might lose virtue and fall.

Just as the foregoing humanistic concepts provided rules of conduct for private individuals, so they also provided a Bible for statesmen on the assumption that "orderly political life must come from orderly private lives." The Confucian philosophy stressed the reciprocal nature of duties and obligations between the ruler and the ruled, and the primary duty of the ruler to give good government to the people. To do this, the ruler himself had to set a high moral standard and select with care the officials who served under him. The Confucian scholar became important because only he, by his knowledge of the rules of right conduct, could advise properly the "Son of Heaven" in his traditional duties of maintaining universal harmony between man and nature.

In the Analects, Confucius said, "When a prince's personal conduct is correct, his government is effective without the issuing of orders. If his personal conduct is not correct, he may issue orders but they will not be followed." Right conduct gave the ruler his power.

On this basis the Confucian scholars established themselves as an essential part of the government. Since the Rites tended to be "what was" rather than "what ought to be" (Confucius himself being a realist), the whole body of Confucian political thought tended to be conservative, stressed legitimacy, avoided the revolutionary, and found in monarchy a convenient instrument to promote a stable society.

The business of making over, so to speak, the early and fluid Confucian philosophy into an effective, applicable body of political dogma was largely the work of Former Han times (202 B.C. to A.D. 9), when the first great Chinese empire was consolidated. It was at this time also that a civil service examination system began to take shape whereby political office was virtually closed to all but Confucian scholars or at least to those who professed to be Confucian.[6]

During the first ten centuries of the Christian era, Confucianism, somewhat discredited by the fall of the eminently Confucian Han dynasty, encountered political rivals in Buddhism and Taoism. Nevertheless, by Sung times the challenge was met in the rise of Neo-Confucianism (the *Li* school of Sung and Ming times). Finally, under the Manchu dynasty the leading Confucian school was known as the Classicists. These modern schools endowed Confucianism with a spirit of inertia and traditionalism in political thought, and thus the doctrine of absolute monarchy tempered by mildness persisted—the stereotyped ideal of the literati, the men who ruled China.[7]

Confucian Political Precepts

Since Chinese government has been affected more by Confucianism than by any other philosophy, it is worthwhile to inquire into the nature of its more important political precepts. These precepts came to be so deeply rooted as to be taken for granted by the ruling bureaucracy.

Among the first precepts was that of unity, both social and political. To Western students familiar with the chaotic and amorphous China of the early twentieth century, it may be surprising to find that Confucius taught: "As Heaven has not two suns, so the people should not have two kings." This was a doctrine frequently invoked when the state was threatened with political division.

---

6 See Têng Ssŭ-yü, "China's Examination System and the West," in H. F. MacNair, ed., *China*, 441-451.

7 See Ch'ien Tuan-Shêng, *The Government and Politics of China*, 27-28.

Closely allied with this concept of political unity was the doctrine of Heaven's Mandate, which appears to have been taught by Confucius, but more particularly by his disciple Mencius. This doctrine taught that the supreme earthly ruler, the emperor, was elevated to his position through the favor of Heaven. The emperor was therefore the Son of Heaven, and by Heaven's Mandate maintained his rule. But Heaven did not lose control of its mandate. When an incapable or wicked ruler ascended the throne, Heaven withdrew the mandate and bestowed it on some righteous noble. It then became the duty of this noble to rebel, to overthrow the emperor, and to ascend the throne himself. In expounding this doctrine, Confucius was really idealizing the method by which dynasties in China were said to have been overthrown.

A number of important implications followed very naturally from this convenient doctrine of the Mandate of Heaven. It could be a justification for rebellion—a very significant point to the practical Chinese mind. It was also a justification for conquest, once the conquest has been achieved successfully. It could sanction submission on the part of a conquered people to the conqueror, since the latter undoubtedly held the Mandate of Heaven.

However, the conqueror might also be resisted, for Mencius, one of the greatest of Confucian adherents, taught that Heaven sees as the people see and hears as the people hear. Therefore a conqueror who did not improve the lot of the people might be resisted. In modern times China has twice applied these political principles. She accepted the rule of the Mongols (1280-1368) and of the Manchus (1644-1912) so long as these foreigners conferred substantial benefits upon her. She overthrew their rule once they had lost the Mandate of Heaven.

The principle of political loyalty was also affected by the doctrine of Heaven's Mandate. Although loyalty in the Confucian code was honored frequently to an extreme degree, it was not an absolute virtue. When the ruler had lost the Mandate of Heaven, it was the duty of the subject to be disloyal. The Western concept of the divine right of kings, demanding absolute loyalty to the throne, did not exist in the Confucian scheme of things. On the contrary, Confucianism called upon the people to pass judgment on their sovereign. Hsün-tzu, one of the great Confucian teachers of the third century B.C., said: "The people are the water and the prince is the boat; the water can support the boat, but it can also sink it."

Again, the doctrine of Heaven's Mandate justified only a very limited use of force by a conqueror, for a conquest was not achieved by fighting but only by securing the favor of Heaven. Hence force was only to subdue recalcitrants against the Will of Heaven. As a result, Chinese, generally speaking, have been pacifists. Mencius taught that there were no righteous wars, although some wars might be better than others. Lao-tzŭ and Mo Ti likewise condemned war. Virtue was more likely to impress Heaven than brute force. Consequently, Confucianism justified military expeditions only when they could be interpreted as designed to restore order and preserve peace in a neighboring state. The record of Chinese history, to be sure, may appear as a contradiction of all this theorizing about peace, for actually the Chinese have warred as generously as other peoples; but their wars of conquest were conducted mostly by rulers who were not Confucians.[8] The Confucian theory alone does not of course explain why the Chinese have in general avoided wars of conquest. Economic considerations have also played an important part. But it does appear that, had there been no Confucian pacificism, China would have warred upon its neighbors to a much greater extent than it has. In general, Old China preferred to let her neighbors alone, provided the neighbors did not meddle in Chinese affairs.

The Political Institutions of Confucian China

1. *The Monarchy*

The political institution of supreme importance in Old China was the monarchy, which operated on the theory of the emperor's unlimited power. In the case of most sovereigns the actual exercise of power could be and often was limited in various ways, but the theory of absolutism remained strong. As a result, in the course of time absolutism was pretty well taken for granted, sterility in political discussion was encouraged, and eventually there was developed the idea that good government is government by men, since under unlimited power there could be no rule of law. Thus, absolutism, the inevitable, was made more palatable by the process of making it humane, on the assumption that man as a ruler could and should be humane whereas an inflexible law could not. In practice, of course,

[8] However, the whole question of Chinese pacificism is a touchy one and cannot be disposed of easily. Most of China's dynasties were set up by brute force, as, for a recent example, the Communist conquest of 1949.

the imperial power was exercised not by the emperor himself but by various ambitious groups: kinsmen, eunuchs, generals, or powerful families.

Under the Manchu dynasty (1644-1912) the emperor was accountable for famine, flood, or pestilence because such things were believed to be a consequence of his misrule. As the father of the nation, he was clothed in theory with autocratic, absolute powers; yet these powers were not to be exercised in an arbitrary manner, but in conformity with customary practices established through the ages. The succession passed in the male line to whichever son an emperor might choose; the offspring of concubines were not excluded. When there was no direct heir, the succession passed to a lateral branch of the family of a younger generation. The new emperor was thus adopted as the son of his predecessor and performed the ancestral rites to the spirits of the departed sovereigns.

The authority of the Manchu emperor was not confined within definitive politico-geographic boundaries as was the case with European sovereigns. The territory over which he exercised direct rule included eighteen provinces, known as China Proper, and four great dependencies: Mongolia, Manchuria (which enjoyed a privileged status because it was the homeland of the dynasty), Tibet (after 1700), and Sinkiang (after 1789). Beyond these dependencies lay the tributary states, varying in number from time to time and recognizing, according to Confucian political ideas, the overlordship of the Middle Kingdom. Payment of tribute was one tangible evidence of inferior status (it was repaid by imperial gifts), and its bearers had come, in the course of Chinese history, from such distant lands as Arabia, Malabar, Ceylon, and eastern India, as well as from the adjacent kingdoms of Indochina, Ryukyu, Sulu, and Korea. The theory and practice in these "foreign" relations will be treated in detail in Chapter 6.

As legislator and administrator, this autocratic Manchu emperor was bound by powerful controls: custom—the unwritten constitution of the Empire—and precedent as defined in the edicts of his predecessors. He was influenced and not infrequently controlled by the opinions of his ministers and by those of his personal attendants within the palace. Under the guidance of these latter, he selected his empress from a group of daughters of Manchu nobles. Secondary consorts might be chosen from the same group. Finally, he might favor himself with an unlimited number of concubines from the families of Manchu nobles and freemen.

The nobility consisted of the imperial clansmen who traced their descent directly to the founder of the dynasty; the hereditary nobility who were direct descendants of the eight princes who co-operated in the conquest of China; and finally, a number of Chinese families, such as the household of the Duke of Yen, a descendant of Confucius.

Usually the function of the metropolitan administration at Peking was negative rather than positive: to check rather than to direct the actions of the provincial officials. In the middle of the nineteenth century, however, increasing contacts with Western states forced the central government, though reluctantly, to assume a more positive responsibility.

2. *Ministers and Departments*

The ministers of state, the immediate official servants of the emperor, varied in title, number, and power. Their ultimate function was to preserve the sovereign's power. Actually, they usurped for themselves whatever powers they could. The net product was the binding of public life to Confucianism. Scholarship led to the civil service examinations. Those who passed the examinations were Confucian scholars. These successful candidates might be appointed to political office. Thus, in normal times, Confucianism alone opened the door to political power.

3. *The Censors*

Among the more interesting political institutions of Old China was the Court of Censors. Originally there were two classifications of censors: (a) those whose function it was to impeach erring officials, and (b) those who might protest against acts of the Court and propose remedies. In general, the censors provided a healthy and useful instrument of government. However, by Ming times (1368-1644), with the full development of monarchical rule, the censors tended to lose their function of remonstrating with the Court. How could a monarch who had become infallible submit to criticism and still maintain his prestige?[9]

---

9 Richard L. Walker, "The Control System of the Chinese Government," *Far Eastern Quarterly,* VII (1947), 2-21.

4. *The Law*

The law of Old China possessed a twofold character. First, it consisted of rather indefinite yet accepted political and ethical ideas, concepts, and principles; for example, the venerable dictum that asserted: "As Heaven has not two suns, so the people should not have two kings." In the second place, the law of Old China was a body of recorded rules and precedents. The distinction should not be pushed too far, since the two forms were not distinct.

The Chinese regarded law as a part of their total cultural heritage handed down by early rulers and distinguished scholars and brought to perfection by Confucius. As a consequence, the law was filled with Confucian ethical and moral precepts and appeared very unlike Western law. This form of the law dealt with the Confucian Rites and Relationships and with the station of the emperor between Heaven above and his subjects below. The law clothed Confucianism with authority.

Law in the second sense noted above was more definite, more enforceable, and somewhat similar to law in the Western World. These laws were sometimes contained in dynastic codes such as the T'ang code of the seventh century, dealing with such matters as the status and the rights of the various members of a family, specifying offences against life and property, and setting forth rules of what the West would term criminal procedure. Here again the Confucian influence is to be noted in that the rules concerned the relations of men, the sanctions of law being mostly penal, and that the concept of civil responsibility was all but lacking. Moreover, the law was customary and not created by legislative process. As a result, it was not fixed but subject to constant change; yet at the same time, since the Confucian foundations remained stable, the law acquired a continuous and a traditional character. Moreover, the principal aim of justice was not to safeguard the individual but to strengthen and support the political and social order. The Western student repelled by the "barbarity" of Chinese punishments would do well to review the history of pre-twentieth century ideas on this subject in the West, and to recall that the Chinese, in fact, were constantly concerned with justice, but they defined it in terms of their own culture and law, not of those of the West.

5. *Provincial Administration*

Under the impressive but rather passive metropolitan administration the provinces of China enjoyed a large measure of autonomy.

So long as the actions of provincial leaders did not run counter to Peking's general instructions and so long as the appropriate revenues were forwarded promptly to the capital, a province was free to administer local affairs largely as it saw fit. This did not mean, however, that Peking had no control in the province. All provincial officials from the highest to the lowest were appointed, promoted, transferred, and dismissed by the central government. Appointment was made usually for a three-year term, and high officials were not assigned to office in the province of their birth. It followed that the personnel was constantly changing and that every official ruled among strangers. Officials sent to a given capital were likely to be chosen from various factions or cliques in order that each might act as a check on his fellows.

The principal official of the provincial administration was a viceroy or governor. With him might be associated a Tartar general in command of the local Manchu garrison. There were also a treasurer who transmitted the revenues to Peking, a judge who passed on appeals from prefectural and district courts, a salt commissioner who controlled both the manufacture and sale of this article, a grain commissioner (in some provinces), and a literary chancellor who supervised the civil service examinations.

6. *Local Government*

For purposes of administration, the province was divided into a number of units, the most important of which was the county. A number of counties (from two to six) formed a prefecture, and two or more prefectures were grouped in a circuit under a supervising official known as the *taotai*. The county (*hsien*) was composed of a walled city and the adjacent country with its towns and villages. In the case of larger cities, only half or a third of the city was included. The magistrate, supposedly a master of all the arts and problems of government, was the chief official. His functions were as many and varied as the problems of mankind. He collected all local revenues, with the exception of special taxes such as the salt tax and *likin,* the latter being an internal transmit levy. He was judge in first instance in cases both civil and criminal. He was registrar of land, famine and pestilence commissioner, and custodian of official buildings. In general, it was his business to preserve law and order and to have a care for both the physical and the moral welfare of his people. It has been said that the functions of the magistrate called for rare ability. Here it may be added that as local administrators the magistrates were free in general to pursue whatever course seemed good so long as they could raise the necessary finances without arousing public protest, and without offending higher officials or the Court. Moreover, some local public functions could be and sometimes were performed by the local gentry. From this circumstance, however, it should not be concluded that Old China enjoyed local self-government. The gentry who performed these functions were not elected or formally appointed, nor did they constitute self-governing councils free from the interference of higher authorities.

Within a county, the towns and villages were governed by their own officials, who were nominated by the village elders and confirmed in office by the magistrate. Within the village lay the real government of China, where the spirit of the family or the unity of the family expressed itself in a larger loyalty to the land that had supported the family or the clan. The government of the village was communal and largely invisible, for there were no mayor and councillors; it was a moral government of the elders based on "custom and usage, the unwritten law." This was the only government that most Chinese knew. As for Peking and the metropolitan administration, the villagers considered that "heaven was high and the emperor far away."

7. *Economic Theory and Taxation*

Economic administration in Old China considered in its narrowest sense was concerned with the problem of extracting enough revenue to maintain the Court and the necessary public services. As in all agricultural societies, most revenue was derived directly from the land, which, though belonging in theory to the emperor, was in reality owned by individuals. At times the entire system of taxation rested on the land tax. Land and taxation, therefore, were major administrative problems. Sometimes, as in the cases of salt and iron, the principle of government monopoly was applied. In general, some degree of economic regulation was regarded as a proper state function, and in times of great natural calamities this principle might be applied rather widely in public works and even in more direct measures of relief.

8. *Education and Government*

Although schools did exist in the China of the Manchus and although some schools were subsidized, formal public education was not regarded as the function or duty of government. The wealthy employed private tutors for their children and in some cases established a free school as an act of benevolence, but the average Chinese boy enjoyed no formal schooling. At the close of the nineteenth century, not more than 3 per cent of the people were literate. However, as Arthur W. Hummel has suggested, the word "literate" is apt to be misleading when applied to a people so compact socially and so deeply rooted in their culture as were the Chinese. A Chinese, for instance, might not be able to read, and yet he could possess extraordinary traditional skills which would make him almost a cultured man.

The small literate group, however, provided the scholars, and scholarship in turn was of high importance, since only through learning could men rise to official position and honor. The basis of education was the Confucian classics and their commentaries, a knowledge of which required a much more extensive scholarship than, for example, a thorough knowledge of English literature. The commentaries, of which there were thousands of volumes, had also to be mastered. In addition, the extensive Chinese histories had to be known. Therefore there was much emphasis on memory. To be able by memory and in appropriate style to apply a classical phrase to the solution of a philosophical problem of politics was the goal of the scholar. Science, mathematics, and the development of independent and critical thought were regarded as of little consequence in fitting a man for the responsibilities of government.

Scholarship achieved its rewards when the candidate had passed one or all of the civil service examinations prescribed and conducted by the metropolitan government. This was the only proper avenue to public office and official distinction. There were four series of examinations, the first being held in the county and prefectural cities twice every three years. In the county only some 2 per cent of the candidates were permitted to pass. These were admitted a few weeks later to the prefectural examinations, where somewhat more than 50 per cent were likely to be successful. These men were now eligible for minor posts and could qualify to enter the provincial examinations held every three years in the provincial capitals. In great examination halls, as many as 14,000 candidates ate the food they brought along, wrote their essays, and slept in their "cells" for three separate sessions of three days each. During these sessions the candidates were permitted no recesses. Once a session had commenced and walls between the rows of cells had been bricked up, the gates of the hall were locked, and none, not even the chief examiner, might enter or leave. Successful candidates in the provincial tests were eligible for the metropolitan examinations in Peking. In these about 6 per cent passed, and they, in turn, might enter the palace examinations held in the presence of the emperor.

The significance of the Chinese examination system can hardly be overestimated. It was the great carrier of tradition. It helped, under the Ming and Manchu dynasties, to freeze the old and rich Chinese culture into a fixed pattern. It encouraged reliance upon the wisdom of the past; it discouraged freedom and independence of thought and thus prepared the way for a cultural decline that was hastened by the concurrent impact of an expanding Europe on China. It was the principal agent by which Confucianism monopolized scholarship, and by which scholarship, in turn, monopolized politics. But it went even further. The examinations became a principal road to wealth as well as to official position. This wealth was usually invested in land. The landed gentry, the silk-gowned, frequently controlled public opinion. The official did well to defer to this class, for he was a member of it either in his person or in his interests, or in both.[10]

9. *Tradition versus Innovation*

The foregoing sketch has suggested briefly the extraordinary influence Confucianism in its broadest aspects has exerted on the government of China. Now, in the middle of the twentieth century, this unique background seems to have vanished. A new China, no longer merely rebellious but openly revolutionary, appears to challenge not only the future but also the hallowed Confucian past. The American student would find this upheaval far more comprehensible if China's revolutionists had patterned their course on models provided by eighteenth- and nineteenth-century America. On the contrary, however, China's revolutionists, whether of *Kuomintang* or Communist persuasion, have striven toward their own peculiar goals. Quite naturally in this striving they will continue to wrestle with prob-

[10] Too frequently there was a wide gulf between theory and practice in the administration of the examination system. In addition to entry into the civil service through the examinations, many officials were admitted through the recommendation of their relatives who had attained high position. While this practice was looked down upon, a considerable fraction of the lesser officials entered office through this *yin* system.

lems of political power and government. No student of history expects that China's dead past will determine the shape of things to come, but it would be equally naive to suppose that political principles by which China has lived for more than two thousand years and by which she was still living in the early years of the twentieth century can be discarded and destroyed as one might throw away an old coat. What, then, are some of the political ways in which China's political past has asserted itself even as that past was being destroyed? In what ways will political tradition continue to reassert itself even in the midst of revolutionary change?

(*a*) *Authoritarianism.* It is clear that the Confucian tradition is one of authority exercised (sometimes humanely) by those who were above upon those who were below. Very little evidence has emerged from twentieth-century China to suggest that this tradition has been weakened seriously. Both the *Kuomintang* and the Communists have used it, the latter with seemingly more effect than the former.[11]

(*b*) *Ideological control.* Confucian China is one of the best examples history provides of a society that operated by ideological control rather than by organized governmental direction. In many respects Confucianism was to China what religion has sometimes been to the West, namely, an agency for control. An ideology that captures the imagination (by whatever means), particularly in times of political corruption and popular distress, enjoys a marked advantage. Chinese Communists have attempted to capitalize on this ideological tradition.

(*c*) *Bureaucracy.* Again, it is to be noted that in Confucian China government was by a bureaucracy. For Americans steeped in the democratic tradition and only recently subjected to problems of bureaucracy, it is difficult to sense the hold which this tradition has had upon China. It was not a tradition of responsible government as the West understands that term, but rather of the responsibility of one official to another. It followed that the people, given the foundation on which bureaucratic rule stood, were not concerned and did not regard it as their business to be concerned with affairs of state. The point is illustrated by an incident in 1851 at the time of the death of the Tao Kuang emperor. The intrepid traveller E. R. Huc, who with his fellow travellers was taking tea at an inn with some Chinese, attempted unsuccessfully to induce the latter into a

---

[11] The authoritarian tradition is discussed ably by John K. Fairbank, *The United States and China* (Cambridge, Mass., 1948), 98-119.

political discussion. Finally, a worthy Chinese laid his hands paternally on Huc's shoulders and said, smiling ironically:

> Listen to me, my friend! Why should you trouble your heart and fatigue your head by all these vain surmises? The Mandarins have to attend to affairs of state; they are paid for it. Let them earn their money then. But don't let us torment ourselves about what does not concern us. We should be great fools to want to do political business for nothing.[12]

Moreover, bureaucracy in a society based on personal relationships lived on standardized forms of corruption practiced so generally and openly as to become accepted institutions.

(*d*) *Chinese humanism.* Although the Confucian tradition was authoritarian, it was also humanistic in that it concerned itself with human relationships and practical patterns of conduct. Although the sovereign was absolute, arbitrary, and without fear of any higher law, there was a constant regard for stability in human relationships. From this one may conclude that the Confucian tradition did not place the state above mankind. There was some regard for the individual. The worth of the individual, however, was measured in social, not in personal, terms. Success was not derived from personal initiative and individual accomplishment but from conformity with right conduct. Confucianism thus left a tradition and a principle not of individual but of social action.

For Further Reading

The student will find it helpful to distinguish as clearly as he may between government as a theory and the realities of government in action.

Bodde, Derk, *China's First Unifier, A Study of the Ch'in Dynasty as Seen in the Life of Li Ssŭ (280?-208 B.C.)* (Leiden, 1938).

Chi Ch'ao-ting, *Key Economic Areas in Chinese History as Revealed in the Development of Public Works for Water-control* (New York, 1936).

Hsieh Pao-chao, *The Government of China, 1644-1911* (Baltimore, 1925).

Kracke, E. A., *Civil Service in Early Sung China, 960-1067* (Cambridge, 1953). The techniques developed for maintaining administrative integrity among government personnel.

Lin Mou-shêng, *Men and Ideas, An Informal History of Chinese Political Thought* (New York, 1942).

Linebarger, Paul M. A., Djang Chu, and Ardath Burks, *Far East Governments and Politics* (New York, 1954). A penetrating comparative study of the governments of Japan and China.

[12] E. R. Huc, *A Journey Through the Chinese Empire* (2 vols., New York, 1859), I, 117.

Mayers, William Frederick, *The Chinese Government. A Manual of Chinese titles categorically arranged and explained with an Appendix* (3rd ed., Shanghai, 1897).

Meadows, Thomas Taylor, *The Chinese and Their Rebellions* (London, 1856). By an able British diplomat and scholar who was in China during the Tai-p'ing Rebellion.

Michael, Franz, *The Origin of Manchu Rule in China* (Baltimore, 1942). A study in the significance of the frontier.

Shryock, J. K., *The Origin and Development of the State Cult of Confucius* (New York, 1932).

4

Ways of Life in Old Japan

THE Japanese and the Chinese are in many ways the product of the single civilization of China. From early times Japan drew heavily upon the profound learning of the Chinese: their arts, letters, and philosophy. It thus came about that there was much common ground in the cultural and intellectual life of these two great oriental states. Yet they did not become one people or one culture, and, indeed, their differences have often appeared quite as arresting as their similarities.

As was pointed out in the two preceding chapters, the impact of the Western world upon China in the past hundred years can be comprehended only by those who have some understanding of the Chinese institutional life upon which this Western impact exerted its influence. So too, in the case of Japan, the impact of the West cannot be separated from the ideas and the institutions by which the Japanese have lived.

An historical sketch of this kind can perhaps best begin with the reminder that geography had its part in shaping the distinctive character of Japan no less than it did in the case of China. Japan's insular position, like that of the British Isles, gave a special character to Japan's life. It was possible, as will be seen, for Japan at various times to avoid the main stream of continental life and thereby to protect its own individuality. On the other hand, Japan as often received invaders, immigrants, and a stream of continental cultural influence. Out of these importations, which they combined with their indigenous traditions, the Japanese fashioned a distinctive Japanese culture and a character which, though belonging to Asia, was unlike that of any other Asiatic people. Moreover, Japan's ancient cultural borrowings were voluntary; they were not forced by military conquest, since the Chinese showed little tendency to expand overseas. Japan was therefore free to reject this or to accept that, and to digest in comparative seclusion those things which she did take from China, permitting them to shape and color her own ideas but never to destroy them. Japan, as a result, has sometimes seemed to present the paradox of a people always ready to consider new teachings yet jealous to retain their own traditions. These circumstances have sometimes led to untenable opinions concerning the Japanese, as, for example, the belief that geography fostered a spirit of isolationism in Japan and a spirit of repugnance toward foreign intercourse.[1]

The history of Japan, measured in terms of China's long past, is a comparatively brief story. When Confucius, around the year 500 B.C., was giving form and purpose to one of history's greatest codes of humanistic behavior (Confucianism), the history of Japan had not yet begun, though the islands may well have been at that time the battleground of rude and barbarous tribes.

The Japanese who peopled the pages of early Japanese history were a product of racial mixture but were also predominantly Mongoloid and certainly akin to their neighbors in Korea and China. Most of them reached Japan through Korea. Some, of course, may have come from the southern coasts of China and Southeast Asia by way of Formosa and the Ryukyu Islands. These Mongoloid folk were preceded in the islands by another people, by the ancestors of the present day Ainu, a people of proto-white stock but of a neolithic culture inferior to the new invaders from Korea. The Ainu, in time, were pushed to the east and north. In the mid-twentieth century a few members of this vanishing race still survived in Hokkaido.

Men of Bronze and Iron

It was about the beginning of the Christian era that Japan was invaded by Mongoloid clans of horsemen who brought with them a superior civilization built on bronze and iron. These were the men who were shortly to set up in central Japan the original Japanese state known as Yamato. These invaders had already known something of the superior culture of China, for they brought into

[1] G. B. Sansom, *The Western World and Japan* (New York, 1950), 167-169. A masterpiece of historical interpretation.

Japan not only the iron sword of northern Asia but also semi-precious stones often found in archaeological remains in Korea, and a round bronze mirror of Chinese origin. These three articles, the mirror, the sword, and the jewel became in time the historic symbols of authority for Japanese sovereigns. At first Yamato was merely one of the many clan states, some of which were ruled by women. The idea of hereditary rights and of the soldier as aristocrat and ruler was probably strong among these people. These ideas were to show a marked capacity to survive in the Japanese mind.

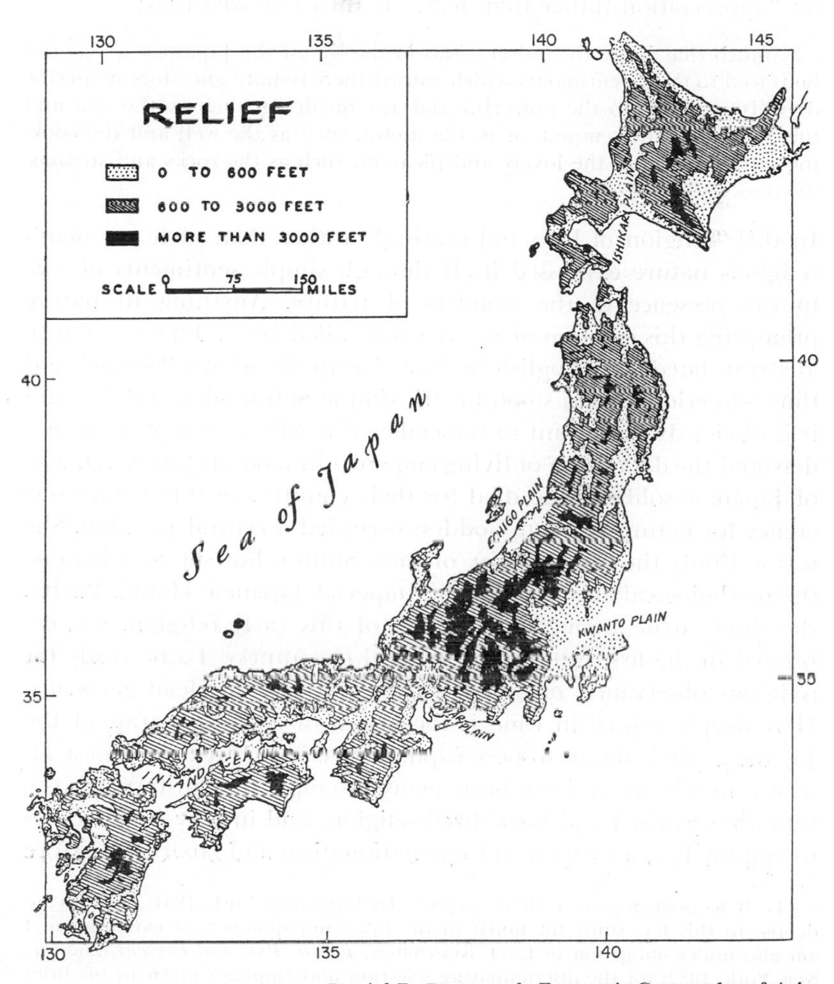

From Daniel R. Bergsmark, Economic Geography of Asia

Religion in Primitive Japan

The religion of this young Japan was a simple nature worship involving, somewhat later under Chinese influence, some concepts of ancestor worship. This religion was Shinto, "the way of the gods," as it came to be known in the sixth century to distinguish it from Buddhism, which by that time had reached Japan from China. If the material culture of this early Japan was crude, its religious and social life were of a comparatively high order, for Shinto was based on "appreciation rather than fear." It thus followed that:

> . . . much that is kindly and gracious in the life of the Japanese to-day can be traced to those sentiments which caused their remote ancestors to ascribe divinity not only to the powerful and awe-inspiring, such as the sun and the moon and the tempest, or to the useful, such as the well and the cooking pot, but also to the lovely and pleasant, such as the rocks and streams, the trees and flowers.[2]

In this "religion of love and gratitude rather than of fear," man's religious nature expressed itself through simple sentiments of awe in the presence of the wonders of nature. Anything in nature prompting this emotion of wonder was called *kami*. This word, usually translated into English as "god," actually means "above" and thus "superior." *Kami* stood for the simple Shinto idea of deity, and it is obviously important to remember this when attempting to understand the deification of living emperors in modern Japan and also of Japanese soldiers who died for their country. In this Shinto reverence for nature the Sun Goddess occupied a central position. She was not only the central deity of early Shinto, but she also became the mythological ancestress of the Imperial Japanese House. Purity, the chief virtue among the concepts of this early religion, was expressed in the first instance in physical cleanliness. To be ready for religious observance, one took a bath and put on clean garments. Here deeply rooted in time is the origin of a modern trait of the Japanese: their desire to be scrupulously clean. During the past fifteen centuries there have been many attempts to transform Shinto into an organized and formalized religion, and in very recent times to employ it as a weapon to forge nationalism and fanaticism. More

---

[2] G. B. Sansom, *Japan: A Short Cultural History* (New York, 1931), 3. I am indebted to this fine study for much in the following summary of early Japan. I am also under obligation to E. O. Reischauer, *Japan: Past and Present* (2nd ed., New York, 1952) for the discriminating selection and emphasis given in his brief history.

will be said on these aspects of the subject in later pages. Meanwhile, it is well to be reminded that the essence of Shinto was appreciation of nature, hardly to be counted an ignoble sentiment.

Political Origins: Yamato

As the migrations from Korea continued through successive centuries, the later invaders pushed and fought their way through the Inland Sea to settle in the Yamato area of central Japan. There a clan emerged, stronger than its neighbors, absorbing some of its rivals until it could claim a shadowy overlordship throughout central and western Japan and in parts of southern Korea. The rise of this Yamato clan did not mean the destruction of all other clans, nor did it challenge their autonomous rights. It did mean that the priest-chief of Yamato assumed priority among all clan chiefs, and the cults of the Yamato clan tended to become the cults of the land as a whole. It was in this way that the Sun Goddess who, according to mythology, was the ancestress of the founder of the Yamato clan (Jimmu) became the supreme diety of Japanese Shinto. Moreover, the chiefs of Yamato by gaining some degree of supremacy over other clan chiefs became the founders of the Japanese imperial family. In a word, the beginnings of the Japanese state go back to a time about the beginning of the Christian era, when the Yamato clan could at least claim some form of suzerainty over a group of lesser but associated clans.

The Foreign Education of Young Japan

This young Japanese nation composed of a primitive clan-conscious people with simple native traditions was soon to be revolutionized by a foreign educational tidal wave that poured in upon it from China. The early Japanese had always had some indirect contacts with China, and new immigrant waves continued to carry the Chinese influence to Japan; but it was not until the sixth century that the Japanese, consciously recognizing how superior Chinese civilization was, sought actively to understand it and make much of it their own. Somewhat earlier, perhaps before the beginning of the fifth century, Japan had some knowledge of the Chinese language and script. In 405 A.D. the arrival of a Sino-Korean scholar, Wani by name, as tutor to the heir apparent of Yamato, meant that the Chinese written language had been adopted officially by the Japanese court. These events paved the way for the general Chinese cultural impact that followed. Buddhism was introduced to the Yamato court in the early part of the sixth century and won numerous converts. Many of these converts journeyed to study in China and returned to Japan as the most effective missionaries of Chinese culture. By 587 these pro-Chinese, pro-Buddhist factions controlled the Japanese (Yamato) court and the way was thus cleared for the radical reforms that followed under the leadership of the crown prince, Shotoku Taishi, sometimes called the father of Japanese civilization.

The conditions of the time called for reform. The old clan system had degenerated under the power of a few families who had failed to understand the new Chinese influence and learning. Supported by the Chinese-Buddhist factions, Shotoku Taishi in 604 issued a code of moral injunctions superior to any political philosophy hitherto known in Japan. This code enunciated a Chinese theory that political power resided with the ruler. Shotoku Taishi and those who influenced him were seeking in Chinese political theory for a unifying force to break the heritage of clan and caste barriers. He was thus attempting to lay the foundations of a new political and economic life in Japan by a frontal assault on the old clan order. The movement was advanced further when, beginning in 607, Shotoku Taishi sent embassies to China accompanied by able young Japanese students, who on their return became promoters of Chinese learning not only in government, but also in the whole range of artistic and cultural life.

By 645 the reformers were committed to remaking the Yamato state in the image of their magnificent neighbor, T'ang China. Some of their ideas toward this end were contained in the *Taikwa* or Great Reform of 645-650. Its edicts contemplated a new system of taxation, of local government, and of land tenure. In theory they all involved a greater centralization of power, but in practice they did not work out ideally. Powerful families who could not be deprived expediently of their lands were confirmed in their titles on the questionable assumption that they now held their lands from the throne. In addition they were given official posts or court rank. The central government also undertook to appoint governors for the provinces; but here too the practice was to confirm the existing authority of the most powerful local chief. Theoretically, all of this amounted to a political reorganization, but in reality the emphasis in the Great

Reform was on the economic rather than on the political. The reformers who controlled the court were not concerned primarily with the extension to remote regions of their direct political control. Their immediate concern was to find a more effective means of collecting wealth from the provinces.[3] By 701-704, in the code of *Taiho* (Great Treasure), the Japanese reformers were attempting to set up an intricate central administration on the elaborate pattern of T'ang China. Of course they did not succeed fully, but the point that will bear remembering is that these early Japanese had the ambition and the nerve to try, and the understanding to succeed as far as they did. Even this early in their history the Japanese were showing an amazing zest for learning, a trait noted many centuries later by the first Europeans to reach Japanese shores. Moreover, these reforming Japanese were now thinking of their state as an empire and of their ruler as an all-powerful monarch in the Chinese tradition. However, in Japan this ruler, while attaining this new stature, retained his original and indigenous character as chief-priest. In this manner Japanese sovereigns came to play a dual role embodied in the single person of the emperor: he was the Shinto high priest of Japan's divine origins as well as an absolute secular ruler such as the Chinese had long had. As an additional product of Chinese influence the Japanese practice that permitted rule by women came to an end, and the position of women in general declined from one of superiority to one of subserviency to men. In some very important cases the Japanese accepted the form of a Chinese idea or institution but rejected its spirit, as when the reformers amid all this Chinese flavor attempted to preserve the interests of a court aristocracy of birth at the expense of other groups. In China the aristocracy was one of learning rather than of birth.

Japan Builds a Chinese City: Nara, 710-784

The ancient city of Nara near the modern town of that name in the Yamato plain stood in eighth century Japan as the most striking tangible evidence of the Chinese influence. Prior to this time the Japanese had not been city builders, nor had they a permanent capital. Nara was their first great city and the first permanent capital. Ch'ang-an, capital of T'ang China and perhaps the greatest city

[3] A basic study is K. Asakawa, *The Early Institutional Life of Japan* (Tokyo, 1903).

in the world at that time, was the model—a rectangle with the imperial palace at the northern end and broad straight thoroughfares intersecting at right angles. Here was the actual design and structure of Chinese architecture transplanted into Japan. The city was not so large as the Chinese model. Nevertheless, some of its Buddhist temples still stand in the twentieth century, the oldest wooden buildings in the world, and the only existing examples of the graceful Chinese architecture of T'ang.

It was at Nara that the imported Buddhism acquired tremendous influence as the new state religion. Buddhism in turn was one of the chief instruments through which the young bureaucratic government sought to strengthen its control by appointing the "right" men as chief abbots of the growing and powerful monasteries. Buddhist temples with their brilliant decorations dotted the near and the distant landscapes. Moreover, the cultured men of the Japanese court were steeped not only in Chinese religion, government, city-planning, and art, but also in the vehicle through which much of this learning came to Japan, namely, the classical written Chinese language. When they discovered that the writing of history had always been an important concern of Chinese governments, these aristocrats of Nara felt that they too must have histories. Their first great chronicles, the *Kojiki* or *Records of Ancient Matters,* and the *Nihon Shoki* or *Chronicles of Japan* were completed in the early years of Nara, probably in 712 and 720 respectively.[4] Both of these chronicles, official histories though they be, are of immense importance in the study of early Japanese history. They have proven to be rather accurate accounts of the years after 400 A.D. For the earlier years, they present a wealth of mythology and tradition from which it has been possible to reconstruct much of that early and simpler Japan which existed before the coming of Chinese learning. However, historians are not always free to be good historians. Sometimes they are under pressure from politicians or from advocates of this theory or that theory to color what they have to say. So it would seem that the rulers of Nara were not content that history should record the simple myths and traditions handed down orally by professional chroniclers. On the contrary, it was thought that matters would be much improved if history should teach that the chiefs of Yamato were the unique and divine rulers of an old Japan no less glorious

[4] B. H. Chamberlain, trans., *Kojiki or Records of Ancient Matters* (2nd ed., Kobe, 1932); W. G. Aston, *Nihongi: Chronicles of Japan* (2 vols., London, 1896).

than its mighty neighbor China. Accordingly the historians created what Professor Edwin Reischauer has called an impressive pseudo-history in which the Sun Goddess, a principal object of nature worship by the men of early Yamato, now became the progenitress of the royal family and the grandmother of Japan's first emperor, who supposedly ascended the throne on February 11, 660 B.C. This date, which, of course, had not the slightest foundation in fact, may have been arrived at by projecting the founding of Japan a full Chinese time cycle of some 1,260 years into the past. In the twentieth century, as we shall see, these early Japanese chronicles were to be revised and used by super-nationalists and super-patriots to serve the ends of a philosophy of 100 per cent Japanism.

In poetry as well as history, Nara was a great age. The great anthology of verse, the *Manyoshu* (Collection of One Thousand Leaves), has never since been surpassed in Japanese poetry.[5]

Politically, Nara witnessed the beginnings of a movement in which the national government, such as it was, practically withered away due to the growth of tax-free estates, both secular and religious. Unlike the Chinese, the Japanese with their strong leanings toward clan loyalty and hereditary rights failed to develop a bureaucracy of education and learning to maintain the national domain and protect the central authority. As a consequence, in Japan, the peasantry and their lands fell under the control of powerful local families with enough influence at the capital to escape the government tax collector. This meant the decline and impoverishment of the royal authority and the ultimate control of the weakened court by some powerful local family such as the Fujiwara clan, which came to the fore in the Nara period. All in all the close of the Nara era did not present a pretty picture. To be sure, artistic triumphs in temples and images were created, but they were the work of a government that lived far beyond its means, and which, through purchasing the favor of the powerful Buddhist priesthood by means of generous gifts from the public domain, reduced the central authority to impotence and the peasants to the level of slaves. While the central authority thus became bankrupt, local officials, families, and Buddhist orders grew wealthy through their control of the land.[6]

---

[5] Nippon Gakujutsu Shinkōkai, *The Manyoshu. One Thousand Poems Selected and Translated from the Japanese* (Tokyo, 1940).

[6] An exhaustive treatment of early Japan is R. K. Reischauer, *Early Japanese History* (2 vols., Princeton, 1937).

Japan in the Heian Period, 784-1185

The four centuries following the Nara period remain to this day in many respects the most fascinating and revealing period in Japanese history. Although the men who ruled at Nara were absorbed in the new learning from China, their successors in the age of Heian had a deeper understanding of the processes of cultural borrowing, and therefore a more critical attitude toward Chinese learning in its new Japanese environment. By the ninth century the undiscriminating zeal for Chinese learning had given place to critical analysis of it which sought to adapt the new ideas to the peculiar background and needs of Japan. In part this more critical point of view was due to the decay of T'ang China and the resulting end in 838 of Japanese embassies to the continent, but it should also be attributed to the growing intellectual maturity of the Japanese. It was in this period that the Japanese first showed their capacity not only to borrow and imitate but also to adapt and develop the ideas and institutions of other lands to their own purposes and in their own particular ways. It was in this period, for example, that Buddhism in Japan became a Japanese rather than an Indian or a Chinese Buddhism. It is worthwhile to note the reasons for and the methods by which this reshaping of the imported institution was effected.

Religion and Politics

At the beginning of Heian, which was to witness the development of a mature native culture, the Buddhist church still retained the power to intimidate government. The capital was moved accordingly to Heiankyo (City of Peace), known today as Kyoto, where it was to remain until the Restoration of 1868. This astute maneuver to escape the political control of a powerful church, the Nara temples, was the work of the Emperor Kammu, who, when he had thus curbed the political power of the Buddhists, set about to fuse the church's religious power with the native cult of Shinto to create a national religion supporting the throne. The task of doing this was entrusted to two learned priest-patriots, Kobo-Daishi and Dengyo-Daishi, who became the founders respectively of the Shingon and the Tendai sects of Japanese Buddhism. Kobo-Daishi reconciled Buddhism with Shinto by a very neat doctrine which stated that the Buddhas had in part revealed themselves in Japan as

Shinto deities. In this way a foreign Buddhism became a patriotic Japanese Buddhism and thus a bulwark of the central government.

Kyoto and the New Japan

The new capital, Kyoto, the most spacious city Japan had yet known, modelled after the T'ang capital of Ch'ang-an, became one of the world's most beautiful cities. Surrounded by and built into natural scenic beauty, it expressed the early maturing of Japanese artistic expression. Here the Japanese Imperial Court, the court nobility (*Kuge*), the men of letters, and, to an even greater degree, the women of letters, created the masterpieces of classical Japanese literature. The second great anthology, the *Kokinshiu* (Poems Ancient and Modern), was completed in 922.[7] The age also brought forth Japan's ablest women of letters: Lady Murasaki no Shikibu, author of the *Genji Monogatari*[8] (*ca.* 1004), and Lady Sei Shonagon, author of the *Makura-no-soshi* (Pillow Sketches).[9] Kyoto was a cultured, refined, and effeminate city. Belles-lettres dominated its great literature. It was the great age of the novel and poetry, of diaries and essays in the sophisticated manner, and written in the native language. The duller pursuits of theology and the law were left to scholars who still wrote in rather bad Chinese.

Japan Creates Her Own Written Language

The flowering of this early native literature in prose and poetry meant among other things that the Japanese had now acquired an adequate system for writing their native tongue. The creation of this system had taken place gradually through the ninth and tenth centuries. The method involved using simpler Chinese characters or parts of them as phonetic symbols usually representing a syllable such as *ka, mi, ku, se,* or *to.* This syllabary or *kana* was and still is written in two forms, the one cursive, the other angular, known respectively as *hiragana* and *katakana.* Although some poetry had been written in Japanese during earlier centuries by using unabbreviated Chinese characters, it was the new syllabary that made a real

[7] T. Wakameda, trans., *Early Japanese Poets. Complete Translation of the Kokinshiu* (Tokyo, 1929). A complete translation but in inferior English.

[8] Monogatari means narrative. It is applied chiefly to fiction and sometimes to histories. Murasaki, like Fielding, created the prose epic of real life.

[9] Waley, Arthur, trans., *The Pillow Book of Lady Sei Shonagon* (Boston, 1929).

and rich Japanese literature possible. It was in the new phonetic medium that the court ladies, Sei and Murasaki and others, wrote their thirty-one syllable poems, their diaries, and their novels. This was a Japanese literature expressive of a distinct Japanese culture in which the Chinese influence was all but completely adapted to Japanese forms.

Chinese Political and Social Institutions Become Japanese

It was likewise in the Heian period that the political and social institutions built in Japan during the previous centuries of Chinese influence were so altered by the Japanese as to leave in some cases little evidence of their original Chinese models. For example, in China the civilian-scholar-bureaucrat chosen through civil service examinations operated in a system in which the educated class, drawn in theory at least from all walks of life, was accepted as the proper ruling class. In Japan, too, as a result of the Chinese learning, the classics were studied and examinations held, but it was clan loyalties and hereditary rights that determined who was appointed to high office. In such a situation there was, as already indicated, no group of public servants whose duty it was to preserve the national domain. The result was that the central government, instead of developing into the stature of its Chinese model, became an empty pretense. The imperial family continued to enjoy great prestige because of its political background and its relation to Shinto, but in terms of actual power it was reduced to a succession of puppet emperors in the control of a powerful family—the Fujiwara. This clan family, which had been a leader of the pro-Chinese factions in the seventh century, had acquired great wealth in lands, and finally gained complete control of the capital and the court by marrying its daughters to the young emperors. Thus the Fujiwaras created a situation in which the clan monopolized the high if empty offices of state. Child emperors, the off-spring of Fujiwara consorts, were placed on the throne, while heads of the Fujiwara house administered what was left of the state as regents (*sessho*) or as civil dictators (*kampaku*). Ambitious and capable men who were not members of the Fujiwara clan had no choice but to seek their fortunes in distant provinces. There, by various means and as a result of varying conditions, many of them acquired great manors and built the foundations of a frontier, military, vigorous society in striking contrast to the civilian effeminacy of the Kyoto aristocracy. These new landed barons had very little concern for the stability of the central government. On the contrary their ambition was to strengthen their own local independence. During the last century of the Heian era, the feudal barons (*buke*) and their hardy soldiers (*bushi*) were beyond the control of Kyoto. The once powerful Fujiwara was forced even to seek the aid of some of these new military upstarts to maintain order in the imperial capital itself. In the conflicts which ensued between the frontier warrior factions of Taira and Minamoto, the old civil government of Kyoto collapsed. Control of the next chapter in Japan's history was settled at the naval battle of Dan-no-ura, 1185, when the Taira were routed by their Minamoto rivals.

Kamakura: The First Military Dictatorship, 1185-1338

Minamoto Yoritomo, the victor, avoiding the mistakes of his vanquished rival, Taira Kiyomori, set up his seat of government not at Kyoto with its effeminate court, but at the seaside village of Kamakura near the principal estates of his relatives and allies in eastern-central Japan, not far from the present-day Tokyo. At Kyoto he permitted the emperor, the Fujiwara, and the court nobility to carry on the forms of their make-believe civil government and to perpetuate the fiction that it was this emperor's government that actually ruled. The fiction was strengthened further when Yoritomo accepted from the emperor the title Shogun (generalissimo), which invested him with supreme command of all military forces. The implication was that Yoritomo commanded the emperor's army. Actually there was no emperor's army. What Yoritomo commanded was a powerful association of knights held together by family ties or by bonds of friendship arising from relations of mutual assistance. This military association under Yoritomo's leadership made up the real power and thus the real government. Moreover, with Yoritomo, the title of Shogun became hereditary and therefore of greatly increased significance. The military administration that came into being at Kamakura as a result of these happenings was known significantly as the *Bakufu* (meaning literally "tent government"), a term used originally to designate the headquarters of an army in the field, and later the administrative headquarters of a military dictator. In addition, this Kamakura administration was not a national government in the modern sense of that term but a simple machinery to control and regulate the affairs of the knights making up the Minamoto faction. Since these knights were scattered throughout the land, many of them as estate managers, Kamakura was in a position to control all areas and classes. During the time of the Minamoto shoguns and their successors, the Hojo regents, the lands of the Minamoto and their vassals were scattered thickly throughout eastern Japan, and more thinly in other areas. Sometimes the lands of a vassal lay within the domain of some independent lord. The authority of the shogun was thus likely to vary from complete military control in some areas to a rather shadowy suzerainty in others. So long as the *Bakufu* retained able administrators its power was for all practical purposes supreme. The Shogun was a military dictator deriving his military power from the Minamoto faction. Within this sphere, the administration of Kamakura was direct and exclusive.

These bold statements, however, require some important shading. Yoritomo, although acting the part of a military dictator, recognized the sovereignty of the throne and considered himself as exercising authority delegated by the throne. The throne therefore did not disappear with the creation of the shogunate, even though the throne did lose all save *de jure* authority. Emperors continued to reign in Kyoto, where the throne retained at times "a certain social prestige and a certain negative authority." In this way the throne expressed rather vaguely a continuing concept of unity. It was significant that the throne should have carried this tradition, since Yoritomo probably did not think of himself as the ruler of all Japan or of Japan as a national unit. The twelfth century had already created a feudal society in which landed barons were virtually independent within their own estates. The barons did not recognize the military power of the throne, for the throne possessed no military power. The barons did recognize the military power of the Shogun, for he had the power, and it was expedient for them to do so. They were the more likely to bow to the Shogun's legal as well as military authority, since the former was derived from the throne and carried with it whatever prestige the throne possessed.

The Meaning of Kamakura

The Kamakura system was of importance for itself alone as a system by which Japanese society of that day was ordered and controlled, but it was perhaps even more important for the influence it was to exert on the Japanese character during the succeeding six centuries of feudalism (until 1871). Kamakura planted firmly in Japan the tradition of military rule, of dictatorship of the peculiar Japanese variety, and of the principle of dual government in which an emperor reigned but a shogun ruled, but it did more than this. It preserved the theory of the political and religious role of the imperial family. In the nineteenth and the twentieth centuries this imperial tradition was to be reasserted as a vigorous force, as we shall see, when Japan emerged as a modern nation state.

The Hojo Regency, 1205-1333

On Yoritomo's death, his wife's family, known by the name of Hojo, disposed of his heirs and proceeded to rule under the title of Regents, acting for puppet shoguns chosen from either the Fujiwara or the imperial families. Japan of the thirteenth century thus presented the amazing spectacle of a country headed by a sovereign who was emperor in name only, whose vestigial functions were assumed by an abdicated emperor, and whose real power was delegated to a hereditary military dictator (the shogun), but wielded by a hereditary regent acting for the dictator. It might be supposed that this absurd appearing system, where the theoretical sources of power were so remote from the agencies exercising real power, would be meaningless and unworkable. Actually, the Hojo regents, men of great capacity, gave Japan a government more stable, honest, and efficient than it had previously known. The period, moreover, was one of spiritual vigor. Great teachers such as Honen (1133-1212), Shinran (1173-1262), and Nichiren (1222-1282), forsaking the classical Chinese for Japanese, touched and quickened the intellectual life of the people and made of Buddhism a popular religion.[10]

In the midst of this moral and political awakening, the regency was called upon to repel the Mongol invasions of Kublai Khan, who in 1263 had become emperor of China. In 1274 and again in 1281, the Mongol armies were driven back by the Japanese, the fleets of the

[10] For Japan's great religious leaders, see Masaharu Anesaki, *History of Japanese Religion* (London, 1930).

invaders being destroyed by providential typhoons. The Hojo regents, their vassals, and their feudal allies had been equal to the military task of defense, but they were unequal to the task of domestic reconstruction that followed the attempted invasions. The shogunate was bankrupt. Increased taxes brought on local rebellions. Vassals who had defended the nation and priests whose prayers had brought the typhoons wanted to be rewarded, as politicians usually do, for these services, but there were no new lands for the Hojo to bestow. In 1333 the Hojo regency was destroyed by an ex-emperor who thought to restore the imperial rule. Instead there followed a new shogunate established by a rebellious general, Ashikaga Takauji, who had assisted in the destruction of the Hojo.

The Ashikaga Shogunate, 1336-1573

Politically, Ashikaga Shogunate had little to recommend it. The Ashikaga shoguns who set up their capital at Kyoto never exercised effective control over the barons and the military caste. The result was incessant feudal strife, while for a time rival dynasties claimed the imperial throne. The disappearance of any real central authority meant that Japan was in the grip of factions seeking to gain control of feudal privileges in the form of lands or vassals.

The Culture of Kamakura and Ashikaga

The cultural life of Japan during the period of Kamakura and Ashikaga was dominated by the rise of the military caste. Moreover, military men continued to rule Japan after Ashikaga on through the nineteenth century. It is not unnatural therefore that the military-feudal patterns of behavior which came to the fore seven centuries ago and which continued to persist should influence and at times dominate Japanese thought and manners even to this day. In a word, much of the Japanese mental atmosphere of the twentieth century can be understood only in terms of what happened in Japan in the days of Yoritomo and his successors.

The new culture of Kamakura, like its new political system, mirrored the warrior class of the provinces who were so unlike the literary dilettantes of the older Kyoto aristocracy. Symbolized by the hard, finely tempered steel of his sword, the ideal of the warrior was a life of self-discipline, Spartan, ascetic. The supreme virtues were the personal loyalties of family ties and a stoical indifference to suffering. Where practiced, these virtues produced men of parochial horizon but of tough fiber. They read a new literature on the military exploits of the Taira and the Minamoto instead of the love diaries and novels of court ladies. With this newer austerity came a new interest in religion, particularly Buddhism, the evidences of which are still present in twentieth century Japan not only in monuments such as the Great Buddha at Kamakura but also in the religious thinking of the modern Japanese. This religious awakening took various forms. It created a popular Buddhism of the people which rested on belief and faith and salvation in an afterlife rather than on philosophic enlightenment. It developed further the doctrine of Zen Buddhism, which cast aside formalized religion and faith in the saving power of a redeemer in favor of the effort of the individual to discover the meaning of the universe. Zen made a special appeal to the fighting men of the *Bakufu*. Zen was self-reliant, did not depend on scriptures, was unencumbered by any intricate philosophy. Its stern injunction to self-examination, its freedom from the emotional, its stress on individualism—each and all of these appealed to the rugged warriors of the *Bakufu*. Zen, the religion of the soldier, became in succeeding centuries a vital influence not only in the lives of military men but also of those whom they influenced and ruled.

Culturally, the Ashikaga period brought about a mingling of the provincial military-feudal society with the older civilian society of Kyoto. The Ashikaga shoguns, unlike their predecessors, set up their residence in Muromachi, a quarter of Kyoto. This meant that the military caste tended to gravitate to Kyoto where it could not but be influenced by the older civilian culture. Military men soon learned to covet the cultural trappings which wealth could buy in the capital. Here, against a background of political chaos, Japan entered upon a period of cultural and economic growth.

Ashikaga was a period of Zen culture. Leading artists were Zen priests who, because of their close contacts with China, brought to Japan new aspects of Chinese art and learning which were soon blended with the native arts. For example, the *No* drama was developed as a major contribution to dramatic art. Japanese painting reached new heights of perfection in Chinese and in native schools. Likewise from Chinese inspiration the Japanese of Ashikaga developed as their own art their unsurpassed landscape gardening, their aesthetic masterpieces of flower arrangement (*ikebana*), and the disciplinary diversion of the tea ceremony (*cha-no-yu*), by the last of which it was held the sophisticated virtues of urbanity and courtesy were fostered.[11]

The period of Ashikaga was marked also by the growth of Japanese trade and industry, by the formation of guilds of merchants. In fostering foreign trade, some Ashikaga shoguns even accepted investiture as "Kings of Japan" from the Ming emperors of China. By the end of the Ashikaga period Japan had developed economically far out of proportion to her political maturity. Thus the picture was not well balanced. Extravagance and dissipation were reflected in vast sums expended on the Kinkakuji (Golden Pavilion) and the Ginkakuji (Silver Pavilion). Wealthy barons rivalled each other in the construction of costly palaces and in indulgence in aesthetic amusements, while in contrast squalor infested the countryside and impoverished emperors sought a subsistence by selling their calligraphy in the market place.

Dictators Reunite Japan

The Ashikaga period, which had brought great economic growth and a brilliant development of the arts, had also fostered the collapse of the central authority, whether of emperor or shogun, and the creation in the domains of the great feudal lords, the *daimyo,* of both the spirit and the reality of complete local independence. To put the matter in other words, during the age of Ashikaga all centralized control withered and was replaced by the local authority of each *daimyo* in his own domain. Each of these domains had become a political unit unto itself, a miniature state, in which the *daimyo* assisted by a bureaucracy of chosen military officers maintained his court and government at a central castle fortress from which he ruled his peasants, merchants, and soldiers as an independent sovereign. The tendency was for each *daimyo* to build up his military strength at the expense of his neighbors and rivals. By this process there emerged finally a few *daimyo* of unrivalled strength who fought for control of the entire nation.

The first of these powerful figures moving toward the re-unification of the land was Oda Nobunaga. By seizing Kyoto in 1568, and

---

[11] See A. L. Sadler, *Cha-no-yu, the Japanese Tea Ceremony* (Kobe, 1934); Jiro Harada, *The Gardens of Japan* (London, 1928).

by destroying the military power of the central Buddhist monasteries, Nobunaga made himself master of central Japan. When he was assassinated in 1582, his ablest general, Hideyoshi Toyotomi, later known as the Japanese Napoleon, carried on the conquest. Wisely recognizing the force of tradition, he instilled new life into the hapless imperial court by having the throne bestow upon him the title of *kampaku,* regent or civil dictator, and won military control of all Japan by defeating the powerful daimyo of Satsuma in Kyushu and his remaining rivals in the east and north. With these victories behind him he embarked on the conquest of China by way of Korea in 1592. His armies, however, numbering at times as many as 200,000, men did not get beyond Korea. Chinese resistance was too powerful, and on Hideyoshi's death in 1598 they were withdrawn.

Hideyoshi's successor as master of Japan was one of his own vassals and generals, Tokugawa Iyeyasu, whose home was at Yedo in east-central Japan. Iyeyasu first defeated Hideyoshi's rivals, then turned upon and destroyed Hideyoshi's family. Since neither Nobunaga nor Hideyoshi had been able to make their rule hereditary, Iyeyasu was consumed with a single ambition—to fashion a political structure that would preserve in the Tokugawa family its newly acquired power. In this ambition Iyeyasu and his successors met with astonishing success. The edifice they erected was the final and greatest of the shogunates, lasting from 1603 to 1868.[12]

This story of Tokugawa Japan and of the institutions which it bequeathed to later generations must be told in another chapter.

For Further Reading

HISTORY AND CULTURE: GENERAL

Honjo Eijiro, *The Social and Economic History of Japan* (Kyoto, 1935) The best single volume social and economic history in English.

Murdoch, James, *A History of Japan* (3 vols.). Vol. I, *From the Origins to the Arrival of the Portuguese in 1542* A.D. (Kobe, 1910). Vol. II, *A History of Japan During the Century of Early Foreign Intercourse (1542-1651),* by James Murdoch in collaboration with Yamagata Isoh (Kobe, 1903). Vol. III, *The Tokugawa Epoch 1652-1868,* rev. and ed. by Joseph H. Longford (London, 1926). Heavy in political matters and weak in interpreting the aesthetic side of Japan.

[12] For the period in biography, see Walter Dening, *The Life of Toyotomi Hideyoshi, 1536-1598* (3rd ed., Kobe, 1930), and A. L. Sadler, *The Maker of Modern Japan, the Life of Tokugawa Iyeyasu, 1542-1616* (London, 1937).

Takekoshi Yosaburo, *The Economic Aspects of the History of the Civilization of Japan* (3 vols., New York, 1930). An English translation of a well-known Japanese work.

SPECIAL STUDIES

Anesaki Masahuru, *Prince Shotoku, the Sage Statesman* (Tokyo, 1948).

Asakawa, K., *The Documents of Iriki, Illustrative of the Development of the Feudal Institutions of Japan* (New Haven, 1929).

Benedict, Ruth, *The Chrysanthemum and the Sword: Patterns of Japanese Culture* (Boston, 1946). An able picture of the patterns of Japanese culture.

Groot, Gerard J., *The Prehistory of Japan* (New York, 1951). Depicts the Stone Age culture and relates it to comparable cultures.

Munro, Neil Gordon, *Prehistoric Japan* (Yokohama, 1911).

Takahashi Siego, *A Study of the Origin of the Japanese State* (New York, 1917). A good brief study.

ECONOMIC AND SOCIAL ORGANIZATION

Brown, Delmer M., *Money Economy in Medieval Japan: A Study in the Use of Coins* (New Haven, 1951). Covers the period 1200 to 1600.

Fukukita Yasunosuke, *Cha-no-yu, Tea Cult of Japan* (Tokyo, 1932).

Hani Setsuko, *The Japanese Family System* (Tokyo, 1948).

Sansom, Katharine, *Living in Tokyo* (New York, 1937). Observations on the manner and tone of Japanese life.

PHILOSOPHY AND RELIGION

Anesaki Masahuru, *Nichiren, the Buddhist Prophet* (Cambridge, 1916).

Eliot, Sir Charles, *Japanese Buddhism* (London, 1935).

LITERATURE

Aston, W. G., *A History of Japanese Literature* (London, 1933). Inadequate, but still the only work of its kind in English.

Bowers, Faubion, *Japanese Theater* (New York, 1952).

Miyamori Asataro, trans., *Masterpieces of Japanese Poetry, Ancient and Modern* (2 vols., Tokyo, 1936). One of the largest and most important anthologies in English.

Redesdale, Lord (Mitford, A. B.), *Tales of Old Japan* (London, 1905). A free translation of early Japanese stories.

Reischauer, Edwin O., and Joseph K. Yamagiwa, eds. and trans., *Translations from Early Japanese Literature* (Cambridge, Mass., 1951). Works of the eleventh to thirteenth centuries.

Sugimoto Etsu, *A Daughter of the Samurai* (New York, 1928).

Waley, Arthur, trans., *The Pillow-book of Sei Shonagon* (Boston, 1929). A fine work of interpretation with a scholarly introduction.

———, trans., *The Tales of Genji: A Novel in Six Parts Translated from the Japanese* (London, 1935). An important translation of Japan's greatest early novel.

ART AND ARCHITECTURE

Anesaki Masahuru, *Buddhist Art in Its Relation to Buddhist Ideals, with Special Reference to Buddhism in Japan* (Boston, 1915).

Minamoto, H., *An Illustrated History of Japanese Art,* trans. by Harold G. Henderson (Kyoto, 1935). A systematized arrangement of reproductions and historical explanation.

5

The West Discovers Eastern Asia

THE history of Western contacts with the Far East is a long and fascinating story. It reaches back into the pre-Christian Era. This study, however, is concerned only with years that are distinctly modern—the nineteenth and twentieth centuries. But modern events find their origins in the remote past. A study of the French Revolution involves some delving into the much earlier society of feudalism And so, in seeking to understand the conflicts between the West and the Far East during the past century and a half, it will be of advantage to review, even briefly, some highlights of earlier centuries. What, then, was this pre-nineteenth century heritage in the relations of Europe and America and the Far East?

The time at which Europe gained its first knowledge of China is not known with certainty. Perhaps it was as early as the sixth or even the seventh century B.C. In 128 B.C. the Chinese emperor Wu Ti dispatched the embassy of Chang Ch'ien into west central Asia. The results of this mission were notable. Force and diplomacy extended Chinese influence west of the Pamir divide; regular communication with western Asia was established; and, finally, an indirect trade between China and Europe developed.[1]

Thus there grew at the beginning of the Christian Era a remarkable overland traffic in silk from China to the Roman World. The direct overland route stretched from Antioch through Samarkand, Kashgar, Lopnor, and across Central Asia to the Sera metropolis of

[1] For a detailed account of early relations between Europe and China, consult G. F. Hudson, *Europe and China* (London, 1931), which covers the period to 1800.

Ch'ang-an in western China. Alternate water routes extended from the Red Sea and the Persian Gulf to western India, whence they joined the land route by way of Khotan, or continued eastward by the sea route as far as the modern Hanoi in Indochina. This traffic was due primarily to the Roman demand for silk, not to any Chinese demand for the products of Rome.

The European demand for Chinese silk continued during the first six centuries of the Christian Era. In the sixth century, however, "the smuggled moth" was producing silk in Europe, where the silk industry had been established at Constantinople. The Roman World, and ultimately Europe as a whole, was freed from dependence on China's silk. The early romance of the China trade was for the time being ended.

The sixth century likewise witnessed the rise in Central Asia of the Turks and their advance westward until they had effected diplomatic contacts with the Roman World at Constantinople. This did not lead to direct Roman contacts with China, but it created in Byzantine Greek literature, from Turkish sources, the most revealing picture of China to appear in European literature prior to the accounts of Marco Polo. This was the work of Simocatta, an Egyptian Greek, writing about 630. But, though Europe had lost its interest in China, the annals of the T'ang dynasty contain much on the population and wealth of Byzantium.

The Nestorian Missions

When Christianity, in one or other of its various forms, first reached China is not known. Tradition would have it that Saint Thomas preached there. More substantial evidence attaches to the work of the Nestorian missionaries. The Persian Church, augmented by Nestorian disciples, who were expelled from the Roman Empire, had by the close of the fifth century become Nestorian in doctrine. Its missionaries were active in Mesopotamia, India, and Central Asia, and from there they finally reached China. The record of this Nestorian effort has been preserved on a monument erected at Sian in 781, though not discovered until the seventeenth century.[2] From this and other sources it now appears that the Nestorians

[2] *Sian* is the generally used modern spelling for Hsian (Wade-Giles romanization). In the spelling *Hsianfu,* the *fu* ending is a Manchu dynasty form that was not used in Nationalist China. Again, the T'ang dynasty name was *Ch'ang-an,* not *Hsian.*

reached T'ang China about 635, where they were honorably received by the emperor. Churches were built in several cities and, though at times the faith was persecuted, it appears in general to have been tolerated for two centuries, until, in 845, the missionaries were commanded by the emperor to renounce their priestly calling and to cease to pervert the institution of the country.

The Arab Trade

In Chinese history the period of the Five Dynasties (907-960) and of the Sung dynasty (960-1279), though marked by political weakness, was nevertheless distinguished for cultural brilliance. The Chinese were moving southward and thereby were increasing the relative importance of the Yangtze Valley and the southern coast. A very considerable foreign trade was conducted at Ch'üan-chou (Zayton) in Fukien, and at Canton in Kwangtung. This trade was both encouraged and rigidly controlled by the Sung emperors, who derived a substantial revenue from it. Most of the foreign merchants in this trade were Moslem Arabs, who in general seem to have been well treated, were permitted to settle in the country, to take Chinese wives, to adjust disputes among themselves according to their own laws, and, in some cases, to hold high office in the state. There was, too, among these southern foreigners a colony of Jews. It was this Arab trade which was to carry eventually to Europe a knowledge of Chinese tea. Meanwhile, Islam straddled the trade routes between Europe and the Far East, while Europe's energies were consumed in the monstrous political failure of the Crusades. Following close upon these disasters came the Mongol invasions of Europe. The time had come when in Europe both church and state would seek an escape from this new challenge from Central Asia.

The Renewal of European Interest in China

Christian Europe was beset in the thirteenth century by unprecedented dangers. On the south and southeast lay the fanatical power of Islam. Directly to the east was the rising threat of the Mongol Empire, whose armies in 1222 invaded Europe and defeated the Russians on the Dnieper. Simultaneously, other Mongol armies were advancing eastward upon North China. Before the close of the thirteenth century, the empire built by Chingiz Khan and his successors sprawled across the map of Eurasia from the western borders of Russia to the Pacific. Trade routes from Europe to China, closed for more than four centuries, were again opened. Europe was soon to expand upon the meager knowledge of China which it had gained in the days of the silk trade. The motives inspiring this new European interest in China and the empire of the Tatars were various. Christian Europe was not averse to the possibility of an alliance with the Mongols and the Chinese against the Moslems. The Crusades, quite apart from their spiritual results, had created a new demand for the wares of the East. Finally, the Roman Catholic Church recognized in some measure the new opportunity to carry Christianity to the pagan world. Faith, fear, and the desire for material gain combined to inspire the embassies which Europe was soon to dispatch into Central Asia and the Far East.

The first ambassador of the Catholic Church was a Franciscan, John de Plano Carpini. He delivered a papal letter to the Great Khan at his Mongolian capital in 1246. The Khan's reply was not encouraging. Instead of agreeing to accept Christianity, he counselled the Pope to proceed to the East and there pay homage to the Mongol power. The next Christian missions to the East were sent by Louis IX of France. The first of these, headed by Andrew of Longomeau and designed to secure a treaty of alliance against the Moslems, was rebuffed in 1249. The second of Louis' embassies, sent in 1252, was in charge of a Flemish Franciscan, William of Rubruck. He, like Carpini, was received at the camp of the Great Khan in Mongolia. Neither of them reached China, though both recorded the information they obtained concerning that country.

The Polos in China

Kublai Khan, as ruler of the eastern Mongol dominions, set up his capital at Cambaluc (Khanbaliq, the modern Peking or Pei-p'ing) in 1264. There the Khan received two Venetian merchants, Nicolo and Maffeo Polo, whose travels in Asia had been prompted by neither political nor religious, but rather by commercial, motives. Now, however, they were commissioned by the Khan with letters to the Papacy asking that a hundred scholarly missionaries be sent to the Mongol capital. The Papacy responded by dispatching two

Dominicans who turned back to Europe before the journey was well begun. The Polo brothers, less timorous than their ecclesiastical brethren, returned in 1275 to Kublai's capital, taking with them Nicolo's son Marco. All three entered the service of the Khan and continued to serve him for seventeen years, enjoying both honor and advancement. *The Book of Marco Polo,* written at the close of the century after the return of these intrepid travellers to Europe, gave to the West its first comprehensive picture of China. Marco records the existence in China of Europeans carried there captive by the Mongols. His, too, was the first European account to record the name Zipangu or Chipangu (Japan).

It was just as the Polos were returning for the second time to Europe that the first zealous Roman missionary, John of Monte Corvino, in 1289, was carrying a papal letter to the Khan. Arriving at Cambaluc about 1293, he was permitted to preach, to erect a church, and to be assisted by missionaries sent subsequently to join him. In 1307 the Pope created him Archbishop of Cambaluc, and when, in 1328, Corvino died, there had been created a Christian community of several thousand enjoying the favor of the Mongol dynasty. This favor was a feature of the Mongol policy of cultivating foreign religions as a counterpoise to the Confucian philosophy of their conquered subjects, the Chinese. With the collapse of the Mongol rule in 1368, the Christian community established by Corvino appears to have vanished. Under the subsequent Ming rulers foreign creeds and isms that had been patronized by the Mongols were suppressed.

The fall of the Mongol power interrupted the revival in the silk trade between China and Europe. It also tended to center the attention of Europe upon the spice trade. During the period when the Mongols controlled Persia, prior to its conversion to Islam, Italian traders were permitted direct access to India. They were able to lower the fantastic prices charged by the Egyptian middlemen in the spice trade. Thus when the Mongol power fell and Europeans could no longer trade directly with India, but on the contrary were subject to the exactions and wars of a hostile Islam, a demand was thereby created for a new route to the land of spices. This demand was created just at a time when the European conception of India and the Far East was overcoming the incredulity which had greeted the accounts of Marco Polo.

The All-Sea Route to China

From as early as 1291 Europe had played with the idea of a sea route to the East. Not until two centuries later was this dream brought to fulfillment when, in 1488, Portuguese navigators reached and passed the Cape of Good Hope. Ten years later (1498-1499), Vasco da Gama reached Calicut in India from Lisbon, and returned with a valuable cargo of pepper. Successors of da Gama reached Malacca in 1511. From these advanced trading posts, which now for the first time could be reached by an unbroken sea voyage, the Portuguese advanced to Java, Siam, Indochina, and the southern coasts of China Proper. Meanwhile, they had, by their naval warfare against the Arabs, become the commercial masters of the Arabian Sea. The Portuguese could contemplate with satisfaction their control of the sea route from Lisbon to Malacca.

The China which Portuguese traders were soon to visit was ruled by the last of the great Chinese dynasties, the Ming (1368-1644). The first century of Ming rule had been a period of commercial and maritime vigor dominated by a forceful naval diplomacy. Chinese fleets penetrated the South China Sea and the Indian Ocean, and tribute-bearing embassies from these areas visited China. After 1421, when the Ming capital was moved from Nanking to Peking, maritime interests were subject to increasing neglect. Yet some remnants of the trade remained, for when Portugal's emissary, Albuquerque, reached Malacca, he found a Chinese trading squadron of five junks.

The Portuguese Reach China

The Portuguese reached China from Malacca in 1514. This was a commercial and unofficial enterprise, and though the mariners were not permitted to land, they disposed of their goods at a considerable profit. This auspicious beginning led in 1517 to an official Portuguese mission headed by Thomas Pires, who was conducted to Canton in a pepper-laden Portuguese squadron commanded by Fernam d'Andrade. The embassy was well received at Canton and permission was requested for it to proceed to Peking. In this it was supported by the Canton merchants whose commercial interests had been furthered temporarily by the arrival of the Portuguese in Malacca. Accordingly, in 1519 Pires was ordered to proceed to

Peking. But no sooner had he reached the capital than he was hustled back to Canton and imprisoned. In 1522 the Chinese attacked and destroyed the Portuguese trading post at Canton, though another was soon established nearby at Lappa and survived for some years. Later, Portuguese traders were driven from Ningpo and Amoy. These misfortunes are not difficult to explain. Reports had already reached the Ming court that the Portuguese, far from being bent solely on peaceful commerce, were intent on conquest. Meanwhile, too, Simon d'Andrade, a brother of Fernam, who had reached Canton with a Portuguese license to trade, had outraged Chinese officialdom by his insolence, and by piratical forays along the coast. Consequently, the Portuguese could blame only themselves for their diplomatic and commercial failure.

The Portuguese Post at Macao

The informal trade and the intermittent conflicts waged by the Chinese and the Portuguese along the coasts as far north as Ningpo gave place in 1557 to a somewhat more formal intercourse. In that year the Portuguese established themselves at Macao, a small peninsula joined by a narrow neck of land to Hsiang-shan, now called Chung-shan, which lies in the delta to the south of Canton. Portuguese occupation of this uninviting spot appears to have been arranged quite informally, though in part it may have been a reward for assistance in the suppression of Chinese piracy. At all events the foreigners were permitted to remain, assisted to this end no doubt by a little well-placed bribery, and later by the payment of an annual rent. Across the narrow isthmus, the Chinese constructed a wall with one gate in order that the movements of the Westerners might be the better controlled. Here the Portuguese traders were under the jurisdiction of the Chinese authorities. They themselves, however, were usually allowed to handle cases involving only their own subjects. Beyond this, Chinese control, territorial, judicial, and fiscal, was absolute.[3] It remained so until 1849, at which time the Portuguese began to persist in a claim to exclusive jurisdiction. Macao, nevertheless, was not recognized as Portuguese territory until the Protocol of Lisbon was signed in 1887. Macao, from the time when the Portuguese first settled there until the cession of Hong-

---

[3] H. B. Morse, *The Chronicles of the East India Company Trading to China* (5 vols., Oxford, 1926-29), I, 8-9.

kong to Great Britain in 1842, remained the summer residence of Westerners engaged in the Canton trade. During the later nineteenth century its importance declined steadily.

China's Policy and the Portuguese Trade

The question naturally arises why China, after her expulsion of the Pires mission and her subsequent experience with the Portuguese lawlessness, tolerated these foreign merchants at all. In part it may be explained by the tendency of the Chinese Imperial Court to assert an authority which it was either unwilling or unable to enforce. Certainly the emperor could not bestow his Imperial favor on surly Western barbarians who had respect neither for the dignity of the empire nor for its control over neighboring tributary states. Yet if there was profit to be derived from a limited commerce with the barbarian, he might be permitted to trade informally at a few ports. This was practical and therefore good Chinese doctrine. Actually the Chinese merchants at Canton desired the trade; there were provincial officials who for a consideration would permit the trade; and at Peking, metropolitan officials, likewise for a consideration, might pretend ignorance that there was any trade with the barbarian at all. The consequence was that the trade prospered while the question of diplomatic recognition was ignored.[4]

The Development of Catholic Missions

The rediscovery of China by Portuguese traders renewed and intensified the missionary interest of the Roman Catholic Church.

---

[4] The system of foreign trade that prevailed under the Mings is the key to the politico-commercial difficulties that were to plague China's relations with the Western powers during the later eighteenth and nineteenth centuries. Under the Mings, foreign trade was considered primarily as an instrument for controlling the vassal states, not as a source of government revenue. Local officials, however, found in this trade a door to great wealth. The system worked very well in early Ming times, but with the arrival of the European barbarians (the Portuguese and those who followed them), who did not consider themselves as tributaries, it was subjected to new and powerful pressures. To high Chinese officials at Macao, the Portuguese, who frequently acted in defiance of all law and custom, were "like a tumour on the back." Teh-ch'ang Chang, "Maritime Trade at Canton during the Ming Dynasty," *Chinese Soc. and Pol. Science Rev.* XVII, No. 2 (July, 1933), 264-282. Note also J. K. Fairbank, "Tributary Trade and China's Relations with the West," *Far Eastern Quarterly*, I (1942), 129-49; and J. K. Fairbank and S. Y. Teng, "On the Ch'ing Tributary System," *Harvard Journal of Asiatic Studies*, VI (1941), 135-246.

Francis Xavier, who, in 1549, introduced Catholicism to Japan, was the first zealot in the new campaign to convert the Chinese. Xavier, however, died off the coast of Kwangtung (1552), thwarted in his ambition to carry Catholic Christianity to China. Several missionaries who sought subsequently to enter the country were denied admittance. From these failures came the resolve to train in the Chinese language a selected group of Jesuits who might appeal to Chinese officialdom not on religious grounds but rather through other scholarly attainments. So it was that Matteo Ricci, an Italian and a student of mathematics and astronomy who had joined the Society of Jesus in 1571, came to Macao in 1582. At first garbed in the robes of a Buddhist monk, he contented himself with winning the interest and respect of Chinese officials through his scientific knowledge. His Buddhist robes were later discarded for the dress of a Chinese Confucian scholar, and not without effect, for in 1601 he received permission to reside and preach in Peking, where he continued to live until his death in 1610.[5]

The religious propaganda of Ricci, his associates, and successors, based on their appeal to the scientific and scholarly interests of Chinese officialdom, met with notable success. Among the converts were many princes of the blood, mandarins, and other courtiers. As aids in their missionary work, the Jesuits employed every intellectual, scientific, and mechanical device which the Europe of their day could suggest: clocks, horological instruments, gauges, glass prisms, mathematical and astronomical instruments, and geographical, architectural, literary, and religious books. Ricci prepared for the Chinese a map of the world, on which he tactfully placed China in the middle; his followers corrected the Chinese calendar; others were appointed by the emperor to the post of state astronomer. A century after Ricci's arrival at Canton, the K'ang-hsi emperor granted freedom of worship to the Roman churches throughout the empire.

Persecution and Its Causes

These official favors did not exempt the missionaries from persecution. In 1616 and again in 1664 some of the Jesuits were expelled from Peking and forced to return to Canton or Macao. In fact it is

[5] K. S. Latourette, *A History of Christian Missions in China* (New York, 1932), 91-98.

surprising that in the seventeenth century there was not more persecution. Neo-Confucianism under the Ming emperors was inclined to be fixed and intolerant; Buddhism and Taoism were permitted but were regulated closely. The Imperial Court under the late Mings and under the first Manchu rulers did not look with favor on an exclusive, authoritarian, and dogmatic religion such as Catholicism. Actually, seventeenth-century China, whatever its limitations may have been, was more tolerant than Catholic Europe. At the very moment when the Papacy was seeking tolerance for its monks in China, Alva, as agent of the Counter Reformation, was seeking to crush by the sword heresy in the Netherlands. A Church that denied tolerance to Europe insisted upon it from the Chinese. And when finally Christianity was proscribed by Peking (1724), responsibility rested upon the missionaries rather than upon Chinese officialdom.

The Rites Controversy

For some fifty years after the arrival of Ricci, the Jesuits were the only Christian missionaries in China, but in the following century they were joined by representatives of the Dominicans (1631), the Franciscans (1633), the Augustinians (1680), and the Paris Foreign Missions (1683). With the arrival of these competing orders, many of the policies toward doctrine and procedure which had been adopted by the Jesuits were attacked by the late comers. These disputes may be classified under three heads, all of importance to the theological mind of the times. They involved the major question whether Christianity as practiced by the Church should compromise with Chinese culture in order to appear less antagonistic to China's political and social institutions. Under the first group of controversies was the question whether Chinese classical terms, such as *T'ien* (Heaven), known to all Chinese scholars, should be used by the missionary and given a Christian connotation. In the second group fell such questions as to whether Chinese converts should be forbidden to engage in ceremonies honoring Confucius and the ancestors. Finally, there were numerous miscellaneous problems. Would the Church permit Masses to "be said for the souls of the non-Christian ancestors of [Chinese] Christians?"[6]

Ricci and his immediate followers had recognized that if Christianity was to make progress in China, it must accommodate itself

---

[6] Latourette, *A History of Christian Missions in China,* 132-135.

to some of the beliefs and practices of Confucianism and ancestor worship. Thus he maintained that the ceremonies to Confucius and to ancestors were civil and not religious acts. Therefore a convert to Catholicism could participate in them without violating his religion. Some of the Jesuits themselves doubted the moral basis of this liberal policy, but by the Franciscans and by the Dominicans such practices were stoutly opposed. Furthermore, the Jesuits permitted use of the Chinese character *T'ien* (Heaven) in referring to the Christian God. The rival orders asserted that *T'ien-chu* (Lord of Heaven) was the correct character. These disputes raged on among the missionaries for the better part of a century, and finally were carried for settlement both to the emperor in Peking and to the Pope in Rome. In 1700, the Manchu K'ang-hsi emperor decided in favor of the Jesuits, while in Rome the Papacy supported their critics. The resulting situation was ludicrous. No missionary could go to China as a representative of the Roman Church unless he accepted the Papacy as the final authority on the true significance of China's religious ideographs; such missionaries as accepted this authority, the Manchu emperor would not receive. The net result of this extraordinary episode was that in 1724 all missionaries, save a few who were retained for scientific work, were expelled.[7] Despite this development, the Church fared better than it deserved. Many of its converts retained their faith, and courageous missionaries more interested in the work of salvation than in theological disputation entered China secretly at the risk of their lives to minister to the faithful and to win new converts.

The Spaniards Reach the Philippines

Less than a decade after the first Portuguese navigators reached Canton, Spanish explorers were crossing the Pacific after rounding Cape Horn. In March, 1521, Ferdinand Magellan, a Portuguese by birth but sailing under the flag of Spain, discovered the Mariana or Ladrone (Robber) Islands, and later in the same month reached Samar in the Philippines. At Cebu, Magellan found a native population engaged in trade with China. Junks from Siam visited in Philippine waters, while in the markets of Cebu brass gongs and a

[7] A full and excellent discussion of the origin and development of anti-missionary feeling and anti-foreignism in China during the seventeenth and eighteenth centuries is given in Earl H. Pritchard, *Anglo-Chinese Relations during the Seventeenth and Eighteenth Centuries* (Urbana, 1931), ch. vi.

variety of articles gave evidence of an extensive trade with the Chinese.

The Spaniards, however, were not seeking the Philippines or China, but the Spice Islands, which lay to the south. As it happened, these islands, by the line of demarcation of 1494, lay, as did also the Philippines, in the Portuguese half of the world. It was not, then, until some years later that Spain undertook conquest and exploration of the Philippines. Manila was founded in 1571, by which time the Chinese trade with the islands was considerable. In this trade the Spaniards were soon involved, for they had failed to find in the Philippines the coveted wealth of the Spice Islands, and they could not trade directly with China, which was recognized as lying within the Portuguese sphere. Herein lies the explanation of the rapid increase in the Chinese commerce with Manila and in the Chinese population of that city.

The Dutch in the Far East

Fresh from their successful struggle for national independence, the Dutch reached the Far East at the beginning of the seventeenth century. Organization of the United Dutch East India Company signalized the emerging commercial supremacy of the Netherlands and its determination, with England, to destroy the colonial and mercantile monopoly of Spain and Portugal. The Dutch attempted to open trade at Canton in 1604, and again in 1607, but on both occasions permission was denied, probably at the instigation of the Portuguese at Macao. In retaliation, the Dutch attacked Macao unsuccessfully in 1622. Subsequent attacks on the Portuguese were conducted from a new Dutch base on the Pescadores Islands near Taiwan (Formosa). Here too the Dutch carried on trade with Chinese from the mainland until, under pressure from Chinese authorities, they were forced to retire to Formosa (1624), where on the west coast of the island they constructed a factory (trading post) and a fort known as Zelandia Castel. Here the Dutch were advantageously situated for the development of their trade between the East Indies and Japan, and for the formalizing of their relations with China. In 1662, however, they were driven from Formosa by Cheng Ch'eng-kung, known popularly as Koxinga, a partisan of the last Ming aspirants who had not yet been suppressed by China's new Manchu rulers. Two decades later the Dutch, who meanwhile had assisted the Manchus in the overthrow of Koxinga's mushroom state (Formosa, Amoy, and part of Fukien), were permitted, along with the English, to trade at Amoy, but such were the exactions of the Manchu military that the trade was soon virtually abandoned.

During the seventeenth and the eighteenth centuries the Dutch sent four embassies to Peking (1656, 1667, 1685-1686, and 1795) seeking formal contacts with the Manchu Court and commercial concessions. The ambassadors were required to perform the humiliating *kotow* (nine prostrations), in return for which they received only meager commercial privileges. After 1729 the Dutch traded regularly at Canton.

The Dutch were the first representatives of the Protestant faith in China. Though they sent no missionaries to the Far East, their traders, who had tasted the bitterness of religious persecution in Europe, did not fail to warn the Chinese against the political and social dangers inherent in the Roman Catholic system, in which the spiritual allegiance of Chinese converts was transferred from Peking to Rome.

The English Reach China

The first English vessel to reach Canton was dispatched in 1635 by the English East India Company. This was followed by a squadron of English vessels, commanded by Captain John Weddell, sent by the Courteen Association. Weddell arrived at Macao in 1637, proceeded to Canton, and at first met with opposition from the Chinese, but was finally permitted to engage in trade. The English sent ships regularly to Canton after 1699, which is the probable date of the beginning of their permanent factory there.

Other European nations played an inconspicuous role in this early China trade. The first French ship to reach Canton arrived in 1698; the first Danish ship in 1731; the first Swedish ship in 1732; and the first Russian ship in 1753. The first American ship, *The Empress of China,* sailed for China in 1784.

First Russian Contacts with China

While western Europeans in the sixteenth and seventeenth centuries were making their first contacts with China by the all-sea route, Russians were moving to the East by way of Siberia. These first adventurers were composed of a motley aggregation of explorers, fur traders, and fugitives from the law. Some of them reached the Pacific slope, while across Siberia appeared permanent settlements at Tobolsk, Tomsk, Yakutsk, Nertchinsk, and other points. In far eastern Siberia there was a natural tendency for the Russians to move south into the valley of the Amur River. Here they came into conflict with tribal peoples who, theoretically at least, recognized the overlordship of China. For some years there was intermittent conflict between the Russians and the Chinese at Albazin, a Muscovite outpost on the upper Amur. Not until 1689 was a boundary settlement effected by the Russo-Chinese Treaty of Nertchinsk, China's first treaty with a Western power. As a result of this settlement, in which the Chinese negotiators were assisted by Jesuit advisers, Peking retained and extended its sovereignty over the Amur Valley. A number of Russian embassies were sent subsequently to Peking during the eighteenth century. A settlement of the Russo-Chinese northwestern boundary was reached in 1727, and permanent trading posts were established on the frontier. Permission was also given for establishment of a Russian church in Peking, and China sent to St. Petersburg her only embassy to a foreign court.

The West Discovers Japan

It was more than two centuries after the travels of the Polos in China before Europeans set foot on the shores of Japan. The account generally accepted relates that in 1542 (Japanese sources say 1543) Portuguese sailors voyaging from Macao to Siam were blown from their course to the shores of Tanegashima, a small island off the southern coast of Kyushu, where they instructed the natives in the use of firearms. These visitors were followed closely by Fernando Mendez Pinto, to whom the discovery of Japan is usually credited. He, too, appears to have impressed the Japanese with the admirable qualities of the gun. More Portuguese ships soon appeared, for the feudal lords of southern Japan took readily to the idea of trade with the foreigners.

These commercial contacts with southern Japan aroused the interest of the Portuguese monks. Francis Xavier, a Jesuit who had been preaching in Goa, Travancore, and Malacca, was inspired to visit the Japanese. In this he was influenced by Anjiro (Yajiro), a Japanese who had been carried to Goa on a Portuguese ship. In company with a brother missionary, Father Fernandez, Xavier landed at Kagoshima in August, 1549. For more than two years he pursued in this new field the most successful mission of his life. The Japanese, far from repelling the foreigner, welcomed both his commerce and his religion.

Other Jesuits followed Xavier to Japan, where their work soon testified to their vigorous spirit and to the tolerance of the Japanese. The missionaries were heard respectfully by all classes of the people, including Buddhist priests. This may be accounted for partly by certain similarities between the rites and ceremonials of Buddhism and Catholicism. Also, since Catholicism was introduced directly from India, many Japanese assumed that it was a reformed Buddhism. Some of the Japanese feudal lords in their official edicts referred to Catholicism as "the New Buddhism from the Western Nations." It may of course be questioned whether many of the Japanese converts possessed any profound understanding of the new Western religion, for it has been noted that "Japanese is a difficult language and Christianity is hard to explain."

Other causes, too, contributed to the early success of Christianity in Japan. The feudal barons desired the profits of the foreign trade, and those in southern Japan, where most of the trade was conducted, were eager to increase their own power at the expense of the shogun's government. These barons observed the deference paid by the Portuguese traders to the missionaries. They concluded that where the missionary was, there too would be the trader. In Kyushu, the barons, on occasion, ordered the mass conversion of their retainers to Christianity and even instigated persecution of the Buddhists; but if no foreign ship arrived, the populace was as often commanded to revert to the native faith. But although the Japanese were attracted by the learning and dignity of the Jesuits, they were at a loss to understand their intolerance. Thus, while gaining many converts through one influence or another, the missionaries aroused bitter opposition to themselves and their creed. Their main strongholds were in Kyushu, but they enjoyed some success in Kyoto, where a group of Jesuits was received by the shogun and also by Nobunaga (1568), who befriended them in his desire to curb the political power of Buddhism.

The Spaniards in Japan

Until 1592 the Portuguese were the only Europeans to reach Japan. When Philip II of Spain ascended the throne of Portugal in

1581, he confirmed his Portuguese subjects in the exclusive right to the Japan trade. Four years later the Papacy conferred upon the Jesuits the sole right to enter Japan as missionaries. It was just at this time (1591) that Hideyoshi, planning the conquest of China, sent an embassy to Manila demanding that the Spaniards there recognize Japan as their suzerain. The Spanish governor sent two missions to Japan, carrying among their number four Franciscan friars, who, in the guise of ambassadors, entered Japan in violation of the papal order. Other priests who soon followed were permitted to remain on the understanding that they should not preach Christianity. Having accepted this prohibition, the priests proceeded immediately to violate it by conducting services in Nagasaki, Kyoto, and Osaka. Hideyoshi had at first been disposed favorably toward the foreign priests, but he had become suspicious of political implications in the Jesuit policy and conduct. In confirmation of his fears, he now observed the Spanish priests openly defying his authority, and promoting, as in China, sectarian feuds with their Jesuit colleagues. Finally, the idle boasting of a Spanish pilot to the effect that the missionary was preparing the way for political conquest led Hideyoshi to act. In February, 1597, six Franciscans, three Japanese Jesuits, and seventeen Japanese laymen were crucified at Nagasaki. In explanation of this vigorous act, it should be noted that ten years earlier, Hideyoshi, after subduing the *daimyo* of Satsuma, where most of the Christians lived, had issued an edict ordering the foreign missionaries to leave Japan within twenty days. This edict was directed against the priests, not against their religion, for the Japanese desired to continue the Portuguese trade. The edict was in consequence modified to permit priests to accompany the Portuguese ships but not to remain in Japan. But for a number of reasons the law was not enforced effectively. Priests defied the law; some of them were protected by friendly barons in Kyushu; Hideyoshi's attention was diverted both by war at home and abroad. Thus, when the first crucifixions occurred in 1597, the Spanish priests could not plead ignorance of the law. Hideyoshi, it will be observed, did not interfere with the Jesuits. Probably he feared stoppage of the valuable Portuguese trade.

The Foreign Policy of Iyeyasu

With the passing of Hideyoshi (1598), political control in Japan passed into the hands of Tokugawa Iyeyasu, the able founder of the last great shogunate. Iyeyasu's views on foreign policy and trade were probably more enlightened than any that prevailed at the time, even in Europe. During his rule the Portuguese, the Spaniards, the Dutch, and the English were all welcomed in Japanese ports. The exclusion edict against foreign priests was not revoked; neither was it enforced. Spanish monks from Manila again entered Japan, and in 1608 the Papacy rescinded the restriction which had granted the field solely to the Jesuits.

In 1600 the first Dutch ship reached Japan. It was one of a fleet of five vessels which had sailed by way of the Straits of Magellan, and, blown from its course, had sought shelter in the Japanese harbor of Bungo. The pilot of the vessel was an English sailor, Will Adams, who, because of his natural wit and ability, was promptly employed by Iyeyasu as adviser in matters of commerce and navigation. Other Dutch ships arrived in 1609, and a Dutch factory was built at Hirado, an island near Nagasaki. News of these successes brought the first English ship to Hirado in 1613. Iyeyasu, influenced by Adams, offered the English a charter for free trade and urged them to construct a factory at his capital, Yedo, the modern Tokyo. The short-sighted English Captain Saris preferred to remain with his factory and trade at Hirado. There the business was handled incompetently and abandoned in 1623, at a time when the Dutch trade was prospering.

Iyeyasu was likewise interested in developing closer commercial relations with Spain. He communicated with the Spanish authorities in the Philippines, offered to open the ports of eastern Japan to Spanish ships, and allowed it to be understood that the edicts against the missionaries would not be enforced. But it soon appeared that Spain was more likely to send missionaries than traders to Japan. The problem, presented in its simplest terms, was that Iyeyasu was suspicious of Spanish motives. The Dutch and English asserted that priests were not essential to trade. Accordingly, in 1612 Iyeyasu proscribed the Christian faith. All the Franciscan churches and many of the Jesuit establishments were destroyed. Some Japanese converts were executed in Yedo (1613), and in the following year suppression of the faith was ordered throughout the empire. However, most of the foreign missionaries were not harmed at this time, and many of the local barons refused to act against the native Christians in their domains. Hidetada, who succeeded Iyeyasu in 1616, executed some Spanish priests, yet the laws were still not fully enforced. The government sought rather to have the priests leave the country voluntarily, whereas native Christians were induced by peaceful means to abandon the faith. Actually this policy failed, for the priests were defiant, and most of the converts clung to their new-found religion.

The Policy of Exclusion and Seclusion

The Catholic priesthood and their converts were, it seemed to the shogun, creating a rival authority in Japan which the shogunate was no longer willing to tolerate. Accordingly, in 1624 the Spaniards were ordered to leave the country. Direct relations between Japan and the Philippines were severed. Then in 1636 Iyemitsu, son and successor of Hidetada, proscribed Japanese trade on the high seas. No Japanese vessel might proceed abroad; no Japanese subject could lawfully leave his country; those doing so and attempting to return would suffer death. For this revolutionary policy, Catholic Christianity was in part responsible. Many Japanese converts had gone abroad to receive instruction at Macao or Manila, whence they returned to propagate the faith in their native land. This practice was now stopped, while at the same time foreigners who were permitted to remain in Japan were sharply controlled. The Dutch were still permitted to trade at Hirado, but at Nagasaki the Portuguese were forced to conduct their commerce virtually as prisoners on a small artificial island known as Deshima.

These forceful measures did not end the trouble. The Shimabara revolt of 1637, a movement occasioned by feudal oppression and Christian persecutions, involved a large number of Japanese converts and was believed to have been incited by the missionaries. The government acted promptly. Spanish and Portuguese subjects were forbidden to visit Japan. Furthermore, it was decreed that if any Portuguese ship came to Japan, the vessel and cargo would be burned and the crew put to death. A Portuguese embassy of 73 persons, seeking to prove Portuguese innocence of the Shimabara revolt, met exactly this fate. A second embassy sent to Japan after Portugal had regained her independence from Spain failed also.

Japan in Seclusion

In this manner Japan entered upon a long period of exclusion and seclusion. The Dutch, to be sure, were permitted to carry on a limited trade confined to the island of Deshima in Nagasaki harbor, and the Chinese could send a few junks annually to the same port. Except for these contacts Japan was excluded from the outside world, and was to remain so for more than two centuries, the centuries (1638-1854) in which the Western powers built and consolidated their colonial empires.

For Further Reading

Appleton, W. W., *A Cycle of Cathay* (New York, 1951). The Chinese vogue in England during the seventeenth and eighteenth centuries.

Boxer, C. R., *Fidalgos in the Far East, 1550-1770: Fact and Fancy in the History of Macao* (The Hague, 1948). A history of early Macao and Portuguese contacts with China.

———, ed., *South China in the Sixteenth Century* (London, 1953). Accounts of Western travelers in China written between 1553 and 1576.

Chang T'ien-tsê, *Sino-Portuguese Trade from 1514 to 1644. A Synthesis of Portuguese and Chinese Sources* (Leyden, 1934).

Hart, Henry H., *Sea Roads to the Indies* (New York, 1950). An account of Portuguese exploration.

———, *Venetian Adventurer* (3rd ed., Stanford University, 1947). Researches on Marco Polo.

Lloyd, Christopher, *Pacific Horizons: the Exploration of the Pacific before Captain Cook* (London, 1946).

Moule, A. C., *Christians in China before the Year 1550* (London, 1930). Of value as a source book.

Plattner, Felix A., *Jesuits Go East.* Translated from the German by Lord Sudley and Oscar Blobel (Westminster, Md., 1952). A record of missionary activity in the East, 1541-1786.

Ricci, Matthew, *China in the Sixteenth Century: The Journals of Matthew Ricci: 1583-1610.* Translated from the Latin by Louis J. Gallagher (New York, 1953).

Rowbotham, Arnold H., *Missionary and Mandarin: The Jesuits at the Court of China* (Berkeley, 1942).

Stein, Sir Mark A., *On Ancient Central-Asian Tracks* (London, 1933).

6

The Canton Trade

THE sixteenth and seventeenth centuries, as noted in the previous chapter, gave promise of a rich and permanent intercourse, both material and cultural, between Europe and the Far East. In China there was an intelligent and on the whole a tolerant audience ready to listen while Jesuits lectured on Europe's science. In Japan, the commercial and economic ideas of Tokugawa Iyeyasu far surpassed in liberality the economic policies of contemporary leaders in Europe. Yet by 1638 Japan had closed her doors to all foreign intercourse save for the annual Dutch ship and a few Chinese junks at Nagasaki. China likewise adopted a policy of cultural if not commercial exclusion. Repelled by the exclusive philosophy of the Catholic Church and by the quarrelsome character of its rival religious orders, the Chinese government expelled the missionaries in 1724. Thus the trade between Europe and Japan was ended, while such trade as remained with China enjoyed only a precarious, unstable existence. This China trade, dominated in the sixteenth century by the Portuguese, passed during the seventeenth century into the hands of the Dutch, who by the beginning of the eighteenth century were in turn surrendering it to their English rivals.

The eighteenth century was in fact notable for two distinct though perhaps related movements in the relations of the West (Europe) and the Far East. The first was the rise and the decline in Europe of a pronounced Chinese influence: artistic, cultural, and intellectual. The second was the development of what was known as the Canton trade. It was this trade, maintained in the curious circumstances which prevailed at Canton from 1750 to 1839, that precipitated the nineteenth-century conflict between the West and the Far East.

CHINA'S INFLUENCE UPON EUROPE

At the beginning of the eighteenth century polite society in Europe spoke of Chinese art with ease and familiarity. The brilliant masquerades of the French court were dominated by the art of China. The work of many of Europe's rococo artists was enriched if not inspired by the elaborate arts of southern China. To Europeans, the word porcelain connoted China; in England it actually was called "china," and still is. Lacquer ware, a rarity in the time of Louis XIV, was almost a commonplace in eighteenth-century France. Europe was influenced not only by Chinese styles in ornamentation, but also by Chinese technical skills in the coloring of silks.

Side by side with these Chinese influences upon the Paris *salon* were others playing upon the intellectual life of so-called "enlightened" Europe. European philosophers such as Leibnitz, La-Mettrie, and Quesnay found in Confucian philosophy support for the rational basis of their systems of "pure thought." The physiocrats derived in part their notions on the economic nature of the state from their conception of conditions in ancient China. Lastly, it may be noted that in the late eighteenth century Europe's "Back to Nature" movement and the development of a sentimental nature-worship found some of their inspiration in the form and symbolism of the Chinese garden. This particular enthusiasm was the final and the most extreme form of China's cultural influence upon Western society. In England the Confucian legend of the good governor appealed to the intellectuals. The Deists liked its materialism. Confucian humanism and the seemingly perfected Chinese way of life were regarded as thoroughly sound by stable Tories and cautious Whigs. Confucius became the symbol of an orderly *status quo*.

As the eighteenth century drew to a close, China ceased to be a source of vital inspiration to either the art or the philosophy of Europe. This was due in part to the altered views and changed status of the Jesuits. To a great degree the intellectual bridge between China and Europe had been built by the Jesuits. They had found in China something akin to the ideal state, and they had so reported it to Europe. But the expulsion of the missionaries by

China and the later dissolution of the Jesuits in Europe destroyed the main carrier of Chinese thought and influence.[1]

Cultural Enthusiasm Becomes Skepticism

With the passing of the Jesuit contact, Chinese cultural influence not only ceased to reach Europe, but such influence as persisted there was subjected to attack. The authenticity of the early Chinese annals was questioned. In England (1790) Chinese philosophy was dismissed by one writer as virtually worthless. Save for a few remnants here and there, the China of art, letters, and philosophy had by 1800 all but disappeared from the European mind. Yet quite another China was already making its appeal to Europe. This was a material China rather than an aesthetic one; an economic China rather than an intellectual one. Unlike the China that had appealed to the intellectuals of the European enlightenment, this was a China that appealed to the moneyed barons of the English East India Company. It was a China of statistics and markets, and, so the barons hoped, of larger and larger profits.

Thus it was that as the later eighteenth century advanced, Europe's cultural interest in China was replaced by a growing commercial interest—an interest that tended more and more to be monopolized by the British, which is to say, by the powerful English East India Company. This did not mean of course that other nationals were excluded from the trade of the China coast, but their share in it was circumscribed by political events. For instance, the Portuguese who had dominated the early trade (1517–*ca.*1600), maintained themselves continuously at Macao during the seventeenth, eighteenth, and nineteenth centuries, enjoying the profits of a small but lucrative, if not always honorable, trade. The Dutch, who dominated the eastern trade in the seventeenth century, failed to maintain this lead against the British in China. France, defeated by Britain in the colonial struggle, was unable to bid seriously for the China trade. So it was that as the eighteenth century advanced, the China trade became more and more the property of the English East India Company. Britain's victories in the colonial wars, her established position

[1] See Adolf Reichwein, *China and Europe* (New York, 1925), for a full discussion of intellectual and artistic contacts in the eighteenth century. Also, W. W. Appleton, *A Cycle of Cathay: The Chinese Vogue in England during the Seventeenth and Eighteenth Centuries* (New York, 1951).

in India, and her primacy in the industrial revolution all served to stimulate her trade with the Far East. In fact, from 1750 until 1834 it may be said that China's relations with Europe were essentially her relations with the English East India Company. For most of this period China's foreign trade was confined to the single South China port of Canton. Thus, this commerce came to be known as the Canton trade. The peculiar circumstances surrounding this trade, the attitude of the Chinese toward the foreign barbarians, and the attitude of foreign barbarians in turn toward the "heathen" Chinese —all these had created by 1839 a crisis in the relations between Great Britain and China. It was this crisis and the wars which followed it that were to determine the relations of China and the West for the succeeding century (1840-1940).

The Canton Trade: Early Development

The trade at Canton in the seventeenth century had been granted by China as a monopoly to the Portuguese, and as late as 1681 the Portuguese, by reason of this grant and because of their establishment at Macao, were still successful in excluding all other nationals from this commerce. However, in 1685, when the emperor of China declared all ports open to foreign commerce, the English East India Company was granted the right to establish a factory—that is, to trade—at Canton.[2] Since subsequent efforts to trade at ports other than Canton did not prove successful, the Company centered its efforts at Canton, to which ships were dispatched regularly after 1715. The increase in the size and value of the trade encouraged the Company to maintain a regular staff at Canton and Macao. The French also set up a factory at Canton. Thus the tendency for the foreign trade to gravitate to Canton was well under way when the Chinese government, in 1757, speeded the movement by decreeing that all the foreign trade should be confined to this city. From this time on the English East India Company's trade prospered. By the close of the century the Canton trade had become in large measure a British trade, monopolized by the English East India Company.[3]

---

[2] On the trade of various countries at Canton, see the tables compiled by Earl H. Pritchard, "The Struggle for Control of the China Trade," *Pacific Historical Review,* III (1934), 280-295.

[3] See the analysis of the eighteenth-century trade with China by Pritchard, *loc. cit.*

The primacy enjoyed by British trade was not, however, a reflection of British satisfaction with the commercial system that prevailed at Canton. On the contrary, the British, like all other foreign traders in China, regarded these conditions as exceedingly irksome. Accordingly, between 1787 and 1816 the British sent three embassies to Peking to establish a more reasonable system of trade. These

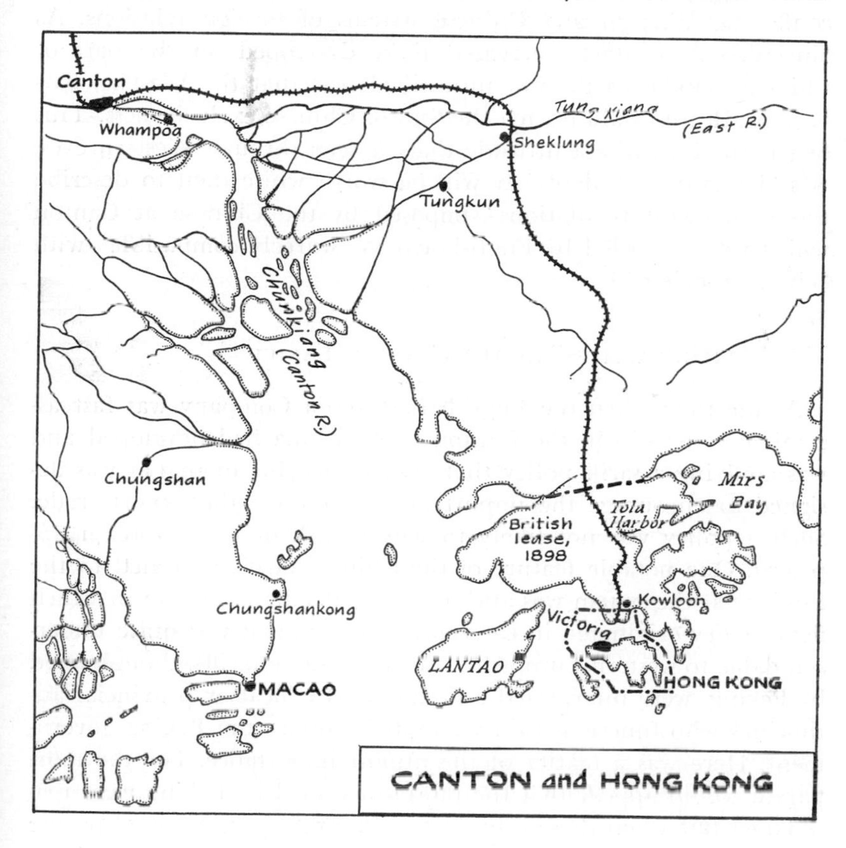

successive embassies, headed by Charles Cathcart (1787), George Macartney (1792-93), and Lord Amherst (1816), all failed.

The failure of the missions and the insults to which the British believed they had been subjected served to clarify the alternatives facing British policy at Canton. To English commercial interests and to the government it was becoming increasingly clear that English trade at Canton might follow one of three policies: (1) complete submission to a commercial system prescribed and controlled wholly by the Chinese; (2) complete abandonment of the trade (an unlikely course, since the trade was profitable even under the worst conditions); and (3) the application of force to compel the Chinese to do business on terms dictated by the West. Certainly a situation had arisen in which if Britishers and Chinese were to do business at Canton some accommodation would have to be found between the conflicting Western and Chinese systems of foreign relations. As Sino-Western contacts increased there developed on the part of Chinese mandarins the not unjustified fear that the Western barbarian culture would breach the wall of Chinese exclusiveness. This fear created a Chinese attitude that, as seen through Western eyes, was "haughty and aloof." It will be worth while then to describe those "arrogant regulations" imposed by the Chinese at Canton which were regarded by Englishmen as "scarcely compatible" with "civilized society."[4]

THE "IRREGULARITIES" OF THE CHINESE TARIFF

At the time when the English East India Company was fast assuming leadership in the Canton trade, China had developed and was applying a tariff policy that was remarkable in that it was designed to encourage the import and discourage the export trade. Such a policy was not likely to win British or other foreign approval. One notable feature of the Chinese tariffs appealed to the foreigners—the system was authorized by Peking. A system in which fiscal policy originated in the central government was quite understandable to western Europeans. But these same tariffs, though fixed by Peking, were interpreted and applied by local or provincial authorities who functioned only nominally under the Peking government. Here was a matter of the utmost importance. For the most part it would appear that the rates sanctioned by Peking were reasonable. But when these rates were interpreted and applied by the local customs authorities, the tariff became far from reasonable—such, at least, was the constant complaint of the foreign traders at Canton.

This complaint was not without some foundation. The chief Chinese customs officials and their staffs had every reason to seek rapid and ready fortunes. Each chief together with his staff enjoyed

---

[4] Earl Pritchard, *Anglo-Chinese Relations during the Seventeenth and Eighteenth Centuries* (Urbana, 1931), 189-190.

only a short term in office. He had paid heavily for the office; he continued to pay for the favor of the higher authorities; he was required to see that fixed contributions reached the Imperial government; and he would indeed be short-sighted not to make provision for his own later days of retirement. All these ends he accomplished by a constant though irregular pressure on the foreign trade. These unpredictable exactions meant fortunes to the customs bureaucracy but were an abomination to the foreign traders.

British traders frequently voiced their protests in Parliament. They complained that from the moment a foreign vessel reached Canton her business was delayed by underlings of the custom house on all manner of frivolous pretexts for the purpose of extorting unauthorized charges. The duty on imports was levied "in an arbitrary manner by low, unprincipled men, who openly demand bribes." The merchants thus claimed that the actual duties paid were of uncertain amount, and that local "exactions" far exceeded the rate prescribed by the Imperial tariff. In general, the merchants held that, although the Imperial rates appeared to be moderate, they were so little regarded in practice that it was scarcely possible to name any fixed charge, save on a few articles.[5] In fact, the policy of the local officials at Canton was to keep the foreigner in ignorance of the actual tariff schedule. In summary, it may be said then that the foreigners disliked a tariff system that was arbitrary and unpredictable, but so long as profits were great they were not likely to do much about it.

The Canton Monopoly—The Co-hong

In the early nineteenth century, British traders, so it was said, found China as difficult to enter as Heaven and as difficult to get out of as Chancery. This was merely a way of saying that the Canton trade was a monopoly, and that the Chinese, at least a favored few of them, were the monopolists. There was of course nothing shocking to the English East India Company in the fact of monopoly. The Company was itself a monopoly. But when Chinese traders exacted monopoly profits at the expense of Western traders, monopoly as a principle lost much of its virtue.

The monopoly system that prevailed at Canton from 1757 to 1842

5 See Stanley F. Wright, *China's Struggle for Tariff Autonomy 1843-1938* (Shanghai, 1938), 1-5.

bore resemblance in some respects to commercial institutions and practices of Europe in the Middle Ages, namely, to the staple and the gild merchant or hanse. In Europe the gild merchant was a society whose primary purpose was to secure and hold a monopolistic privilege of carrying on trade. In China, the Co-hong, which corresponded to the gild merchant, was an instrumentality of Imperial politics as well as of trade.

The origins and character of the Co-hong are not without interest. At the beginning of the eighteenth century, although the foreign trade had gravitated to Canton where it was restricted in many ways, it was not subject to any *consistent* regulation. Private bargaining had a good deal to do with what each ship was required to pay in the matter of fees. But in 1702 Peking appointed a single Canton merchant, who might be called the emperor's merchant, charged with handling the entire business of the foreign traders. This system satisfied no one save the emperor's merchant. Therefore he soon found it expedient to admit other Canton firms, on payment of a fee, to share in the foreign trade.

Against the power of these Chinese firms and of the Hoppo (the commissioner of customs at Canton), the foreign traders found no redress from what they considered to be their legitimate grievances. They were denied liberty to trade with whom they would. They were not free to engage Chinese servants in the factories. They were restricted in buying provisions for the factories and the ships. Sometimes they were denied the privilege of re-exporting unsold goods duty free.

In 1720 the Canton merchants who shared in the foreign trade formed themselves, presumably with the approval of local officials, into one body, the Co-hong, in order the better to control the price that might be demanded from the foreigners for cargoes of silk and tea. Exactions and monopolistic controls on the trade thus continued to increase. A practice had arisen by 1736 whereby every foreign vessel was to be "secured"; that is, it was to be assigned to a security merchant who was to be responsible not only for the sale of the inbound cargo and provision of an outbound cargo, but also for every operation connected with the arrival and departure of the ship. Imperial decrees of 1755 required that in future only Hong merchants could act as security merchants. After 1782 "The Twelve," later "The Thirteen Security Merchants," or Co-hong, was more closely controlled by the government, being directly subject to the Hoppo, and was made the instrument for exacting a great revenue from the foreign trade for the benefit primarily of the Hoppo and, indirectly, through him, of the Canton officials and the Court of Peking.[6] The Co-hong was to insure that foreigners observed the rules of the government and was to act as the sole medium of communication between the government and the foreign traders. These functions were thus superimposed on its monopolistic control of the trade itself. Thus this merchant gild, the Co-hong, "operated in close touch with the agents of government, receiving their full support on the one hand, and on the other serving as the channel through which was transmitted the stream of wealth in which the officials [of government] expected to share largely."[7]

The End of the Company's Monopoly, 1833

In 1833 occurred an event of great significance. The English East India Company's monopolistic charter giving it exclusive control of English trade at Canton expired and Parliament did not renew it. So far as England was concerned, the trade was now open to any British merchant who had a mind to engage in it. This change foreshadowed grave complications in the commercial relations of Chinese and foreigners. Prior to 1833 the English traders at Canton had been under the control of a mere commercial agent, the chief factor of the Company there, but after 1833, with the abolition of the Company's monopoly, His Britannic Majesty was to be represented in the Canton trade by a "commissioned officer not only as a protector of his subjects and an overseer of their commercial activities, *but as a political and diplomatic representative*" of the British Crown.[8] The Crown was not likely to bow without protest to those real or supposed indignities and to the "exactions" under which, at China's will, the *Fan-hwei* (foreign devils) had previously traded

[6] Pritchard, *Anglo-Chinese Relations*, 141-142. The Hong merchants were among the world's greatest businessmen and traders of this period. Most popular with the American traders at Canton was the Hong merchant, Houqua (Wu Ping-ch'ien). He is described by Thomas W. Ward of Salem as "very rich," "just in his dealings," "a man of honour and veracity," who "loves flattery and can be coaxed." Joseph Downs, "The American Trade with the Far East," in *The China Trade and Its Influences* (New York, 1941), 15.

[7] H. B. Morse, *The Gilds of China* (2nd ed., Shanghai, 1932), 78. See also John Barrow, *Travels in China* (Philadelphia, 1805), 414. Barrow was private secretary to the Earl of Macartney during the latter's mission to China.

[8] The italics are mine. See W. C. Costin, *Great Britain and China 1833-1860* (Oxford, 1937).

at Canton. This change in the status of British traders and of the agent who was to represent British interests at Canton set the stage for the ensuing Anglo-Chinese troubles that resulted finally (1839-1842) in the first Anglo-Chinese war, sometimes called the Opium War.

On December 10, 1833, Lord Napier, a Scottish peer of distinction, received a royal commission as First Superintendent of (British) Trade at Canton.[9] On his arrival at Macao (July, 1834), he proceeded to carry out his instructions, which, although they appeared proper enough from the Western point of view, were, if pressed, bound to result in conflict. Napier was required to announce his arrival "by letter to the Viceroy." He interpreted this to mean that he could not communicate through the Hong merchants. At the same time he was instructed not to arouse Chinese prejudice or to endanger the trade; he was not to call for armed assistance save in "extreme cases"; yet he was advised by Lord Palmerston that "the establishment of direct communications with the Imperial court at Peking would be desirable." Neither Palmerston nor Napier appears to have realized that all these diplomatic eggs could not be carried in one basket with safety. A foreign naval officer and a representative of the British king simply could not be recognized by the Chinese unless he came as a bearer of tribute, as Napier did not.

Accordingly, at Canton, Napier announced his arrival by a letter to the Viceroy, which, of course, the latter refused to receive. This refusal was natural enough, for Napier had violated three important rules by which the Chinese controlled the foreigners. He had proceeded from Macao to the Canton factories, which were located on the bank of the river outside the walled city, without asking and receiving China's official permission; he had attempted direct communication with the Viceroy, instead of using the medium of the Hong merchants; finally, he had termed his communication a *letter* instead of a *petition,* the form required by China of inferior tributary or vassal states. During this impasse Napier sickened and died,

---

[9] He was assisted by Sir John Francis Davis and Sir George Best Robinson as Second and Third Superintendents, respectively, both of whom succeeded to the post of First Superintendent in the years following Napier's death. The fact that these officials were Superintendents of Trade precluded any possibility of their being treated as diplomatic equals by the Chinese officials. A merchant as such did not enjoy a station of honor in the official social scale of either Chinese or Japanese society.

and for the ensuing five years (1834-1839) both the British and the Chinese governments followed a policy of indecision and drift. This procrastination merely put off slightly the day of crisis, for these were the years of the opium boom and the confusion and lawlessness it produced.

The Legal Problem of Jurisdiction

The abolition of the English East India Company's monopoly at Canton precipitated in aggravated form another problem of long standing. This was the question of legal control over foreigners engaged in the trade. The problem was by no means academic, since some of the foreign traders and the crews of the foreign ships could scarcely be classed as the cream, so to speak, of Western society. Both traders and seamen were, by and large, a rough and ready lot, and at times they might well be described as an intractable crowd. Remembering, then, the suspicions and prejudices of the Chinese populace toward the foreigners, and the jealousy of the Mandarins, it is not surprising that truculent foreign sailors on shore after the long and irksome sea voyage should become involved in altercations sometimes resulting in serious injuries and even death. Before 1833 the East India Company had controlled its licensed traders by the threat of withdrawing their license, but after 1833 Napier exercised no such authority.

More serious in Western eyes were those cases in which the Chinese demanded the surrender to Chinese justice of a foreigner accused of homicide in which a Chinese was the victim. There is a long history of cases in which the Chinese and the foreigners clashed on this point. One of the most notorious cases illustrative of the jurisdictional conflict was the Terranova affair. Terranova was an Italian seaman serving on the American ship *Emily* of Baltimore. In 1821, he was accused by the Chinese of having caused the death of a Chinese woman. Although convinced of his innocence and thoroughly aware that the Chinese would not give him a fair trial according to Western standards, the American merchant consul at Canton and the officers of the ship surrendered Terranova after the Chinese had stopped all American trade. Terranova was strangled and the credit of the American merchants was saved.

In this conflict of jurisdictional interests all the faults or misunderstandings were by no means on one side. It would appear that the Chinese authorities had no fixed desire to shield their own nationals from punishment; but they insisted that justice should take its course according to well-established Chinese ideas and methods. These the foreigners regarded as barbarous. At least until 1844 American traders generally adopted the view that they must abide by Chinese law. The settled British policy after 1784 was never to surrender one of their nationals to Chinese justice. The foreigners came more and more to the view that whatever merits Chinese law might possess in theory, its practice was entirely unsuitable to Westerners.

The contrary Chinese view is equally understandable. Prior to the coming of the Westerners, China's foreign relations were confined substantially to bordering vassal states which acknowledged their inferiority. If Chinese law had been accepted by these vassals, there seemed to be no good reason why special legal concessions should be made to the Western barbarians.

Again it should be noted that the foreigners, who considered themselves extremely practical, argued that no matter what China's legal theories might be, her courts were utterly corrupt. In cases involving foreigners, money, it was said, was more effective than evidence. A Chinese judge was disposed to give more credence to the testimony of a "civilized" Chinese than to that of an "uncivilized" barbarian. Furthermore, torture was applied inevitably to any victim who refused to confess. This method of extracting a confession, by no means unknown in the Western world at the time, appeared more sinister when applied by "yellow" men against "white."

Finally, it should be observed that the Chinese legal theory of responsibility was thoroughly obnoxious to the English and other foreigners at Canton.

> The Yellow River bursts its banks; the governor of Honan begs the emperor to deprive him of his titles, since he is responsible. A son commits an offence; the father is held responsible. A bankrupt absconds; his family are held responsible in body and estate. A shopman strikes a blow and goes into hiding; his employer is held responsible for his appearance. A province is overrun by rebels; its governor is held responsible. . . . The result is that nothing which occurs goes unpunished; if the guilty person cannot be found, convicted, and punished, then the responsible person must accept the consequences—father, family, employer, village, magistrate, or viceroy.[10]

---

[10] H. B. Morse, *The International Relations of the Chinese Empire* (3 vols., London, 1910-1918), I, 56.

Social Restraints on the Foreigner at Canton

If the foreigner was aggrieved when China dictated the terms on which he might conduct his trade, he was exasperated when his personal life was treated in like manner. At Canton, the foreign factories were situated on the river bank just outside the walled city. To this city the foreigner was denied access. His movements at Canton were confined to the narrow limits of the factory grounds. He was denied the use of sedan chairs—the most honorable conveyance for travel. He could not row on the river and only on rare occasions was he permitted to visit the flower gardens on the opposite bank. The markets of the walled city, with their variety of wares, were as far removed from his view as though they had been on the opposite side of the globe. He could hire Chinese servants only by connivance, not by right. Neither wives nor other foreign women could accompany the traders to Canton. These were required to remain at Macao, to which all the traders were also forced to return at the close of the trading season.[11] Official China, which made these rules, looked upon the foreigner as a lower order of being and treated him accordingly. Since there were virtually no contacts between the foreign traders and the officials, there was little hope of such barriers being lowered. And yet, in contrast with these imposed social restraints, there were frequently the most friendly and intimate relations among the traders, their Chinese agents, and the Hong merchants. At times the foreigner did become restive, yet he was also timid. Despite all its impositions the Canton trade was profitable. On the whole, the foreign trader was inclined to bear exasperating regulations rather than risk stoppage of the trade. If he desired or sought the diplomatic support of his government, he was also fearful of what the consequences of government interference might be.

The Canton trade was, in brief, much more than a mere rivalry of merchants. It was a clash between essentially different commercial, legal, and political systems. To the foreigner, as Arthur Smith observed, it was "one long illustration of the Chinese talent for misunderstanding." Yet to the complaints of the foreigner the Chinese had a ready and plausible answer.

---

[11] See Charles T. Downing, *The Fan-Qui or Foreigner in China* (2nd ed., London, 1840), III, 199-200.

Why do you come here? We take in exchange your articles of produce and manufacture, which we really have no occasion for, and give you in return our precious tea, which nature has denied to your country; and yet you are not satisfied. Why do you so often visit a country whose customs you dislike? We do not invite you to come among us; but when you do come and behave well, we treat you accordingly. Respect then our hospitality, but don't pretend to regulate or reform it.[12]

The Chinese System of Foreign Relations

Moreover, the Canton trade as it had developed by the 1830's was both an example of and a challenge to China's theory and practice of foreign relations. The traditional Chinese system of foreign relations was one between China—the Middle Kingdom, the universal empire, and therefore the superior—on the one hand, and lesser peoples—the outer barbarians and therefore the inferiors—on the other. In the Chinese view, the relationship was not one between equals. Historically, China had rarely been confronted by equals, but she had never been lacking in enemies on her borders, particularly in her great land frontier on the northeast. Foreign relations was therefore the problem of controlling the barbarians culturally even in those periods when the barbarian was able to invade and conquer China. The Chinese concept of their own superiority was one of culture rather than of physical or material power, and this concept derived conviction from the Confucian emphasis on the power of example. Thus the idealized relationship between China and the outer barbarians required that the barbarian recognize the unique position of the Son of Heaven as the ruler of mankind and be submissive to him, while the emperor in turn was to be generous and benevolent to lesser peoples who showed him proper respect. This respect for and acceptance of Chinese suzerainty was given ritualistic expression and a measure of reality through the institution of *tribute* (usually native produce). The presentation of tribute at Peking by both the barbarians and also by the provinces of China itself signified membership in the Chinese Confucian society of peoples. In this ritual the tributary envoy might receive a patent of appointment, appointment to noble rank, and an imperial seal in addition to the hospitality of the Chinese court. In return the tributary performed the *kotow* (knocking the head upon the ground) a symbol of submission. As elaborated at the Chinese court

12 John Barrow, *Travels in China,* 413.

the *kotow* consisted of three kneelings each involving three prostrations before the emperor. It was a ceremony that left no doubt as to who was above and who was below. To Westerners recently imbued with ideas of equality it was a repugnant performance, but to men of the Confucian order it was no more than good behavior. The emperor himself performed the *kotow* at the altar of Heaven and to his parents.

The tribute system and its missions had survived because it served the interests of both the superior and the inferior, of China and the outer barbarians. It served the Chinese rulers as evidence that they did hold the mandate of Heaven. This prestige was important to the dynasty not only in controlling the barbarians but also in maintaining its rule over its own people, the Chinese. It was also China's medium of diplomacy, the process by which she kept in touch with the outside world. On the other hand, the barbarians conformed to the tribute system and were prepared to accept inferior status partly because there was no alternative, but to an even greater degree because the tribute missions became an instrumentality for conducting commerce. Over the years the expanding tributary trade, even in the anti-commercial and self-sufficient Confucian society, could be rationalized as a benevolence to less fortunate peoples. But whatever the rationalization, China's system of foreign relations by the nineteenth century involved two inseparable factors—tribute and trade.

This background on the Chinese theory of foreign relations is an important key to understanding the explosive conditions created as Western traders congregated at Canton. What mattered to the rulers of China was the ethics of tribute; what mattered to the Western barbarians was the profits of trade and, after 1834, the concept of equality. Herein lay a fundamental conflict between Confucian and Western society.[13]

The Economics of the Canton Trade

In spite of all the irritations that surrounded it, the Canton system of trade had been a profitable venture both for the English East India Company on the outside and for Chinese merchants and officials on the inside. So picturesque indeed was this meeting of

[13] J. K. Fairbank, *Trade and Diplomacy on the China Coast* (2 vols. Cambridge, 1953), I, 23-53.

East and West in search of profits from teas and silks that the story of the old Canton trade before 1834 has often taken on the glamour of a fabulous and ideal age where merchants met as gentlemen. There is of course evidence to justify within some limits this glorification. At the same time, the early years of the nineteenth century were a threshold on which the Canton system tripped and fell. The economic reasons for this collapse must be treated in some further detail if there is to be an understanding of what followed.

A very conspicuous feature of the old Canton trading system was the pressing need for cargoes outbound to China to pay for exports of silk and tea. This need operated at the beginning of the nineteenth century in a complex of evolving and contradictory pressures. The Macartney (1793) and the Amherst missions (1816) signified, under the influence of the industrial revolution, Britain's need for wider markets for increased manufactures. Yet in these same years the fortunes of the Company tended to be in decline. As a monopoly it was inclined to accept the Canton restrictive system rather than to press for reform and the expansion of markets. The way out of this contradiction came in part through what was known as the "country" trade.

As exports of silk and tea were growing rapidly between 1760 and 1800, there developed a distinctive British commerce, the "country" trade between India and China conducted by private individuals licensed by the Company in India and under its control at Canton. This country trade made up the third side of what was in reality a triangular commerce between Canton, London, and India. But it did far more than that. The country trade took over in large measure the old native Chinese junk trade of the Southeast Asia seas, carrying to Canton articles the Canton market would buy, such as cotton piece-goods and opium from India, and tin, camphor, and spices from the East Indies and Malaya. In this way imports to China were provided to pay for exports. Equally important was the fact that the growth of this private trade and the ingenuity of the private traders in performing all manner of services (acting as the agents of private firms in London in banking and insurance, and as selling agents, etc.) meant that the Company's monopoly was becoming nominal rather than real. The private traders with their agency houses were therefore deeply involved in the Canton system while officially the monopoly of the Company still prevailed.

The Opium Traffic

To the foregoing picture of the Company's declining monopoly in the face of the resourceful pressures of the private traders was added the disrupting influence of opium, to the importation of which into China the private traders turned much of their skill.

The first cause of this traffic lay in the unexplained development of a Chinese demand for opium. Since extensive cultivation of the poppy within China did not occur until after 1850, the demand could be met only by importation. Thus the demand within China plus the constant need at Canton for imports to balance the tea trade provided the economic bases for the growth of the traffic. As the Chinese demand grew, Indian opium came to surpass Indian raw cotton in balancing the trade. In time, too, opium production in India became an important source of government revenue there, thus tending to insure opium's place in the China trade. As it happened, the phenomenal growth in the opium trade came just at the time the Company lost its monopoly at Canton. The two circumstances' coinciding brought on what may be called the Canton crisis of 1834-1840. The stimulus to this illegal traffic extended the opium business along the entire southeastern China coast to the mutual financial benefit of both foreign and Chinese merchants and of Chinese officials.

The rise of the opium trade presented the Peking government not only with a grave social problem but also with perplexing questions of regulation of the foreign trade, which was supposed to keep itself nicely confined at Canton between the Co-hong and the foreign merchants. Nevertheless, the smuggling of opium was as prevalent at Canton as it became elsewhere. The dangers of opium, of course, had long been recognized by Peking. Importation and sale had been prohibited as early as 1729. In 1799 the ban on importation was renewed and cultivation of the poppy in China was proscribed. But these edicts were of no avail. The fact was that Chinese officials from the highest to the lowest "all connived at the continuous breach of the law provided only that they found therein their personal profit."[14]

Although Indian opium bulked largest in the trade and although the British occupied a conspicuous place as the carriers, all the foreign nationals represented at Canton were involved. Portuguese,

---

14 Morse, *The International Relations of the Chinese Empire,* I, 56.

French, American, and other ships carried Persian and Turkish rather than Indian opium. Indeed, prior to 1820 American cargoes of the Persian and Turkish drug were regarded as a threat to the East India Company's interest in the trade.[15]

From the record summarized briefly in the pages of this chapter, it must be clear that by 1834 the meeting of the West with China at Canton had produced complexities and tensions of the gravest import. The Canton system, contrived to meet the limited contacts of the eighteenth century, could not control the expanding contacts of the nineteenth. The system was no longer a vehicle for legitimate Western commerce or a shield for China's theory and practice of foreign relations.[16]

For Further Reading

Augur, Helen, *Tall Ships to Cathay* (New York, 1951). An account of a New England firm's efforts to establish an Oriental trading company.

Clark, Arthur H., *The Clipper Ship Era. An Epitome of Famous American and British Clipper Ships, Their Owners, Builders, Commanders, and Crews, 1843-1869* (New York, 1910).

Clyde, Paul H., *United States Policy Toward China, Diplomatic and Public Documents, 1839-1939* (Durham, N.C., 1940).

Collis, Maurice, *Foreign Mud* (New York, 1947). A popular account of the opium dispute at Canton and of the Anglo-Chinese war that followed.

Coupland, R., *Raffles, 1781-1826* (London, 1926). An excellent study of the founder of Singapore.

Dennett, Tyler, *Americans in Eastern Asia* (New York, 1922). Superseded by later research but still useful.

Foster, William, *England's Quest of Eastern Trade* (London, 1933).

Greenberg, Michael, *British Trade and the Opening of China, 1800-1842* (Cambridge, 1951). One of the best treatments of the subject.

Keeton, G. W., *The Development of Extra-territoriality in China* (2 vols., London, 1928).

Kuo, P. C., *A Critical Study of the First Anglo-Chinese War (with Documents)* (Shanghai, 1935). The first work in English resting primarily on Chinese official sources.

Morse, H. B., *The Trade and Administration of the Chinese Empire* (3rd rev. ed., London, 1920). Treats of Chinese institutions having a bearing on the foreign trade.

---

[15] Charles C. Stelle, "American Trade in Opium to China prior to 1820," *Pacific Historical Review,* IX (1940), 425-444.

[16] See J. K. Fairbank, *Trade and Diplomacy on the China Coast* (Cambridge, 1953), 57-73.

Pelcovits, Nathan A., *Old China Hands and the Foreign Office* (New York, 1948). Presents the thesis that the British government resisted efforts of its merchants to make the Middle Kingdom another India.

Pratt, Sir John, *The Expansion of Europe into the Far East* (London, 1947).

Rydell, Raymond A., *Cape Horn to the Pacific: The Rise and Decline of an Ocean Highway* (Berkeley, 1952). An account of voyages made into the Pacific by merchants and missionaries prior to the opening of the Panama Canal.

7

China Submits: The Treaty System

THE clash of interests and purposes in Anglo-Chinese trade at Canton and on the southeast China coast had become fundamental by 1835. The issues were not simple. Beyond the matter of profits in trade, whether legitimate or contraband, these issues, to mention only the more striking, revolved about such things as: (1) the British desire for diplomatic representation and equality as against China's assumptions of superiority; (2) the free-trading aspirations of the foreigners against the controlled economy of the Co-hong; and (3) the rights of the individual in Western law as against Chinese concepts of collective responsibility. When to these basic conflicts were added the abolition of the Company's monopoly (1834) and the rapid expansion of the legal and the contraband trade, there was created a degree of confusion in Canton waters which neither the British nor the Manchu government could long ignore. The policy of drift following Napier's death (1834) could not be prolonged indefinitely. When and how would Britain and China act?

China's immediate contribution to the coming crisis came from its anti-opium movement, which, in turn, was first a moral protest against the drug evil as expressed in imperial edicts against the traffic, and second and more particularly an economic protest resting on the somewhat mistaken belief that opium was the cause of the government's fiscal troubles. The general Chinese belief of the time was that as opium moved into China, silver, which was often used to pay for it, moved out. Although in some degree this was so, there were many other factors inducing the silver shortage. To the government, this shortage was a matter of grave concern. The Chinese people, who used copper coins in everyday transactions, were required to convert these to silver for purposes of tax payments. Thus, when silver became more valuable in terms of copper, the taxpayer suffered, and the government, in turn, had to choose between facing popular resentment or accepting reduced tax revenue.[1] As a result the government resolved to end the opium trade, and for this purpose sent to Canton in 1839 a determined official, a rare character in the Chinese bureaucracy of the time, as Imperial Commissioner. This was the famous Lin-Tse-hsü, known to the foreigners as Commissioner Lin.

Lin Acts; The British React

Commissioner Lin was a man of action, but not always of well-considered action. A product of China's ignorance of barbarian power, he thought to reform the Canton system on China's own terms by attacking the problem unilaterally through the single target of opium. Accordingly, within a week of his arrival Lin had imprisoned the foreign traders in the factories and demanded delivery of the opium in their possession. The traders, through Captain Elliott, Superintendent of British trade, eventually surrendered some twenty thousand chests. To the astonishment of the foreign community this comfortable fortune, later valued at $6,000,000, was mixed with salt and lime and sluiced into the river. War was now certain, for whereas Lin seems to have felt that his mission was accomplished, the British government could not do less than seek reparations or reprisals.

The first Anglo-Chinese war, which followed in 1840-1842, involved two campaigns. In the first (1840), the British took Canton only to withdraw in favor of an expedition up the China coast where they attacked Chinese garrisons and blockaded the mouth of the Yangtze. This advance brought the removal of Lin and the appointment of a Manchu, Ch'i-shan, to negotiate. He induced the British to return to the south where in January, 1841, an abortive convention was signed which included the cession of Hongkong to the British, the conceding of diplomatic equality, an indemnity to

[1] J. F. Fairbank, *Trade and Diplomacy on the China Coast* (Cambridge, 1953), 75-76.

the British, and provision for resumption of trade. For their trouble Ch'i-shan was promptly disgraced and Elliott promptly recalled. In the view of their respective governments, Ch'i-shan had gone too far; Elliott, not far enough. Accordingly, the war was renewed in a second campaign (August, 1841-August, 1842). The victory of a British garrison at Ningpo in March, 1842, finally brought the Manchu court to consider negotiation.[2]

Meanwhile, Sir Henry Pottinger had arrived off the coast as Britain's chief representative. A British fleet moved northward, meeting no effective resistance. Early in August, 1842, Nanking, the southern capital, was at the mercy of British guns. The war was ended. The military defeat of China was decisive. A small British force, never more than 10,000 effectives, had broken what remained of Manchu military prestige. It was the beginning of a century of military defeats for China. Helpless and humbled, she sought peace on the deck of a British battleship, the *Cornwallis,* as it lay in the river off Nanking. Legally, the days of China's exclusiveness and superiority were at an end. During the ensuing century the "barbarians" would dictate the terms on which China might trade and enjoy peace.

The Nanking and Bogue Treaties

The formal settlement of the first Anglo-Chinese war was embodied in two treaties: the Treaty of Nanking, August 29, 1842, and the supplementary Treaty of Hoomun Chai, signed at the Bogue, October 8, 1843.[3] The two treaties contained the basic principles that were to govern China's international status for a century. Later treaties between China and foreign states modified or amplified details, but the basic structure of principles contained in the first treaties remained with little change until the end of the unequal treaty system in 1943.

Five ports, Canton, Amoy, Foochow, Ningpo, and Shanghai, were opened to the residence and trade of British merchants. Britain was to appoint consular officers to these ports.

---

[2] P. C. Kuo, *A Critical Study of the First Anglo-Chinese War* (Shanghai, 1935), 194-199. See also D. E. Owen, *British Opium Policy in China and India* (New Haven, 1934), 167-175.

[3] For texts of all important nineteenth-century treaties with China, see China, the Maritime Customs, *Treaties, Conventions, etc., between China and Foreign States* (2 vols., 2nd ed., Shanghai, 1917).

The island of Hongkong was ceded to Great Britain "in perpetuity."

The Co-hong was abolished, and British merchants were "to carry on their mercantile transactions with whatever persons they please."

China was to pay a total indemnity of $21,000,000–$6,000,000 for the surrendered opium; $3,000,000 to cover debts owed by Hong

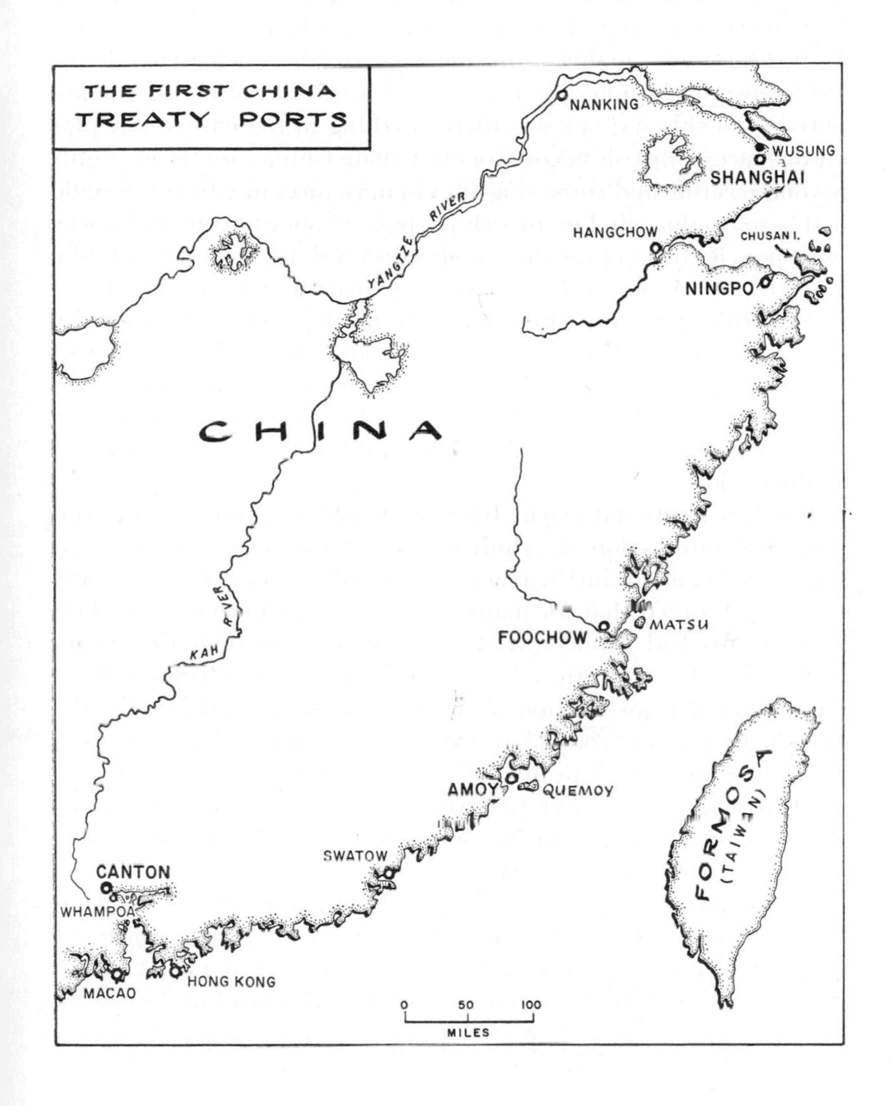

merchants to British subjects; $12,000,000 for expenses occasioned by the war.

Correspondence between the chief British representative and high Chinese officials was to be under the term "a communication," not "a petition."

China agreed to a uniform and moderate tariff on exports and imports, which came to be known as the 5 per cent ad valorem treaty tariff. The duties fixed at this time were not to be increased save by mutual agreement. Thus, for the ensuing 88 years—that is, until 1930—China was unable to fix her tariffs of her own free will. In 1842, however, it should be noted that China did not realize the importance of this act; nor was there anything in the nature of a plot on the part of British negotiators to violate China's sovereign rights beyond meeting and correcting the circumstances in which the trade had been conducted. The British purpose was not to control China's fiscal policies but to provide a *modus operandi* for the foreign trade. Since this trade was still relatively small, and since isolation was still China's prevailing philosophy, the principle of tariff autonomy had at the time little of the significance it acquired in later years.[4] Another motive behind the tariff clause of the treaty was the aggressive free trade philosophy that existed in Britain. In general the free traders felt that they had a divine mission to impose their creed on the world.

The first treaty settlement likewise included provision for extraterritorial jurisdiction in criminal cases (Treaty of the Bogue, Art. IX)—a second major infringement on China's exercise of sovereignty. It will be recalled that for many years the foreign traders and their governments had condemned Chinese notions of both the theory and the practice of justice. At Macao the Portuguese had sought to retain exclusive jurisdiction over their nationals, and in 1833 the British, by order-in-council, provided their own court at Canton with criminal and admiralty jurisdiction. In this matter, as in the tariff, it was only in later years that China awoke to the full implications of harboring in her seaports a foreign population over which her courts had no power.

Although China regarded opium as the primary cause of the war, the first treaty settlement, aside from stipulating the payment of $6,000,000 for the opium seized, mentioned the traffic not at all. In the British view, China was free to legalize and control imports or to

---

[4] S. F. Wright, *China's Struggle for Tariff Autonomy* (Shanghai, 1938), 45-48.

prohibit them, but enforcement of the latter course would be China's responsibility. The Chinese would not agree to legalization, and thus the treaty was silent on this important question.

Finally, Britain secured the principle of most-favored-nation treatment. Art. VII (Treaty of the Bogue) stated "that should the Emperor hereafter, from any cause whatever, be pleased to grant additional privileges or immunities to any of the subjects or Citizens of such Foreign Countries, the same privileges and immunities will be extended to and enjoyed by British Subjects."

The new status enjoyed by Great Britain and her traders in China prompted other powers to seek treaty relations. Between 1844 and 1847 three treaties were concluded by China: with the United States (July 3, 1844); with France (October 24, 1844); and with Norway and Sweden (March 20, 1847). Of these, by far the most important was the American. Its significance may best be seen by reviewing briefly the growth of American interests in China in the decades following the Revolutionary War.

Early American Interests in China

Even before the days of independence some American intellectuals had expressed themselves on China. Benjamin Franklin (1771) hoped America would increase in likeness to her. Thomas Jefferson (1785) held that China's policy of non-intercourse was ideally adapted to American use. John Quincy Adams (1822) praised the Chinese for recognizing the virtues of the decimal system. But to most Americans, certainly prior to 1830, China was merely a vast and remote empire—as much a curiosity as if it had belonged to another planet.

John Ledyard, an American who accompanied Captain Cook to the Pacific (1776-1781), was among the first to tell his countrymen how furs from the northwest coast of America sold in Canton at enormous profit. The result was a voyage by the *Empress of China*, the first American ship to sail direct for Canton (1784).[5] The trade, thus begun, soon prospered. The Americans, like the European traders, sought Chinese silk and tea, and they encountered the same difficulties as the Europeans in finding an outbound cargo. Furs,

[5] The *Empress of China*, 360 tons, carried as cargo "furs, foodstuffs, and ginseng—a wild root worth its weight in gold in the Orient as the 'dose of immortality.'" Robert Morris financed the voyage. Joseph Downs, "The American Trade with the Far East," in *The China Trade and Its Influences* (New York, 1941), 13.

ginseng, sandalwood, opium, and silver constituted main items in the China-bound cargoes, and various routes were followed by the ships in the early American trade.

Between 1784 and 1811 Americans were the most serious rivals of the British in the tea trade at Canton. Their ships were neither so large nor so numerous as those of the English East India Company, yet in the season 1805-1806 they carried from Canton 11 million pounds of tea in 37 ships, as against British exports of 22 million pounds in 49 ships.[6]

The position of the Americans at Canton contrasted in some respects with that of the British. The Americans traded with greater individual freedom, but they possessed neither the financial backing nor the prestige of the English company, nor did they enjoy any naval protection from their home government. The first official representative of the United States in China was Major Samuel Shaw, who, after a number of voyages to the Far East, was named consul, without salary, at Canton by the Continental Congress acting on the recommendation of John Jay. It would seem that the early American trader felt little need for official support so long as he was permitted to trade on equal terms with his British rivals. But as the tension grew between the British and the Chinese after 1834, the indifference of American merchants to official backing disappeared. In May, 1839, after Lin had forced the surrender of foreign-owned opium, a group of Americans at Canton memorialized Congress to send a commercial agent to negotiate a treaty, and a naval force to protect persons and property.[7] Although expressing no sympathy with the opium traffic, they found no excuse for the "robbery" committed on the British. They foresaw that England would use armed force, and they believed "that this is necessary." They recommended that the United States take *joint* action with England, France, and Holland to secure: (1) resident ministers at Peking; (2) a fixed tariff on exports and imports; (3) the liberty of trading at ports other than Canton; and (4) Chinese assent to the principle that, until their laws are made known and recognized, punishment for offences committed by foreigners against Chinese or others shall

---

[6] See K. S. Latourette, *History of Early Relations Between the United States and China (1784-1844)* (New Haven, 1917).

[7] For a selected group of representative documents on American policy, see Paul H. Clyde, *United States Policy Toward China: Diplomatic and Public Documents, 1839-1939* (Durham, N.C., 1940).

not be greater than is applicable to a like offence by the laws of the United States or England.

When the opium crisis broke at Canton, the Americans turned over their opium to the British superintendent for surrender to the Chinese; but when the English withdrew to Macao, and later to Hongkong, the Americans remained at Canton, conducting the while a lucrative business in carrying to Canton cargoes of British goods when British ships were no longer permitted to enter the river. These events during 1839-1840 focussed for the first time American public attention, both official and non-official, on the Canton trade.

In the broad sense, Americans appeared ill-prepared to formulate a political policy toward China. A fair proportion of Americans who thought about China at all harbored all manner of distorted, if not fantastic, notions concerning her. The most prevalent opinion was that the Anglo-Chinese war was "another item in the sad catalogue of [British] outrages on humanity." When in 1841 John Quincy Adams suggested in an address that the principle of equality among states was the real cause of the war in China, the idea was so shocking to the editor of the *North American Review* that he refused to print Adams' manuscript. After the first American Protestant missionaries, Elijah C. Bridgman and David Abeel, were sent to Canton in 1829, the missionary press dwelt heavily on the vices of the "heathen Chinese." The Chinese were frequently pictured as masters of deceit, of cruelty, of gambling and rioting, of indolence and superstition. Worst of all was their preference for rice rather than for salvation. To many religious Americans there was a shocking satisfaction in the thought that China's "depravity" offered an unlimited field for American missions. Nor were these opinions merely the fulminations of fanatics. After seventeen years in China, S. Wells Williams, one of the ablest of missionaries, succumbed at times to the prevalent conclusion.

> It is much easier [he wrote] loving the souls of the heathen in the abstract than in the concrete encompassed as they are in such dirty bodies, speaking forth their foul language and vile natures exhibiting every evidence of depravity.[8]

Many an American was at a loss to know what to believe about China. He could read that the Chinese had "some very esteemable qualities" but were "false, dishonest and distrustful"; that they

[8] F. W. Williams, *The Life and Letters of Samuel Wells Williams* (New York, 1899), 174.

were "base" yet "more civil" than Americans; that their government was a system of unwarranted oppression in a society remarkable for its thrift and industry.

The First Enunciation of American Policy

Out of the background of these confused and inadequate ideas on China there was to emerge an official policy which, surprising as it may seem, expressed so exactly what Americans believed their interests to be that it survived for a century. President Tyler, on December 30, 1842, four months after the Treaty of Nanking had been signed, asked Congress to authorize appointment of a resident commissioner in China to protect the commercial and diplomatic affairs of the United States. This post was conferred upon Caleb Cushing of Massachusetts, brilliant lawyer, member of the Committee on Foreign Affairs, and intimate friend of the President. To Daniel Webster, Secretary of State, fell the task of preparing Cushing's instructions. The American envoy was to secure entry of American ships and cargoes into the open ports on terms as favorable as those enjoyed by the English. He was to employ the utmost tact; to impress the Chinese with the peaceful character of his mission; to visit Peking if possible; but in no case was he to perform the *kotow*. The instructions were concluded with these significant words—the essence of American policy:

> Finally, you will signify, in decided terms and a positive manner, that the Government of the United States would find it impossible to remain on terms of friendship and regard with the Emperor, if greater privileges or commercial facilities should be allowed to the subjects of any other Government than should be granted to the citizens of the United States.

Cushing reached Macao on February 24, 1844, welcomed neither by the Chinese, nor by the British, nor by the American communities. The treaties of Nanking and the Bogue were already in operation. Also, the Manchu negotiators had already applied, in 1842-1843, the old and well-established idea of equal treatment for all barbarians, so that the Americans enjoyed most-favored-nation treatment in fact without the asking. Thus the question arose as to what Cushing could do that had not already been done.[9]

---

[9] The Manchu emperor's formal approval of the equal extension of trading privileges had been given November 15, 1843, before the arrival of Cushing in China. Kenneth Ch'en, "The Cushing Mission: Was It Necessary?" *Chinese Soc. and Pol. Science Rev.,* XXIII (1939), 3-14.

In the face of Chinese procrastination on the subject of a treaty, Cushing intimated that he would proceed to Peking. This threat brought an Imperial commissioner to Macao, and soon thereafter the first American treaty was signed (Treaty of Wang-hsia [Wang Hiya], July 3, 1844).[10] Although this treaty followed in general the principles contained in the British treaties, it was superior in point of clarity and in extending the principle of extraterritoriality to include civil as well as criminal cases (see Arts. XXI, XXIV, XXV). Thus the American treaty rather than the British became the basic document in China's foreign relations until the treaties of Tientsin were signed in 1858. Whereas the commercial policy set forth by Webster was in the main approved by American opinion, criticism of the Cushing mission was not lacking, although for the most part it was political in character—directed at the gold braid and plumes worn by the "pompous" Cushing rather than at the purposes of the mission. Journals such as *Hunt's Merchants' Magazine,* which a few months previously had bitterly denounced England's motives in China, reversed themselves, found excuses for England's behavior, and supported her policy of treaty relations. And in Congress there was spirited support for Cushing, since no one knew "just how much of our tobacco might be chewed [in China] in place of opium."[11]

These more favorable reactions were not unanimous. There was a strong current of opinion that the China trade did not merit the publicity given it. Americans, it was said, might better direct their attention to the internal development of their own country. This was doubtless a very natural reaction in an America in the full tide of expansion on the frontier. Perhaps, too, the very positive character of this pioneer society reinforced the general American tendency to judge things Chinese solely in terms of American values, a tendency that contributed to tragic results in the twentieth century.

The Franco-Chinese treaty (October, 1844) followed the model of the British and American treaties. The French diplomats, however, appeared also in the role of "protectors" of Catholic missions. Their

---

[10] For a scholarly editing of this treaty, see Hunter Miller, ed., *Treaties and Other International Acts of the United States of America* (Washington, Department of State), IV. The prompt conclusion of the American treaty, once negotiations were begun, was due to Chinese "abhorrence of Cushing's intention to go to Peking." Ping Chia Kuo, "Caleb Cushing and the Treaty of Wanghia, 1844," *Journal of Modern History,* V (1933), 51. China was represented by Ch'i-ying.

[11] *Congressional Globe,* 27th Cong., 3rd sess., 325.

request that permission be granted to build Roman Catholic missions at the five treaty ports, and for toleration to Chinese and foreign Christians, was granted by the emperor, though not as a part of the treaty. These concessions were extended later to Protestants.

The Reception of the First Treaties

The first treaty settlement viewed in retrospect reveals graphically its deep significance, but it must not be assumed that all this was clear to the contemporaries of Lin, Ch'i-ying, Pottinger, and Cushing. The fact that a handful of British troops and a small fleet had forced the Manchu court to terms did not signify necessarily that all was now well. The treaties themselves were an experiment. Would they in practice satisfy either the foreign traders and their governments or the reluctant Manchu court? Behind this question was a broad and vital problem. Did China's signature of the first treaties mean that she had broken positively and willingly with the past? Would her doors now be opened widely to Western influence, or, by evasion of the treaties, would she await the day when these doors might be closed again to a presumptuous, barbarian world? Answers to these basic questions involve consideration of China's developing attitude toward the foreign barbarian and the means she employed to implement these attitudes, especially in the years 1838 to 1861.

China's Management of the Barbarians, 1839-1861

The period from the First Anglo-Chinese War until the settlement of the second war (1861) illustrates nicely the persistence of the Chinese view that all Westerners were "irritating intruders." Confident of the greatness and self-sufficiency of her own rich culture, China was still confident that she could control the intruders and preserve her own integrity. The defeat in the "Opium" War and the imposition of the treaties were considered temporary reverses, unfortunate, even frightening, but not fatal. Within this over-all official Chinese attitude were the more particular reactions of the ruling Manchu dynasty. This dynasty, already weakened in the nineteenth century by the declining capacity of its emperors, was confronted by recurring rebellion at home as well as by the intrusions of the Westerners at the ports. Faced by these distressing trials, the Manchus attempted at times to use the lesser trading powers,

France and the United States, in an effort to thwart the main antagonist, Great Britain. The mass of memorials that flowed to Peking from high officials at Canton and later from Shanghai insisted that the barbarian problem could best be handled by adroit "management." Accordingly, the emperor created a Barbarian Affairs Bureau (*I Wu Chu*) to collect all records and information concerning foreign affairs, thus indicating that the government knew it was faced with a new problem.

The United States by 1842 occupied a somewhat distinct position as the most important "neutral" state involved in the Anglo-Chinese struggle. Since the Americans had not joined Britain in the war, and appeared to show some liking for things Chinese, a number of Chinese officials played with the idea of "utilizing the American barbarians" in a general scheme of "using barbarians to curb barbarians." Indeed, throughout the remainder of the nineteenth century, China, for understandable reasons, relied heavily on the technique of playing one power against another in her effort to resist the Western impact and to preserve her political and cultural system.[12]

How the Chinese Handled Foreign Affairs, 1841-1861

It will be recalled that the Treaty of Nanking (1842) had ended the old Chinese system of dealing with the foreigners through the Co-hong and the factories at Canton. This development did not mean that China's foreign relations were patterned immediately on the Western model. In the strict sense of the term there really were no official Chinese foreign relations before 1841, nor were there to be any, even in a semi-orthodox sense of the term, until the establishment of the Tsungli Yamen (Foreign Office) in 1861 and the opening of Peking to residence of ministers of the treaty powers. Thus China's foreign affairs from 1841 to 1861 were in a formative stage.

The embryonic organization China used to deal with the barbarians in these years was briefly as follows: The most important official dealing directly with the foreigners at the five recently opened treaty ports was the *tao-t'ai,* or Intendant of Circuit, who had jurisdiction over two or more prefectures and who served as an

---

[12] Earl Swisher, *China's Management of the American Barbarians: A Study of Sino-American Relations, 1841-1861, with Documents* (New Haven, 1953), 1-54.

intermediary in diplomatic intercourse with the foreigners while he also usually served as superintendent of customs, a post formerly held by the "hoppo," or superintendent of customs at Canton.

A second official concerned with foreign affairs was the provincial governor (*hsün-fu*). Although the governor did occasionally receive the representative of a foreign state, he more frequently merely memorialized the throne on negotiations between the *tao-t'ai* and the foreigner, or shifted the problem down to the *tao-t'ai* or up to the governor-general.

More important, therefore, in handling foreign affairs in the new treaty period was the governor-general (*tsung-tu*), whom Westerners usually called the "viceroy." His prominence in foreign affairs was due partly to the American treaty of 1844, which stated that communications to the court were to be transmitted through this official.

The highest official outside of Peking who dealt with foreign affairs was the imperial commissioner (*ch'in-ch'ai*). Ranking above the governor-general and with a direct commission from the emperor, he might be instructed to cope with any new or alarming crisis such as the one that occurred when Lin Tse-hsü was sent to Canton in 1839 to deal with the opium affair. When the Treaty of Nanking abolished the Co-hong as the agency for dealing with foreigners, the "diplomatic" function was taken over by the governor-general at Canton under the new title of "Imperial Commissioner charged with the superintendence of the concerns of foreign nations with China." All of the above mighty officials were served by a host of underlings who were supposed to know something about foreign affairs but whose knowledge, in this period at least, was anything but impressive or accurate.[13]

The Central Machinery of Foreign Affairs at Peking, 1841-1861

Throughout the nineteenth century Western diplomats in China felt, more often than not, that China's handling of foreign affairs was a colossus of purposeful evasion and neglect, capped with downright administrative incompetence. Evasion of foreign purposes there certainly was, but the charge of administrative incompetence has subsequently been overdrawn. Actually Peking's handling of foreign affairs was centralized and orderly. All such matters were

13 Swisher, *China's Management of the American Barbarians,* 1-7.

dealt with directly by the emperor and the highest organ of state, the Grand Council (*Chun Chi Ch'u*). Originally set up in 1729 to handle secret military affairs, the Council, as a kind of inner, intimate staff of the emperor, acquired the power to interfere with any political matter. It had become indeed an agency of dynastic power negating traditional Chinese restrictions on imperial authority. This small group, usually five or six, responsible personally to the emperor, was obviously not a foreign office, for it dealt with matters of all kinds. Moreover, in the period 1841-1861 the Council was declining in character and initiative. In this picture it is clear that the emperor's authority was final; however, the degree of initiative he exercised and the degree of judgment exercised by the Councillors are by no means clear, and indeed could vary greatly.

The working of this machinery for foreign affairs was regular and efficient according to the Chinese standards of that day. The foreign diplomat presented his credentials to the governor-general and imperial commissioner at Canton, or, if this had been done, he might, in specific cases of diplomatic business, deal with a governor-general, governor, or *tao-t'ai* at one of the treaty ports. The next step was a memorial from the high Chinese official to the emperor setting forth and reporting upon the business at hand. The important point is that the Western diplomat was dependent upon the case presented by the memorialist.

Chinese "Diplomatic" Officials

The Chinese official at the ports who dealt with representatives of the Western treaty powers was separated from them culturally by barriers of language, tradition, philosophy, and custom. He was therefore apt to be in the opinion of the foreigner an inscrutable enigma or a thoroughly perverse and unreasonable being. There was, however, a Chinese side to this picture that was not always comprehended by Western envoy, merchant, or missionary. What manner of men were these Chinese officials, and what ideas concerning the foreigners did they entertain in the twenty years following the first treaty settlement?

Since these Chinese officials were numerous and held posts of varying importance, from the exalted station of the imperial high commissioner down the scale of rank to semi-official and even unofficial underlings, it is only possible to give here by a few selected examples some impression of their quality as men. Among the more prominent names known to the foreigners were those of Lin Tse-hsü (1785-1850), who seized the opium, and Ch'i-ying or Kiying (d. 1858), who negotiated the first treaty settlement.

Lin Tse-hsü, a native of Fukien, had first acquired fame as judicial commissioner in Kiangsu, where his judgments were regarded as so able he came to be known as "Lin, Clear as the Heavens." When, as his reputation grew, he memorialized the throne in 1838 on the opium question, he was called to Peking, and, following nineteen audiences, was appointed imperial commissioner with full powers to examine and stamp out the evil of opium at Canton. The reader already knows what Lin did at Canton. However, when China was defeated in the war that followed and a British fleet lay off Tientsin, Lin was dismissed and ordered to Peking. Following a period of banishment to Chinese Turkestan, he was recalled in 1845 and thereafter served in a number of provincial posts. His fame rests not solely on his general administrative career or on his virtuosity in the opium drama at Canton. Beyond these accomplishments he was a pioneer in recognizing the power of the West. He advocated the study of Western geography and the introduction by China of Western methods and weapons of warfare as means of restoring Chinese power.

Ch'i-ying, known to contemporary Westerners as Kiying, was a Manchu imperial clansman. It was he who concluded the Treaty of Nanking with Great Britain in 1842, the Treaty of the Bogue in 1843, and the American Treaty of Wang-hsia in 1844. He also signed the later treaties with France and Sweden-Norway in 1844 and 1847 respectively. His power in China's relations with the West was unrivalled until 1850, when, under a new emperor, he was denounced as having "oppressed the people to please the foreigners." Degraded in rank he committed suicide in 1858. He was the victim of an uncompromising court party, and of the unpopularity of the first treaties.

Indeed, the Manchu failure of 1842 was due in considerable measure to ignorance of the West. Even some of China's most distinguished dignitaries thought "it was because England had only a queen" that many of her subjects dared to be so unruly in China. Chinese scholars found the barbarian character "unfathomable," since it would do anything for profits. But there were reasons other than ignorance and misunderstanding for China's capitulation. The

Manchu military structure had been designed to control the Chinese people, not to resist invasion from the sea. In Peking, the court, ever sensitive to public opinion, feared rebellion in the provinces—always an indication that the dynasty was losing the Mandate of Heaven.

The New Treaty Ports

The laboratory in which the new treaties were to be tried consisted of the five treaty ports: Canton, Amoy, Foochow, Ningpo, and Shanghai. In all these ports save Canton, the foreigner was a stranger, and to the vast population in the interior he was all but unknown. China and the Powers were entering upon a very unpredictable experiment. In the first years, 1843-1845, the way was paved for initial application of the Treaties by Ch'i-ying's policy of appeasement toward Pottinger. Thereafter, 1845-1853, there was to follow a progressive breakdown of the Treaty system. This was to lead in 1854 to the creation of the Foreign Inspectorate of Customs at Shanghai, one of the most significant developments in the evolving Sino-Western system of the nineteenth century.

Only two of the first treaty ports were destined to develop as great centers of the foreign trade—Shanghai and Canton. For a few years, commerce, particularly in black tea and in contract coolie labor to Cuba, flourished at Amoy. Trade at Foochow was negligible. Until the middle of 1844 not a foreign ship had entered its harbor. As a port Foochow suffered because its harbor was poor, its population, under official encouragement, was anti-foreign, and its location was too close to Amoy. In the same way Ningpo was too close to Shanghai. Ningpo's later fame was due to missionary rather than commercial enterprise.

Shanghai was opened to foreign trade on November 17, 1843. Situated on the Whangpoo River about twelve miles from where it joins the Yangtze at Woosung, and having a native population of some 270,000, it was already an important center of China's inland and coastal trade. Here traders were no longer hampered by such monopolistic agencies as the Co-hong. There were business and opportunity for all. In 1844 forty-four foreign ships of a total tonnage of more than 8,000 entered Shanghai. Eight years later the number of ships was 182, with a total tonnage of 78,000. Shanghai exports were valued in 1846 at $7,000,000; in 1853, at $23,000,000. By 1852 Shanghai accounted for more than half of China's export trade. Many factors contributed to this rapid growth. The city bordered the great silk-producing areas; its situation at the mouth of the Yangtze was ideal for both the import and the export trade; its inhabitants were free from the unhappy memories and the violent anti-foreignism so pronounced at Canton.

Origins of the Shanghai International Settlement

The treaty status under which foreign merchants lived at the new ports was a peculiar, not to say unique, system. At Canton and at many of the ports opened subsequently, the treaty powers obtained from China—that is, from the emperor—grants of land known as "concessions," where the traders could erect commercial structures and residences. The concession was leased by China to the foreign power concerned; the power subdivided the land into lots, granting these on long-term leases to its subjects and in some cases to other foreigners. Sometimes, as later at Tientsin, there were at one time in one open port as many as eight separate foreign "concessions." The foreign community of each concession provided, under authority of its home government, its own municipal government for the concession. Over this municipal government the consul of the given power presided. Thus at a treaty port there came to exist, in contiguous concession areas, a number of separate municipal governments, each exercising independent authority.

Shanghai met the problem in its own way. Since the local Chinese authorities there objected to the concession system, the first British consul accepted a plan whereby the Chinese authorities set apart an area of land on the river bank in which British subjects might acquire lots from Chinese owners. A British purchaser, having reached an agreement with a Chinese owner, reported it to the British consul, who in turn reported it to the Chinese local authority, the *tao-t'ai*. This latter functionary then issued to the British subject, through his consul, a title in the form of a perpetual lease, under which the foreign buyer paid a nominal annual rent to the Chinese government, the theory being that all land belonged to the emperor and could not be alienated by outright sale.[14]

The Shanghai "settlement," as this area and its peculiar system

[14] *Report of the Hon. Mr. Justice Feetham to the Shanghai Municipal Council* (4 vols., Shanghai, 1931-32), I, 27.

came to be known, was at first restricted to British control. Foreigners of non-British nationality secured land therein through the consent of the British consul. This proved particularly objectionable to Americans, and so in time the right of all foreigners to lease land within the settlement and to register such land at their own consulates was recognized. In this manner a system developed whereby each consul exercised jurisdiction over his own nationals in the common settlement area, and at the same time participated with his fellow consuls in supervision of settlement affairs.[15]

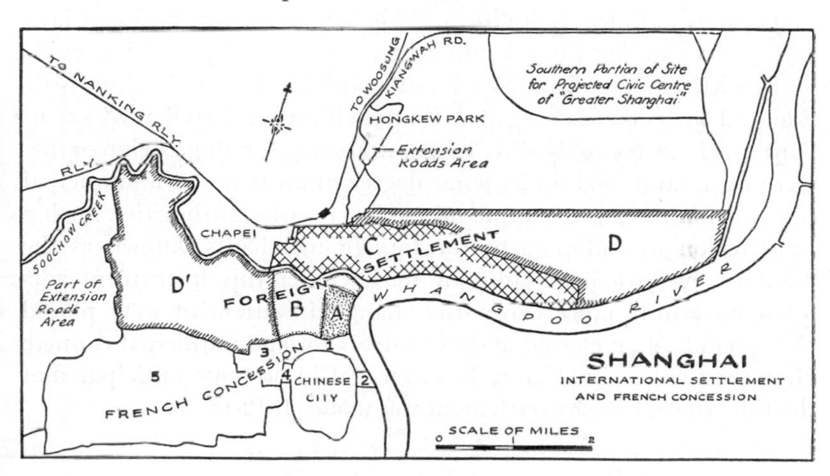

A. Original boundaries of the foreign settlement.
B. Extension of the settlement boundaries, 1848.
C. The "American Settlement," 1863; incorporated with the foreign settlement the same year.
D. Further extension of the settlement, 1899.
D1. Extension of 1899.
1. Original French concession, 1849.
2. Extended, 1861. 4. Extended, 1900.
3. Extended, 1900. 5. Extended, 1914.
The projected civic center of Shanghai is a project of the municipal government of the Chinese city.

When the Shanghai settlement was first established, it was supposed that the area would be inhabited exclusively by foreigners, and for some eight years this was so. In 1853 there were only 500

[15] For a brief period, separate American and French settlements existed at Shanghai, but in 1863 the American was merged with the British, forming the basis of what was to be known as the International Settlement. The French area continued to remain separate and came to be known as the "French concession," though the term is not strictly accurate.

Chinese residents, most of whom were servants or shopkeepers supplying the needs of the 200-odd foreign residents. In this same year, however, Chinese authority in areas adjacent to the settlement having broken down completely as a result of rebellions and civil war, the foreign area was soon swarming with homeless and often destitute Chinese refugees. By 1854 the Chinese population of the settlement exceeded 20,000. In this manner the whole character of the settlement was changed, and it became imperative that this unorganized community consisting of groups of foreigners belonging to different nations, each group living under its own national laws and subject to the jurisdiction of its own consul, should provide itself with effective municipal authority for internal administration and for protection against the rebellions and civil wars on its borders. To accomplish this it was necessary for the foreign settlement community to acquire some degree of unity under a municipal constitution having the approval of the consular authorities. Such a constitution was adopted by the foreign merchants (known as the "renters" of settlement land) in 1854. Under this instrument adequate governing powers over the Shanghai Settlement were placed in the hands of an elected and exclusively foreign municipal council. Here then was a situation unforeseen and in no sense anticipated at the time the first treaty settlement was made (1842-1844).

Foreign Relations at Canton

While the new foreign trade at Shanghai grew rapidly under conditions that were generally amicable, its corresponding growth at Canton was marked by friction, mob violence, and open armed conflict. To understand this contrast, one should recall that at Canton the foreign traders and some Chinese had long been in contact and in many cases had made fortunes; but also at Canton had arisen the grievances, real and imaginary, and the hatreds that had finally produced war. At Canton the foreigner had been subjected to "insults" by the populace and by high-handed Chinese officials. At Canton these same officials had bowed outwardly at least before the power of British guns. Now that the war had been won, the British proposed to assert after their own fashion their newly won privileges of equality. But the Chinese populace and many of the officials were by no means prepared to concede all this. The issue was soon drawn. No sooner had the city been officially opened in its new status as a treaty port (1843) than the intensity of its anti-foreignism became apparent. The mere presence of Caleb Cushing in South China and his threat to proceed to Peking called forth a popular manifesto from Canton: "Ye men of America may truly dread local extermination." Foreigners were not permitted access to the walled city, and Governor Davis of Hongkong regarded this "degrading" exclusion as a factor "provoking the insolence of the people." The treaties, to be sure, did not provide explicitly for entrance into the city, but the British claimed that denial of the privilege violated the spirit of the treaties and indicated the resolve of both officials and populace to preserve the old exclusive superiority. Because of this intensity of feeling, it was agreed in 1846 to postpone the "opening" of the city. The temper of the populace, however, did not improve. Foreigners, including Englishmen and an American, were stoned in a nearby village in 1847; a British fleet attacked the Bogue Forts and blockaded the river; the viceroy thereupon agreed to open the city in April, 1849, but this settlement was not approved by the emperor. Peking in fact was torn between the demands of the foreigners and those of its own people. Until 1848, Ch'i-ying at Canton attempted at least to keep the local people within the strict limits of the treaties, but his successors, Hsü Kwang-chin and Yeh Ming-ch'en, as will be seen, encouraged anti-foreignism and thus contributed to a second war, which was already in the making.[16]

In summary it may be said that the First Treaty Settlement was merely the beginning, not the consummation, of a new order between China and the West. By 1852 it had become merely a matter of time until Britain (this time aided by France) would demand the enforcement of the treaties and the addition of new and greater commercial privileges. This result was the more certain because Chinese leadership had neither the power nor the will to concede fully what had already been granted. There were at this time three factors in the Chinese intellectual tradition shaping her resistance to the Western impact: (1) the beginnings of a nationalistic ideology created by Chinese scholars who had long resented the alien Manchu dynasty; (2) the existence of a well-established anti-Western political tradition, in part the product of Jesuit efforts in the seventeenth and eighteenth centuries to plant Western technology and religious philosophy in Chinese soil; and (3) the determination of the Manchu

[16] T. F. Tsiang, "New Light on Chinese Diplomacy 1836-49," *Journal of Modern History,* III (1931), 590-91.

court to apply to the Western barbarians, as it always had applied to the barbarians of inner Asia, the Chinese theory of the Middle Kingdom as the universal empire to which all outsiders were to come as inferiors and bearers of tribute. Thus China's initial response to the modern West was one of complete intellectual resistance.[17]

The intellectual limitations noted above which conditioned China's response to the West in the mid-nineteenth century revealed themselves of course in the opinions commonly held by the scholar-officials about the foreigner barbarians. In the Chinese documents of the time the conventional phrases applied to Britons, Frenchmen, and Americans were vigorous and colorful. The barbarians were inherently cunning and malicious, impatient and with no understanding of values, insatiable and avaricious, self-seekers with the feelings of dogs and sheep, fickle and inconstant, and perverse in words. If there was any fine distinction to be drawn concerning the Americans, it was that they were weak and might therefore be used in turning one barbarian against another. As for the America from which some of these barbarians came, the best that was known about it by the scholar-officials was that it was "maritime, uncultivated, and primitive."[18]

For Further Reading

Abend, Hallett, *Treaty Ports* (New York, 1944). A popular account.

Allen, George C., and Audrey G. Donnithorne, *Western Enterprise in Far Eastern Economic Development: China and Japan* (New York, 1954). Methods and policies pursued by Western firms.

Ch'en, Gideon (Ch'i-t'ien), *Lin Tse-hsü, Pioneer Promoter of the Adoption of Western Means of Maritime Defense in China* (Peiping, 1934). A valuable study of the Chinese official whose actions precipitated the Opium War.

Dulles, Foster Rhea, *China and America, the Story of Their Relations Since 1784* (Princeton, 1946). One of the best general surveys.

Eitel, E. J., *Europe in China. The History of Hong Kong from the Beginning to the Year 1882* (London, 1895).

Kuo, P. C., *A Critical Study of the First Anglo-Chinese War (with Documents)* (Shanghai, 1935).

---

17 Têng Ssŭ-yü and John K. Fairbank, *China's Response to the West* (Cambridge, 1954), 6-21.

18 Swisher, *China's Management of the American Barbarians*, 44-48.

Lanning, George, and Samuel Couling, *The History of Shanghai* (2 vols., Shanghai, 1921-1923).

Mayers, William Frederick, N. B. Dennys, and Charles King, *The Treaty Ports of China and Japan, a Complete Guide to the Open Ports of Those Countries . . . Forming a Guide Book and Vade Mecum for Travelers, Merchants and Residents in General, with 29 maps and plans . . .* (London, 1867).

Têng Ssŭ-yü, *Chang Hsi and the Treaty of Nanking, 1842* (Chicago, 1944). An annotated translation of a diary kept during the opium war.

Wu Wen-Tsao, *The Chinese Opium Question in British Opinion and Action* (New York, 1928).

8 *China: 1848–1860*

The New Sino-Western Order in East Asia

THE first Sino-Western treaties, of which an outline has been given in the preceding chapter, formed the beginnings of a new order for East Asia. These agreements called for treaty relations based on a theory of the equality of states to replace a theory of Confucian relations between peoples that were unequal. A victory of British arms had ordained a new order to regulate the meeting and the mingling of Western states with China's Confucian society. The creation of treaty ports, the arrival of consuls, the appearance of concessions and settlements, the application of the new treaty tariff and of extraterritoriality gave tangible evidence that an old order was passing and that a new one was appearing. These obvious changes from the procedures of pre-treaty days are easily stated, but in themselves they present no adequate picture of the conflict in manners and values between Confucian China and an equable-minded West. Britain had won a war, but the settlement she had imposed was to operate in an alien environment where the Western barbarian, asserting his equality and thereby assuming the role of reformer, was not welcome. He was feared because of his military power, but he was not respected for his appreciation of values. Thus the opening of the ports, the arrival of the first consuls and merchants, and the setting apart of concessions were merely the preliminary steps in the application of a new order the future of which was as yet unpredictable. Would this order, even if China observed the treaties, satisfy the commercial ambitions of the Westerners?

How far and how speedily could the Manchu government go toward enforcing a treaty system so repugnant to traditional Confucian concepts of foreign relations and trade? Answers to these and to related questions form the basic history of the turbulent years in Sino-Western relations from 1848 to 1860. The outcome, as will be seen, was a compromise, acceptable but not satisfactory to either side.

The crisis confronting the Manchu Empire in the decade 1850 to 1860 was perhaps no less acute than that faced by Commissioner Lin at Canton in 1840. Great Britain had won the first war but there was some doubt as to who was winning the peace. By 1850 most of the foreigners in the five ports regarded the first treaty settlements as inadequate if not a complete failure. The major question was whether this settlement could be revised by diplomacy or would require resort to arms. This problem was resolved ultimately by conditions of political disintegration within China: conditions that, in a sense, deprived the Manchu government of both the will and the power either to enforce the treaties and their broad implications upon its subjects or to repudiate them completely. The days of the great K'ang-hsi emperor (1662-1722) and the Ch'ien-lung emperor (1736-1796) were long since past. With all her vast population, China lacked great leadership.

Thus in the mid-nineteenth century China possessed neither the power to repel the "barbarian" nor the leadership to create a new China adjusted to a new world. Future conflict was inherent in these facts. This conflict was to develop out of three major sources: (1) the decline of Manchu power, hastened by the T'ai-p'ing and other rebellions; (2) the incapacity of the official hierarchy to adjust itself to the new order of foreign intercourse with its broad social and economic implications; and (3) the growing co-operation and strength of the treaty powers in their quest for wider and more stable commercial relations with The Middle Kingdom.

The T'ai-p'ing Rebellion

Rebellion is an old institution in China, sanctioned by Confucian philosophy and essential in the theory of the Mandate of Heaven. When a dynasty, for whatever reason, lost its ability to rule, it was obvious that Heaven had withdrawn the mandate. The duty of the subject to rebel was then clear. This ancient theory was to enjoy wide application in nineteenth-century China. In the two decades that preceded the first British war, revolts had occurred with alarming frequency in Kwangsi, Shansi, Kweichow, Kiangsi, Hainan, Hupeh, and Formosa. All were indicative of growing political discontent. These revolts also aggravated the Manchu problem of dealing with the troublesome foreigners. While pirates swarmed and looted along the coasts, floods in the Yellow River Valley drove thousands to brigandage. Secret political societies bent on rebellion flourished as rarely before.

Fundamentally the causes of unrest in the mid-nineteenth century lay in the fact that in China "economic change had outrun the growth of social theory." Population had increased out of proportion to the land under cultivation. As a result of this, of the growth of internal and foreign trade, and of the inequalities of an antiquated tax system, the peasant was degraded to virtual serfdom. Thus a permanent, floating "population of paupers" provided the raw material for rebellion.[1]

In these circumstances there appeared one Hung Hsiu-ch'üan, a native of the Canton district, the youngest and brightest son of a farm family. Young Hung passed the local examinations, but failed repeatedly in the provincial tests. To this background of disappointment and failure were added illness, visions, and some contacts with the Reverend Issachar Roberts, an American Baptist missionary at Canton. With the mental and spiritual equipment thus provided, Hung resolved that he was commissioned to restore the worship of the true god. His original organization, the *Pai Shang-ti Hui* (Association of God Worshippers), soon recruited an enormous following from disaffected elements in Kwangsi. At first the movement appeared as religious and iconoclastic, and, superficially at least, seemed to bear some resemblance to Protestantism. As the movement grew, its devastating armies moved north to the Yangtze and captured Nanking, where its capital was established in 1853. Meanwhile Hung had bestowed upon himself the title, *T'ien-wang* (Heavenly King), professed to rule over the *T'ai-p'ing T'ien-kuo* (The Heavenly Kingdom of Great Peace), and had set for his purpose the overthrow of the Manchu dynasty. In this new theocracy God was the Heavenly Father; Christ, the Divine Elder Brother; the *T'ai-P'ing Wang* (Hung, himself), the Divine Younger Brother. The Christian factor in the movement was, in the main, the first five

---

1 G. E. Taylor, "The Taiping Rebellion: Its Economic Background and Social Theory," *Chinese Soc. and Pol. Science Rev.*, XVI (1933), 545-549.

books of the Old Testament. Such was the notable achievement of this "soured and disappointed member of the learned proletariat."

The Rebellion and the Foreign Powers

During the winter of 1853-1854, Hung and his rebels advanced to the north and reached the outskirts of Tientsin. They were unable to reach Peking. Yet for another decade they dominated the Yangtze Valley in defiance of Manchu authority. A rebellion so wide-spread and promoting a government that threatened to rival, if not over-

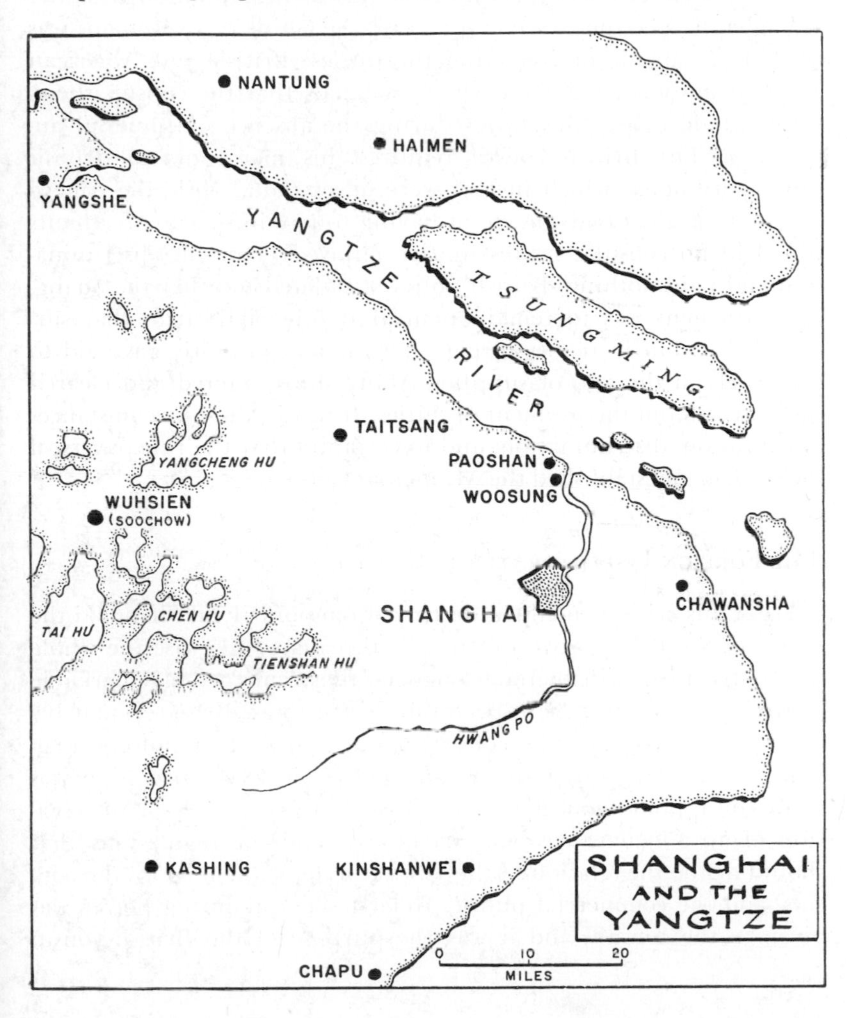

throw, the Manchus could not but command the attention of the foreign powers. If the T'ai-p'ing were Christians, would they not be more amenable than the Manchus to foreign treaty relations, to the commercial, social, and political concepts of the Westerners? This importance of defining their relation to the rebels was brought home to the powers in 1853, when the Chinese walled city of Shanghai, on the very border of the foreign settlements, was captured by a rebel band known as the "Small Swords." Civil war had thus reached the edge of the settlements, and retreating Imperial authorities deserted the Shanghai customs house. This raised the question whether Shanghai had become a free port, since the Chinese government was no longer capable of collecting the duties. British and American consular authorities notified their nationals that the consuls themselves would collect the duties during the absence of Imperial authorities. The British consul required his merchants to deposit promissory notes, which in fact were never paid, while the Americans were at the disadvantage of having to pay in specie. Merchants who had no consular representative enjoyed favorable discrimination and paid nothing. British policy stipulated too that the Shanghai settlement was to remain neutral in the civil strife that surrounded it; but in reality foreign merchants constantly gave aid to the rebels in the sale of supplies. Many ships entered and cleared the port without the payment of duties. It was in these circumstances of confusion, discrimination, and uncertainty that the rate-payers of the settlement established the Municipal Council.

The Foreign Inspectorate of Customs

From this crisis, which had destroyed temporarily at Shanghai the power of the Peking government and threatened likewise the whole treaty structure built by the foreigners, there emerged a remarkable institution—the Foreign Inspectorate of Customs. By agreement between the *tao-t'ai* and the consuls of the three treaty powers, England, the United States, and France (June 29, 1854), provision was made for appointment of a board of foreign inspectors, for the creation of an adequate customs machinery, and for regulations that should define the relation of the Inspectorate to the *tao-t'ai,* the consuls, and the commercial public. At first the appointing power was given to the consuls, and it was the purpose of the British consul

(Alcock) that the British should control the new Inspectorate, but within a year the British Foreign Office had ruled that the foreign inspectors were officials of China and not the nominees and delegates of foreign countries. Thus was formed the nucleus of a new Chinese customs administration, officered by foreign inspectors, which, in 1858, was extended to all the treaty ports, where it became a model of efficient government.[2]

Thoughout these early years of the T'ai-p'ing revolt the efforts of the major treaty powers to determine what policy they should follow relative to the T'ai-p'ings were hampered by the uninformed yet often positive attitude assumed by segments of public opinion in Europe and in America toward the rebellion. In the United States, where "Manifest Destiny" had become the slogan of the decade, journalists and other writers found evidence of a divine plan in the opening of China to Western trade and in the subsequent rebellion of the T'ai-p'ings, which, as God's instrument, was destined to overthrow the Manchu dynasty and hasten the advent of a Chinese Christian republic. Once the T'ai-p'ings had prepared the way, so it was said, China would progress to republicanism and Christianity aided by the educational forces of commercial intercourse and Christian missions. There appears to have been little disposition to evaluate or to question the evidence on which these comforting predictions were based. It was enough that the predictions were in line with what many Americans wanted to believe.

The Obligations of Extraterritoriality

The growing crisis in the treaty system was not due solely to Chinese obstructionism or to her political decline. The Western governments were at times notably negligent in their obligations toward China. The application of extraterritoriality was a case in point. In acquiring extraterritorial jurisdiction over their nationals

---

[2] For detailed studies of the customs problem at Shanghai in this period, see: J. K. Fairbank, "The Provisional System at Shanghai," *Chinese Soc. and Pol. Science Rev.*, XVIII (1934-35), 455-504, and XIX (1935-36), 65-124; "The Creation of the Foreign Inspectorate of Customs at Shanghai," *ibid.*, XIX (1935-36), 469-514, and XX (1936-37), 42-100; "The Definition of the Foreign Inspector's Status (1854-55): A Chapter in the Early History of the Inspectorate of Customs at Shanghai," *Nankai Social and Economic Quarterly*, IX (1936), 125-163; and *Trade and Diplomacy on the China Coast,* 371-461.

in China, the treaty powers had won a legal right of the greatest consequence. The practice of extraterritoriality, however, carried with it grave responsibilities, which for many years most of the powers treated with shameful disregard. At first only the British recognized and sought to meet their extraterritorial obligations.

Since under the extraterritorial grants China had surrendered the power of her own courts over foreigners, it became the duty of the treaty powers to provide competent consular courts in the treaty ports, and jails where criminals might be incarcerated. Prior to 1857, Great Britain alone took adequate steps to meet this need. A British criminal court, provided for in 1833, functioned at Canton after 1839. By act of Parliament (1843) British legal jurisdiction was authorized on foreign soil, as a result of which machinery was provided for the administration of extraterritoriality in China, including provision for jails. In contrast, habitual American criminals in the China ports could be confined only on a national ship, or, as frequently happened, by courtesy in a British jail. In 1858 American criminals were released from the British jail in Shanghai because the American consul had no funds for jail expenses. Two years later the United States provided its first appropriation for consular jails in China.[3]

The Growth of the Opium Trade

Since 1842 the opium trade had continued to grow and to prosper. Although opium had provided the occasion for the first Sino-British war, the subsequent treaties had evaded the problem of control. Thus, although the importation of opium was still prohibited by the laws of China, foreigners and Chinese conspired to flood the market with this contraband and demoralizing drug.[4] It has been estimated that between 1840 and 1858 the annual imports increased almost 300 per cent. The effects upon the Chinese were devastating; but so long as the Chinese government would not or could not enforce its laws, there was little hope that the foreigners would forego a trade so profitable.

---

[3] For an extended treatment, see G. W. Keeton, *The Development of Extraterritoriality in China* (2 vols., London, 1928).

[4] *The Times* correspondent reported, 1857: "At present the [opium] trade is as open and as unrestrained in all the cities of China as the sale of hot-cross buns on Good Friday is in the streets of London." Cooke, *China . . . in 1857-58,* 179.

DEMANDS FOR TREATY REVISION

By 1854, despite the growth of profitable trade at Shanghai and Canton, it was evident that the relations of China and the treaty powers were far from healthy. The abuses of extraterritoriality, a flagrant traffic in coolies to servitude in Cuba, the opium trade, and the gun-boat policy (whereby one did the shooting first and the talking afterwards) at Canton, all served to reinforce the official Chinese view that the foreign barbarians were an uncouth and troublesome lot with whom China should have as few dealings as possible. On his part, the foreigner, both merchant and consul, was convinced that China had no respect for treaties and no understanding of the benefits of free commerce and free access to markets. The foreigners now regarded the treaties of 1842-1844 as inadequate not only because China had frequently evaded them but also because under these treaties foreign trade was confined to the five ports: the foreign trader was still a stranger to China's vast interior; the foreign diplomat was still a stranger to Peking. Both the American and the French treaties of 1844 provided for revision after twelve years, and the British claimed this same privilege on the basis of most-favored-nation treatment. Under this claim the British held that the Treaty of Nanking would be subject to revision in 1854.

The scope of Britain's policy of treaty revision was contained in instructions from Clarendon to Bowring (February 13, 1854). The British government insisted on China's recognition of the *right* of immediate revision, but the actual revision might be delayed at Bowring's discretion in view of China's domestic strife due to the T'ai-p'ing Rebellion. Meanwhile, Bowring was to seek co-operation with the Americans and the French, whose treaties would also soon be subject to revision. In his negotiations with China he was to seek "access generally to the whole interior of the Chinese Empire as well as to the cities on the coast: or failing this, . . . free navigation of the Yangtze Kiang and access to the cities on its banks up to Nanking. . . ." He was to effect legalization of the opium trade, in order that it might be limited and controlled, and to seek abolition of internal transit duties on goods imported or purchased for export. He was also to secure suppression of piracy and regulation of the coolie trade. Finally, the British government desired "the permanent and honourable residence at the Court of Peking of a Representative of the British Crown" or provision for direct and unobstructed correspondence with that government. These official British objectives also represented approximately those general principles that were beginning to appear in French and American policy.

The desire of the British to be represented diplomatically at Peking indicated, among other things, that they were no longer willing to tolerate the Chinese system whereby the Canton viceroy was entrusted by Peking with the actual conduct of foreign affairs. With this official alone the foreigners were expected to deal, and their experience had not recommended the system. In 1848 John W. Davis, the American commissioner, after great difficulty secured an interview with the viceroy for the purpose of presenting his credentials. He was treated "with extreme rudeness" by both viceroy and governor. In fact, after 1852 "the practice of ignoring the foreign representatives became a part of the settled policy of the Chinese government."[5]

A French diplomat remained at Macao fifteen months vainly awaiting a personal interview with a qualified Chinese official. Of the various successors of Davis in the period to 1855, none succeeded in securing an interview. The high commissioner was always "too busy," and in any event would have to await the dawn of "an auspicious day." Two American commissioners, Humphrey Marshall and Robert McLane, went to Nanking hoping to make direct contact with responsible officials, only to be referred back to Canton. Thus in 1854, when Clarendon instructed Bowring on British policy, the foreign traders and most of their consular and diplomatic associates were of a mind not only to extend their commercial rights but also to convert China, forcibly if necessary, to Western concepts of international law, diplomacy, and commercial intercourse in general.

Limited Co-operation Among the Powers

England's plan for treaty revision did not imply an immediate resort to war. There was to be no precipitate action. Actually the British government hoped for a co-operative policy with France and the United States.

Among American merchants in the treaty ports there was very general support for Britain's policy of treaty revision. This was natural because the interests of British and American traders were in many

[5] H. B. Morse, *The International Relations of the Chinese Empire* (3 vols., London, 1910-1918), I, 411.

respects identical. Some support for British policy was contained, too, in the dispatches of various American commissioners in China.

In view then of the general harmony between British and American expressions of policy, England's proposals through Lord Napier to Secretary Cass (March, 1857) for a three-power alliance (the United States, France, and Great Britain) to effect revision of the treaties were not surprising. These proposals were of course declined, yet the dangers threatening American interests in China did prompt the appointment of William B. Reed as envoy extraordinary and minister plenipotentiary to the court of Peking.

By the early autumn of 1856, with the crisis of the Crimean War already past, Great Britain had determined on a diplomatic and naval move toward Peking to hasten revision of the treaties, to expand commercial intercourse, and to destroy the exclusiveness of Chinese policy at Canton.

A So-called Judicial Murder

In this forward policy Britain could count on the support of France, for in February, 1856, a French Catholic missionary, Auguste Chapdelaine, had been put to death by Chinese authorities at Sinlin in Kwangsi. Chapdelaine and some of his converts had been arrested on a charge that they were rebels—a natural enough charge, for Kwangsi had witnessed the beginnings of the T'ai-p'ing Rebellion with its frosting of Christian flavor. The arrest, torture, and execution of the foreign priest and his followers are thus understandable according to official Chinese ideas of the time. The Chinese magistrate could likewise rest his case on the fact that under the treaties no foreigners were allowed beyond the treaty ports. Furthermore, the testimony of Catholic missionaries themselves reveals that they indoctrinated their Chinese converts with the idea of looking to "France as their support and liberator" against persecution.[6] China's fault of course lay in the fact that the execution of the priest violated the extraterritorial rights of France.

News of this so-called "judicial murder" reached Canton in July, 1856. It was not unwelcome to Napoleon III. France was now in a position not only to assist Great Britain in forcing, if need be, a revision of the treaties, but also to aid the Catholic Church by political

6 *Missions Etrangères* (Paris), Vol. DL. Quoted by W. C. Costin, *Great Britain and China* (Oxford, 1937), 202.

means in the spiritual conquest of China. By October, 1856, France and England were able to agree upon a common policy of force.

The Affair of the Lorcha *Arrow*

The incident that was to precipitate hostilities between Great Britain and China found its origin in a system by which Chinese coasting vessels acquired temporary register under foreign flags. During 1853-1854 southern Chinese rebels held positions so strong in the regions of Canton and Kowloon that communications between Whampoa (the Canton anchorage) and Hongkong were frequently broken so far as the passage of Chinese vessels was concerned. Even commissioner Yeh asked help from the despised foreigners. In 1855 English and American authorities, in order to maintain trade between Hongkong and Canton, believed it was necessary to grant "English and United States flags with a passport to Chinese lighters for a single trip to and from Canton and Whampoa to be immediately returned and filed at the consulates by which they were issued." Out of this situation arose various ordinances of the colonial government of Hongkong permitting residents of the colony, including Chinese, under prescribed conditions, to use the British flag on their vessels for this limited purpose. In time this right by ordinance was abused. Some vessels used the protection of the British flag to engage in the smuggling trade; others carried the flags of various foreign powers with no authority whatsoever for doing so; sometimes merchant consuls, without authority from their governments, issued foreign registry to native craft. As a result it was soon difficult for Chinese authorities to distinguish between the legitimate and the illegitimate use of foreign flags by native craft.

The lorcha *Arrow,* owned by a Chinese who had resided in Hongkong for ten years and commanded by a British subject, was boarded by Chinese police (October 8, 1856) while it was lying at anchor in the river at Canton. Twelve of her Chinese crew of fourteen were arrested on charges of piracy and removed to a Chinese war-junk. Harry Parkes, British consul at Canton, promptly demanded release of the captives on the ground that the *Arrow* was a British ship carrying colonial registry from Hongkong, that she had been boarded without communication first having been made to the British consul, and that the British flag had been hauled down by the Chinese police. Sir John Bowring supported Parkes by demanding an apology and guarantees for the future. The prisoners were eventually handed over by Yeh (October 22), but Consul Parkes refused to accept this release, since the captives were accompanied neither by a Chinese officer of rank nor by an apology. British naval forces therefore attacked the forts guarding the approach to Canton. On October 29, the walls of the city were breached, but though the British could attack the city, they had insufficient forces to occupy it. In the heat of these proceedings the American flag too was fired upon by Chinese forts—a fire that was returned by American ships of war. Trade was now at an end, yet Commissioner Yeh refused all concessions.

In England, Bowring's actions were approved despite vigorous criticism from the Opposition; and now that France was prepared for full co-operation in treaty revision, the British government appointed Lord Elgin to head Her Majesty's special embassy. Elgin's mission was not merely to solve local grievances at Canton or elsewhere. He was to extend the opportunities for foreign trade and to establish diplomatic representation at Peking. In other words, he was to revise the treaties thoroughly.

War was now certain. The "murder" of the French priest and the affair of the *Arrow* were the convenient pretexts for armed action, the real causes of which were far more fundamental than these incidents. China's obstructive policy was regarded by Britain as a menace both to her actual and to her potential commercial interests, while the conduct of Chinese officials—that of Yeh in particular—was looked upon as an insult to the Crown. Napoleon III was happy to be associated with the British policy that derived from these sentiments. A victorious war in China would appeal to French business, and, by avenging the death of a priest and providing religious guarantees for the future, would not be unwelcome to French Catholics or to the Papacy. In extenuation of these official views it may be noted that the powers and their nationals had suffered grave indignities in China. The treaties had been consistently broken by China, though she was not the sole offender in this respect. In addition, her officials had given little evidence of adjusting themselves to a world of Western trade and law. Yet this was not surprising. Nations rarely recognize voluntarily the need for change or appreciate their own attitude as an obstacle to change. It was natural and it was easier for China to see the foreigners as barbarians to be repelled, not as envoys of a "superior" or more powerful civilization.

After much delay due to diversion of British contingents to suppress the Indian Mutiny, British and French forces bombarded and captured Canton in December, 1857. British marines seized the venerable but proud and obstinate High Commissioner Yeh as this portly gentleman sought to escape over the back wall of his yamen. Fifteen months later he died, a prisoner of war, in India. Until 1860, Canton was ruled by Chinese officials acting at the command of a British and French commission.

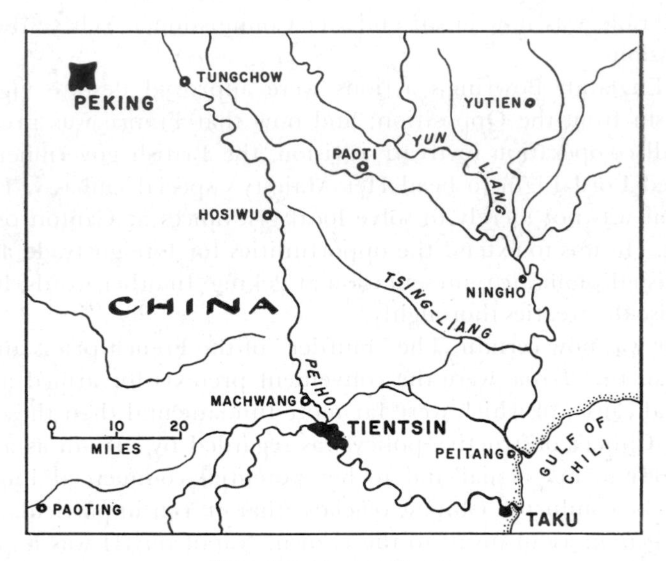

THE APPROACH TO PEKING

Britain and France, on February 11, 1858, were joined by the representatives of the United States and Russia, William B. Reed and Count Putiatin, respectively, in simultaneous notes to Peking making clear the united demand of the powers for treaty revision and religious toleration, and suggesting negotiations at Shanghai. To the Chinese demand that negotiations be conducted at Canton, the representatives of the powers replied by sailing north to the mouth of the Pei-ho, at the very gateway to Peking. Alarmed by this manoeuvre, the Chinese court appointed the viceroy of Chihli to negotiate, but his powers were regarded by Lord Elgin and Baron Gros (France) as inadequate. It was their view that only an advance to Tientsin would bring the Chinese to terms. To this end they demanded the surrender of the Taku forts guarding the mouth of the river, and when this was refused, the forts were stormed and taken (May 20). Peking thereupon promptly appointed officials whose powers were regarded as adequate. Negotiations leading to new treaties were now conducted with all four powers, concurrently but separately. Before the end of June, 1858, the four treaties of Tientsin had been signed: the Russian on the 13th, the American on the 18th, the British on the 26th, and the French the following day.

The Treaties of Tientsin, 1858

The treaties of Tientsin were a revision and an enlargement of principles and practices set forth in the first treaties of 1842-1844. Since England and France had employed force, it was their treaties that embodied the new and valuable concessions, which, however, by reason of the most-favored-nation clause would be enjoyed likewise by Russia and the United States.[7] In this sense the four treaties constituted a single settlement having a profound influence upon China's relations with the West.

The new and significant privileges won by the treaty powers in the Tientsin Treaties included:

1. The right to maintain a resident minister at Peking, or the right of the minister, at the discretion of the British government, to visit the capital. The British minister should "not be called upon to perform any ceremony derogatory to him as representing the sovereign of an independent nation on a footing of equality with that of China."

2. The right of travel in all parts of the interior under passports issued by the foreign consuls and counter-signed by the local Chinese authorities.

3. The right of foreign ships to trade on the Yangtze River, and the opening of additional treaty ports.[8]

4. The right of missionaries to protection by the Chinese authorities, since "the Christian religion, as professed by Protestants or Ro-

[7] It has been stated with some justification that "it became ingloriously, yet very profitably, the role of the United States pacifically to follow England to China in the wake of war, and to profit greatly by the victories of British arms." Tyler Dennett, *Americans in Eastern Asia* (New York, 1922), 159.

[8] To the five ports opened by the treaty of 1842 were added Chefoo in Shantung, Chinkiang in Kiangsu, Hankow in Hupeh, Kuikiang in Kiangsi, Kiungchow in Hainan, Newchwang in Manchuria, Swatow in Kwangtung, Wenchow in Chekiang, and Nanking in Kiangsu.

man Catholics, inculcates the practice of virtue, and teaches man to do as he would be done by."[9]

The Tientsin Treaties were of such moment as to justify a further statement on the policy embodied in them. It is to be noted that they represented a common policy on the part of the four powers, for although England and France alone had used force, the United States and Russia insisted on most-favored-nation treatment.

The most striking concession was the right of residence of foreign ministers at Peking, or at least the right of these ministers to visit the capital. The delay and evasion that China had practiced constantly in dealing with the foreign governments would now be more difficult.

The grant of toleration to Christians, to missionaries, and to their Chinese converts has been a subject of much controversy. To toleration in principle there could be no objection; but in 1858 toleration was won as a result of war, and was granted in the clause of a treaty exacted as a result of war. The missionaries, particularly the Catholics, were already well aware that many elements in Christian doctrine had proved disruptive of China's cultural heritage; yet, since the object of the missionaries was to make this heritage subservient to Christianity, it was natural that they should welcome the new treaty status for themselves and for their religion. Neither is it surprising that after 1858 many Chinese felt quite justified in regarding Christianity as a political as well as a religious weapon of the West.

The right of foreigners to travel in the interior was another concession on which interpretation has differed widely. The traders of 1858 had complained bitterly of the restrictions that confined them to the treaty ports. They were businessmen intent on profits, and these same profits, they felt, would depend in turn on freedom of access to the entire country. Against this point of view the Chinese could argue that the people were not yet ready to receive foreigners beyond the port towns, and that because the foreigner enjoyed extraterritoriality and would when in the interior be far removed from his nearest consul, China could exercise over him only an ineffective control.

Since the powers were now bent on expanding their commerce with China, the opening of additional treaty ports (nine in China

---

[9] All quotations are from the British treaty. In addition, the extraterritorial rights of foreigners were further defined in criminal cases. Indemnities demanded by the British totalled four million taels; by the French, two million taels.

and one in Formosa) could not long be delayed. Nevertheless, the opening of the additional ports did occasion trouble, and in the case of Nanking the port was not opened until 1899. In addition, the admission of foreign vessels to the trade of the Yangtze could not be easily defended. It was the great artery to the richest areas of China. The fact that the foreigners could demand and be granted access to China's coasting and inland trade is the most eloquent testimony to the decay of the Manchu dynasty.

Legalization of the Opium Trade

Following the Tientsin settlement, negotiations were adjourned to Shanghai, where a revised schedule of rates in the conventional tariff was adopted, providing for a general 5 per cent duty on exports and imports. But more significant than this revision was the legalization of the opium trade at a duty of 30 taels per 100 catties.[10] This new legal status of opium was a triumph for British policy, which, since 1842, had been consistent, and probably sound, despite the fact that it appeared to support a nefarious traffic. The British argument ran as follows: Since the Nanking settlement, the importation of opium, a contraband trade, had increased rapidly. Although most of the opium was produced in India, other sources of supply were available, and therefore prohibition by the British authorities was not likely to prove effective in stopping the trade, though it would materially reduce Indian revenue. It was the business of China to enforce her laws against an illicit traffic. England would not give protection to subjects violating China's laws, but neither would she undertake to enforce the laws for China. Since China had failed to enforce the law against opium, the trade should be legalized at a fixed duty and supervised strictly.[11]

The attitude of the United States at this time to the opium ques-

---

[10] One catty equals 1⅓ lbs.

[11] J. F. Fairbank, "The Legalization of the Opium Trade before the Treaties of 1858," *Chinese Social and Political Science Review,* XVII (1933), 215, points out that although the Imperial government in Peking took no steps to levy an official impost on opium trade before 1858, nevertheless "the unofficial or private taxation of the traffic by local [Chinese] authorities, . . . appears to have been put gradually on a more regular basis." Thus the taxing of opium was applied by the Chinese authorities at some of the ports before the legalization clause was written into the treaties of 1858. Legalization served two purposes: it provided China with needed revenue, and it stabilized an important item of the foreign trade by placing it on a treaty basis.

tion is also of interest. Minister Reed had been instructed that his government would not seek legalization of the opium traffic, and thus the treaty that Reed signed at Tientsin made no mention of opium. But later, in discussions with Lord Elgin, Reed came to the view that "any course is better than that which is now pursued." He therefore supported the principle of legalization, and his action in this respect was accepted by his government. American business in general approved of the Tientsin Treaties, since it was believed that, as trade with China continued to increase, cotton alone would probably more than repay the annual deficits on the imports of tea and silk.

The Renewal of Hostilities

The treaties of Tientsin were approved by the Chinese government in 1858 before the British and French forces left Tientsin. They were not to become effective, however, until ratified copies had been exchanged *at Peking*. This was done without difficulty in the case of the Russian treaty. The new Russian minister, General Ignatiev, proceeded to Peking by the old overland route and was promptly received. The British, the French, and the American envoys, accompanied by ships of war, arrived at the mouth of the Pei-ho in June, 1859. Here it was discovered that the Chinese had strengthened the forts at Taku and had blocked the river's mouth. The envoys were informed, but only when it was too late, that they would be received at P'ei-t'ang ten miles farther north on the coast, but that China would repel any attempt to enter the river at Taku. The British and French therefore attempted to storm the forts and break the barrier—an attempt in which they failed utterly, and accordingly were forced to return to Shanghai.[12]

Hostilities had thus been precipitated and a second chapter in the *Arrow* War was now inevitable. Again it should be noted that the question of responsibility is difficult to assess. The British envoy, Frederick Bruce, had been instructed that it would be desirable for him to "reach Tientsin in a British ship of war," but that since defi-

---

12 During the engagement, the commander of the American naval forces, whose country was neutral, had nonetheless come to the assistance of his British cousins, explaining his action with the statement that "blood is thicker than water." This was doubtless scientifically true, but it had little bearing on the commander's official instructions.

nite rules of procedure could not be laid down in London the envoy was to use discretion when "to give way" and when "to stand firm." Thus Bruce, faced with dilatory Chinese correspondence and evasion followed by the blocking of the river at Taku, had come to the conclusion that this was the time "to stand firm." When he insisted on the approach through Taku and Tientsin he was not violating his instructions, but he *was* demanding something not granted by the British treaty. Actually neither British nor French policy in this instance could be justified in law. Both the policy and Bruce's decision were political. They rested on the conviction, for which there was considerable ground, that the Peking government had no intention to honor the extensive new concessions it had been forced to grant at Tientsin the previous year.

Meanwhile, John E. Ward, the American envoy, not restricted to any route or place for the exchange of his country's treaty, proceeded to P'ei-t'ang. At Tungchow the Chinese provided carts that carried him and his mission to Peking.[13] This was unfortunate for the dignity of the United States. Ward, a native of Georgia, was a Southern gentleman of some distinction, but being sadly ignorant of the finer points of Oriental procedure he permitted the Chinese to take full advantage of his inexperience. He should have demanded sedan chairs, the mode of conveyance used by high Chinese officials. The cart in which he did ride was the kind of vehicle used to carry Korean and other tribute-bearers to the Chinese capital. Over this cart floated banners describing Ward as a tribute-bearer from the United States. This of course was further evidence that the Manchu Court did not accept the Tientsin treaties in letter or spirit.

Arrived in Peking, Ward was requested to perform the *kotow,* which of course he refused to do, and with what must have been a splendid dignity informed the Chinese officials that "although he was willing to 'bend the body and slightly crook the right knee,' he was accustomed to kneel only to God and woman."[14] Thoroughly disgusted, Ward returned to P'ei-t'ang, where copies of the ratified American treaty were exchanged.

Meanwhile, British and French reinforcements reached the Pei-ho. On August 21, 1860, the Allies stormed the Taku forts and advanced on Tientsin and Peking. The Chinese retired in confusion, and

[13] The Ward correspondence is in U.S. Sen. Ex., doc. 36-1:(30), 569 ff.

[14] Tyler Dennett, *Americans in Eastern Asia* (New York, 1922), 342.

when the foreigners entered the capital, the degenerate Manchu emperor had already fled with his court to Jehol, ostensibly on a hunting trip. During the Allied march on Peking, thirty-nine foreigners (twenty-six English and thirteen French, including the private secretary of Lord Elgin, who had replaced Bruce as Britain's plenipotentiary) were captured by the Chinese. At the time, the victims were presumably protected by a flag of truce, but the Chinese appear to have believed that by holding these hostages they would bring the Allies to adopt a more moderate policy. Twenty of the prisoners were already dead when the remaining survivors were released. As a result, Lord Elgin ordered the burning of the emperor's Summer Palace (Yüan Ming Yüan) situated outside the city, an architectural monument which the French troops had already occupied and looted.[15] In Elgin's view China would have no peace with Britain until by the destruction of the Summer Palace a price had been paid for her "foul deed."

The Peking Convention, 1860

With the Chinese capital now at their mercy, the Allied envoys proceeded to the exchange of the ratified treaties of 1858, and to exact new concessions embodied in the Conventions of Peking, 1860. The Emperor of China expressed "his deep regret" that a "misunderstanding" had occurred at Taku the previous year; agreed that the British minister might "reside permanently" at Peking, consented to additional indemnities and to the opening of Tientsin as a treaty port, legalized the coolie trade under regulation, and consented to the cession of Kowloon on the mainland opposite Hongkong. The French convention secured the restoration to the Roman Catholic Church of all property confiscated since 1724, a provision that was to work great hardship on Chinese who had acquired the property. The fact does not appear to have troubled the French government or the Church. Both found a convenient justification for taking the property in an Imperial edict of 1846, which had promised restoration of religious establishments to Roman Catholics. The Chinese text of the French convention (which was not authoritative) also contained

---

15 The Summer Palace extended over an area more than six miles in length, situated at the foot of the first range of hills some five miles to the northwest of Peking. The grounds, which might be described as a great private park, included residences, temples, pagodas, gardens, and artificial hills, some of them 300 feet in height, surrounding a lake.

a troublesome provision allowing French missionaries to rent and purchase land and to erect buildings in all provinces.[16]

The most curious phase of events in China during 1860 remains to be told. It was in this year that rebel bands associated with the T'ai-p'ing were threatening to advance upon the wealthy and populous city of Shanghai with its growing foreign settlement. In this extremity the Chinese authorities appealed to the English and French for protection, and these latter agreed to defend the Chinese city and the foreign settlement against any attack. On August 21, 1860, the British troops, assisted by some French, repelled the rebels from the walls of Shanghai. It was on this very day that British and French troops in the north were storming the Taku forts and beginning their march on Peking.

The new order in Sino-Western relations formalized by the Tientsin Treaties, 1858, and the Peking treaties, 1860, has often been explained exclusively in terms of imperialism, a Western movement imposing itself upon a helpless and unco-operative China. This Western impact interpretation is sound but it is not the entire explanation. Between 1840 and 1860 imperialism did work its way with China. There was also, however, a concurrent and complementary movement by means of which the Chinese state, long skilled in handling the barbarians of Inner Asia, adjusted itself to the new nineteenth-century Western intruders by drawing upon institutional devices fashioned from long experience. From the Chinese point of view there is evidence to suggest that the treaty system was added to the traditional tribute system with the idea of bringing the foreigner under the influence of the universal Confucian state. The new order was therefore not an exclusively Western creation. Seen in the perspective of Chinese historical experience with outer barbarians, the treaty ports were modern reflections of the stations assigned for ancient tributary trade. Consular jurisdiction could be compared to the method by which the chief of Arab traders was responsible for the actions of his countrymen in China (see page 80). The most-favored-nation principle could be interpreted as contemporary evidence of the benevolence of the Confucian sovereign toward all barbarians to the end of playing one against another. The treaty tariff, so antagonistic to potential Chinese industry, had its

[16] For a full discussion of the social and political complications arising from this alleged right of Catholic missionaries, see Paul H. Clyde, *United States Policy Toward China* (Durham, 1940), 107-112.

forerunner in the older and onerous Manchu policy of taxation on production and trade. Finally, the employment of foreigners in Chinese government service had many precedents in China's history. Thus the period 1840 to 1860 witnessed the achievement of a compromise settlement which took the form of a joint Chinese-Western administration in the treaty ports. Pre-eminent as an example of an institution of this dual administration was the Foreign Inspectorate of Customs at Shanghai. Imperialism alone does not explain what happened to Chinese-barbarian relations in the nineteenth century.[17]

For Further Reading

Boardman, E. P., *Christian Influence Upon the Ideology of the Taiping Rebellion* (Madison, Wis., 1952). A study of the part played by Christianity in initiating and shaping the rebellion.

Ch'en Ch'i-t'ien, *Tseng Kuo-fan,* trans. by Gideon Chen (Peiping, 1935).

Collins, Charles, *Public Administration in Hong Kong* (London, 1952). A well-documented account of the development of administrative machinery in the British colony.

Fox, Grace, *British Admirals and Chinese Pirates, 1832-1869* (London, 1940). The influence of the Admiralty on British policy towards China from 1832-1869.

Hail, W. J., *Tseng Kuo-fan and the Taiping Rebellion* (New Haven, 1927).

Kotenev, A. M., *Shanghai: Its Mixed Court and Council* (Shanghai, 1925).

Meadows, Thomas Taylor, *The Chinese and Their Rebellions* (London, 1856). By a British diplomat and scholar who was present during the Taiping Rebellion.

———, *Desultory Notes on the Government and People of China and on the Chinese Language; Illustrated with a Sketch of the Province of Kuang-Tung, Showing Its Division into Departments and Districts* (London, 1847).

Michael, Franz, "The Military Organization and Power Structure of China During the Taiping Rebellion," *Pacific Historical Review,* Vol. XVIII, No. 4, Nov., 1949.

Michie, Alexander, *The Englishman in China* (2 vols., Edinburgh, 1900). The life in the Far East of Sir Rutherford Alcock.

Murphey, Rhoads, *Shanghai, Key to Modern China* (Cambridge, Mass., 1953). The geographic and economic influences which made Shanghai a great port.

Oliphant, Laurence, *Narrative of the Earl of Elgin's Mission to China and Japan in the Years 1857, '58, '59* (New York, 1860).

---

[17] Fairbank, *Trade and Diplomacy,* 462-468.

Têng Ssŭ-yü, *New Light on the History of the Taiping Rebellion* (Cambridge, 1950). An important bibliographical survey of historical studies with an excellent brief account of the rebellion itself.

———, and John K. Fairbank, *China's Response to the West: A Documentary Study, 1839-1923* (Cambridge, Mass., 1954). Excerpts from the writings of Chinese statesmen and reformers, dealing with the history of China's attempt to comprehend the West and adjust to it.

Wu, James T. K., "The Impact of the T'ai-p'ing Rebellion Upon the Manchu Fiscal System," *Pacific Historical Review*, 19, Aug., 1950, 265-276.

9

The Russo-Chinese Frontier to 1860

THE longest and perhaps least generally known land frontier in the history of modern political geography is a tortuous line that lies between China and Asiatic Russia. From the northern tip of Korea, a few miles from Vladivostok and the Korean port of Yuki, it runs northward along the Ussuri River to the junction with the Amur, then up the course of that river and on westward through a vast expanse of desert and mountain that divides in uncertain fashion Mongolia from Siberia. Far to the west it veers southward into the heart of Central Asia between Sinkiang (Chinese Turkestan) and Kirghiz (Russian Turkestan). Until very modern times this boundary was little more than a species of geographical mystery winding its often unchartered way through a remote continent. But during the past century the Russo-Chinese frontier has given to history some of its most significant chapters. Russian commerce, imperialism, and communism have all crossed this frontier to play their part in the Western World's impact on China and Japan.

Russian expansion eastward across the Ural Mountains into Siberia began in the sixteenth century in the time of John the Dread (1533-1582). Cossack adventurers, seeking to escape the law, fled to Siberia, conquered the native chieftains, and, with these territorial prizes taken in the name of Russia, purchased pardons from the tsars. Russian peasants sought relief from oppressive government by migrating to the Siberian frontier. By 1638 a motley crew of these hardy pioneers had pushed eastward as far as the Lena River, where

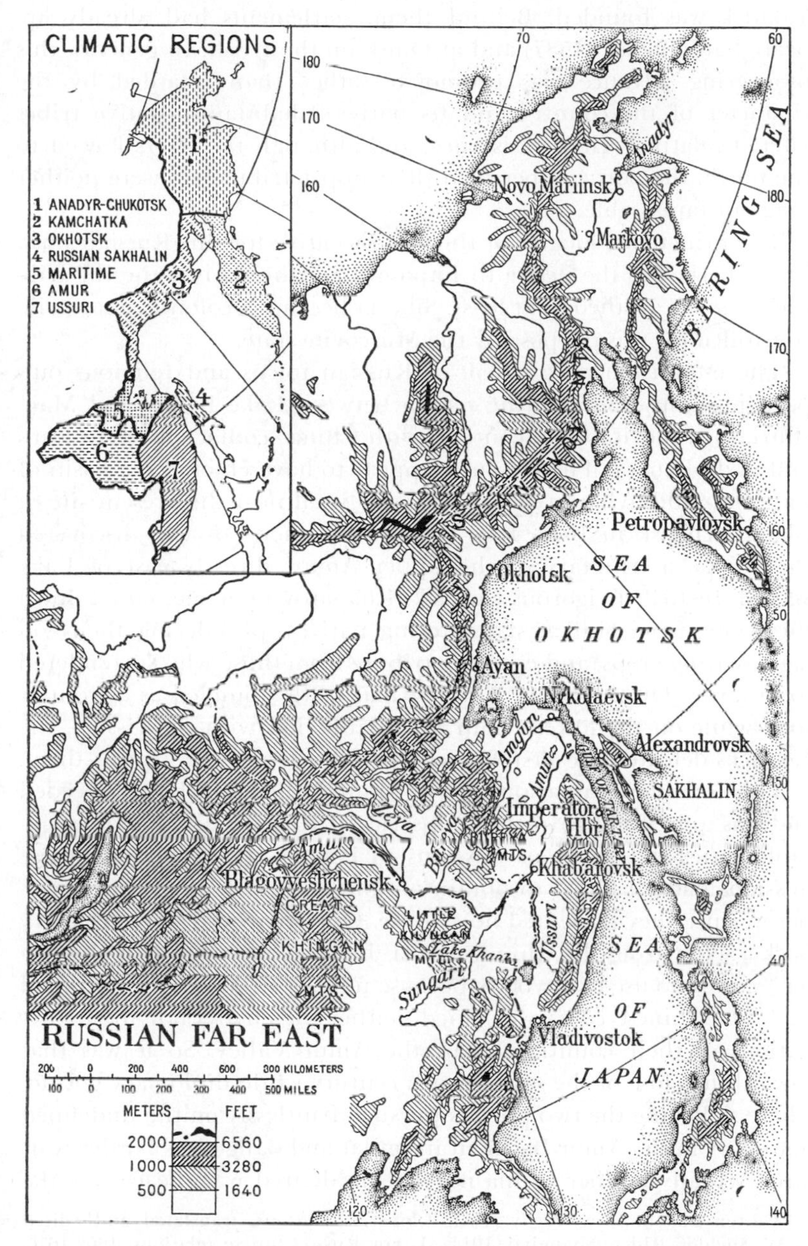

Courtesy of the Geographical Review, *published by the American Geographical Society of New York.*

Yakutsk was founded. Behind them, settlements had already appeared at Tobolsk (1587) and at Omsk on the Irtish. In general, this pioneering advance was promoted rather than retarded by the character of the country and its native inhabitants. Native tribes offered relatively little resistance, and although the rivers flowed to the north, the portages between their upper tributaries were neither long nor impassable.

The principal though not the sole incentive for this Russian push into Siberia was the desire to impose upon the natives the fur tribute, or *iasak*. In theory, at least, Siberia became a colonial enterprise controlled for this purpose by the Muscovite state.

The establishment by 1650 of Russian towns and religious outposts in Trans-Baikalia (the region between Lake Baikal and Manchuria) led inevitably to contacts with China—contacts both in arms and in diplomacy. The Cossacks appear to have entered the basin of the Amur and to have reached the river itself near the present site of Blagoveschensk in 1643. Five years later other Cossacks discovered the Shilka, a tributary of the upper Amur, directly east of Lake Baikal. In 1649 a vigorous Cossack, Khabarov by name, sailed down the Amur from Shilka, slaughtering natives, plundering their villages, seizing crops, and exacting tribute from those who surrendered to his arms. On the upper Amur, Albazin was founded as a frontier fort, while on the lower Amur, at its junction with the Ussuri, the Cossacks defeated the first Manchu-Chinese force sent against them.

This forcible occupation of the Amur Valley had been preceded and was to be followed by a long series of Russian diplomatic, semi-diplomatic, and religious missions to Peking. The earlier of these missions had all failed to obtain an audience with the Chinese emperor, since they presented no tribute. One envoy did however carry back a letter from the Chinese court, but it is recorded that this letter "was of no use to anybody because nobody in Moscow could read it."[1] The Chinese court welcomed neither the envoys nor the depredations of their countrymen in the Amur Valley. So it was that toward the close of the seventeenth century while diplomacy got nowhere at Peking the two powers pursued fruitlessly on the undefined boundary in the Amur Basin an irregular and dangerous border warfare. Actually neither China nor Russia desired war. Peace was the

[1] Gaston Cahen, *Some Early Russo-Chinese Relations,* translated and edited by W. Sheldon Ridge (Shanghai, 1914), 1. For Russo-Chinese relations, 1602-1676, see the monumental work by John F. Baddeley, *Russia, Mongolia, China . . .* (2 vols., London, 1919).

objective of both powers, but the ends for which peace was sought were not identical. Russia sought commerce: the exchange of furs for Chinese products. China sought, not commerce, but the stabilization of her traditional suzerainty over the principal people (Turguts, Kalmuks, and Eleuths) forming border or tributary states between herself and Russia. The problem of reaching an understanding was complicated further by Russo-Chinese ignorance of the extent and power of their respective empires, and when the Treaty of Nertchinsk was finally concluded (1689), Latin was chosen as the language of official intercourse, a fact which gave to Jesuit missionaries at Peking strategic posts as indispensable interpreters.

The Treaty of Nertchinsk (1689)

The immediate origins of this famous treaty, the first concluded by China with a Western power, are found in two letters in Latin from the K'ang-hsi emperor of China which reached the tsar in 1685. These letters gave evidence of a conciliatory policy to which Russia responded by the appointment of Theodore Alexievitch Golovin as "High Ambassador Plenipotentiary" to meet the representatives of China and with them to fix the frontier and determine commercial relations. It was not, however, until nearly four years later that the envoys of the two powers met in the summer of 1689 at Nertchinsk, east of Lake Baikal and about 180 miles from the present city of Chita. The Russian negotiators had about 1,000 troops to reinforce their diplomatic arguments; the Chinese had about 10,000, plus a fleet of river boats and artillery. This disparity in military strength was not without effect on the subsequent negotiations. The treaty that resulted was for China a diplomatic triumph.

The treaty provided: (1) that the boundary should be at the Argun River, the Gorbitsa (left bank tributary of the Shilka), and along the watershed between the basins of the Lena and the Amur to the sea;[2] (2) Albazin was to be destroyed and its garrisons withdrawn; (3) deserters were to be subject to extradition; (4) commercial relations

[2] Actually the frontier was fixed specifically only at one point. "There was no clear delimitation of any part of the region to the northeast of Nertchinsk, for the simple reason that it was quite unknown. . . . The country to the southwest of Nertchinsk, Trans-Baikalia and all the remainder of Siberia was left without delimitation of frontiers." Cahen, *Russo-Chinese Relations*, 16.

were to be maintained by the merchants of both countries provided with official letters.

By this agreement the Manchu dynasty achieved a settlement of its northern frontier that was to prevail with little change for more than a century. For the time being the Russians were excluded from the Amur Valley, but they had won an important concession in the right of their merchants to enter China for trade.

For many years following the Nertchinsk settlement the Amur Valley played only an insignificant role in the affairs of Russia and China. Russian ambitions were centered for the time in Europe. China was engaged in the conquest of border states such as Mongolia, Turkestan, Tibet, and Indochina. Meanwhile the center of such Russo-Chinese trade as there was shifted to Kiakhta, from which a subsequent treaty settlement (1727) takes its name.[3]

The Treaty of Kiakhta defined the frontier westward from the Gorbitsa; future deserters were to be extradited and punished; a Russian commercial caravan of 200 men was to be admitted every three years to Peking; several frontier posts were designated where commodities might be exchanged; ambassadors and diplomatic mail were to be received with dispatch; Russia might maintain in Peking a church, a priest, three curates, and five language students. These modifications were important in themselves, but in addition they signified a change in Russian policy: the decline of Russian state commerce and the triumph of the private traders.

In the broadest historical sense these early years of limited Russo-Chinese intercourse were full of deep significance for later generations. From them China had learned virtually nothing of Russia, whereas Russia used every returning embassy and caravan as the carrier of ideas as well as commodities.

There were few developments of importance in Russo-Chinese relations from 1727 until well into the nineteenth century. Yet these intervening years did forecast the renewal of rivalry on the Amur. By 1795, when the Ch'ien-lung emperor abdicated, the Ch'ing

---

[3] See William Coxe, *Account of the . . . Commerce between Russia and China* (London, 1780), 211-215.

Russo-Chinese commerce in these early years was one of barter. Russian exports included furs (sea-otter, beaver, fox, sable, ermine, gray squirrel) and cloth of various types. Russian imports from China included raw silk (smuggled into Kiakhta), raw and manufactured cotton, teas ("much superior in flavor and quality to those which are sent to Europe from Canton"), and porcelain "of all sorts."

(Manchu) empire, having reached the height of its power, was already suffering from internal decline. The Pai-lien Rebellion, suppressed in 1804, was the first major evidence that the dynasty was losing the Mandate of Heaven. Later rebellions were to cripple its power permanently, coinciding as they did with the impact on China of the Western maritime powers (Opium War, 1840; *Arrow* War, 1857). It is notable, then, that in these same years (1847-1860) China was called upon to meet new problems on her northern frontier. Russia had determined on a territorial advance, which could be made only at the expense of China.

THE CH'ING POLICY IN MANCHURIA

Although China had won a diplomatic victory at Nertchinsk (1689), she failed in the years following to consolidate her hold on the Amur country. While the Manchus themselves tended to migrate southward to China, Chinese migration to Manchuria was prohibited. Therefore the Amur Valley persisted as an uncolonized, undeveloped, and unprotected frontier.

It was not until 1847 that Russia undertook seriously the task of advancing the frontier beyond the unsurveyed line of the Treaty of Nertchinsk. It was in this year that the tsar appointed Count Nicholas Muraviev governor-general of eastern Siberia, with instructions to pursue special investigations of the Amur question. This renewed Russian interest in the Far East had been prompted by a number of developments. The British as a result of the Opium War had opened a new maritime door to the China trade, eclipsing the Russia caravans at Kiakhta. The activities of the British navy in the Pacific spurred the Russians with the desire to establish ports on their own Pacific coastline. Both eastern and western Siberia had grown in importance to Russia, particularly after 1825. The growth of settlements in Kamchatka, the expanding activities of the Russian-American Company in Alaska, and the development of the whaling industry in the Bering Sea—all these prophesied the growing importance of Russia's Pacific and China frontier. It is hardly surprising therefore that between 1847 and 1854 Russia reached a number of decisions that were to launch her on the new policy of the "Easterners" under the leadership of Muraviev.[4]

---

[4] T. C. Lin, "The Amur Frontier Question between China and Russia, 1850-1860," *Pacific Historical Review,* III (1934), 1-27.

The Policy of Muraviev

The new governor-general applied his policy with promptness and decision. His first agents sailed down the Amur in 1848. This river, it will be recalled, was wholly within the territory of the Manchu empire according to the terms of the Treaty of Nertchinsk. The following year Russian officers explored the coasts of the Sea of Okhotsk as far south as the mouth of the Amur. This was a preliminary survey in Russia's general plan to prevent occupation of the area by potential enemies: Great Britain and France. Nikolaievsk was founded at the mouth of the Amur (August, 1850). These were the first major violations of the Nertchinsk Treaty. They were to be followed by a vigorous pursuit of the new policy. Russian posts were founded at De Castries, Mariinsk, and Imperatorski Bay in 1852. Sakhalin Island was annexed in 1853.[5]

Up to this point China paid little attention to the Russian advance and seems to have ignored the deep significance of the new aggressive policy. Chinese border authorities were negligent, and most of the Manchurian troops had been withdrawn by 1853 to meet in China Proper the threatening northward march of the T'ai-p'ing rebels. Even had this not been the case, China's position in 1853 did not appear on the surface at least to be threatened seriously on the northern frontier. Officially the policy of the Russian government was still one of respect for the terms of the Nertchinsk Treaty. Nevertheless, by 1854 Muraviev had received the tsar's mandate to settle directly with Peking all questions concerning the eastern boundary. He was thus freed from all interference by the "Westerners" in the Russian ministry of foreign affairs. He was free to pursue his own grandiose scheme of making Russia a power on the Pacific, and, if need be, "the protector of China."[6]

The Crimean War had already broken out in Europe. In the Pacific the two great commercial pioneers, the Hudson's Bay Company and the Russian-American Company, had agreed to remain neutral, but this did not deter Great Britain and France from attacking Russia's Pacific base at Petropavlovsk. The real value of the Amur as a road for the transport of Russian supplies to the Pacific could no longer be denied even by the "Westerners." As a result, in April, 1854, Muraviev, on the pretext of military necessity, the defense of

[5] *Ibid.*

[6] Anatole G. Mazour, "Dimitry Zavalishin: Dreamer of a Russian-American Empire," *Pacific Historical Review*, V (1936), 26-37.

Kamchatka, sent his first major expedition down the entire length of the Amur. No attempt was made by the Chinese frontier forces to question or stop the Russians. More troops and munitions of war descended the river the following year, and the tsar informed Muraviev that the left bank of the Amur was now indispensable to Russia.

Now that Russia had occupied the river with her transports, contacts with the border Chinese authorities were inevitable. The first direct Russo-Chinese negotiations at Mariinsk in 1855 proved abortive. In 1856 Muraviev ordered his third major expedition down the river. The Chinese authorities protested, but the Russians replied with the stationing of garrisons at strategic points on the left bank of the river.

The Mission of Count Putiatin

Meanwhile Russia was preparing a double diplomatic assault on Peking. While Muraviev was yet on the Amur, Count Putiatin was sent to Peking to secure for Russia whatever commercial concessions should fall to England and France as a result of the *Arrow* War. He was also to seek a settlement of the Amur question. Putiatin was refused entry at Kiakhta but reached the mouth of the Pei-ho in August, 1857, by way of the Amur and the ocean route. To his overtures, the Chinese replied tersely that Russia should observe her treaty obligations. Blocked in his mission, Putiatin joined the British, French, and American envoys at Canton and proceeded north again with them to Tientsin, where in June, 1858, the four commercial treaties were signed. His influence on the Amur question was negligible. Not so with that of Muraviev.

During the progress of the *Arrow* War, Muraviev had not been idle in the north. Early in May, 1858, he succeeded in bringing the Chinese into conference at Aigun, where he demanded the river boundary which was to divide Manchuria from Siberia. China's protests received but scant consideration. On May 28, 1858, the Aigun Treaty was signed. In it Russia acquired all the territory on the left or northern bank of the Amur, while the land lying between the Ussuri River and the sea (the present Maritime Province) was to be held in joint control by both powers.[7] The Aigun agreement was

[7] The Chinese text of the treaty refers, in the case of territory to be held in common, only to the right bank of the Amur from the Ussuri to the sea, and not to the entire Maritime Province as is implied in the Russian text. T. C. Lin, "The Amur Frontier Question . . . ," 21.

thus signed two weeks before Putiatin signed the Russian Treaty of Tientsin, and without his knowledge.

Although China was in no position to dispute successfully Muraviev's advance, she refused to accept the Aigun Treaty in its entirety. China was prepared to cede those territories north of the Amur not already occupied by Chinese subjects, but she was not prepared to dispose of the Ussuri country. The local Kirin provincial authorities were accordingly commanded to prevent Russian encroachments. But this gesture was of no effect. When these officials failed, Peking might, and in fact did, order punishment of these helpless underlings. She might declare null and void the joint-control clause of the Aigun Treaty. Actually, China's impotence and Russia's strength remained unchanged.

Having thus pushed her boundary to the river, and having commenced penetration of the Trans-Ussuri region, Russia now directed her final attack through diplomacy in Peking. Early in the summer of 1859 General Ignatiev had reached the Chinese capital to exchange the ratified copies of the Russian Treaty of Tientsin. In addition it was his purpose to cultivate Russian interest in other ways. In his first diplomatic overtures he sought additional commercial privileges and the outright cession to Russia of the Trans-Ussuri lands. These requests were promptly refused, and the envoy was informed that China did not regard the Aigun settlement as binding. Here matters might have rested until such time as Muraviev was again prepared to use force. But, happily for Russia, other powers came unwittingly to her aid. By October, 1860, the British and French Allies, having broken Chinese resistance between Peking and Taku, had occupied the capital. The Manchu Dynasty appeared to be on the verge of total collapse. The T'ai-p'ing rebels were laying waste the central coast; the capital lay at the mercy of British and French arms; the Summer Palace had already been looted and burned, while a cowardly emperor and his renegade court had fled to the mountains of Jehol. Baffled and perplexed by the misfortunes that pursued the dynasty, Prince Kung, brother of the emperor, remained in Peking to seek a settlement with the victorious "barbarians."

Here was Russia's opportunity. Ignatiev played on the fears of the frightened Prince. He would intervene, so he said, with the Allies, and thus save Peking itself from the destruction that had already consumed the Summer Palace. For these services to China he would ask only an insignificant return: the rectification of a frontier, the cession of the Trans-Ussuri country. Prince Kung was not deceived, but assuredly he was defeated. On November 14, 1860, he signed with Ignatiev the convention that, among other things, ceded the Manchurian coastline to Russia.

In large part Muraviev's dream had now been realized. By the close of 1860, Russian policy in China had enjoyed a success unparalleled by that of any other state. Like the United States, she had not participated as a belligerent in the *Arrow* War, yet she was to reap all the advantages, commercial and diplomatic, won by England and France in the Treaties of Tientsin. In the north, through a policy of force, but without declaration of war, she had opened the Mongolian frontier to her traders and had advanced her boundary along the course of the Amur and far south along the Pacific coast to the northern tip of Korea. By conquest and colonization, yet without war in the legal sense, she had deprived the Manchu empire of 350,000 square miles of territory. Manchuria was cut off from the sea on the east, whereas Russia possessed a new and broad road to the ocean. Before Ignatiev signed the convention that transferred the Maritime Province, Russia proceeded to consolidate her new lands. At the southern extremity of the new coastal territory Muratiev selected the harbor and site of Russia's future fortress on the Pacific. The founding of Vladivostok, "dominion of the East," was a fitting culmination to the work, aggressive, unscrupulous, but successful, of one of Russia's greatest empire-builders.

For Further Reading

Dallin, D. J., *The Rise of Russia in Asia* (New Haven, 1949). Traces the rise of Russia as an Asiatic power in the nineteenth and early twentieth centuries.

Frank, V. S., "The Territorial Terms of the Sino-Russian Treaty of Nertchinsk, 1689," *Pacific Historical Review,* XVI, Aug., 1947, 265-270.

Golder, Frank A., *Russian Expansion on the Pacific, 1641-1850* (Cleveland, 1914). A basic work by a distinguished American scholar.

Kerner, Robert J., *The Urge to the Sea: the Course of Russian History* (Berkeley, 1942).

Lobanov-Rotovsky, A., *Russia and Asia* (New York, 1933). A popular general survey.

Mandel, William, *The Soviet Far East and Central Asia* (New York, 1944).

Norins, Martin, *Gateway to Asia: Sinkiang Frontier of the Chinese Far West* (New York, 1944).

Pasvolsky, L., *Russia in the Far East* (New York, 1922).

Raeff, Marc, *Siberia and the Reforms of 1822* (Seattle, 1956).

10

1600–c.1840

The Making and Breaking of Tokugawa Japan

DURING the past one hundred years, certainly until well into the twentieth century, there was in all Eastern Asia only one great nation that appeared to think and act in the spirit and the manner of the modern age. That nation was Japan. The story of her remarkable entry into the modern world will be told in later pages. That story, however, can hardly be seen in its varied shapes and shadings until it is recalled that this modern, aggressive, restless Japan came of cultural parents very unlike the forebears of modern Europe or the United States. For example, in the seventeenth century when Europe had already set its course toward geographical discovery and expansion, toward far-flung trade and settlement, toward a liberal philosophy of man's rights and of respect for the individual, Japan was setting her course with determination against these infatuations of a modern age, was turning inward upon herself, was closing her doors to either entry or exit, while consolidating a political and social structure whose virtues were stability and rigid conformity to orthodox values and habits of behavior.

Japan, in a word, was entering upon the period of the great, if parochial, Tokugawa Shogunate, 1603-1867. For Japan it was to be an age of isolationism, of 100 per cent Japanism, an heroic attempt lasting for more than two centuries to resist the modern world. It ended, of course, in failure, for in the nineteenth century Japan broke through the bonds of her isolation and forsook the traditions of stability to join and compete with a modern world that had left her far behind. Yet—and this should be remembered—as she entered upon that adventure, her spirit and her form were often the spirit and the form of the old Tokugawa culture she could not wholly discard. As a result, the Japanese of the twentieth century were by no means as modern as they often thought themselves to be. They were children not only of the modern Western impact but also of the Tokugawa inheritance. To the age of Tokugawa, then, we must turn if we are to know what manner of men created modern Japan.

The Tokugawa: Men Who Knew Their Own Minds

The *Bakufu,* it will be recalled, had achieved its mastery of Japan in battle and, within a few decades, had sealed the country from foreign influence. These steps were in a sense merely preliminaries to their major ambition, which was to create a political and social system that would preserve in their own hands and in those of their descendants this newly won power. The means they employed toward these ends were not a loose set of expedients or defensive measures designed to combat opposition where and when it might arise, but rather an integrated design of authoritarian rule for the entire nation. Under this plan the military power of the shogunate would remain so complete that no one would dare to challenge it. The result would be an age of unbroken peace and political stability buttressed by a social order resting on clearly defined and rigidly maintained class lines—that is, a society of status. In achieving this ambition of authoritarian stability the *Bakufu* could at first rely on a large measure of popular support. The efficient exercise of centralized power leading to peace and order was welcomed as a relief from the intolerable disorders of the late Ashikaga period. Stable absolutism was considered a refuge from the uncertainties of unstable feudalism that threatened to bring complete anarchy.

The political edifice built by the Tokugawas often appears at first glance as a kind of government by paradox, for it involved the rehabilitation of feudalism under which the *daimyo* or great lords ruled with relative independence in their own domains, while at the same time it created effective centralized authority in the shogunate to which in the final analysis all the *daimyo* were subservient. To begin with, the Tokugawas reverted to Yoritomo's system of two capitals. The emperor's court was preserved at the old imperial city of Kyoto where, surrounded by the civilian aristocracy, the *Kuge,* the emperor continued to preside over priestly affairs, etiquette, and the conferring of titles. The shogun's headquarters, the center of political power, was in Yedo, the home of Iyeyasu. There Iyeyasu and his successors, although receiving the title of shogun from the emperor, created not merely the military and administrative capital but in addition the economic and the cultural heart of Japan.

Yedo (Now Tokyo) and the Control of Japan

Yedo was a strategic location, economic and military as well as political. From its great castle surrounded by a series of high stone walls, huge embankments, and wide moats (the inner parts of which may still be seen in what is now the Imperial Palace grounds in Tokyo), the Tokugawas held central Japan directly, or controlled it through branches of the family or through feudal lords who had been Tokugawa allies in the civil wars of 1600. Here was much of the best land of Japan and most of the richer commercial centers, the cities, which at first were of great importance to the shogunate though eventually they became a principal agent in the downfall of the Tokugawas and their system. The shogunate was therefore protected by the lands it held directly, then by the lands of its branch families, and lastly by the lands of its feudal allies known as the *fudai* or hereditary vassals, who numbered at that time one hundred and seventy-six. Beyond these areas, principally in western Japan, were the *tozama,* or Outside Lords, who had submitted to the Tokugawas only after defeat in battle. They numbered eighty-six, and included such names as Satsuma and Choshu. Much will be heard of them later on in this story under the name of the Western clans.[1]

Although these *daimyo,* both *fudai* and *tozama,* were, in the main, independent petty sovereigns within their own domains, the Tokugawas insured their continued subservience and good behavior by an elaborate system of controls. Each *daimyo* was required to declare his loyalty to Yedo. Each was required to maintain a residence at great expense in Yedo, to divide his time between this residence and his fief, and to leave his wife and family in Yedo as hostages when he was absent. This was known as the rule of *sankin*

[1] The transition from the pre-Tokugawa to the Tokugawa era is ably presented in E. O. Reischauer, *Japan: Past and Present* (2nd ed., revised, New York, 1953), 62-95.

kotai, alternate attendance. Movement from fief to fief, especially when it involved the *tozama,* was severely restricted.

The Blossoming of Bureaucracy

Back in the days of Nara and Heian, Japan, for reasons that have been suggested, developed no adequate body of administrative officials loyal to or appreciative of a stable and healthy central government. By 1600, however, there was a body of educated men that Yedo could call into government service, and this the Tokugawas proceeded to do.

At the high level of policy-making the Tokugawas relied heavily on their Council of Elders (*toshiyori*). A member of this Council acted as regent when the shogun was a minor. This Council was all important in fixing the relationships of the shogunate with the emperor's court and the feudal lords. The lesser vassals of the Tokugawa were regulated by a lower Council of Junior Elders. Under these high-ranking bodies was a large civil service, the bureaucracy proper, comprising executive, administrative, and judicial officials together with their still more numerous underlings handling all the various aspects of government. This personnel, as might be expected, was drawn, usually on an hereditary basis, from the Tokugawa and the *fudai* families. Among these officials there was in general a lack of any precise definition of responsibility, a circumstance which, although it can be explained in part on grounds of custom, was also a matter of intentional policy whereby the individual was prevented from building his own little empire of power. In reality it added up to a system of government by council, not by individuals. This feature was common in government in all the various feudal domains and even in the local government of the peasant village as well as on the high plane of the shogunate. Indeed, government in the fiefs of the great lords varied little in organization from that of the shogunate. Each fief made its own laws and collected its own taxes very much on the pattern set by the Tokugawas. At the extreme local level, the village, government was directed and administered by village headmen and councillors under the watchful eye of district officers of the *daimyo.*

Society's Social Structure

The foregoing details will have suggested that the machinery of government in Tokugawa Japan was comparatively simple. It was possible and logical for this to be so because in Old Japan, as in Old China, the ordering and the controlling of society was sought through social rather than through political principles and agencies. This being so, it is essential to take careful note of the social orders or classes as they existed in Tokugawa times. As will be seen later on, the influence of this social class structure often exerted itself after Japan had become a modern and partially Westernized state. This class system, moreover, was deeply rooted long before the Tokugawas came to power at the beginning of the seventeenth century. What the Tokugawas did was to distinguish the classes in elaborate detail and to encourage a rigid crystalization of them through more than two centuries of peace.

First in rank and in social prestige among the classes of society was the Imperial Family and the emperor's immediate vassals, the court nobles or *kuge*. The emperor, to whom land and income was granted by the shogunate, bestowed titles, including that of shogun, performed ceremonial functions, and retained a real if somewhat uncertain traditional influence, but his political power had become a matter of theory only, and his court nobility subsisted on less income than that enjoyed by the poorest feudal lords. Theirs were the vaporous satisfactions of honor, not the tangible rewards of wealth.

Second in the social scale but first in power and privilege were the military men, the *samurai*. These made up the ruling class in Japan's military-feudal dictatorship. Within this class was a vast array of gradations from the shogun at the top to the foot soldier at the bottom. The principal ranks within this powerful caste in descending order of grade were: (1) the *daimyo* or great lords, some two hundred and seventy in number who were classified according to wealth, and all of whom enjoyed an annual rice income exceeding ten thousand *koku* (a *koku* is 4.96 bushels); (2) direct retainers of the shogun, known as *hatamoto* and *gokenin,* some of whom lived in Yedo performing civil or military duties; (3) *baishin,* who were retainers of *daimyo* or *hatamoto,* and who according to grade within their own class served as government advisers, administrative officials, or as foot soldiers, which last category was the most numerous within the *samurai* class; (4) *ronin,* or soldiers unattached to any lord; and (5) *goshi,* or *samurai*-peasants who acquired the status of active soldiers only in time of war. At the beginning of the Tokugawa period Japan's entire population was about thirty million, and of these the *daimyo* and their vassals numbered about two million, the *ronin* about four hundred thousand.

The court nobility and the *samurai* belonged, in a society of status, to what may best be called the privileged classes. They were not permitted to engage in common manual labor. All others, and this included the vast majority, can hardly be said to have had no privileges, but certain it is that their privileges were few and, as we would think today, quite unimpressive.

Heading, in the Confucian sense, this multitude of the common man was the farmer or peasant who, like his betters in privileged society, was ranked and graded by various standards within his own class. The first rank among these plebians were the village headmen and councillors. In second rank came those farmers who owned their land. Finally there was the landless peasantry, the most numerous and poorest of all. It was from this group that the laboring force of the growing cities was recruited.

Differentiated from the farmer but of about the same social rank among common men were the artisans or craftsmen. They fashioned the simplest articles of daily use or created the marvellously tempered two-handed sword known as the soul of the *samurai*. Neither the farmer nor the craftsman was a person of power, but since they fed and armed the *samurai* they were accorded a measure of honor as useful members of society.

Ranking as the commonest of common men was the merchant or *chōnin* class. In the feudal-military society of early Tokugawa days, the merchant was thought to perform no worthwhile function, since he depended upon others for his money. He was therefore regarded as a parasite hardly to be tolerated by right-thinking men. Long before the close of the Tokugawa era, however, this despised merchant was to acquire an influence wholly out of proportion to his lowly social status.

Finally, if one scraped the bottom of the social barrel, one discovered the sub-stratum of mankind, the untouchables, as it were, known as the *senmin,* who were divided into two classes, the *hinin* and the *eta*. The *hinin* were professional entertainers, executioners, beggars. One could be born into this class or be consigned to it as punishment for some crime. The *eta,* regarded as even more degraded, tended to the killing of animals and the manufacture of leather and leather goods. Districts were set apart where they were required to live unto themselves, since they could not even act as servants to commoners. In fine, they were classified as animals rather than humans, for they were not even included in the census.

The Business of Being Fed

Japan in the Tokugawa period was overwhelmingly an agricultural society. About 80 per cent of the people belonged to the farming population. Rice was the great crop on which the nation lived, and the great majority of farmers were self-sufficient save for a few essentials such as metal wares, salt, medicines, etc. It was this farmer of course who fed the nation, and he did this in large part by turning over between 40 and 50 per cent of his crop to his local lord as taxes. This revenue supported the idle *samurai* class and maintained the government. The idea was that the peasant would be left just enough and no more. The Tokugawas knew perfectly well how important the farmer was, and they exerted great efforts to improve farming methods, but the peasant did not share the fruits of this greater efficiency. On the contrary, he tended in time to be labored with even greater burdens occasioned by the financial ineptitude of both shogunate and *daimyo*. This chronic economic distress was locally the common lot of the peasantry and the occasion of frequent peasant uprisings.

The Philosophy Directing Tokugawa Society

The goal of Tokugawa government, it will be recalled, was stability, but in seeking this end the shogunate did not confine itself to defining social classes, to collecting high taxes from farmers, and to spying upon its enemies. It went beyond these matters to prescribe in minute detail the morals and the behavior of the entire populace. In the Western World morals had usually been left to the management of some church, but in Japan, as in China, ethics were the concern of government, and thus moral and political philosophy became one. As a consequence the fundamental laws of the shogunate were really codes of moral injunction, such as, for example, "Avoid what you like, and attend to unpleasant duties." Life was not considered to be the pursuit of happiness, but rather the performance of obligation. There was no place for freedom of thought because duty called for unqualified loyalty and obedience. The idea of progress was also excluded because this was a society of status in which each man occupied his proper place and was expected to stay in it. A more conservative philosophy would be difficult to imagine.

The intellectual cornerstone upholding this Tokugawa scheme of government and society was Confucianism in its most conservative aspects, in which stress was laid on the "proper" relations between ruler and ruled. The Buddhist church had already been reduced to obedience to the state by Nobunaga and Hideyoshi, and the first Tokugawa shoguns had suppressed Christianity. Therefore, the way had already been cleared for the secular morality of the Confucians. The trend actually was not entirely new. *Samurai* had long prided themselves on their regard for courage, self-sacrifice, disregard of material wealth, and loyalty to one's lord. In theory, at least, all of these qualities had been the moral stock-in-trade of the soldier since long before the Tokugawas came to power. They were qualities that the shogunate wished to strengthen. But the problem was not as simple as this would suggest. The shogunate recognized that the *samurai* warlike spirit could, in times of peace, be inconvenient and even dangerous to the rulers. They therefore attempted also to turn the minds of military men toward peaceful undertakings. What the consequences were to be we shall discover shortly.[2]

Such then was the pattern or permanence the Tokugawas tried to impose. At first their success seemed complete. For a long time the basic character of Tokugawa institutions remained substantially without change. Yet, almost from the beginning, processes of change were at work. Indeed, the advent of unbroken peace and the closing of the country to foreign intercourse created conditions that forced the Tokugawas to tolerate and even to encourage changes in a policy that was designed to resist change.

---

[2] The prescribed philosophy of Tokugawa times especially as it applied to the *samurai* or ruling caste is sometimes referred to as *Bushido,* the Way of the Warrior, a term of comparatively recent origin though the set of ideas for which it is the label are quite old. These ideas are not unlike those in the code of early European chivalry. Historically the code was the expression of early ideas on the duty of the soldier. Since Japan had been controlled by soldiers since the time of Yoritomo, there had been both the need and the opportunity to develop a set of principles on the duty of the soldier. These principles varied in degree from time to time and had not been highly conventionalized until well into the Tokugawa period, and then, in part at least, under the Confucian influence. In general, *Bushido* extolled "rectitude, courage, benevolence, politeness, sincerity, honor, disdain of money, and self-control" as ideals to be followed by the *samurai.* Since virtue is only as strong as those who profess it, this code was the measure of what a *samurai* was supposed to do, not of what he sometimes actually did.

The foregoing outline of Tokugawa government, class structure, and politico-moral philosophy suggests that Japan had fashioned for herself a way of life that must have been very bleak indeed. Nevertheless, could a Westerner have visited Yedo, Kyoto, or Osaka in, let us say, 1700, he would doubtless have been impressed not so much by the coldness of life as by its warmth, its vitality, its apparent prosperity, and its color. However gloomy the moral injunctions of shogun or *daimyo* might be, it was very evident that the city dwellers of this Japan, whether they knew it or not, were much concerned with the idea of progress and the pursuit of happiness. The processes of change so repugnant to Tokugawa philosophy were already in operation, and something of the nature of these changes must now be described.

The Economics of Peace

It was in the field of economics and commerce that the processes of change first became apparent. When military Japan settled down to a life of peace in the early 1600's, it was possible for trade to grow to proportions previously unknown. In peace, too, there was also less reason for local commercial restrictions, so that even though the country was still divided into the many domains of this or that lord, the tendency was for the whole to become one economic unit. This tendency acquired strength from the nature of the shogun's government at Yedo, to which city under the decree of *sankin kotai* came all the *daimyo* with their families and a host of retainers. This official and aristocratic populace of government officials, *daimyo,* and *samurai* created a demand for goods and services which only artisans and tradesmen could furnish. In these circumstances the relatively simple rice economy of the individual feudal domain gave way more and more to a money and credit economy managed by merchants, brokers, and bankers who controlled the rice markets and storehouses of such cities as Osaka and Yedo. The *daimyo* when in residence at Yedo converted his rice revenue into cash, spending the proceeds on elaborate furnishings, dress, and lavish entertainment. Since his income in rice did not vary greatly, and since keeping up with the Joneses in Yedo was an expensive business, it was not difficult for a *daimyo* to find himself in debt to his social inferior the merchant—not a healthy or comfortable status for members of a ruling class.

Two points need to be emphasized in explaining how the mercantile class that had relatively limited legal rights and no military power could reach a point where it was able to exploit the military classes and the farmers. The first of these was the further development of Yedo as a large city which had to be supplied in part by imported food and which demanded a large supply of manufactured luxuries. These factors encouraged further the use of money and made the merchant indispensable. Yedo's growth, as indicated, resulted from the growth of government and the enforced residence there of the *daimyo* and their families. Had the *daimyo* remained in their castle towns, their consumptive habits and those of their retainers would have developed and changed much more slowly, and likewise the use of money and the growth of a merchant class to cater to these expensive habits would have been retarded. In the second place, the military class by reason of its new consumptive habits became more and more dependent on the merchant. Once a taste for luxury had been acquired, the nobility was prepared to mortgage its future to the merchant rather than be eclipsed in the rivalry of social living. The merchant was not liquidated because without him the necessary food and luxuries would not have been forthcoming.

It thereby came about that by 1700, roughly a hundred years after the Tokugawas had first risen to power, Japan had not only modified her economy but had also acquired in her larger cities a prosperous middle class of which it has been said that they had money in their pockets and were determined to spend it in ways of their own choosing. Side by side then with the extravagance of the *daimyo* and their followers to maintain the elegance to which their social position appeared to entitle them, there appeared a new world of well-to-do merchants and their hirelings who had their own particular ideas on how to have a good time with the money they had made. These merchants and their associates, who were regarded by the *samurai* as uncultivated persons of low and vulgar taste, soon created through their demands for entertainment a whole new world of popular arts in literature, in the theater, in painting, and in color prints.

Amusement for the Tired Businessman

The new art was distinguished from older forms by its subject matter. It was an art that dealt with the doings and the aspirations of the newly rich commoners, their own common but colorful everyday life. Here were street scenes, the theaters, the tea-houses, or taverns of that time, the actors who had risen to stardom, and, as Sir George Sansom has said, the easy-going ladies of the world of entertainment. The patrons of this new art were the tradespeople. In time they developed their own standards and critics, so that eventually the old aristocratic monopoly over art was broken. The processes of change were in motion.[3]

In literature and in the theater, as in art, the city folk were not satisfied wholly with the classical romances and stage plays that were the traditional fare of the military class. The tastes of the city commoners, robust and sensuous, called forth a new group of authors whose stories and plays had a wide contemporary appeal. All of this brought books and plays and an appreciation of literature and acting to a growing populace of city dwellers. Yedo literature is important historically because it was another indication of change in the Tokugawa changeless pattern, and because the vacuous character of Yedo writing explains in some measure the easy inroads made by European literary influence and thought in the Meiji period, when Japan had opened her doors to Western intercourse.

These bright and attractive colors in Yedo's life of business and of the new arts need to be appraised against a background of contention—both social and economic. It has been suggested that the long period of peace the *Bakufu* was able to impose opened the way for a new society which in turn destroyed eventually the social and political order Iyeyasu had founded and laid the foundations for a new state and nation. This new society, far from being confined to the markets and pleasure haunts of Yedo, made itself felt in every aspect of the nation's life. Although the Tokugawas, as the reader knows, did not set out to build a modern national state, Japan during most of the Yedo period was taking the first steps in the direction of modern nationalism and industrialization. The Tokugawa period saw the beginnings of prolonged struggles between a rice agriculture and industry, between a local barter economy and a national money economy, between a feudal and military aristocracy

---

3 Hishigawa Moronobu was one of the great painters of this popular new art. The work of such men was the forerunner of the famous Japanese color print which testified to the widely developing artistic sense of the urban classes. The great print artists (Hiroshige, for example) became popular idols. They were the creators of *Ukiyo,* or Floating World. *Ukiyo-e* was a picture of the passing world of pleasure.

and the power of commercial and then industrial capital, between the food supply and the population that had to be fed, between what was traditional and what was not. There was much dislocation and much suffering before the birth pains of this new society with its creeping capitalism had passed.

Since every society must provide a means of feeding and clothing itself, it follows that economic conditions are often a barometer of a society's contentment and therefore of its stability. Stability was a primary goal of the Yedo *Bakufu,* but the history of the period is a story of growing dissatisfaction with economic conditions. These dissatisfactions played their part in the gradual undermining of that "massive stability" which describes the early years of the Tokugawa system. The most obvious signs of unrest occurred in the countryside among the peasantry. Peasant uprisings were not peculiar to Tokugawa times, but they increased under the Yedo *Bakufu* in number and violence. Their causes were very complex and it is possible here to suggest only a few of the conditioning factors.

First of all was the important fact that the peasant was the only regular taxpayer. A large part of his rice crop he owed to his feudal lord for the support of the whole military aristocracy. Whatever new burdens the *Bakufu* might lay on the military or business classes were passed on by them to the peasant in the form of additional direct taxation or through currency or market manipulations. Since a peasant paid more to his lord in a good crop year than in a bad one, a bumper crop was a questionable blessing. Although the peasant did not "own" the land he cultivated his tenure was secure through laws that prohibited transfer of land under cultivation. Nevertheless, with the appearance of a merchant class with funds for investment, ways were found to get around these laws and thus to create a new landlord class of city merchants who shared in the revenue derived from land on which the whole feudal state rested.

Closely allied to the burden of peasant taxation was the distressing problem of population. For the first half of the Tokugawa period population increased rather rapidly. Through the second half it remained practically stationary at about thirty million. The initial increase bore heavily on food supply. The growth of cities contributed to shortages of farm labor, which in turn contributed to falling production and to increased poverty in rural areas. The problem was aggravated by Japan's dependence on a single food crop, rice, and her isolation from the outside world. In periods of crop failure there was no foreign trade, no imports and exports to relieve the crisis, and no effective means by which the price of rice could be controlled. In a fluctuating market it was the merchant who understood such matters who profited. Those who paid were the military caste and, most of all, the peasants.

The stability of the *Bakufu* was also undermined by its failure to pursue sound policies in public finance. It should be recognized of course that the Yedo government faced extraordinary difficulties. Its military triumph at the beginning of the seventeenth century imposed upon it responsibilities that were really national in scope, while in a state organized in the pattern of feudalism the *Bakufu* derived regular revenue largely from its own domains only. The consequence was a state of chronic deficit relieved but little by drastic economic policies effected from time to time. Because of the country's political organization there could be no recourse to national loans. Instead, the *Bakufu* resorted to emergency measures. Since the peasant was already taxed to the limit that agriculture could bear, and since forced "gifts" from the *daimyo* could not be demanded too frequently, most of the special emergency levies fell upon the merchant class in the large cities under Tokugawa control. Although these levies were called loans, they were frequently not repaid. When these levies, as was often the case, failed to meet the government's financial plight, it could and did resort to debasement of the coinage. These expedients, which at best could only postpone the day of judgment, aggravated economic conditions that were already bad by encouraging wild fluctuations of prices.

It will be recalled that the intellectual-philosophical basis on which the Tokugawa system rested was an official school promoting orthodox interpretations of Confucianism, though this did not mean that all studies save those having the official benediction were always proscribed. Indeed, some researches on the nature of loyalty which were undertaken in the territories of those lords least susceptible to *Bakufu* censorship led to a questioning of the shogun's position. If loyalty was to be accorded to the shogun, Confucian concepts of loyalty demanded that he be worthy of loyalty, that is, that his position be legitimate.

Along with these Confucian scholars were others who were devoted to historical studies in the native Japanese classics. The researches of these men into Japan's political history revealed the chain of events that in times past had shifted political power from the throne into the hands of feudal dictators. On the positive side these studies formed the beginnings of a new Japanism that was essentially anti-Confucian, promoted a revival of Japan's ancient religion of Shinto, and amounted ultimately to an intellectual attack upon the shogun as a usurper of the throne's legitimate function.

As they developed, all these various conditions, trends, changes, and schools of thought destroyed gradually but surely the Tokugawa pattern of permanence and created in its place a society whose formal structure of feudal dictatorship with its peculiar and rigid class lines was no longer an adequate vehicle by which what was now a young nation could live and move and have its being. Tokugawa feudalism had become a façade behind which went on the strivings and struggles of a disgruntled people. No class was exempt from the disturbing effects of these varied dislocations. In summary they added up to a complex anatomy of maladjustments:

1. At the top of the politico-social scale, many of the *daimyo* were plagued by the same financial ailments that beset the shogunate.
2. The *samurai* posed the perplexing problem of what to do with an idle standing army in a prolonged period of unbroken peace. As the finances of shogun and *daimyo* went from bad to worse, there was the irresistible tendency to cut the allowances of their *samurai* retainers. As a net result, the *samurai* had too little money and too much time on their hands.
3. The farmers, as the Tokugawa era moved into the nineteenth century, continued through peasant uprisings to protest against economic grievances magnified by periodic natural calamities of flood and famine. In general the farmer's mood was one of desperation induced by taxes even his strength and patience could not bear.
4. The merchants, even with their wealth, were vulnerable and insecure. They were never free from the vexatious interference by government which amounted often to confiscation. They dared not show open hostility to the *Bakufu,* yet they were ready to promote its downfall should the occasion arise. Most of all they resented the lowly social status from which their wealth had not freed them.

At the beginning of the seventeenth century, the Tokugawas had fashioned a society of "massive stability." For a time their plan was eminently successful. In the end, the regime of peace which they themselves had created was their own undoing. By the end of the eighteenth century, stability was a memory. The political framework of the past still stood, but the society it was supposed to represent was no longer essentially feudal. The first steps toward modern nationhood had been taken. What would the next steps be? Could the shogunate survive a major crisis if and when it came?

For Further Reading

Borton, Hugh, "Peasant Uprisings in Japan of the Tokugawa Period," *Transactions,* Asiatic Society of Japan, Second Series, 16 (1938), xv, 219. A thorough study using original sources.

Bowers, Faubion, *Japanese Theatre* (New York, 1952).

Boxer, C. R., *The Christian Century in Japan,* 1549-1650 (Berkeley, 1951). Political developments in Japan, as seen by Jesuit missionaries.

———, *Jan Compagnie in Japan: 1600-1850, an Essay on the Cultural, Artistic and Scientific Influence Exercised by the Hollanders in Japan from the 17th to the 19th Centuries* (2nd rev. ed., The Hague, 1950).

Cary, Otis, *A History of Christianity in Japan* (2 vols., New York, 1909). The basic work in English.

Hall, John Whitney, *Tanuma Okitsugu (1719-1788) Forerunner of Modern Japan* (Cambridge, 1955). A penetrating history of the period.

Kaempfer, Engelbert, *The History of Japan, Together with a Description of the Kingdom of Siam, 1690-92* (3 vols., Glasgow, 1906). By a German physician attached to the Dutch embassy in Japan.

Keene, Donald, *The Japanese Discovery of Europe; Honda Toshiaki and Other Discoverers, 1720-1798* (New York, 1954). An account of the first Japanese travelers in Europe and the ideas they took back to Japan.

Norman, E. H., *Ando Shoeki and the Anatomy of Japanese Feudalism* (2 vols., Tokyo, 1949). On the writings of an eighteenth century philosopher and critic of feudalism.

Paske-Smith, Montague, *Western Barbarians in Japan and Formosa in Tokugawa Days, 1603-1868* (Kobe, 1930).

Sadler, Arthur Lindsay, *Cha-no-yu: the Japanese Tea Ceremony* (London, 1934).

———, *The Art of Flower Arrangement in Japan. A Sketch of its History and Development* (New York, 1933). The basic work on the subject.

———, *The Maker of Modern Japan: The Life of Tokugawa Iyeyasu (1542-1616)* (London, 1937). The life of the founder of the Tokugawa shogunate.

Satchell, Thomas, trans., *Hizakurige* (*Tokaido Circuit*) (Kobe, 1929). An excellent translation of the famous roisterous adventures on the Tokaido of two irresponsible, comic characters.

Smith, T. C., "The Introduction of Western Industry to Japan during the Last Years of the Tokugawa Period," *Harvard Journal of Asiatic Studies*, XI, June, 1948, 130-152. Explains in part Japan's later transformation.

Takizawa Matsuyo, *The Penetration of Money Economy in Japan* (New York, 1927). Traces the decline of feudalism to the effects of money on political and social institutions.

11

1840–1865

Japan: The Collapse of Isolation

JAPAN experienced during the nineteenth century a revolution the consequences of which it would be difficult to exaggerate. There were two major effects of this revolution which are of importance to this narrative. As a result of the first (the subject of this chapter), the 250-year-old policy of exclusion and seclusion was ended and replaced by a broad policy of intercourse with the West. As a result of the second (treated in Chapter 12), dual government, the shogunate, and the system of feudalism were replaced by a centralized administration, carried on in the name of the Mikado, and clothed in 1889 with a constitution deriving its form, if not its spirit, from Western political models.

The collapse in the middle of the nineteenth century of Japan's policy of isolation was a result not only of external pressures exerted by foreign states, but also of revolutionary social pressures within Japan itself. To put the matter another way, when in 1854 the Japanese signed a treaty with the United States, they were not reacting solely to American naval power; they were reacting also to the fundamental needs of their own society. For nearly 250 years the Tokugawa shoguns had sought to maintain a planned and fixed social economy. Their initial success and their ultimate failure have been discussed in the previous chapter. Thus, by mid-nineteenth century, Japan was living under a regime that was no longer adequate to meet new conditions. A new policy, both internal and external, was imminent.

It will be well perhaps to recall that while Japan was living within the exclusive walls of the Tokugawa dictatorship, Western states were developing a new society, new theories of government, new conceptions of national wealth, and new colonial empires. Between 1638 and 1854, the period of Japanese seclusion, Europe witnessed the Glorious Revolution in England, the perfecting of the absolute monarchy in France, the victory of England over France in the great colonial wars in America and India, the revolt of the thirteen English colonies, the French Revolution, the wars of Napoleon, and the beginnings of the Industrial Revolution with its emphasis on economic doctrines of *laissez faire.* By the first half of the nineteenth century, popular middle-class nationalism had triumphed over the crumbling edifice erected by Metternich. Both Europe and the United States (the latter had become a power on the Pacific with the acquisition of the Oregon Territory in 1846) were prepared for a new era of commercial and industrial expansion. Western commerce was already invading every area of the globe. It certainly could not by-pass Japan for long. Already, in 1840-1842, England had fought successfully her first commercial war in China.

Japan's knowledge of this changing and threatening Western world was imperfect and colored by lack of perspective. Yet the shogunate was by no means in complete ignorance of external affairs. Some considerable body of information had entered Japan through the medium of the Dutch at Nagasaki and through Chinese merchants.

Early Attempts to Open Japan

Late in the eighteenth and early in the nineteenth centuries a number of Western powers made half-hearted efforts to open Japan to trade. All of these attempts failed, for prior to 1850 no Western power was of a mind to force the issue with Japan. Yet by 1850 the United States was becoming as interested in Japan as it had previously, since 1842, been interested in China. Shipwrecked American seamen from the North Pacific whaling fleet cast upon Japanese shores were often treated as criminals. Some died from exposure; others were required to trample and spit on the Cross; all were exhibited in cages to the public gaze. Furthermore, America's expanding trans-Pacific trade from San Francisco to China passed through Japanese waters. Japanese ports were needed as coaling stations for the new trans-Pacific steamships. American business was already anticipating the opening of a lucrative trade with Japan.

Influenced by these various motives, by petitions to Congress, and by what appeared to be an influential public interest, President Fillmore in 1852 selected Commodore Matthew C. Perry, a distinguished naval officer and a brother of the hero of Lake Erie fame, to command a naval expedition designed to open Japan to trade.

Public reaction to the mission was divided. While optimists hoped for its success, the pessimists referred to it as a "romantic notion" and "a matter of ridicule abroad and at home." A contributor to *Putnam's Magazine* thought Perry the instrument of a divine plan. Trade would follow Perry's mission and thus the merchants would open "a highway for the chariot of the Lord Jesus Christ. . . ." There were also voices that cautioned care lest the United States become involved in a war with Japan. The fact that the Japanese were "rude, intractable, selfish, and unsocial" was not sufficient reason for going to war with them. These reactions are not surprising, since both in the United States and Europe inadequate knowledge had produced strange and varied opinions of Japan and the Japanese. Estimates of Japan's area ranged from 9,000 to 266,000 square miles; of population density, from 184 to 4,000 per square mile; and of total population, from 15,000,000 to 50,000,000. Yedo alone was said to have a population of at least 10,000,000. The Japanese of the "lower orders" were said to have a yellow complexion, "like the color of cheese." Only a few years later, in 1860, American "authorities" were proclaiming the comparative values of Japanese and Chinese culture. The previously imagined virtues of China disappeared while those of Japan became more substantial. China was described as "so palsied, so corrupt, so wretchedly enfeebled by mis-government, as to be already more than half sunk in decay" while Japan showed "vigor, thrift, and intelligence."

With a fleet of four ships, Perry entered Yedo (later Tokyo) Bay and anchored off Uraga, July 8, 1853. His arrival did not take the Japanese by surprise, for they had been warned of his coming by the Dutch, yet the appearance of the American squadron precipitated one of the great crises of Japanese history. While unaware of the real nature of this crisis, Perry proceeded to the task before him with firmness, dignity, and tact. He impressed the officials of the shogun's government with the power of his fleet—it contained the first steamers seen in Japanese waters—and with his own good will.

He refused to retire to Nagasaki or to deal through the Dutch there. He demanded treatment suitable to the representative of a great power. In this behavior he was justified when, in opposition to Japanese law, President Fillmore's letter was received by two high officials of the shogun's court. Then Perry sailed away, but not without informing the Japanese that he would return the next year with a more powerful fleet to receive their answer.[1]

The Shogun's Dilemma

Perry's visit confronted the shogun with the most serious decision ever faced by the Tokugawas. An Iyeyasu would have decided the matter on his own responsibility. Now, however, the shogunate had come on sorry days, and, faced with an issue of unparalleled importance, it took the unprecedented step of seeking the advice not only of the leading *daimyo*, but also of the emperor. The preponderant opinion favored repelling the foreigner, but some few recognized the futility of armed opposition.

Perry was already hastening his return, spurred by rumors that French and Russian squadrons planned to visit Japan. This time with an augmented fleet of seven vessels, he entered Yedo Bay on February 13, 1854. Fortunately, the far-sighted minority at the shogun's court had prevailed, and so at Kanagawa the negotiation of a treaty proceeded amid social activities of the utmost gaiety. Gifts presented to the Japanese by the United States included a miniature railway, telegraph, books, and a variety of liquors. All these delighted the Japanese no end.[2]

The treaty signed by Perry and the representatives of the shogun, March 31, 1854 (Treaty of Kanagawa), viewed superficially, was in many respects a disappointment. In reality it was little more than a convention covering shipwreck and supply. It provided for peace, for the opening of two ports for supplies (Shimoda immediately and Hakodate a year later), for good treatment for shipwrecked American sailors, for a limited trade under Japanese regulations, and for supplies for American ships—really a treaty of friendship. Yet the

---

[1] Payson J. Treat, *Diplomatic Relations Between the United States and Japan* (2 vols., Stanford University, 1932), I, 11.

[2] See Francis L. Hawks, compiler, *Narrative of the Expedition of an American Squadron to the China Seas and Japan, Performed in the Years 1852, and 1854, under the Command of Commodore M. C. Perry, United States Navy* (published by order of Congress, A. O. P. Nicholson, Washington, 1856), 375.

treaty Perry did secure was a remarkable achievement viewed in the light of more than two centuries of Japanese exclusion. His success was due to many factors: his own "firmness, sagacity, tact, dignity, patience, and determination"; the strength of his great naval squadron, the like of which the Japanese had never before seen; and his declaration that more ships would be sent if the just demands of the United States were not met. Reinforcing these attributes of Perry the diplomat were others over which he had no control, but without which he might well have failed: the recent frequent appearance of Russian vessels in Japanese waters, Japanese knowledge of China's defeat in 1842, and, above all, those internal developments, described in the preceding chapter, which had made Japan ripe for revolution. Any estimate of Perry as naval officer, diplomat, or statesman should consider not only his success in Japan but also the broader pattern of Pacific policy which he had in mind. To Perry the opening of Japan was not an end in itself but rather one in a series of steps toward creating American maritime power in the Pacific. This pattern would include coaling stations and naval bases throughout the Pacific and especially in the Bonin Islands, the Liu-ch'iu (Ryukyu), and Formosa. Perry has sometimes been called the first American imperialist. He foresaw and supported a policy to which little heed was given while he lived, but which was implemented in great detail in the century after his death.

Perry's success was one of the most significant events in American history, though it was not so recognized in the United States at the time. Little attention was paid to it in the press, and it was almost ignored by President Pierce in his annual message to Congress, perhaps because it had been the work of a Whig government. Almost the only interest shown by Congress took the form of a protest that the cost of printing the report of the Perry mission was "outrageously extravagant." Moreover, the book was "full of pictures and most costly engravings of shells, and birds, and snakes, and bugs in Japan, with God knows how many maps that are appended to its surveys." Actually, Japan's exclusion policy had been ended. The decision that effected this momentous change was made by the shogun's government, but the United States had provided the occasion that forced the decision.

Representatives of other powers soon followed Perry to Japan and secured treaties similar though not identical with that of the United States. A British admiral, Sir James Stirling, negotiated a treaty at

Nagasaki (October, 1854). The Russian Admiral, Count Putiatin, secured his treaty at Shimoda (February, 1855).[3] Finally the Dutch were released from their commercial confinement at Nagasaki and given a new treaty (January, 1856). The most-favored-nation clause made the provisions of each treaty the common property of the four powers, and expanded somewhat the rights Americans had won in the Perry treaty. These total and enlarged rights held by the four powers in 1856 included: (1) permission to secure supplies at Shimoda, Hakodate, and Nagasaki; (2) permission to trade through Japanese officials and under their regulations at these ports; (3) right of male residence at Nagasaki; (4) permission to appoint consuls at Shimoda and Hakodate; and (5) a limited extraterritorial jurisdiction.

Three of these treaties (the American, the British, and the Russian) were approved by the emperor in February, 1855. The importance of this was not realized at the time by the foreign powers. The treaties had been negotiated with the shogun's government and they were signed under the title of "tycoon" (great lord). By the foreigners it was assumed that the shogun was the proper authority to control diplomatic affairs. This of course was so, but what the foreigner did not know was the extent to which the authority of the shogun had already been weakened by internal dissension. This explains why the shogunate, when Perry arrived, was unwilling to accept full responsibility for signing a treaty. It had therefore referred the matter for approval to the emperor. Since the shogun's influence with the Imperial Court was still strong, the Imperial approval was given. With this approval the shogun could for a time silence the powerful opposition to the new policy.

The Imperial approval insured general acceptance of the treaties, but the fact that the shogunate almost failed to secure the throne's favor revealed how the might of the *Bakufu* had declined. It had not been the habit of the Tokugawas or their predecessors to consider the will of the throne. They did so now because their old supremacy was little better than a political fiction, because they recognized the power of their feudal enemies, the *tozama* lords, and because there was bitter dissension within the Tokugawa clan itself. Indeed, even

---

3 See George A. Lensen, "Russians in Japan, 1858-1859," *Journal of Modern History,* XXVI (1954), 162-173; "The Russo-Japanese Frontier," *History and Literature,* Florida State University Studies, No. 14, 1954, 23-40; and *Russia's Japan Expedition of 1852 to 1855* (Gainesville, 1955), 111-126; W. G. Beasley, *Great Britain and the Opening of Japan* (London, 1951), 113-144.

among those elements that favored signing the treaties, the feeling was strong that no further concessions should be made to the foreigner—no general trade would be permitted and foreign contacts would be held to the bare treaty minimum.

Townsend Harris in Japan

Shortly after the Perry treaty was concluded, the American government sent its first consul general to reside at Shimoda. He was Townsend Harris of New York, a merchant familiar with the Far East and a man of excellent mind and character. Harris travelled by way of Siam, where he negotiated a treaty granting extraterritoriality and a conventional tariff. He reached Shimoda on August 21, 1856.

The village of Shimoda, some 60 miles from Yedo, on the southern extremity of the Izu Peninsula southwest of Yedo Bay, was possessed of an exceptionally poor harbor that had been all but ruined by a tidal wave the previous year. The town, shut off from the hinterland by ranges of hills, was remote from the high roads and markets, and, in a word, was peculiarly ill-adapted to the needs of Harris. The Japanese had hoped to isolate the consul, if one came, and the selection of Shimoda was admirable for this purpose. Here Harris was in virtual quarantine not only from the United States but also from Japan. Fourteen months elapsed before he was visited by an American naval vessel, and eighteen months before he received additional instructions from the Department of State. On one occasion he wrote in his journal that for ten months he had not received a letter from the United States, that his supply of Western food was exhausted, and that he had lost so much weight it appeared that a vice-consul had been cut out of him. His position was described as "one honest man against a host of liars."

The principal objective of the Harris mission was to secure a full commercial treaty. The prospects of success were small. From the moment Harris landed, the Japanese used every device of obstruction and deceit to discourage and defeat him. They asserted that he had no right to land, since Japan had not approved his coming. With reluctance they assigned him an old temple as a residence. It was infested with mosquitoes, cockroaches, and large rats. The market sold him roosters that were too tough to eat. Police constantly guarded the temple on the pretext of protecting him. Wherever Harris or his Chinese servants went they were spied upon with the utmost suspicion. Japanese officials lied to him in the most flagrant manner. All this and much more Harris bore with patience, until after some months he was able to write in his journal: "The Japanese officials are daily becoming more and more friendly and more open in their communications with me. I hope this will grow and lead to good results by and by." This turn for the better in the relations between Harris and the shogun's officials must be attributed in large part to the patience, firmness, and unfailing honesty of this lonely bachelor American diplomat. He had set for himself a high goal. He proposed to serve the interests of his own country by leading Japan to a policy of full commercial intercourse, yet in so doing he was resolved not to take advantage of Japanese ignorance and lack of experience in international affairs. Harris, indeed, had become Japan's first instructor in world politics.

In June, 1857, Harris witnessed the first official fruits of his labors when the Japanese signed a convention that, among other things, granted formally to the United States all that was contained in the British, Russian, and Dutch treaties. This was merely a preliminary. The great work still remained. Harris had asked for an audience with the shogun in Yedo at which he would present a letter from the President. After much delay the request was granted. Harris himself described the astonishment of the officials as he stood in the presence of the shogun and looked "the awful 'Tycoon' in the face," spoke "plainly to him," and heard his reply—all this without any trepidation, or any "quivering of the muscles of the side."[4] Without the support of gunboats or marines Harris had won a diplomatic victory of the greatest magnitude.

It now remained for Harris to approach his main task—negotiating a full commercial treaty. He sought to convince the shogunate that the limited intercourse established by the first treaties was no longer adequate or practical. By January, 1858, the shogunate had agreed to the principal terms of a treaty. As the details of the treaty were perfected, Harris continued to act as instructor to the Japanese in diplomacy and international law. He continued to be that rare type of patriot who believed that the honor of his own country depended on its consideration for the rights of others.

When the treaty was completed, Harris waited impatiently month after month for the Japanese to sign. In July an American warship

[4] See M. E. Cosenza, ed., *The Complete Journal of Townsend Harris* (New York, 1930); and Carl Crow, *He Opened the Door of Japan* (New York, 1939).

reached Shimoda bringing news of the Tientsin Treaties recently forced upon China. Harris saw in these reports both a danger and an opportunity. If the Europeans now turned their guns on Japan, his own policy would be in jeopardy. Could this potential threat from English and French warships be used to frighten the shogunate into signature of the new treaty with America? Harris believed it could, and in this he was right. Despite bitter division of opinion in the shogunate, the treaty was signed July 29, 1858. It was a great personal victory for Harris, and a great diplomatic victory for his country. The treaty provided for diplomatic representation at the capitals of both powers, for the opening of new treaty ports where consuls might be stationed, for extraterritoriality, civil and criminal, for prohibition of the opium trade, for the freedom of foreigners to practice their religion, for a conventional tariff, and for the principle of most-favored-nation treatment.

The Harris treaty became the fundamental document in Japan's foreign relations until 1894. European powers accepted it as a model for their new treaties concluded in the months immediately following: the Dutch, August 18; the Russian, August 19; the British, August 26; and the French, October 7.[5] Ratifications of the Harris treaty were exchanged in Washington in 1860 by the first modern Japanese embassy to the Western World. Members of this embassy, the first Japanese to see the wonders of the Western World, were influential promoters of Japan's subsequent modernization.

Domestic Politics and Foreign Affairs

The shogunate had signed the Harris treaty. Could it enforce acceptance of the new policy by its enemies at home? These latter included not only the *tozama* lords but also powerful leaders within the Tokugawa family itself. During 1857 powerful opposition against the pro-foreign policy of the shogunate had again reasserted itself. Thus, when the shogunate sought the emperor's consent to signature of the Harris treaty, the request was denied. This explains why Harris was kept waiting. Furthermore, his treaty represented a new policy adopted by the *Bakufu without the consent of the Mikado.* The enemies of the Tokugawas were quick to see that by opposing this liberal foreign policy of the shogunate they could ap-

5 For the Harris treaty and conventions, see Hunter Miller, ed., *Treaties, etc.* . . . (Washington, 1931-), VII, 598-648, 947-1170.

pear as loyal supporters of the "divine" emperor against a "usurping" shogun. It was clear too that the balance of power in Japan had so shifted as to enable the Imperial court to issue orders to the *Bakufu*. Therefore the shogun was told by the court that the new treaties could be accepted only until such time as the foreign barbarians could be expelled and the old policy of exclusion resumed. In this way the Imperial court at Kyoto became the center of an anti-foreign, anti-*Bakufu* party, deriving its support from the *tozama* lords (the so-called "western clans"—Satsuma, Choshu, Hizen, and Tosa), from disgruntled allies of the Tokugawa clan, and from branch families of the Tokugawa house itself, such as the Mito group. Japan was on the brink of a civil war in which the new treaty rights and the very lives of the foreigners would be subject to attack.

July, 1859, was a critical month both for the shogunate and for the new treaty powers. So great was the danger of murderous attacks upon foreigners that the shogunate, refusing to open Kanagawa, which lay on the *Tokaido* highway between Yedo and Kyoto, encouraged the foreigners to settle at Yokohama, farther down the bay and destined soon to become one of Japan's great seaports. The immediate danger was twofold. So-called ultra-patriots, *samurai* and *ronin*, who had detached themselves from their clans, were anxious to embarrass the shogunate by attacking foreigners. Many of the foreigners in turn had come directly from residence in China, where too frequently they had acquired the habit of regarding the Oriental as an inferior to be treated with little respect. This being so, it is surprising that in the years 1859 to 1865, when foreigners were denounced by every fanatical supporter of the throne, only twelve Westerners were killed. Two cases that had important repercussions on foreign relations may be mentioned. When in January, 1861, the interpreter at the American legation, Heusken by name, was murdered, the foreign representatives, with the exception of Harris, retired from Yedo to Yokohama in protest against the shogun's failure to give the legations adequate protection. Harris took the broader view that the administration was doing everything in its power to protect them. He therefore remained in Yedo, where for a time he was the only foreign diplomatic representative.

The second case had more serious consequences. In September, 1862, C. L. Richardson, a Britisher visiting from Hongkong, was killed on the highway near Yokohama while riding with three compatriots, two men and a woman. The assassins were *samurai* in the feudal procession of the father of the Lord of Satsuma, a leader of the anti-shogun and anti-foreign party supporting the throne. This influential personage had just served upon the shogun a summons ordering him to appear in Kyoto to explain his conduct before the throne. There are various accounts as to what happened. There is no proof that Richardson intended to be offensive. Nevertheless, he and his companions failed to dismount while the feudal procession passed by. For this he sacrificed his life, and his companions were wounded. Although foreigners in Yokohama demanded immediate military action, saner counsel prevailed. Early in the following year (1863), the British government made the following demands: (1) payment of an indemnity of 100,000 pounds; (2) an indemnity of 25,000 pounds to be paid by the Satsuma clan, and (3) trial and execution of the assassins in the presence of a British naval officer.

These demands came at a most unhappy moment in the shogun's career. He had already been summoned to Kyoto to explain his conduct, which could mean only that those opposed to his government and his policy were now in control of the throne. This proved to be true, for the emperor ordered that all ports be closed to foreign commerce. Meanwhile, the negotiations on the British demands continued at Yokohama, where the British and the French now offered to use their naval forces on behalf of the shogun against the anti-foreign lords. This offer the shogun declined. On June 24 the British indemnity was paid and the powers were notified of the emperor's exclusion decree. Their reply declared that the treaties must be enforced, which, of course, the shogun fully realized. For the moment his policy would be one of delay, while he entertained the hope that some change could be effected in the attitude of his domestic enemies.

According to the Imperial decree, the expulsion of the foreigners and the discarding of the treaties were to be carried out by the shogun's government. However, the Lord of Choshu, a *tozama daimyo* whose lands controlled the western entrance to the inland sea, fired on an American ship lying off Shimonoseki. Later, French and Dutch vessels were also fired upon. Consequently, one American and several French war vessels hastened to attack the Choshu forts. It was evident that the shogun was unable to control the western barons. The British had already determined to take action against Satsuma to enforce compliance with the demands arising out of the

Richardson affair. Accordingly, a British squadron appeared at Kagoshima in August, 1863. Here negotiations broke down, and the resulting bombardment, assisted by a typhoon and fire, resulted in the destruction of more than half the town. Without securing acceptance of their demands, the British sailed away. Three months later envoys from Satsuma called upon the British *chargé,* agreeing to pay the indemnity and to continue the search for the guilty. They also requested assistance in securing in England a naval vessel for their clan. The significance of the incident is obvious. Anti-foreignism in Satsuma was in part a cloak hiding a determination to destroy the shogunate.

And now events took an unusual turn at Kyoto, where the anti-foreign and anti-shogunate forces were in control. Dissension appeared in these councils, where Choshu leaders were accused of attempting to seize the person of the emperor. Choshu troops were therefore ordered to leave the capital, and when they attempted a *coup d'état,* the shogun was ordered by the emperor to deal with the rebellious clan. At this juncture, Sir Rutherford Alcock, the British minister, returned to Japan determined to unite the foreign powers in a joint expedition against Choshu. The purpose of this was to give support to the shogunate in the hour of its need and to demonstrate to the hot-headed clans that it was no longer safe to tamper with the treaty rights of foreigners. Alcock's plan was supported by his diplomatic colleagues, and so, contrary to his instructions from London, he set about to organize a joint naval expedition, consisting of British, Dutch, and French ships, and one small American vessel, which sailed from Yokohama in August, 1864. No negotiations preceded the engagement off the Choshu coast. The fleet went straight to the task of silencing the batteries. On Choshu this lesson was as effective as the previous affair at Kagoshima. Clan leaders agreed to open the straits, not to repair the forts or to build new ones, and to pay an indemnity covering the cost of the expedition. This clan, too, now turned to the West for armaments and advice that would create an effective military machine. Since the shogun could not permit the foreign powers to negotiate with a single clan, a convention was soon concluded whereby the indemnities were assumed by the shogunate. Payment of large sums, however, proved most embarrassing to the government, and since the powers were more interested in new treaty ports and new concessions, the opportunity was favorable for a second naval demonstration.

Under the leadership of the new British minister, Sir Harry Parkes, it was planned to assemble the naval forces of the powers at Osaka, close to Kyoto, where pressure could be most effectively brought to bear upon the anti-foreign forces surrounding the throne. This time no American vessel participated, for none was available. The demands stated that two-thirds of the Shimonoseki indemnity would be remitted if Hyogo and Osaka were opened immediately, if the emperor gave his approval to the treaties, and if the tariff were reduced to a general 5 per cent. The reply was delivered on the final day permitted by the Allies' demands. The emperor—and this was most important of all—had agreed to ratify the treaties, the tariff would be reduced, and the full indemnity would be paid, for Japan was not prepared to open Hyogo and Osaka until 1868. Thus the most serious problem, the opposition of the imperialists to the treaties, was disposed of. The western *daimyo* were no longer aligned against the foreigners, but their determination to overthrow the shogunate and restore the emperor still remained.

The first phase of Japan's nineteenth-century revolution was now complete. The two-centuries-old policy of exclusion and seclusion had been abandoned not only by the weakened shogunate but also by the throne, which derived its power from the vital western clans. Japan had now accepted full treaty relations with the major Western powers. These treaties, as in the case of those with China, imposed certain serious limitations upon Japan's sovereignty—extraterritoriality and the conventional tariff.

Finally it should be observed that Japan's anti-foreignism in these early years of contacts with the West should not be considered merely the emotional outburst of military patriots. Anti-foreignism did have deep cultural and political roots, but its appearance after Perry's arrival is to be explained also by the economic results of the opening of Japan to foreign commerce. The cost of living was increased by large exports of consumer goods. The price of tea soon doubled; that of raw silk tripled. Before 1867 the price of rice, Japan's main food, had increased twelvefold. This disastrous revolution in prices was induced in part by the outflowing of Japan's gold supply due to the high and fixed price of silver in Japan. Hardships resulting from this price revolution supported the case of those factions that, for whatever reasons, regarded anti-foreignism as a patriotic duty.

For Further Reading

Cole, Allan B., ed., *A Scientist with Perry in Japan, the Journal of Dr. James Morrow* (Chapel Hill, 1947).

———, ed., *Yankee Surveyors in the Shogun's Seas: Records of the U.S. Surveying Expedition to the North Pacific Ocean, 1853-56* (Princeton, 1947).

Fukuzawa Yukichi, *The Autobiography of Fukuzawa Yukichi,* trans. by Eiichi Kiyooka (Tokyo, 1934).

Graff, Henry F., ed., *Bluejackets with Perry in Japan, A Day-by-Day Account Kept by Master's Mate John R. C. Lewis and Cabin Boy William B. Allen* (New York, 1952).

Gubbins, J. H., *The Making of Modern Japan* (London, 1922). A general survey, 1850-1919.

Harrison, John A., *Japan's Northern Frontier: A Preliminary Study in Colonization and Expansion with Special Reference to the Relations of Japan and Russia* (Gainesville, Fla., 1953). The story of Japanese fears of Russia and Britain to 1882.

Jones, F. C., *Extraterritoriality in Japan and the Diplomatic Relations Resulting in Its Abolition, 1853-1899* (New Haven, 1931).

Lensen, George A., *Report from Hokkaido: The Remains of Russian Culture in Northern Japan* (Hakodate, 1954).

Nakamura Katsumaro, *Lord Ii Naosuke and New Japan* (Tokyo, 1909). A biography on an important Tokugawa leader.

Reischauer, Edwin O., *The United States and Japan* (Cambridge, 1950). An excellent survey of U.S.-Japanese relations.

Satow, Sir Ernest, *A Diplomat in Japan* (London, 1921). Observations of a diplomat on the Restoration.

Treat, Payson Jackson, *Japan and the United States, 1853-1921* (rev. and continued to 1928, Stanford University, 1928). A standard survey.

Walworth, Arthur, *Black Ships Off Japan, The Story of Commodore Perry's Expedition* (New York, 1946).

Yanaga Chitoshi, *Japan Since Perry* (New York, 1949). A rich, factual survey.

12

1865–1889

Japan: The Divine and the Constitutional

By 1865 the contending clan factions that controlled political power in Japan had accepted as a basic plank in the national policy the principle of diplomatic and commercial intercourse with the West. This, as already stated, was the first phase of the nineteenth-century revolution. But by whom should this new policy be controlled and carried on? The general economic distress, the weakness of the shogunate, its lack of national confidence, and more specifically its bankrupt prestige in the eyes of the western *tozama* clans —all these and other factors foreshadowed the need for sweeping changes in the whole structure of Japanese government if the nation was to acquire a position of strength in its relations with the foreign commercial powers. Neither dual government, nor the shogunate, nor military feudalism was designed to serve Japan adequately in her new relation with the outside world. Indeed, it will be recalled that these institutions had long since ceased to provide an adequate political vehicle for a Tokugawa society in process of evolution. The need was for a strong national government capable of controlling the clans and of creating a unified political structure that might deal with the foreigners on terms of equality.

The most vigorous and effective spokesmen of all elements disgruntled with the existing social and economic order, whether *daimyo, kuge, samurai, ronin,* merchants, or peasants, were certain able *samurai* of the western clans, who by capacity and experience had already become the real controllers of clan policy, the *daimyo* being reduced to the role of mere puppets.

It was men of this stamp who planned and executed in its initial stages the political revolution which, between 1867 and 1889, destroyed the shogunate, stripped the Tokugawas of their lands and power, restored the emperor as the supreme ruler, abolished the feudal order, and bestowed upon the nation a centralized and constitutional but not a democratic government. This revolution, effected in scarcely more than twenty years, was destined to place Japan before the turn of the twentieth century in that exclusive company known as "the Great Powers." It was a political, an economic, and in some degree a social revolution of transcending importance not only to Japan but also to China, Europe, and the United States.[1]

The End of the Shogunate

The first step in these revolutionary changes occurred in 1867, when the *daimyo* of Tosa demanded the resignation of the Tokugawa shogun and the restoration of all power to the emperor. Since this demand was supported by the *daimyos* of Satsuma, Choshu, and Hizen, and by the strongest branch families of the Tokugawa clan itself—the *daimyos* of Owari and Echizen—the shogun was forced to comply, consoled by the thought that he would doubtless be chosen as chief adviser to the emperor under the new regime. This, however, was not the purpose of the revolutionists. These men were impelled by a number of motives: (1) their newly found loyalty to the Throne, (2) their hatred of the Tokugawa family, and (3) their own personal clan ambitions for power. Therefore, when the Tokugawas and their allies realized that the western clans were bent on their total destruction, they resorted to arms. In the brief civil war that followed, they were defeated. This was the end of Tokugawa power, and likewise the end of the shogunate and the ancient system of dual government. These stirring events opened the way for the restoration to full sovereign power, at least in theory, of a boy emperor, Mutsuhito, fourteen years of age, who was destined to go down in history as one of Japan's greatest rulers. He bore with dignity the reign-name of *Meiji* (enlightened government) from 1867 to 1912.

---

[1] Here we are concerned with the political revolution. Its economic and social features will be discussed in Chapter 13.

THE IMPERIAL OATH, 1868

The question is frequently asked: "Why did not the young, revolutionary *samurai* who engineered this Restoration, particularly those representing the powerful clans of Satsuma and Choshu, erect a new shogunate under their own control?" There was a time indeed when the Restoration was interpreted largely as a product of clan ambition and intrigue. Local and personal ambitions were indeed present, but they formed only a part of the larger revolutionary picture involving economic and social maladjustments that could not be met merely by substituting one shogunate for another. It must be remembered that if the younger *samurai* provided the personal leadership of the Restoration, the big merchants of Osaka and Kyoto financed it. Such a movement cannot be interpreted solely within the narrow view of feudal clan rivalries. Moreover, the emperor was the logical person to wear the official mantle of authority under the new regime. Though often neglected by the shoguns and sometimes relegated to a position of abject poverty, the emperor, or rather "the magic power of the Throne," was "such as to evoke the most passionate feelings of loyalty which were never completely dissipated."[2] This loyalty was soon developed by the Restoration leaders into a cult of emperor-worship deriving its immediate background from historical studies that stressed the "divinity" of the Imperial Family and the "illegitimate" character of Tokugawa rule. Fundamentally the new emperor-worship rested on what has been called a revival of "pure Shinto"—a Shintoism which, purged of Buddhist influence, was to stress as never before the emperor as the central and supreme deity of the nation.[3]

Since many of the *daimyo* and the *samurai* feared that power in the new regime would be monopolized by a few younger revolutionary leaders, these latter caused the young emperor, Mutsuhito, to issue in June, 1868, an Imperial Oath setting forth the principles on which the new Imperial rule was to rest. This charter, a sort of Japanese Declaration of the Rights of Man, recognized, sometimes in ambiguous terms, the principles of public discussion and debate by both the high and the low, and called for the abandonment of "absurd" practices of former times and for the pursuit of knowledge

---

[2] E. Herbert Norman, *Japan's Emergence as a Modern State* (New York, 1940), 27.

[3] D. C. Holtom, *Modern Japan and Shinto Nationalism* (Chicago, 1943, rev. ed., 1947), chs. i and ii.

wherever it might be found in order that the nation might be strengthened.[4] Although the framers of this charter had in mind the *samurai* and not the people as a whole, it was to this same charter that the liberals of later nineteenth-century Japan appealed in their struggle for representative government. In 1868, however, these gropings of new political forces were extremely vague, and the framework of the new political order had not taken definite shape even in the best Japanese minds. For some fifteen years after the Restoration, one temporary administration followed another. All these passing executive councils were headed nominally by Imperial princes, by *kuge* or by *daimyo,* but the real power remained in the hands of younger *samurai* advisers among whom the personnel of real leadership was remarkably cohesive.

The Abolition of Feudalism

It has already been pointed out that for many years economic and social adjustments had been taking place extra-legally in Japanese society, adjustments that revealed the incapacity of the feudal structure to meet new needs. The Restoration of 1868 in bestowing political power on the young *samurai* leaders of the western clans gave them also the opportunity to destroy political feudalism and thus to clear the ground for a truly national government.

The initiative in this development came again from the western clans of Satsuma, Choshu, Hizen, and Tosa, whose *daimyo* in 1869 returned their feudal domains to the emperor. These lords had been advised by their *samurai* leaders, who now controlled the emperor, that they were surrendering power only to receive greater power. Indeed the western lords were ordered to take up their residence in Tokyo, the former Yedo, to which the emperor had moved, and place their troops at the disposal of the sovereign's government. Thus strengthened in their position, the young *samurai* leaders were able through the emperor "to invite" the remaining *daimyo* to surrender their lands, and to follow this "invitation" with an Imperial rescript (1871) abolishing fiefs and clans. Feudalism as a political structure was thus destroyed.

This sweeping change in the political edifice affected materially

---

[4] For text of the Imperial Oath, see W. W. McLaren, "Japanese Government Documents," *Transactions of the Asiatic Society of Japan,* XLII, Pt. 1 (Tokyo, 1914), 8.

every class of society. Most of the *daimyo* viewed the change with apprehension, but they knew better than to oppose the great western clans. Then, too, they were consoled with annual pensions of one-tenth of the nominal revenue from their former fiefs. Indeed, their financial position was greatly improved because (1) the nominal income was higher than the actual income; (2) they were no longer burdened with the support of their *samurai;* and (3) their debts in most instances were assumed by the new central government or were cancelled. However, none of the *daimyo* won political distinction in the new government.

Far different were the effects upon the *samurai.* This class numbered about 450,000 families in 1871. The *samurai's* income from his feudal lord, measured in rice, was already small. This income was cut in half; but he was permitted to lay aside the badge of his class, the two swords, and to enter the field of business or finance. All this, however, was highly bewildering to men whose sole profession had been that of bearing arms, who regarded the fief as owing them a living, and whose mental horizon was restricted to the military philosophy of *Bushido.* They now faced a society that deprived them of half their income, deprived them of their monopoly in bearing arms (the new conscript national army was made up largely of commoners), and, worst of all, directed them toward the despised walks of business. Some of the lesser *samurai* adjusted themselves with relative ease to the new order. Some indeed were to emerge as the leaders of modern Japanese business. But the majority could not make the adjustment. These malcontents, and their intellectual descendants, as we shall see, were destined to play a significant role in Japan's later bid for world power.

Capitalistic groups—bankers, rice brokers, and wealthy merchants—welcomed the Restoration and the abolition of feudalism. Among these groups were families such at Mitsui and Sumitomo, who had helped to finance the Revolution of 1868-1871. For these services they were not to go unpaid. Many of the debts owed to these capitalists were assumed by the new government.

Most significant of all the effects stemming from the abolition of feudalism were those directly touching the farmers. In 1871 probably 80 per cent of Japan's population was composed of farmers, a majority of whom were independent cultivators. Yet within a few years "tenant land occupied 30 per cent of the area cultivated," a tendency that was accelerated in later years. In a word, the surreptitious acquisition of land by the new capitalistic landlord class, which had been going on before the Restoration, was now legalized; the peasant was freed from feudal obligations and became nominally a free-holder paying, not a tax in kind on the value of his crop, but a money tax on the value of his land. When in feudal days taxes were collected, the principle followed was "to see that the peasants had just enough to live on and no more." Thus under the "paternal" care of the feudal lord, the peasant "neither died nor lived." "In the new society [after 1871] they [the peasants] were free to choose their own fate; to live or die, to remain on the land or sell out and go to the city."[5] Thus the way was opened for the dispossession of the peasantry and the creation of "modern Japanese agriculture with its unique tenant-landlord relations."

The Era of Enlightened Government (Meiji)

The Restoration and the abolition of feudalism, together with the earlier adoption of the new policy of commercial intercourse with the great Western maritime powers, were an essential prelude to the creation of a new Japan.

Prior to the Restoration, foreign travel had been forbidden. Japan's knowledge of the Western world was confined to what she had learned from the Dutch at Nagasaki, from the foreigners who had come in the wake of Perry, and from the limited company of Japanese who had gone abroad with or without government approval. It was a new and strange world that they saw. The scope of the impressions carried back to Japan by the first travellers in these years is illustrated by the report of the shogun's mission to the United States in 1860. Its observations covered every human activity from the constitutional position and behavior of the President to the plumbing and etiquette of the bathroom.

The New Education

Significant among the reforms of early Meiji were those in education. Here Japan's enthusiasm for the new world of the West appeared to recognize no barriers. Following the mandate of the Im-

---

[5] For population estimates and vocational distribution, see Ryoichi Ishii, *Population Pressure and Economic Life in Japan* (London, 1937), and A. E. Hindmarsh, *The Basis of Japanese Foreign Policy* (Cambridge, 1936).

perial Oath (1868) that knowledge should be sought wherever it might be found, a department of education was set up (1871) under a law which proclaimed that "all people, high or low, and of both sexes, should receive education, so that there should not be found one family in the whole empire, nor one member of a family, ignorant and illiterate." This was a radical departure from previous policy and practice. Education in feudal Japan had been restricted to men of privileged society; now elementary education was to be compulsory. It was based on a modification of the American primary and secondary systems. Boys and girls, six years of age, were required to attend a four-year, later increased to a six-year, course. They were given instruction in elementary subjects plus special character training closely associated with reverence for and loyalty to the emperor. Secondary education prepared students for an immediate vocation or for entrance into a university. Normal schools turned out an ever-increasing supply of elementary teachers, and in a few years the personnel needs of Japan's expanding trade and industry were met by commercial schools. Elementary training for girls was similar to that for the boys; secondary education, however, stressed woman's role as wife and mother; and it was not until 1902 that the government made provision for higher education for women. Yet in this limited program for women, Japan was in advance of many Western states. In the organization of her universities for men Japan tended to follow the French model, and throughout the entire educational system the German insistence on vocational training was notable.

From whatever angle it be considered, this was a revolution in education, quite as striking as the political and economic revolutions of 1867-1871. The Japanese clamored for the new education with an unbounded but at times undiscriminating enthusiasm. Many mistakes were made, laws were frequently altered, and hurriedly trained teachers taught what they themselves did not understand. It was above all an educational system founded and shaped by the new Restoration government, a system that imparted to Japan's rising generations the strength and likewise the weakness of her revolutionary leaders. Two positive accomplishments are traceable to the new education: it created a literate people, and a nation that was technically abreast of the modern mechanical world of science. But as a purely intellectual force, the new education in the late nineteenth century did not create—in fact, was never intended to create

—a democratic philosophy for free men. There was no Thomas Jefferson in Japan's historical heritage. Consequently, although Japan imported precipitately a thousand forms and techniques of American education between 1870 and 1890, the spirit and ideals of this education did not thrive in the new environment. From the standpoint of the leaders of post-Restoration Japan, education could be useful only as it helped in the transition from a mediaeval to a modern autocratic state, only as it prevented "the predatory powers of America and Europe" from gaining "a stronghold in the economic life of the islands." Therefore education was limited to specific purposes: "national unification, unquestioning loyalty, the acquirement of modern scientific and economic technique, and the perfection of national defense."

The Material Transformation

The technical, material transformation of Japan was rapid and dramatic. Every Western mechanical device of the time in trade, business, commerce, and transportation soon found its place in the Japanese scene. Foreign architecture and city planning appeared first in the seaports of Yokohama and Kobe. Japanese in foreign trade put on foreign dress, and, even in later days of the twentieth century, those who were not too discriminating might be seen taking their summer evening stroll through the bazaars of Yokohama clad in a hard straw hat, white cotton gloves, a cane, native *geta* (wooden clogs), and, for the finishing touch, a suit of American model BVD's. A postal system and telegraph were in use by 1868. In 1872 the first railroad, 18 miles long, began business. In 1897, 3,000 miles of railroad, mostly government owned, were in operation. In all these activities and many others the initiative of the government was evident either through organization or subsidy. Shipping lines such as Nippon Yusen Kaisha (Japan Mail) (1885), and Osaka Shosen Kaisha were organized. Tonnage increased from 59,000 in 1885 to 1,115,000 in 1907. The textile industries were promoted by every modern means designed to improve and standardize the product and to assure its acceptance by the public. To meet the needs of currency reform and national credit, national banks, after the American model, made their appearance after 1872. The Central Bank of Japan was formed in 1882 as the financial bulwark of the government. This was followed among others by the Yokohama Specie Bank (1887) to finance foreign trade and to control exchange.

Appearance of Representative Institutions

The overwhelming enthusiasm of the Japanese for the newly discovered Western world was affected naturally enough by Western political philosophy and especially by the dominant liberalism of

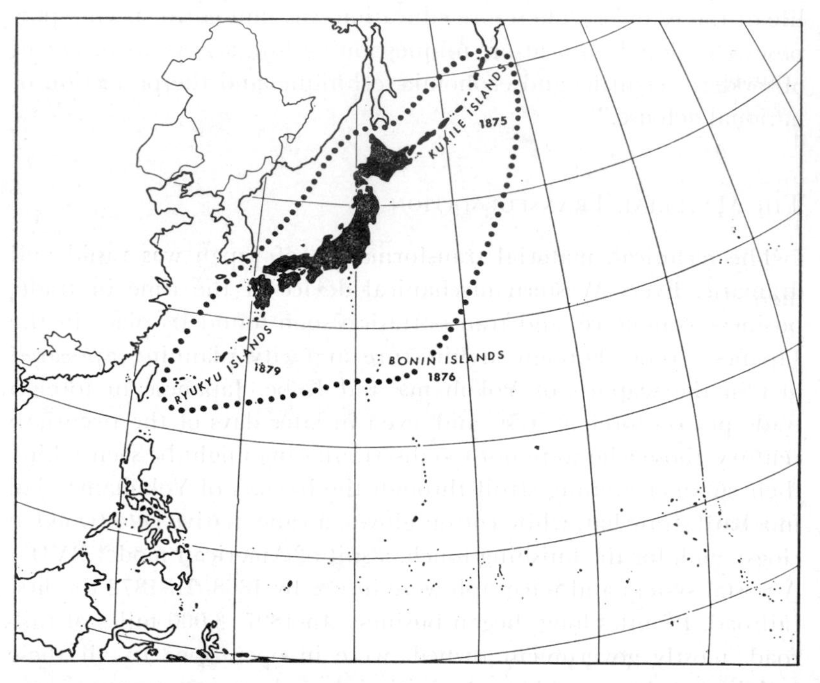

JAPAN, 1875-1890. *Reproduced from* A War Atlas for Americans, *Simon and Schuster, Inc., New York, 1944, by permission from Simon and Schuster, Inc., and from the U. S. Department of State, Division of Map Intelligence and Cartography.*

the nineteenth century. What philosophy and structure of government would Japan erect on the foundations of her Meiji Restoration? Her new educational program indicated already that the new government would be nationalistic and centralized in a peculiarly Japanese sense. Would it also be democratic, based on a popular constitution, a bill of rights, a broad franchise, political parties, and economic individualism as understood by powerful industrial and middle class groups in the Western democracies?

The answer to these questions must be found in the sphere of domestic Japanese politics following the return (1873) of the Iwakura mission from Europe and America. Impressed by the strength of the West, the members of this mission soon emerged as leaders of a so-called peace party in opposition to a war party composed of more belligerent *samurai,* who, for reasons to be explained later, desired a foreign war in Korea and Formosa. The war party soon withdrew from the government and thus formed a nucleus of potential political opposition. To strengthen its position, the government created a Ministry of Home Affairs, which had immediate control over prefectural and city governments. The opposition then attempted to assassinate Iwakura and demanded a national elective assembly. This the government refused, and a series of rebellions followed. As a concession, the government did call an Assembly of Local Governors (1875), which proved to be a rubber stamp for approval of government policies.

While the government continued to live under the protection of press censorship, it succeeded in defeating a desperate rising by opposition leaders from Satsuma (1877). The Satsuma Rebellion, led by Saigo Takamori, was a protest against the general policy of the government—against the conscription law (1873), against the importance of capitalistic interests in the new government, and against the refusal of the government to employ the ex-*samurai* in foreign war—a composite policy that threatened the very existence of *samurai* traditions. When, however, despite suppression of the rebellion, further assassinations of government leaders followed, prefectural assemblies (*fuken-kai*) were established. This was a step toward representative government, but it was a faltering one, because the franchise in the assemblies was limited; prefectural governors initiated and could veto all bills, leaving to the assemblies nothing but the privilege of discussing budgets and finding new ways to raise new taxes. Nevertheless, these assemblies encouraged the opposition to agitate for a national assembly. In response to the incessant demands of Itagaki, the government, while opposing anything in the form of a national parliament, did permit (1880) the calling of municipal assemblies.

A Constitution Promised; Political Parties

The immediate origins of the Imperial edict granting a national parliament involved among other things the financial corruption of the Satsuma and Choshu ex-*samurai* who controlled the government. When these practices were exposed publicly in 1881 by Okuma Shigenobu, there was mob violence in Tokyo. Government property was destroyed and the police were defied. A frightened government sought refuge behind the Imperial apron strings, while an Imperial rescript announced that a national parliament would be created in 1890. For this turn of events the Satsuma and Choshu leaders had only themselves to blame. They had excluded from office or had relegated to minor posts their colleagues from the less powerful clans such as Itagaki Taisuke and Goto Shojiro of Tosa. It was this disgruntled but able opposition that now used the pretext of graft in high places to force the issue of a national parliament and its natural concomitant, political parties.[6]

A so-called Liberal Party (*Jiyuto*) was organized by Itagaki in 1881, and a so-called Progressive Party (*Kaishinto*) by Okuma in 1882. These parties issued elaborate platforms. The *Jiyuto* advocated a one-house legislature, universal suffrage, a "strong" foreign policy, and many features of the French system of government. Some members of the party leaned toward republican ideas. The *Kaishinto* favored a bicameral legislature, limited manhood suffrage, administrative reform, and a national but non-imperialistic foreign policy. A third party, the Imperialist (*Rikken Teiseito*), also appeared in 1882, sponsored by the government. It favored absolute monarchy. Organized by Fukuchi Genichiro, it accepted literally the idea of restoring full power to the emperor. Thus in theory these parties represented widely divergent views on the future constitution: the *Jiyuto* stood theoretically for popular sovereignty after the manner of Rousseau; the *Kaishinto* wanted a more restricted constitutional regime on the British model; the *Teiseito,* if it had to agree to a constitution, wanted essentially the Prussian system.

It cannot be said that these platforms were completely meaning-

[6] It is not to be assumed that Itagaki and Goto were concerned primarily with the purification of Japanese politics. They, like many members of the government, began as poor if high ranking *samurai* and died immensely wealthy. Moreover, opposition came from within as well as from without. Okuma was in the government in 1881 when he did the exposing.

less, theoretical as they were. Historically they represented the first unsteady gropings of the Japanese toward modern and liberal government. Yet it must be remembered also that these first platforms had no solid foundation in the traditions of Japanese thought. In reality, therefore, the parties did *not* represent political principles as set forth in the platforms. Instead they were personal followings of particular political leaders. In this sense they were patterned after the Oriental idea that government is a matter of men rather than of law.

Constitutional Preparations

Meanwhile, as the political parties clamored for a popular and liberal constitution, the government set about the task of drafting a document that would preserve the power of oligarchy. It created a commission on constitutional investigation headed by Ito Hirobumi. In 1884 a new nobility was created to draw together and unify the conservative and aristocratic elements that were to dominate the new government. It was also decided to fashion the executive department prior to the adoption of the constitution. This would enable the executive to become a functioning organism familiar with its duties before it would be required to adjust itself to a parliament. Accordingly, a cabinet (*nai kaku*) was set up in 1885 modelled on the German cabinet of that day. Then in 1888 a new privy council was named with Ito, head of the constitutional commission, as president. As further preparation for the constitutional regime, a merit system was introduced into the civil service and new codes were prepared in both public and private law.

Japanese law of the earlier Restoration period had been derived from early Japanese law, which in turn had been borrowed from China in the seventh and later centuries and codified extensively in the Tokugawa feudal society. As the Western powers entered into treaty relations with Japan, they objected to submitting their nationals to Japanese law and consequently demanded and secured extraterritorial jurisdiction, as they had also done in the case of China. The Restoration government in its desire to preserve the national independence was quick to recognize that the abolition of extraterritoriality would depend on the speed and effectiveness with which Japan adopted principles of jurisprudence acceptable to Europeans and Americans. Accordingly, a penal code and a code of criminal procedure, begun in 1873 and completed in 1880, were adopted in 1882. They were strongly influenced by French law. Revisions of the code of criminal procedure appeared in 1890, and of the penal code in 1908. The larger task of constructing a civil code, begun in 1870, was completed and put into effect in 1899, in which year extraterritoriality was terminated. The basis of the civil law was also French, though it drew contributions also from German and other law. A code of civil procedure was operative as early as 1891, and the commercial code, German in origin, was adopted, as was the civil, in 1899.

The Drafting of the Constitution

From the foregoing it will be noted that some of the more important instruments of a new government had been created and were in operation before the constitution itself was created. Although this procedure lent stability to political affairs in a period of transition, it also enabled the ruling faction, headed by Ito, to maintain its monopoly of power.

The foundations of a constitutional regime had been laid as early as 1868, when the Charter Oath was proclaimed. Two years later, in 1870, Ito visited the United States, where he studied the American constitutional system, delving deeply into the pages of the *Federalist*. More important in shaping Ito's ideas, however, was the advice of General Grant, given in 1879, that Japan in designing a constitution should give full regard to her own peculiar traditions. Then, in 1882, a year after the emperor had promised a constitution, Ito studied in Germany, where the successes of Bismarck had brought new prestige to the political philosophy and institutions of Prussia. Back in Japan and commissioned in 1884 to draft a constitution, Ito called on the services of three able assistants, all of whom had travelled abroad: Inouye Kowashi, Ito Myoji, and Kaneko Kentaro. With Ito these men constituted a bureau attached to the Imperial Household, thus precluding political pressure from the liberals. When the draft of the constitution was completed, it was ratified by the Privy Council, which was created by Ito for this specific purpose and was to be maintained under the constitution as the highest advisory body to the sovereign. Finally, when the work was complete, Emperor Mutsuhito on February 11, 1889, the anniversary of the traditional founding of the state of Yamato in 660 B.C., bestowed the constitution as a royal gift upon his people. Every precaution had already been taken to insure an obedient and peaceful acceptance by the people at large. Tokyo under a special Peace Preservation Ordinance was subject to a sort of quasi-martial law. Most of the radical newspapers had already been suppressed, while the press in general was under strict instructions to refrain for the time being from all critical comment. As a consequence the public reception was peaceful.[7]

The Basic Character of the Constitution

The Constitution, drafted by a small group of Meiji leaders, bestowed as a gift by the emperor and accepted obediently by the people, denied any opportunity for criticism. It has been most aptly described by a Japanese student of politics, Uyehara, as "a document embodying Japanese political principles under the cloak of representative institutions." To the aristocrats of the Privy Council viewing Ito's work in the light of Japan's traditional political ideas, the Constitution may well have appeared as a singularly progressive affair, but, as Uyehara again remarks, the aristocrats had not only "defeated the extreme doctrines of Liberalism, but also had lost sight of the true principle of representative institutions." They had, in fact, created a framework of government which all but denied any "available avenue for democratic development," and which was admirably designed to perpetuate "the oligarchical absolutism in which it began its career." What then were the essential principles in the new constitutional political order?

The Essentials of Japanese Government

1. *The Law and the Constitution of 1889*

The fundamental law of the Empire consisted of the Constitution, the Imperial House Law, Imperial ordinances, statutes, and international treaties.[8]

---

[7] W. W. McLaren, *A Political History of Japan* (New York, 1916), 186; G. E. Uyehara, *The Political Development of Japan* (London, 1910), 109-123. The official interpretation of the constitution is by Hirobumi Ito, *Commentaries on the Constitution of the Empire of Japan,* trans. by Myoji Ito (2nd ed., Tokyo, 1906).

[8] For an excellent and concise summary of the organization of Japan's government, on which I have drawn heavily, see R. K. Reischauer, *Japan: Government—Politics* (New York, 1939), ch. iv.

The nature of the Constitution was best revealed by the position of the emperor. Since the Constitution was a gift of the Throne, only the emperor could initiate amendments. These required the consent of the House of Peers (*Kizoku-in*) and the House of Representatives (*Shugi-in*). Interpretation of the Constitution rested with the courts, and, in a case of dispute, with the Privy Council.

The Imperial House Law occupied a unique position. It could not be affected by legislation, was beyond the control of the Diet, could be amended only by the emperor with advice of the Imperial Family Council and the Privy Council. The Imperial House Law, not the Constitution, determined the succession.

Great powers were exercised by the emperor through Imperial ordinances of three kinds: (1) prerogative—Imperial House Law; (2) administrative—executive acts in the interest of the general welfare; (3) emergency—to meet emergencies when the Diet was not in session. These last required at time of issue approval by the Privy Council (*Sumitsu-in*), and ultimately approval by the Diet, unless repealed before a new session. It is thus clear that in a very large field the ordinance powers of the emperor were beyond legislative control.

Statutes were enacted by majority vote of both houses of the Diet, whose powers over legislation were the same, save that money bills were to be presented first in the lower house. The emperor's veto power over all laws was made absolute. In practice, most legislation was initiated by the government.

Treaties were to be ratified by the emperor with the consent of the Privy Council. Treaties were to be regarded as superior to ordinary law: they were not subject to change by ordinance, but could not be in conflict with the Constitution or the Imperial House Law.

2. *The Power Elite and the Constitution*

Japanese government was dominated after 1889 by a power elite composed of the Imperial Family, the *Genro* (Elder Statesmen), and the House of Peers. In this group were the former *kuge* (the civilian court nobility), the *daimyo* (the former great feudal lords), those *samurai* who engineered the Restoration in 1868, wealthy merchants and capitalists who financed the Restoration, and, finally, a select few from the professional classes.

The emperor's powers as defined by the Constitution were extremely broad. He possessed the rights of sovereignty and exercised them within the Constitution, convoked and prorogued the Diet, dissolved the House of Representatives, issued ordinances, determined the organization of the government, and acted on appointments and dismissals of all officials, save in those cases where other provision was made by the Constitution. He exercised the administrative and command powers over the army and navy, declared war, made peace and concluded treaties, proclaimed martial law, conferred all high official ranks and honors, appointed and removed judges. All these constitutional powers and prerogatives of the emperor were to be exercised *only* on the advice of his advisers, whether ministers of state, ministers of the Imperial Household, or chiefs of the general staffs of the army and navy. The emperor, in a word, reigned but did not rule. The problem for the student of Japanese government in any period after 1889 is to discover which individuals and groups ruled through the sovereign.

The Genro (elder statesmen). From shortly after the promulgation of the Constitution until 1931, the most powerful group in Japanese government and politics was the *Genro*. This group was extra-constitutional. It was composed of trusted and tried statesmen who had assumed leadership in the making of the new Japan, approximately in the years 1880-1900. These men exercised the real power in government under the Constitution. No important decisions were made without their consent. In fact they made the decisions. Although the power of the *Genro* was contested as early as 1913, it was not until about 1922 that their supreme control in all important affairs of state, domestic and foreign, began to be questioned. The *Genro* illustrate clearly the fact that although constitutional government in Japan often appeared to be Western in structure and performance, actually it was not so. The *Genro* as personalities, not as constitutionalists, were the real makers of the new Japan in the later years of Meiji. They included Ito Hirobumi (Choshu), maker of the Constitution, Yamagata Aritomo (Choshu), the builder of Japan's modern army, Inouye Kowashi (Choshu), influential in the drafting of the Constitution and reforms in taxation, Oyama Iwao (Satsuma), a great soldier, and Matsukata Masayoshi (Satsuma), of great prominence in taxation and finance. These were the original members. Later, General Katsura Taro (Choshu) and Saionji Kimmochi (Kuge) were added.[9]

---

[9] Ito was assassinated, 1909; Katsura died, 1913; Inouye, 1915; Oyama, 1916; Yamagata, 1922; Matsukata, 1924; Saionji, 1940. It is significant that no *Genro* was ever assassinated in Japan or by a Japanese. But as indicative of the weakening prestige of the group, attempts were made on the life of the aged Saionji.

The House of Peers. This body, the upper house of the legislature, included: (1) all Princes of the Blood who had reached majority; (2) princes and marquises twenty-nine years of age; (3) representatives of counts, viscounts, and barons, elected by their orders for terms of seven years; (4) Imperial appointees selected for life because of distinguished service to the state or in recognition of scholarship; (5) representatives of the Imperial Academy elected by their colleagues for seven-year terms; and (6) elected representatives of the highest taxpayers from each prefecture. This was a body distinguished for its conservatism of blood, wealth, and title. Its power was guaranteed by the Constitution.

3. *The Bureaucracy*

The bureaucrats were the civil office holders. Their position was based on ability and on appointment. Their loyalties were to the aristocrats rather than to the common people. Of first importance among the bureaucratic elements was the Imperial Household Ministry. The Lord Keeper of the Privy Seal and the Minister of the Imperial Household headed this group. Both, because of their close personal relationship with the emperor, had great influence as advisers of the throne. It was through them that audience with the sovereign was secured. These ministers were appointed by the emperor on the advice of the Prime Minister.

The Privy Council. The second group in the bureaucracy was the Privy Council. Created, as already noted, in 1888, it was designed to review and accept the Constitution and to be the highest constitutional advisory body to the emperor. Its membership numbered twenty-six, appointed for life by the emperor on the advice of the Prime Minister and with the approval of the President of the Council. Ministers of state were *ex-officio* councillors. The Council proved itself an effective curb against democratic or representative tendencies.

The Civil Service. The great body of civil servants—the rank and file of bureaucracy, numbering nearly half a million members—was selected by competitive examination. Usually the most rigid application of these examinations was in the Foreign Office (*Gaimusho*), whereas in the Home Ministry they have been less effective in competition with the spoils system.

4. *The Militarists*

In no modern state, save perhaps Prussia, has the professional soldier played so influential a role in politics as in Japan.[10] His influence was exercised through a number of military boards and officials. The Board of Field Marshals and Fleet Admirals (*Gensuifu*) was most significant in wartime, since usually (Yamagata was an exception) only Imperial princes were raised to these supreme ranks in times of peace. Much more important was the Supreme War Council (*Gunji-Sangi-in*), consisting of the field marshals, fleet admirals, chief of the general staff, chief of the navy staff, minister of war, minister of the navy, as well as additional high-ranking officers appointed by the emperor. It was this Council that controlled the policy of the fighting services. After 1900 both service ministers were required to be high-ranking officers on the active list. They were selected by the premier but only with the approval of the respective chiefs of staff. The services thus had the power to destroy any cabinet by forcing the resignation of the service ministers and refusing to nominate new ones.

5. *The Politicians and the House of Representatives*

The Constitution provided for a bicameral legislature or Diet, which the Japanese called *gikai*. The purpose of the framers was to prevent the legislators from indulging in hasty legislation and to give decisive legislative power (in the House of Peers) to the aristocracy. The House of Representatives, according to the Commentaries, was to regard itself as "representatives of the people of the whole country," though prior to 1925 there were high property qualifications both for candidates and for the franchise. The Constitution required annual sessions of the Diet, which were supplemented frequently by extraordinary sessions caused by frequent dissolutions. Originally the House of Representatives consisted of

---

[10] The army and the navy liked to think of themselves as unique guardians of the throne and of the so-called "national spirit." In practice, however, they were the most flagrant violators of the commands of the throne. An Imperial rescript addressed to service men (1882) set forth that: "Service men should not involve themselves or interest themselves in politics." Under the Constitution they did not vote. Nevertheless, no group in Japanese society was more jealous of its political fortunes than the military. See the concise discussion of this subject in K. W. Colegrove, *Militarism in Japan* (Boston: World Peace Foundation [World Affairs Books No. 16], 1936); see also E. E. N. Causton, *Militarism and Foreign Policy in Japan* (London, 1936), and O. Tanin and E. Yohan, *Militarism and Fascism in Japan* (New York, 1934).

Special Powers of Emperor

Supreme Commander Army and Navy.
Rules Affairs of Imperial Household under Imperial House Law.
Confers Honors on advice of Minister of Imperial Household.
Promulgates Imperial ordinances which are executed by Cabinet.
Controls foreign affairs which are conducted by the Cabinet.
Convokes and prorogues Diet.
Appoints some members of House of Peers.
Dissolves House of Representatives.

Privy Council

Appointed by Emperor; the highest constitutional adviso body to the Throne. Cabinet ministers are ex-officio members Advises Emperor on both domestic and foreign affairs. Appointments for life on nomination of Prime Minister.

The Imperial Diet

All statutes require a majority vote of both houses, but are subject to the Emperor's veto; most bills are presented by the Government, not by a member of the Diet; power to approve or reject Imperial ordinances; has no control over Imperial House Law; power to approve but not to initiate amendments to the Constitution.

House of Peers

Membership: Princes of the Blood, Princes and Marquises; representatives of Counts, Viscounts, Barons; Imperial appointees for life selected because of special service to the State; representatives of Imperial Academy; representatives of the highest tax payers. Legislative powers equal to those of House of Representatives.

House of Representatives

Members elected for 4 years (manhood suffrage after 1925). Convoked annually by Emperor. Has power, usually not exercised, to initiate legislation. Financial bills introduced first in House of Representatives. Has no control over "fixed" expenditures in budget. Membership representative of varying political parties. "Party" cabinets more or less responsive to House of Representatives prevailed 1918-1932.

The people elect. Manhood suffrage after 1925.

PRINCIPAL FEATURES OF THE GOVERN

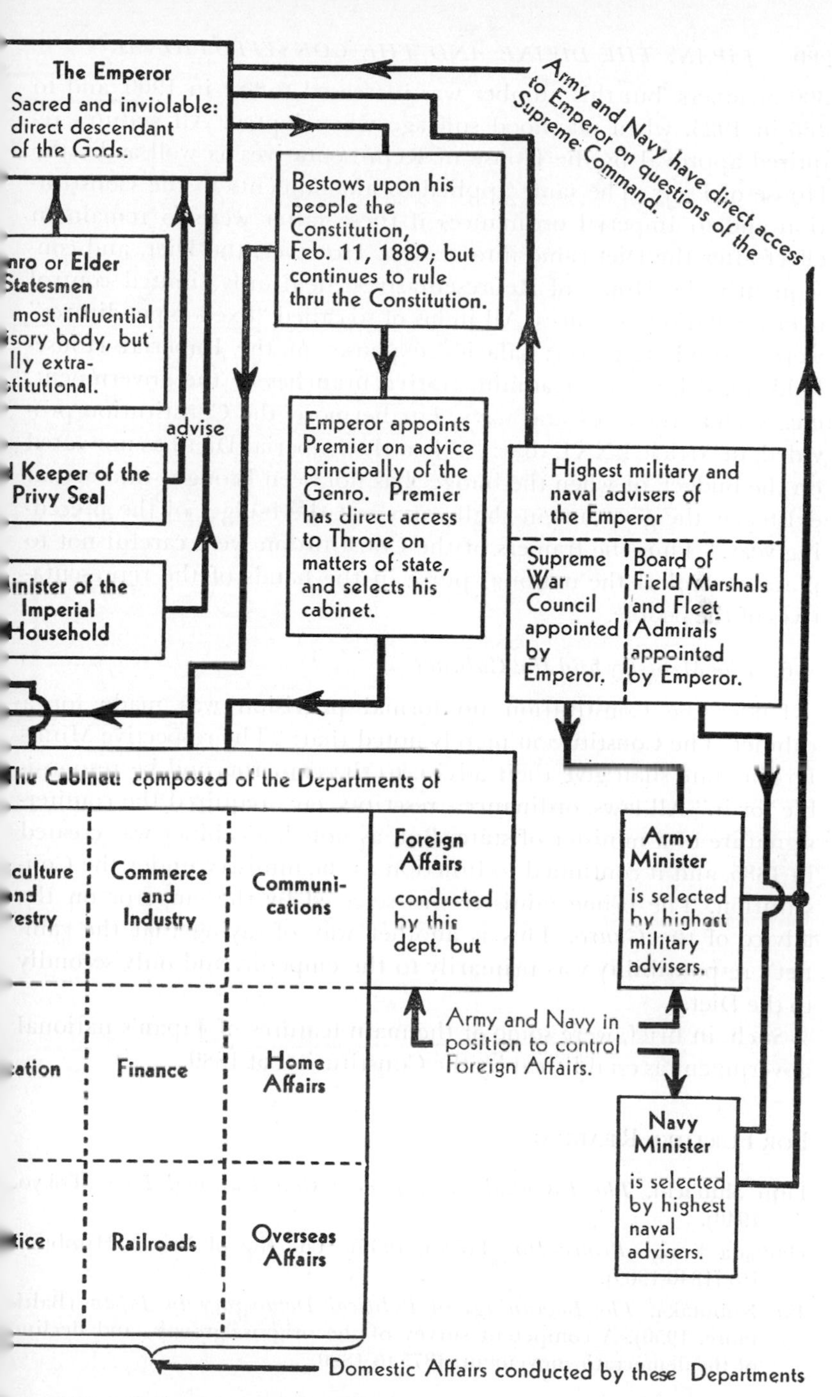

AN UNDER THE CONSTITUTION OF 1889

300 members, but this number was increased to 381 in 1900, and to 466 in 1925, when manhood suffrage was adopted. All statutes required approval by the House of Representatives as well as by the House of Peers. The same applied to amendments to the Constitution and to Imperial ordinances if these latter were to remain in effect after the Diet came into session. However, the Diet, and consequently the House of Representatives, held only limited control over the nation's finances. All items of so-called "fixed expenditures" were beyond its power: salaries, expenses of the Imperial Household, fixed budgets of administrative branches of the government, etc., such as the army and navy. Furthermore, the Constitution provided, in Article LXXI, that: "When the Imperial Diet has not voted on the budget, or when the budget has not been brought into actual existence, the government shall carry out the budget of the preceding year." Thus the framers of the Constitution were careful not to place control of the national purse in the hands of the representatives of the people.

6. *The Ministry and the Cabinet*

Under the Constitution no formal provision was made for a cabinet. The Constitution merely noted that: "The respective Ministers of State shall give their advice to the emperor, and be responsible for it." All laws, ordinances, rescripts, etc., required the countersignature of a minister of state. But, as noted, a cabinet was created in 1885, and it continued to function as the ministry under the Constitution. The prime minister was selected by the emperor on the advice of the *Genro*. This is another way of saying that the cabinet's responsibility was primarily to the emperor, and only secondly to the Diet.

Such, in brief, were some of the main features of Japan's national government as established by the Constitution of 1889.

For Further Reading

Fujii Shin'ichi, *The Essentials of Japanese Constitutional Law* (Tokyo, 1940).

Hamada Kengi, *Prince Ito* (Tokyo, 1936). The life of Prince Hirobumi Ito (1840-1909).

Ike Nobutaka, *The Beginnings of Political Democracy in Japan* (Baltimore, 1950). A competent survey of the origins, growth, and decline of the democratic movement, 1875 to 1890.

Mounsey, A. H., *The Satsuma Rebellion: An Episode of Modern Japanese History* (London, 1879). An account of the revolt of 1877.

Mushakoji Saneatsu, *Great Saigo, the Life of Takamori Saigo,* adapted and trans. by Morishi Sakamoto (Tokyo, 1942).

Nakamura Kaju, *Prince Ito, the Man and Statesman, A Brief History of His Life* (New York, 1910). A biography of the leader of the Japanese constitutional movement.

Norman, E. Herbert, *Soldier and Peasant in Japan: The Origins of Conscription* (New York, 1943).

Quigley, Harold Scott, *Japanese Government and Politics, an Introductory Study* (New York, 1932). Valuable as a reference work.

13

Japan: Economic and Cultural Bases of Meiji

THE political history of Japan between the years 1853 and 1889, recounted briefly in the foregoing chapters, is the record of an extraordinary revolution under equally extraordinary leadership which was designed to bring Japan into the modern world, to transform overnight, as it were, an isolated, feudal society into a modern, centralized state and nation. This transformation from feudalism to centralization and from military dictatorship to constitutionalism would have been much more difficult had it not been for the foundations laid in the later years of the Tokugawa era in which Japan's traditional society had already outlived its usefulness. Nevertheless, it may be said that in point of rapidity of change in the nature of the Japanese state, the Meiji revolution was unique. Although the concept of constitutionalism, as it appeared in late nineteenth-century Japan, was imported from the West, the political society created by this revolution cannot be described adequately by saying that it too was Western. On the contrary, it was a peculiarly Japanese product colored, to be sure, by Western influence, shaped in some respects by Western forms, and here and there partaking of the Western spirit, but its intellectual and philosophic foundations were, in the main, Japanese, deriving principally from Japanese historic ideals and institutions both political and social and from conditions then prevailing within Japan. In a word, the political revolution of early Meiji acquires historical meaning only when it is placed in a setting of the economic, the social, and the intellectual Japan that emerged in the four decades following Perry's expedition.

It will be convenient to deal first with some economic foundations that underlay this Meiji transformation. In this connection it will be recalled that by 1871, with the framework of feudalism already destroyed, Japan was creating a new and unified political regime that would make invasion from abroad too dangerous and too uncertain an undertaking. This new Restoration government derived part of its economic power from the financial backing of the merchant-capitalists, and its leadership from the lesser but capable *samurai* of the Western Clans. In the face of violent domestic opposition, these leaders pursued steadfastly until 1894 the goal of internal reconstruction—political, economic, and social. Only after the foundations of the new economic, social, and political Japan had been laid did they venture into the field of foreign expansion.[1] What, then, were the economic and social foundations of the new state?

Foundations for Industrialization

At the close of the Tokugawa period, although rice was still the standard of exchange, money had become the principal means of exchange. In the great castle towns (eighteenth-century Yedo had a population of some 1,300,000) there was a thriving trade in the products of the skilled handicraft industries of Kyoto and other centers. A division of labor was also becoming apparent between those who produced raw materials and those who produced the finished products. This division, however, was restricted by the dominance of household industry which prevailed, though in lesser relative degree, into contemporary, twentieth-century Japan. Commercial capital was concentrated in the hands of traders and usurers, dominated by the *fudasahi* (rice brokers) of Osaka, among whom were numbered such families as Mitsui. In general, the economic system that developed was a kind of primitive monopoly mercantilism between the great cities and the adjacent rural areas.

In Japan the young capitalist class, far from dispensing with the

[1] For detailed treatment of the decay of feudalism, of the rise of the merchant-capitalists, and of the lower *samurai* as political leaders of early Restoration Japan, see E. Herbert Norman, *Japan's Emergence as a Modern State* (New York, 1940), 1-104; Sansom, *Japan: A Short Cultural History,* ch. xxiii; Eijiro Honjo, *Social and Economic History of Japan* (Kyoto, 1935). W. W. Lockwood, *The Economic Development of Japan 1868-1938* (Princeton, 1954), 3-37, gives a comprehensive summary of the foundations of industrialism in the Meiji period.

crutch of state absolute power, leaned more completely upon it in the Meiji era than in the days of the Tokugawas. The reasons for this are readily discernible. In the first place, early Meiji Japan, intent upon overtaking the Western states in point of industrial progress, did not possess any great reservoir of skilled labor. In the second place, the merchant-capitalists who had financed the Restoration and who were in a financial position to set up factory industry on the Western model, hesitated to assume the vast risks involved. As a result, factory industry was undertaken in early Meiji *by the government itself* drawing its capital from merchant loans and from the labor of the peasants in the form of land tax revenue. Private capital, in contrast, tended to remain in the field of trade or in banking, where it found a safe and profitable outlet in government loans. This policy of government-in-industry was followed closely until 1880, when the principle of "direct control" began to give place to "indirect protection." It was at this time that the government, which had carried on the initial development of industry, began to turn over some specific enterprises to the financial oligarchy, the *Zaibatsu,* "at amazingly low rates." By this means, industrial as well as financial capital came to be concentrated in the same hands. Finally, it may be added that the economic structure of nineteenth-century Meiji Japan was fashioned without a major resort to foreign loans.

The Strategic Industries

In applying the economic policy outlined above, the interest of the Meiji government was centered first upon those industries directly concerned with the armed defense of the nation. This course was taken to save Japan from the unhappy plight of China. These industries were the *strategic* industries, and "from the very first in modern Japan they were government owned and inextricably interwoven with the military problem."[2] The same principle was followed in transportation. The principle of nationalization of railroads was recognized in 1892, and by 1906 most of the lines were nationalized. As early as 1872, the nationalization of telegraphs was

---

[2] Note in particular three chapters in Shigenobu Okuma, ed., *Fifty Years of New Japan* (2 vols., London, 1910): (1) Yamagata Aritomo, "The Japanese Army"; (2) Yamamoto Gombei, "The Japanese Navy"; and (3) Oura Kanetake, "The Police of Japan."

likewise recognized on strategic grounds.[3] These developments do not necessarily suggest that Meiji Japan from the beginning was bent on an ultimate policy of foreign conquest. They do suggest, however, that the leaders of Meiji were conscious of the "political necessity" of defending the Restoration government from attack, foreign or domestic, and that, as a result, industrialization and strategic security became not a dual but a unified single concept. Another consequence was that, contrary to what had occurred in the West, in Japan it was the heavy rather than the light industries that first assumed importance.

The Place of *Zaibatsu*

There was, therefore, a strong and peculiar focus of economic power which implemented Japan's modern industrialization. Although in modern Japanese industry the small technical unit was typical of a wide range of enterprise, these small units, more often than not, were dependent on larger concerns which, in turn, were controlled, if not owned, by a very few financial-industrial groups having manifold interests. This state of affairs was encouraged because the Meiji and later governments were determined to hurry by industrialization the creation of national power and security in a country that lacked adequate material resources and technical experience. Scarcity of capital and entrepreneurial skill tended to concentrate industrialization in a few immense concerns, which, as noted, were known as the *Zaibatsu.*

The principal *Zaibatsu* were the families of Mitsui, Mitsubishi, Sumitomo, and Yasuda. Lesser but powerful groups often referred to as *Zaibatsu* included: Okura, Asano, Kuhara, Ogawa-Tanaka, Kawasaki, Shibusawa, Furukawa, and Mori. Mitsui were great financiers and traders far back in Tokugawa times. Mitsubishi, founded by the *samurai* family of Iwasaki, dated its greatness only as far back as the Formosan affair of 1875, when it had provided the ships for the government's expedition. Sumitomo mined copper and traded in rice in Tokugawa times; Yasuda were money lenders under the last shogunate. The modern rise to power of all four *Zaibatsu* is explained (1) by their capacity to aid the government industrially and financially, and (2) by the choice privileges which the govern-

[3] See Kenjiro Den, "Japanese Communications: The Post, Telegraph and Telephone," in Okuma, *Fifty Years of New Japan,* I, 408-423.

ment in return bestowed upon them. In short, they were principal instruments of national policy in the creation of national power.[4]

The economic control, direct and indirect, exercised by the *Zaibatsu* was a product of their diversified interests. They owned and/or controlled banks, trust companies, insurance companies, and leading firms in every line of industry. They also placed heavy investments in undertakings which they did not own or control. In some areas their position was monopolistic. The extent of this concentration of *Zaibatsu* power is suggested by the fact that, together, Mitsui, Mitsubishi, and Sumitomo, prior to World War II, controlled one-third of the copper production, one-half the coal, more than one-half of the merchant marine and a major proportion of the cargoes carried, large interests in oil importing, half the warehouse capacity, one-third of Japan's foreign trade, nearly all of the paper industry, more than 70 per cent of the flour milling, and about 40 per cent of raw and refined sugar. Holdings such as these could have a profound effect on many other industries.

Big Business and the Family

From the point of view of modern Japanese politics as shaped by older historical patterns, it is important to observe that the *Zaibatsu* were family concerns. Control was in a family partnership; the capital was owned exclusively by the family or sometimes by a group of families all having a common ancestor. By the holding of shares and by the appointment of managers and directors in the various concerns, the partnership or family council could direct all matters of policy. At times actual control was vested by the family in *Banto,* or managers, who were not regarded primarily as hired officials but rather as fellow members of the clan serving their overlord.

This pattern of industrialization for early Meiji Japan was applied, however, in a society that was overwhelmingly agricultural. It is not surprising therefore that the leaders of Meiji applied themselves to the agricultural settlement with the same revolutionary vigor they were showing in politics and industry. The importance of their agricultural settlement can scarcely be overestimated, for it fashioned the unique features of much of Japan's twentieth-century social, as well as economic, structure.

---

[4] The four *Zaibatsu* proper were distinguished from the lesser groups by reason of their supremacy in finance as well as in industry and commerce.

In the later years of the Tokugawa *Bakufu,* the illegal alienation of land to a new landlord class had gone on at a considerable rate. Then, after 1867, the Restoration legalized the sale of land. Although this made the peasant a nominal free-holder, it also created the means through which he could be dispossessed through foreclosures on mortgaged land. This was a matter of significance, since in 1870 many of the peasants were small, independent cultivators. Meanwhile, the Restoration government was seeking a unified and workable system of taxation to provide the revenue with which it hoped to carry the burden of military expenditure, and the capital necessary for the new strategic industries. The answer was found in the land tax policy of 1873, which effected a radical revision in previous methods of taxation. It involved three principal changes: (1) the tax was to be fixed by the *value* of the land, not, as formerly, by the yield of the harvest; (2) the tax would be at a fixed rate (3 per cent), not adjustable, as it had been in feudal times, to good or bad seasons; and (3) the tax would be paid in money and not, as formerly, in kind (rice).

The Land Tax and the Peasantry

How did the new policy of taxation affect the peasant? It meant in general a steady dispossession of the landowning peasantry and the accumulation of land in a new, wealthy, landowning class. Yet, unlike the eighteenth-century enclosures in England, this did not mean that the Japanese peasantry deserted the countryside and moved to the cities. Since from the beginning Japanese landlords were able to collect excessively high rents, they preferred to retain the tenant on the land rather than to oust him and exploit the land themselves as capitalists. Thus the tradition and habit bound peasant remained upon the land, paying exorbitant rents and sinking deeper and deeper into poverty. During Meiji Japan his economic decline, caused principally by fantastic rents, was aided and abetted by other factors: (1) the decline of the older household industries, and (2) a marked increase in the rural population. The resulting conditions of extreme agricultural poverty were closely related to developments marking the expansion of the Japanese textile industries in the twentieth century. The younger generation in the tenant households, the girls in particular, moved to the cities seeking to increase the *family* income. The textile industry was thereby provided with extremely low-cost labor.

Again, the depressed position of the peasant was conditioned by the size of the average unit of land cultivated by a single household. The growth of tenancy in Japan was not accompanied by any marked increase in the size of the lots cultivated. In 1874 the average holding cultivated by a peasant household was 2.35 acres. In 1909 it was 2.38 acres, and in 1914 (including the larger individual holdings in Hokkaido and Ryukyu) it was 2.61 acres. These figures, covering both paddy and dry fields, were considerably larger than the averages for paddy field holdings alone. The perpetuation of small holdings was partly traceable to Japanese topography, but it was also a direct result of the agrarian settlement made in the early Meiji period. Furthermore, although the Japanese tenant-farmer assumed all the risks involved in crop raising, the landlord, through high rent, took most of the profit. The composite results of this subsistence economy were far-reaching. The peasant could no longer resort to the common lands for fodder, wood, implements, etc. His household cotton industry was destroyed first by imported cotton and then by the rise of the urban industry in Japan; thus he was forced to turn chiefly to sericulture as the principal supplementary household industry. The partial destruction of the old domestic industry created a home market for the products of Japan's new factory industries, but this expanding home market was subject to limitations such as lack of purchasing power in the home market. This limited purchasing power of the Japanese home market became in the late nineteenth as in the twentieth century one of the chief factors impelling Japanese industry to seek foreign markets for its goods and the Japanese nation to use war to this end. Japan's case was not of course unique. Nevertheless, the direction of her national policy could not remain unaffected by the fact that the masses of rural labor and unskilled industrial labor were unable to buy the products of their nation's industry.

Political Parties in Meiji Japan

The reader will recall that three important political parties appeared in late nineteenth-century Japan: the *Jiyuto* (Liberal Party), the *Kaishinto* (Reform Party), and the *Teiseito* (Constitutional Imperial Party). All these parties boasted of their adherence to stated political principles and platforms. These principles and platforms, however, were usually exceedingly vague and broad, and, in any case, were of secondary importance, since in Japanese political thought the emphasis was on the political leader rather than upon any body of principles. It followed then that political parties tended to be aggregations of individuals bound by personal loyalty to a particular man, as was the case in feudal times, rather than a group held together by loyalty to any set of political principles.[5] Although this was the generally prevailing tendency, it should not be assumed that Western political theory in terms of constitutionalism, liberalism, etc., played no part in the thinking of Japanese politicians and intellectuals, for indeed quite the contrary was the case. Yet, at the same time, it would be a mistake to assume that Japanese political parties were inspired primarily by Western concepts of constitutionalism, or that the early "liberal" in Japanese politics was a replica of the nineteenth-century English liberal. From 1881, when the first party appeared, until about 1900, there appears to have been some genuine enthusiasm among some politicians for the principles of responsible government. But after 1900 and on until 1918 the power of the *Genro* and the special groups that supported them—aristocrats, bureaucrats, and militarists—was so entrenched that in general the party politicians gave up the struggle for liberal principles (for which there was no long background of tradition as there was in England), and sought the spoils of office by selling their parliamentary support to the oligarchy. In turn, oligarchs such as Ito Hirobumi and militarists such as Katsura Taro accepted the presidency of major political parties. Considering such leaders, it becomes obvious why the parties could no longer stand effectively for liberal or responsible government.

The Economic Base of the Meiji Parties

The *Jiyuto,* or Liberal Party, of 1881 presented the seemingly incongruous spectacle of liberalism promoted by a class of rural landowners. This was due to the peculiar character of Japan's rural economy in the Restoration era. Landed proprietors occupied a dual position. They collected the profits of agriculture in the form of land rent paid by tenants in rice. These profits, which the pro-

[5] R. K. Reischauer, *Japan: Government—Politics* (New York, 1939), 29-30, 95-97. Parties were at times a means of opposing government.

prietors converted into money at the best possible rate, were usually invested either in land or in rural industries such as the manufacture of *sake* (rice wine) or *miso* (bean paste). Thus the landowner became a local rural industrialist, or rice-broker, or merchant. He thereby combined the functions of "semi-feudal landlord" with those of the commercial capitalist. It was in this latter capacity of commercial capitalist that the manufacturing-landlord entered politics in 1881, combining his efforts with other groups in the formation of the *Jiyuto.* He did so because he was opposed to the government's policy of financing its military and naval program by increasing taxation on the products he manufactured, and because he objected to paying the bulk of the nation's income in the form of the land tax while the government bestowed its favors and protection on the financial oligarchy of the cities. Other rural groups also had their special complaints. The tenant cultivator wanted reduction in his rent. Those who owned their land were already threatened with dispossession at the hands of larger landowners. Thus from these various groups, particularly from the landed, rural manufacturers, came the crusade for "Liberty and the People's Rights" with its subsequent development into the constitutional movement that culminated in the Constitution of 1889. In this sense Japanese liberalism sprang from the countryside and not from the cities. In contrast the ideological leadership of the movement came from quite a different group. This was a nucleus of *samurai* from Hizen and Tosa who had been pushed out of the new government bureaucracy by the *samurai* politicians of Satsuma and Choshu. These men of Tosa and Hizen, no longer enjoying office, became the ideological leaders in the demand for a people's assembly.

The second and rival political party, the *Kaishinto,* led by Okuma, included in its membership other disgruntled bureaucrats who were out of office, a scattering of liberal intellectuals who favored the British parliamentary system, and, significantly, from the economic point of view, some of the wealthier urban merchants and industrialists, including representatives of the Mitsubishi interests. In ideology, the *Kaishinto* was a mild reflection of the then current English liberalism and utilitarianism.

From 1880 until 1918 the oligarchy, led by the *Genro,* was able to channel within narrow limits all movements of political liberalism, and thus to uphold its authoritarian concepts on the economic and social structure of society. It accomplished this in a number of ways.

It neutralized the parties by playing one against another. It won over to its own fold some of the party leaders by various means, not excluding that of bribing them with offices. Freedom of speech and of the press were seriously hampered long before the Constitution was promulgated. The Press Law of 1875 and the Peace Preservation Law of 1887 were the nineteenth-century manifestations of what came to be known in the twentieth century as the control of "dangerous thoughts." The first liberal political parties were for a time suppressed entirely, thus depriving the economically and socially depressed masses of any political leadership. What is more, when the resurrected Liberal Party (*Jiyuto*) took its place in the first Diet of 1890, it had been shorn of its liberalism and its democratic ideology. By 1900, when it became the *Seiyukai,* it was the party of the great landlords and rural capitalists. As such, it became a bulwark of the rural economic settlement that impoverished the small farmer.[6]

The Political Philosophy of Meiji

The political and economic settlement which the Meiji leaders devised in the late nineteenth century was much more than an opportunistic design to meet a coterie of practical and pressing problems. It was also a product of deeply ingrained Japanese values and habits of thought. What the Japanese did in the Meiji era was occasioned by and often colored by the Western impact, but the intellectual and cultural bases of their actions were rooted in Japanese concepts. Their approach to the problem of government was no exception to this generalization. Since early times, Japanese ideas on government have been, for the most part, exceptionally uniform. The makers of Meiji Japan were themselves a product of these traditional values. What then were the principal tenets of Japan's traditional political creed?

First in importance was the idea, derived from Confucianism, of unity. Whether it was the family, the clan, or the family-state, the individual was merely a part of these larger units, and only through them did his life acquire meaning and become an expression of what has sometimes loosely been called the Japanese spirit. In the

[6] G. E. Uyehara, *The Political Development of Japan, 1867-1909* (London, 1910), 89-106, 215-253; Yusuke Tsurumi, "The Liberal Movement in Japan," *The Reawakening of the Orient* (New Haven, 1925), 68 ff.; W. W. McLaren, *A Political History of Japan during the Meiji Era, 1867-1912* (New York, 1916), 153-177.

West in modern times, science, philosophy, literature, even religion have struggled to free themselves from control by church or state. This quest for new and free roads to individualism has produced many types of individuals and all manner of standards of values with the resulting changes and conflicts between them: Christian versus Atheist, Protestant versus Catholic, Liberal versus Conservative. This self-seeking diversity did not make sense to the traditional Japanese mind in which philosophy, religion, and politics were one and indivisible. Consequently, a Japanese was a Confucian, a Buddhist, and a Shintoist at one and the same time. Nothing, it was believed, should be permitted to interfere with this idea of oneness. There could be no place in the old Japanese society for the rugged individualism of the capitalist, the parochial school of an exclusive church, the class struggle of the Communists, or even the conflicting platforms of political parties.

The application of this principle of unity to practical politics was best exemplified by the Japanese attitude toward the emperor-system. In Shintoism the emperor was the descendant of the gods; in Buddhism, of the supreme Buddha; and in Confucianism, he was the fountain of the great virtues from which good government would come. He symbolized the complete unity of the family-state in its philosophical, religious, and mundane affairs.

An American school child learns at a tender age that "all men are created equal." Japanese children, however, learned to recognize inequality as a principle that is both self-evident and natural. Again, as in the case of unity, the doctrine of inequality was sanctioned by the dominant systems of thought. Shintoism explained inequality in terms of blood, the emperor being what he was because of his direct descent from the Sun Goddess. The respective stations of all persons in society were determined by the stations of their divine ancestors. Buddhism gave equal stress to the inequality of men as they struggled toward salvation. Confucianism rated men as having superior or inferior virtue. One man was, therefore, not as good as another. Within the circle of Japanese culture he held a particular station that was determined by nobility of blood, Buddhist enlightenment, and Confucian virtue. Moreover, these stations or classes in which men found themselves were regarded as the natural strata of society, necessary to the life of the whole state. This theory of society, it will be noted, would not harmonize easily with *laissez-faire* capitalism, with theoretical communism, or with democracy.

The Union of Religion and Politics

Although the separation of church and state dated back to the beginnings of American history, the principle was maintained only at the price of constant vigilance by the democratic community. In Japan, again in contrast, church and state were regarded as one, or, to put the matter as the Japanese saw it, politics was a phase of ethics. The Japanese sovereign, descended directly from the gods, was both priest and emperor to his people. He was also a manifestation of the spirit of Buddhism. Confucianism, taken over by the Japanese from China, pictured him as the exponent of the Will of Heaven. In a word, good and just government could not be independent of Heaven's Will, nor could it arise from any source other than Heaven's sovereign whose ideas obviously could not be subject to question, since God was on his side.

Freedom under constitutional law is a familiar concept to young American students, for it is the ideal of the American system of government. It stresses regulation arrived at in democratic fashion through the legislative process. It implies that law is the essential factor in safeguarding equal opportunity and the common good. A traditionally minded Japanese, however, did not see good government in this light. Because of his indoctrination with unity, inequality, and ethics, he looked to man as the answer to good government. In other words, it was the will of the sovereign that was important to the welfare of society. Laws were simply an expression of what the sovereign believed to be best at a given time. Their purpose could not be the protection of individual freedom because it would violate the principle of unity. Furthermore, a society based on inequality meant that there were rulers and those who were ruled. Written law was considered a guide to the former rather than a protection of the latter. Since rulers were men of superior virtue, their judgment was also superior to any fixed and arbitrary rule or law.

With the foregoing principles in mind, the student will more readily see the Japanese analogy between the family and the state in terms of governmental theory and practice. In both all members were supposed to subordinate themselves to the interests of the whole. The result would be unity. In both, each member was expected to accept his particular station with its particular responsibilities and rights. Here was inequality according to status. The head was expected to rule with superior virtue, and therefore with equity. Such was the theory. But in Japan, as in other lands, performance was often far short of the ideal. Nevertheless, it must be remembered that this Japanese political faith was even more hallowed by habit and indoctrination in the Japanese mind than contrasting democratic ideals have been in the minds of Americans, and, as a result, the Japanese struggle to break politically with the past has been particularly difficult.

Moreover, these traditional Japanese political principles provide a key to an understanding of what the Meiji leadership was attempting to do. Because Meiji Japan had set her course vigorously toward modernization, the West often assumed that the result would be a Westernized Japanese state expressing itself through democratic principles and institutions.

However, the leadership of the Restoration movement was directed by able young *samurai* convinced that their own political power, as well as the safety of the state, could best be assured by the material products of modern industry and by the political ideals of an ancient and in part mythological past. Accordingly, while industrialization was fostered by all modern techniques, including government ownership and subsidization, "the system of beliefs and values . . . was pushed back, as it were, to an earlier age." A modern system of communication and education, employing thought control, propaganda, and censorship, was used to counter democratic ideals surging in from the West, and to revitalize traditional notions on unity, inequality, government by man, and the patriarchal state.[7]

This dual course, dictated by the Meiji leadership, toward what was materially modern but spiritually ancient has, of course, been present in varying degree in all modern societies. In Meiji Japan, as the student is aware, freedom of speech and of investigation asserted themselves stubbornly. Nevertheless, the material success of the Meiji leaders and their resulting and growing prestige enabled them to insist on public orthodoxy in social and political matters. At no time was the atmosphere congenial to freedom of thought, to free public discussion, or to the formation of political parties that might challenge the views of the oligarchs. The appearance, therefore, of political associations in mid-nineteenth-century Japan must

[7] For an effective treatment in detail, see Nobutaka Ike, *The Beginnings of Political Democracy in Japan* (Baltimore, 1950), 195-201.

be examined through Japanese eyes, not as they might appear to an American hoping to see democracy arise in Japan.

Meiji political parties were associations rather than parties. Parties in the true sense of the word only exist where there is a keen *public* consciousness—a sense of the *public* and the *public welfare* or of *society* and its welfare. These concepts as Americans understand them did not exist in Japan, where, in place of "public servants," there was something quite different, namely, the emperor's officials, and where a man's obligations were to family and to state but not to society. When a man did step outside of the circle of family and state, he tended to be on an uncharted road with no sign-posts to guide him. In these circumstances he tended to fall back on a pattern which he did understand—the pattern of the family. He sought the protection and security of some prominent individual. There was thus established between the two a sort of son and father relationship, as in the family. The existence of this kind of relationship bore heavily, of course, on the character of Japan's political parties.

Some of the consequences as far as political parties were concerned may be summarized briefly. The acceptance of principles held in common had less bearing on an association of this kind than did general congeniality or birth in the same town. Obedience to the leader was far more important than discussion, analysis of issues, and the taking of a stand because it represented principle. Since criticism was not welcome, there was little room for individual responsibility. Therefore, despite the fact that feudalism was abolished formally in 1871, the essential character of the relationship between feudal lord and retainer lingered on in the new Japan and placed its stamp on the political parties.

The Disintegrating Family Structure

It is not proper, however, to dismiss the subject of Meiji political parties by saying that they were mere relics of familial relations and feudalism. In the Meiji period and even after it, these influences were undoubtedly dominant, but they were not exclusive. The Meiji leaders, to be sure, attempted to reimpose family structure and discipline of the *samurai* type on the entire population. In this, they enjoyed a large measure of success, but the success was not unqualified. One explanation is apparent. Industrialization and population growth created a shifting population, disrupting the compact family circle. During and after Meiji, rural Japan had a higher birth rate than urban Japan, yet rural population remained relatively stationary. With young men and women flocking to the city, family ties were weakened though by no means destroyed. Meiji literature was filled with the resulting conflict between family and individual.

The means by which traditional Japanism was made the inspiration of Meiji's modernization was best exemplified in the use made of the old and indigenous cult of Shinto. From the beginning of Meiji there was a conscious, deliberate, and organized effort not only to perpetuate old cultural values but also to give them new strength. These efforts created in the late nineteenth and twentieth centuries (perhaps it would be better to say re-created) out of Japan's mythological past a foundation for the modern Japanese state that was essentially religious in character. Marked by a high degree of organization and formalization, these religious foundations were clothed with a sanctity that made them immune to free debate or criticism. Since they were concerned essentially with the political origins of the state, their authority could be invoked at all times to stifle criticism and thereby negate the principles of democratic practices. This state religion, so intimately a part of modern Japanese nationalism, was commonly known as State or Pure Shinto to distinguish it from popular sectarian cults of Shinto that had no formal official standing.

THE NATURE OF STATE SHINTO

For many centuries after its early, simple flowering, Shinto had been all but submerged by Buddhism, just as was Confucianism in China. But, with the rise of military feudalism, Shinto, taking on a new intellectual vigor, not only freed itself by degree from Buddhist control but even asserted its superiority over Buddhism. This regeneration of Shinto, strongly nationalistic, sang the praises of early Japan as it was before the coming of Confucianism and Buddhism. In Tokugawa times, although the shoguns patronized Chinese learning and although Buddhism was the established religion, Shinto scholars nevertheless were able to revive interest in the *Kojiki,* to make it a Bible of nationalism and a proof of Japan's unique superiority. During the early nineteenth century, the popular appeal of the Shinto myths was revealed in the rise of numbers of Shinto sects which eventually attracted many millions of adherents from among the common people, thus testifying to the inadequacy of modern Japanese Buddhism as a popular religious vehicle. One of the early decisions of the Meiji leaders involved the disestablishment of Buddhism and the re-establishing and revitalizing of Shinto. An Office of Shinto Affairs became one of the highest organs of the new state. By this means it was possible to reinvigorate Shinto and to use it consciously as the spiritual foundation of the new national state.

The nationalistic values in Shinto mythology were exploited to the full. From Japan's ancient myths re-emerged a pantheon of deities headed by the Sun Goddess, who was now ministered to by thousands of priests at tens of thousands of sacred places. Elaborate ceremonies, along with sacred texts and their dogmas, completed the picture of an institutionalized and official religion of the great and unique family state. The dogma of State Shinto cannot be treated here in detail, but its character may be suggested by three essential tenets of this politico-religious faith.

The first was the dogma, extolled in the first and third articles of the Meiji Constitution, of unbroken, divine, imperial sovereignty. The emperor was divine because he was the living embodiment of the divine ancestors of the race.

The second dogma of State Shinto, closely related to the first, was the belief in Japan as the land of the gods. Here the concept was that Japan, far from being merely the product of ordinary geographical and historical forces, was peculiarly endowed with grace by the divine ancestors. The very existence of this dogma was not unrelated to the fact that the Japanese as a race are an exceedingly sensitive people, peculiarly conscious of themselves as Japanese.

The third dogma was the belief in Japan's benevolent mission or destiny. Modern Japanese were taught that the land of the gods, uniquely formed, was possessed of a divine mission to extend its righteous sovereignty over less fortunate peoples. This idea became the national doctrine of Japan, the savior of mankind.

It need hardly be stressed further that the dogma of divine descent, of the land of the gods, and of benevolent destiny, all served to reinforce traditional Japanese political thought, and, by so doing, to create a climate inhospitable to democratic ideas.[8]

---

[8] The subject of Shinto nationalism is treated in great detail in D. C. Holtom, *Modern Japan and Shinto Nationalism* (Chicago, 1943, rev. ed., 1947).

Imports from the West: Economics

Although the Meiji period, for all its profound changes, was built on political foundations that were peculiarly Japanese, the occasion for these changes was the impact of the West and the response of the Japanese to this impact. When, after 1865, the question of exclusion and seclusion was no longer a political issue, and when in 1868 the Charter Oath proclaimed that "wisdom and knowledge shall be sought in all parts of the world," Japanese students turned to things Western with a boundless and often undiscriminating enthusiasm. This crusade in search of Western learning was at first directed mainly to those fields of learning considered most essential in creating a modern state: Western ideas and techniques in economics, finance, and commerce. Free trade versus protection was a lively issue among Japanese policy-makers as early as the decade of 1870. It was resolved finally in favor of protection under German and American influence, especially through the writings of Friedrich List (*National System of Political Economy*), and the ideas of Henry Charles Carey (*Principles of Social Science*). Moreover, interest in Western economic thought and its systems stimulated research in Japan's own economic history which was at first carried on by the government but later developed by independent scholars.

Philosophy and Law

General Western philosophy and science were also introduced in the early years of Meiji. Leaders in Japanese thought read John Stuart Mill (*System of Logic*), Jeremy Bentham (*Principles of Morals and Legislation*) and widely in the writings of Herbert Spencer (*Social Statistics*), whose advice, particularly on sociological matters, was often sought by the Meiji government. The influence of German idealistic philosophy was felt particularly after 1880 through the works of Nietzsche, Schopenhauer, and Hegel. In psychology Spencer's *Principles* were well known. In law, the Tokyo Imperial University, founded in 1886, offered instruction in English, French, and German jurisprudence. Japan's pioneer student in the field of constitutional and administrative law was Hozumi Yatsuka, and in international law Ariga Nagas, later well known in the West. In the drafting of Japan's modern criminal code French influence was strong, since a French jurist, Gustave Boissanade, was legal adviser to the government. The later civil code, however, was framed under German direction, and a German scholar at Tokyo Imperial University, Herman Roessler, was adviser to the drafting committee for the Constitution of 1889. Also, the legal framework for local government was patterned in some degree on the Prussian system as outlined for the Japanese by Albert Mosse.

History and Science

In their search for the secrets of Western progress, the Japanese also turned to Western historical literature: Guizot's *History of Civilization in Europe,* and Buckle's *History of Civilization in England.* During the Tokugawa period Japan had learned something of Western medicine through the Dutch at Deshima (Drs. Carl Thunberg and Philip Franz von Siebold). Japanese interest was further stimulated in 1860 by Dr. J. C. Hepburn, the first American medical missionary in Japan. After 1871, with the appointment of two German doctors to the faculty of Tokyo Imperial University, the influence of German medical science was pronounced.

Christian Missions and Education

Even before the Restoration government removed in 1873 the two-centuries old ban against Christianity, British and American Protestant missionaries in some numbers had been well received. In 1875 the founding of Doshisha English School (later Doshisha University) in Kyoto marked the beginnings of Christian education by Japanese converts. Five additional Christian schools and colleges had been founded by 1890. At first the Christian movement was welcome, perhaps for itself but also because it contributed to Westernization. In time it met opposition from: (1) advocates of English empiricism who taught evolution and agnosticism, (2) zealots of Buddhism and Shintoism, and (3) extreme disciples of the new nationalism who held that Westernization was being carried too far. Although Christian theology made only a limited imprint in Meiji Japan, the influence of Chrstian principles of social responsibility and humanitarianism was, though indeterminate, by no means inconsiderable. In particular it was a revitalizing force upon Japanese Buddhism.

New Customs in a Bewildered Society

The social and intellectual temper of Japanese life from 1870 to 1900 was not only complex; it was also subject to constant and bewildering change. In the earlier years there was, as indicated, a mad mania for Westernization: a willingness to replace everything that was native with anything that was foreign. Confusion in thought was followed by confusion and contradiction in action. The dictum of the Charter Oath of 1868 that "absurd customs" would be discarded was at first taken very literally. Class distinctions were abolished. Buddhist priests were told to take wives, to raise families, and to eat beef. Since beef eating was common in the West, it was inferred that it must be a symbol of advanced civilization. Married women and former court nobles (kuge) were told to stop blackening their teeth and shaving their eyebrows. For men, the Western haircut, instead of long hair done in a top knot, came to symbolize that the wearer was modern and progressive. Former *samurai* gradually gave up the wearing of their swords.

Particularly in the early years of their new contacts with the West, the Japanese showed a deep sensitivity to Western opinion. Since they were determined to be well thought of by the "more advanced" Europeans and Americans, there was a general scramble to discard or to hide institutions and customs that might subject them to ridicule or moral scorn by the foreigners. Abortion and infanticide, both common practices in Tokugawa times, for quite understandable reasons, were now prohibited. Mixed bathing at public bath houses, the social clubs of feudal times, met a similar fate.

By 1885, however, although the mania for things Western remained strong, it was countered by a conservative reaction—a demand for the preservation of Japanese values. On the eve of the constitutional era nationalism had come of age. Western influence was still strong, but it was no longer unopposed.

Literature and the Arts

Because the Meiji period was one of planned Westernization it was natural that in the early years its literature was centered on translations of European and American works. Many of the translators were not professional writers but students of politics, economics, and government, and the first translations were from the classics in these fields. In time literary as well as political and economic classics appeared in Japanese: *Ernest Maltravers, Hamlet, Aesop's Fables, The Lady of the Lake, The Arabian Nights, Julius Caesar,* and a host of others. In time these Western masterpieces together with the fast march of events in Japan itself produced a new creative Japanese literature. Side by side, too, with Westernization came a literary reaching back to the ideals of *Bushido* as extolled in *kabuki.*

The Temper of Meiji Japan

It must be clear that Meiji Japan compresses itself into no easy historical nutshell. Indeed, it has much in common with Stephen Leacock's hero who rode off in all directions. This is not to imply that there was no purpose in the Meiji revolution. In fact, the purpose—to enable Japan to overtake the West and become overnight a powerful national state—was never in doubt. If there were confusions and contradictions, these were the natural garments of a people torn between the old and the new, between what was indigenous and what was foreign, between a native heritage they understood and alien cultures they could scarcely comprehend. Historically, the point to observe is that before the turn of the nineteenth century the pattern of the new Japan had been made and applied. In material things and purposes it was a modern and even a Western Japan, where politics was constitutional, where wages replaced kinship and loyalty, and where businessmen wore coats and trousers instead of the kimono. At the same time, the leaders directing this revolution were men of the *samurai* tradition, and they preserved and invigorated that tradition as the moral and spiritual foundation of the new nation.

An understanding of late nineteenth century Japan involves among many problems the measurement of Western penetration and influence. This task is beset by many pitfalls. For example, it has often been assumed that Germany provided Ito with the model for the Meiji constitution. Certainly, Ito saw merits in the German structure, but it should not be forgotten, as Sir George Sansom notes, that Japan, it would seem, even without the German experience to draw upon, would have produced a political system almost precisely like the one adopted.[9] In Meiji Japan, Westernization and modernization were not always the same thing.

For Further Reading

Allen, G. C., *Modern Japan and Its Problem* (New York, 1928). Excellent essays on many aspects of Japanese life.

———, *A Short Economic History of Modern Japan, 1867-1937* (London, 1946). The best short economic history.

Causton, E. E. N., *Militarism and Foreign Policy in Japan* (London, 1936). Valuable background material.

Ike Nobutaka, "Western Influence on the Meiji Restoration," *Pacific Historical Review,* XVII, February, 1948, 1-10. Develops the political hopes of the last shogun to preserve his power.

Itani Zenichi, "The Economic Causes of the Meiji Restoration," *Transactions of the Asiatic Society of Japan,* 2nd series, vol. XVII, 1938, pp. 193-207.

Kincaid, Zoe, *Kabuki, the Popular Stage of Japan* (London, 1925). A detailed study based on secondary sources.

Kishimoto Hideo, *Japanese Religion in the Meiji Era,* trans. and adapted by John F. Howes (Tokyo, 1956). A survey covering all religions.

Kokusai Bunka Shinkokai, *Introduction to Contemporary Japanese Literature* (Tokyo, 1939).

Kublin, Hyman, "The 'Modern' Army of early Meiji Japan," *Far Eastern Quarterly,* IX, 1949, pp. 20-41.

Kunitomo Tadao, *Japanese Literature Since 1868* (Tokyo, 1938).

Lockwood, William, *The Economic Development of Japan: Growth and Structural Change, 1868-1938* (Princeton, 1954). An erudite and comprehensive pioneer work.

Okazaki Yoshie and V. H. Viglielmo, *Japanese Literature in the Meiji Era* (Tokyo, 1955).

Smith, Thomas C., *Political Change and Industrial Development in Japan: Government Enterprise, 1868-1880* (Stanford, 1955). Emphasis on the role of the middle-class peasantry.

Takekoshi Yosaburo, *Economic Aspects of the History of the Civilization of Japan* (3 vols., London, 1930). Rich in significant materials.

---

[9] Sir George Sansom, *The Western World and Japan* (New York, 1950), 358-363.

14 China: *1860–1890*

Cold Wars for Hot

In returning to the story of the Western impact on China, it will be remembered that the years 1840 to 1860 had confronted the Ch'ing dynasty with unprecedented crises in its relations with the Western powers. Within the compass of twenty years China had suffered humiliating defeat in the so-called Opium War and the *Arrow* War, had seen its capital invaded by British and French armies, and, far more significant, had pledged itself in treaties to conform to a theory of international relations founded on a concept of equal and sovereign states. To put the matter in other words, Manchu-Chinese society in 1860 was faced with the business of revolutionizing its outlook upon and its approach to the "barbarian" society of the West. In reality, the Ch'ing dynasty had no alternative other than to meet and comply in some measure with the demand for a new world. The record of how China sought in the late nineteenth century to adjust to these new facts of life is a story of consuming interest and complexity. In the interest of understanding, it will be presented here in two parts. This chapter will discuss some aspects of China's diplomacy in the three decades after 1860, her problems with the powers and what was done about them. In the next chapter some attention will be given to the inner intellectual revolution within the Chinese mind. What impress, if any, was made by the Western impact on China's traditional values, on her hopes for the future, and on how they might be achieved?

In 1861, as the first ministers of the treaty powers took up their residence in Peking, it seemed that the days of the Manchu dynasty might well be numbered. Nevertheless, the end of the dynasty was not yet to be. Indeed, during the T'ung-chih period (1862-1874), there was a short dynastic revival called the "Restoration." This

"Restoration" must therefore be examined in the context of the continuing pressures of the Western treaty powers on the coast and of the T'ai-p'ing rebels in the interior.

Peking in 1860 was a "deserted" city—deserted by its emperor and his court. The Imperial entourage had fled to the mountains of Jehol when the British and French advanced on the capital. When the panic passed, the Court had to return to set up an administration capable of enforcing the new treaties of 1858 and 1860. To this nervous capital came also, in the spring of 1861, Frederick Bruce and M. de Bourboulon, the British and French Ministers, respectively. Anson Burlingame, the new American Minister, arrived a few months later. These ministers were permitted to set up permanent residence in Peking, but when a representative of Prussia appeared, the Chinese, although granting him the commercial privileges won by the treaty powers, refused him residence at the capital. This refusal was significant because it revealed the power still exercised by the extreme anti-foreign party at court. Even while members of this court were in virtual exile at Jehol in 1860, they still clamored for the impossible—the execution of all foreign prisoners. It was evident then that many members of the nobility had not learned the lesson that the *Arrow* War was supposed to have taught.

The newly arrived envoys of the Western powers were met in Peking by I-hsin, usually known as Prince Kung (1833-1898), a half-brother of the fugitive Hsien-feng emperor who had been left behind to deal as he could with the victorious British and French. Faced with the humiliation of signing the supplementary conventions of 1860, Prince Kung was convinced that China had no alternative but "to act according to the treaties and not allow the foreigners to go even slightly beyond them." His conclusion combined both wisdom and naivete: wisdom in seeing that the treaties must be accepted and observed; naivete in the assumption that the powers would remain satisfied with what the treaties contained.

To implement this new policy of treaty observance there was created, on the recommendation of Prince Kung and with imperial sanction, the Tsungli Yamen, a special body under the Grand Council which was to deal with all matters relating to the Western powers. The creation of this special board, which was often staffed with able and powerful officials, was a major step toward a ministry of foreign affairs (Wai-wu-pu), which was not established until 1901. Prince Kung, although not a statesman of great stature, had sensed the futility of China's blind resistance. Accordingly, as head of the Tsungli Yamen, he set about to improve relations with the foreign ministers in Peking, organized the beginnings of a Westernized Manchu army, revitalized if he did not reform the Peking administration, acted as regent for the child T'ung-chih emperor (1862-1874), and until his dismissal from the Tsungli Yamen in 1884 directed his influence toward maintaining peace with the Western powers on the theory that only through peace could China gain strength. A vital weakness in Prince Kung's policy was his inability, for reasons that will be apparent later, to reassert the influence of Peking in the provinces after the defeat of the T'ai-p'ings. Nor was Prince Kung able to free himself wholly from the stifling influences of an ignorant, retrograde, and anti-foreign Manchu court.[1]

The Collapse and Defeat of the T'ai-p'ing Rebellion

The T'ai-p'ing rebels had continued to threaten the life of the Manchu dynasty from 1851 until 1863, the years in which the pressure of the foreign powers on the coast had been most severe. The rebellion, as the reader is aware, had its origins in economic and social conditions within China and in pseudo-Christian influence deriving from the Western impact. Since this rebellion was the opening phase of the revolutionary process that possessed China in the twentieth century and culminated in the rise of Chinese communism, its basic foundations and the reasons for its failure are noteworthy.

The causes of the rebellion, exceedingly complex, may be summarized briefly. Basic to the revolutionary process were economic, mili-

[1] Something of the atmosphere of this court is suggested by events of 1861. The Hsien-feng emperor, a mental and physical degenerate, had died at Jehol in August. Two court factions seeking control promptly appeared. The one was headed by reactionary Manchu princes; the other by an equally reactionary and anti-foreign concubine who in 1856 had borne the sovereign his first and only son. Anti-foreignism, characteristic of the Court during the entire Hsien-feng period, left ample room for factionalism, and so it came about that under the influence of her enemies, the emperor had at his death named an administration from which she and Prince Kung were excluded. These circumstances drove the former concubine, now the junior Empress Dowager Tz'u-hsi, and Prince Kung to join forces. The princes were ruthlessly crushed. Since Prince Kung had saved the throne for her son, Tz'u-hsi repressed her violent anti-foreign views, perhaps in gratitude, perhaps because it was expedient. Such was the uneasy court alliance on which Prince Kung was required to base his policy of peace with the powers.

tary, and social infections arising from a common source that may best be described as chronic and general political corruption. Political resentment against the alien Manchus, and their harsh conquest, again found expression in the old Chinese cyclical theory of a period of peace followed by a period of disorder. Rebellion against Manchu oppression, against official "squeeze" of public funds, was regarded as justified and inevitable, and found its traditional expression in secret revolutionary societies. Between 1774 and the outbreak of the First Anglo-Chinese war of 1840 some scores of secret societies had fomented rebellions that touched almost every province of China. All had been suppressed, with great slaughter. These movements were the forerunners of the T'ai-p'ing rebellion. Political discontent was aggravated by economic depression, by the accumulation of land in large holdings, by the concentration of grain in the hands of merchants who could hold it until the price was right, by an increase in population without a corresponding increase in crop land, and by the consequent growth of a rabble of paupers, brigands, and criminals. The First Anglo-Chinese War had completed this picture of social instability by destroying the last shreds of morale of the Chinese army, so much so that retreat on the eve of battle was considered standard procedure. In these appalling conditions lay the opportunity for the T'ai-p'ings.

The failure of the T'ai-p'ing revolt cannot be ascribed to a single cause. Like the Manchus whom they sought to overthrow, the T'ai-p'ing leadership found the recesses of the harem more congenial than the edifice of political reform. Beginning as the promoters of a social-economic revolution against the traditional and decadent Confucian order, they were themselves recaptured by the traditions and the abuses against which they fought: provincialism, familism, and nepotism. Indeed, the loss of their revolutionary ardor coincided with the revival of dynastic spirit at Peking under Prince Kung. Moreover, the T'ai-p'ings did not solve the problem of recruiting and training young leaders to perpetuate the new order. In addition T'ai-p'ing military strategy was weak. During the northern march it failed to concentrate on Peking when the capital was in panic. The later T'ai-p'ing attacks in 1860 and 1862 on Shanghai only served to encourage foreign assistance to the imperial forces. Finally, the T'ai-p'ings failed in leadership and in education to convert either the scholars or the peasants to the new ideology—a curious mingling of Christian, Confucian, and Taoist ideas encrusted with a primitive communism. In a society that had always been ruled by ideological controls rather than by rules of law, this failure was fatal.[2]

If China was slow in meeting the threat of the T'ai-p'ing, she was not wholly without resolve. It was the T'ai-p'ing revolt that brought into prominence two of China's all too few great nineteenth-century leaders, Tsêng Kuo-fan of Hunan and Li Hung-chang of Anhui. These men, unlike so many of their colleagues, had fought the rebellion from its beginnings; but it was not until after 1860 that they achieved, with foreign assistance, any major success.

Among the foreigners who entered the Chinese military service to fight the T'ai-p'ing were Frederick Townsend Ward, an American soldier of fortune of Salem, Massachusetts, organizer of a Chinese force known as the "Ever Victorious Army"; and Major Charles George Gordon of the British army, who took command of the "Ever Victorious Army" in 1863 after Ward's death. The military campaigns of Tsêng, Li, and their foreign colleagues, together with the aid of the British and the French governments, resulted in the slow but sure destruction of the rebel military power on the lower Yangtze. The city of Soochow, one of the strongest rebel bastions, fell in December, 1863. One year later the T'ai-p'ing "Heavenly King," debauched and degenerate, committed suicide when his capital Nanking fell before the armies of Tsêng Kuo-fan. So ended the T'ai-p'ing Rebellion. During its course through the middle decades of the century, twelve of the richest provinces were devastated, some 20 million people were exterminated, and poverty and despair made an unprecedented conquest. In short, the movement was an agrarian revolt, a religious and moral movement, and a rebellion against a dynasty that appeared to have lost the Mandate of Heaven. In some respects the rebellion played a decisive part in the relations of China and the West. It helped to encourage European intervention in China. For instance, the conclusion of the treaties of 1858 and 1860 stamped the T'ai-p'ings as rebels. They could be regarded no longer as potential allies of the Western powers, nor as potential successors to the Manchus. Furthermore, the indemnities for the *Arrow* War depended on the fate of the Peking dynasty.[3] These were

[2] Ssŭ-yü Têng, *New Light on the History of the Taiping Rebellion* (Cambridge, 1950), especially 35-73. Eugene P. Boardman, *Christian Influence upon the Ideology of the Taiping Rebellion, 1851-1864* (Madison, 1952), especially 41-105.

[3] G. E. Taylor, "The Taiping Rebellion," *Chinese Social and Political Science Rev.*, XVI (1933), 612-614; W. J. Hail, *Tsêng Kuo-fan and the Taiping Rebellion* (New Haven, 1927), 290.

not inconsequential factors in the decision of the foreign powers to intervene in support of the moribund Manchu rule.

China's Military Establishment

The final suppression of the T'ai-p'ings after more than a decade of unspeakable pillage and suffering is a reminder that the Confucian dynasty, which had already suffered military defeat by the British (1842) and by the British and French (1858-1860), had narrowly escaped destruction from domestic foes. How, then, had it come to pass that Peking could show so little capacity to meet her enemies at home or from abroad? This question involves some probing into the history of China's military establishment.

When the crises of the mid-nineteenth century befell China, her military establishment, set up by the Manchus some two centuries earlier, was all but useless as a fighting force. Prior to the conquest of China (1644), the Manchus had been organized in military-administrative groups, known as "banners," that served the civil and economic as well as the military activities of the Manchu rulers. After the conquest of China, the Manchus sought to rule their new subjects in a Chinese way while, at the same time, preserving their own identity as Manchus. The banner organization was thus maintained and banner garrisons were placed throughout the Empire. These garrisons were heaviest about Peking, along the northwestern frontier, and in the provincial capitals and larger cities. Although some Chinese, mainly from the northern frontier, had been admitted to the banners, these military units and their families remained a class apart from the conquered people.

With the consolidation of the Manchu conquest, the bannermen emerged as a hereditary privileged military group or caste, excluded from trade and labor though not always from the civil service. Like the *samurai* in Japan under the Tokugawa dictatorship, they were perpetuated through generations of comparative peace, losing their character and capacity as warriors and lapsing into the role of "tragic and useless idlers."

The Manchus had also maintained in the provinces a second and Chinese military force known as the Army of the Green Standard. This force was descended from certain Chinese armies that had assisted the Manchus during the conquest. Some of these forces had been taken into the Banners, but for the most part, especially in the south, they remained separate and formed the beginnings of a separate Chinese army under the Manchu rule and closely controlled by Peking.

Some of the Green Standard was used to assist the Banner garrisons on the northwestern frontier or to help suppress rebellious factions in various parts of the Empire, but the far greater portion appeared to be devoted to the detection and prevention of robbery and other crimes, of protecting government property, or of escorting criminals from one locale to another. The Green Standard could thus hardly be counted an army as the West understood that term. Nevertheless, it was an integral part of the central bureaucratic administration through which the Manchus ruled China, and in the earlier and more vigorous years of the Dynasty the Green Standard had served understandable purposes.

As the leadership and competence of the Manchu dynasty declined in the late eighteenth and the nineteenth centuries, the military services, both the bannermen and the Green Standard, no longer served effectively the original purposes for which they were designed, and were next to useless against the guns and disciplined troops of the Western powers. Worst of all, corruption had sapped the services of whatever morale they once possessed. As the dynasty no longer led the nation, so the officers of the Green Standard no longer led their troops. It had become common practice for officers to use their men as servants, to ride in sedan chairs when an infrequent march was undertaken, to withhold soldiers' pay for their own use, to charge the government for companies at full strength when actually no more than a handful of men were really in service. In times of emergency or for purposes of some official inspection, units were hastily recruited to full strength by gathering in a rabble of bandits, idlers, and criminals who could be discharged just as promptly once the inspectors had moved on. Thus it was that Chinese diplomacy at Nanking in 1842 and at Tientsin and Peking in 1858 and 1860, respectively, operated in a vacuum: there was no effective military power behind it. This same lack of military power also had much to do with the early successes of the T'ai-p'ings and with their ability to remain in occupation of so much of central China long after their movement had lost direction and momentum.

As some few abler members of China's ruling class, the scholar gentry, witnessed this spectacle of crisis, it would seem that it was rebellion at home rather than the barbarian in the Treaty Ports that occasioned the more intense alarm. The immediate, and presumably the ultimate, purpose of the barbarians was trade, and this, it was assumed, could eventually be confined and controlled, whereas the T'ai-p'ing rebels, entrenched in the heart of China, were pseudo-Christian, anti-Confucian, anti-Manchu, and thus a positive and immediate threat not only to the established governmental system but also to the personal vested interests of all who enjoyed the favor of those in power. Against this threatened calamity, some members of the official scholar gentry were moved to action in the interest of the dynasty, of the social-political system, and of their own stake therein.

In the beginning the resultant movement to create regional armies was nothing more than an effort by some of the gentry to organize local militia for the defense of their home communities against the T'ai-p'ings. Since the regular troops, the bannermen and the Green Standard, had failed to destroy the rebels, the central government was in the unhappy position where it must accept and even encourage this kind of local initiative. Accordingly, in 1852 the emperor ordered Tsêng Kuo-fan, who had a reputation for scholarship and experience as an official at Peking, to organize forces in his native Hunan to fight the T'ai-p'ings. In a Confucian society Tsêng's lack of military background was considered no drawback. He soon justified the Confucian theory that scholarship and virtue fit a man for any public service. His Hunan army, as it came to be known, was built on quality rather than numbers. His recruits were hardy loyal peasants, not the dregs of the slums and jails. Moreover, these soldiers were well paid and were led by officers selected for character and ability to lead. Early in its career this army gained its first battle training suppressing banditry in its home province, Hunan. This strategy gave Tsêng control of the province from which his financial support had to come, demonstrated to the populace the value of the army, and guaranteed the necessary replacements in troops. Moreover, what was done by Tsêng in Hunan was repeated by Li Hung-chang in Anhui and by Tso Tsung-t'ang, Chou Sheng-po, and Sung Ch'ing in other areas.[4]

---

[4] Among the important studies on the military power under the Manchus is Franz Michael, *The Origin of Manchu Rule in China* (Baltimore, 1942). On the new military leaders of the nineteenth century, see Arthur W. Hummel, ed., *Eminent Chinese of the Ch'ing Period, 1644-1912,* 2 vols. (Washington, D.C., 1943). On politico-military aspects during the T'ai-p'ing rebellion, see Franz Michael, "Military Organization and Power Structure of China during the Taiping Rebellion," *Pacific Historical Review,* XVIII (1949), 469-483; James T. K. Wu, "The Impact of the Taiping Rebellion on the Manchu Fiscal System," *Pacific Historical Review,* XIX (1950) 265-275; and Ralph L. Powell, *The Rise of Chinese Military Power, 1895-1912* (Princeton, 1955).

Implications of Regional Militarism

It was armies such as these which, bolstered with some foreign assistance, finally destroyed the incubus of the T'ai-p'ing. The military importance of these armies in preserving the life of the Manchu dynasty was thus immediate and apparent. It was not so apparent, of course, that while these armies were saving the dynasty from the T'ai-p'ings they were not saving the dynasty from itself. This was so because, unlike the traditional armies, the banners and the Green Standard, which were closely integrated with the central political authority, the new nineteenth-century armies were not one national army; they were regional armies recruited from and financed by local areas. The financing of these armies by the local authorities who organized them meant that new sources of revenue had to be found by these same local authorities. One such source was a new tax called *likin* (literally one thousandth). *Likin* was a commercial tax on goods in transit imposed and collected by provincial or other local authorities.

The point to be noted in particular is that Peking had little part in conceiving, directing, or controlling these matters. China was saved from the T'ai-p'ings, but it was not the dynasty that did the saving. All that was left for Peking was to acquiesce in what local leaders of initiative were doing by appointing them, as Prince Kung did, as governors or governors-general of provinces, and by placing its seal of approval on their selection of subordinates, on the local laws they passed, and on the taxes they collected. This meant, in a word, that Peking was losing its power of control as the local and regional administration was being taken over by provincial leaders of the new militia armies, which were loyal to their local commanders. It meant, in addition, that after 1860 the nice balance which the dynasty had maintained between Manchu and Chinese officials began rapidly to favor the Chinese, many but not all of whom were of the scholar-official class. From 1861 to 1890 the number of Manchu governors-general appointed was ten, while the number of Chinese was thirty-four. Manchu governors appointed during the same period numbered thirteen, while the Chinese totalled 104.

The conclusion is inescapable that the structure of political power within China was altered radically during and following the T'ai-p'ing period. The centralized military organization effective in the early years of the dynasty had lost its practical power. Actual power, no longer centralized, was diffused at the military level in various provincial and therefore local areas. With this diffusion of military authortity went also a comparable diffusion of fiscal authority and ultimately of Peking's administrative control. A governor or governor-general who owed his position to a local army, to local taxation, and to his control of local administration was not a mere servant of the dynasty. These beginnings in a conflict between centralism and regionalism were to continue, and in the twentieth century they were to have far-reaching results. These shiftings within China in the politico-military focus of power had a very direct bearing on China's relations with the foreign powers. The military impotence of Peking was a constant invitation to the Treaty Powers to take advantage of China's treaty violations to demand further treaty concessions.

The Co-operative Policy, 1861-1867

Nevertheless, in a number of ways the years following the Peking settlement of 1860 gave promise of peaceful and constructive adjustment in China's relation with the powers. This was due very largely to the personalities of the four principal ministers who had established their legations in Peking: Anson Burlingame of the United States; Sir Frederick Bruce of Great Britain; M. Berthemy of France; and General L. de Balluseck of Russia, known popularly as the "Four B's." In this group Burlingame soon achieved a leadership that was the more remarkable because his own country was involved in civil war and because he himself was a novice in the diplomatic techniques of commercial imperialism.

Since Burlingame was under instructions to "consult and co-operate" with his diplomatic colleagues, he described for Secretary Seward in 1862 the principles through which the United States might apply a "co-operative" policy. These principles, approved by Seward, included:

1. No acquisition of Chinese territory by the United States.

2. No interference "in the political struggles of the Chinese further than to maintain our treaty rights."

3. Active assistance, in co-operation with other powers, to Chinese authorities in maintaining treaty rights against pirates, bandits, and rebels to the end that should the other powers "menace the integrity of the Chinese territory then the very fact that we had acted with

them for law and order would give us greater weight against such a policy."

To Burlingame the danger of continuing foreign aggression in China was very real.

> Here are over three hundred millions of people who are without arms—industrious, patient and wealthy and who, it is thought would be but too happy to submit to any power that would protect them.

To meet this danger Burlingame reiterated a principle already expressed by Humphrey Marshall nearly a decade earlier.

> If the treaty powers could agree among themselves to guarantee the neutrality of China and together secure order in the treaty Ports and give their moral support, at least, to that party in the Empire which would most favor a stable government—the interests of humanity would be subserved. The Treaty powers are practically doing this now, but how long they may remain in agreement it is impossible to imagine.

From 1862 until he retired as American Minister in 1867, Burlingame and his three colleagues applied the co-operative policy with notable success. In essence the policy achieved two things. First: China, confronted by united diplomatic action from the powers, was held to a stricter observance of the treaties, and this lessened the danger of resort to the gunboat policy. Second: as a result of this increased diplomatic stability, there was less temptation to individual powers to take advantage of China's weakness. The co-operative policy, so long as it was applied, served to protect China's integrity at the hands of foreign aggressors. However, China's ills in the decade of 1860 could not be laid solely at the door of foreign commercial exploitation. China also suffered grievously from a paralysis of initiative in her own bureaucracy.

Chinese Missions Abroad

Since the Ch'ing court had excluded foreign envoys from Peking until forced to admit them in 1860, it is understandable that China was not represented in the West. Yet here, too, there were signs of what the West liked to call progress. At Peking after 1860 some members of the new Tsungli Yamen sought the advice of Burlingame and other foreigners on many matters of foreign affairs. But when in return the suggestion was made that China would be better informed by sending her own diplomats abroad, it was met by a chorus of objections and excuses. Finally, in 1866, as a kind of temporary substitute for regular diplomatic intercourse, the court approved a semi-official mission headed by an elderly Manchu official of low rank, Pin-ch'un. Since he was a person of little consequence, indignities he might suffer abroad could be ignored. Pin-ch'un visited widely throughout Europe. He paid little attention to political affairs but was impressed greatly by the spotless hotels, the brightly lighted streets that did not become muddy in the rain, and by Queen Victoria "unable to act without the sanction of a parliament." Although the mission had little if any influence on its return, it was China's first modern diplomatic effort.[5]

The Burlingame Mission

Far more significant was China's invitation in 1867 to Burlingame, who was about to retire as American minister at Peking, to serve as one of China's first official envoys to the Treaty Powers. Prince Kung and his colleagues took this unprecedented action in the hope that misunderstandings might be removed, that there might be closer contact with foreign governments, and, most important, that in the approaching revision of the treaties the powers might be persuaded to show forbearance on the theory that China was already "progressing" as rapidly as could be, and that demands for further concessions would be inexpedient. Burlingame had so won the confidence of Peking that he was considered the ideal envoy to achieve these ends. Associated with him on a basis of equality in the mission were Chih Kang, a Manchu, and Sun Chia-ku, a Chinese.

The Burlingame mission was doubtless due in some measure to the fact that after 1861 Prince Kung, Wên-hsiang (his chief assistant), Tsêng Kuo-fan, and Li Hung-chang, "while no more favorably inclined toward revolutionary changes than their predecessors," were able to see that China must make adjustments to the West if she hoped to survive. Indeed 1861 was a key year. The death of the infamous Hsien-fêng emperor, and the establishment of the Tsungli Yamen opened the way for Prince Kung and others to make some limited headway against a "seemingly hopeless combination of blind conservatism and inertia." It was against this background that the Tsungli Yamen in 1867 required the provincial governors to give

---

[5] Knight Biggerstaff, "The First Chinese Mission of Investigation Sent to Europe," *Pacific Historical Review*, VI (1937), 307-320.

Peking their views on what should be done when the foreign powers pressed for further treaty revision. The replies of these officials are of importance historically, since they reveal the attitude of high Chinese officials to the problem of foreign relations in general and to specific questions in particular, and thus provide an approach to the history of China's foreign relations during the next half century. In general the views expressed in this secret correspondence with Peking in 1867-1868 are a fair indication of the rough road China was to travel in foreign affairs. For the most part the opinions from the provinces may be summarized as follows: (1) foreigners and the countries from which they came were still held in low esteem; (2) no further treaty concessions should be granted to foreign merchants; and (3) no further expansion of foreign missionary activity should be permitted. Only three high officials who engaged in this correspondence (Li Hung-chang, Tsêng Kuo-fan, and Shên Pao-chên) showed any understanding of the possible values to China of railways, telegraphs, steamships, and mining machinery. Perhaps not more than five of these officials sensed the gravity of the political problems posed for China by an aggressive and powerful Western World.[6]

The Burlingame mission was received in America with an enthusiasm not unlike that small boys accord a circus. Burlingame, an idealist and above all an orator, gave free reign to his own eloquence. He pictured China, the oldest nation, seeking Westernization and progress through America, the youngest of nations. He pictured a China that stood with arms extended to receive "the shining banners of Western civilization"—strange-sounding words to the conservative ears of Prince Kung and his associates in Peking. Many an American editor assumed that Burlingame's words meant what they said. The *Farmer's Cabinet* of Amhearst, New Hampshire, was moved to observe that China's exclusiveness was ended. This "must give an enormous development to our trade, and the interests of Christianity will be more effectively promoted by this action of the Chinese Emperor, than by any other political event of the last two centuries." Although Burlingame's intentions were of the best, he laid the foundations of a species of oratorical reporting on China that was thoroughly acceptable to an uninformed American public, for it was

---

[6] Knight Biggerstaff, "The Secret Correspondence of 1867-1868: Views of Leading Chinese Statesmen Regarding the Further Opening of China to Western Influence," *The Journal of Modern History,* XXII (1950), 122-136.

precisely what that public hoped to hear. The validity of the conclusions reached by the *Farmer's Cabinet* was not questioned.

In Washington, Burlingame and his Chinese colleagues were received by President Johnson and the Congress. Their presence, said the Speaker of the House, was a sign "of closer commercial and international intercourse." Burlingame replied that it was for the West to say whether "it was sincere when it . . . invited China to more intimate relations." Was it extending "a fair and open policy or one founded upon that assumption of superiority . . . not justified by physical ability or moral elevation."[7]

Burlingame and Secretary Seward then concluded (July 28) eight supplementary articles to the American Treaty of Tientsin. These articles provided that China might appoint consuls at United States ports, that Americans in China and Chinese in the United States should enjoy complete freedom of religion, and that rights of residence and travel were to be open to the nationals of both countries. Moreover, the United States disavowed "any intention or right to intervene in the domestic administration of China in regard to the construction of railroads, telegraphs or other material internal improvements," China being conceded the right to determine the time for such improvements; and, finally, China and the United States recognized "the inherent and inalienable right of man to change his home and allegiance. . . ."[8]

On September 19 the mission reached London, where it received Lord Clarendon's assurance that the British government would show forbearance in seeking further commercial concessions and would deal only with the central government in seeking redress for wrongs to British subjects. From London the mission visited Paris, Belgium, Prussia, Denmark, Sweden, Holland, and Russia. While in Russia, on February 23, 1870, Burlingame died of pneumonia. Meanwhile, although the foreign press in the treaty ports had heaped abuse on the mission, declaring that it did not represent the real purposes of Peking, the Chinese government did ratify the Seward-Burlingame articles, thus demonstrating its faith in an envoy who, though ex-

---

[7] *The Congressional Globe,* 2nd Sess., 40th Cong., 1867-68, 2970, 3215.

[8] For the Burlingame mission, see Knight Biggerstaff, "The Official Chinese Attitude toward the Burlingame Mission," *American Historical Review,* XLI (1936), 682-702; and Knight Biggerstaff, "A Translation of Anson Burlingame's Instructions from the Chinese Foreign Office," *Far Eastern Quarterly,* I (1942), 277-279.

ceeding the stricter limits of his instructions, had presented China's case with ability and enthusiasm.

It required another ten years, however, before the Manchu court established its first diplomatic mission in Britain (1877). This mission provided a nice example of the processes by which China was learning, slowly, to comprehend the West. When Kuo Sung-tao, the first Chinese minister at London, returned to Peking, he said, to the astonishment of his colleagues: "Confucius and Mencius have deceived us." By this he meant not that he was converted to Western ideas, but that he had learned there were ways other than the Chinese of governing civilized countries. For a distinguished Chinese official to acknowledge that there were barbarian governments untouched by Confucian culture that were both "civilized and rational" was unprecedented if not subversive. In the United States the first Chinese legation was opened in 1878 by Ch'en Lan-pin and Yung Wing, who had been in charge of an educational mission. Other legations were also established in Germany in 1877, in France in 1878, in Russia and Spain in 1879, and in Peru in 1880.

The Problem of Treaty Revision

The British Treaty of Tientsin was subject to revision in 1868, but, as already noted, Lord Clarendon had assured Burlingame that the British government would exercise forbearance. This was significant. Chinese officialdom was convinced that the treaties offered too much; the British, and most of the foreign merchants in the ports, that they conceded too little. There was always the danger, too, that attacks upon foreigners by lawless and anti-foreign elements of the Chinese populace would lead to a resumption of the gunboat policy. Americans, like all foreigners, were subject to these attacks. In 1866, for example, the American vice-consul at Newchwang in South Manchuria was entrusted with arms and ammunition so that the American community there might protect itself from armed ruffians.

Skillful diplomacy was needed if the legitimate rights of the powers were to be observed, if the uncompromising demands of the merchants were to be curbed, and if Chinese officialdom was to be convinced that its best interests would be served by educating its people to a fuller observance of the treaties. A few Chinese officials did have some understanding of all this. Li Hung-chang, for example, advocated a more progressive policy. Discarding the view that foreigners were a plague on Chinese soil, he observed with brutal frankness that "The outrageous craft and malignity of the Chinese exceeds even that of the foreigners." It was good sense for China to adopt those modern instruments of industry and politics which had given strength to the West.

The foreign merchants in the treaty ports and Hongkong also had their ideas on what should be done. They were appealing already to their home governments on the subject of treaty revision to redress their real or imagined grievances. However, Sir Rutherford Alcock, British Minister at Peking, believed that China could better be induced to adopt a progressive policy if coercion were not applied. He recognized that a moderate policy would never satisfy the merchants, and he added that they had no claim to consideration, since they refused to appreciate the difficulties of reform and progress in a land as old as China and since they themselves were guilty of "fraudulent practices and want of good faith." Accordingly, Lord Clarendon decided to delay pressing for treaty revision until 1872-1873, when the young T'ung-chih emperor would attain his majority. In this decision the other treaty powers concurred. This evidence of Western forbearance has not always been recognized.

The Development of Christian Missions

The question of treaty revision and in fact the larger problem of China's relations with the West were connected intimately with the so-called missionary problem. The reader is already familiar with some aspects of Roman Catholic missions in China during the sixteenth, seventeenth, and eighteenth centuries. In the nineteenth century, coincident with the opening of China and Japan, Protestant Christendom became active in the field of foreign missions. In 1805 the London Missionary Society sent Robert Morrison to China. He travelled on an American ship, because the English East India Company, fearful of offending the Chinese, refused him passage on a Company ship.[9] The American Bible Society also entered the field. During the first year of its work in China (1822) the Society distributed 500 copies of the New Testament. Eighty years later it was giving away more than half a million copies, including an elegantly bound edition to the far-from-pious Empress Dowager on her six-

---

[9] See K. S. Latourette, *A History of Christian Missions in China* (New York, 1929), 212.

tieth birthday. After 1830, American Protestantism was represented in China by an expanding group of churches and missionary societies.

The Treaty Status of Missionaries

Christianity and those who preached it had acquired an international legal status in China as a result of the toleration clauses of the Tientsin Treaties of 1858; the Russian and the French treaties permitted the missionaries *to travel* with passports in the interior. The Chinese text of the Franco-Chinese Convention of 1860 conceded the right of missionaries *to reside* in the interior, to acquire land, build churches, schools, etc., and to propagate Catholic doctrine without hindrance. The French text, which was the authoritative text, contained no such concession, and was kept secret from the other legations at Peking for ten years. Whatever the explanation of this discrepancy in the texts of the Franco-Chinese Convention, its effects were explained clearly by Frederick F. Low, American Minister at Peking in 1870:

> The missionaries of this [Roman Catholic] Religious Faith have, in addition to the right of residence as Bishops and Priests, assumed to occupy a semi-official position which places them on an equality with the native officers where they reside. They also claimed the right to protect the native Christians from persecution, which practically constituted the missionaries the arbiters of their disputes and the judges of their wrongful acts, and removed this class from the control of their native rulers. The absolute right of the Roman Catholic Clergy to exercise, in the name and by the authority of the French Government, a protectorate over native Christians was claimed . . . and insisted upon by some of the earlier representatives of France in China.[10]

Chinese officialdom feared and resented these pretensions of the missionaries. Not only did the official see immediate political implications involving his own power, he was also suspicious of Christianity because it was an alien and exclusive faith that was frequently in conflict with fundamental concepts of Chinese social and religious life. It will not be difficult, then, to understand how easily the ignorant and superstitious masses might be aroused to attacks upon missionaries and their property. All classes of the Chinese found ample evidence to support their distrust of the foreign mis-

[10] Low to Secretary of State, Hamilton Fish, Peking, Dec. 5, 1870. Printed in Clyde, *United States Policy toward China,* 108-112.

sionary. His fundamentalist and intolerant dogmas could scarcely be reconciled with Chinese philosophy, which was essentially tolerant, practical, and mundane. Christian love and Christian intolerance were difficult for many Chinese to reconcile. Christian theory did not seem to be practiced with much vigor by the foreign merchants in the ports. From these critical conclusions grew others less critical, born of ignorance and fanaticism. It was common belief that Christian hospitals and orphanages purchased from indigent mothers hapless infants, whose eyes were extracted to compound direful drugs which when taken converted the victim to Christianity.

From a background of such suspicion, hatred, and fear came the so-called Tientsin Massacre of 1870. A Chinese mob destroyed a Roman Catholic orphanage and adjoining church, and killed the French consul, two priests, ten nuns, three Russians, and some thirty Chinese servants. Alarm soon spread to many of the treaty ports, and French, British, and American warships appeared off Tientsin. The demands of France led to the death penalty or banishment of some of the perpetrators. China paid an indemnity of 250,000 taels and sent a mission of apology to France. Peking proposed a number of rules to govern and safeguard the work of missionaries, but only the American Minister was willing even to discuss them.

Thus less than ten years after Burlingame had reached China, and two years after negotiation of the Burlingame-Seward Treaty, the policy of patience and forbearance was headed for rough weather. The responsibility for the Tientsin Massacre cannot be laid at the door of one country or one group of individuals. It was an ugly creation of Chinese officials and agitators, and of foreign missionaries, their church, and their governments.

During the remainder of the nineteenth and on into the twentieth century China's relations with the West continued to be complicated by the political and other implications of the Christian missionary movement. A balanced picture of the missionary at work must of course give full weight to the sincerity and humanity with which the missionaries labored. Many of them lived in almost complete isolation, and sacrificed themselves willingly in the cause of Christianity. The educational and the medical work of the missions brought forth the highest praise. Nevertheless, George F. Seward, while American Minister at Peking (1876-1880), found that the majority of the grievances with which the legation was called upon to deal concerned missionaries. He regretted a situation that made the diplomatic agent of the American government the right arm of the propagandists of the Christian faith.

Treaty Revision and the Margary Affair

Foreign traders in the Far East had long speculated on the possibilities of reaching China's western provinces of Kweichow, Yünnan, and Szechuan by way of the Burma border. One expedition from British India had proceeded to Bhamo on the upper Irrawaddy in 1868; a second expedition, under the command of Colonel Horace A. Browne, was organized in 1874 to enter Yünnan. The British legation in Peking was asked to secure passports and an interpreter from the consular service. For this post Minister Wade selected Augustus Raymond Margary, who, travelling overland with six Chinese, reached Bhamo on January 17, 1875.

In February the Browne expedition left Bhamo. It was preceded by Margary and his Chinese, whose purpose was to discover whether the route might be travelled in safety. The answer to this question was given when Margary and five of his Chinese associates were killed by what seems to have been the premeditated act of armed Chinese. Responsibility for this outrage is not easily placed. The Burmese sovereign was opposed to the opening of trade routes, as were also the local Chinese authorities in Yünnan. The border tribes were irresponsible and frequently beyond Chinese control; yet the local Chinese authorities could scarcely be absolved of negligence if not connivance. What is really significant is that the murder of Margary was seized upon by British Minister Wade as an appropriate incident to be used in forcing a settlement with Peking of all outstanding Anglo-Chinese questions.

Wade formulated his demands promptly: (1) China to send a mission of investigation accompanied by British officers; (2) permission for a second expedition from India; (3) 150,000 taels to be placed at the British Minister's disposal; (4) the emperor to grant a fitting and satisfactory audience to Her Majesty's Minister; (5) British goods to be freed from all *likin* taxation; and (6) all British claims to be satisfied at once. On second thought Wade reduced his demands to the first three. In London the government approved one and two but reserved judgment on point three.

The Chinese government accepted the demands in principle but objected to the blunt manner of Wade's diplomacy. It was not until

August, 1876, that Wade met with Li Hung-chang at Chefoo, where on September 13 an agreement known as the Chefoo Convention was signed. It was ratified by China four days later, but not by Great Britain until July, 1885, which delay suggests that governments sometimes have difficulty in making up their minds.[11]

The Chefoo Convention was an impressive document embodying three sections. The first, which dealt with the Yünnan-Margary case, provided for the issuance of proclamations in the provinces, for the drawing up of regulations for the Burma-Yünnan frontier trade, for a second mission from India, for the stationing for five years of British officers at some city in Yünnan, for an indemnity of 200,000 taels for the families of those murdered, for expenses incident to the whole case, and for the claims of British merchants. Finally, China was to send a mission of apology to London.

Section two of the Convention dealt with "Official Intercourse." China was to invite the foreign powers to consider with her a code of procedure and official etiquette designed to insure proper treatment of the foreign ministers at Peking and of the consuls at the treaty ports. China was also to invite the powers to consider with her means of insuring more effective administration of justice at the treaty ports.

Section three, dealing with trade, provided for the opening of additional treaty ports (Ichang, Wuhu, Wenchow, and Pakhoi), for stationing a consul at Chungking, and for the opening of several ports of call on the Yangtze. Other clauses provided for defining more clearly the foreign settlement areas in the ports.

In general it may be said that the Chefoo Convention was a substantial supplement to Britain's treaties of 1842, 1858, and 1860, in that it secured practically all the concessions the British Minister had been demanding over a period of nearly two years, the major exception being the failure to have Viceroy Tsen and others brought to trial. However, the Convention was not well received by representatives of the other treaty powers. There were objections from the Russians, the Germans, and the French, which was a point of importance, since by the nature of its content most of the Convention required the ratification of these powers also. In general, British merchants were also opposed to it, on the ground that it would be

---

11 For text of the Chefoo Convention, see China, The Maritime Customs, *Treaties* (2 vols., 2nd ed., Shanghai, 1917), 491-505. Note S. T. Wang, *The Margary Affair and the Chefoo Agreement* (New York, 1940).

better to hold China to a strict observance of the 1858 settlement than to require new concessions of her. The Chefoo Convention illustrated not only how pressure was exerted on China to revise the treaties but also how difficult it was to attain agreement among the foreign powers themselves. Burlingame's co-operative policy had already been shelved.

IMMIGRATION: PRINCIPLE AND PRACTICE

While these problems of treaty revision and interpretation were still being debated, China's relations with the United States were disturbed by the results of the emigration of Chinese laborers to California. During the nineteenth century Chinese emigration had been of two kinds: free emigration of coolie laborers, for the most part to California and Australia, and contract-labor emigration to Cuba and Peru, known as the coolie trade. After 1862 the coolie trade was prohibited to American ships, and was brought under rigid regulation in British vessels sailing from Hongkong. Nevertheless, until 1874 this nefarious trade continued to flourish from the Portuguese settlement at Macao. S. Wells Williams wrote in 1866 from Peking that "the most flagitious acts have been committed by the [Chinese] natives upon each other, under the stimulus of rewards offered by foreigners to bring them coolies." Burlingame reported that in the season 1865-1866 there were sent to Cuba alone, mostly from Macao, 13,500 coolies at a cost of nearly $3,000,000.[12] Until this vicious traffic was brought to an end in 1874 there was no logic in Western moralizing on the shortcomings of China in international affairs.

In contrast with the pitiable condition of the Chinese coolie laborer in Cuba and Peru, the free laborer who went to California enjoyed a personal and an economic freedom he had not known in China. So relatively prosperous, indeed, was the lot of these immigrants that by 1880 there were 75,000 Chinese in California—9 per cent of the population. They had been attracted by news of the rich opportunities offered in the gold fields, by the demands for labor in the building of the first transcontinental railroad, and by the retail trade in San Francisco and other towns. At first the Chinese were welcome laborers. They provided cheap convenient labor,

[12] United States, Department of State, *China Despatches,* Vol. 23, No. 27, and Vol. 24, No. 130, printed in Paul H. Clyde, ed., *United States Policy toward China* (Durham, 1940), 76-79.

able to live on "the smell of a greasy rag." In the beginning, too, their qualities of industry and docility were thought of as virtues. This attitude prevailed until the great depression of the seventies, at which time the cry was raised that the "Chinaman" was robbing the white man's dinner pail and destroying his standard of living. The "Chinaman's" virtues now became vices. The New York *Nation* noted derisively in 1883 that on the Pacific Coast the Chinese were perpetuating "those disgusting habits of thrift, industry, and self-denial. . . ." It became clear, to those who wished so to think, that the Chinese had many other vices. They lived to themselves, frequently in hovels. They were impervious to the beneficent influence of Americanization. They gambled. They smoked smuggled opium, and, since they had no wives with them, they consorted with prostitutes. There was some truth in all these charges, but no evidence has yet been unearthed to indicate that in these respects the Chinese were any worse, or better, than virile immigrant "Americans" of Irish and other foreign descent who at this time made up the vociferous element on the Pacific Coast.

Violence against the Chinese in word and deed reached a shameful intensity in 1877. San Francisco harbored the backwash of the depression of 1873: the scum of the labor market, rowdies, and political adventurers. In this group were many Irish, naturalized and unnaturalized, who readily accepted the leadership of one Denis Kearney, an Irish-born, recently naturalized agitator, famous for his hypnotic power over the mob. It was Kearney who shouted as he held a noosed rope in his hand, "The Chinese must go!" "Christian" followers of Kearney held that the Chinese didn't have souls, and even if they did, they weren't worth saving. So the Chinese were attacked, their store windows broken, their freshly laundered clothing trampled in the gutter, their queues snipped with scissors, their bodies kicked and stoned. Finally, there were boycotts of Oriental labor, and cold-blooded murdering of some of the Chinese.[13]

The Chinese Become a Political Question

What was basically an economic and sociological problem soon became political. Western politicians and members of Congress were

13 See M. R. Coolidge, *Chinese Immigration* (New York, 1909), chs. i-vii; R. W. Paul, "The Origins of the Chinese Issue in California," *Miss. Valley Hist. Rev.*, XXV (1938) 181-196; and the study by H. F. MacNair, *The Chinese Abroad* (Shanghai, 1924).

determined to be rid of the Chinese. The attitude of the eastern states was one largely of indifference. To the rather sanctimonious East, a western editor wrote:

> Let a colony of these Asiatic brethren, with souls to save, camp down beside Boston Common, with their filthy habits, their criminal practices, and their nasty vices, and how long would it be before Beacon Hill would sniff the polluted atmosphere, and all the overgodly of New England would send up their prayers for relief.[14]

This political uproar against the Chinese had its background. As early as 1855 a governor of California was denouncing the Chinese to satisfy his constituents, anti-Chinese memorials were in circulation, and anti-Chinese bills were being offered in the legislature. Charges were made that the Chinese in California, like those in Cuba and Peru, were under servile contracts. The Civil War quieted the agitation for a time, and the transcontinental railroad construction that followed absorbed all available Chinese labor. The Central Pacific was finished in 1869, at which time the roads were employing nearly 10,000 men, of whom some 9,000 were Chinese who were noted to be "peaceable, industrious and economical, apt to learn and quite as efficient as white laborers." However, in defiance of all forecasts, the completion of the railways did not usher in prosperity. On the contrary, land values failed to rise, thousands of white and Chinese laborers were thrown out of employment, the California State Democratic platform of 1869 was rabidly anti-Negro, anti-railway, and anti-Chinese. The Republicans too found it expedient politically to be nominally anti-Chinese. In 1876 the California Senate sent to Congress, in the guise of an impartial investigation of the Chinese, a viciously partisan document designed to inflame race prejudice and win an election. Against this testimony were the words of a former American Minister at Peking, J. Ross Browne, usually regarded as severe in his judgments of the Chinese:

> [The Chinese] do not seek to interfere in our political struggles; they are peaceful and law-abiding; they are always willing to bear their equal burden of taxes; and all they ask is to be treated with common humanity. It is a noticeable fact that the only strenuous opposition to them is from an alien population [the Irish], who upon the principle of discrimination urged against the Chinese would themselves be excluded. But the fault is

---

14 *San Francisco Argonaut,* II, 5 (Jan. 19, 1878), quoted by Bailey, *A Diplomatic History,* 430.

not so much with the laboring classes who pour into our country from Europe, as with the political charlatans who mislead them.[15]

The unhappy fate of the Chinese on the Pacific Coast made it abundantly clear that Seward and Burlingame had misjudged not only the future but also the nature of Sino-American relations when in 1868 they had written into their Sino-American treaty "the inherent and inalienable right of man to change his home and allegiance." It now appeared either that this principle itself was not valid or that many Americans were not so closely wedded to it as had been supposed. At any rate, the American government was faced with the embarrassing task of informing China that her people were not wanted here.

Prompt action by the federal government could not be delayed, for in 1879 Congress passed a law prohibiting any ship from bringing to the United States more than fifteen Chinese on any one trip. President Hayes vetoed the bill on March 1, 1879, on the ground that it was virtual exclusion and therefore in violation of the Burlingame Treaty. In the West, Hayes was burned in effigy, while the East greeted his act as "wise and manly." Thereupon the President sent to China a commission composed of James B. Angell, William H. Trescot, and John F. Swift. One who is unfamiliar with the background traced in the preceding paragraphs, and who reads only the instructions of Secretary Evarts to the commission, June 8, 1880, might well suppose that in that year it was the United States rather than China that suffered injury. The commissioners were to concern themselves with: (1) "making our [commercial] privileges more clear, more secure and more extensive"; (2) impressing upon the Chinese that if they could collect *likin* and other "discriminatory" taxes, they could also prevent their collection; (3) entertaining any ideas the Chinese might have for reconciling the systems of jurisprudence, American and Chinese, in applying extraterritoriality in China; and (4) explaining to the Chinese why "this Government finds great public interests to require in our relations to China and the movement of its population to our Pacific coast, what may appear to be a modification of our universal hospitality to foreign immigration."[16] On November 17, 1880, the commission signed two treaties with China, the one commercial, the other giving the United

---

15 United States, Department of State, *China Despatches,* Vol. 25, No. 1.

16 United States, Department of State, *China Instructions,* Vol. 3, No. 1.

States the right to "regulate, limit or suspend" but not to "absolutely prohibit" the immigration of Chinese laborers. When in response to this new treaty status Congress suspended Chinese immigration for twenty years, President Arthur vetoed the measure, April 4, 1882, as "unreasonable," that is, not within the meaning of a "suspension." Again East and West were divided, but compromise was found in a second bill, in 1882, suspending Chinese immigration for ten years, a measure which the President accepted. The law of 1882 was amended and strengthened in 1884, and two years before it was due to expire in 1892 it was made more rigid, on the eve of a presidential election. Chinese exclusion had become a national policy.

Even this diplomatic settlement and the legislative program against the Chinese did not for a time put an end to anti-Chinese riots in the United States. Twenty-eight Chinese were murdered in Wyoming in 1885; the federal government was powerless to intervene in what was purely a state matter. The best that Congress could do was to vote an indemnity.[17]

The facts of the Chinese immigration question in the late nineteenth century lead to conclusions that are not pleasant. On a number of points the evidence is perfectly clear. Most of the Chinese in the United States were here legally; as a group they were industrious and peaceable; their vices may have been different but it would be a wise man who could affirm that they were worse than those of other immigrants, or for that matter of native-born Americans. Indeed, the Chinese had been encouraged to come to the United States not only by economic opportunity but also by the diplomacy of two Americans, Seward and Burlingame. Burlingame was undoubtedly influenced by idealism, Seward by the more mundane considerations of cheap labor. Their combined motives resulted in the writing of a treaty in 1868 which embodied the ideal and the principle of free immigration. Within twelve years this ideal had become unworkable. Thereupon the problem was permitted to fall into the hands of demagogues, agitators, political hoodlums, and others who thought of themselves as "100 per cent American." By them the Chinese question was never considered upon its merits. Their policy of total exclusion was as barren in statesmanship as was the naive "free immigration" of Burlingame and Seward.

---

[17] Coolidge, *Chinese Immigration,* chs. ix-xvii.

FOR FURTHER READING

Bales, W. L., *Tso Tsung-t'ang, Soldier and Statesman of Old China* (Shanghai, 1937). An able study and description of the campaigns of the T'ai-p'ing Rebellion.

Chen Ch'i-t'ien, *Tso Tsung T'ang* (Peiping, 1938). A brief biography of one of China's first industrialists.

———, *Tseng Kuo-fan, Pioneer Promoter of the Steamship in China* (Peiping, 1935).

Chiang, Siang-tseh, *The Nien Rebellion* (Seattle, 1954).

Mason, Mary Gertrude, *Western Concepts of China and the Chinese, 1840-1876* (Durham, 1939).

McKenzie, R. D., *Oriental Exclusion* (Chicago, 1928). An extensive work covering the entire field.

McLeod, Alexander, *Pigtails and Gold Dust: A Panorama of Chinese Life in Early California* (Caldwell, 1947).

Pelcovits, Nathan A., *Old China Hands and the Foreign Office* (New York, 1948). Refutes view that mercantile interests shaped British China policy after 1858.

Sandmeyer, E. C., *The Anti-Chinese Movement in California* (Urbana, 1939). Notable for its stress on the conflict between local and federal jurisdiction.

Tansill, C. C., *The Foreign Policy of Thomas F. Bayard, 1885-1897* (New York, 1940). See ch. v for discussion of diplomatic aspects of Chinese immigration after the treaty of 1880.

Wright, Stanley F., *Hart and the Chinese Customs* (Belfast, 1950).

Wright, Mary C., *The Last Stand of Chinese Conservatism: the T'ung-chih Restoration, 1862-1874* (Stanford University, 1957).

15

China: 1860–1890

New Questions but Old Answers

CHINA'S record in the new world of Western diplomacy, 1860 to 1890, as suggested in the preceding chapter, does not lend itself to easy analysis either by the contemporary participants or, for that matter, by posterity. The general failure to understand what was really happening in China was shared by both Chinese and foreigners. The contemporary official reaction on China in both America and Europe vacillated between hope and despair: hope that China would soon accept the virtues of Western modernization, and despair that she would ever free herself from the dead hand of her past. Even so astute an observer as John Russell Young, American Minister at Peking, 1882-1885, saw only the surface manifestations of China's troubles. His dictum that China had largely herself to blame for her woes, that she had no government worthy of the name, and that her efforts in foreign affairs amounted to simple "trifling" was substantially true, but it did not touch the core of China's real problem. The essence of that core was the intellectual reaction of the scholar-official class, the ruling bureaucracy, to the Western assault not simply upon China's seacoast but, more important, upon her institutions and the ideas and values from which they sprang. Of this intellectual reaction, the West knew almost nothing. The ways through which China's educated men sought to fathom the alien and powerful West and to protect their own culture from its contagion is therefore the subject to which this chapter now turns.[1]

[1] The pioneer collection of documents on this subject on which I have relied heavily is Ssŭ-yü Têng and John K. Fairbank, *China's Response to the West* (Cambridge, 1954).

The Role of Questionable Assumptions

The historical puzzle posed by the character of China's response to the West was complicated from the first by the Chinese attitude of superiority and exclusiveness, and perhaps even more by the capacity of Americans (and of Europeans to a lesser degree) to approach the Chinese question armed only with questionable assumptions on what the Chinese were, what ideas they entertained concerning the West, and what they wanted to be. Burlingame, it will be recalled, had told his American audience of a China bent on mastering the fundamentals of Western civilization. These were sweet words to Americans in an era of Manifest Destiny. They carried the implication that, given the chance, China would forsake gladly her own outmoded ways for the modern manners of America. As will be seen later, this slender thesis was to intrude itself repeatedly into American thought on China from that day to the present, with results that shall be examined later in these pages. It will be important therefore to discover whether the assumptions were valid, and to note the depth of their roots in American thought. Certainly evidence from the later nineteenth century suggests that what many Americans chose to believe concerning China was fanciful, though well intentioned. Yet, in sharp contrast, the testimony of J. Ross Browne, who succeeded Burlingame as American Minister at Peking, 1868, was a direct and explicit denial of what many Americans thought Burlingame had said. Browne's words, however, did not reach the American public. They were for the confidential ears of Secretary William H. Seward.

An impression [said Browne] seems to have obtained in the United States that the Government of China is peculiarly friendly to our country, and that great advantages to our commerce are about to accrue from this preference. Enthusiastic expectations are entertained that the [Manchu] Empire, so long isolated from the world, is on the eve of being thrown open to American enterprise; that important concessions will soon be made granting special privileges to our citizens.

I need scarcely say these anticipations are without foundation. The Government of China may have preferences; but it has no special regard for any foreign power. The dominant feeling is antipathy and distrust towards all who have come in to disturb the administration of its domestic affairs. But little difference is recognized between one power and another. The concessions obtained by force of arms have been accepted by all.[2]

[2] United States, Department of State, *China Despatches,* XXV, No. 7, November 25, 1868, quoted by Paul H. Clyde, *United States Policy toward China, 1839-1939* (Durham, 1940), 93-94.

There was indeed a wide gulf between the China that was and the China that, in America, was thought to be.

China's First Response: Force Tempered with Persuasion

The Canton crisis of 1834-1840 revealed China's original and basic intellectual response to the West. This response was pre-eminently Chinese. It did not assume that China might profit through learning from the West, and this was natural, since the Chinese tradition was self-sufficient and less disposed to borrow abroad than was, for instance, the Japanese tradition. At Canton, therefore, in 1839, Lin did what any able and traditional Chinese could be expected to do. He applied force against the British while at the same time, by letter, he delivered himself of a sermon to Queen Victoria exhorting that lady to control her subjects within the bounds of Confucian virtue. This formula of force plus persuasion was the traditional method by which China had controlled the barbarians on her borders. Lin, however, although traditional, was also observant. The subsequent debacle at Canton convinced him that China should purchase and manufacture Western armaments, translate Western books, hire foreign technical advisers, and train Chinese technical personnel; but these ideas were so revolutionary that he confided them only to his most intimate friends.[3] China was to wait another twenty years before embarking on these ventures. Meanwhile, the Chinese response, particularly at Canton, took the form of bitter and violent anti-foreignism, which meant anti-Westernism. Although in some limited measure this movement may have been a spontaneous reaction to foreign arrogance at Canton, it was also encouraged and led by the scholar-gentry with the approval of the Peking government.

The Policy of Conciliation

Although Lin's policy failed and Chinese arms met defeat, China's traditional diplomatic arsenal was not thereby exhausted. If an enemy could not be forced and persuaded, it was good traditional

[3] Lin's letter to Queen Victoria and his comments on Western arms, etc., is in Ssŭ-yü Têng and J. K. Fairbank, *China's Response to the West, a Documentary Survey, 1839-1923* (Cambridge, 1954), 23-30. See this source for other documents referred to in this chapter.

policy to conciliate him through negotiation, and this was what the Ch'ing dynasty did when it accepted the first treaties of 1842-1844 and 1858-1860. Under this strategy the treaties were regarded officially as temporary devices for pacifying the barbarians and thereby bringing them under control. The great exponent of this policy was the imperial Manchu clansman, Ch'i-ying, who negotiated with Sir Henry Pottinger of Great Britain (1842), Caleb Cushing of the United States (1844), and Th. de Lagrené of France (1844). The policy of conciliation was not regarded as a concession to Western ways or as a reform of Chinese ways. It was traditional procedure. At the same time, the agent of conciliation, even so distinguished an official as Ch'i-ying, was in constant danger of being denounced to the court as subversive on the theory of guilt by association. The barbarians being untouchable, there was a fine line of distinction between conciliation that was appeasement and conciliation that was not. Thus conciliation was not regarded as surrender. It was a delaying tactic designed to hold and then to divide the enemy, to "manage" him adroitly by playing one barbarian against another.[4]

The period of conciliation, 1842-1860, involving unavoidable contacts with the unwelcome foreigner, produced, in time, a new type of Chinese official, a man familiar with the barbarians and presumed to know how to deal with them. Among these scholar-officials were the authors of the first Chinese books describing the world from which the barbarians came. Some of these new type officials were on friendly terms with foreigners, but it is important to note that their memorials to Peking continued to denounce the barbarian, his opium, his ignorance, and his religion.

The "Restoration" of T'ung-chih, 1862-1874

The invasion of Peking by British and French troops in 1860 together with the pitiful flight of the dynasty to Jehol brought forth the first tangible evidence that at least a handful of Chinese and Manchus saw the dire plight of the nation and were stirred to do something about it. The first efforts, as the reader knows, resulted in new Chinese institutions, such as the Tsungli Yamen, and the expansion of the customs service to cope more effectively with foreign affairs. Foreign advice and personnel were sought and accepted in

[4] Earl Swisher, *China's Management of the American Barbarians, 1841-1861* (New Haven, 1953), 1-54.

the suppression of the T'ai-p'ings. After the collapse of the rebellion, civil administration was re-established in former rebel areas. There were even efforts at rehabilitation and relief from excessive taxation. These promising measures seemed to suggest that a new leadership, capable of adjusting to the aggressive West, was in command at Peking and in some of the provinces. Such was not the case. These hopeful signs were a "Restoration," not a revolution. The intellectual temper was a revival of good but traditional Confucian ideas whereby through scholar-government and the practice of virtue China, it was said, would again become strong. It was a theory of self-strengthening propounded by scholar-officials who were not Western and who had no desire to become Western or to model their state on Western precedent and example.

One of the notable creators of the "Restoration" mentality was Feng Kuei-fen, a Soochow scholar, versed in the classics, experienced in government, and possessed of a keen and cosmopolitan interest in modern scientific knowledge. As an associate of such men as Tseng Kuo-fan and Li Hung-chang he knew many foreigners, and was instrumental in opening a school of Western languages and science at Shanghai (1863). His essays, written about 1860 but not widely distributed until 1898, revealed him as perhaps the first to understand that Western pressures were a complex of ideas and power unlike any invasion China had previously known. He thereupon concluded that Western languages and sciences must be acquired and used to supplement Chinese knowledge. The superiority of Confucian ethics was not questioned. These would remain as the foundation and the principal structural form of Chinese society. Within technological limits Western learning could be useful. There was no thought of concessions to Western learning in general; indeed, Western books "which expound the doctrine of Jesus are generally vulgar, and not worth mentioning." This idea that there was a place for some Western knowledge within a Chinese way of life had also been present in the contemporary and abortive reform program of the T'ai-p'ings which held that calligraphy, footbinding, and long fingernails had less value than ships, railroads, and guns.

THE APPEAL OF WESTERN TECHNOLOGY, 1860-1870

The theory of Feng Kuei-fen that Western "know-how" should become the servant of a Confucian society was shared and sometimes applied by the leaders of the "Restoration." It was also opposed. Tseng Kuo-fan, Li Hung-chang, and Tso Tsung-t'ang, the great administrators of the period, were all advocates of Western science.

At the time of the downfall of the T'ai-p'ings, Tseng Kuo-fan (1811-1872) was probably the most influential man in China. He had employed foreigners and their weapons in his fight against the rebels. Long before the *Arrow* War (1857-1858) he had urged the building of a Chinese navy. He built arsenals in the provinces of Hunan and Kiangsi and, together with Li Hung-chang, the Kiangnan arsenal at Shanghai (1865). In these matters of armament Tseng was a Western convert. Yet he never deserted the Confusian ideal of the good statesman. His formula for dealing with the foreigners was to treat them with Confucian virtue. In treaty revision, for example, what could be conceded should be conceded; that which could not be conceded should be resisted with resolution. "We should never hem and haw [literally, half spit and half swallow]."

T'ung-wen Kuan, or Interpreters' College

Like Tseng, Li Hung-chang not only approved the use of Western arms but also took practical steps to secure them through the training of Chinese personnel in Western mathematics as applied to engineering. An Interpreters' College, T'ung-wen Kuan, had been approved at Peking and opened in 1862. Later its curriculum was expanded to include science and mathematics, since, as Prince Kung said, science was the secret of Western strength. Meanwhile, additional language schools had been founded at Shanghai (1863), at Canton (1864), and at Foochow (1866).

These innovations met opposition from high places at court led by a Grand Secretary, Wo-jen by name, who was a Mongol scholar of great reputation, a tutor to the emperor, and head of the Hanlin Academy. His objections to Western learning expressed the conservative traditionalism that was still dominant. Wo-jen declared that if mathematics was to be taught by Westerners the damage to China would be great. The way to establish and strengthen a nation, he said, was to lay emphasis on propriety and righteousness (Confucian virtues), not on power and plotting. No nation, he asserted, had ever raised itself from decline by the use of mathematics. As for other aspects of Westernism, he pointed out that Christianity had already deceived many ignorant Chinese. Therefore, China's only defense was to explain to the people the power of the Confucian tenets.

Tso Tsung-t'ang's Reforms

Another great advocate of self-strengthening through Western methods and Chinese values was Tso Tsung-t'ang (1812-1885), the son of a Hunan peasant family. Tso became first a student and school teacher, but after failing three times to win his degree in the metropolitan examinations he turned from the classics to knowledge for "practical use." When his experimental steamboat built by native craftsmen and mechanics proved unsatisfactory, he sought the advice of French engineers. As one of the first advocates of a Chinese navy, he was author of the plan for a Foochow shipyard. In his later government career in the far northwest (Shensi, Kansu, and Sinkiang), he introduced a program of modernization in agriculture, transportation, and fiscal policy, and the suppression of graft. Tso's formula was to learn from the barbarians, but not to rely on them. Comparing Japan's mastery of Western knowledge of shipbuilding with China's ignorance, he likened it to a race where Japan rode on a steed and China on a donkey.

Chinese Students Abroad

Among the most revealing episodes in China's intellectual response was the effort to educate young Chinese in the United States, Britain, and France. The training of Chinese in science and mathematics had already been undertaken at the T'ung-wen Kuan in Peking and elsewhere, but ultimately the need for young Chinese to study abroad gained some recognition. Two principal student missions followed. The first sent one hundred and twenty Chinese students to the United States between 1872 and 1881; the second sent thirty students to England and France for technical training in 1876. As in other matters it was Tseng Kuo-fan and Li Hung-chang who implemented these missions. Their memorial of 1871 to the Tsungli Yamen declared that there was no way to master Western ideas, techniques, and machines "unless we have actually seen them and practised with them for a long time." Or, as the Chinese proverb put it, "To hear a hundred times is not as good as to see once."

In the United States the education of these Chinese students gave promise of significant results. The way for them had been paved by the enthusiasms of Yung Wing (1828-1912) (Yale '54), the first Chinese to graduate from an American university. Then the venture ended as suddenly as it had begun. In 1881 the students were recalled for reasons that bear directly on China's intellectual response in this period. In part this premature death of China's efforts in foreign education was hastened by jealousies among those Chinese who administered the program in America, but more important, it would appear, was the discovery that the students were mastering American studies to the exclusion or at least the neglect of Chinese studies. This revelation was too much for the traditionalists in Peking, and even Li Hung-chang felt that China had gone too far, though there was a touch of understanding in his remark that it was hard for young Chinese abroad "to avoid indulging in foreign customs." Again the evidence suggests that in this period the men who guided Peking had no thought of making China less Chinese.

Prince Kung and Western International Law

At the same time there were occasional suggestions that a knowledge of Western government and law might be a good thing, not because Western law was good in itself or superior to Chinese law, but because China might use it to confound the barbarians with their own rules. A very delightful case in point was Prince Kung's discovery of the marvels of international law. In a memorial of 1864 the Prince recounted how a barbarian scholar[5] had shown him some volumes of foreign laws translated into Chinese which the barbarian had said "should be read by all countries having treaty relations with others. . . . Your ministers [the Prince wrote] forestalled his attempt to get us to follow the book, by telling him at once that China has her own laws and institutions and that it is inconvenient to consult foreign books. . . . Your ministers find [moreover] that the contents of this book of foreign laws do not entirely agree with the system in China, but there are occasional passages which are useful. For instance, in connection with the case this year of the Danish ship captured by Prussia outside of Tientsin, your ministers used as arguments some sentences from this book without expressly saying so. The Prussian minister immediately acknowledged his mistake and said nothing further." The happy re-

[5] An American, W. A. P. Martin, later president of the T'ung-wen Kuan.

sult of this episode was that Prince Kung honored the request made by the barbarian scholar for five hundred taels to publish this wonderful book.

The Audience Question

The thirteen-year period from 1860 to 1873 had shown that the Ch'ing dynasty in its relations with the West as directed by Prince Kung was capable of some faltering steps toward reform and adjustment to the new world of the West. At the same time this Manchu-Chinese capacity to take one step forward was countered more often than not by a genius for taking two steps backward. The granting by the emperor in 1873 of the first official audience at Peking to the ministers of the foreign powers resident there suggests how this genius worked. When a minister from a treaty power reached China, he would, if Western practice prevailed, be received in audience by the emperor to present his credentials. However, such an audience would imply that the Son of Heaven was a mere equal of Western sovereigns, an admission conservative Peking could not bring itself to make. As late as 1867 the Court had been most careful in its instructions to the Burlingame mission to guard against committing the emperor on this point. Consequently, all requests for audience made by the envoys in Peking had been denied. From 1861 to 1873 the Tsungli Yamen was able to evade and delay a decision on the ground that the emperor was a minor. But this excuse could not be used indefinitely. The powers were in general agreement that eventually the audience must be insisted upon.[6] It seemed that 1873, the year of the emperor's coming of age, would be the appropriate time.

The date for the first audience was finally set for June 29, 1873. During the previous months the ministers of the Tsungli Yamen and the foreign envoys had engaged in an unprofitable wrangle, the former demanding that the foreigners kneel before the throne. Three bows were finally accepted as a substitute. Then came the appointed day when the T'ung-chih emperor entered the *Tzu Kuang*

[6] The Chinese attitude toward the audience question may be stated in this way: Apparently the Court was not unwilling to grant Imperial audiences during the 1860's. It merely demanded that foreign envoys conform to certain ceremonial usages to which the foreign envoys objected. Hence came the desire of the Chinese to postpone grappling with the question. Note W. W. Rockhill, *Diplomatic Audiences at the Court of China* (London, 1905).

Ko (Throne Hall of Purple Effulgence) located in an Imperial park adjacent to but not in the Imperial Palace. The Japanese ambassador, Soyejima, outranking his European colleagues, was received first and alone. Then the representatives of the Western powers were led in together by Prince Kung: General Vlangaly of Russia, Frederick F. Low of the United States, Thomas F. Wade of Great Britain, M. de Geofroy of France, and M. Ferguson of the Netherlands. All bowed three times as they advanced to the center of the hall and placed their letters of credence on the Dragon Table. After the reading of a congratulatory address in French the emperor acknowledged receipt of the letters by a slight inclination of the head and a few words in Manchu addressed to Prince Kung. The envoys now stepped backwards bowing repeatedly until they had reached the entrance to the Hall. The entire ceremony had taken less than half an hour.

So ended the first audience granted the foreign powers since the establishment of treaty relations. It was an event of primary importance to the powers, for, as Minister Low had said, friendly relations could not be cultivated unless the "arrogance and conceit" of high Chinese officials was curbed by a ceremonial recognition that China was not superior to the foreign barbarians. On the surface therefore the powers could pride themselves on a diplomatic, ceremonial victory. Their triumph, however, was not so complete as they supposed. The Manchu-Chinese Court had succeeded in snubbing the foreigners at the very moment their equality was seemingly recognized. The *Tzu Kuang Ko* was a pavilion used for receiving tribute missions from the rulers of lesser kingdoms such as Korea, Burma, and the Ryukyu Islands. Furthermore, the envoys were not permitted to enter the grounds by the main gate but through a side entrance, just as lesser officials were required to enter at the side gate of a yamen. Finally, the Chinese account of the audience notes particularly that the foreign ministers were admitted "after an interval of some duration"; that is, after they had been kept waiting, a favorite method of making a caller feel his inferiority.

In reality, therefore, the audience had accomplished very little, for the Peking authorities were convinced that they had succeeded in maintaining their superior position. Moreover, a year and a half later (January 12, 1875) the T'ung-chih emperor died of smallpox. Under the influence of the Empress Dowager Tz'u-hsi, and against all precedent, the Court named as successor Tsai-tien, a child of the same generation as the deceased monarch. The new sovereign, the Kuang-hsü emperor (1875-1908), was a son of Tz'u-hsi's sister and of Prince Chun, her most ardent supporter in the Imperial Family. For the next fourteen years Tz'u-hsi, as regent, was again the ruler of China in fact and in name. This development did not bode well for China's relations with the treaty powers.

Efforts Toward Industrialization

The emphasis that Chinese leadership was placing in the late nineteenth century on the problem of defense against the West led inevitably to concern with industrialization. Here there was a natural train of thought, beginning with the idea that China must use Western arms and armament and ending with the conclusion that China herself must manufacture these arms. Mention has already been made of the building of arsenals and shipyards. In 1872, organization of the China Merchants Steam Navigation Company led to the need for opening the Kaiping coal mines near Tientsin. Transportation of the coal from mine to port called for railroad construction.

Here it may be helpful to recall that the idea of industrialization, already a century old in Europe, was still a very new idea in the China of Tseng and Li. It was therefore something to which the scholar-official mind of China had yet to be converted. When indeed it was discovered that the first steamships built in China cost more than was anticipated and proved to be inferior to foreign ships, there were officials who advised abandoning the whole business. Li Hung-chang's protest against this proposed retreat from industrialization was expressed in a memorial of 1872. "Our scholars and officials," said Li, "have confined themselves to the study of stanzas and sentences and are ignorant of the greatest change of the last several thousand years." The seeming security of the "Restoration" had bred complacency. "That is how this talk of stopping steamship construction arose. . . . The Westerners rely upon the excellence and efficacy of their guns, cannon, and steamships, and so they can overrun China. . . . The sailing boats, rowboats, and the gunboats which have been hitherto employed cannot oppose their steam-engined warships. Therefore we are controlled by the Westerners. . . . Furthermore, the building of ships, cannon, and machinery will be impossible without iron, and then we shall be helpless without coal."

As a result of the energy and foresight of Li and Tso a great variety of industrial enterprises were planned and some were actually established between 1863 and 1890. These included technical schools, arsenals, shipyards, machine factories, Western fortifications, coal and iron mines, a steamship company, a telegraph from Taku to Tientsin in 1879, plans for a navy and a naval school, the building of railroads and a dockyard, and the establishment of textile mills. Yet for all its variety the movement toward industrialization was slow and ineffective.

Government Supervision; Merchant Operation

This failure of the early industrialization effort to meet China's goal of self-strengthening and defense was not due primarily to the advantages enjoyed by and the competition of the foreigners. In the same period Japan faced similar competition but succeeded in creating a strong industrial foundation based on initial government capital, operation, and control.

In China quite a different system of control and management was followed, one derived from traditional methods of economic administration. Under this system merchants provided a part of the capital, while the manager was apt to be of official status with influence enough to deal with local authorities in the matter of securing special privileges such as exemption from taxation. There might even be two managers, one to run the business, the other to manage the government. Thus, management was half business, half politics. Initially the purpose of the system was to enlist private capital from merchant sources. What happened more often than not was that officials, using the names of merchants, invested in these semi-government enterprises and placed their own relatives in charge as managers. The whole system went under the name of "official supervision and merchant operation."

The evils that resulted from this mingling of Confucian bureaucracy and Western business were described vividly in 1892 by a contemporary Chinese compradore-scholar, Cheng Kuan-ying, who knew many foreigners and much Western literature.

> In recent days [he wrote], although the court has ordered the governors-general and governors to develop commerce and open all kinds of manu-

facturing bureaus, and authorized the inviting of merchants to manage them, yet the officials and merchants have habitually been unable to get along together. . . . Businessmen who have undertaken many affairs, although they understand clearly that there are profits to be made, nevertheless hesitate to accept the invitation to manage government enterprises. . . . If a surplus or profit is made by the company, all the local officials request some contribution and overstep their proper duty to meddle in the company's affairs.[7]

The Nature of Chinese Leadership, 1860-1890

By the year 1890, China had passed through three decades of effort in "self-strengthening." What had the movement achieved? During the '60's there were signs that a new order was in the making, but during the 70's and 80's signs of self-strengthening were not easy to discern. The movement appeared to lose rather than to gain in strength. In explanation it may be noted that the entire period was in general one of peace in which the Western powers used the pressures of negotiation rather than of war, and it would appear that this softer policy was interpreted by the great majority of the scholar-bureaucrats to mean that the crisis was passed. If the crises of 1840 and 1860 were not forgotten, at least their forebodings seemed less ominous. The stirrings toward reform during the "Restoration" seemed less urgent after 1870. In 1872 Li Hung-chang complained that scholars and officials "are accustomed to the temporary security of the present, and so they forget . . . [the] suffering of twenty or thirty years ago [the Opium War]." Thus the crusade for Western techniques to bolster Chinese values lost its early momentum while it was far short of giving China the power to defend herself from the West.

How shall this lack of sustained purpose be explained? History has not as yet given definite answers to this question, but some of the factors involved are reasonably clear. Basic among these was the nature of the Confucian leadership which the mid- and later nineteenth century had produced. It was not that China had no men of political stature. Prince Kung, Tsêng Kuo-fan, Li Hung-chang, Tso Tsung-t'ang and others were administrators of ability who perceived the danger of foreign control and sought their defense against it through Western scientific techniques. Beyond this point,

[7] From the writings of Cheng Kuan-ying, *ca.*1892, printed in Têng and Fairbank, *China's Response,* 113-114.

however, they were unprepared to go. Their answer to the West was to use Western science to make China more Confucian. When it appeared, as in the case of Chinese students abroad, that Confucian values would thereby suffer, even China's most progressive leaders drew back. The students were recalled. Mastery of Western techniques was less important than preservation of the Confucian heritage. No responsible Chinese statesmen of the period perceived or accepted the idea that if China were to arm herself against the West, she might be called upon not only to import Western technology but also to make critical appraisal and perhaps revolutionary reforms in the structure and institutions of the traditional Confucian state.

The Quality of Leadership at Peking

There were two areas in which Chinese leadership, or the lack of it, were of the greatest import: (1) at Peking in the Manchu court and the metropolitan administration, and (2) in the provinces, where vigorous administrators such as Tseng and Li held office.

At Peking the hopeful course set by Prince Kung in 1860 was soon abandoned. For five years as a member of the regency and as head of the Grand Council and of the Tsungli Yamen, he had shown an awareness of China's plight and had wielded sufficient influence to direct policy accordingly. When, however, by 1865 the immediate threat of dynastic collapse had passed and the T'ai-p'ings had been suppressed, the incubus of court conservatism reasserted its power in the person of Tz'u-hsi, the Empress Dowager (1835-1908). This able and ambitious Manchu woman, a concubine of the Hsien-feng emperor (ruled 1851-1861) and mother of the T'ung-chih emperor (1856-1875), had become co-regent with the first wife and with Prince Kung when her son ascended the throne in 1862. Some reference has already been made to the uneasy alliance between Prince Kung and this remarkable woman. On the death of her childless son in 1875 she adopted and placed on the throne the son of Prince Kung's brother, Prince Chun, and her own sister, thereby maintaining her power as regent for the new child emperor, Kuang-hsü (ruled 1875-1908). From then on until her death in 1908, except for a brief period, 1889-1898, she was the greatest power in the Peking government.

Two principal traits highlighted the character of this woman as a ruler. By the power of her inflexible will and her knowledge of human frailty she dominated the court and thereby the metropolitan administration. She won or controlled officials of court and government by an amazing assortment of methods. According to the need of the moment, and in this her judgment rarely erred, she exhorted, flattered, bribed, commanded, or pleaded to get what she wanted. By placing an increasing number of Chinese in high provincial office she strengthend the loyalty of the scholar-bureaucrats to the Manchu monarchy. At the same time the high price she placed on her official favors raised the fine art of bribery (gifts to the Empress Dowager) to new and fantastic levels. By these means she sought to revive and protect the dynasty.

Against her limited success in reviving the loyalty of Chinese officialdom was her incapacity to face repeated crises in foreign affairs. Though she usually followed the advice of her ministers, she hated the foreigners and their works. Moreover, there were few who could advise her with intelligence. As Li Hung-chang wrote in 1881: "The stupidity and confusion of our scholar-officials, and the lack of men of ability in the court are really ridiculous."

From these circumstances came the stupid confusion of the Empress Dowager's rule. Under her authority vast sums had been collected to give China a modern navy. The money was spent in rebuilding the Summer Palace. Such was the leadership provided by Peking in the crusade for self-strengthening. The warnings of Wen-hsiang, one of the able assistants of Prince Kung, were like a small voice calling in the wilderness: "When Your Majesty is concerned to work diligently, then your ministers . . . dare not follow their traditional dawdling habits. Otherwise . . . the disaster will be unspeakable." These were prophetic words, but the Empress Dowager did not understand them.

In the provinces the prospect for leadership had more substance. The efforts of Tsung, Li, and the others who have been mentioned meant that there was some awakening among the scholar-bureaucrats. At the same time this awakening was so hedged about by mental obstructions and the carrion weight of traditionalism that not even Li saw the alternatives among which China might choose. The time had not yet come for Chinese-Manchu leadership to question the dead hand of the past. Moreover, and this is historically quite understandable, history had not bequeathed China a sense of political patriotism. The urge to adopt Western technology and science was seen, more often than not, as a means whereby officials and merchants might make profits for themselves rather than as a method of saving the country from foreign aggression. In addition, such limited leadership as did appear in the provinces did not and could not compensate for the vacuous leadership of Peking. Although the progressive governors were for the most part steadfast in their loyalty to Peking, their local successes in provincial finance and military affairs were at the expense of central authority and therefore at the expense of a unified and coherent effort to save the empire through self-strengthening.

A Nineteenth-Century Contrast

The ways in which China on the one hand and Japan on the other responded in the nineteenth century to the Western impact form an arresting study in contrasts. As an historical problem these contrasts have continued to perplex statesmen and students. How did it come about that, of all the far eastern peoples, the Japanese met the Western intrusion with vigor, seeking survival in strong, independent nationhood that readily employed modern science and technology to refashion traditional Japanese society on industrial foundations, while the Chinese in the same years of the nineteenth century made no positive, constructive response at all? Satisfying answers are the more elusive because what actually happened was just the reverse of what informed contemporaries might well have predicted. They might well have noted that Japan was at a grave disadvantage physically in the struggle for power and wealth. Her farmlands were crowded, her minerals scanty. She was not well located either as to materials or to markets. In mid-nineteenth century she was still bound by feudalism and by the self-conscious power of a warrior caste wholly antagonistic to modernization. In contrast China might have seemed ready for the modern world. In location and wealth she was superior. She had traditions of freedom and social mobility, of private property, of pragmatism and materialism, of humane political ideals, and of knowledge as the key to office. All in all China appeared uniquely equipped to adopt "the secular, rational, utilitarian democratic culture of the West." Yet it was Japan, not China, that embraced the modern world in the nineteenth century. No simple explanation can explain why and how this occurred but the following factors are suggestive of the processes at work.

1. Traditional philosophical attitudes, especially those attributable to Confucianism and Taoism, with their emphasis on indirection, may well have conditioned the Chinese response. In Japan the code of the *samurai* taught that an enemy was met by direct action, and, of course, Japan's Meiji leaders were *samurai*.

2. Most important in Japan's response was her capacity to combine the two essential conditions of successful adaptation and growth: (a) leadership in technological and social change, and (b) teamwork and discipline in organization giving order and momentum to the process of change. The fitness of the leaders to rule and the willingness of the majority to follow characterized Japanese organization.

3. Japan's response was aided by the fact that her society, above the family, was more pluralistic in structure than was China's. Initiative in Japan thus tended to be dispersed among a number of centers. Particular groups such as the business elite, barred from the hereditary aristocracy, had built their own money power undermining the ruling caste; or particular families such as the Western clans became the pioneers in Western technology and later the leaders of political revolution.

4. Japan's response was more vigorous because her internal crisis, unlike that of China, was potentially revolutionary. Within Japan the mid-century tensions were such that powerful elements of the ruling class were ready to adopt modernization even if it meant the downfall of feudalism and the liquidation of their own class.

5. Historically Japan was a frontier society, a cultural borrower, and, as it happened, the Western impact reached her shores at the precise moment when internal frictions had already prepared the way for great changes in her society.[7]

For Further Reading

Bland, J. O. P., and E. Backhouse, *China Under the Empress Dowager* (Philadelphia, 1910).

——, *Li Hung-chang* (London, 1917).

[7] W. W. Lockwood, "Japan's Response to the West: the Contrast with China," *World Politics,* IX (1956), 37-54.

Chang Chung-li, *The Chinese Gentry. Studies on Their Role in Nineteenth-Century Chinese Society* (Seattle, 1955). A study of local leadership.

Creel, H. G., *Chinese Thought, from Confucius to Mao Tsê-tung* (Chicago, 1953). A survey that can be understood and enjoyed by the beginner.

Douglas, Sir Robert Kennaway, *Li Hung-ch'ang* (London, 1895).

Fei Hsiao-t'ung, *China's Gentry,* rev. and ed. by Margaret Park Redfield (Chicago, 1953). A study of political and social classes in China, stressing the disruptive influences of Western commerce.

Hughes, E. R., *The Invasion of China by the Western World* (London, 1937). A pioneer appraisal of the influence of Christian missionaries, Western political thought, science, and medicine.

Levenson, Joseph R., *Liang Ch'i-ch'ao and the Mind of Modern China* (Cambridge, Mass., 1953). An intellectual history of modern China centering on one of the most articulate and influential men of the period.

Levy, Marion J., *The Rise of the Modern Chinese Business Class* (New York, 1949).

———, *The Family Revolution in Modern China* (Cambridge, 1949). An important study of change in the past 100 years.

Little, Mrs. Archibald, *Li Hung-chang, His Life and Times* (New York, 1903).

Wright, Arthur F., Hellmut Wilhelm, and Benjamin Schwartz, "Chinese Reactions to Imported Ideas, a Symposium," *Journal of the History of Ideas,* Vol. XII, No. 1, January, 1951, pp. 31-74.

Lin Yu-t'ang, *A History of the Press and Public Opinion in China* (Chicago, 1936).

16

China and Her Dependent States

It has already been suggested in these pages that the increasing nineteenth-century contacts between Westerners and the Chinese involved forces more complex than the balance sheet of a trader, the catechism of a missionary, or the etiquette of a diplomat. In their various callings, trader, missionary, and diplomat carried to China a Western civilization that was well on its way to Europeanizing the world. It was a vigorous and an aggressive civilization which assumed that man's material and, in some degree, even his spiritual, salvation rested on the national state and the colonial empire, on the Industrial Revolution and the development of commerce, on the conversion of the heathen to Christianity, and on the acceptance by "remote and backward peoples," such as the Chinese, of Western ideas of international law. But all these concepts were foreign to the traditional thought of nineteenth-century China. She could accept them only through changes which, in the light of her civilization, would be in the broadest sense revolutionary; and, as was indicated at the close of the preceding chapter, China was not yet prepared to undertake a revolution.[1]

[1] The traditional Chinese view of history had something to do with the slowness of Chinese modern adjustment. According to the traditional view, "dynasty succeeded dynasty, each following the same cycle of rise in virtue and decay in vice—the same play presented over and over again, but each time with a new cast. It was this view of Chinese history which T. T. Meadows had in mind in mid-nineteenth century when he coined his famous description of the Chinese as the most rebellious but the least revolutionary of peoples. A change of dynasty meant new personnel, not new institutions." Meribeth Cameron, "The Periodization of Chinese History," *Pacific Historical Review,* XV (1946), 173.

It is true that the Seward-Burlingame Treaty (1868) had conceded to China "the right to decide the time and manner and circumstances" of westernization; but treaties fail frequently to control "the march of events." So it was that between 1870 and 1895 China's position in the Far East was challenged by the powers not only at Peking but also on the borders of the Empire in the "vassal" or "tributary" or, to use a better term, dependent states. During this period the Middle Kingdom lost whatever control *de facto* or *de jure* it had exercised previously in the Ryukyu Islands, in Indochina, in Burma, in Korea, and in other areas.[2] Thereby a fundamental principle of Chinese government—the relation between the superior and the inferior state—was destroyed. States that had recognized the overlordship of Peking were to become either independent or colonies of foreign powers. To understand how this came about, and the consequences to China resulting from it, one must review briefly certain Chinese concepts of government.

Confucian International Theories

The Confucian system of China in its bearing on international relations rested on the principles of familism and the inequality of nations. The world was regarded as a unit, natural rather than legal in organization. China Proper, the Middle Kingdom, was the controlling center area where men were civilized and thus understood and lived by the Confucian rules of propriety. All who lived outside this area were "barbarians," a term denoting anything from savagery to a state of civilization different from and therefore inferior to China's. As border states became civilized—that is, Confucianized—the Confucian system was extended to them. The relation between China and these border, Confucianized states was that of the elder and younger brother. It was a relation not always definite or uniform, but it was apt to include the following: (1) China, the superior, taught and admonished the lesser state; (2) the lesser state might be under close supervision or the contacts might be largely ceremonial; (3) the lesser sovereign received investiture from the Chinese emperor; (4) the lesser state could be required to furnish men and supplies when China engaged in mis-

[2] In some cases (e.g., Burma, Sikkim, Annam) China had not exercised any control for a very long time, so that despite theoretical dependence upon China, these states were really independent *de facto*. This was one reason why France and Britain paid little attention to Chinese claims of overlordship.

sions of "correction"; (5) tribute-bearing missions from the lesser state were sent to China, thereby recognizing the primacy of China in the Confucian family of nations.[3]

In theory, and generally in practice, China did not seek through these means to control directly the internal affairs of the border states. In fact, the border states were largely autonomous so long as their rulers kept the peace, lived with their peoples on the Confucian model, and performed the ceremonial and other duties of their inferior status. In practice, however, many of the men who have controlled China have been politicians rather than pure Confucian theorists. It was possible for such men to use the theory of the superior and the inferior state to serve the ends of what today would be called power politics, and thus to make the border states mere satellites of the Middle Kingdom.

With all influence flowing outward, with no competing cultures or authority against which the barriers of definite boundaries need be raised, China had no need for the legal concept of the state or of sovereignty. Its control was through ideas that could be confined within no physical boundaries. The marking off of a certain territory within which its word was the highest law and beyond which its precepts were unrecognized was not contemplated in Chinese theory. Not only was the field of Chinese influence unlimited by physical boundaries, but its field of action embraced the entire social life of man, not certain fields that were deemed public.

These controls were applied "through propaganda, appeal to reason, and example, not through the enactment of law, enforced by the authority of the state." None of this was understood by the Western powers when in the nineteenth century they sought to open relations with China's border states. To the West it appeared that China was the "suzerain" over various "vassal" or "tributary" states. This was of course so; but these terms did not connote identical forms of control in the Western and in the Chinese system of things.

While China remained the center and the superior in a Confucian community of nations, and while China had no vital contacts with other civilizations, all was well; but when in the nineteenth century Western states sought relations not only with China but also with the border states, such as Korea, they precipitated a

---

[3] I have here drawn heavily upon M. Frederick Nelson, *Korea and the Old Orders in Eastern Asia* (Baton Rouge, 1945). Tribute-bearing missions usually received in return gifts of greater value than those they had brought.

conflict between the Confucian theory and Western concepts of international law and the legal equality of states. In Korea, for instance, they found a people "which to them was neither sovereign enough to conduct independent relations nor subject enough to throw responsibility for its actions on China."

The Case of the Ryukyu (Liu-ch'iu) Islands

The island kingdom of Ryukyu, the chain of small islands reaching from Kyushu in southern Japan southward to Formosa, had sent tribute to China since late in the fourteenth century, a fact that placed it in the Confucian community of states over which China presided. However, feudal Japan also exercised certain political claims over Ryukyu. The royal family of Ryukyu was said to be related to the Minamoto clan; this may explain why it was that the Ryukyuans sent tribute to Japan in the fifteenth century. Early in the seventeenth century the Japanese *Daimyo* of Satsuma attacked the islands, brought the northern group under his immediate control, leaving the southern group semi-independent, a species of tributary status. Thus in the middle of the nineteenth century the unfortunate little state found itself tributary to both China and to Japan. In 1871 some Ryukyu islanders, wrecked on the shores of Formosa, were murdered by the aborigines. When China in response to Japanese overtures disclaimed responsibility for acts of the Formosans, Japan sent a military expedition to Formosa (1874). In addition, the Japanese continued to occupy a portion of the island, pending a settlement of the dispute with China. This was finally secured through British mediation; China agreed to indemnify the families of the murdered men and to pay for the roads Japan had built in Formosa. The significant implication of this settlement was that Japan was able to establish a legal claim to be protector of the Ryukyu islanders. For a time China refused to accept this view, and Ryukyu continued to send tribute missions to Peking. Attempts at mediation by General U. S. Grant in 1879 also failed, but in that year the Ryukyuan king was removed to Tokyo, where he was granted a title of nobility, and the islands were incorporated into Japan as a prefecture under the name of Okinawa. In 1881 China accepted a situation which she was powerless to alter.[4] The Ryukyu

[4] Payson J. Treat, *Diplomatic Relations between the United States and Japan 1853-1895* (2 vols., Stanford University, 1932), I, 473-475, 568-569; II, 71-78, 98-

incident is important because in this case Japan had succeeded in breaking the Confucian concept of international relations and in substituting for it the Western code of state responsibility.

THE CASE OF KOREA

The case of Korea was to be of far greater international consequence than that of Ryukyu. The earliest European contacts with Korea had occurred in 1593 when the Spanish Jesuit, Gregorio de Cespedes, administered spiritual consolation to Japanese Christian soldiers during Hideyoshi's abortive invasion. A number of Dutch sailors were shipwrecked on Korean shores in the seventeenth century and later escaped to Japan. Some attempts were made to open trade toward the end of the eighteenth and the beginning of the nineteenth century. During these developments Catholic Christianity reached Korea by way of the Jesuit mission in Peking, and, later, French priests entered the country surreptitiously. The conflict between Christianity and Confucianism, and the increase in the number of converts (there were 9,000 in 1839) led in that year to persecution and to the death of many converts and three priests. When in 1846 France sought explanations, she was informed that Korea was subordinate to China, to whom all questions of foreign relations must be referred. By this statement Korea was attempting to avoid relations with the West rather than to describe accurately her own status, for actually she had negotiated directly with foreign states such as Japan, though not with other states that were outside the Confucian system.

After 1860 a number of powers attempted to trade with Korea: the British and the Russians in 1861, the French the following year. To a second Russian mission in 1866 the Koreans declared that they were a dependent state of China. This Korean policy, in so far as it was followed from 1863 until 1898, may be ascribed to the regent, father of an infant king, who was vigorously anti-Western and anti-Christian, and who carried the title Tai wun kun.

FRANCE IN KOREA, 1866

In 1866 a great wave of anti-Christian persecution virtually wiped out the Christian community of some 18,000 converts; only three of a

104, 126-127, 141-144. Hyman Kublin, "The Attitude of China During the Liu-ch'iu Controversy, 1871-1881," *Pacific Historical Review,* XVIII (1949), 213-231, presents a detailed account of Sino-Japanese negotiations on Liu-ch'iu.

score of French priests escaped with their lives. A French force from China prepared to attack Korea, and the Peking government was informed that, since China disclaimed any authority over Korea, France herself would seek satisfaction. The military-naval expedition that followed suffered a decisive defeat, and for a time France abandoned any further action. The fact that China did not assume any responsibility for the acts of Korea confirmed France in the belief that China had voluntarily surrendered any claim to suzerainty over this former vassal or tributary state.

The United States and Korea

The United States, too, showed an official interest in Korea in 1866, when Secretary of State William H. Seward, thinking that Korea was about to be partitioned, proposed a joint Franco-American expedition. The French had brought back from Korea word that an American merchant ship, the *General Sherman,* had been wrecked on the Korean coast and that the natives had burned her and killed the crew. To Burlingame's inquiries at Peking, China replied that her connections with Korea were only "ceremonial." Seward's joint expedition was not undertaken, but American naval vessels did some charting on the Korean coast, and it was decided to seek a treaty with Korea for the protection of Americans shipwrecked on her coasts. When the American naval expedition reached Korea in May, 1871, it was fired upon. In retaliation, it destroyed a number of Korean forts, but got no treaty.[5] Indeed, the Koreans made it clear to China that they hoped to continue the old Confucian relationship, and they hoped China would make this clear to the barbarians. This, China made little effort to do. Thus American diplomats in Peking, like their French colleagues, continued to hold the view that China had recently renounced control over Korea's foreign affairs in order to avoid responsibility for Korea's involvements with Western powers.

Japan and the Opening of Korea

Japan sent a mission to Korea in 1868 to announce the restoration of the emperor and to seek the re-opening of relations. This mission and subsequent ones in 1869 and 1871 were treated with scant re-

[5] C. O. Paullin, *Diplomatic Negotiations of American Naval Officers, 1788-1883* (Baltimore, 1912), 282-328.

spect by the Tai wun kun's government, since Japan was regarded as a traitor to Confucian society because of her adoption of Western ways. However, in 1875 a Japanese gunboat engaged in marine surveys on the Korean coast was fired upon. Here, then, was an incident that could serve to bring Korea into treaty relations with Japan and at the same time detach Korea from its Confucian dependency on China.

Mori's Mission to China, 1876

Recognizing, however, that her success in Korea might well depend on the attitude of China, Japan first dispatched to Peking a mission under Mori Arinori to seek a more definite Chinese avowal of Korea's independence. China however continued to maintain that the relationship was that of "dependence yet no control." Nevertheless, Li Hung-chang agreed to aid Japan in securing a friendly reception at Seoul.

The mission that Japan sent to Korea soon secured a treaty (February 26, 1876) which opened three Korean ports to trade and provided for diplomatic intercourse. In English translation, Article I reads: "Chosen, being an independent State (tzu chu), enjoys the same sovereign rights as does Japan." Some Chinese historians have, however, translated this article more favorably to China. For instance: "Chaohsien [Chosen or Korea] being an autonomous (tzu chu) state, shall enjoy the rights of equality with Japan."[6] Nevertheless, despite arguments over the precise meaning of Article I, certain points are quite clear. The Japanese at this time intended by their treaty to make Korea "independent" as the West understood that term, whereas China on the other hand had no intention to alter the ancient relation in any way. As for the Korean government, the best that can be said is that it signed a "Western treaty" with Japan, making at the same time a mental reservation to continue the old Confucian relation with China.

The Dependencies of Ili, Annam, Burma, Sikkim

Korea's status, hanging as it did at this time between an ancient Confucian ideology and a modern Western one, was soon to be

[6] Shuhsi Hsu, *China and Her Political Entity* (New York, 1926), 109. Tzu chu is usually translated "self-governing" or "autonomous," rather than "sovereign" or "independent."

clarified by events in China's other dependencies. In 1881 the inroads of Russia in the northwest resulted in the loss by China of the western part of Ili, which was ceded to Russia. In 1885 the long story of French penetration into Indochina, dating back to the days of Louis XVI, was completed. In that year Annam, which had been a dependent state of China since Han times, fell completely under the control of France. At virtually the same time, Burma ceased to be a dependency of China. It had been a vassal state of China since its conquest by Kublai Khan in 1284. Lower Burma had passed to British control in 1862. Now, in 1886, the British extended their jurisdiction over all Burma. China recognized British sovereignty in Burma, and Britain agreed that Burma might continue to send decennial tribute missions to Peking. Only one mission, that of 1895, was ever sent. Finally, in 1890, China recognized a British protectorate over Sikkim. All of these treaties concerning Ili, Annam, Burma, and Sikkim revealed that the old Chinese relationship to these states (dependence yet no control) was giving place to a new Western and legalistic relationship in which these states were recognized by China as the colonies or protectorates of Western powers. It was therefore apparent that Japan's attempt to establish the independence of Korea in 1876 was not an isolated occurrence but rather a part of a larger movement by which the dependencies of China were being detached from dependence on Peking.

The New Chinese Policy Toward Korea

China was not slow in recognizing the danger of losing her ancient Confucian control over Korea. Following the loss of Ryukyu, Li Hung-chang noted that: "We can no longer refrain from devising ways and means for the security of Korea." Accordingly, China adopted a threefold course of action: she urged Korea to strengthen her military forces; she increased her diplomatic contacts with Korea in the hope of exercising greater influence at Seoul; and she urged Korea to conclude treaties with those powers which, unlike Japan and Russia, would be unlikely to have territorial ambitions. Of these powers the United States was the first to show a renewed interest in treaty relations with Korea. Commodore Robert W. Shufeldt was sent by the Navy Department to seek, with Japanese aid, a commercial treaty. The mission failed, but Shufeldt was encouraged by Li Hung-chang to seek a treaty through China's good offices. In 1882 the first American-Korean treaty was concluded. It provided among other things for the exchange of diplomatic and consular officers, for trade with Korea on the most-favored-nation principle, and included the provision:

If other Powers deal unjustly or oppressively with either Government, the other will exert their good offices, on being informed of the case, to bring about an amicable arrangement, thus showing their friendly feelings.

Li had asked, and Shufeldt had refused, to include a clause acknowledging the dependence of Korea upon China. This matter was disposed of by a letter from the Korean king to the President acknowledging the subservient status. However, the United States took the position, stated by Frederick T. Frelinghuysen, the Secretary of State,

that we have not regarded the aid lent to us by Chinese officials in bringing about this treaty as in any way an assertion of China's administrative rights over Corea . . . but that we regarded Corea as *de facto* independent, and that our acceptance of the friendly aid found in China was in no sense a recognition of China's suzerain power.[7]

The principal European powers were quick to follow the example of the United States in securing treaties through China's good offices: Great Britain, November 26, 1883; Germany, November 26, 1883; Italy, June 26, 1884; Russia, June 25/July 7, 1884; and France, June 4, 1886. In each case Korea, while negotiating as a sovereign power in terms of the treaty, set forth in accompanying letters her dependent position upon China.

Korean Politics and Chinese Relations, 1882

Prior to the conclusion of these treaties, the international status of Korea had been affected by other developments. The first of these was China's intervention in a palace revolution at Seoul; the other, the conclusion of certain Sino-Korean trade regulations.

There were two major factions at the Korean court: the one, led by the family of the queen, favored relations with foreign powers; the other, led by the Tai wun kun, was, as already noted, intensely anti-foreign. The rivalry of these two factions, together with bad

[7] United States, Department of State, *China Instructions,* Vol. 3, No. 30.

economic conditions, led to a conspiracy (1882) to do away with the queen. The plot failed, but in the course of the fighting Korean mobs attacked the Japanese legation and drove its occupants to the coast, where they were rescued by a British ship. Both Japan and China now stepped into the picture by sending troops to restore order. China, claiming to act in her traditional Confucian capacity, seized the Tai wun kun and sent him to Tientsin for punishment. Japan on her part exacted from Korea an agreement providing for an apology, an indemnity, the right to station a legation guard at Seoul, and the right of travel in the interior. To the Western powers all this was thoroughly confusing. Here was China intervening in the internal affairs of Korea, for which she professed to have no responsibility, using troops to restore order, issuing proclamations in the name of the king, and carrying off a member of the Royal House to answer for his deeds. On the other hand, here was Japan ignoring the Chinese and dealing directly with Korea.

The second development of 1882 was the conclusion by China and Korea of new regulations on trade. This agreement, although asserting that there was no change in Korea's status "as a boundary state of China," gave to the Chinese discriminatory advantages over other foreigners in matters of residence, travel, trade, and import duties. These advantages were granted exclusively to China because Korea was a tributary kingdom. Again the question before the Western powers was how this sort of thing could be reconciled with their own Korean treaties negotiated on the assumption that Korea was now independent.

It was evident after 1882 that Chinese control over and intervention in Korea was becoming more pronounced. High Chinese military officers even proposed the annexation of Korea and war with Japan. Li, however, adopting measures short of this, sent P. G. von Mollendorff to Korea as Inspector-General of Korean Customs. He also sent a number of Chinese "commercial agents" who would "actually assist the King to decide political issues" under the guise of their title. Indeed, Korea had ceased to be merely a Confucian appendage of China, for Li Hung-chang was now asserting, "I am King of Corea whenever I think the interests of China require me to assert that prerogative."[8]

---

[8] United States, Department of State, *China Dispatches,* Vol. 65, No. 230, Young to Frelinghuysen, Aug. 8, 1883.

The Tientsin Convention, 1885

Japan too had become active in Korea. She gave her support to the progressive or reform party. By 1884 the Japanese minister at Seoul openly criticized the policies of China, adding that Japan would welcome complete Korean independence. In December, 1884, the Korean Progressives seized the king and called upon the Japanese for military protection. Yüan Shih-k'ai, commanding Chinese troops, promptly drove the Japanese to the coast and restored the king to his conservative counsellors. For this affair, the Japanese exacted from Korea a mild treaty including an indemnity; but they also sent a mission headed by Ito Hirobumi to Tientsin to discuss the Korean question with Li Hung-chang. The treaty of Tientsin (April 18, 1885) which resulted was a partial though not a complete victory for Japan. The two powers agreed to withdraw their troops from Korea, and, in the case of future disturbances, neither would send troops *without notifying the other*. Thus, Japan gained a position of equality with China in the matter of military intervention.

Korea: A Chinese "Protectorate," 1885-1894

Between 1885 and 1894 Li Hung-chang so strengthened his control over Korea that the country became a Chinese protectorate rather than a dependent state in the old Confucian sense. Li accomplished this end by various means. To the control which he already exercised through foreigners in the employ of the Korean government and through Chinese commercial agents, he added the appointment of Yuan Shih-k'ai as Chinese Resident in Korea, a post superior to that of a mere diplomatic representative. By the control which he exercised through these agents, Li attempted to destroy any idea in the minds of the powers that Korea was fully sovereign. Li also sought economic as well as political influence at Seoul. In 1885 China obtained a monopoly in the Korean telegraph, and attempted to get control over future loans sought by the Korean government. So successful was Li's policy that in 1892 even Japan approached Korea through China when seeking satisfaction for losses occasioned by certain Korean embargoes on the exportation of beans to Japan.

Immediate Background of the Sino-Japanese War

The issue between China and Japan concerning the international status of Korea was clear by the early months of 1894. Summarized briefly, it was this: (1) the impact of the West had already deprived China of her principal dependent states, Burma, Annam, Ili, and Sikkim—Korea alone remained; (2) Korea too appeared to be headed toward what the West called "sovereign independence" (this was indicated by the Japanese treaty of 1876, the American treaty of 1882, and the European treaties of 1883 and after); (3) Li Hung-chang, however, was determined to preserve China's influence in this strategic peninsula against the designs of either Japan or Russia, and to do so by Western as well as Confucian techniques if necessary; and, finally, (4) since no one of the Western powers, despite their treaties, was prepared to assert the fact as well as the principle of Korean independence, the way was left open for Japan to do so. And when the time at last came for Japan to implement her policy of upholding Korean independence, she enjoyed a special advantage. It was relatively easy for her to give the impression that her motives were benevolent—to rescue Korea from China and Russia, and to bestow upon the Hermit Kingdom the independence, the sovereignty, and the progressive outlook which Japan herself enjoyed. It is perhaps needless to add that Japan's motives relative to Korea were no more benevolent than those of any other power.

Korea: A European Problem

However, even in 1894 Korea was not a question concerning Japan and China alone. It had already become "a sort of focal point for great European rivalries, as well as for Asiatic antagonisms."[9] When in 1885 it was rumored that Russia was to seize Port Lazarev, the British occupied Port Hamilton, an island off southern Korea; but Russia pursued a cautious policy, mildly supporting Japan and the United States against Chinese pretensions. England's policy in these years was dominated by the idea of preventing "the Russians from encroaching on Korea and from securing an ice-free port." It was against this background of European rivalries that the Japanese policy of 1894 was launched.

By 1894, Japan's political position in Korea was woefully weak, but her economic position was showing steady growth. Ninety per cent of Korea's foreign trade was with Japan. Li had made strenuous efforts to counter Japan's economic advance. He was slowly acquir-

[9] William L. Langer, *The Diplomacy of Imperialism,* 1890-1902 (2 vols., New York, 1935), I, 168. Note ch. vi for a discussion of European aspects of the crisis.

ing an army and navy, and was creating at Port Arthur a respectable naval base. He was also planning a railway from Shanhaikwan to the Manchurian border near Vladivostok. News of this latter project created considerable excitement in Russia, where in 1891 the decision was made to build the Trans-Siberian Railway. This was looked upon in Europe as a decision of the utmost importance, and it was viewed with misgivings by both China and Japan. The Japanese believed that if Russia completed her system of communications, her advance into eastern Asia could not be stopped; yet they also believed that Korea must be independent or controlled by Japan if the Empire was to be secure. The Japanese also had domestic worries on their minds. The constitutional government inaugurated in 1890 was not going well. Cabinets that considered themselves responsible only to the emperor were faced with a succession of recalcitrant Diets that refused to accept naval estimates presented by the government until appealed to directly by the emperor.[10] With young and inexperienced parliamentarians in this mood, some of the bureaucrats and militarists in the government were ready to welcome a foreign war that would unite the political home front in bonds of patriotism.

Immediate Preliminaries to War

From 1871 until 1894 the peace party in Japan, headed in the later years by Ito Hirobumi, maintained its ascendancy over the militarists, and consequently there was no war over Korea. But after 1890 the "obstructive" tactics of the Diet gave the war party its opportunity. Only a pretext was needed, and this was soon forthcoming. The *Tong Hak* ("Eastern Learning Society"), originally a Korean religious sect, had acquired a political complexion, had drawn into its membership the politically oppressed, and had assumed a program that was anti-foreign, anti-Christian, and anti-Japanese. When as a result rebellion finally occurred in the southern provinces, Korean government troops sent to quell the disturbance were themselves defeated. Acting on the advice of Yüan, Li Hung-chang promptly decided to send Chinese troops (June 6, 1894), and, in accord with the Tientsin Convention, notified Japan that he was doing so. Untactfully, China's notice referred to "our tributary

[10] Tatsuji Takeuchi, *War and Diplomacy in the Japanese Empire* (Garden City, 1935), 109-110.

state." Japan replied the same day that she too would send troops owing to the "grave nature" of affairs in the peninsula, and added that she had "never recognized Korea as a tributary state of China." By the time the Chinese and the Japanese troops arrived, the Koreans had already suppressed the revolt. Two hostile foreign armies faced each other before Seoul. A miracle perhaps could have prevented a clash, but miracles were not happening at Seoul. Japan proposed joint Sino-Japanese action to effect financial, administrative, and military reforms in Korea. China replied that she would not interfere in the internal administration of Korea and added that Japan had no right to do so. Japan then turned to the Korean government, demanding a declaration indicating whether or not Korea was tributary to China. When Korea's reply proved unsatisfactory to the Japanese, their troops seized the king, and a reorganized Korean government ordered Japan to expel Chinese troops. The Sino-Japanese War had begun. The declarations were issued on August 1, 1894.

The War

The diplomatic front was by no means favorable to Japan when she embarked on a policy of war. Britain, having supported China, indicated that she would not agree to Japanese annexation of Korean territory. Russia too gave her diplomatic support to China, seemingly on the theory that it was better to have Korea controlled by a weak China than by a young and vigorous Japan. As a result, Japan gave assurances to the powers that she had no designs on Korean territory, was interested only in Korean reform, and, in the interests of European commerce, would refrain from attacking Shanghai. These assurances were accepted, probably because it was believed generally in the West that Japan would be defeated. But these early forecasts were shattered by the September victories of Japanese arms at Pingyang and the Yalu. It soon became evident that Chinese forces were no match for the small but relatively efficient Japanese military machine.

Indeed a diplomatic revolution was already under way. British opinion, reacting to the Japanese victories, contemplated a complete reorientation of British far eastern policy. On October 6, the British invited France, Germany, Russia, and the United States to intervene jointly to seek a settlement that would include Korean independence, a European guarantee to Korea, and indemnity for Japan. The proposal was dropped when Germany and the United States refused to join. Li Hung-chang himself also sought the support of Europe and America to end the disastrous war before China was completely humbled. During the winter months of January and February, 1895,

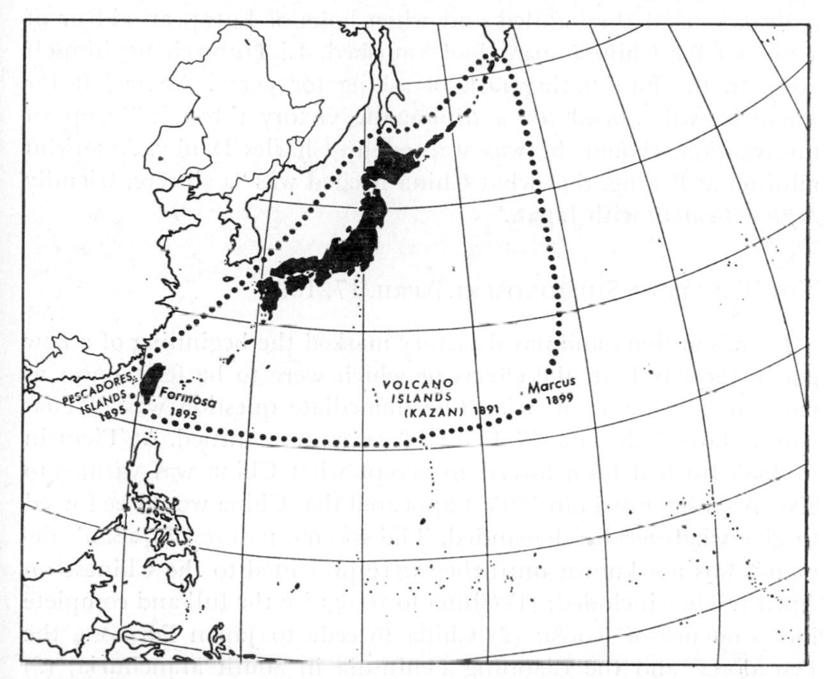

JAPAN, 1891-1904. *Reproduced from* A War Atlas for Americans, *Simon and Schuster, Inc., New York, 1944, by permission from Simon and Schuster, Inc., and from the U. S. Department of State, Division of Map Intelligence and Cartography.*

the Japanese had taken Wei-hai-wei; their armies were crossing southern Manchuria; and in early March they had occupied Newchwang and Yingkow, from which they might soon advance on a frightened and humiliated government in Peking. Here the Empress Dowager, instead of building a navy, had employed government funds to rebuild the Summer Palace, now embellished with an atrocious triumph, the Marble Boat, which was made mostly of wood. But the Marble Boat was small comfort to Chinese Admiral Ting Ju-Chiang, who committed suicide at Wei-hai-wei when forced to surrender to the Japanese, who had not spent their money on marble boats. When at this juncture the United States offered its good offices to both belligerents, Japan replied significantly that her objectives would not be reached "until China finds herself in a position to approach Japan directly on the subject of peace."

Indeed Li did send a succession of peace missions to Japan. Finally, when all these failed and when hope of European aid or of a victory for Chinese arms had vanished, Li Hung-chang himself accepted the humiliating task of asking for peace. As he left for Japan he still hoped for a diplomatic victory through European intervention, though he was warned by Charles Denby, American minister at Peking, that what China needed was "a sincere, friendly *rapprochement* with Japan."

The Treaty of Shimonoseki, April 17, 1895

Japan's military and naval victory marked the beginning of a new era in the Far East, the effects of which were to be felt almost as much in Europe as in Asia. The immediate question was: "What will be Japan's demands?" The tables were now turned. At Tientsin in 1885 Ito had been forced to accept what China was willing to give. At Shimonoseki in 1895 it appeared that China would be forced to give whatever Ito demanded. The specific nature of Japan's demands was not known until they were presented to the Chinese on April 1. They included: (1) China to recognize the full and complete independence of Korea; (2) China to cede to Japan Formosa, the Pescadores, and the Liaotung Peninsula in South Manchuria; (3) China to pay an indemnity of 300,000,000 taels; (4) China to conclude with Japan a new treaty of commerce, granting among other things most-favored-nation treatment to Japan and opening seven new treaty ports. Since neither Europe nor the United States was prepared to come actively at this time to China's aid, Li was forced to accept Japan's terms with some modifications. The treaty of Shimonoseki (sometimes known as Bakan) was signed April 17, 1895.

The efficacy of war as a stabilizer of Japanese politics was immediately evident. By the declaration of war Ito and Japan's Elder Statesmen achieved notable results. The nation was unified; peace prevailed between the government and the Diet; huge war budgets (one of 150,000,000 yen) were passed without a dissenting vote; in February a resolution was adopted unanimously to appropriate any amount of funds needed for the prosecution of the war. Japan had indeed taken the first step in what was to be a vigorous policy of expansion on the Asiatic continent. With Port Arthur and the Liaotung Peninsula in her possession she could look forward to a controlling influence at Peking. In short, she had made it clear that both territorially and diplomatically she proposed to be a part of whatever imperialistic pressures were exerted upon China.

For China the results of the war were no less momentous. The

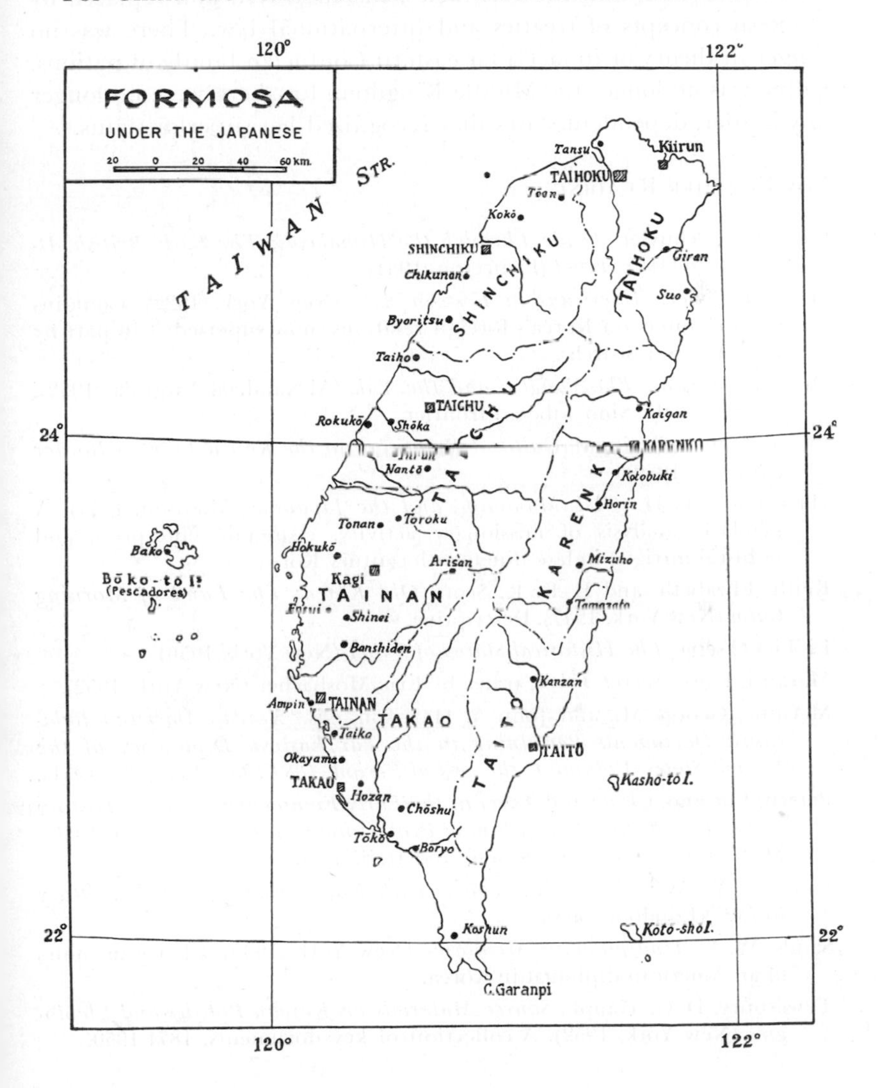

proud Middle Kingdom had been defeated by a people looked upon not only as inferior but also, by reason of their Westernization, as traitors to the Confucian family of nations. In naval, military, and political affairs the Manchu government was revealed as inefficient and corrupt. To a few thoughtful Chinese it already appeared that the dynasty had lost the Mandate of Heaven. Now with Japan's victory the old Confucian theory of international relations, which China had maintained for centuries, was destroyed and replaced by Western concepts of treaties and international law. There was no longer in theory or in fact a far eastern Confucian family of nations. China was no longer the Middle Kingdom, for there were no longer any border, dependent states that recognized her superior status.

For Further Reading

Cammann, Schuyler, *Trade Through the Himalayas: The Early British Attempts to Open Tibet* (Princeton, 1951).

Dennett, Tyler, *Americans in Eastern Asia* (New York, 1922). Contains good chapters on Korea's foreign relations, now superseded in part by more recent research.

Duncan, Marion, *The Yangtze and the Yak* (Alexandria, Virginia, 1952). A study of the Sino-Tibetan frontier.

Ekvall, Robert Brainerd, *Cultural Relations on the Kansu-Tibetan Border* (Chicago, 1939).

Harrington, F. H., *God, Mammon, and the Japanese* (Madison, 1944). A scholarly analysis of missionary activity, economic enterprise, and political intrigue in late nineteenth-century Korea.

Keith, Elizabeth, and E. K. R. Scott, *Old Korea: The Land of Morning Calm* (New York, 1947). Descriptive.

Li Tieh-Tseng, *The Historical Status of Tibet* (New York, 1956).

Maraini, Fosco, *Secret Tibet,* trans. by Eric Mosbacher (New York, 1952).

McCune, George M., and John A. Harrison, eds., *Korean-American Relations: Documents Pertaining to the Far Eastern Diplomacy of the United States, Volume I: the Initial Period, 1883-1886* (Berkeley, 1951).

Petech, Luciano, *China and Tibet in the Early Eighteenth Century: History of the Establishment of Chinese Protectorate in Tibet* (Leiden, 1950). Makes use of Tibetan, Chinese, and Italian sources.

Rockhill, W. W., *China's Intercourse with Korea from the XVth Century to 1895* (London, 1905).

Sands, W. F., *Undiplomatic Memories* (New York, 1930). Chatty memoirs of an American diplomat in Korea.

Tewksbury, D. G., compl., *Source Materials on Korean Politics and Ideologies* (New York, 1952). A collection of key documents, 1871-1950.

17

1895–1899

China and the Powers

THE Treaty of Shimonoseki placed Japan in the company of the so-called Great Powers; but it did much more than this. It precipitated a new and a dramatic era in the relations of China and the West. Until 1895, the major interest of the Western states in China was commerce. The traders had purchased China's silk and tea, and in return they had sold to China silver, opium, ginseng, sandalwood, furs, and, in the later years of the century, an expanding assortment of manufactured textiles, flour, and kerosene. There had been little penetration by the trader *into* China. Business was conducted in the treaty ports on the coast. Here, to be sure, the foreign merchants and their governments had surrounded themselves with certain protective agencies—the conventional tariff, extraterritoriality, concessions, and settlements—but apart from these guarantees to commerce, neither governments nor merchants had been concerned primarily with China as a great frontier for capital investment or with the political controls that might be imposed upon China to that end. Between 1895 and 1899 much of this was changed, for in these years China did become a market for the investment, principally, of railroad capital. This development, considered so vital by the industrialized states of the West, took the form of an international scramble by the powers for exclusive economic concessions and spheres of political interest. For a time it appeared that a complete political partitioning of China was imminent. The roots of this movement antedate of course the Sino-Japanese War, but it was Japan's victory in that war and her threat to dominate North China by the annexation of Port Arthur and Liaotung which precipitated the movement and endowed it from this time on with the full flavor of power politics.

The Triple Intervention

The ink was dry, but no more than dry, on the seals of the Treaty of Shimonoseki, when six days after its conclusion—that is, on April 23, 1895—the representatives of Russia, Germany, and France in Tokyo presented to Count Hayashi, deputy foreign minister, notes which said that

> . . . the possession of the Peninsula of Liaotung, claimed by Japan, would be a constant menace to the Capital of China, would at the same time render illusory the independence of Korea, and would henceforth be a perpetual obstacle to the peace of the Far East.

The three powers, protesting that in this manner they were giving new proof of their friendship, "advised" Japan to renounce possession of Liaotung. For a week the diplomatic scales hung in uneasy equilibrium. On May 1, Japan offered to give up all of Liaotung save the southern tip with Port Arthur. This offer the three powers refused, and on May 5 Japan accepted their "advice" without qualification. She asked, however, that the Treaty of Shimonoseki be ratified in its original form prior to the retrocession, and that she be given additional indemnity. This the powers granted. Ratification took place at Chefoo, May 8, where, significantly, a Russian squadron, wearing the gray paint of war and with its decks cleared for action, lay at anchor. The Liaotung Peninsula was returned to China by a convention signed November 8, 1895, in which China agreed to pay an additional indemnity of 30,000,000 Kuping taels.

The Triple Intervention ended the temporary truce in Japan's domestic politics. During the Shimonoseki negotiations Prime Minister Ito and Foreign Minister Mutsu knew that an unfriendly European intervention was in the making. Accordingly, Mutsu, in an effort to forestall action by the powers, had insisted that Japan make no territorial demands on the mainland, but he was overruled by pressure of the military and naval staffs. The generals were determined to have a strategic foothold on the continent. Therefore, when the Japanese public, elated with the news of military and naval triumphs, learned that its government had bowed to a European intervention, indignation was widespread, and was not quieted until May 10, when the emperor sanctioned an Imperial rescript stating that the retrocession in no way compromised the dignity or honor of the nation. Actually, the government was well aware that Japan had won the war but had lost the peace. For the brief duration of the war she had bid for and had held diplomatic leadership in the Far East. (It will be remembered that none of the Great Powers was willing to intervene to "save" China during the war.) Then, with military victory achieved, Japan made certain her diplomatic defeat by permitting the militarists to have their way in demanding a territorial concession from which Japan could dominate Peking.

European Background of the Intervention

The reasons that led to this dramatic three-power intervention are now reasonably clear to the historian, as are also the reasons why Britain did not participate. Up to the time of the war, English policy had been decidedly pro-Chinese. However, it also favored independence for Korea while opposing any thought of Japanese annexations on the continent. Japan's demands were therefore disturbing to the British, for they upset whatever balance of power there was in the Far East; yet at the same time the British admired Japan's aggressive efficiency, and they were not insensible to the fact that the commercial clauses of the peace settlement would be very profitable to British business in China.

Russia's problem created by the Japanese peace terms could not be rationalized so easily. In general, Russian policy in the long view was aiming at acquisition of an ice-free port on the Pacific. For Russia, the Sino-Japanese War had come too soon: the Trans-Siberian Railway was not completed and Russian plans were as yet immature. As a result of Japan's victory, Russia was forced to decide whether to seek a temporary understanding with Japan, or by diplomatic pressure and the threat of war to force the Japanese out of Manchuria at once. Under the guidance of Count Witte and with the assurance of German and French support, Russia adopted the latter policy. The Russians saw numerous advantages in this course. It would exclude Japan from any share in the partition of China (a partition which the Japanese were already considering), and it would make Russia appear as the savior of China, which would thus dispose Peking favorably to subsequent Russian territorial demands.

Germany's participation in the intervention is explained largely by the fear that a partition of China was possible and that it would be well to be active in the events leading to that end. The Germans already had their eyes on several bases in the Far East, and the views of the German Foreign Office were influenced by von Brandt, who for a quarter of a century had been the leading German diplomat in the Orient. Furthermore, anything that encouraged the Russians to become involved in eastern Asia would presumably react to German advantage in Europe.

The participation of France is explained by "considerations of general policy." France feared that the Japanese would resist, and that they would be joined by the British, which would thus precipitate a general conflict. Therefore, France favored letting the Japanese have their gains while the powers would seek their own territorial compensation elsewhere in China. When, however, Russia decided to act, France joined her in the interest of the Dual Alliance.

Financing the War and the Peace

While Japan paid for her diplomatic defeat with humiliating loss of her territorial gains in Manchuria, China paid for her unpreparedness with cold cash. Her efforts to float domestic loans during the war had failed. Chinese bankers had little interest in Li Hung-chang's Korean or Manchurian policies. Consequently, the Peking government financed the war with two loans totalling some £4,-635,000 from the British Hongkong and Shanghai Bank. After the war, China was confronted with the Japanese indemnity totalling 230,000,000 Kuping taels (about $172,000,000 gold). The Russians were particularly anxious that this bill should be paid and thus effect the Japanese evacuation of Liaotung; but they were equally concerned that the indemnity be met in such fashion as to leave China in a kind of politico-financial dependence upon Russia, which thus would prevent the extension of British financial influence at Peking. The Germans and the French shared in this desire. The result was a Franco-Russian loan to China, July 6, 1895, of 400,-000,000 francs. The political motive behind the loan was indicated by China's pledge not to grant to any foreign power any right of supervision or administration over any of its revenues, unless the same rights were extended to the Russian government. Witte, Russia's minister of finance, had won the first round in the financial battle for dominance at Peking. The Germans, who had not been admitted to the Franco-Russian loan, now joined the British bankers in a loan of £16,000,000, March 23, 1896. Two years later, March

1, 1898, the Anglo-German banking group extended another loan in the sum of £16,000,000. The era of international European rivalry to finance and to control China had begun.

The Russo-Chinese Agreements of 1896

The indemnity loans, virtually forced upon China by Russia and France in 1895, were not of course to be considered as adequate compensation for "the diplomatic aid" these powers had given Peking. The shape of future Russian policy was made clear during 1896. Since 1891 the Russians had been engaged in construction of the Trans-Siberian Railway. It was obvious that such a huge undertaking involving a line some 5,000 miles in length was not designed primarily to connect European Russia with Vladivostok or any other port which, like it, was ice-bound four or five months each year. What Russia wanted was a port in southern Korea or Manchuria; but in the months immediately following the peace this was out of the question unless she was prepared to fight Japan. However, by February, 1896, Russian fortunes in Korea took an unexpected turn for the better. The Koreans had not taken kindly to Japan's energetic suggestions on reform, and, when the Japanese Minister was implicated in the murder of the Korean queen, the king fled to the Russian legation in Seoul, from which for some time he ruled the country. Even this development did not result in immediate Russian seizures in Korea.

In Europe, Witte was developing Russia's far eastern plans with deliberation. In December, 1895, he chartered the Russo-Chinese Bank, ostensibly a private corporation but officially approved and inspired. Baron Rosen called it a "slightly disguised branch of the Russian treasury." The capital came from French banks. The new concern was to be the financial arm of the new Trans-Siberian Railway. Its powers were notable in that it could collect taxes, finance the business of local government, coin money, and secure commercial and industrial concessions such as railroads. Its founders likewise assumed, unofficially of course, that the granting of special concessions to Russia would be promoted by a judicious bestowal of "financial gifts" upon suitable Chinese officials in Peking.

Another phase of the Russian far eastern plan concerned the route of the Trans-Siberian Railway from Lake Baikal to Vladivostok. To run the line wholly in Russian territory north of Manchuria and the Amur would entail 350 miles of additional construction through difficult terrain. If, however, it were run directly across Central Manchuria, it would be the first step to Russian control of all Manchurian commerce and to the present and future railroad systems of North China. For a time, however, the Russians made little headway at Peking. The Chinese Minister at St. Petersburg was without authority; Li Hung-chang was under a temporary shadow; some of the Peking officials were leaning toward the British and the Germans, so that when Count Cassini, the Russian Minister at Peking, began to push the Trans-Siberian project in March and April, 1896, he met with no encouragement from the Chinese. The latter were well aware that the Russian railway demands could not be pushed aside, but they hoped to strike a better bargain by sending Li Hung-chang to the coronation of the new tsar. Actually this arrangement was exactly what Witte wanted. Li was met at Port Said by Witte's agent, Prince Esper Ukhtomskii, whose colorful writings on the cultural and philosophical unity of the Russians and the Asiatics were well known. It was the role of the Prince to prepare Li for Witte's more practical proposals on Russo-Chinese industrial unity in Manchuria. The argument as presented to Li was that Russia had plenty of territory and therefore no designs on that of China; that culturally the tie between the two nations was great; that by building the railroad across Manchuria, Russia would be in position to aid China against attack; and finally that China herself was not in a position to finance or build the road. There seems little doubt that Li was bribed handsomely by Russian agents, but his decision was probably made basically on other grounds. He had given up hope of aid from England after the "desertion" of 1895; he hated Japan intensely. Therefore, an alliance with and concessions to Russia seemed the natural answer.[1]

Moreover, Li was not alone in wishing to play Russia against Japan and other powers. Japan's victory in 1895 as will be noted in greater detail later had awakened and alarmed the Chinese scholar-official mind as had no crisis in the previous half century. The Sino-Japanese War illumined the empty pretense of the program of self-strengthening and hustled the high command of the Confucian bureaucracy back again to the older weapon of playing one power against another, of using barbarian to fight barbarian. Even among

---

[1] A. Yarmolinsky, ed., *The Memoirs of Count Witte* (New York, 1921), of great value but incomplete and unreliable in Witte's estimates of his own role.

Li's rivals there were supporters of his Russian policy, such, for example, as Chang Chih-tung (1837-1909). In 1895 Chang wrote that Russia was China's natural ally, "because England uses commerce to absorb the profits of China, France uses religion to entice the Chinese people, Germany has no territorial boundary with us, and the United States does not like to interfere in others' military affairs." As a result, China got the Russian alliance she wanted, but she did so by granting concessions which within two years precipitated the threatened break-up of the Empire.

The Russo-Chinese secret alliance, known as the Li-Lobanov Treaty, was signed on June 3, 1896. It was to remain in force for fifteen years. Among other things it provided: (1) for mutual assistance against any Japanese aggression, (2) for the use of Chinese ports by Russia in the event of war, and (3) for China's consent to the construction of the Trans-Siberian Railway across Manchuria, construction and operation of the road to be accorded to the Russo-Chinese Bank. Although rumors of this agreement soon became public, it was not until many years later that the exact nature of the alliance was revealed.

The Chinese Eastern Railway Agreements, 1896

What the public did learn was that on September 8, 1896, the Russo-Chinese Bank and the Chinese government had agreed to the construction and operation by the Chinese Eastern Railway Company of a line of railway from Manchouli on the western border of Manchuria to Pogranichnaya (Suifenho) on the southeast border near Vladivostok. The statutes of the new Chinese Eastern Railway Company were to conform to Russian law; the president was to be named by China; but the Russian general manager would exercise the greater power. The political nature of the line was indicated by the fact that over the "lands actually necessary for the construction, operation, and protection of the line" the Company was to have "the absolute and exclusive right of administration." China was to grant reduced tariff rates to goods entering or leaving by the line; there was to be no interference with the movement of Russian troops or munitions; and the Company was to have "the complete and exclusive right to operate the line."

These terms were confirmed in December, 1896, when the Russian government sanctioned the statutes of the Chinese Eastern

Railway Company. These statutes in addition obligated the Company to construct telegraph lines and to carry Russian mails free. Although the Chinese government was to adopt measures for the protection of the line, the statutes provided that "the preservation of law and order on the lands assigned to the railway and its appurtenances shall be confided to police agents appointed by the Company." After eighty years the railroad was to become Chinese property without payment. Thirty-six years after its completion China could purchase it by paying to the Company the full outlay with interest. Construction of the Chinese Eastern Railway was completed in 1904. From this great trunk line, nearly 1,000 miles in length, Russia hoped to build a political and commercial empire, providing easy access to the Pacific and insuring Russian economic dominance in North China. This was the Russian policy that Witte called "peaceful penetration."

The Yamagata-Lobanov Agreement, June 3, 1896

Li Hung-chang was not the only distinguished Oriental guest at the Russian coronation in 1896. Japan was represented by Yamagata Aritomo, the most powerful of the Choshu clansmen, father of the modern Japanese army, and, in his day, the leading exponent of the military tradition. The Japanese wanted a compromise settlement of Russo-Japanese rivalry in Korea, a compromise that would maintain the balance until the army and navy expansion program could be effected. Accordingly, Yamagata proposed to the Russians that the two powers divide Korea at the 38th parallel into a northern Russian sphere and a southern Japanese sphere, an arrangement that would give the Japanese control of Seoul, the capital. But the Russians turned down the offer. For the present they regarded it as good policy to play along with England and the United States, respecting the integrity of Korea. In the long run, they hoped to get control of the entire peninsula, especially the more highly developed and richer south with its strategic naval harbors of Fusan, Gensan, and Masampo. As a result, two general and unsatisfactory compromise agreements were reached. At Seoul the Russian and Japanese representatives advised the Korean king to return as soon as possible to his palace from his refuge in the Russian legation. The Japanese were to withdraw most of their troops. This understanding reached at Seoul (May 26) was supplemented by the Yamagata-Lobanov

Agreement made at Moscow (June 9). Both powers would support the Korean king's efforts to restore and maintain order; both would guarantee foreign loans so that adequate police could be maintained and foreign intervention avoided. Korea was thus recognized as a Russo-Japanese joint problem. A secret article provided that in case it became necessary to send troops to Korea, the two powers would consult with a view to fixing a neutral zone between their spheres of action. This meant that Korea had become a kind of joint protectorate.[2]

Germany and the Far East

The German intervention against Japan in 1895 had been prompted not only by the desire to involve Russia in the Far East and thus weaken the Franco-Russian alliance in Europe, but also by the German ambition to secure a naval and commercial base in China. All during the last quarter of the nineteenth century, Germany had possessed very able scientific as well as diplomatic representation in the Far East. To the diplomatic and political knowledge concerning Asia from such men as von Brandt was added scientific, geographic, and social-economic data from such authorities as Ferdinand von Richthofen, perhaps the outstanding European authority of the time on China. It was he who dramatized for Europe the dire consequences that must follow when Asiatic labor was turned loose upon the world. It was he also who first pointed out the strategic and economic advantages of Kiaochow on the South Shantung coast; but for a time Germany appeared to be more interested in various islands on the Korean coasts, in Wei-hai-wei, Chusan, Woosung, Amoy, Samsah Bay, and Mirs Bay.[3]

The German decision to take Kiaochow was made in the summer of 1897. This decision rested on the enthusiasm of the Kaiser, on the reports of Admiral von Tirpitz, who was in command of the German far eastern fleet in 1896, and on the reports of German harbor-construction engineers. To avoid any collision with Russia,

---

[2] William L. Langer, *The Diplomacy of Imperialism, 1890-1902* (New York, 1935), I, 405-407.

[3] German commercial and colonial activity in the Pacific area dates back to the activities of Hamburg merchants in Samoa (1857); by 1885 Germany had possession of a large section of New Guinea, and of the Bismarck and the Marshall Islands.

whose fleet had already wintered at Kiaochow, thus setting up a sort of priority in the place, the Kaiser appealed to the tsar and was seemingly given a green light. In September, Germany notified China of her need for this harbor. Apparently the plan was for the German fleet, uninvited, to winter at Kiaochow—a friendly but unmistakable gesture calculated to bring the Chinese to terms. But the way was made easier when, on November 1, 1897, two German Catholic missionaries were killed by Chinese robbers in southern Shantung. On November 14, Admiral von Diederich landed German troops at Kiaochow Bay. For a time the Chinese government refused to come to terms. The mandarins were encouraged by the Russians to resist, but by January, 1898, the Russian opposition had subsided, and on March 6 Germany secured her agreement with China. This convention was prefaced with the remark that "The Imperial Chinese Government consider it advisable to give a special proof of their grateful appreciation of the friendship shown to them by Germany." How deep this "friendship" was, and how significant its results, may be judged from the terms of the convention. It provided, among other things: (1) for a so-called "neutral" zone 50 kilometers wide surrounding Kiaochow Bay, in which zone China would permit the free movement of German troops, and in which China would take no measures without the consent of Germany; (2) for the lease to Germany for 99 years of both sides of the entrance to Kiaochow Bay, including the port of Tsingtao as a naval base; (3) for the exercise by Germany during the term of the lease of sovereign powers over the leased area; (4) that should Germany return the territory to China prior to the expiration of the lease, China would "cede to Germany a more suitable place"; (5) that Germany should not "sublet" the territory to another power; (6) that Germany might construct two railways in Shantung, construction and operation to be handled by a Sino-German company in which the nationals of both powers might invest; (7) that German nationals might mine coal within 30 *li* (10 miles) of the railways; and, finally, (8)

> the Chinese Government binds itself in all cases where foreign assistance, in persons, capital or material, may be needed for any purpose whatever within the Province of Shantung, to offer the said work or supplying of materials in the first instance to German manufacturers and merchants engaged in undertakings of the kind in question.

RUSSIA LEASES PORT ARTHUR

Germany's descent upon Kiaochow necessitated changes in Russia's plans. She had considered taking Kiaochow herself in the winter of 1895-1896, and her Foreign Minister, Muraviev, was violently opposed to the German occupation. Although the Germans had taken the one good naval harbor in North China, there were still plenty of harbors in Korea. Back in Moscow in 1896 Li Hung-chang had even advised the Russians to take a Korean port. But when in late 1897 Russia turned to Korea and attempted to make a Russian the financial adviser of the king and to oust a Britisher, M'Leavy Brown, from control of the Korean customs, she was met with the appearance of a strong Anglo-Japanese squadron in the harbor of Chemulpo. Accordingly, late in November, 1897, the Russian government began to consider occupation of the harbor of Talienwan on the Liaotung Peninsula in South Manchuria a few miles northeast of Port Arthur. In Peking, the Chinese government, though petitioned by some of the most powerful viceroys, such as Chang Chihtung, to seek an alliance with Japan and England, had already determined on a policy of surrender. And so, on March 27, 1898, less than three weeks after Germany had leased Kiaochow, China leased to Russia for twenty-five years the southern tip of the Liaotung Peninsula containing Port Arthur and Talienwan (Bay). This was the spot from which Russia, France, and Germany had ousted Japan three years earlier. North of the leased area was to be a neutral zone stretching to the base of the peninsula. Finally, the convention granted to the Chinese Eastern Railway Company the right to connect Talienwan by rail with the main line in Central Manchuria. Thus, to use the terms of the agreement, Russia's naval forces had secured "an entirely secure base on the littoral of northern China," and the two sovereigns had fulfilled their desire of still further strengthening the friendly relations existing between the two Empires.

FRANCE LEASES KUANG-CHOU WAN

During the winter of 1897-1898, when Germany and Russia were maturing their plans at Kiaochow and Port Arthur, France did not appear disposed to play an active role in China. French political leaders were paying lip service to the principle of China's integrity.

Yet it was obvious that France was not unaffected by the German and Russian moves. Since 1885 France has possessed a great empire of colonies and "protectorates" in Indochina. In that year China had renounced sovereignty over Annam, had agreed to respect Franco-Annamite agreements, and had promised to open two cities in Yünnan to French commerce. In 1895, French influence, now more strongly entrenched in northern Indochina (Annam and Tongking), was looking to industrial concessions across the frontier in China's southern provinces. Within a month of the famous Triple Intervention of that year, France reaped her first reward. On June 20, 1895, it was agreed that

> . . . for the exploitation of its mines in the provinces of Yunnan, Kwangsi, and Kwangtung, [China] may call upon, in the first instance, French manufacturers and engineers . . .

The principle that the railways of Annam might be extended into China was also agreed upon. Following close on the heels of this agreement, France in June, 1896, secured from China a concession to construct a railroad in Kwangsi from the border of Tongking to Lungchow. In the same year a French expedition explored the interior of the island of Hainan, and in January China promised France never to alienate it to any other power. It is not surprising, then, that France was ready with new demands on China once Germany and Russia had taken action at Kiaochow and Port Arthur. The gains of France were extensive. On April 10, 1898, China agreed not to alienate any of her territories on the border of Tongking (northern Annam). On the same day China agreed: (1) to grant France a concession for a railroad from Tongking to Yünnan-fu; (2) to lease to France for 99 years the bay of Kuang-Chou as a naval station and coaling depot; and (3) to appoint Frenchmen as advisers to the newly proposed Chinese postal service. These measures were designed not only to give France a strategic foothold and industrial concessions in South China, but also to draw Chinese commerce away from British influence at Hongkong and Canton and to center it under French control in the Gulf of Tongking.

GREAT BRITAIN: KOWLOON, THE YANGTZE VALLEY, WEI-HAI-WEI

The British government during 1897-1898 had failed to place any effective restraints on the development of German, Russian, or French policy in China. British policy had been basically commercial rather than political, but it could hardly remain unaffected by the new position now occupied in China by the other great European powers. In other words, if leaseholds, preferential concessions, and special spheres were to be the order of the day, it behooved England, so ran the argument, to have her share. From February through July, 1898, the British and China concluded a series of agreements of the utmost importance. China agreed: (1) never to alienate any territory in the Yangtze Valley (February 11); (2) that the Inspector-General of the Chinese Maritime Customs should be a British subject so long as British trade predominated (February 13); (3) to lease Wei-hai-wei to Britain as a naval harbor "for so long a period as Port Arthur shall remain in the occupation of Russia" (July 1); (4) to extend the British territory of Kowloon by a lease for 99 years of the entire peninsula lying between Deep Bay and Mirs Bay (June 9). With this British advance should be noted also the Anglo-German loan to China (March 1, 1898) in the amount of £16,000,000, and various preliminary agreements between the Hongkong and Shanghai Banking Corporation and Chinese authorities concerning the financing of the Shanghai-Nanking Railway (May 13) and the Peking-Newchang Railway (June 7). By November, 1898, the British had secured nine railroad concessions totalling 2,800 miles; the Russians, three concessions, 1,500 miles; the Belgians, one concession, 650 miles; the French, three concessions, 300 miles.[4] This scramble intensified the desire of the powers to define more specifically the limits of the spheres that were claimed by each. Diplomatic pressure was continually exerted on Peking to this end.

These developments, culminating in the spring and summer of 1898, made it quite clear that the integrity of China was worth very little. Germany, Russia, and France had all expressed great respect for this principle, but their leaseholds and their railroad and non-alienation agreements made it perfectly clear that these protestations were not to be taken too seriously. It was clear that an era of special and exclusive privilege was dawning in China. Britain disliked the tendency, for she had more to gain in an open market where all traded on terms of equality. But no power, not even the United States, would align itself with the British. Consequently, Downing

---

[4] Details on railroad concessions in E-tu Zen Sun, *Chinese Railways and British Interests, 1898-1911* (New York, 1954).

Street, having protested, decided to join the robbers.[5] In London, opponents of this policy of imitation spoke in sarcastic terms of "Port Arthur Balfour" and "a triumph of diplomatic incompetency." The Opposition called Wei-hai-wei, "Woe! Woe! Woe!" The fact was that the four great powers of Europe had begun the serious business of tampering with Chinese sovereignty. To be sure, each of the leasehold agreements carefully reserved to China her full sovereignty in the leased areas. But as Langer has said: "This was mere camouflage and the statesmen knew it." The most serious phase of the business was that in 1898 there was no unity of purpose within China herself, no constructive program of reform and resistance, and no able leadership.

For Further Reading

Ballard, G. A., *Influence of the Sea on the Political History of Japan* (New York, 1921). A naval rather than an historical analysis.

Clyde, Paul H., *International Rivalries in Manchuria* (rev. ed., Columbus, 1928). A general survey of international relations affecting Manchuria.

Gerard, Auguste, *Ma Mission en Chine, 1893-1897* (Paris, 1918). Very important for both French and Russian policy.

Inspectorate General, Chinese Maritime Customs, *Treaties, Conventions, etc. between China and Foreign States* (2 vols., 2nd ed., Shanghai, 1917).

Joseph, Philip, *Foreign Diplomacy in China, 1894-1900* (London, 1928).

Kent, Percy Horace, *Railway Enterprise in China* (London, 1907).

Mayers, William Frederick, ed., *Treaties between the Empire of China and Foreign Powers* (5th ed., Shanghai, 1906).

McCordock, R. Stanley, *British Far Eastern Policy 1894-1900* (New York, 1931).

MacMurray, John van Antwerp, *Treaties and Agreements With and Concerning China, 1894-1919* (2 vols., New York, 1921).

Pooley, A. M., ed., *The Secret Memoirs of Count Tadasu Hayashi* (New York, 1915).

Remer, C. F., *Foreign Investments in China* (New York, 1933). The best estimate of Japanese investments in China up to 1930.

Treat, Payson J., *Diplomatic Relations between the United States and Japan* (3 vols., Stanford University, 1932 and 1938).

"Vladimir" (Z. Volpicelli), *The China-Japan War* (Kansas City, 1905). A useful contemporary account.

[5] Of British policy at this time it should be said that the only way to stop Russia in Manchuria was to fight her, and Britain had no intention of doing this. For one thing, it would have been a doubtful war fought at the end of sea lines of communication 2,000 miles long. Geography would have favored Russia. Britain preferred the maintenance of China's integrity, but she had no intention of going to war to uphold it. There was little chance that she could stop Russia, since no other great power was prepared to join in the crusade.

18

1898–1913

The Philippines

It has been said that in the months and the years that preceded May 1, 1898, no idea was perhaps so remote from the mind of the American people as the conquest and acquisition of the Philippine Islands. Yet within the year that followed this date, the United States had taken unto itself a great Asiatic territory 6,000 miles from San Francisco across the Pacific, had projected itself into the main currents of world politics; and had discarded, so it seemed, some of its most deeply rooted traditions. It was as though the habits and dress of an old century had given place to the more modish styles of the new.

To Americans there was, to be sure, nothing new in the simple acquisition of contiguous territory. That was an old American custom. The nineteenth century was filled with the territorial advance of Americans through Louisiana and Florida, through Texas to the Rio Grande and California, and across the plains of Kansas to Oregon. The movement was completed by mid-century. The natural limits of westward continental expansion had been reached. Was it not now the business of Americans to remain at home to develop what they already possessed? Nevertheless, a new extracontinental, overseas expansion had already been foreshadowed and was soon to begin. The interruption was only temporary. In Seward's purchase of Alaska, 1867,[1] there was the suggestion of the earlier ideas of Commodore Perry in Japan and Peter Parker in China that the United States needed coaling and naval stations on far eastern

[1] On the Alaska purchase, see V. J. Farrar, *The Annexation of Russian America to the United States* (Washington, 1937); F. A. Golder, "The Purchase of Alaska," *American Historical Review,* XXV (1920), 411-425; T. A. Bailey, "Why the United States Purchased Alaska," *Pacific Historical Review,* III (1934), 39-49; and the popular account in F. R. Dulles, *America in the Pacific* (Boston, 1932), ch. vi.

islands: Formosa, the Ryukyus, and the Bonins. As early as 1854 President Pierce and Secretary of State Marcy tried but failed to annex the Hawaiian Islands by treaty. The Midway Islands were easier marks. A thousand miles northwest of Hawaii, they were occupied by an American naval force in August, 1867. In 1878 the American Navy acquired the use of a harbor in the far distant Samoan Islands of the South Pacific, and a decade later the State Department resisted German encroachment there with vigor.[2] This official American interest in Samoa and the harbor of Pago Pago, 5,600 miles from Panama, was significant because it was an

> . . . assertion by the United States, not merely of a willingness, but even of a right to take part in determining the fate of a remote and semi-barbarous people whose possessions lay far outside the traditional sphere of American political interests.[3]

And, if Americans had not been seriously interested previously in annexing Hawaii, the Senate in 1887 secured an equivalent, the exclusive right for the United States to use Pearl Harbor as a naval station, and by 1893, Americans were debating with a good deal of heat the proposals of the Harrison administration to bring the island under the American flag. Against the pro-expansionist arguments of Captain Alfred T. Mahan, that the islands controlled the commerce of the North Pacific and were strategically essential, were those of the anti-expansionists and anti-annexationists: men such as Carl Schurz, E. L. Godkin, editor of *The Nation,* and James Gordon Bennett, Jr., publisher of the Democratic *New York Herald.* This triumphant opposition to expansion expressed views running the gamut from the constitutional and ideological objections of Schurz to the polemics of Godkin, who asserted that if Hawaii were admitted to the Union,

> men would come into our Senate worse than those from Nevada, Wyoming and Idaho and which will be sent from Utah, Arizona, New Mexico and Oklahoma after they are admitted into the Union.[4]

Blocking the New Manifest Destiny

It is thus proper to note that in the decades immediately preceding the Spanish-American War the American mind as it contem-

[2] George H. Ryden, *The Foreign Policy of the United States in Relation to Samoa* (New Haven, 1933) chs. vii-x.

[3] John Bassett Moore, in *Cambridge Modern History,* VII, 663.

[4] E. L. Godkin, "Hawaii," *The Nation,* 56 (1893). 96.

plated the Pacific had not kept pace with "the march of events." The official arm of the United States had already carried the Stars and Stripes far out into the Pacific, to Alaska and the Aleutians, to Midway and to Samoa, and finally to Pearl Harbor. Yet the vast majority of politically minded Americans had no interest in these places, no understanding of why their government was projecting itself into foreign fields, and certainly no thought of setting up a colony in Asia itself. Disciples of the New Manifest Destiny, of imperialism, there were, but they were few compared with those Americans who followed the more timid and conscientious philosophy of Grover Cleveland, called by the expansionists "the Buffalo lilliputian!"[5] Even American "big business," usually considered the spearhead of imperialism, was, in the main, content to stay at home. In 1893 no less a person than the vice-president of the Great Northern Railroad was saying publicly that

> he [the Chinaman] is as poor as a rat, and has nothing with which to pay for our high-priced products except silk handkerchiefs and bamboo pipes. . . . The Great Northern is coming here to do business with the Pacific slope, not with Asia.

The New Far Eastern Policy in the Making

Nevertheless, on the eve of the Spanish-American War a new far eastern policy for the United States was taking shape in the minds of a handful of Americans. Policy up to this time had been shaped by commercial rather than political aims.[6] The new policy, although by no means nation-wide as yet in its appeal, gained ground rapidly after 1890 under the leadership of a group of dynamic spokesmen.

The patron saint of the new and large policy of expansion, John Louis O'Sullivan, close associate of Polk, Pierce, and Buchanan, and coiner of the phrase "Manifest Destiny," died in 1895, but his philosophy was kept alive by John W. Burgess of Columbia University,

---

[5] For further readings on the beginnings of American imperialism in the Pacific, see J. W. Pratt, *Expansionists of 1898* (Baltimore, 1936), ch. i, "The New Manifest Destiny"; H. W. Bradley, "The American Frontier in Hawaii," *Proceedings,* Pacific Coast Branch, American Historical Association, 1930, 135-150; Allan Nevins, *Grover Cleveland* (New York, 1934), ch. xxx; C. C. Tansill, *The Foreign Policy of Thomas F. Bayard, 1885-1897* (New York, 1940), ch. xii; A. T. Volwiler, "Harrison, Blaine, and American Foreign Policy, 1889-1893," *American Philosophical Society Proceedings,* LXXIX (1938), 637-648.

[6] A. Whitney Griswold, *The Far Eastern Policy of the United States* (New York, 1938), 8.

under whom Theodore Roosevelt sat as a student, and Captain Alfred Thayer Mahan, whose lectures at the Naval War College were later published under the title, *The Influence of Sea Power upon History*. The composite doctrine that emerged from the writings and speeches of these men and others was that the United States had come of age; that it could no longer be held within the old continental borders; that the commerce of the world was beckoning to American enterprise; that benighted areas and backward people were calling to the beneficent forces in American civilization; in a word, that we could no longer ignore the responsibilities of the "white man's burden" to civilize, to Christianize, and (it was added by a few) to commercialize less fortunate peoples.

To a notable though limited degree, therefore, the stage was already set for new adventures in American foreign policy when, on April 19, 1898, the Congress of the United States passed the joint resolution that precipitated the Spanish-American War. Actually, the roots of this war were connected only remotely, if at all, with the white man's burden and the larger policy it entailed. There were few Americans indeed in the spring of 1898 who entertained any notion that the war with Spain would place the United States among the great colonial powers, much less that the principal new colonies would lie on the fringe of Asia some 7,000 miles from San Francisco. There was in fact no official suggestion that, if war came, it was to lead to colonies at all. On the contrary, the war resolution voiced traditional principles associated with the Monroe Doctrine. It stated that Cuba was and ought to be free "of right"; it demanded the withdrawal of Spain; it instructed the President to secure these ends by use of the armed forces; and it expressly denied any intent on the part of the United States to annex Cuba.

The Popular View of the War

Most Americans viewed the outbreak of war as the inevitable result of what they called Spain's long record of corrupt, oppressive, and cruel rule in the island of Cuba. Then came the destruction of the *Maine* in Havana harbor on February 15, 1898 with a loss of more than 250 officers and men. While some sections of the American press called for restraint, the yellow journals yelled for war and a "Free Cuba." The demands for war came from mass meetings, from university students, and from members of the clergy. Responsi-

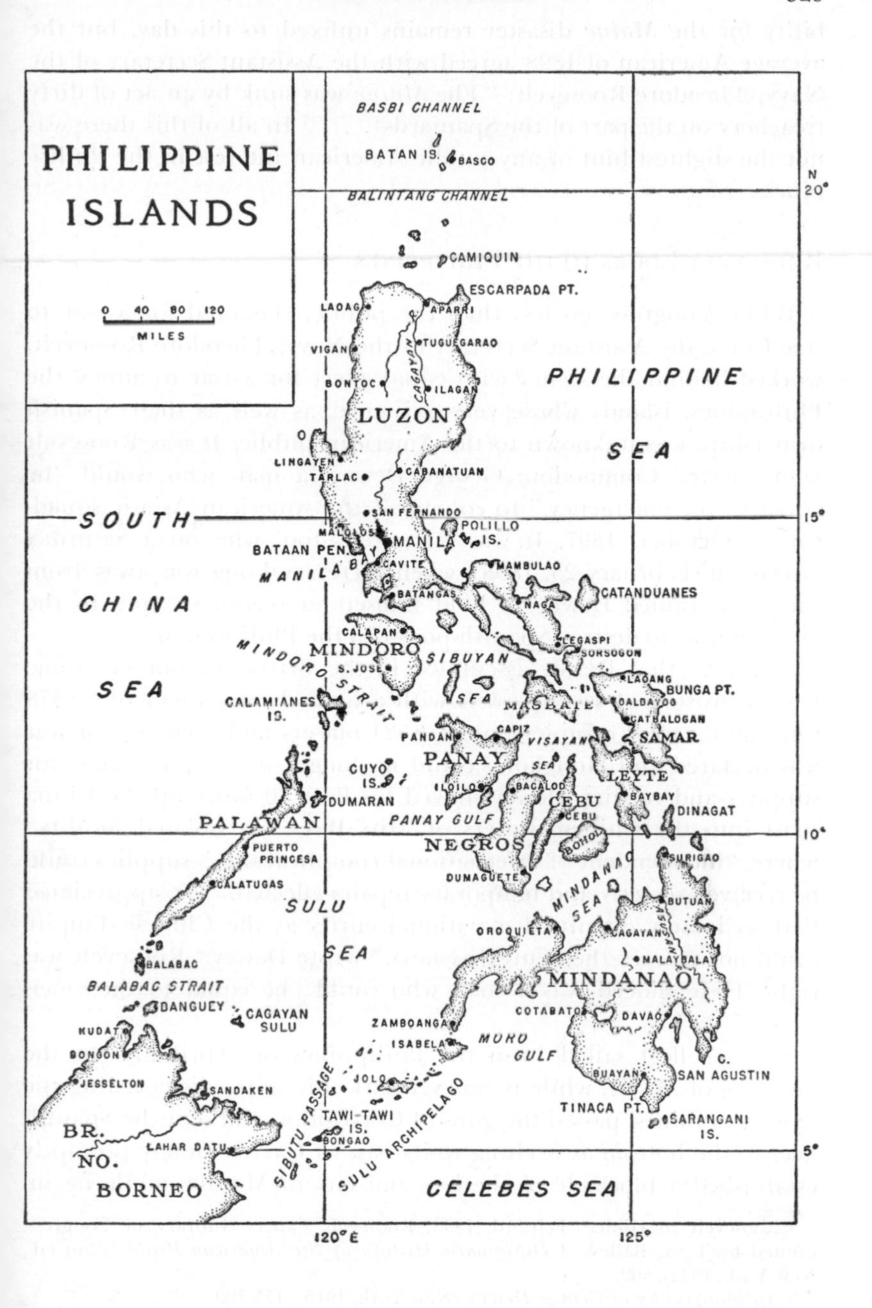
PHILIPPINE ISLANDS
0 40 80 120
MILES
BASBI CHANNEL
BATAN IS.
BASCO
BALINTANG CHANNEL
N
20°
CAMIQUIN
ESCARPADA PT.
LAOAG
APARRI
TUGUEGARAO
VIGAN
CAGAYAN
BONTOC
ILAGAN
PHILIPPINE
LUZON
SEA
LINGAYEN
TARLAC
CABANATUAN
SAN FERNANDO
SOUTH
15°
MALOLOS
POLILLO IS.
BATAAN PEN.
MANILA
MANILA BAY
CAVITE
MAMBULAO
BATANGAS
CATANDUANES
CHINA
NAGA
CALAPAN
LEGASPI
MINDORO
SORSOGON
MINDORO STRAIT
SIBUYAN
S. JOSE
LAOANG
SEA
BUNGA PT.
CALAMIANES IS.
SEA
MASBATE
CALDAYOG
CATBALOGAN
PANDAN
CAPIZ
SAMAR
VISAYAN
PANAY
SEA
LEYTE
CUYO IS.
ILOILO
BACALOD
BAYBAY
DUMARAN
CEBU
DINAGAT
PALAWAN
PANAY GULF
CEBU
NEGROS
BOHOL
10°
PUERTO PRINCESA
SURIGAO
DUMAGUETE
MINDANAO
CALATUGAS
SEA
BUTUAN
SULU
OROQUIETA
CAGAYAN
AGUSAN R.
SEA
MALAYBALAY
BALABAC
MINDANAO
BALABAC STRAIT
BANGUEY
CAGAYAN SULU
COTABATO
DAVAO
KUDAT
ZAMBOANGA
ISABELA
MORO
BONGON
GULF
C. SAN AGUSTIN
JESSELTON
JOLO
BUAYAN
SANDAKEN
SIBUTU PASSAGE
TINACA PT.
TAWI-TAWI IS.
SARANGANI IS.
BR. NO. BORNEO
LAHAR DATU
BONGAO
SULU ARCHIPELAGO
5°
CELEBES SEA
120° E
125°

bility for the *Maine* disaster remains unfixed to this day, but the average American of 1898 agreed with the Assistant Secretary of the Navy, Theodore Roosevelt: "The *Maine* was sunk by an act of dirty treachery on the part of the Spaniards . . ."[7] In all of this there was not the slightest hint of any public American interest in the Philippines.

Roosevelt Looks to the Philippines

While Congress, no less than the public, clamored for a war to free Cuba, the Assistant Secretary of the Navy, Theodore Roosevelt, worked behind the scenes with equal effect for a war to annex the Philippines, islands whose very existence, as well as their Spanish ownership, was unknown to the American public. It was Roosevelt who selected Commodore George Dewey, a man who would "be equal to the emergency," to command the American Asiatic squadron in October, 1897. It was Roosevelt, too, who on a Saturday afternoon (February 25, 1898), when Secretary Long was away from the office, cabled Dewey to hold himself in readiness, and, in the event of war, to destroy Spanish power in the Philippines.

The fleet that Dewey assembled in the British harbor of Hongkong consisted of seven vessels with a total displacement of 20,378 tons, and a total complement of 1,524 officers and men. When war was declared and Hongkong could no longer be used as a base for supplies and repairs, Dewey moved his fleet 30 miles up the China coast into the Chinese waters of Mirs Bay, "an isolated locality" where, "independent of international complications," supplies could be received secretly and temporary repairs effected. "We appreciated that so loosely organized a national entity as the Chinese Empire could not enforce the neutrality laws," wrote Dewey.[8] Roosevelt was right. Here indeed was a man who could "be equal to the emergency."

Dewey's fleet sailed from the Philippines on April 27. On the morning of May 1, while it was yet dark, his ships, disregarding the danger of mines, passed the guns of Corregidor, and sent the Spanish fleet to the bottom as it clung to its base at Cavite. Dewey promptly established a blockade of the bay and city of Manila, while he in-

---

[7] Roosevelt to Diblee, Feb. 16, 1898, Roosevelt Papers, Library of Congress, quoted by T. A. Bailey, *A Diplomatic History of the American People* (2nd ed., New York, 1942), 502.

[8] *Autobiography of George Dewey* (New York, 1916), 175-190.

formed Washington that the city could be taken but that 5,000 men would be needed to hold it. In Washington, the decision to send troops to the support of Dewey involved many questions. No political policy as to the future of the Philippines had yet emerged, and even the future of the immediate military policy, now forced upon the consideration of the government by Dewey's victory, was in a formative and tentative stage. For what specific purposes were the troops to be sent? Were they to engage in the conquest of the entire archipelago? How many troops would be sent? Illogically, the last question was answered first. The fact was that Dewey's dramatic victory had taken the country by surprise. Neither the government nor the people were prepared for the vital decisions that the victory demanded. What is more, Theodore Roosevelt, who was more responsible than anyone else for Dewey's presence in Manila Bay, was now a colonel commanding a regiment of Rough Riders. Thus McKinley's cabinet, groping for an immediate and future policy, dispatched troops to Manila, where by the end of July some 8,000 had arrived. This was to make possible the eventual capture of Manila, but it did not clarify the political atmosphere in the islands. Filipino nationalists with American encouragement and assistance had taken the field against Spain, and with Dewey's approval harassed the outskirts of Manila while the American commodore awaited the arrival of an American army.

Nationalism in the Philippines

Who were these Filipino patriots, who, like the Americans, were fighting against Spain?

Prior to the Spanish conquest of the islands in the sixteenth century there was no strong national or political structure in the Philippines. With the completion of the Spanish conquest, which by the close of the sixteenth century reached all parts of the archipelago save Palawan and the Moro country, the islands passed under a unified control. Slavery was abolished in law if not in fact, and the natives were converted speedily to Christianity. However, economic progress under the Spanish regime was slow. Agricultural methods remained antiquated until well into the nineteenth century, while excessive restrictions on trade hampered commercial development. Under remnants of feudal theory, Spain at first controlled all the land, conducting its administration through the *encomienda* system.

With the failure and subsequent abolition of this system, the control of local affairs passed largely into the hands of the regular clergy (known as the friars). This was natural enough at the time. The clergy, as missionaries, were close to the natives; they had mastered the native tongues, and had frequently protected their converts from the injustice of the *encomenderos*. In addition, the union of church and state in the Philippines "was apparently even more intimate" than the corresponding union in Spain. Thus, while in law the governor general might appear all-powerful, he acted, and usually wished to act, in close collaboration with the hierarchy of the religious orders. The system contributed much by bringing Christianity to the Filipino, but it also meant that he lived "through more than two centuries of political stagnation."[9]

The nineteenth century saw the beginnings of a political awakening in the Philippines which drew its inspiration from liberal movements in Europe and the democratic struggle within Spain itself. In part, too, the movement was a revolt against the increasingly oppressive rule of the friars.

Leaders of the Philippine Revolt

The last quarter of the nineteenth century produced a number of Filipino students, writers, and political agitators who became aggressive in their demands for reform. Marcelo H. Del Pilar attacked the friars as the principal enemy of both the church and the state. Jose Rizal wrote political novels revealing the social, political, and economic backwardness of his people. These books, though condemned by the friars, found their way secretly into thousands of homes. Rizal, a man of education, culture, and letters, who had studied abroad, founded in 1892 the Liga Filipina, through which he hoped to raise the economic, social, and educational life of his people. Whether he contemplated political revolution is a matter of dispute. Far more radical in method and purpose were Andres Bonifacio and Emilio Aguinaldo, who were associated with a new secret society, the Katipunan. This organization, definitely plebeian and revolutionary, contemplated destruction of the power of Spain, of the friars, and of the great landlords. Discovery of its plans resulted in a premature revolt in 1896. Rizal, unjustly accused of in-

---

[9] Maximo M. Kalaw, *The Development of Philippine Politics, 1872-1920* (Manila, 1926), 1-19.

spiring the rising, was executed, and thereby was to become the Philippine national hero. During 1897 the revolt was suppressed. Several of the rebel leaders who were paid to leave the islands claimed that Spain had promised reforms. These were not forthcoming, whether promised or not. The result was that on the eve of the Spanish-American War sporadic revolts were again occurring even though most of the leaders were in exile.

The Return of Aguinaldo

Aguinaldo, one of the exiles, was at Singapore when Dewey entered Manila Bay. The Commodore, advised of this fact by an American consul, first encouraged and then actively aided Aguinaldo's return to Manila on an American dispatch boat. At Manila, Aguinaldo was assisted further with supplies and rifles from the Cavite arsenal in recruiting a new revolutionary army. On May 24, 1898, five days after his arrival, Aguinaldo proclaimed his revolutionary government and announced his purpose to liberate the islands from Spain. On June 23, the revolutionary government named Aguinaldo president, and adopted a constitution proclaiming independence. On August 6, this government petitioned foreign powers for recognition of its belligerent status and for recognition of independence in the Philippines. A week later, after the newly arrived American troops had occupied lines that Aguinaldo's insurgents had thrown about the city, Manila capitulated to the American forces. This occurred only a few hours after a protocol of peace had been signed at Washington by the United States and Spain, August 12, 1898 (August 13, 5:30 A.M. Manila time).

The Embarrassments of Victory

From May 1, 1898, the date of Dewey's naval victory, until February 6, 1899, when the Senate ratified the Treaty of Paris by a margin of only two votes, the government and the people of the United States were embarrassed by an unforeseen naval victory which had given them a tropical archipelago and some six or seven million "little brown wards." At first the experience was intoxicating. When the news came of Dewey's triumph,

> the country went wild with excitement. "Dewey Days" were celebrated in the principal cities. Streets were renamed for Dewey. Young women wore "Dewey" sailor hats, sipped "Dewey" cocktails, chewed "Dewey Chewies"

—a new brand of gum—and wrote letters on "Dewey blue" stationery. Men smoked cigars made of Sampson [Havana] filler and Dewey [Manila] wrappers, while those who were so inclined resorted to the corner saloon and called for Dewey brand whiskey. Meanwhile the President notified Congress that: "At this unsurpassed achievement the great heart of our nation throbs, not with boasting or with greed of conquest, but with deep gratitude that this triumph has come in a just cause . . ."[10]

When this tumult and shouting had subsided somewhat, the country was faced with the serious problem of what to do with these Oriental fruits of victory.

The Emergence of a Policy

Any uncertainty in the original intent of Roosevelt and other supporters of a policy of expansion was swept away by Dewey's victory. The expansionists now wanted annexation of all the Philippines. While Roosevelt led his Rough Riders to Cuba in late May, Senator Henry Cabot Lodge urged the larger policy on a hesitant McKinley and his Secretary of State, Judge William R. Day, but with little immediate success. Then, early in July, the Congress, by joint resolution, annexed the Hawaiian Islands, and by the time Manila fell, public opinion and pressure groups, always effective instruments on government, were swinging definitely toward the larger policy. There were petitions to Congress and to the State Department picturing the Philippines as the key to far eastern commerce. Publications of the Protestant churches favored annexation almost unanimously, for church editors saw God's hand and new mission fields in Dewey's victory.

Powerful forces in international politics also played on the uncertain views of McKinley and his cabinet. Great Britain and Germany were dominated by their bitter colonial rivalry. Each was determined that the Philippines should not fall into the hands of the other if by chance the unpredictable United States turned them loose. Great Britain, whose attitude when the war began was in doubt, later urged retention of the islands by Washington. England did not wish to be placed in a position where she would have to oppose German claims directly. Unquestionably, the Germans were interested. They had hoped to prevent the war. They were alarmed by signs of Anglo-American friendship and the prospects of Ameri-

---

[10] H. R. Lynn, *The Genesis of America's Philippine Policy* (Lexington, University of Kentucky, 1935), in manuscript, 8.

can commercial rivalry in Asia. During the war German public opinion, favorable to Spain, again aroused the suspicions of Americans, who were still sensitive over the Samoan affair. Then, too, there was a story, widely believed, that at Manila the German admiral, von Diederich, had interfered with Dewey's blockade, and had withdrawn only when threatened by Captain Chichester of the British squadron. This was a far cry from what actually happened, but the incident served none the less to arouse American resentment, and so to support the advocates of American annexation.[11] Japan's attitude at the time was not very significant. She was not as yet a great power. Her influence, such as it was, was added to England's urging American annexation. If the United States did not take the islands, Japan, while not refusing them herself, would accept an international protectorate in which she should share.

The Protocol of Peace, drawn up by McKinley's cabinet and signed with Spain, August 12, was diplomatically vague concerning the future status of the islands, though it foreshadowed occupation of at least part of them. It stated (Article 3) that:

> The United States will occupy and hold the city, bay, and harbor of Manila pending the conclusion of a treaty of peace which shall determine the control, disposition, and government of the Philippines.

The implications of the Protocol were soon reflected in the appointment by McKinley of a peace commission that was dominated by expansionists. Whitelaw Reid and Senators Cushman K. Davis of Minnesota and William P. Frye of Maine were definite for annexation. Judge William R. Day, who gave up the State Department to be on the commission, was uncertain. Senator George Gray of Delaware opposed annexation to the last. While the commissioners sailed toward Paris, John Hay was crossing from the London embassy to become Secretary of State and to be one of the decisive influences on McKinley's final decision (October 26): "The cession must be of the whole archipelago or none."

The Treaty of Paris was not signed until December 10, 1898, for Spain's opposition to relinquishment of the Philippines was persistent and bitter. The Spanish commissioners had not been slow to point out that in their view the United States could not claim the Philippines by right of conquest, since Manila had been captured

---

[11] T. A. Bailey, "Dewey and the Germans at Manila Bay," *American Historical Review,* XLV (1939), 59-81; L. B. Shippee, "Germany and the Spanish-American War," *American Historical Review,* XXX (1925), 754-777.

several hours after the signing of the Protocol of Peace. Thus the Treaty, which set up American sovereignty in the Philippines, Puerto Rico, and Guam and provided for Spain's withdrawal from Cuba, also stipulated that the United States pay Spain $20,000,000.

One more hurdle remained: ratification of the Treaty by the Senate. This was secured February 6, 1899, by the dangerously narrow margin of two votes. It was preceded by some of the most dramatic debates in the Senate, in the press, and on the public platform. The arguments centered primarily on the Philippines. In Congress the opposition to expansion and imperialism was led by Senator Hoar (Representative from Massachusetts). His eloquence opposing imperialism failed to curb the popular enthusiasm for empire either within or outside Congress. Even then the result was in doubt until news of the outbreak of the Filipino insurrection against American control (February 4) raised the issue of national honor and strengthened the hands of the annexationists. Certainly one of the most momentous decisions of American history had been made. The United States had acquired a dependency—a dependency that was already in armed revolt against its new master. Truly, this country was entering the arena of world politics the hard way. She had fought a war to free Cuba; she had won a distant archipelago whose people did not welcome her. For the Filipino patriot, it was a case of a new master for an old.

The Beginnings of American Government in the Philippines

The McKinley administration took prompt action in assuming its new responsibilities in the Philippines. An American military government of occupation was instituted immediately after the fall of Manila. Local civil authorities were soon functioning under American military supervision in Manila and Cavite. Meanwhile, in January, 1899, before ratification of the Treaty of Paris, McKinley appointed a commission of investigation headed by Dr. J. G. Schurman of Cornell University. The preliminary and final reports of this commission, submitted to the President in November, 1899, and January, 1900, respectively (in published form the report filled four large volumes), were a comprehensive and, on the whole, accurate picture of the Philippine problem. While in the islands, the commission had attempted to make clear "the liberal, friendly, and beneficent attitude of the United States," coupled with the fiat that its "supremacy . . . must and will be enforced." Back in Washington, it recommended a territorial form of government, since "the Filipinos are wholly unprepared for independence, and if independence were given to them they could not maintain it." Acting on the report, McKinley now took steps, through appointment of the second, or Taft, Commission, to provide a government in which there should be a gradual swing to civilian in place of military government. In addition to William Howard Taft, its president, the second commission, a truly distinguished body, included: General Luke E. Wright of Tennessee, a gracious Southern gentleman, learned in the law; Henry C. Ide from New England, who had been chief justice in Samoa; Dean C. Worcester, who had served with the first commission; and Bernard Moses of the University of California, a mature student of history and economics.

The reception of the Commission, unlike the climate at Manila, was distinctly chilly. A month before its arrival, General Arthur MacArthur, who had been at Manila since 1898, had been made military governor. He was absorbed in the task of putting down the insurrection. As a professional soldier, he saw the complex question of the Philippines as a simple matter of crushing the insurgents with rifle and bayonet and then enforcing law and order by military discipline. He resented the arrival of a civilian commission which was soon to take over all legislative authority, including control of appropriations.

In these unfavorable and discouraging circumstances the Commission began its work. Many minds had contributed to the Instructions which the Commission was required to apply. Judge Ide was responsible for keeping appropriations out of the hands of the army, and thus for curbing the militarists. In the main, the Instructions were the work of the Secretary of War, Elihu Root, and the President of the Commission, Taft. On questions of fundamental, immediate concern, the policy was definite, even arbitrary. In the Philippines the United States was supreme. No promise of independence was to be given.[12] With the exception of trial by jury and

[12] For many years after Dewey had assisted Aguinaldo's return to Manila, there was bitter debate on the question: Did the United States promise independence to the Philippines at that time? The answer would seem to be "that the United States by properly accredited agents made no promises of independence, but that the actions of certain Americans led the Revolutionists to draw inferences, exaggerated by their hopes." Malcolm, *The Government of the Philippine Islands*, 121-122. See also Dean C. Worcester, *The Philippines Past and Present* (new ed., New York, 1930), ch. ii.

the right to bear arms, the Filipino was to enjoy all the guarantees of the American Bill of Rights. From this point the policy was subject to broad interpretation. The Filipino was to be given the greatest possible influence and participation in government for which his education and increasing experience would fit him. Americans today may take pride in the words of the Instructions which reminded the Commission that the system of government it was to build in the islands was

> . . . designed not for our satisfaction, or for the expression of our theoretical views, but for the happiness, peace and prosperity of the people of the Philippine Islands, and the measures adopted should be made to conform to their customs, their habits, and even to their prejudices, to the fullest extent consistent with the accomplishment of the indispensable requisites of just and effective government.

Where, however, local customs interfered with "the rule of law and the maintenance of individual freedom," custom must give way.

The second Philippine commission carried out its instructions with vigor and, on the whole, with tact. The period of transition from a military to a full civil administration remained complicated by the fact that the military governor retained the executive power until July 4, 1901, when Taft became the first civil governor. Taft's appointment was a victory not only for himself but also for the American principle that civil government should be established as rapidly as possible. From the time of his arrival in Manila, Taft had held that the army was a necessary evil but not an agent to encourage the establishment of a well-ordered civil government. Actually, long before July, 1901, the major task of the army, suppression of the insurrection, had been completed in all save remote districts. Aguinaldo had been captured by General Funston's forces on March 23, and on April 19 he took the oath of allegiance to the United States. The way had thus been paved for the rapid extension of local civil government.

Firm in its conviction that for decades the Filipinos would be incapable of self-government, and that independence was not to be thought of, the Taft Commission was equally determined to avoid the charge that a handful of Americans were running the islands without consulting their little brown brothers. Accordingly, to the American membership of the Commission were added three Filipinos of wealth who were not advocates of independence: Benito

Legarda, Jose R. de Luzuriaga, and T. H. Pardo de Tavera. Legarda and de Tavera were among the organizers of the native Federal Party, which favored peace, allegiance to the United States, and eventual admission to the Union as a state. The inclusion of Filipinos on the Commission was by no means welcome to all Americans, but Taft, as governor, was less concerned with exploitation of the material resources of the islands than with understanding the character and potentialities of the Filipinos. He was quick to note that they were proud, sensitive, and resentful of any suggestion that their race was inferior. While there was a tendency for some Americans to regard the Filipinos as "niggers," there was no color line in the Philippine policy of the Commission. It maintained a paternal if not always democratic attitude toward the Filipino; an attitude which Taft liked to express in the phrase "our little brown brothers." This made no appeal either to MacArthur's staff or to the rank and file of the American army of occupation. Soldiers of this young army of imperialism sang with gusto a refrain which ended:

> He may be a brother of William H. Taft,
> But he ain't no friend of mine![13]

The Period of the Taft Policy

The administration of the United States in the Philippines from 1901 to 1913 may best be described as the period of the Taft policy. Taft, first as Civil Governor, then as Secretary of War, and finally as President, gave direction and continuity to these years. The Taft slogan, "The Philippines for the Filipinos," was applied as a political doctrine with the utmost caution. By 1907, however, Filipino political aspirations were given some recognition with the election of the first Philippine Assembly, which, as the lower house, was to share the legislative power with the Commission. Since the governor-general (previously the civil governor) did not possess the power of veto, the principal check on legislation rested in the power of Congress to nullify. Taft described the political development of the whole period when he said that it was a process of making a paternal government less paternal.

---

[13] Mrs. William Howard Taft, *Recollections of Full Years* (New York, 1914), 125.

The American People and the Philippines

The relationship of the American people to American policy in the Philippines, 1898-1913, has not yet received definitive treatment by the historian. Nevertheless, some features of the story are reasonably clear. To summarize, its origins are to be found in the ambitions of the small but articulate Roosevelt-Lodge group to direct the United States toward colonial empire and sea-power. McKinley's government, the Congress, and the American people, all engaged in fighting a war to free Cuba, had no interest in and little knowledge of these ambitions until Dewey's victory revealed new vistas in Manifest Destiny. Even then the popular enthusiasm barely carried the treaty of annexation through a divided Senate, and in later years McKinley felt it necessary to place responsibility for annexation on Divine Providence. Perhaps he might better have attributed it to his desire to follow the popular clamor. Thus the Philippines were taken, not in pursuit of a well established national policy, but because "the march of events rules and overrules human action." Nevertheless, the issue of empire was not yet settled. Though anti-imperialism was the slogan of the Democrats in the presidential campaign in 1900, the sweeping victory of the Republicans was not a mandate on imperialism, for the campaign was a confusion of many issues. Back in 1897-1898, as McKinley pondered over the problem of an American empire, his mind had travelled between political extremes. Before the war he had seen annexation as "criminal aggression"; after the fall of Manila he came to view annexation as "benevolent assimilation." It was Taft, not McKinley or the American people, who found and applied in the Philippines a middle course between these extremes.

For Further Reading

Abelarde, Pedro E., *American Tariff Policy towards the Philippines, 1898-1946* (New York, 1947).

Bailey, T. A., "Japan's Protest against the Annexation of Hawaii," *Journal of Modern History,* III (1931), 46-61.

———, "Why the United States Purchased Alaska," *Pacific Historical Review,* III (1934), 39-49.

Barrows, David P., *History of the Philippines* (rev. ed., Yonkers-on-Hudson, 1924).

Blair, Emma Helen and James A. Robertson, ed., *The Philippine Islands, 1493-1898* (55 vols., Cleveland, 1903-1909). An exhaustive compilation covering the history of the Philippines to the end of the Spanish regime.

Conroy, Francis Hilary, *The Japanese Frontier in Hawaii, 1868-1898* (Berkeley, 1953). Gives an account of the establishment of the Japanese community in Hawaii prior to annexation.

Elliott, C. B., *The Philippines: to the End of the Commission Government* (Indianapolis, 1917). An exhaustive analysis of American government in the islands, both federal and local.

———, *The Philippines: to the End of the Military Regime* (Indianapolis, 1917). Treats of the Spanish colonial system as well as the American military occupation.

Forbes, W. Cameron, *The Philippine Islands* (rev. ed., Cambridge, 1945).

Grunder, Garel A., and William E. Livezey, *The Philippines and the United States* (Norman, Okla., 1951). A study of the development of American colonial policy and colonial administration.

Jenkins, Shirley, *American Economic Policy toward the Philippines* (Stanford, 1954).

Pratt, Julius W., *America's Colonial Experiment* (New York, 1950). Presents ably the rise and decline of imperialistic sentiment in the United States.

Sargent, Nathan, *Admiral Dewey and the Manila Campaign* (Washington, 1947).

19

China: 1890–1901

Artless Reform and Blind Reaction

CHINA in the last decade of the nineteenth century was a pitiful shadow of a great Confucian civilization. The comfortable and once realistic concept of China as the center of a natural world order, fringed with weaker satellites unable to compare with her in power, wealth, culture, and virtue, had become an empty pretense. For half a century, since 1840, the Manchu-Chinese scholar-officials had fumbled with the task of saving and revitalizing their Confucian vehicle for government and power. To this end they had used the means or weapons that were familiar to them: force plus persuasion, conciliation, enticing barbarian to fight barbarian, and finally the long but uneven effort in self-strengthening. All had failed. The onerous defeat at the hands of the despised Japanese, 1894-1895, mocked the very idea of the Middle Kingdom.

Indeed, there was evidence that China, or rather the Ch'ing dynasty, had made its bargain with the West. It had come to accept the foreigner, however unwillingly, with his treaty ports, his settlements and his concessions, his treaty tariffs and extraterritoriality, and his management of the great Imperial Maritime Customs Service under Sir Robert Hart. It was not a happy acceptance, but it was a profitable one for the merchant, whether Chinese or foreign, and there was the possibility that, if the powers were reasonable, acceptance might even strengthen the dynasty. The late nineteenth century was the great day of commercial development between China and the West. It was the era especially of great British prosperity in the treaty ports. These commercial good times were shared also by the Chinese merchants of the ports and by political leaders such as Li Hung-chang. Then, too, it was the continuing support (albeit always for a price) which the powers had given to Peking since the T'ai-p'ing threat and the treaties of 1858 that had enabled the dynasty to live on in smug senility. Thus the bargain was more than a bargain. It was an uneasy and delicate balance of pressures. It was a balance personified by the foreign trader naturally concerned with profits, by the Chinese trader and official torn between profits and cultural humiliation, and by a resourceful concubine in Peking who, having made herself master of the dynasty, was intent on the single purpose of preserving her court and her power. This temporary equilibrium explains why it was that in 1880 or in 1890 there appeared to be no Chinese response to the West, no answer to the barbarian challenge other than stagnation, no thought of a new China to meet a new world.

These complacent trends were the mood of official China when in 1894 the Japanese struck in Korea, ushering in the scramble of the powers to divide the spoils.

Yet at the same time the picture involved more than stagnation. There were men in China who were not content to let time take its course, men who perceived that China's salvation lay in ideological and institutional reform. Their influence was becoming positive as the end of the century drew near. There is reason, then, to note who these men were, to examine the nature of the reforms they proposed, and to observe the fate that befell their efforts.

Reform and Christian Missions

The complex processes through which Western influence stimulated a reform movement in China are known as yet very imperfectly, but it is clear that the Christian missionary, particularly English and American Protestants, played an important part. What the missionary said and did shaped in some major degree the ideas that the Chinese held concerning the West. Moreover, the Protestant missions, especially, came to have a broad social as well as a religious purpose. They were concerned to improve, through education, the lot of the convert in this world as well as in the world to come. From the earliest days schools were regarded as an essential part of the missionary establishment. Shortly after 1830 two of the first American Protestant missionaries at Canton, David Abeel (1804-1846) and E. C. Bridgman (1801-1861), opened a school and began publication of the later famous *The Chinese Repository* (1832-1851). The first American missionary hospital and medical school at Canton was the work of Peter Parker (1804-1888). After the second treaty settlement (1858-1860), which legalized inland missions, there was a marked expansion in both the Catholic and the Protestant establishments. English and American Protestant missionary scholars took the lead with the assistance of Chinese associates in publishing Chinese translations and digests of Western books on history, literature, and science. Among the Britishers contributing to this cultural invasion were William Muirhead (1822-1900), Joseph Edkins (1823-1905), Alexander Wylie (1815-1887), James Legge (1815-1897), translator of the Confucian classics, and Timothy Richard (1845-1919), who at the invitation of Li Hung-chang edited a Chinese daily at Tientsin. Some of the Americans included W. A. P. Martin, S. Wells Williams, John Fryer (1839-1928), and Young J. Allen. Fryer and Allen compiled and translated into Chinese the first textbook in science for Chinese students.[1]

However, the cultural influence of the missionary in support of reform was limited in many ways. His direct contacts were confined to the treaty ports and a few inland posts. He reached only a handful of the scholar-official and gentry classes. By the officials and gentry as a whole, the missionary was regarded as a subversive influence, especially when he sought to protect his converts from the course of Chinese justice, a practice especially notable among Catholic missionaries. Furthermore, the religious role of the missionary became in the Chinese mind inseparable from Westernization in general. The consequence was that the growing anti-missionary movement from 1890 onward retarded the entire process of learning from the West, and thereby retarded any genuine reform movement.

The First Chinese Reformers

The pioneer Chinese reformers were men of agile intellect, though their knowledge of the West was usually very imperfect. The earliest and most striking among these men was Wang T'ao (1828-1897), an able journalist who was closely associated with the foreigners at Shanghai and later, when in exile, at Hongkong. Wang assisted Legge in the translation of *The Chinese Classics,* spent two years in

---

[1] In this background of the reform movement I have relied heavily on the useful summaries of Teng and Fairbank, *China's Response to the West,* 133-193.

Europe, wrote a book on the Franco-Prussian War, delivered a lecture at Oxford in 1868, visited Japan, and founded his own newspaper in Hongkong in which he launched his editorial attacks on the Manchu-Chinese administration of the time. While never losing his love of Confucian civilization, he became an ardent admirer of Western law and constitutional government on the British model. Though his comments on Western politics were often acute, his observations on social matters were at times overdrawn, as when he wrote that "most women in the state of Massachusetts have preferred to get concubines for their husbands."[2]

Also an advocate of basic reform was Hsueh Fu-ch'eng, successively secretary to Tseng Kuo-fan and Li Hung-chang, and later a member of China's diplomatic service at London and Paris, where he kept a diary. Hsueh remained a staunch opponent of those Western social customs, such as freedom of choice in marriage, which he thought honored woman but degraded man, but, like Wang, he saw in constitutional government the answer to China's ills. In these views Wang and Hsueh went far beyond the mere material and technological reforms proposed by their predecessors. Hsueh, like many of the reformers who followed him, was also concerned with a philosophical problem. This was the problem of finding precedent in Chinese history for institutional reform. If such precedent were there, then China could safely learn from the West without surrendering her own foundations. The argument as it is found in Hsueh's writing is suggested by the sentence: "Mathematics had its beginning in China and yet it has reached its highest development in Western lands." For those who clung to the traditionalism of the sages, Hsueh remarked that: "We cannot expect to excel others [the Westerners] merely by sitting upright in a dignified attitude."

K'ang Yu-wei and Other Reformers

China's first heroic efforts toward radical reform are associated with K'ang Yu-wei (1858-1927), a Cantonese, and others influenced by him. K'ang was a utopian who had buttressed his Confucian learning with reading of Western books in translation. Perhaps the most significant point in his political philosophy was his interpretation of Confucius as a reformer. Therefore he concluded that all intelligent Confucians in a time of troubles should be reformers.

---

2 See excerpts from Wang's writings, Têng and Fairbank, *China's Response to the West,* 137-140.

Most notable among K'ang's associates was his student Liang Ch'i-ch'ao (1873-1929), who became a great scholar and a widely read author. In his early career he was an ardent reformer seeking a constitutional basis for China's government. In 1896, as editor of a Shanghai newspaper, he attracted the favorable attention of some of the more progressive provincial governors. One of his famous themes was to liken China to a thousand-year-old mansion, decayed and broken. Threatened with collapse of their home, the indifferent inmates merely awaited their doom with weeping or sought to patch up a few holes in the hope that good fortune would catch up with them. Like K'ang Yu-wei, Liang believed that modern reform could be built on Chinese foundations. He attempted to re-evaluate Chinese tradition so that the tradition would justify Western reform. In this pursuit he convinced himself that Confucian teachings had been distorted by faulty texts and dishonest commentators. If the real Confucius were known, it would be obvious that he foretold the coming of science, democracy, and prosperity, the very ideals for which the West stood.[3]

Other important advocates of reform were Huang Tsun-hsien (1848-1905), Yen Fu (1853-1921), T'an Ssu-t'ung (1865-1898), and Wang K'ang-nien (1860-1911).

CHANG CHIH-TUNG

Reformers at the close of the century did not belong exclusively to the lesser ranks of journalists, poets, philosophers, and minor officials. Some of their number belonged to the high and mighty, such as Chang Chih-tung (1837-1909), one of the great Chinese statesmen of the period. Indeed, the diversity of status among the reformers added to the diversity of diagnoses of the disease and the remedies proposed to cure it.

Chang Chih-tung, with all the advantages of a Chinese classical education, was for many years the most powerful and distinguished official in the provinces, where he was governor-general of Kwangtung-Kwangsi (1884-1889) and Hupei-Hunan (1889-1907). In these capacities he was one of the essential advisors of Peking not only on domestic but also on foreign affairs. His fame rested on his capacity as an administrator and his proposals for reform expressed in fre-

---

[3] Joseph R. Levenson, *Liang Ch'i-ch'ao and the Mind of Modern China* (Cambridge, Mass., 1953), 1-2.

quent memorials to the throne. Of him it has been said that he "was both a liberal official who worked for reforms and a conservative scholar who objected to parliamentary government."[4] In his philosophy, Chang Chih-tung reflected with greater maturity the earlier thought of Feng Kuei-fen. Chang took the position that China's troubles would be remedied by "Chinese learning for the fundamental principles, Western learning for practical application." Behind this approach was the fact that he did not admire Western political theory and philosophy. He proposed to save China by a threefold assault on her ills. By the first, the Manchu dynasty to which Chang was loyal was to be saved by a revival of Confucianism, with which he found democracy incompatible. The purpose would be to harmonize Confucianism with Western technology and political methods as opposed to political institutions. By his second approach, Chang proposed to rescue China through education, which he promoted unceasingly. Here the limiting factor was that to Chang the goal of education was mastery of the classics and loyalty to the throne. Chang's third approach was to create a new China through industry. His work in this field was notable. He was responsible for the first modern Chinese mint, for the Han-Yeh-p'ing steel mills at Wuhan, and the Peking-Hankow railway.

The Hundred Days Reform

It was the march of events—China's defeat in the war of 1894-1895 and the subsequent scramble for leaseholds and spheres, 1896-1898—rather than the power of the reform movement itself that plunged K'ang Yu-wei and his associates into power and as rapidly into defeat and exile or death. In the spring of 1898 the question of reform as presented in the memorials of K'ang and others touched the imagination of a few progressive officials at the Peking court and, more important, of the Kuang-hsü emperor himself, the nephew of Tz'u-hsi, the Empress Dowager. Since 1889 this weak, ineffectual, and inexperienced but well-intentioned young sovereign had been ruling in his own right. Frightened by the tidings of disaster, and emboldened by the urgings of the reformers, the emperor announced the need for reform by a decree of June 11, 1898. K'ang Yu-wei, Liang Ch'i-ch'ao, and others were appointed to advise the sovereign on proposed reforms, and K'ang was allowed to submit memorials di-

[4] Têng and Fairbank, *China's Response to the West,* 164.

rectly to the throne. The result was an unparalleled flood of ill-devised reform decrees known as the "Hundred Days of Reform." The problems tackled were as varied as the ills of this sick civilization. China was to have able diplomatic representation abroad, and officials were ordered to recommend men "who are not enveloped in the narrow circle of bigoted conservatism." China was to have a new order in which all the nation would unite in a march to progress. High conservative officials were advised to seek education in Europe. The old education was to be replaced by "practical" subjects; modern schools and colleges were to be established in every province; a transportation and mining bureau would be set up in Peking; the army would be reorganized; useless government posts would be abolished; foreign works on politics and science would be translated. From June to September, some forty decrees attempted to remake an old people into a new. It is small wonder that the effort failed. The reformers lacked experience, and the young emperor was not a magician. Undoubtedly he was well-intentioned, but he was emotionally unstable and intellectually diffuse. He possessed no adequate appreciation of the practical difficulties of constructive reform or of the conservative forces, personified by the Empress Dowager, that would oppose him.[5]

Recognizing that their plans of reform would certainly fail unless this conservative opposition were removed, the reformers conspired to seize the Empress Dowager and Jung Lu, her most trusted adviser and commander of the northern army, and, though the evidence here is conflicting, perhaps to do away with both of them. The plot, however, was discovered; K'ang and some of the reformers fled; and on September 21 the Empress Dowager again seized control of the government. The attempted reform had failed because of the impetuous ineptitude of the reformers, the worthy but misdirected zeal of the emperor, the determined opposition of most of the conservatives, and finally the fact that "the lethargic mass of the people was not stirred" by any popular understanding of, or desire for, reform. Many of the reformers suffered summary execution. But the leaders, K'ang Yu-wei and Liang Ch'i-ch'ao, escaped to British Hongkong, where in safety they could read the decrees condemning them to death by "slicing." For ten years the Kuang-hsü emperor lived on, a prisoner of the Regent Empress Dowager. That he was permitted

[5] For a full discussion of the reforms of 1898, see Meribeth E. Cameron, *The Reform Movement in China* (Stanford University, 1931), ch. ii.

even this existence was due, among other things, to the intervention of the powers, the Regent's fear of provoking the southern liberals, and the desire to hide the fact that China was again ruled by a woman.

The Reaction Again in Power

The collapse of the reform movement of the Hundred Days gave renewed evidence of the stubborn power and "the elegant perfumed ignorance" of the court reactionaries. Furthermore, the conflict at Peking for and against reform was merely one aspect of a complex struggle for power between Manchus and Chinese, between Northern and Southern factions at court, and between the personal ambitions of rival officials to insure their own futures. In this context the Empress Dowager symbolized the craving for personal and dynastic power and the aroused inertia of the system-bound eunuchs and officials through whom her influence was maintained. In the provinces high officials with rare exceptions opposed reform while pretending to implement the decrees.

In the closing months of 1898 it was the fashion among the foreigners in Peking to dismiss Kuang-hsü's reforms as a case of misguided zeal, in the light of which fact it is easier to understand the determination of the Chinese conservatives to have their way, while the Empress Dowager never ceased to protest her own enthusiasm for reform. Judged to be practical results of her efforts were the recruiting of additional men for the army by questionable methods, and an audience which the Empress Dowager held for the wives of foreign diplomats in Peking. The ladies noted the "courteous amiability" of the Empress Dowager, and that was all.

The return of the Empress Dowager to power could not be interpreted as a victory for progressive or patriotic forces in Chinese life, but it was coincident with a stiffening of the government's opposition to further foreign demands. In March, 1899, when Italy demanded the lease of San Men Bay and the setting aside of the greater part of Chekiang province as a sphere of influence, she received a polite but firm refusal. In fact, no further major concessions were secured by the powers during 1899 or the early months of 1900.

Nevertheless, as the last days of the year 1899 and of the nineteenth century approached, the far eastern situation was filled with dire forebodings. In addition to the naval leaseholds secured by

Germany, Russia, France, and Great Britain, hardly a square foot of Chinese territory remained which was not already claimed or about to be claimed as a sphere of influence. The Russians claimed Manchuria and were extending their influence into Mongolia. From Shantung the Germans were looking westward into the northwest provinces. Great Britain was firmly entrenched in the great Yangtze Valley. France was encroaching on concessionary rights in Yünnan, Kwangsi, and the greater part of Kwangtung. Japan, though not as yet a serious contender, had secured, on April 26, 1898, China's assurance not to alienate any portion of the province of Fukien opposite Japanese Formosa. In the view of many a Chinese editor the time was not far distant when Europe would "slice China as a ripe melon."

The Threatened Partition of China

It has been noted (Chapter 17) how the Sino-Japanese War, 1894-1895, precipitated a train of events, resulting, in 1896-1898, in a movement threatening the partition of China. This movement, against which the spineless Manchu government seemed helpless, had, by 1899, reduced strategic areas in China to a semi-colonial

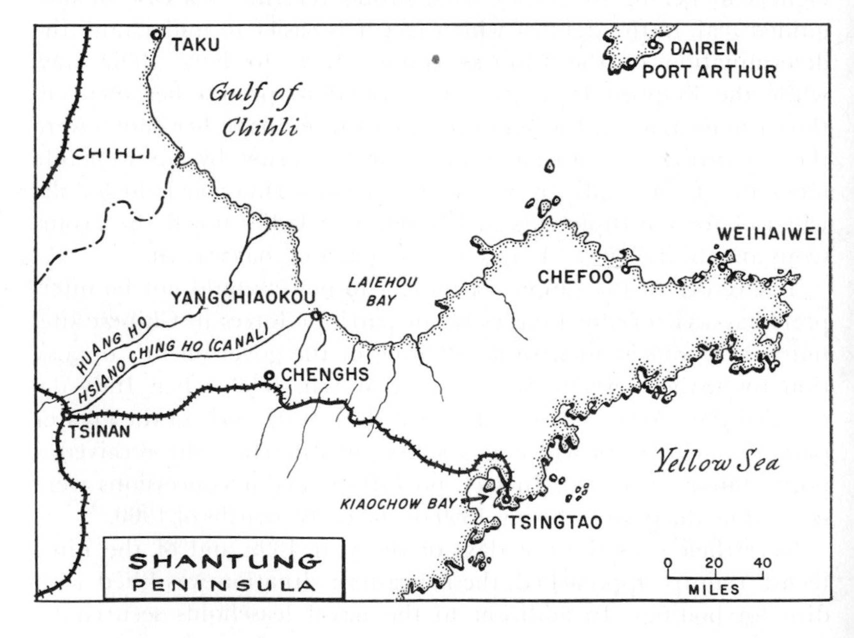

status. For example, Tsingtao, under lease, had become a German city protected by a German squadron; the Chinese derived such consolation as they might from the fact that sovereignty in the abstract was reserved to Peking. Beyond Tsingtao throughout populous Shantung province, the birthplace of Confucius and thus China's Holy Land, German capital had acquired a practical monopoly in railroad and mining development. The stage was thus set in China for an era of special monopolistic privilege for German capital in Shantung, for Russian capital in Manchuria, for British capital in the Yangtze Valley, and for French capital in the areas bordering Indochina.

This state of affairs, whereby large areas of China had fallen into a sort of industrial-investment servitude to the great powers of Europe, would not have come about but for the inability of Peking to protect its territory and to enjoy the respect that power invites. In reality, Peking was not only weak, it was growing weaker. There was no intelligent leadership in China's capital, and popular discontent among the masses suggested that the dynasty had lost the Mandate of Heaven, and that the foreigner, with his leaseholds, his railways, and his Christianity, was not looked upon by the Chinese people as an adequate substitute for Heaven's favor.[6] After 1898 the political and military impotence of Peking and the lack of a national consciousness served as constant invitations to the great powers in their quest and rivalry for markets that could be controlled politically. Thus, once the first steps had been taken in 1897-1898 to cut the Chinese melon, once the leaseholds and spheres had been acquired, the powers were under the temptation to cut deeper—to make "spheres" into protectorates, and protectorates into annexations. This threat to China's sovereign existence was, it should be remembered, an important by-product not only of China's weakness but also of that intense European imperialistic rivalry which was to result finally in the World War of 1914. Against the background of this rivalry among the great powers, and of incompetency at Peking, the United States sought to protect its interests by proposing a doctrine designed to create a commercial market in China that was free and open to all comers.

[6] For background manifestations of political weakness, anti-dynastic, and anti-foreign reactions, see Paul H. Clyde, *United States Policy toward China* (Durham, 1940), ch. xxix.

The Open Door Policy

The major interest of the powers in China during the nineteenth century had been in the main commercial. After the first treaty settlement of 1842-1844, these commercial interests were pursued by the powers within the limitations imposed by the most-favored-nation clause contained in all the treaties. Commercial privileges or concessions extended by China to one power were thus automatically enjoyed by all. As a result, the principle of equal commercial opportunity was maintained with a fair measure of support from all the powers, and in particular from the United States and Great Britain.[7] When in the winter of 1897-1898 Germany and Russia launched the scramble for naval leaseholds and spheres of influence, the British at first opposed the idea. They were confident that a free and open market for British commerce and capital was the best guarantee of their continued economic supremacy in China. Realizing, however, that it could not hope for success by playing a lone hand, the British government appealed to the United States in March, 1898, and again in January, 1899, for some form of joint action to maintain an open door.[8] Neither President McKinley nor Secretary of State John Sherman was disposed to act on the British suggestion. Neither possessed any deep understanding of previous American policy in China, and, anyway, American eyes were turned toward Cuba, not Kiaochow or Port Arthur. Accordingly, Britain, as we have seen, went into the business of leaseholds (Kowloon extension and Wei-hai-wei) and spheres of influence (Yangtze Valley) on a magnificent scale.

The Revival of American Policy

One may well ask why any administration could be so unresponsive to the call of historic American policy. The principle of most-favored-nation treatment was as old as American independence itself and had been applied in European as well as in far eastern treaties. The State Department had been advised repeatedly by Ambassador John Hay in London and Minister Charles Denby in Peking that the leaseholds and the spheres threatened not only equal opportunity in commerce but the territorial and political integrity of China as well.

---

[7] The background of the British attitude is given in Lord Charles Beresford, *The Breakup of China* (New York, 1899).

[8] The relevant correspondence is treated in A. L. P. Dennis, *Adventures in American Diplomacy 1896-1906* (New York, 1928), ch. viii, with documents.

Only on the basis of a number of factors can this costly mistake of 1898 in failing to defend the principle of equal opportunity be explained. Principal among these were: (1) Sherman's incompetence in diplomacy and his fear of being "used" by the British; (2) the preoccupation of government and people with Cuba and the war; and, finally, (3) the fact that the material American commercial stake in China was small—hardly 2 per cent of the total United States foreign trade.

Slowly, and with hesitant steps, the American government moved to reassert its interests and its historic policy in China. In the winter of 1898-1899 Lord Charles Beresford, returning to England from China, aroused his American friends with a picture of China preserved by an Anglo-American open door policy. The idea fitted well into the new and larger concepts acquired by American businessmen after Dewey's victory of May, 1898, at Manila Bay.[9] The reasonableness of the picture depended on preserving China as a free market. The American government began to react to the pressure of these ideas in the early fall and winter of 1898. The Anglophile John Hay was now Secretary of State. McKinley told the Paris Peace Commission (September 16) and the Congress (December 5) that the sale of American products in China could not be prejudiced by exclusive treatment. But the President was still uncertain of his course, for the second British overture for joint action on the open door was rebuffed in January, 1899, despite the fact that more than 1,000 American missionaries in China were at one with American business in wanting a "strong" policy from Washington.

The antecedents from which the reassertion of American policy in China was to emerge must be related here in some detail, since these antecedents and American reactions to them were to exercise an extraordinary influence on twentieth century American policy in the Far East. Principal among these antecedents was the threat to British commercial supremacy in China brought about by the success of the Russian, German, and French drives to create for themselves special positions in China through their respective spheres of influence in Manchuria, Shantung, and Kwangtung-Kwangsi. The British government had reacted to this threat by approaching Washington, as noted, seeking a joint open door declaration, but at the same time it considered seriously, if reluctantly, the creation of its own sphere in the Yangtze Valley. Indeed, it was argued that in the new era of railroad and mining enterprise in China there was logic

[9] See Julius W. Pratt, *Expansionists of 1898* (Baltimore, 1936), 278.

in a system of spheres of concentration as against an open door where the powers would be milling around jostling each other in the scramble for concessions. In other words, so the official British argument ran, it would be useful to keep the open door open in matters of trade in consumption goods while protecting future capital investment through the principle of spheres. As a result, the British government was not particularly disturbed when Sherman turned them down in March, 1898; but John Hay, American ambassador in London, was disturbed. Hay knew nothing about China, but he thought it poor business to rebuff the British needlessly. The net result was that when Hay became Secretary of State in the summer of 1898 his thoughts were moving toward an open door policy at the very moment when unbeknown to him the British government, while giving the idea lip service, was actually moving away from it by appropriating a Yangtze Valley sphere and by leasing the Kowloon extension across from Hongkong.

It was at this point that an Englishman, Alfred Hippisley, second ranking official of the Chinese Imperial Maritime Customs Service, returned to England on leave and urged upon his friend W. W. Rockhill, Hay's new adviser on far eastern affairs, that the United States do something to preserve an open door for commerce in China. The spheres, he said, might as well be accepted as realities, and, if they applied only to railroads and mines, might do little harm. What he feared was that the sphere-holding powers would tamper with the Chinese customs administration as the British had already done at Kowloon. These ideas made a strong impression on Rockhill and Hay. At Hay's suggestion, Rockhill prepared recommendations for a policy based on the Hippisley ideas, which was approved by the President.[10]

The Hay Open Door Notes

These were the antecedents that produced the Hay Open Door Notes sent to Britain, Germany, and Russia, September 6, 1899.[11]

---

[10] For the background of the Hay open door policy, see George F. Kennan, *American Diplomacy, 1900-1950* (Chicago, 1951), 21-37.

[11] Similar though not identical notes went to Japan (Nov. 13), to Italy (Nov. 17), and to France (Nov. 21). See A. Whitney Griswold, *The Far Eastern Policy of the United States* (New York, 1938), ch. ii; texts of the Hippisley memorandum, Rockhill memorandum, and drafts of the final notes are in Griswold, 475-500.

These prosaic notes that were to plague American diplomats for half a century began with some background of Hippisley's and Rockhill's ideas and with a denial of any American recognition of the spheres, though both Hippisley and Rockhill accepted as axiomatic that the spheres were facts whose existence could only be challenged by force. The real substance of the notes was a three-point technical formula by which each power within its alleged sphere was requested: (1) not to interfere with the administration of treaty ports; (2) not to impede the equitable administration of the Chinese Customs; and (3) not to charge discriminatory railroad rates or harbor dues. It would appear that there was no attempt by the government in Washington to appraise the formula in terms of what its practical application in China was likely to be. Actually, the formula seems to have been an expression of what the Chinese Imperial Maritime Customs Service wanted at that particular time. Hippisley had secured the support of the United States without Rockhill or Hay realizing the degree to which their formula might be contrary to the real purposes of the British government.

By the powers to which they were addressed, the Hay Open Door Notes were received with no enthusiasm, and their replies were plainly evasive. The British response, the most favorable of any, was clearly conditional, accepting the formula in so far as others might accept it. The Russians did not wish to reply at all, and when they did they were completely evasive. As a consequence the replies were really worthless. Nevertheless, Hay, on March 20, 1900, announced he had received "satisfactory assurances" from all the powers and that he looked upon these responses as "final and definitive." This piece of sheer diplomatic bluff did not deceive the powers, but it did deceive the American people. It created the impression that the American government by a stroke of diplomatic genius had saved China from the evil purposes of predatory powers.[12]

It is not belittling the Hay policy of 1899 to say that it was inadequate to protect either immediate American commercial interests or the historic American principle of equal opportunity. One need only recall that "in the Far East the powers were dealing with the fate of an empire of upward of three hundred million souls and no

---

12 Paul H. Clyde, "Historical Reflections on Continuity in United States Far Eastern Policy," *Southeast Asia in the Coming World,* Philip W. Thayer, ed. (Baltimore, 1953), 17-24.

less than five major states were disputing the spoils."[13] This was not the sort of thing to be arrested by polite diplomatic notes. The spheres were still there, and they were designed to give preferential treatment in railroad, mining, and investment concessions.[14]

THE BOXER CATASTROPHE

Close on the heels of Hay's timid efforts came the catastrophe of the Boxer rising in North China. The origins of the Boxer movement are not entirely clear, but it is credited generally to a secret society that dated back to the eighteenth century and was known as the *I-ho-ch'üan,* or Harmonious Brotherhood.[15] Actually, the origins of uprising, sometimes called the Boxer rebellion, involved far more than the conspiracy of a secret society, since the Manchu court itself was involved in what was soon to transpire. Faced with the imminent breakup of the empire into foreign-controlled spheres and with mounting Chinese antagonism to Manchu rule, the Empress Dowager, having crushed the reforms and the reformers of 1898, threw the weight of her power behind the parties of reaction at court that were bent on the suicidal policy of directing the rising tide of discontent away from the throne and against the foreigners and all their works: their railroads, their churches, their religion, and their converts. This strategy was all too successful.

In June, 1900, the violence, organized and unorganized, began. Boxers by thousands, superstitious and fanatical, and prompted by conservative officialdom, joined in a debauch of slaughter and de-

---

13 William L. Langer, *The Diplomacy of Imperialism* (New York, 1935), II, 677.

14 It is Langer's conclusion that to this point "the efforts of Hay, then, had no practical bearing on the situation as it was at the turn of the century." *Ibid.,* II, 688. Tyler Dennett, *John Hay* (New York, 1933), 295, gives the following comment on the whole negotiation: "It would have taken more than a lawyer to define what new rights had been recognized, or acquired, or even what had actually been said."

15 *Ch'üan* signifies defensive calisthenics, hence boxing or boxers. In areas such as Shantung, where the government encouraged the organization of militia to resist the Germans, the Boxers by infiltration acquired a semi-official status as militia. The Boxers were local groups organized to destroy Chinese Christians. Later, under official encouragement, they became the core of a desperate antiforeign movement. The movement was opposed in varying degrees by Li Hungchang and Yuan Shih-k'ai in the north, and by powerful governors in the Yangtze provinces, such as Chang Chih-tung and Liu K'un-i. Chester C. Tan, *The Boxer Catastrophe* (New York, 1955), is a corrective to earlier studies.

struction in Shantung, Chihli, Shansi, and Manchuria. They tore up railroads and telegraphs, burned churches, and murdered Christian missionaries and their converts. This lunacy reached the heart of the Manchu court itself on June 20, when the government declared war on the foreign powers and permitted the Boxers to lay seige to the foreign legations in Peking. A British relief expedition from Tientsin was forced to retire and the siege dragged on until August 14 when an allied army of Americans, British, French, Germans, and Japanese entered Peking. Again, as in 1858, China's inability to adjust to the West, and the blind reaction of court and officialdom, had opened the gates of Peking to foreign armies. This time, however, the threat to China's integrity was far greater. In 1858 it was a question of a few commercial concessions. Now in 1900 it was a question whether China as a state should continue to be.

The Boxer outbreak, following closely on the "final and definitive" assurances Hay had received from the powers, meant that if in 1899 there was little structure on which to hang the open door, there was even less in 1900. The powers were moving toward armed intervention at Peking. The Russians were soon to occupy strategic areas in Manchuria as a result of the Boxers' attack on the Chinese Eastern Railroad, which forced the Russians out of Mukden and Tsitsihar and put Harbin under siege. Kuropatkin, the Russian Minister of War, had exclaimed when he heard of the Boxer outbreak: "This will give us an excuse for seizing Manchuria." By October, 1900, Russia was in complete military control of the Three Eastern Provinces. Certainly there was nothing that was "final or definitive" in what was happening in North China. Moreover, in a presidential election year there was no disposition in Washington to become embroiled with the powers in China, particularly as nobody knew what, if anything, had best be done. During the first half of 1900, Edwin H. Conger, American Minister at Peking, while reporting to his government on the chaos in North China, had co-operated with his diplomatic colleagues in joint protests to the Chinese government. This procedure was in line with the Hay notes of 1899 and had precedent in Burlingame's co-operative policy of the 1860's. Yet between March and June operational procedures were reversed and Conger was told to act "singly and without the co-operation of other powers." Then, on the eve of the attacks on the Peking legations, Rockhill told Hay that the Boxer movement was not likely to "cause any serious complications," and the Department, again partially reversing itself, told Conger that he might act "concurrently" with other powers "if necessity arises."

China's Political Integrity

To Hay the time seemed ripe for a clarification of American policy. On July 3, 1900, in a circular to the powers he said in words that were designed to be quieting that the United States had no thought other than

> . . . to seek a solution which may bring about permanent safety and peace to China, preserve Chinese territorial and administrative entity, protect all rights guaranteed to friendly Powers by treaty and international law, and safeguard for the world the principle of equal and impartial trade with all parts of the Chinese Empire.

This principle of China's territorial integrity was not new in the language of American policy. It had been expressed by Humphrey Marshall in 1853, and by Anson Burlingame in 1862. It had been absent from, if not repudiated by, the Hay policy of 1899, which tacitly acknowledged the reality of leaseholds and spheres. Now in July, 1900, it was revived in a new and stronger form. Hay invited not only "respect" for China's integrity but also suggested "a collective guarantee" by the powers—a guarantee that was not forthcoming, since, with the exception of Great Britain, none of the powers even replied to the July circular.

Yet the important point is that in late 1900 the threatened partition of China was again arrested temporarily. Why was this? The note-writing of Hay probably had some psychological effect, but it does not appear to have been the determining factor. The determining factor again was the rivalry and the mutual jealousy of the powers, and their retreat from the co-operative policy to bilateral negotiations. England and Japan were slowly drawing together to stop Russia in Manchuria and in the Middle East. Germany's equivocal position in Shantung between Russia and England had, to be sure, resulted on October 16, 1900, in an Anglo-German agreement favoring the open door and the integrity of China, but this was an innocuous affair. John Hay referred to it as "a horrible practical [German] joke on England." He failed, it would seem, to realize that if this were so, it was an equally horrible joke upon himself and everything he had been attempting to do in China. In a word, there was no conversion of the powers to the idea of China's integrity. The business of melon-cutting was stopped temporarily because each of the potential aggressors, fearful of the debacle that would follow, hesitated to make the first move. Then, ironically, in the midst of this lull, Hay himself joined the concession hunters. In December, 1900, under pressure from the American Navy, he sought a naval coaling station at Samsah Inlet, north of Foochow on the coast of Fukien province. Japan, when consulted, blocked the move, reminding Hay, presumably with some delight, of his own recent efforts to preserve the territorial integrity of China.[16] The incident did not strengthen in subsequent years the moral influence of the United States in the Far East.

The International Boxer Settlement

With the defeat of the Boxers and the occupation of Peking by an international army the powers set about the long drawn out business of deciding how to punish China and how to provide security for the future. The final settlement embodied in the Peace Protocol of September, 1901, was achieved only after prolonged and involved negotiations. The jealousies of the powers being as they were, it was with the utmost difficulty that agreement was at length reached on the kind and degree of punishment China should suffer.

During the advance of the international relief expedition on Peking there was relative harmony, for the plight of the besieged foreigners in the capital was desperate. The international relief army was one of the most remarkable ever assembled: 8,000 Japanese, 4,500 Russians, 3,000 British, 2,500 Americans, and 800 French. Available German troops were held back to protect Kiaochow and the coast. The honor of commanding the allied forces had been given, to please the Kaiser, to Field-Marshal Count von Waldersee, who, perhaps fortunately, did not arrive until after Peking was in allied hands. This was a severe blow to German imperialistic pride.

---

16 Hay consulted Japan because the latter regarded the province of Fukien, opposite Formosa, as a Japanese sphere of influence. The Chinese Foreign Office in response to a Japanese note had pledged itself, April 26, 1898, never to "cede or lease" any part of the province (MacMurray, *Treaties*, I, 126). Hay's effort to secure Samsah was not made public until 24 years after the event (United States, *Foreign Relations*, 1925, 113-115). The Navy again urged the project on Hay in December, 1901, and in May, 1902 (Griswold, *Far Eastern Policy of the United States*, 83-84.)

The Kaiser, who was somewhat rabid on the subject of the yellow peril, had instructed his troops "to give no quarter and take no prisoners," and was now forced to see the glory of leadership go to General Linievitch, the Russian commander. The general tension was increased during the autumn and winter of 1900-1901, when the powers became convinced that Russia was preparing to control not only Manchuria but also the metropolitan province of Chihli. This led to all manner of attempts by the powers for additional concessions. In these unhappy circumstances, suggesting another partition of the empire, the Boxer Protocol was concluded, September 7, 1901.

The terms were severe and humiliating. The wisdom of the settlement has often been called in question. From the standpoint of the powers it could be argued that Peking's responsibility was great. The Manchu government had regarded itself as at war and therefore must now pay the price of its defeat and its treachery. The terms therefore were dictated against a background of punitive expeditions against many localities where foreigners had been attacked, and allied troops occupied the Imperial City within Peking itself.[17]

In the long view the Boxer uprising was to exert a profound influence upon China's political future. It hastened the end of the Manchu dynasty and the creation of the Republic. In this respect it was a dynamic step in the progress of China's revolution. To be sure, the Boxers were inspired by little more than a "blind and ignorant patriotism," while their patron and defender, Yü Hsien, the Manchu governor of Shantung, was distinguished by nothing save a "policy of blind reaction." The Boxers had no constructive program of re-

[17] The terms of the Protocol may be summarized as follows: (1) apology to Germany and Japan for the murder of the German minister and the Japanese chancellor of legation, and erection of a memorial to von Ketteler on the spot where he was assassinated; (2) punishment of responsible Chinese officials; (3) erection of monuments in desecrated foreign cemeteries; (4) official examinations to be suspended in all cities where attacks had occurred; (5) China to pay an indemnity of $333,000,000, to create an effective 5 per cent tariff, and to prohibit for at least two years importation of arms, ammunition, and materials for their manufacture; (6) the Taku forts to be destroyed, and a legation quarter to be created in Peking under exclusive control of the powers, which they might make defensible; (7) right of the powers to occupy 13 places as a guarantee of free communication with Peking; (8) China to agree to the amendment of commercial treaties, and to create a ministry of foreign affairs; (9) China to publish preventive edicts against further outbreaks; (10) the right of the allies to maintain legation guards at Peking. The American share of the indemnity, $25,-000,000, was, as in the case of all the powers, far in excess of justifiable claims. Substantial portions of it were returned to China in 1907 and 1924.

form to offer. They merely attributed China's ills to the "foreign devils" who must be destroyed along with their machines and inventions, "their strange and intolerant religion, their insufferable airs of superiority."[18] Yet, with all its weakness, its lack of constructive program, its blind fanatiscism and reaction, the Boxer movement was an unmistakable symptom of China's growing unrest, of her resentment against foreign intrusion and exploitation, and of her will to resist.

For Further Reading

Chang Fêng-chên, *The Diplomatic Relations Between China and Germany Since 1898* (Shanghai, 1936).

Clyde, Paul H., "The Open Door Policy of John Hay," *The Historical Outlook*, XXII, May, 1931, 210 214.

Ho Ping-ti, "Weng Tung-ho and the 'One Hundred Days of Reform,'" *Far Eastern Quarterly*, X, February, 1951, 125-135.

Powell, Ralph L., *The Rise of Chinese Military Power, 1895-1912* (Princeton, 1955). Deals with military reorganization and modernization and its political effect.

Remer, C. F., *Foreign Investments in China* (New York, 1933).

Steiger, G. N., *China and the Occident, the Origin and Development of the Boxer Movement* (New Haven, 1927).

Treat, P. J., *Diplomatic Relations Between the United States and Japan, 1895-1905* (Stanford University, 1938).

Varg, Paul A., *Open Door Diplomat: The Life of W. W. Rockhill* (Urbana, Ill., 1952).

Willoughby, W. W., *Foreign Rights and Interests in China* (2 vols., rev. ed., Baltimore, 1927).

Zabriskie, E. H., *American-Russian Rivalry in the Far East* (Philadelphia, 1946).

---

[18] R. F. Johnston, *Twilight in the Forbidden City* (London, 1934), 44.

20 China: 1901–1910

The Empress Dowager Tries Reform

UNTIL the imminent collapse of the dynasty during that "midsummer madness" known as the Boxer Rebellion, the Empress Dowager had set her face steadfastly against any significant reform. The failure of the One Hundred Days in 1898 was due directly to her. Her return to power in the capacity of regent signalized an intensification of reaction. This tendency was given its fullest expression in the policies and actions of the court as the Boxer movement got under way. The Empress Dowager was in full sympathy with the anti-foreign, anti-Christian philosophy of the blind Boxer patriots. It was not by accident, therefore, that "government troops under Tung Fu-hsiang and other sympathizers with reaction were allowed by the Court to join forces with the Boxers."[1] In a word, the Empress Dowager had set her course not only against reform at home but also against the treaty powers that personified the impact of all things Western.

When, in the midst of the Boxer troubles, foreign armies again entered Peking, the Empress Dowager fled for a second time, as in 1860, from the capital. Before her return to Peking in January, 1902, Tz'u-hsi professed to be a converted woman. She had not become a liberal, far less a democrat, for she had no understanding of such things, but she was converted to "reform," at least as she defined that term. From 1901 until her death in 1908, the Regent, and therefore the dynasty, turned in principle to a program that bore striking resem-

[1] R. F. Johnston, *Twilight in the Forbidden City* (London, 1934), 46.

blance to the reforms she had so ruthlessly suppressed in 1898. During 1902, as indicative of things to come, reform edicts removed the ban on intermarriage between Chinese and Manchus, advised the Chinese to abandon the practice of binding the feet of their women, ordered the sending of intelligent Manchus abroad for study, and abolished a number of sinecures. All this seemed to indicate that the Empress Dowager was intent on a thorough housecleaning. There was still, however, the question of the depth and sincerity of her conversion, and whether this masterful but unscrupulous woman had the capacity to rebuild the fortunes of the dynasty and the people it ruled.

The Manchu Reform Program, 1902-1911

Thus it was that the Manchu dynasty, which had already done so much to lose the Mandate of Heaven, attempted in the years 1902 to 1911 to reverse its course through a program of reform designed on the surface at least to remold the structure of Chinese society. These reforms were to involve the educational system, the army and navy, the form of government, and a great array of miscellaneous matters including a crusade against the opium traffic.

The Reform in Education

The decision to reconstruct China's educational system involved a revolutionary departure from the past. Some rather futile efforts in this direction had already been made in the late nineteenth century. They were important first steps in spite of their failure. The traditional Confucian education leading to the civil service examinations with their eight-legged essays had been sanctified by a thousand years of history and guarded jealously by the ruling scholar-bureaucrats as the fortress of their position and power. A few progressive scholars had dared to say that the classical education alone was no longer adequate for a China harassed by the modern world, but it was not until 1887 that mathematics became a subject for examination. Even then the weight of tradition was so strong that few candidates prepared for it. In 1897 a special examination on political economy was suggested in order that some candidates might be encouraged to learn about current affairs. At the time of the fateful One Hundred Days of Reform, 1898, Liang Ch'i-ch'ao and more than a hundred other progressives asked for abolition of the whole traditional civil service examination system. Nothing came of these preliminaries until 1903, when Chang Chih-tung, governor-general at Nanking, and Yuan Shih-k'ai, governor-general at Tientsin, suggested the gradual abolition of the system. The weight of their prestige encouraged other memorialists, with the result that an imperial decree, September 2, 1905, announced the immediate and permanent end of the examinations.

The Boxer Protocol (1901) had already suspended for five years the civil service examinations in cities where foreigners had been attacked. In 1901, too, an Imperial edict had called for the building of a national school system. Instruction was still to be primarily in the Confucian classics, but it was also to include Chinese and Western history, government, and science. In 1904 this educational plan was revised and extended on the model of the educational system then prevailing in Japan. It was designed to provide for kindergartens, primary schools, middle schools, high schools or provincial colleges, and an Imperial university at Peking. There was a notable lack of provision for the education of women.

There was substantial evidence that many Chinese accepted the new educational reforms with enthusiasm if not always with understanding, but there was also persistent opposition. Fitful waves of reaction followed the first waves of reform. While temples were being turned into schools, and the Empress Dowager was curtailing her theatricals to equip an academy for girls, some of the erstwhile reformers turned conservative, re-emphasized Confucian studies, and belittled the Western learning. Still greater opposition came from the local mandarins. Peking might decree reform in education, but it would remain a dead letter until the local officials were prepared to implement it. Even where the local official attitude was favorable, the educational effort frequently dissipated itself in the construction of colleges rather than primary schools.

Of equal difficulty were the problems of financing the new schools and staffing them with trained teachers. Finance was left to the ingenuity of the local community with results that were "precarious and unsatisfactory." In the teacher problem, the missionaries and the native graduates of the mission schools offered the greatest hope. The missionaries, however, were deterred from accepting appointment by a rule forbidding the teaching of religion in government schools. As a result, a large proportion of the new teachers came from

Japan. These worked for lower salaries than Westerners, and culturally they fitted more easily into the Chinese environment.

Meanwhile, in 1905, the Empress Dowager, intent on building through education a new body of public servants capable of strengthening the dynasty and resisting the pressure of the foreign powers, urged more students to study abroad. At one time there were probably 15,000 Chinese students in Japan. Some undoubtedly profited by the experience, while others were mere adventurers, seeking the prestige that a few months of foreign residence would give. A lesser number of students went to Europe or to the United States. Those who came to America were assisted through Boxer Indemnity funds which the American government returned to China after 1907.[2] On the eve of the Revolution of 1911 there were some 800 Chinese students in the United States and about 400 in Europe.

These were encouraging signs. In the years 1909-1910 China could point to 57,267 schools, 89,362 teachers, and 1,626,529 enrolled students. In the light of only ten years of educational reform the figures seem reasonably impressive until one recalls that China's population was in excess of 400,000,000, of whom some 65,000,000 were children of school age.

The New Army: Plans versus Performance

The need for military reform, for the creation of a national Chinese army worthy of the name, was obvious even to the Manchus. China's military humiliation had reached a new height in the Sino-Japanese war and in the Boxer uprising, while during the Russo-Japanese war, as will later be seen, the hapless dynasty had no alternative but to open Manchuria to the battling armies of two great foreign powers. There could be little respect for the dynasty at home or for the nation among the powers so long as this military impotence continued.

It will be recalled that China had acquired in the days of the T'ai-p'ing rebellion a number of excellent regional armies that suppressed the rebellion but which in so doing weakened the central government at the very moment they were saving it. The effectiveness of these armies against the T'ai-p'ings naturally suggested a

[2] In 1908 the American Congress by joint resolution authorized President Roosevelt to reduce the United States share of the Boxer Indemnity from $24,440,000 to $13,655,492. The original figure had far exceeded American claims. (United States, *Foreign Relations, 1907,* Pt. I, 174-175; *ibid., 1908,* 64-65, 71-72.)

means by which China in time might defend herself against the Western powers. Accordingly Li Hung-chang and others among the new Chinese scholar-militarists had set about to buy arms and munitions from the West, to seek Western military advisers, and to establish arsenals. All this, however, was without pattern or plan so that, as one observer noted, a small body of troops might carry thirteen kinds of rifles and even more brands of ammunition. The picture, of course, was not wholly negative, but as so often in nineteenth-century China, what the right hand gave the left hand took away. What was learned in the classroom was rarely applied in manoeuvres, either because young officers scorned the drill field or because their old-fashioned commanders blocked reform. Since the reform spirit rarely penetrated to Peking, progress, if there was any, was confined at the local level. In the end, the militia armies tended to degenerate once the T'ai-p'ings had been suppressed until with some exceptions they were not much better than the defunct Banners and the Green Standard. Military reform, it would seem, was "fashionable only when disaster was imminent."[3]

China's humiliating defeat in the Sino-Japanese war, 1895, and the subsequent scramble of the powers for leaseholds opened a new chapter in the nation's stumbling search for military power. In the first place, there was evidence of some popular demand among the Chinese for reform. In the second, even the Manchu court was no longer wholly blind to the dangers from within or from abroad invited by its military weakness. The central figure in the new military reforms was Yuan Shi-k'ai, who, it will be recalled, had been Li Hung-chang's agent in Korea in the years before the Sino-Japanese war. Yuan, born in Honan, 1859, in a family of the smaller landed gentry, had failed the literary examinations, and therefore had to purchase his first post and rank in government. He appears to have decided quite early that in the China of his day a career primarily military was the surest path to power. In any event, he became a staff officer in 1880, and between 1882 and 1894 through service in Korea established a reputation as a military man and a diplomat. By 1895 he had formed high connections at Peking with such Manchu officials as Prince Ch'ing and Jung Lu, the Manchu president of the Board of War, and was promptly placed in command of an army corps in which many of the young officers were graduates of Li Hung-chang's

---

[3] Edward L. Jones, *The Development of Regional Militarism in China, 1850-1927* (Duke University, 1953, in manuscript), 38.

military school at Tientsin. Yuan set about to make his corps the best-trained, equipped, and disciplined army in China. But it is important to note that because of the political circumstances in which he operated, Yuan was not building a national army but rather was reviving a pattern of principles which had appeared earlier in the days of the T'ai-p'ings, that is, of personal armies operating with Western training and Western arms. From these beginnings there was soon to emerge what was essentially Yuan's own army (the Peiyang army, as it was known) and his own politico-military cabal of followers, the so-called Peiyang clique.

The One Hundred Days of 1898 made possible Yuan's complete ingratiation with the Manchu dynasty. By this time Yuan had also formed connections with Chinese reformers as well as with the conservatives of the court. His role in the events of 1898 has never been entirely clear, but it is generally assumed that he betrayed the reformers and thus opened the way for the suppression of the reforms and for the return to power of the Empress Dowager. Whatever the truth, Yuan from that time on until 1908 had the confidence of the Manchu court and of the masterful "Old Buddha."

Indeed, Yuan's position at the turn of the century was compounded of the play of multiple forces in delicate balance. He was a Chinese, described by Lord Charles Beresford in 1898 as intelligent, well-informed, patriotic, and deeply concerned for the fate of his country. At the same time Yuan was an individual ambitious to achieve for himself military and political power. His advancement up to 1900 had been due to his ability, his energy, and his liaison with an ailing dynasty. Yet he had also had close association with Chinese who wanted reform, and, when the Boxer troubles occurred, Yuan displayed a notable independence of judgment. Far from aiding the dynasty in its ill-advised support of the Boxers, Yuan, who had recently been named governor of Shantung, gave no quarter to the Boxers, maintained order in the province, protected the foreigners, and thus, enjoying the favor of the foreign powers, aided in the return of the fugitive court to Peking after the Boxer settlement. Here then lay the background of the Empress Dowager's new-found ardor after 1901 for military reform, and for the role of Yuan Shi-k'ai in implementing the program.

The Manchu military reform program, 1902-1911, like the other efforts of the dynasty to rebuild its prestige and power, was notable in purpose rather than in performance. Under decrees inspired by the Empress Dowager provincial governors were ordered to modernize their troops. Military schools were to be reformed and the entire program was to be directed by a Commission for Army Reorganization headed by Prince Ch'ing. Meanwhile, Yuan Shi-k'ai, on the death of Li Hung-chang, had been named governor-general of the metropolitan province Chihli and was entrusted with the direction of military and foreign affairs in North China. His own army, now expanded to something between 50,000 and 80,000 men, was commanded by officers who were Yuan's men. Many of these politico-military subordinates were later to hold high office during the early years of the Republic.[4]

It was at this point that the plan of the Manchu court to enforce the general principle of governmental centralization of authority in Peking affected the military reform program. In his rise to power Yuan had made enemies at court, particularly among high Manchu officials. These same officials now found in the idea of centralization a means of wresting from Yuan the command of his army. In 1907, control of some two-thirds of the Peiyang army was assumed by the Ministry of War. A few months late Yuan was isolated further from military power when he was appointed Minister of Foreign Affairs and elevated to the Grand Council. When in 1908 the Empress Dowager died, Yuan was dismissed from office and sent into retirement. With Yuan out of the way, the Ministry of War attempted to organize a national army under its immediate direct control. All manner of elaborate plans were drafted setting forth the control, equipment, and training of this force, including the necessary military industries of munitions and supply. Some progress in fact was made. In 1909 about 700 young Chinese were being trained as officers in Japan. The army itself, however, grew very slowly.

However, these abortive attempts in military reform, like other reform efforts of the Manchus between 1902 and 1911, cannot be appraised in the simple language of success or failure. For example, army reform was not merely a belated effort by the Manchus to preserve the dynasty. It was also a response to a new interest in the de-

---

[4] Fêng Kuo-chang was president, 1917-1919; Tuan Ch'i-jui, several times premier and provisional president 1924-1926; Wang Shih-chen, premier, 1917-1918; Hsu Shih-chang, president 1918-1922; Ts'ao K'un, president 1923-1924. Yuan's military schools graduated other men who figured largely in the subsequent struggle for power: Wu Pei-fu, Sun Chuan-fang, and Feng Yu-hsiang, the "Christian general." Chiang K'ai-shek was at Yuan's Paoting officers' school in 1906.

fense of China against the foreign powers. The failure of military reform after 1865 and again after 1901 can only be explained when account is taken of: (1) the decay of the traditional Manchu military organization; (2) the regional and personal character of the newer militia armies; and (3) the lack of national leadership in the belated Manchu reform program. Nevertheless, the Chinese response to the attempted army reforms signified the beginnings, however feeble, of a new military spirit within China. The soldier was beginning to climb in social status; the profession of arms, as well as of scholarship, could now attract even the sons of the wealthy. This was a China in the process of change.

Constitutional Reform

It is perhaps understandable that the Empress Dowager, her frightened dynastic household, and her chief advisers came to grips with the problem of political reform not as a means toward enlightened government but rather as a desperate effort to save the dynasty. As early as January, 1901, "Old Buddha," while still an exile at Sian, had decreed that the best methods of foreign countries should be studied. The idea was that "there must be some germ of strength in Occidental governments" which, if known would give China strength and re-establish her position of superiority.[5] Accordingly, in 1905 she sent official missions to Europe and the United States to study constitutional government. The reports of these commissions, given to the throne in 1906-1907, revealed the limited steps the dynasty was prepared to take toward constitutional government. Constitutionalism, in so far as it might be adopted, was to be justified on practical rather than theoretical grounds. The commissioners argued that a constitution would make the emperor's powers more effective, that to give the people some role in political affairs would make of them more responsive and productive subjects, thus increasing production and revenue.

The commission was particularly impressed by what it saw in Japan. To the investigators it seemed clear: (1) that Japan's strength was due to her adoption of Western institutions, and (2) that Japan had provided herself with a constitution without sacrificing the power of the Imperial House. Why then could not the Empress Dowager by similar reforms satisfy her subjects, strengthen the Em-

[5] Harold M. Vinacke, *Modern Constitutional Development in China* (Princeton, 1920), 54.

pire, and preserve her own power? She therefore proceeded on the assumption that real power was to be reserved to the throne, with the people tendering advice when requested to do so through their representatives. Furthermore, she proposed to act slowly in order to placate the conservative opposition. By the close of 1907 three cautious steps had been taken on the road to constitutional government: (1) the principle itself had been accepted; (2) a commission had been created to advise on procedure; and (3) an edict had been issued authorizing a national assembly and also provincial assemblies.

During 1908 these cautious preliminaries assumed more tangible shape. The throne approved specific regulations for provincial assemblies that were to meet within a year. Underlying principles of the future constitution were decided upon and promulgated. A national parliament was to meet after nine years, and a preliminary constitutional program to that end was adopted. The new provincial assemblies were to be an integral part of the national machinery, their powers in no case infringing the Imperial prerogatives—an indication that the official reformers were under the influence of the Japanese and German models. The assemblies were conceived as sounding boards of provincial opinion. Furthermore, in large part, their discussions were to be limited to matters submitted to them by the viceroy or governor. The right to vote for electors who in turn would choose members of the assembly was strictly limited by property or scholastic qualifications. As time was to show, these assemblies were to make their presence felt in two ways: (1) they reflected a considerable degree of public opinion, and (2) they checked the efforts of the central government to increase its own power.

On the subject of constitutional principles the court reformers were perfectly clear in their position. "The government of China," so said a memorial, "is to be constitutional by Imperial decree. . . . The principles of the constitution are the great laws which may not be lightly altered. . . . The constitution is designed to conserve the power of the sovereign and protect the officials and the people." All legislative, executive, and judicial authority was reserved to the Manchu sovereign.

> Parliament was given power to propose legislation . . .; it might adopt measures of government; and it might impeach ministers for illegal acts, but no action it took had any weight or validity save that derived from the Imperial sanction.[6]

---

[6] Vinacke, *Modern Constitutional Development in China,* 77.

As W. W. Rockhill, American Minister at Peking, commented, the purpose of the Imperial reformers was "a perpetuation of the existing system under a thin veil of constitutional guarantees."[7]

Application of this program of political reform was to take place gradually over a period of nine years. In 1909 the provincial assemblies met for the first time, conducted themselves with considerable dignity, and led in the public agitation for the early calling of a parliament. The following year the National Assembly held its first meeting (October 3, 1910). Of the 200 members, 100 were chosen by the throne, the remainder by the provincial assemblies from their own members. Contrary to expectation, this Assembly, far from proving a mere rubber stamp, forced the government's decision to convoke a parliament in 1913 instead of 1917. It also forced the throne to consider concessions toward establishment of a responsible ministry. In general it showed a remarkably progressive attitude.

The Revolutionary Reformers

The independence shown even by this hand-picked National Assembly of 1910 suggested the appearance of a more general political awakening than the Empress Dowager and her political advisers were willing to acknowledge. This awakening was already taking the form of an embryonic Chinese nationalism stimulated by the writings of Liang Ch'i-ch'ao, the most effective publicist of the period and an exile in Japan from 1898. In a more radical form this awakening was showing itself in a revolutionary reform program and movement led by still another political exile, Sun Yat sen.

Liang Ch'i-ch'ao

After his escape to Japan in 1898 from the wrath of the Empress Dowager, Liang as a philosopher, writer, and editor moved rapidly forward from the conservative reform philosophy of his teacher K'ang Yu-wei. Political and social reform were no longer enough for Liang. These things, he said, would have meaning only when the Chinese became a "new people," reborn by a new patriotic and cultural movement. By the force of his reputation as a scholar, and by the vigor of his pen, Liang became the first great teacher of modern Chinese citizenship. He was among the first of the scholar elite to

[7] Quoted by Vinacke, *op. cit.*, 79.

free himself from the Confucian tradition. Probably no Chinese of the time was so influential in popularizing modern knowledge, especially among the student class. There was little place in Liang's doctrine for the feeble reformism of the Empress Dowager.[8]

Sun Yat-sen

Of lesser prestige in the eyes of Chinese intellectuals at the turn of the century but of growing influence abroad was the political revolutionary, Sun Wen, or, as he is better known to history, Sun Yat-sen. Sun was born in 1866 at Hsiang-shan in the Canton delta of southern China, which had nurtured the T'ai-p'ing Rebellion in the neighboring province of Kwangsi. After his early schooling at Honolulu, where he acquired a knowledge of English and was converted to Christianity, he studied medicine at British Hongkong. What Sun had acquired in these years abroad was not primarily a knowledge of medicine but a picture of two contrasting worlds: (1) a Western world of powerful national states, and (2) a moribund China clinging to the Confucian theory of a world community.

As a political agitator, Sun's early political methods followed a conventional Chinese pattern: the formation of a small group of followers, petitions to the authorities, and finally terroristic attacks and flight into exile. By the time of the Sino-Japanese War, 1894-1895, Sun's revolutionary organization had become "modernist, nationalist, and antimonarchial, instead of merely patriotic and antidynastic."[9] His original revolutionary organization, Society for the Regeneration of China (*Hsing Chung Hui*), 1894-1905, drew much of its strength from overseas Chinese. By 1905, when the Empress Dowager was in the midst of her reform program, the Society was reorganized as the League of Common Alliance (*T'ung Mêng Hui*), 1905-1912, and was acquiring the rudiments of a republican ideology. The object had become the overthrow of the Manchus, the establishment of a republic, and control of the parliamentary regime that would follow. At this stage, Sun's political ideas were still far from mature. His education had been more Western than Chinese, and because of his political exile his audience was composed in the main of overseas Chinese. As a consequence his revolutionary thought

---

[8] For an interpretation of Liang, 1898-1911, see Joseph R. Levenson, *Liang Ch'i-ch'ao and the Mind of Modern China* (Cambridge, 1953), 55-169.

[9] P. M. A. Linebarger, *Government in Republican China* (New York, 1938), 34.

sprang from an undefined intellectual frontier that lay between China and the West.

There was much of the cloak and dagger atmosphere in Sun's early revolutionary career. Following some abortive revolutionary efforts in 1885, Sun had moved his base of operations to Japan where, like Liang, he was associated with Japanese Pan-Asiatic liberals interested in promoting the Chinese revolution. From 1896 to 1898 Sun was in Europe, where he was released from detention in the Chinese legation in London through the intervention of friends and the British Foreign Office itself. During the Boxer troubles Sun was appealing in vain to Li Hung-chang to break with the Manchus and support a democratic republic. From 1900 on, Sun's political aims were republicanism and national; the means would be revolution by force. These ends and means were set forth in the Manifesto of the *T'ung Mêng Hui* proclaimed at Tokyo in 1905, the year in which the Empress Dowager abolished the Confucian examinations. The Manifesto was one of the great landmarks in Sun Yat-sen's career, for it voiced what was to be the central theory of China's first modern political revolution: (1) the concept of land redistribution, and (2) the three stages in the revolutionary process: (a) the period of force and military control, (b) the period of political tutelage during which the people would be instructed in the responsibilities of citizenship, and (c) the final achievement of democratic, constitutional government. It should be quite clear how far these ideas were removed from the controlled reforms acceptable to the Empress Dowager.

Economic Reform

Side by side with the Manchu reform program and the revolutionary agitations of Liang and Sun, China witnessed in the first decade of the twentieth century the beginnings of an economic development unlike anything she had known previously. After 1896 nationals of the Treaty Powers enjoyed the right not only to trade, as previously, but also to engage in industry and manufacturing in the treaty ports. The appearance of this new foreign-owned factory industry employing cheap Chinese labor coincided with the appearance of the foreign naval leaseholds and the spheres of influence in 1898. This industrial activity, so threatening to China's rural handicraft industries, stirred the Manchu-Chinese government to encourage Chinese as opposed to foreign industry. Invention was invited by the offer of patents and monopolies. By 1906 a Ministry of Agriculture, Industry, and Commerce had been created at Peking; codes of commercial and company law were issued; some high officials encouraged or undertook industrial enterprises. As a result, there was a pronounced growth of Chinese factory industry, including cotton textile mills, electric plants, flour mills, match and tobacco factories, steel mills and silk filatures, and the construction of railroads. Financing of these enterprises was aided by the founding of the first modern Chinese banks to compete with the great foreign banking houses of the Treaty Ports. These developments, the beginnings of modern Chinese industrialization, were obviously of great significance. They were the complement of the political and other reforms emanating from Peking. At the same time they were wholly insignificant as compared with the foreign-controlled commerce, industry, banking, and shipping of the Treaty Ports.

Opium Suppression

One of the most notable Manchu efforts in reform was directed against the opium traffic which for a century and a half had played havoc with the physical and intellectual well-being of the Chinese people. Under the legalized trade after 1858, importation had continued to increase, reaching 77,966 piculs (a picul equals 133⅓ pounds) in 1888. After this date importations declined substantially but were replaced in part by production within China. The difficulties of the Chinese government in controlling the business were many. Even if it could have suppressed domestic cultivation in the provinces, which is doubtful, the deficit would have been promptly made up by foreign importation which under the treaties China was powerless to control. Furthermore, Peking needed the revenue derived from the import duties and from the taxes on domestic production. In India, from which most of the foreign opium came, the British government saw no reason to discourage production merely to enrich Chinese growers and venal officials. In China there was no disposition to suppress domestic cultivation merely to enrich foreign producers and traders. The heart of the trouble was the Chinese willingness to use opium, and little improvement could be expected until moral sentiment could be linked with effective administrative reforms.

The Chinese program of reform which took shape in the first decade of the twentieth century drew its inspiration from a number of sources. Chinese public sentiment against the drug was stimulated by the report of an American committee seeking to control the traffic in the Philippines. The Indian government, responding to moral sentiment in Britain, showed a disposition to co-operate with China. The first practical step was taken by the Imperial government in 1906, when it adopted a policy of taxing domestic opium out of existence. This was followed almost immediately by a policy designed to stop by gradual prohibition both the cultivation and use of opium. By 1907, encouraging progress had been achieved. Then, as a result of Anglo-Chinese negotiations, an agreement was reached in January, 1908, whereby Britain would decrease annually the opium exports to China. The arrangement was to run for three years, and to be continued for an additional seven if it was found that China had meanwhile continued effective measures of suppression at home. In 1911 the British government consented to renew the agreement. As a result, too, of findings of an official opium commission, which met at Shanghai in 1909, the International Opium Conference at The Hague, December 1, 1911, reached an agreement among the powers having treaties with China whereby they agreed to take more effective measures to stop the smuggling of drugs into China, to close shops and dens in the foreign-controlled areas, and to prevent opium passing through the foreign post offices in China.

It was just at this moment, when a victory over opium appeared in prospect, that the Revolution of 1911 occurred, turning, for the time being at least, the thoughts of the nation from social reform to political revolution.

A Decade of Reform in Summary

China in the years 1901 to 1911 experienced one of the most critical periods in her modern history. Her government faced social, political, economic, and international problems of great magnitude. In the main these problems had been occasioned by the inability of old Confucian China to adjust her society to the nineteenth-century Western impact. The Manchu dynasty failed to recognize the need of adjustment and also to provide the leadership to execute it. When the need was finally recognized by the Manchus, it was too late. The prestige of the dynasty had already been destroyed. Its conversion was at best half-hearted—an eleventh hour attempt to preserve itself.

At the same time its program of reform, though failing to save the dynasty, was at least a preface to revolutionary changes to come.

For Further Reading

Backhouse, E., and J. O. P. Bland, *Annals and Memoirs of the Court of Peking* (London, 1914).

Cantlie, Sir James, *Sun Yat-sen and the Awakening of China* (London, 1912).

Hu Shih, *The Chinese Renaissance* (Chicago, 1934).

Jansen, Marius B., *The Japanese and Sun Yat-sen* (Cambridge, Mass., 1954). Studies the relations between Chinese revolutionaries and their confederates in Japan, 1895-1915.

Latourette, Kenneth Scott, *A History of Christian Missions in China* (New York, 1929).

Levy, Marion J., *The Family Revolution in Modern China* (Cambridge, Mass., 1949).

Morse, H. B., *The Trade and Administration of China* (3rd ed., London, 1921).

Powell, Ralph L., *The Rise of Chinese Military Power, 1895-1912* (Princeton, 1955).

Reid, John Gilbert, *The Manchu Abdication and the Powers, 1908-1912* (Berkeley, 1935). The basic study.

Reinsch, Paul S., *Intellectual and Political Currents in the Far East* (Boston, 1911).

21

1902–1910

Manchuria and Korea

THE formal diplomatic settlement of the Boxer affair did not stabilize in any permanent sense China's relations with the powers, nor did it end the threat to the American policy of the open door and of China's integrity. The renewed and immediate attack upon these policies came from Manchuria, which had been occupied by Russia in 1900 as a result of the spread of Boxer outbreaks to areas where the Russians were completing construction of the Chinese Eastern Railway. Before the end of 1900 it was clear that Russia was secretly pressing China for a separate Manchurian agreement that would add greatly to her exclusive rights within her Manchurian sphere. This news was disturbing to Britain, to Japan, and particularly to the United States, for these three powers had regarded the Boxer negotiations at Peking as providing a common and all-inclusive settlement between China and the powers. A separate settlement by Russia covering Manchuria would not only destroy this principle, it would also render nugatory the Hay policy contained in the July, 1900, circular. The case was so urgent that Hay again circularized both China and the powers (February 19, 1901), warning the former

> . . . of the impropriety, inexpediency, and even extreme danger to the interests of China of considering any private territorial or financial arrangements, at least without the full knowledge and approval of all the Powers now engaged in [the Boxer] negotiations.[1]

In April, Hay asked Russia for specific assurances that American enterprise in Manchuria would not suffer discrimination. For a brief period this diplomatic pressure was successful; the Russian pressure

[1] Dennis, *Adventures in American Diplomacy*, 243. For texts of most of the agreements referred to in this chapter, see MacMurray, *Treaties*, I.

was withdrawn. But in November, 1901, the Russian Minister at Peking was standing over the deathbed of Li Hung-chang attempting to extort the dying viceroy's signature on a new Manchurian convention. So matters stood on January 30, 1902, when Great Britain and Japan signed the first Anglo-Japanese Alliance, an agreement which by effecting a complete readjustment in the balance of power was to have momentous influence on the future of Europe and the Far East.

The Anglo-Japanese Alliance pledged the signatories in support of "the *status quo* and general peace in the Extreme East," of the

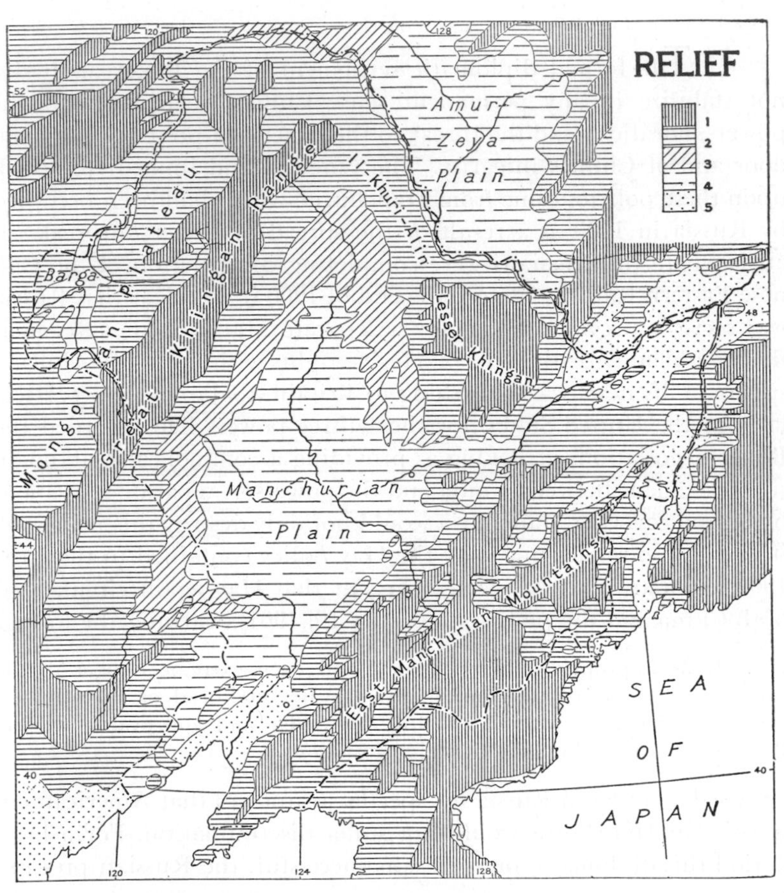

MANCHURIA. The numbers refer to (1) mountains, (2) uplands and higher foothills, (3) lower foothills, (4) plains, and (5) lowlands. *Courtesy of the* Geographical Review, *published by the American Geographical Society of New York.*

"independence and territorial integrity" of China and Korea, and of the open door there. This was the diplomatic window dressing. The real importance of the alliance was stated in Clause I, which recognized the *special interests* of both powers in China, and the *special interests* of Japan "politically as well as commercially and industrially" in Korea. This was a victory for the principles of spheres of influence; it was an equally obvious defeat for the American policies of the open door and co-operative action for its maintenance. The alliance went on to pledge each signatory to neutrality if the other was at war, and to come to the other's assistance if attacked by more than one power.[2] Since it was clear that the alliance was aimed at St. Petersburg, Russia and France replied with a declaration and agreement (March 16, 1902) taking cognizance of the alliance and reaffirming their adherence to the *status quo* and the integrity of China.

FOUNDATIONS OF THE ANGLO-JAPANESE ALLIANCE

How may the appearance of this vital alliance be explained? Certainly it was not born of far eastern considerations alone. In the broader sense "the treaty was Britain's first success in the effort to end her isolation."

In contrast with the British attitude, Japan accepted the alliance for considerations that were predominantly, if not exclusively, far eastern—primarily, to advance her interests in Korea, to protect those interests from the Russian threat arising in Manchuria, and, as with the British case, to end her own diplomatic isolation. Even with these interests at stake there was much Japanese opposition to the English alliance, led by Ito, who believed that a settlement should and could be reached with Russia.[3] Ito's plan was defeated by a small group of able and vigorous leaders in both London and Tokyo who preached the end of isolation and the need for an Anglo-Japanese arrangement.[4]

---

[2] Full text of the alliance in G. P. Gooch and H. W. V. Temperley, *British Documents on the Origins of the War, 1898-1914* (London, 1926-1938), II, 115-120.

[3] For Ito's views and his attempts to reach a settlement with Russia on the eve of the Alliance, see Tatsuji Takeuchi, *War and Diplomacy in the Japanese Empire* (Garden City, 1935), 124-128.

[4] The work of the alliance propagandists is ably portrayed by C. N. Spinks, "The Background of the Anglo-Japanese Alliance," *Pacific Historical Review*, VIII (1939), 317-339.

The Alliance and American Interests

The key to official American reactions to the alliance and to American policy in the Far East, 1902-1904, is suggested by the fact that Secretary Hay, inadequately informed by his diplomatic service, was taken by surprise. When Russia, responding to the pressure of the alliance, agreed (April 8, 1902) to evacuate her troops from Manchuria within eighteen months (that is, by September 8, 1903), Hay appeared to be satisfied. In a letter to President Roosevelt (May 1, 1902), the Secretary of State discussed the purposes of American policy in terms of ungarnished realism.

> We are not in any attitude of hostility towards Russia in Manchuria. On the contrary, we recognize her *exceptional position in northern China.* What we have been working for two years to accomplish, and what we have at last accomplished, if assurances are to count for anything, is that, no matter what happens eventually in northern China and Manchuria, the United States shall not be placed in any worse position than while the country was under the unquestioned domination of China.[5]

There were grounds for some of Hay's optimism, for had Russia carried out her convention with China by withdrawing her troops from Manchuria, "there would have been no war. Not a single major power concerned would have disputed the Russian [sphere of] influence" in Manchuria. Furthermore, withdrawal of the Russian troops would have removed the greatest danger to Japanese interests in Korea, thus depriving Japan's warhawks of one of their most effective arguments.

However, Russia did not withdraw. After a partial and temporary retirement, she re-occupied Manchuria, while at Peking she pressed new secret demands upon China.[6] These demands, which if granted would have ended any pretense of an open door and China's integrity in Manchuria, were the result of a conflict over policy between two factions at St. Petersburg. One group, headed by Witte, favored a gradual economic penetration of Manchuria which could be achieved without unduly alarming the powers. The second group, which controlled the tsar, favored immediate, aggressive economic

---

[5] Roosevelt Papers, printed in Tyler Dennett, *Roosevelt and the Russo-Japanese War* (New York, 1925), 135-136. Italics are mine.

[6] By these demands China would have agreed among other things: (1) not to create new treaty ports or admit additional consuls in Manchuria; (2) to employ no foreigners save Russians in Manchuria; (3) that the Newchwang customs receipts be deposited in the Russo-Chinese Bank. United States, *Foreign Relations, 1903,* 53-54.

and political pressure, backed by military force if necessary, to make Russia's position thoroughly secure in Manchuria, and to challenge eventually Japan's position in Korea.[7]

The failure of Russia to carry out the evacuation, and her presentation of new demands implementing the aggressive policy of Bezobrazov, *et al.*, threatened to make the Manchurian question an exclusive Russo-Chinese concern and to nullify the negotiations for a new Sino-American treaty of commerce already under way. However, the treaty was signed, October 8, 1903, opening Antung and Mukden in Manchuria as treaty ports. Yet Hay still faced great obstacles. He knew that Count Cassini, the Russian ambassador in Washington, was a "lying diplomat," that little useful intelligence could be expected from American diplomatic representatives in St. Petersburg, whom the President termed "cloth dolls," and that the Russian government had made "mendacity" a "science." These were poor materials with which to build a policy of the open door and the integrity of China. Throughout the Manchurian dispute Hay played a cautious game, and when China appealed for American good offices, the Secretary declined to be drawn in.

Japan and Russia

So it was that the way was left open for Japan, backed by the prestige and power of her new alliance with Britain, to challenge Russia, and to do so, ostensibly at least, in defense of the open door. In July, 1903, she opened direct negotiations with Russia for an understanding on both Manchuria and Korea. She proposed an arrangement whereby: (1) Chinese sovereignty and integrity in Manchuria would be respected; (2) the administration of Manchuria would be restored to Chinese hands, Russia retaining only railroad guards; (3) Japan would recognize Russian rights in Manchuria based on recognized treaties; and (4) Russia would recognize Japan's political as well as commercial and industrial interests in Korea as already set forth in the Anglo-Japanese Alliance.

The Russian response was at first dilatory, and when in January, 1904, its official attitude softened, conceding most, if not all, of what Japan had asked, the gesture had no effect, since at the same time

[7] The moving spirit of the group was State Councillor Bezobrazov, supported by many of the grand dukes, the militarists, and Admiral Alexieff, who was later appointed Viceroy of the Far East, in which capacity at Port Arthur he was able to act independently of Count Lamsdorff and the Foreign Office.

Bezobrazov and those who were in control at Port Arthur were insisting that Russia would not get out of Manchuria and that there would be no open door there. This meant war.

Japan's Decision

Japan's policy toward Russia had been fixed with some certainty as early as the spring of 1903. At that time it had been determined "to grant Russia a priority right in Manchuria" while insisting on Japan's unique status in Korea. When negotiations were undertaken with Russia in July, 1903, the Japanese cabinet had already decided "to resort to arms, should such negotiations fail." Although this decision was opposed by Ito, it had the vigorous support of General Yamagata Aritomo. Meanwhile, Japanese public opinion loudly demanded that Russia's advance in Manchuria be stopped. By November, 1903, there was little opposition to this popular, though inspired, public demand, and on February 4 the government reached its decision to sever diplomatic relations on February 6. On February 8 a Japanese squadron delivered a surprise attack on Port Arthur. War was declared on February 10. To neither power did it come as a surprise. Nor does history present a better example of a war fought by both powers for imperialistic ends; but, in assessing the relative responsibility, if this be possible,

> . . . it can at least be said for Japan that her policy was based upon a real need. The argument for self-preservation is in her favor.[8]

The War and American Policy

The outbreak of war re-intensified the so-called Chinese question. There was, to be sure, little danger that other European powers would enter the conflict. For either France or Germany to have done so would have endangered their European frontiers; but since the war was to be fought on Chinese territory, there was very real danger both to the open door and to China's integrity. Accordingly, President Roosevelt reasserted the Hay policy of 1900, asking the powers to respect "the neutrality of China and in all practical ways her administrative entity." Since circular notes had little effect prior to hostilities, even less could be hoped of them after war had begun.

[8] W. L. Langer, "The Origins of the Russo-Japanese War" [from the original English manuscript], *Europäische Gespräche* IV, 279-335 (Hamburg, 1926).

Nevertheless, "the conception of *de jure* Chinese sovereignty over Manchuria was restored to American diplomacy . . ." by these notes. In this sense American policy in China was reinforced at least formally, but at the same time it was weakened by evident American willingness "to follow Great Britain's example and abandon . . . [Korea] to its Japanese fate." Russia was quick to ask why the United States opposed her in Manchuria while giving Japan a green light in Korea.[9]

At the same time, in far western China the American policy of China's integrity was rebuffed by the British. The State Department had been disturbed by implications of the British Younghusband mission to Tibet. In the course of Anglo-American discussions on the subject, the British referred to Chinese sovereignty in Tibet as a "constitutional fiction" and a "political affectation," and when the United States asked that China's territorial integrity be respected there, no assurance was forthcoming from Lord Lansdowne.

While the Russo-Japanese War was yet in progress, the United States made two more efforts to keep alive the principle of China's integrity. The first of these was a diplomatic circular, January 13, 1905, similar to that of the previous year. The Russian response gave no satisfaction. The second case was President Roosevelt's demand upon Japan for assurance that she "adhere to the position of maintaining Open Door in Manchuria and restoring that province to China." Without this assurance the President was not prepared to act as mediator. These efforts closed what may be called the first chapter in the history of the twin American principles of the open door and the integrity of China. Ethically sound, these principles were also in keeping with traditional aspects of American policy, such as, for example, the most-favored-nation principle. It would, however, be foolish to ignore the fact that the open door and the integrity of China meant little to other powers or that they were given more than diplomatic lip-service. Until such time as the United States was prepared to attack the spheres directly, its policies of the open door and China's integrity were destined to savor of the doctrinaire. The American government was not in a position to implement its policy with anything save diplomatic notes and circulars. There is no evidence to indicate that American public opinion

---

9 Griswold, *Far Eastern Policy of the United States,* 96-97. American diplomats in eastern Asia—Griscom at Tokyo, Allen at Seoul, as well as Hay and Rockhill —looked to Japan as the only, if not the most desirable, solution of the Korean problem.

would have sanctioned stronger measures even had the Department of State wished to apply them. Finally, American policy did not always remain true to its own doctrinaire principles. Hay himself became a concession hunter. What is more, he conceded that Chinese integrity in Manchuria was not essential so long as American treaty rights in the area were not infringed. Recognizing these basic weaknesses and periodic lapses, the historian must also note that the twin principles of American policy did enjoy a very limited success. They did restrain the powers in some measure, and they helped to keep alive the ideal of China's nationhood and of free enterprise at a time when both were in serious danger.

The Stakes of the Russo-Japanese War

The Russo-Japanese War transformed the political complexion of the far eastern question. Admiral Togo's naval assault on Port Arthur employed every device of *surprise* attack, preceding, as it did, by two days the formal declaration of war.[10] However, the war that followed was a surprise only to those who had failed to appreciate the growing intensity of imperialistic rivalry in the Far East since 1895.

The issues involved in the war were not exclusively far eastern. They involved the interests and policies of all the great European powers and the United States. For the moment, however, the complexities of the scene as a whole were overshadowed by the specific purposes of Russia and Japan in Korea and Manchuria. These purposes encompassed the question of Korea's independence and of China's territorial integrity. These questions in turn had already been prejudiced in the case of China by the widespread creation after 1897 of spheres of economic and political interest, and in the case of Korea by Britain's recognition there of Japan's primary interests as expressed in the first Anglo-Japanese Alliance. Control of Manchuria and Korea was the key to control of China. After 1902, Japan held in Korea the advantage given her by the Anglo-Japanese Alliance. After 1900, Russia held in Manchuria the advantage bestowed upon her by the Boxer troubles. She was in a position not only to claim Manchuria as a *de facto* sphere of influence but also to proceed to its political conquest. She was not pre-

---

[10] Edwin A. Falk, *Togo and the Rise of Japanese Sea Power* (New York, 1936), 278-306.

pared to acknowledge Japan's exclusive primacy in Korea. Japan in turn was unwilling to share her political interest in Korea with any power. As to Manchuria, though Japan's interests and purposes there were still in the formative stage it is clear that she wanted a Manchurian foothold. The chance of securing this foothold in the future could be safeguarded only by confining Russia's Manchurian interests within the narrowest interpretation, thus blocking any Russian scheme for a protectorate or for annexation of Manchuria. Consequently, as in 1899 and 1900, Japan became for the moment the spokesman of the open door and the integrity of China in the Three Eastern Provinces.

Military Campaigns in Manchuria

A major peculiarity of the Russo-Japanese War was that it was fought in Manchuria, a territory that was under the sovereignty of China, hence neutral territory. However, since Russia after 1900 was in partial military occupation of Manchuria, and since Peking lacked the military power to defend the Three Eastern Provinces, there was nothing for China to do but recognize this part of her territory as an area of hostilities and thereby to imply her consent to military operations by the belligerents in her territory.[11]

Only a few of the military events of the war need be mentioned in passing. Japanese troops landed in Korea at Chemulpo, February 8 and 9. Other forces landed at Gensan on Korea's northeastern coast. General Kuroki's army crossed the Yalu River into Manchuria, May 1. A week later a second Japanese army under General Oku landed in South Manchuria (Liaotung) near the Russian leased territory, while another army under General Nodzu landed further east. On May 26 the Japanese cut the Russian lines at Nanshan, thus forcing them to withdraw on Port Arthur, July 31, and a month later the remaining Japanese armies (123,000) faced the main Russian forces (158,000) under General Kuropatkin south of Mukden. At the Battle of Liaoyang (August 23-September 3), the Russians were forced back, but were not routed. At Sha-ho (October 9-17) the Russians attacked but failed to break the Japanese lines. The campaign was then halted during the bitter Manchurian winter, save at Port

[11] Sakuye Takahashi, *International Law Applied to the Russo-Japanese War* (London, 1908), 250; and Amos S. Hershey, *The International Law and Diplomacy of the Russo-Japanese War* (New York, 1906), in particular, ch. ix, on China's neutrality.

Arthur, which fell to the Japanese at terrific cost, January 2, 1905. Japan was thus able to reinforce her northern armies for the Battle of Mukden (February 23-March 10, 1905), in which for the first time she had superiority in numbers (400,000 to 325,000). Again the Russians were forced to retire, this time to Tiehling, north of Mukden. At his own request Kuropatkin was replaced as commander-in-chief by General Linievitch. Two months later came Russia's most severe reverse—the destruction of her Baltic fleet in the Sea of Japan.

The United States and the Problem of Peace

Efforts to find a basis for peace had been undertaken early in the war. Although she had won technical military victories on land and had destroyed Russian sea-power, Japan had failed to destroy the Russian armies. Each victory removed Japanese armies further from their base. At home the nation's economy had been strained to the point of danger. In a military sense, Russia's position showed some improvement as the war dragged on, but her funds were exhausted and French bankers were not disposed to extend further credits. In addition, revolutionary movements within Russian threatened the entire war effort.

Nevertheless, it was Japan that made the first formal proposal for peace on May 31, 1905, when she requested President Theodore Roosevelt on his own "initiative to invite the two belligerents to come together for the purpose of direct negotiation." Roosevelt's subsequent approach to the tsar was accepted June 6, and two days later the United States sent formal invitations to the belligerents, offering good offices, which were accepted. Roosevelt had acted because, as he said in a letter to President Wheeler of the University of California:

> I believe that our future history will be more determined by our position on the Pacific facing China than our position on the Atlantic facing Europe.[12]

It is unnecessary here to treat in any detail the preliminaries of the peace settlement at Portsmouth, New Hampshire: the appointment of delegates, Witte and Rosen for Russia, Komura and Takahira for Japan; the death of Secretary Hay, July 1, 1905; the renewal of the Anglo-Japanese Alliance, August 12, 1905, recognizing Japan's

[12] Quoted by A. L. P. Dennis, *Adventures in American Diplomacy, 1896-1906* (New York, 1928), 406.

"paramount political, military, and economic" interests in Korea; the signing of the secret treaty of Björkö between the kaiser and the tsar; the alleged success of Witte in capturing American sympathy for Russia's case; the capacity of the Japanese "by their stiff-

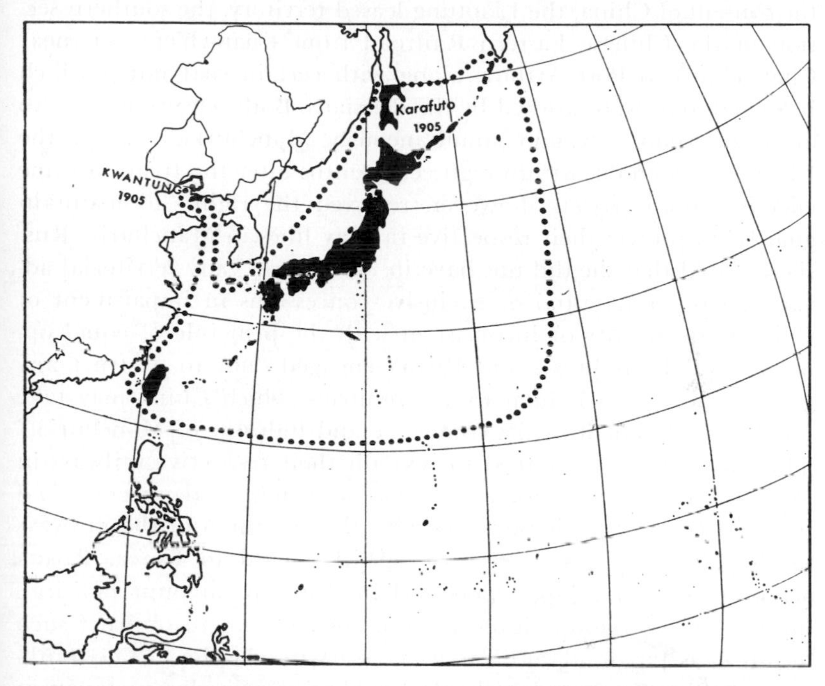

JAPAN, 1905-1909. *Reproduced from* A War Atlas for Americans, *Simon and Schuster, Inc., New York, 1944, by permission from Simon and Schuster, Inc., and from the U. S. Department of State, Division of Map Intelligence and Cartography.*

ness and taciturnity" to lose in the negotiations the advantage won by their military and naval victories; and the other repeated crises into which the negotiations fell.[13]

---

[13] For detailed discussions of these matters, see Tyler Dennett, *Roosevelt and the Russo-Japanese War* (New York, 1925), and Dennis, *Adventures in American Diplomacy,* ch. xiv. In regard to American public opinion and the Portsmouth Peace Conference, a study of the leading American newspapers shows that there was no "overnight" change in American public opinion. Indeed, the American public held to well-established pro-Japanese sympathies. See W. B. Thorson, "American Public Opinion and the Portsmouth Peace Conference." *American Historical Review,* LIII (1947-1948), 439-464.

The Treaty of Portsmouth

The Treaty of Portsmouth, September 5, 1905, was destined to become one of the most consequential agreements in the modern history of the Far East. By it Japan acquired from Russia, subject to the consent of China, the Liaotung leased territory, the southern section of the Chinese Eastern Railroad from Kuan-ch'eng-tzu (near Changchun) to Port Arthur, along with certain coal mines which belonged to or were worked by the Russians. Both powers agreed "to evacuate completely and simultaneously Manchuria," except the Liaotung leasehold, within eighteen months after the treaty became effective. Both powers, however, reserved the right "to maintain guards" to protect their respective railway lines in Manchuria. Russia declared that she did not have in Manchuria "any territorial advantages or preferential or exclusive concessions in impairment of Chinese sovereignty or inconsistent with the principle of equal opportunity." Both Japan and Russia engaged "not to obstruct any general measures common to all countries, which China may take for the development of the commerce and industry of Manchuria." The two powers also agreed to "exploit their respective railways in Manchuria exclusively for commercial and industrial purposes and in no wise for strategic purposes with the exception of the railways in the Liaotung leased territory." With regard to Korea, Russia acknowledged that Japan possessed in Korea paramount political, military, and economic interests, and engaged not to obstruct such measures as Japan might deem it necessary to take there. The southern half (Karafuto) of the island of Sakhalin was ceded to Japan in lieu of a war indemnity, and Japan was granted fishing rights in certain territorial waters of Siberia on the Pacific.

Japan's New Position in Korea

Prior to 1905 Japan considered her primary interests to be in Korea rather than Manchuria. The decade 1894-1904 had been a period of intense but intermittent Russo-Japanese economic rivalry in Korea. During the preliminary conversations leading to the first Anglo-Japanese Alliance, Count Hayashi told Lord Lansdowne that Japan's primary purpose was "protection of its interests in Korea," and the subsequent alliance (1902) recognized that Japan was "interested in a peculiar degree politically as well as commercially and industrially in Korea." By 1903 Japan's instructions to her ministers abroad were referring to Korea as "an important outpost in Japan's line of defense." With the outbreak of the Russo-Japanese War, Korea proclaimed her neutrality but took no steps to defend it, believing, it would seem, that benevolent protection would come from the United States and the great powers of western Europe. Japan, however, was no longer concerned with Korean neutrality or Korean independence. In the military sphere, Korea was now looked upon as a necessary base of operations against Russia, and in the political sphere the peninsula was soon to be subjected to intimate Japanese control. The process was to be the removal of a legal fiction. Japanese forces occupied Seoul (February 8, 1904) the day Togo attacked Port Arthur, and a protocol signed February 23 laid the groundwork for the subsequent Japanese protectorate. Korea was to place "full confidence" in Japan and to "adopt the advice of the latter with regard to improvements in administration." Japan would "definitely guarantee the independence and territorial integrity" of Korea and to this end might interfere in Korean affairs. Korea was pledged not to conclude with third powers any agreement "contrary to the principles" of the protocol. In additional agreements (August 19-22, 1904), Japan was empowered to appoint advisers to the Korean departments of finance and foreign affairs. By the beginning of 1905 Japan had assumed responsibility for policing the Korean capital and had placed a Japanese police inspector in each province. International sanction was promptly given to Japan's new position in Korea. William Howard Taft, Roosevelt's Secretary of War, in conversations with the Japanese Prime Minister, General Count Katsura, gave his approval, later confirmed by the President, to a Japanese suzerainty in Korea.[14] In August, the renewed Anglo-Japanese Alliance referred to Japan's "paramount" interests at Seoul, and in September, Russia likewise acknowledged Japan's "paramount" position (Article II of the Treaty of Portsmouth). With this international sanction, Japan, through pressure exerted at Seoul, secured from the Korean government an agreement giving Japan control of Korea's foreign relations and the right to appoint a Japanese resident-general at Seoul. On the following day the United States instructed its Minister at Seoul to close the legation. Willard Straight described this diplomatic retreat as "like the stampede of rats from

---

[14] H. F. Pringle, *Theodore Roosevelt* (London, 1932), 384. Japan in turn satisfied Roosevelt by a disavowal of any aggressive purpose in the Philippines.

a sinking ship." The establishment of the Japanese protectorate in Korea was thus complete. Having consolidated her position at Seoul, Japan was prepared to implement in South Manchuria the new position there which the Treaty of Portsmouth had given her.[15]

Steel Rails and Politics in Manchuria

The Treaty of Portsmouth was the herald of far-reaching changes in Manchuria. After 1905 it became convenient to refer to "North Manchuria," where Russia still claimed a sphere of influence, and to "South Manchuria," where Japan was about to create a sphere.[16] Since Japan had professed to be fighting for the open door and the integrity of China in Manchuria, the conclusion of peace was greeted with general popular enthusiasm in Europe and America, but "American investors and merchants in the Far East disapproved of the treaty because they were afraid that Japan would now curb their own activity in the Orient," particularly in the promising frontier area of South Manchuria. In its simplest form the question was whether under Chinese sovereignty and administrative integrity Manchuria was to be open on terms of equality to the commerce, industry, and capital of all nations, or whether it was to be an exclusive economic preserve of Russian and Japanese capital, buttressed by Russian and Japanese political control in derogation of Chinese sovereignty and administration.

Military Occupation of Manchuria

Although ratifications of the Treaty of Portsmouth were exchanged at Washington (November 25, 1905), the former belligerents had agreed to an 18-month period in which to complete evacuation of their armies. This meant that for more than a year Manchuria remained partly under military occupation. Although agreements of this type were common at the termination of hostilities, they were often the subject of abuse or of misunderstanding, and in the case of South Manchuria as early as March, 1906, the United States called to Japan's attention charges from American interests in China that

---

[15] For a Japanese account of the Korean negotiations, see Tatsuji Takeuchi, *War and Diplomacy in the Japanese Empire,* 160-162.

[16] The line of demarcation between these spheres (North and South Manchuria) was defined in the secret Russo-Japanese treaties of 1907, 1910, and 1912. See E. B. Price, *The Russo-Japanese Treaties of 1907-1916. . . .* (Baltimore, 1933).

> . . . action of the Japanese authorities in Manchuria during Japanese [military] occupation is so generally directed towards establishing Japanese commercial interests in the principal towns, and toward acquiring property rights for Japanese in all available quarters as to leave little or no opening for other foreign trade by the time the territory is evacuated.

Thus within six months of the conclusion of peace the United States was calling upon Japan, as it had previously called upon Russia, to respect the principle of equal commercial opportunity.

The Sino-Japanese Treaty of Peking

The Treaty of Portsmouth had provided that the transfer to Japan of Russian territorial, railway, and other rights in South Manchuria was to be conditional on the consent of China. This consent was secured by Japan's Foreign Minister, Baron Komura, in negotiations with Yüan Shih-k'ai at Peking in a treaty dated December 22, 1905. An additional Sino-Japanese agreement of the same date contained important provisions: (1) China agreed to open 16 cities in Manchuria to international residence and trade; (2) Japan agreed to withdraw her troops and railway guards (if Russia would withdraw her railway guards) when "China shall have become herself capable of affording full protection to the lives and property of foreigners"; (3) Japan secured the right to maintain the military railway she had built from Antung on the Korean border to Mukden; and (4) China consented to formation of a Sino-Japanese corporation to exploit the Yalu forests.

Moreover, this formal Sino-Japanese treaty and additional agreement were later claimed by the Japanese government to be supplemented by secret "protocols," the most important of which pledged the Chinese government not to construct any mainline railway "in the neighborhood of and parallel to" the Japanese South Manchuria Railway (running from Changchun to Port Arthur and Dalny, now Dairen), or any branch line "which might be prejudicial" to the Japanese line.

The South Manchuria Railway Company

To manage the railroad and the other properties acquired from Russia in South Manchuria the Japanese government created the South Manchuria Railway Company—a joint stock company in which the Japanese government owned one-half of the capital stock and controlled appointment of the principal officers. Shareholders were limited to the Chinese and Japanese governments and to subjects of these two countries. The president and vice-president were responsible to the Japanese prime minister. The company was empowered to engage in subsidiary enterprises such as mining, water transportation, electric power, real estate, and warehousing within the railway zone. In addition, the company possessed broad civil administrative powers and authority to collect taxes within the railroad zone. Until 1931 this company was an amazingly effective agent of Japanese penetration in Manchuria. Protection of the railroad was provided by the government of Japan's leased territory of Kwantung (Liaotung), which was under a governor-general of high military rank who also exercised civil administrative power in the leased territory. After the Russo-Japanese War, the development of South Manchurian resources resulting from the capital, the energy, and the efficiency of the South Manchuria Railway Company not only excited the jealousy of other foreign nationals, principally British and American, but also inspired the fear that Japanese railroads using the S.M.R. as the trunk would branch out east and west to the exclusion of all non-Japanese enterprise.

Jurisdiction in Manchuria after 1905

Among the more significant features of Japan's emerging special position in South Manchuria after 1905 were certain jurisdictional powers. Within the Kwantung leased territory she possessed all rights of administration pertaining to sovereignty except the power to alienate the territory. In addition, Japan and Russia exercised special jurisdictional powers in their respective railway zones. The railway zones, defined as lands "actually necessary for the construction, operation, and protection" of the original Chinese Eastern Railway, were areas in which Russia and, after 1905, Japan (in South Manchuria) exercised very broad administrative powers, the validity of which was often questioned. Powers *exercised* by Japan included: ordinary rights of administration pertaining to sovereignty, taxation, police, and transfer of real property; employment of a limited number of railroad guards to protect the railway; and the exercise of ordinary police power and of customary functions of municipal and local administration. Over and above the foregoing powers, Japan enjoyed, as did also other "treaty powers," extraterritoriality and consular jurisdiction long established in China's treaties with foreign powers. Japanese consular police, attached to various Japanese consulates in Manchuria, exercised authority beyond the railroad zones.

In general, Russia's special position in North Manchuria remained unchanged by the Russo-Japanese War.

Intensification of International Rivalry

Although in Manchuria after 1905 China's sovereign rights were specifically reserved in the Kwantung territory and the various railway zones, *de facto* administration was exercised by Russia (the Chinese Eastern Railway) in North Manchuria, and by Japan (the

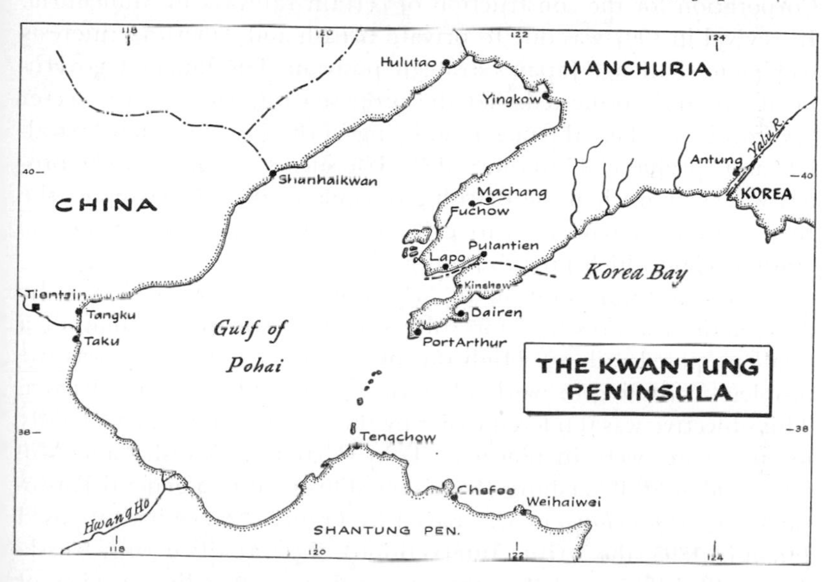

Government General of Kwantung and the S.M.R.) in South Manchuria. Far from decreasing foreign (Russian) control in Manchuria, the Russo-Japanese War had paved the way for Sino-Russian and Sino-Japanese agreements by which two powers instead of one claimed spheres of influence there. In these circumstances the future of the open door doctrine and the integrity of China appeared quite as dim as when Russia was the sole intruder. Foreign business interests in China, British and American in particular, had anticipated great opportunities for their goods and capital in South Manchuria once peace was restored. These opportunities had not appeared, and the powers were therefore concerned to discover how far Japan and Russia were bent on a policy of preference, if not monopoly, for their own commerce, industry, and capital. A test case was soon forthcoming.

Britain and France in Manchuria, 1907

The Chinese government in November, 1907, contracted with a British firm, Pauling and Company, to build a short railroad from Hsinmintun to Fakumen. In its origins this contract was an outgrowth of agreements made as early as 1898 between the Chinese government and the (British) Hongkong and Shanghai Banking Corporation for the construction of certain railways in Manchuria. Its revival in 1907 was due to private British and American interests seeking to challenge Japan's strategic position. The Japanese government promptly protested that the proposed line violated the secret "protocols" of 1905, the new road being in the Japanese view "parallel" and "prejudicial" to the S.M.R. The success of the Japanese protest was assured when the British government refused to support the British concessionaires or to call in question the validity of the "protocol" on which Japan's protest was based.

Japan's post-war position in Manchuria was reinforced, too, by diplomatic measures far more fundamental than the blocking of a small proposed railway. High on the list of Japanese aims was the problem of coming to workable terms with her late enemy, Russia. This objective was rendered easier by the fact that statesmen friendly to an entente were in power at Tokyo (Saionji, Hayashi, and Motono) and at St. Petersburg (Iswolsky). This road to a general Russo-Japanese *rapprochement* was paved by France. France had opposed Japan in 1895 (the Triple Intervention); she was allied with Russia during 1904-1905; and therefore it was now good policy, in view of Japan's victory, for France to clarify her relations with Tokyo, and to aid in creating a Russo-Japanese entente. The Franco-Japanese treaty, which materialized on June 10, 1907, and which was to provide the formula for subsequent Russo-Japanese agreements, is notable ". . . for its complete *sang-froid,* its subtle implications, and its bold assumptions."[17] The two powers, after agreeing "to respect

---

[17] E. B. Price, *The Russo-Japanese Treaties concerning Manchuria and Mongolia* (Baltimore, 1933), 26-31.

the independence and integrity of China, as well as the principle of equal treatment in that country for the commerce and subjects or citizens of all nations," went on to assert that they possessed "a special interest" in preserving peace and order "especially in the regions of the Chinese Empire adjoining the territories where they possess rights of sovereignty, protection or occupation." These two powers then proceeded to constitute themselves as the guardians of peace in vast areas of China which they later defined as including, in the case of France, the Chinese provinces of Kwangtung, Kwangsi, and Yünnan; and, in the case of Japan, Fukien and "the regions of Manchuria and Mongolia."

Following promptly this remarkable Franco-Japanese treaty came important Russo-Japanese agreements. These included a treaty of commerce and navigation and a fisheries convention,[18] and two political conventions, one public, the other secret. The public convention subscribed, as always, to the "independence and territorial integrity of the Empire of China," and pledged the signatories "to sustain and defend the maintenance of the *status quo* and respect for this principle by all pacific means within their reach." The secret convention (not revealed until published by the Soviet government, 1918) established precedents of the greatest importance:

1. It drew a line of demarcation between North and South Manchuria (the Russian and the Japanese spheres).
2. North of this line Japan undertook not to seek for herself or her subjects, nor to obstruct Russian efforts there to secure, concessions for railroads or telegraphs.
3. Russia undertook neither "to interfere with nor to place any obstacle in the way of the *further development*" of the "relations of political solidarity between Japan and Korea."
4. Japan, "recognizing the special interests of Russia [in Outer Mongolia, undertook] . . . to refrain from any interference which might prejudice those interests."[19]

The United States and Manchuria, 1905-1910

The Franco-Japanese and the Russo-Japanese agreements of 1907 presented a clearly defined threat to the American doctrine of

---

[18] MacMurray, *Treaties*, I, 643-648.
[19] Text in Price, *The Russo-Japanese Treaties*, 107-111.

China's territorial integrity and its corollary, the principle of equal opportunity, popularly known as the open door. The efforts of the American government in the earlier years 1899 to 1905 to insist on the integrity of China had been sporadic, periods of positive assertion being followed by silence and even admissions denying the principle. The Franco-Japanese treaty (1907), asserting that it was the business of Japan and France to maintain peace and order in large areas of China, contemplated possible occupation of Chinese territory, a circumstance not to be reconciled easily with China's integrity. And as for the open door in Manchuria after 1905, its status has never been described more realistically than by ex-President Roosevelt to his successor, President Taft:

> . . . As regards Manchuria, if the Japanese choose to follow a course of conduct to which we are adverse, we cannot stop it unless we are prepared to go to war. . . . The "Open Door" policy in China was an excellent thing, and I hope it will be a good thing in the future, so far as it can be maintained by general diplomatic agreement; but as has been proved by the whole history of Manchuria, alike under Russia and under Japan, the "Open Door" policy, as a matter of fact, completely disappears as soon as a powerful nation determines to disregard it, and is willing to run the risk of war rather than forego its intention.[20]

The foregoing explains why the American government under the presidency of Theodore Roosevelt was not prepared to lead any offensive against Japan's claim to special interests in South Manchuria. There were Americans, however, both in and outside government who did attempt to challenge the Japanese position, sometimes from motives of private and corporate profits and sometimes from the higher ground of national policy and principle. In 1905, E. H. Harriman, hoping to build a round-the-world transportation system, reached an understanding with Ito and Katsura to finance the reconstruction of the railway (S.M.R.) which Japan hoped to acquire from Russia at the end of the war. After peace came, Japan dropped the scheme. In Tokyo it seemed better policy to secure funds in London, where the Anglo-Japanese Alliance had recently been renewed, than in the United States, against which Japanese public opinion had been embittered by the Portsmouth Treaty, which had denied to the "victors" a war indemnity.

Far more active than Harriman in furthering American commerce

---

[20] Roosevelt to Taft, December 22, 1910, quoted by A. W. Griswold, *The Far Eastern Policy of the United States* (New York, 1938), 132.

and capital in Manchuria was Willard Straight, Consul-General of the United States at Mukden, 1906-1908. Straight was convinced that the weakness of the United States in the Far East was due to the relatively small American capital investment in China. He saw with much concern the growth of Japanese interests in Korea and Manchuria. A Sino-American publicity bureau which he inspired was so active that the Japanese protested and the bureau was liquidated. Straight made little progress with his official superiors so long as Roosevelt remained in the White House. Indeed, the President was less concerned with Japan and American capital in Manchuria than he was with the possibility of hostile Japanese action against the Philippines. Roosevelt's ideas were shaped in part by the crisis of 1906 in American-Japanese relations when the San Francisco School Board segregated Oriental students in the city schools. The "Gentleman's Agreement," 1907-1908, restored in part a sense of diplomatic calm, but war talk was such in the summer of 1907 that the President sent General Leonard Wood, commanding the troops in the Philippines, special instructions for meeting a Japanese attack, while Taft was again sent to Tokyo (October, 1907), from where he reported that Japan was anxious to avoid war. To meet the crisis in more fundamental ways, Roosevelt decided on two lines of action: (1) he sent the American fleet on a world cruise including Japanese ports (March 16, 1907, to February 22, 1909); and (2) he refused to take the offensive against Japan's position in Manchuria. The cruise of the American fleet signalized the arrival of American sea power, and pleased both the Canadians and the Australians.[21]

While the American fleet pursued its course in foreign waters the President employed the less provocative arts of diplomacy with the Japanese in Washington. A five-year arbitration treaty was concluded with Japan (May 5, 1908). It was an innocuous affair excluding all questions of "vital interests," but nonetheless a peaceful gesture. This treaty was followed by an exchange of notes between Secretary of State Root and the Japanese Ambassador, Takahira (November 30, 1908), which "was as important for what it left unsaid as for what it definitely stipulated." Since the phraseology of the notes was delightfully general there was ground for the belief that the exchange meant more than appeared on the surface. Certainly it would seem that the Root-Takahira exchange gave some

---

21 T. A. Bailey, *Theodore Roosevelt and the Japanese-American Crises* (Stanford University, 1934), chs. xi, xii.

sort of moral sanction to the special position of Japan in Korea and Manchuria. At the same time there is nothing to indicate that Root intended to give Japan a free hand in Manchuria. To the American government the notes meant guarantees on the Philippines, Hawaii, and Alaska, a reiteration of the open door and integrity of China, and a quieting of war talk. To the Japanese the notes gave assurance of peace, a guarantee of Formosa, and acceptance by the United States of the treaties giving Japan a special position in Eastern Asia.[22]

The Shift to Dollar Diplomacy

The Roosevelt-Root policy toward Japan and Manchuria was soon to give place to a new American strategy. William Howard Taft and Philander C. Knox became President and Secretary of State respectively at a time when American capital was to look increasingly to foreign fields for investment. Government was sympathetic, and, as Taft said later, its policy substituted "dollars for bullets" and combined "idealistic humanitarian sentiments" with "legitimate commercial aims." The commercial machinery of the Department of State was enlarged, and from November, 1908, until June, 1909, its Far Eastern Division was headed by Willard Straight, who worked incessantly to maintain Harriman's interest in Manchurian railway finance and to enlist the interest of New York bankers. Early in 1909 these efforts bore fruit. At the instance of the State Department a banking group was designated "as the official agent of American railway financing in China," with Straight as its Peking representative. The Department then demanded of China that the American bankers be admitted to the Hukuang railway loan then under negotiation between China and three bankings groups representing British, French, and German interests. The new American policy was thus striking at European financial monopoly in China Proper as well as at the Japanese in Manchuria. This was in line with the objectives of Taft and Knox "to force American capital by diplomatic pressure" into a region of the world where it would not go of its own accord. Also it meant that Secretary Knox was to attempt what was diplomatically impossible, to "smoke Japan out" of her position in Manchuria despite the fact that Japan by 1907 "had

22 T. A. Bailey, "The Root-Takahira Agreement of 1908," *Pacific Historical Review,* IX (March, 1940), 19-35.

given general notice of her determination to dominate as much of Manchuria as she could."[23]

The Chinchow-Aigun Railway Project

Implementation of the smoking-out experiment was begun by Straight and Harriman, who in 1909 were also attempting to buy the Chinese Eastern Railway from Russia. What Harriman really wanted was the Japanese S.M.R., but the Japanese had refused to sell. Therefore Harriman would force the sale by buying the Russian road and connecting it with the Gulf of Pechihli by a new line parallel to the S.M.R. from Chinchow (near Shanhaikwan where the Great Wall meets the sea) to Aigun on the Amur. If the threat of construction did not bring the Japanese to terms, then actual construction of the Chinchow-Aigun line would be undertaken. "He [Harriman] would smash competitors in Manchuria exactly as he had smashed them at home."[24] But Harriman died on September 10, 1909, and although Straight secured from the Manchurian government a preliminary agreement to finance (by the American group) and construct (by Pauling and Co.) the Chinchow-Aigun line, the bankers in New York without Harriman's leadership became timid. Harriman's railroad politics had failed.

The Knox Neutralization Proposal

It seemed therefore that if dollar diplomacy had any resources left, this was the time to use them. Accordingly, on November 6, 1909, Secretary Knox made two striking (some would say fantastic) proposals to Great Britain: (1) that the foreign-owned Manchurian railways (C.E.R. and S.M.R. systems) be "neutralized" by providing China with funds to purchase them through a great multi-power loan, during the life of which the railroads would be under foreign, international control; (2) in case "neutralization" proved impracticable, that Great Britain join with the United States in supporting the Chinchow-Aigun project and in inviting powers "friendly to complete commercial neutralization of Manchuria to participate." These propositions were nothing if not Gargantuan.

---

[23] J. G. Reid, *The Manchu Abdication and the Powers* (Berkeley, 1935), 75.

[24] Griswold, *Far Eastern Policy of the United States,* 152-153; Reid, *Manchu Abdication,* 42.

Sir Edward Grey approved "the general principle" of the neutralization proposal but thought it "wiser to postpone" any consideration of its application. As to the Chinchow-Aigun proposal, Sir Edward thought nothing should be done until China had agreed to Japanese participation. With this British approval in principle, but refusal in fact, Knox approached the Chinese, French, German, Japanese, and Russian governments. Russia and Japan, after consulting with each other, rejected the neutralization scheme in notes that showed a marked similarity. In addition they warned China that they must be consulted before foreign capital was employed in Manchurian railway enterprise. As a result, France and Great Britain gave notice that they would not support the United States in the Chinchow-Aigun line. The Gargantuan plans of Harriman, Straight, and Knox had miscarried. But this was not all. Secretary Knox, in the view of the British government, had hastened, if he did not actually cause, a tightening of the Russian and the Japanese spheres in Manchuria. On July 4, 1910 (of all days!), Russia and Japan signed two conventions, again, as in 1907, one public and the other secret. They announced to the world "the perfecting" of their connecting railway service in Manchuria. They refrained from any mention of China's integrity and the open door, but engaged publicly, in case the *status quo* should be menaced, to decide "the measures that they may judge it necessary to take for the maintenance of the said *status quo*." Secretly the two powers reaffirmed the line of demarcation drawn between their spheres in 1907, and strengthened their "special position" by recognizing "the right of each, within its own sphere, freely to take all measures necessary for the safeguarding and the defense of those interests." Neither would hinder "the consolidation and further development of the special interests of the other," while each would "refrain from all political activity" within the other's sphere. Finally, the secret convention provided for "common action" in defense of their special interests. The significance of dollar diplomacy as practiced by Knox in this instance is that it had not opened—on the contrary, it tended to close—the door to American capital in Manchuria.

Summarized in broad perspective, the years between the end of the Russo-Japanese War and the close of the Taft administration formed a chapter in American Far Eastern diplomacy distinguished for virility if not for judicious purpose and method. Japan was creating a new balance of power in Eastern Asia. In China the collapsing Confucian order was giving place to impotency and revolution. Into the tumult of these changes stepped American finance and its government seeking to play a decisive role in Eastern Asia. Leadership was provided by the brilliance of young Willard Straight, hero or evil genius according to interpretation. Although possessed of personal and intellectual charm, Straight was a pathetic failure as diplomat, financial agent, and judge of men and nations. He set the American pattern in anti-Japanese thought which was to be of such consequence in later years. Although an artist himself, he had no concept of political shadings. In a word, all the efforts of Harriman, Straight, Knox, the bankers, and the so-called Manchurian wing of the Department of State failed to reverse the pattern set by the Root-Takahira exchange. On the contrary, dollar diplomacy in the Far East stimulated the very things it was designed to destroy —Japan's and Russia's spheres of influence.[25]

The Annexation of Korea

It will be recalled that by 1905 Korea had become a Japanese protectorate, and was so recognized internationally. Roosevelt had written to Hay (January 29, 1905): "We cannot possibly interfere for the Koreans against Japan. They could not strike a blow in their own defense." Nevertheless, the emperor of Korea persisted in the belief during 1905 that the United States would come to his country's rescue because of the "good offices" clause in the Korean-American treaty of 1882. The Department of State, however, had taken the view that the earlier Japanese-Korean agreements of 1904 had already created a Japanese protectorate, which Korea had not protested; she had thus deprived herself of any further grounds for appeal under the good offices clause. Such was the legal status of the case. But these legalities did not present an adequate picture of the political aspects of American policy in 1905. In the political sense, American policy was not opposed to Japanese control of Korea. Roosevelt held that realistic politics demanded the sacrifice of Korean independence, and that a Korea controlled by Japan was preferable to a Korea controlled by Russia.

Despite the fact that by 1907 the Korean royal palace was guarded by Japanese police, an official Korean delegation, bearing credentials

[25] For an extended study, see Charles Vevier, *The United States and China, 1906-1913* (New Brunswick, N.J., 1955), especially 35-170.

from the emperor and advised by H. B. Hulbert, an American teacher long resident in Korea, arrived at the Hague Peace Conference. The mission was to make known "the violation of our [Korean] rights by the Japanese" and to re-establish "direct diplomatic relations" with the powers. Neither the Conference nor the Dutch government would receive the mission. Japan acted promptly. The Elder Statesmen felt that "the hour had not yet come to push to extreme limits [annexation] the chastisement for the felony committed." Instead "the [Korean] emperor king was forced to abdicate the throne in favor of his son" and a new agreement was concluded "whereby the Japanese resident-general became a virtual regent." Under this agreement all matters of internal administration as well as foreign relations were to be controlled by the resident-general.

With Japanese control tightening its grip on the entire Korean administration, the Korean problem as seen by the Japanese government again became an integral part of the larger Manchurian scene, where, as noted, Japan and Russia had come to an understanding (in the 1907 and 1910 secret treaties) in order to block the policies of Straight, Harriman, and Knox. As early as the spring of 1909 Foreign Minister Komura had secured the approval of Premier Katsura and Prince Ito to a memorandum "strongly recommending" Korean annexation, a proposal which soon had the approval of the cabinet and the emperor. Meanwhile, Ito, having resigned as resident-general (June 14, 1909) to become president of the Privy Council, went to Harbin (October, 1909) to meet Russian Minister of Finance Kokovtseff and to prepare the way for a closer understanding with Russia. On July 12, 1909, Viscount Sone, who had replaced Ito in Korea, had already secured an agreement placing the administration of Korean courts and prisons under direct Japanese control. Indeed, every preparation had been made for executing the predetermined policy of annexation. The assassination of Ito by a Korean (fanatic or patriot?) in Harbin (October 26, 1909) served only to increase the popular and public demand in Japan for immediate annexation. Then on June 24, the day on which the draft Russo-Japanese treaties of July 4, 1910, were shown to the British and French governments, the Korean police were placed under the command of the Japanese resident-general and minister of war. General Terauchi, Minister of War, "under heavy guard," reached Seoul on July 23. "All organs of public opinion" had been "suspended or ruthlessly suppressed." In the audience that followed, Terauchi presented the young Korean sovereign with a face-saving means of escape: a request for annexation from the emperor of Korea to the emperor of Japan. The treaty of annexation was signed August 22, 1910, and proclaimed seven days later. In Japan annexation was "acclaimed as a great achievement."

For Further Reading

Asakawa Kanichi, *The Russo-Japanese Conflict, Its Causes and Issues* (Boston, 1904). An important contemporary Japanese view of the causes of the war.

Blakeslee, George H., *Japan and Japanese-American Relations* (New York, 1912).

Campbell, Charles S., *Special Business Interests and the Open Door Policy* (New Haven, 1951). An examination of pressures exerted on the American Government by business engaged in China trade.

Chang Chia-ao, *China's Struggle for Railroad Development* (New York, 1943).

Chung, Henry, *Korean Treaties* (New York, 1919).

Clyde, Paul H., *International Rivalries in Manchuria* (rev. ed., Columbus, 1928).

Kublin, Hyman, "The Japanese Socialists and the Russo-Japanese War," *The Journal of Modern History*, XXII, No. 4 (December, 1950), 322-339.

Kuno, Yoshi S., *Japanese Expansion on the Asiatic Continent* (2 vols., Berkeley, 1937-1940). An uncritical survey.

Lattimore, Owen, *Manchuria: Cradle of Conflict* (rev. ed., New York, 1935). Manchuria's regional relationship to China.

Romanov, B. A., *Russia in Manchuria, 1892-1906*, trans. by Susan Wilbur Jones (Ann Arbor, 1952). Translation of a Russian study that first appeared in 1928.

Sun E-Tu Zen, *Chinese Railways and British Interests, 1898-1911* (New York, 1954). A reliable account.

Williams, W. A., *American-Russian Relations, 1781-1947* (New York, 1952).

Young, C. Walter, *Japanese Jurisdiction in the South Manchuria Railway Areas* (Baltimore, 1931).

———, *The International Legal Status of the Kwantung Leased Territory* (Baltimore, 1931).

———, *Japan's Special Position in Manchuria: Its Assertion, Legal Interpretation and Present Meaning* (Baltimore, 1931). The above three studies present a legalistic interpretation almost devoid of other historical considerations.

Zabriskie, Edward H., *American-Russian Rivalry in the Far East: A Study in Diplomacy and Power Politics, 1895-1914* (Philadelphia, 1946).

22 *China: 1911–1916*

The Gray Dawn of a Republic

In 1911 the Manchu dynasty had ruled China for 267 years. Like other successful conquerors of the Middle Kingdom, it had recognized the superior cultural attainments of the conquered people, and it had associated Chinese with Manchus in government. Thus the dynasty not only held the Mandate of Heaven but also ruled at times with distinction. By mid-nineteenth century, however, the Manchus faced economic dislocation at home and the impact of the Western world of ideas on their seaboard. These conditions called for radical adjustments in China's political, economic, and social structure—adjustments which the Sino-Manchu political hierarchy could neither conceive nor execute. To be sure, in the face of impending disaster, the aging and incompetent Empress Dowager sought refuge in reform, but her conversion was more apparent than real. To the last it was her purpose to give the shadow and not the substance of reform.

A series of events that may be described as the immediate causes of the impending Revolution of 1911 began with the year 1908. There was the death of the unfortunate young emperor, Kuang-hsü, followed shortly by the passing of the old Empress Dowager herself. She had already provided for the succession by unwisely placing an infant on the throne, with the Manchu, Prince Ch'un, as regent. Thus, when death removed the strong, if unscrupulous, hand of Old Buddha, the helm of state was in the keeping of a child directed by a regent who, though well-meaning enough, was to prove himself almost completely devoid of political wisdom. The seriousness of these events should be considered in relation to the complete Chinese picture during the first decade of the century: the abortive reforms of 1898, the disasters of the Boxer revolt, the inroads of the Western powers and Japan, the use of Chinese soil as battlegrounds in the Russo-Japanese War, and the reduction of Manchuria to the status of Russian and Japanese spheres of influence. All of these events called for the appearance of dynamic and far-sighted leadership at Peking. Adding to the political void at Peking was the forced retirement of Yüan Shih-k'ai. Yüan had been the main support of the Empress Dowager. Among the high officers of the court and the metropolitan administration, he almost alone had some appreciation of the need of reform and some capacity to carry it into effect. With Yüan, there also went into retirement many of the abler lesser officials whom he had trained and who were responsive to his leadership. In October, 1909, Chang Chih-tung, the great Yangtze viceroy, died. The result was that, while officially the reform program was continued, it became little more than a succession of edicts and blueprints.

The National Assembly, created by the Manchu reforms and designed to be a willing tool of the dynasty, had met for the first time in October, 1910, but, to the chagrin of the court and in spite of all its hand-picked conservatism, it showed a remarkable spirit of independence. It forced the government to promise a parliament in 1913 instead of after the longer nine-year period of preparation provided in the reform program. It threatened to impeach members of the government, and attacked its fiscal and administrative policies with vigor. Early in 1911 it demanded a responsible cabinet, winning the demand, in principle at least, before adjournment.

THE RETURN OF FLOOD AND FAMINE

Evidence of revolutionary stirrings, however, were not confined to Peking. Pressure of population on the means of subsistence together with recurring crises of famine occasioned by flood and drought were not a new feature of the Chinese scene. Such disasters had occurred many times in Chinese history, and, in the modern period, they had returned with startling frequency. In the twenty-five years preceding the Revolution of 1911, population had increased by perhaps as many as 50,000,000 persons, and while some of these found new homes in Manchuria and other sparsely populated areas of the empire or migrated abroad to Indochina and the Malay States, these movements provided no relief for the basic problem of livelihood. The years 1910 and 1911 marked the culmination of a series of bad seasons. Floods and drought in varying degree of intensity destroyed crops over a wide area. Hundreds of thousands died, and several millions were on the verge of starvation. Those who survived were psychologically prepared for any movement, rebellious or otherwise, that promised relief.

Throughout China discontent had also been fanned by rising taxes. Every measure in the reform program of 1901 and after had called for more revenue: the new army, new railroads, the new educational system. In addition, there were the charges on the Japanese war indemnity of 1895, and the more onerous charges of the Boxer Indemnity of 1901.

Centralization versus Provincial Autonomy

Closely linked with popular criticism of tax policies was the hard fact that the reform program encroached on the traditional autonomy of the provinces. In so far as the reform program possessed a real purpose other than that of saving the dynasty, it was to give China a national progressive government capable of holding the sovereignty of the state, and of protecting it from foreign encroachment. This objective required the sacrifice in large measure of the autonomy of the provinces, where vested local interests were loath to part with the prerogatives which time and custom had given them. It was the time-honored question of centralization versus decentralization, and the mores of China leaned heavily toward the latter.

The issue came to focus on the question of financing and thus controlling proposed trunk line railroads designed to be the first step in solving China's problem of communications. In the midst of the general agitation for reform after 1905, usually known as the "rights recovery" movement, there had been a strong demand for railroad construction on a provincial rather than a national basis, and for financing these lines with Chinese rather than foreign funds. It was a natural reaction to foreign concession grabbing and foreign financial control, while at the same time it was an equally natural expression of traditional Chinese political habits. But it was an impractical policy. The huge sums necessary could not be raised in the provinces, and even such sums as were collected were dissipated in wild speculation or unadulterated graft. Likewise, it was beginning to dawn on the Peking government that a program of national reform, if it were to be dominated by Peking, must presuppose national communications such as railroads. Accordingly, early in 1911 Peking began to prosecute with vigor its policy of railroad centralization. Foreign loans were contracted for the Hankow-Canton and Hankow-Szechwan trunk lines. At the same time the government sought to reach a settlement with the provincial interests involved. This proved to be difficult. Although the bonds with which Peking proposed to recompense the provinces represented a reasonably liberal settlement, it did not satisfy the local interests. Official protests were lodged at Peking, and in Szechwan there were public demonstrations on a wide scale. Discontent took the form of an open, though a minor, rebellion. It was a situation in which Peking, fearful lest the movement spread to other provinces, hesitated to act.

The Revolution of 1911

While the Imperial government was debating measures to settle the railroad troubles in Szechwan, an event of momentous import occurred in the central Yangtze Valley. At Hankow, in early October, an explosion occurred within the Russian concession in a bomb factory operated by followers of Sun Yat-sen. Investigations led to the arrest and execution of a number of republican revolutionaries. These events precipitated a military revolt among troops at Wuchang across the river from Hankow, where leaders of the revolt dragged their commander, Colonel Li Yuan-hung, from under his bed and presented him with the choice of immediate death or leadership of the rebellion. Being a practical man, though at the time far from a revolutionist, Colonel Li chose the latter. Within a brief period the three major cities of the middle Yangtze—Hankow, Hanyang, and Wuchang—were in rebel hands.

From this center, the revolt spread rapidly, particularly in the provinces south of the Yangtze. Although revolts occurred in some regions of the north, such as Shensi, Shantung, and Chihli, generally speaking the north remained loyal to the Imperial government. The pattern was one of a series of local and largely bloodless rebellions seemingly unco-ordinated and without unified leadership or a predetermined national plan.[1] While the Wuchang group was attempting to co-ordinate the movement by requesting provinces which had declared their independence to send delegates to a Wuchang revolutionary council, the revolution spread to Shanghai, where a new rebel government, led for the moment by Wu T'ing-fang, a Cantonese and former Minister to the United States, attempted to speak for the revolution as a whole. Interrevolutionary politics was thus making its appearance. The Shanghai group was dominated by Cantonese who were determined that leadership in the rebellion should not remain with the Yangtze provinces centered at Wuchang. Fortunately, all the revolutionary groups were at one in their determination that the Manchus must go. This and Li Yuan-hung's willingness to give way to Shanghai's so-called "military government" prevented an open break and permitted the Canton elements to lead.[2]

Effects of the Revolution in Peking

Peking, fearful of dealing vigorously with the revolt against its railway policies in Szechwan, was even less capable of meeting the anti-dynastic revolts begun at Hankow. The government was embarrassed not only by rebellion, which was spreading to practically every region of South China, but also by the reconvening on October 22, less than two weeks after the Wuchang rising, of the National Assembly. Heartened by the general spirit of rebellion, the Assembly forced the dismissal of those who had pushed the national railroad policy; again demanded responsible cabinet government; and insisted that a constitution be adopted only with the consent of the Assembly, and that political offenders be pardoned. Since many of the northern troops refused to move south to suppress the rebellions until these questions had been settled, the government had no recourse other than to grant the demands. On November 3, the dynasty gave its approval in edicts establishing a constitutional monarchy. Meanwhile the regent, Prince Ch'un, had induced Yüan Shih-k'ai to return to Peking by promising him unlimited powers. Yüan promptly resumed his command of the military forces, and on November 8 the National Assembly elected him premier.

1 P. M. A. Linebarger, *Government in Republican China* (New York, 1938), 145.

2 H. M. Vinacke, *Modern Constitutional Development in China* (Princeton, 1920), 102.

The Policy of Yüan Shih-k'ai

Yüan Shih-k'ai's critics have dealt harshly with his record. He has been characterized as "a soldier and diplomat from the North, narrow in outlook, altogether a tradition-bound official despite his up-to-date ideas—an opportunist and a realist in politics." Actually, Yüan was far more than these. While he had his limitations, and they were exceedingly large, he had shown genuinely progressive tendencies. He was an opportunist and a realist but he was not altogether tradition-bound. Some of his non-military ideas were as up-to-date as his military ones. He was a progressive, capable of carrying out needed reforms, as the previous decade had shown, and a tried administrator in civil and particularly in military affairs. He was not a republican and did not believe in 1911 that republicanism was the answer to China's ills, in which view he was by no means alone among China's abler men. Like many other Chinese of sober thought, Yüan seems to have held to the view that it would be fatal for China to attempt a complete break with the spirit or the political machinery of the past, and that the stability of reform would depend in some major degree on Confucian mores and not exclusively on the adoption of Western ideologies.[3] Now that he was invested by the dynasty with supreme powers, and endowed by the National Assembly with the post of prime minister, Yüan's task was to put a stop to rebellion and then to carry on the constitutional reforms of the Assembly. Yüan, however, appears to have entertained purposes more subtle than these. Although he was not as yet seeking the destruction of the dynasty, Yüan was willing to permit the spread of the southern rebellions in order to force the Manchus to accept and play the role of the passive, constitutional monarchy. There appears to be no doubt that Yüan's Imperial forces were superior in every respect to the revolutionary armies of Li, yet the northern armies were never permitted to push their advantages to ultimate and decisive victory. So long as these conditions prevailed, Yüan was able to impose his will in Peking and also in the subsequent negotiations with the republican rebels.

Opposed to Yüan, to the dynasty, and to the National Assembly stood the republican rebel armies of Li Yuan-hung, the so-called "military government" (Cantonese) at Shanghai, and the southern provinces that had declared their independence. On October 9,

3 A. M. Kotenev, *The Chinese Soldier* (Shanghai, 1937), 82-83.

when the Hankow incident occurred, Sun Yat-sen, the ideological leader of the southern republicans, was in the United States. Not until two months later (December 24, 1911) did he reach Shanghai.

The Peace Negotiations

The return of Sun Yat-sen, although inspiring to the revolutionists, did not alter the fact that they were incapable of carrying the revolution to a successful conclusion or of holding its leadership. The balance between the hoary traditions of dynastic rule and the mysteries of republicanism was held not by Sun Yat-sen but by Yüan Shih-k'ai. With a subtle appreciation of his political and military advantage, Yüan attempted to negotiate a settlement with Li Yuan-hung, finally agreeing with Li's consent to deal with the republican group at Shanghai. This was in December, 1911. Meanwhile, at Li's suggestion, delegates from the "independent" southern provinces assembled at a national convention in Nanking and elected Sun Yat-sen provisional president. It was this more unified republican regime that finally concluded the peace settlement with Yüan's representative, T'ang Shao-yi, an American-educated Cantonese. In these negotiations the monarchy was brought to an end and a republic, in name at least, was created. Sun Yat-sen stepped down from the presidency, and at his suggestion the Nanking Convention elected Yüan Shih-k'ai first provisional president of the Republic of China. Sun's relinquishment of the presidency may have been due in some degree to his desire to remain solely the ideological leader of the new China, but the more decisive factor in his decision was the political and military power of Yüan.

The new Republic was to be inaugurated with the arrival of Yüan at Nanking. However, Nanking represented the south and was controlled by the southern Republicans, while Yüan's armies were in the vicinity of Peking. This explains why a military mutiny engineered by Yüan near Peking made it inconvenient for the new president to leave the old capital. By this means Yüan was able to force the Republicans to come to Peking, the home of tradition and conservatism. Furthermore, the abdication edicts, dictated by Yüan himself and promulgated on February 12, 1912, implied clearly that the new president derived his power by transfer from the throne rather than by mandate of the Republic.

The Foreign Powers and the End of the Dynasty

The end of the Manchu dynasty and the emergence of Yüan Shih-k'ai in a new position of power as president of the Republic were not due solely to the political and military advantages enjoyed by Yüan within China. Both the Republic and Yüan's leadership therein were in part the creation of the great foreign powers. From 1908, and even earlier, the fate of the Manchu dynasty rested on its capacity to prevent further disintegration, to arrest foreign concession hunting, and to forestall the partition of the empire by the foreign powers. In those crucial years between 1908 and 1912 the powers failed both singly and collectively to support the Imperial government to these ends. Indeed, the rivalries of the powers in their efforts to control China politically and economically weakened what little prestige was left to the dynasty and thereby invited provincial opposition to Peking's national railway policies. Again, the reforms which Peking planned for the border territories of Tibet, Mongolia, and Manchuria—reforms designed eventually to bring these areas into a national China—were frowned upon by Britain, Russia, and Japan. From the Wuchang rebellion in October, 1911, until the abdication edicts of February 12, 1912, the powers did nothing to prevent the collapse of the Imperial regime. On the contrary, they assisted Yüan Shih-k'ai in his ambitions to head the new Republic. As a result of conflicting power-interests and of commitments from some of the powers, Yüan was able to count on diplomatic and foreign financial support before the conclusion of his negotiations with the southern republicans and before he had been elevated to the presidency.

Early Phases of Yüan's Government

With the establishment of the Republic, China did not enter an era of republicanism but rather one of militarism. This is accounted for by a number of considerations. The national army organized by Li Hung-chang and Yüan Shih-k'ai was a northern army; it was not national; its officers thought of themselves as lieutenants of Yüan, not of the State. In the southern provinces during the revolution, authority had shifted to provincial leaders who could command the personal allegiance of troops in their respective areas. Thus, both during and succeeding the Revolution, military authority was also political authority. Since as a result of revolutionary conditions the number of men under arms increased rapidly, there were few checks upon the power of these personal, and in most cases irresponsible, armies.

Not being in a position to destroy or disband these independent provincial armies, Yüan's only recourse was to make allies of them. This he did by appointing their commanders as provincial military governors. Eventually he hoped to replace them by civil administrations responsive to his Peking government. This would be done by coaxing the provincial militarists into various government posts in the capital, thus separating them from their armies, the source of their strength. In these circumstances China was in the grip not of republicanism, but of militarism.

Meanwhile, the new government was attempting to get under way at Peking under the terms of a Provisional Constitution adopted at Nanking in March, 1912. Being the product of southern republicanism, this Constitution was shaped with the idea of making the president subject to parliamentary will. Under it, the Nanking Convention or Council was to act as a parliament until elections had been held. Yüan's first cabinet represented a compromise between his own wishes and those of the parliamentarians, but as early as the summer of 1912 the clash between executive and legislature was apparent. In August, Sun Yat-sen announced organization of his new political party, the *Kuomintang,* to which Yüan replied by organizing his own Progressive Party, the *Chinputang.* When a National Assembly under the Provisional Constitution met early in 1913, the *Kuomintang* held the strongest position but did not have absolute control. In July, a second southern republican revolt was suppressed by Yüan. Yet on October 10, 1913, the Assembly removed Yüan's provisional status by electing him president of the Republic. Less than a month later, November 4, Yüan suppressed the *Kuomintang.* Then by presidential decree, January 10, 1914, he "suspended" the Assembly and replaced it with his own Constitutional Council. This body brought forth on May 1, 1914, its own constitution, known as the Constitutional Compact. It created a "presidential government," and "legitimatized" Yüan's dictatorship.

In this manner Yüan was attempting to pave the way for a restoration of monarchy with himself on the throne. There was much to support the idea that constitutional monarchy as proposed in 1898 by K'ang Yu-wei was more likely to succeed than republicanism. This view was presented to Yüan in a memorandum, August 9, 1915, by his constitutional adviser, Professor Frank Goodnow. Goodnow pointed out the desirability, viewing China's problems of government in the abstract, "of establishing a constitutional monarchy *if* there was general demand for it rather than of maintaining the trappings of Republicanism without operative democracy." As a result therefore of "a circus of plebiscites and constitutional councils," constitutional monarchy was proclaimed in December, 1915. It was short-lived. No considerable body of the Chinese people had any understanding of the relative merits of constitutional monarchy or republicanism, but there were provincial and republican leaders with following enough to oppose Yüan as a monarch of any kind. Revolt promptly flared in Yünnan and spread rapidly through the south. Yüan renounced the throne in March, and died three months later, on June 6, 1916.

Dollar Diplomacy and the Revolution

The collapse of the Manchu dynasty, as noted, was due in part to the acquiescence of the powers. In like manner, the hope of a stable regime under Yüan appeared to depend on the financial policies of the same great powers. The new republican government of 1912 was "without funds and with increasing unpaid obligations."[4] China's quest for foreign financial aid, however, could not be divorced from implications of foreign political control. It should be recalled that the Revolution of 1911 was, among other things, a reaction and protest against the foreign scramble for concessions which followed the Sino-Japanese War of 1894-1895, and which continued with increasing intensity until the outbreak of the Revolution. Indeed, the politico-financial rivalry of the powers was so great that they themselves began to favor pooling certain types of loans to China through an international banking agency called the consortium. This agency was to be composed of groups of bankers designated by their respective governments. Thus, loans made through the consortium would be subject to a double test: their acceptability to the bankers on economic grounds, and to the powers on political grounds. In its embryonic stage in 1909 the consortium included only British, French, and German banking groups that were proposing to finance and construct for the old Manchu-Chinese govern-

[4] C. F. Remer, *Foreign Investments in China* (New York, 1933), 126.

ment the so-called Hukuang railways in Central and South China.[5] An American group was admitted in 1911 after President Taft had appealed to the Chinese regent.

With the progress of the Revolution and the establishment of the Republic, the interest of the consortium, on the surface at least, was directed toward providing the impecunious government at Peking with funds to maintain itself and to create stable conditions throughout the empire. In principle, the Republic was to be assisted through international financial co-operation. However, the road to this objective was beset with many obstacles. Russia and Japan, though borrowing countries, demanded admission to the consortium, and their banking groups were admitted in June, 1912. However, in the view of the Chinese government and of many foreign bankers not included in the various groups, the consortium was an attempt to create a monopoly controlling the Chinese loan market.

In the midst of this complicated political-financial wire-pulling at Peking, the Wilson administration came into power at Washington. The timid American banking group asked whether it would continue to enjoy in its China investments the active support of the Department of State. President Wilson replied on March 18, 1913, withdrawing official support from the American group because he found the control measures of the proposed reorganization loan "to touch very nearly the administrative independence of China itself." Taft had pushed American bankers into China to preserve the open door. Wilson refused to support them there because their activities, along with the activities of the other groups, threatened China's independence. The Reorganization Loan Agreement was concluded without American participation on April 26, 1913.

Separatist Movements in Border Territories

The transition from Manchu empire to Chinese republic was the occasion too for various rebellions and "independence" movements in the former empire dependencies of Mongolia and Tibet. During the decade preceding the Revolution of 1911, the Mongol nobility had grown restive as Chinese settlers encroached on Inner Mongolia and as Peking attempted to extend the government of China Proper to this area. Mongol disaffection was encouraged by

---

5 Charles Vevier, *The United States and China* (New Brunswick, 1955), 88-110.

Russia, whose agents fostered Mongol nationalism. In December, 1911, an independent Mongol government came into being at Urga. China combatted the movement by attempting to re-establish her authority in Inner Mongolia, only to be countered by Russian recognition of the Urga government in November, 1912. A year later (November, 1913) Russia and the Republic of China agreed that Outer Mongolia was "autonomous" but not "independent." Nearly two years later (June, 1915), Mongolia accepted this status in an agreement between herself, Russia, and China.

The Revolution of 1911 was also the signal for trouble in Tibet. The Tibetans drove the Chinese garrison from the country, and, as independent people, proceeded to conclude an agreement (January, 1913) with the new and independent Mongolian government. When Yüan Shih-k'ai sought to re-establish by force China's authority at Lhasa, he encountered British diplomatic opposition. It was not until 1914 that an agreement was worked out among Tibet, China, and Britain whereby western Tibet (Tibet proper) was to be autonomous, the Chinese maintaining a resident and small guard at Lhasa, while in eastern Tibet the authority of China was to be retained. Although this convention was not ratified by China, it set the pattern for future political controls in Tibet.

Analysis of the Old First Republic

The four years, 1912-1916, surveyed in the preceding pages of this chapter, were but a prelude to even more dismal things to come before the final collapse of the old First Republic in 1928.[6] Indeed, it had fallen to Yüan Shih-k'ai to lead one of the most fantastic failures in modern political history. The Chinese republican revolution, 1911-1912, was an attempt to set aside the Confucian monarchy and to replace it with a parliamentary constitutional republic. On paper this republic appeared to have everything needed for success: constitutions, parliamentary procedures, codes of law. But the constitutions were not understood, the parliamentary procedures were not followed, and the law codes were never enforced. What the republic did not have was much more important than what it possessed. It did not have a people who understood parliamentary institutions, government by law, or the rudiments of democratic responsible citi-

[6] The story of the final years of the old First Republic, 1917-1928, will be found in Chapter 29.

zenship. When at the beginning of the revolution in 1911 a council of representatives was convoked by the southern republicans, these representatives were not elected: there was no election machinery in the provinces, and anyway no one knew what an election was. Sun Yat-sen, visionary, genius, Christian, and for the moment provisional president, prayed to his Christian God but also supplicated the spirits of the Ming emperors, the last Chinese rulers of China. Yüan Shih-k'ai rose to the presidency over Sun Yat-sen not by any Mandate of Heaven or mandate of the people but by double-crossing both the dynasty and the republicans through his military power supported later by foreign loans. He dispersed the republican parliament and acquired one that would do his bidding. Then, not content with the realism of this presidential dictatorship in a nominal republic, Yüan became a romantic. The scheme to restore the monarchy with himself as monarch failed not because it was a move away from democracy, as so many Americans then and later imagined, but because Peking did not have enough power to suppress southern insurrection. By 1916, when Yüan Shih-k'ai joined the spirits of his ancestors, the old first Republic of China had already been perverted into an immense failure.[7]

For Further Reading

Brunnert, H. S., and V. V. Hagelstrom, *Present Day Political Organization of China* (Shanghai, 1912).

Chen, Stephen, and Robert Payne, *Sun Yat-sen: A Portrait* (New York, 1946). A useful brief introduction to Sun's career and his thought.

Curry, Roy Watson, *Woodrow Wilson and Far Eastern Policy 1913-1921* (New York, 1957).

Holcombe, A. N., *The Spirit of the Chinese Revolution* (New York, 1930). A discussion of political theory in China's revolution in which the author attempts to find theory through a study of personalities.

Hsu, Leonard (Shih-lien), *Sun Yat-sen, His Political and Social Ideals* (Los Angeles, 1933).

Li T'ien-i, *Woodrow Wilson's China Policy* (New York, 1952).

Linebarger, P. M. A., *The Political Doctrines of Sun Yat-sen* (Baltimore, 1937). Shows the difficulty of applying the concept of democracy against the background of Chinese traditional thought.

MacNair, H. F., *Modern Chinese History: Selected Readings* (Shanghai, 1923).

[7] P. M. A. Linebarger, Djang Chu, and Ardath W. Burks, *Far Eastern Governments and Politics* (New York, 1954), 120-132.

———, *China in Revolution* (Chicago, 1931).

Martin, Bernard, *Strange Vigour* (London, 1944). A biography of Sun Yat-sen. Uses the Cantlie papers and press notices.

Pan Wei-tung, *The Chinese Constitution* (Washington, 1945). A study of forty years of Chinese constitution making.

Peake, Cyrus H., *Nationalism and Education in Modern China* (New York, 1932).

Price, Francis, trans., *San Min Chu I, The Three Principles of the People* (Shanghai, 1928). A translation of Sun Yat-sen's lectures.

Restarick, Henry B., *Sun Yat-sen: Liberator of China* (New Haven, 1931).

Sharman, Lyon, *Sun Yat-sen: His Life and Its Meaning* (New York, 1934). This and the study by Restarick are the most satisfactory biographies of the revolutionary leader.

23

1914–1918

Japan and China in World War I

CONSIDERED in terms of its immediate causes and its military and naval campaigns, World War I was primarily a European conflict. No major battles were fought on Asiatic soil or in Asiatic waters. Nevertheless, at one time or another all the major lands and peoples of Asia were aligned with the Allied and Associated Powers. By their participation in the war, the peoples of eastern Asia were united, formally at least, with the Western democracies in the crusade against German militarism, and, after 1917, in the Wilsonian crusade to "make the world safe for democracy." Thus eastern Asia became a participant in the war despite the fact that it was not intimately concerned with the war's immediate causes.

In contrast with the immediate causes, the more remote causes of the war involved the Far East intimately just as they came eventually to involve the interests of the United States. These remote, underlying causes involved "the psychology of fear, and all other factors which go to make up the somewhat vague conceptions of 'militarism' and 'navalism' as causes of war."[1] They involved the powerful forces of nationalism as they developed in the century following the French Revolution, encompassing the political and prejudicial questions of race, religion, democracy, and education.

These underlying causes of conflict had taken root in the political, the economic, and the cultural soil of the Far East. In 1914 all the great peoples of Asia, the Japanese excepted, were in colonial or

[1] For a detailed discussion of underlying causes, see Sidney B. Fay, *The Origins of the World War* (2 vols. in one, New York, 1931), I, 32-49.

semi-colonial status to one or more of the great Western powers or Japan. Therefore, although the Far East could and did remain in relative isolation from the military conflict, it could not be isolated from the consequences of war or from the aspirations which the war or the peace aroused in the minds and hearts of ordinary men and women.

Japan Enters the War

Japan's entrance into World War I derived its sanction from a double basis: the nation's commitments under the Anglo-Japanese Alliance, and the larger political and military purposes of Japan's emerging Asiatic policy.

Prior to Great Britain's entry into the war, Japanese public opinion, regarding the conflict as purely a European affair, favored, as did public sentiment in the United States, a policy of neutrality. But as Britain entered the conflict, the Japanese press assumed a new and militant tone. It recalled Germany's role in the Triple Intervention of 1895; it reminded the public of Japan's obligations to Great Britain under the Alliance, and to France and Russia under the treaties of 1907 and later; it charged that German naval power in the Pacific was a threat to all neutral shipping, and that German military preparations at Kiaochow were a menace to the peace of the Far East; and finally, it advocated attack on Germany's far eastern possessions.[2] Moreover, the Japanese press, never free from official inspiration, also found cause for entering the war because of the Anglo-Japanese Alliance, the preamble of which was dedicated to the maintenance of peace and the territorial rights of the signatories and their special interests in eastern Asia and India. Great Britain, however, approached the matter of Japanese assistance under the Alliance with the utmost caution. On August 4, Britain declared war, and three days later, August 7, she requested Japan to destroy the German fleet in Pacific waters. The decision of the Japanese government, made August 8, was to demand of Germany not only surrender of its armed ships in Asiatic waters (thus complying with the British request), but also to demand surrender of the Kiaochow leasehold in Shantung. This momentous decision to join Great Britain in the war (as explained by Count Kato Takaaki, the Foreign Minister) was not based on legal obligations of the Anglo-Japanese

[2] The campaign of the Japanese press is summarized in "Why Japan Attacks Germany," *The Literary Digest,* XLIX (September 19, 1914), 502.

Alliance, for "the general conditions were not such as to impose upon Japan the duty to join the war under treaty obligations," but "as a voluntary expression of friendship toward Great Britain under the alliance."[3] What Japan meant was that she welcomed "an opportunity to destroy the German influence from eastern Asia and to enhance the international position of Japan."

The inclusion of Kiaochow in the Japanese reply brought prompt reactions in London. The British felt that a Japanese attack on Kiaochow would imply a full extension of the war to Chinese territory, adversely affecting British commercial interests there. Therefore Britain hoped Japan would confine her activities "to protection of the sea trade and postpone her declaration of war." Japan countered that her Kiaochow proposal was conceived as the best means of safeguarding this sea trade. Britain thereupon reversed her position completely; on August 11, she withdrew her request for assistance under the Alliance.

It was then Japan's turn to be embarrassed. Public opinion favored war; the cabinet had already made its decision, sanctioned by the throne; and tension had been heightened by reports that the German ambassador in Tokyo had used threatening language at the foreign office. To have reversed its decision would have rendered untenable the position of the Okuma cabinet.[4] From this dilemma Kato was partly relieved on August 13, when Grey, again reversing himself, agreed to a Japanese ultimatum to Germany for surrender of armed vessels and also of Kiaochow. Grey requested, however, that Japan confine her zone of activity "to the German base and the neighboring China seas," and that this limitation be stated in the ultimatum to Germany. However, on August 15, with Britain's consent the Japanese ultimatum was dispatched without the reservation. It reviewed the peaceful aims of the Anglo-Japanese Alliance; it advised Germany to withdraw all armed vessels from Chinese and Japanese waters, to disarm any that could not be withdrawn, and to deliver to Japan by September 15 "without condition or compensation," the Kiaochow leasehold "with a view to eventual restoration of the same to China."[5]

---

[3] Tatsuji Takeuchi, *War and Diplomacy in the Japanese Empire* (Chicago, 1935), 169.

[4] See the detailed discussion by Charles Nelson Spinks, "Japan's Entrance into the World War," *Pacific Historical Review,* V (1936), 297-311; also Thomas E. LaFargue, *China and the World War* (Stanford University, 1937), 3-27.

[5] Spinks, "Japan's Entrance into the World War," *op. cit.,* 308-309.

Barring an improbable German acceptance of the ultimatum, Japan was committed to war, yet the British government made a further effort to limit the sphere of Japanese action. In a press release, August 18, it described the ultimatum as designed "to protect the general interests in the Far East contemplated by the Anglo-Japanese Alliance," and referred in particular to the independence and the integrity of China. The statement continued:

> It is understood that the action of Japan will not extend to the Pacific Ocean beyond the China Seas, except in so far as it may be necessary to protect Japanese shipping lines in the Pacific, nor beyond Asiatic waters westward of the China Seas, nor to any foreign territory except territory in German occupation on the Continent of Eastern Asia.[6]

The implications of this statement brought forth from Premier Okuma a denial of territorial ambitions and the assurance that Japan's war activities would be limited to "self-defense." At the same time Kato protested the British statement, and, as a result, the British government gave public assurance that Japan's purpose was to eliminate German influence from China, thereby removing a menace to the peace of the Far East. "She [Japan] harbours no designs for territorial aggrandizement and entertains no desire to promote any other selfish end."[7]

On August 23, Germany having ignored the ultimatum, Japan entered the war. From August 7, when Great Britain first requested assistance, the eventual entry of Japan was never in doubt. It is equally clear that Britain's hope of limiting Japan's field of action was foredoomed to fail. As noted, Kato's policy was not confined to considerations of the Anglo-Japanese Alliance. Of equal, if not greater, weight was the opportunity to destroy German influence in the Far East "and to enhance the international position of Japan."

The Neutrality of China and the Pacific

The outbreak of war in Europe had aroused great alarm in Peking. China's interests, reasoned Peking, would best be served by exclusion of her territories and waters from the zone of hostilities. Consequently, Yüan attempted to enlist American diplomatic action as

---

[6] *The Times* (London), August 18, 1914, quoted by Spinks, "Japan's Entrance into the World War," *op. cit.*, 309.

[7] *The Times* (London), August 21, 1914.

an instrument of China's national policy. He proposed, August 3, 1914, that the United States "endeavor to obtain the consent of the belligerent European nations to an understanding not to engage in hostilities either in Chinese territory and marginal waters or in adjacent leased territories." On the assumption presumably that the neutrality of China was closely linked with the principle of territorial integrity dear to American official policy, Secretary of State Bryan approved the neutralization of foreign settlements and concessions in China but not of leased territories, and he approached the European powers on an even more ambitious scheme designed to neutralize the entire Pacific Ocean as well as China and its adjacent waters. None of the belligerents favored the idea save Germany. Furthermore, the United States was not prepared to enforce neutrality with sanctions.

Kiaochow

Following promptly on her declaration of war, Japan proceeded to the investment of the Kiaochow leased territory and its port of Tsingtao. With this port under naval blockade, Japanese military forces, landing on Chinese soil far to the north, moved to attack Tsingtao from the rear and to occupy the railway zone reaching from Tsingtao to Tsinan far in the interior of the province.[8] As in previous cases, China was unprepared to defend her neutrality. Having formally declared her neutrality she protested Japan's action, but she followed this protest with a proclamation delimiting a war zone in areas adjacent to Kiaochow. In so doing she was following the precedent established in Manchuria in 1904 at the suggestion of the United States. Since Japan promptly ignored the war zone, it was again patent that China could neither keep the war from her shores nor control its course within her borders.[9]

Kiaochow surrendered, November 10, and Japan proceeded to take over not only the leased territory but also all German interests

8 A small British force was also engaged for "token" purposes.

9 Both the Allies and Germany ignored the fundamental issue of China's neutrality. The Germans used the Tsingtao-Tsinan Railway to carry troops from Tientsin and reservists from other areas into the leased territory. The European powers also used Chinese railroads to reach their fighting fronts. For the Germans at this time it should be said that they were going to defend Tsingtao from attack and not to launch an offensive, as were Japan and Britain, across Chinese neutral territory.

in Shantung, including the Tsingtao-Tsinan Railway. Japan also took over from the Chinese, on the plea of military necessity, the policing of the railroads outside the leased territory. Japanese replaced Germans in the Chinese customs office at Tsingtao. Indeed, the ousting of Germany was thorough and complete. Then, on January 7, 1915, China cancelled the war zone on the ground that it was no longer necessary. This cancellation, it will be seen, was to provide the pretext for further Japanese action.

Nature of the German Rights in Shantung

Since the ultimate disposition of the German rights in Shantung was later to claim worldwide attention, and since these German rights were typical of the system of special privilege, particularly economic privilege, in spheres of influence after 1898, the nature and scope of these rights which Japan was to claim as a result of her military victory are matters of importance. They included among others the following: (1) China had conferred upon Germany a 99-year lease of both sides of Kiaochow Bay, on which Germany erected fortifications and in which Germany had exercised "rights of administration"; (2) within a zone of 50 kilometers of the bay, German troops held the right of freedom of passage, and Chinese administration was subject to German approval; (3) Germany acquired the right to construct certain railroads in Shantung, a provision that resulted in the building of the Tsingtao-Tsinan Railway by a Sino-German concern, the Shantung Railway Company; (4) Germany also acquired the right to mine coal within 30 *li* of the railroads; (5) if Germany desired to return Kiaochow to China before the expiration of the lease, China engaged to lease "to Germany a more suitable place"; (6) Germany had engaged not to sublet the territory to another power, but there was no provision regarding the transfer of the territory by Germany to another power as a result of conquest such as the Japanese action of 1914; (7) if assistance in the form of capital or services or materials were needed for any undertaking in Shantung province, China had agreed to approach German nationals. Under these concessions, Germany had built a modern port at Tsingtao, had extended a railroad far into the interior of the province, and had developed broad commercial undertakings, while at Kiaochow she had created a naval base for her Pacific squadron. Her position in this respect was comparable in its political implications with that of Great Britain at Kowloon, with France at Kwangchow, and with Japan at Port Arthur.[10]

Japan's Naval Operations

While Japanese naval and military forces were engaged in the reduction of Tsingtao and in taking over other German interests in Shantung, units of the Japanese navy were operating in the Pacific and Indian Oceans in co-operation with the British against German commerce raiders. Early in these operations, while the Australians were occupying German colonies and islands south of the equator, the Japanese occupied the German islands north of the equator. These included the Marianas (excepting Guam), the Carolines, and the Marshalls. From the beginning of 1915 Japan's relationship to the war became essentially non-military. On one hand, Japanese factories equipped the Russian armies on the eastern European front; on the other, Japan's policies in China became a nightmare not only to Western commerce but also to political principles emerging in the pattern of Allied war aims.

The Background of the Twenty-one Demands

On January 18, 1915, Japanese Minister Hioki at Peking presented to President Yüan Shih-k'ai a group of twenty-one demands designed to "insure" Japan's position in China at a time when Europe was preoccupied with war. The fundamental policy behind the demands was not new, for it dated back to the beginnings of Japanese expansion in the 1870's. The distinction was that Japanese policy as it was to reveal itself in 1915 was a brazen, far-reaching application of the principles of power politics which, although employed by European powers against China on numerous occasions, had never been used with the spirit of reckless abandon which was to characterize the Twenty-one Demands.

After the annexation of Korea in 1910, both the Japanese government and the Japanese public had become vitally concerned with the status and future of Japanese interests in Manchuria. As early as January, 1913, Count Kato Takaaki, before leaving London to become Foreign Minister in the Okuma cabinet, informed Grey that

[10] The British at Kowloon did not have the extensive economic rights in the Chinese hinterland that Germany had in Shantung.

"Japan entertained vital political and psychological concern in the Kwantung Peninsula . . . and South Manchuria"; that Japan was "determined to maintain a permanent occupation of the Kwantung Province"; and that if a "psychological moment" arrived, Japan would seek to extend her leasehold and concessions there.[11]

A second phase of Japanese policy in 1915 concerned itself with the nation's position and influence south of the Great Wall in China proper. In the scramble there for railway and mining concessions, Japan as a debtor nation was at a disadvantage against European and American competitors. Moreover, as Japanese pressures on China had increased after 1905, so China had sought increasingly to protect herself through American intervention. When, for example, it was apparent Japan would attack in Shantung in 1914, China intimated to the United States that the Root-Takahira notes of 1908 established in favor of the United States a *right* to be consulted by Japan before the latter embarked on any military action affecting Chinese territory. Although the American government entertained no such view of its "rights," many "serious and responsible" Chinese were convinced by a campaign of rumors (many of which originated in Japan) that the United States was preparing to act in opposition to Japanese interests in China. Upon this delusion, China "founded extravagant hopes that the United States would undertake to guarantee China against any territorial aggression or disregard of its sovereignty."[12]

It was against this background that China on January 7, 1915, abolished "abruptly and without previous notification" the war zone in Shantung province. It was against the same background that Japan responded, declaring that China's action revealed a lack of "international good faith" and disregard of "friendly relations." The "psychological moment" of which Kato had spoken two years previously had arrived. Japan was ready to use it not only to adjust what were regarded as specific grievances but also to establish if possible a general and paramount influence over all China.

---

[11] Tatsuji Takeuchi, *War and Diplomacy in the Japanese Empire,* 183-185.

[12] United States, *Foreign Relations, 1914* (Supplement), 186-7. How fantastic these Chinese hopes were was revealed by Acting Secretary of State Lansing when he informed the American legation in Peking that although the United States was prepared to promote China's welfare by peaceful methods, "it would be quixotic in the extreme to allow the question of China's territorial integrity to entangle the United States in international difficulties." *Ibid.,* 190.

Specific Objectives of the Demands

The Twenty-one Demands, as presented to President Yüan Shih-k'ai on January 18, 1915, were divided into five groups: Group 1 concerned the disposition of the former German rights in Shantung; Group 2 related to Japan's position in South Manchuria and eastern Inner Mongolia; Group 3 dealt with a program for Japanese industrial capital in regions of the Yangtze Valley; Group 4 concerned the non-alienation of Chinese coastal territory; and Group 5 included a variety of subjects, designated as "requests" rather than "demands."

Group 1: Shantung

In these demands, China was required to assent to any subsequent German-Japanese agreement disposing of German rights in Shantung; to agree not to cede or lease any part of Shantung "to any other power"; to agree to Japanese construction of a railroad connecting Chefoo with the Tsingtao-Tsinan line; and finally to consent to the opening of certain cities to "the residence and commerce of foreigners." By these provisions Japan would preclude the return of Germany to Shantung at the close of the war.[13]

Group 2: South Manchuria

In Group 2 Japan demanded that the lease of Port Arthur and Dairen be extended from 25 to 99 years, as also her agreements covering the South Manchurian Railway and the Antung-Mukden Railway; that Japanese subjects be permitted "to lease or own land" for "commercial and industrial uses or for farming"; that Japanese subjects be accorded "liberty to enter, reside and travel" in South Manchuria and eastern Inner Mongolia; that Japanese subjects be accorded the right to engage in mining; that China engage to secure Japan's consent before granting to any third power a concession to construct railroads or to extend industrial credits in these areas; that Japan be consulted first if China required foreign advisers in these areas; and finally that control and management of the Kirin-Changchun Railway be placed in Japan's hands for 99 years. These were perhaps the most important of all the Japanese demands. Their purpose was to fulfill a policy that had been pursued since 1904:

[13] The Triple Intervention of 1895, and the Portsmouth Conference of 1905, were usually considered by Japanese statesmen as instances of diplomacy depriving Japan of the rewards of military victory.

namely, to establish beyond question Japan's *paramount* interests in these regions.

Group 3: The Han-Yeh-p'ing Company

The third group in the Twenty-one Demands was designed to insure Japan a more adequate source of iron ore by making the Han-Yeh-p'ing Company a Sino-Japanese concern, and by giving the Company a mining monopoly in certain regions of the Yangtze Valley. This Chinese company owned some of the richest iron and coal properties in Central China. Japanese concerns had made extensive purchases of these ores since 1899.

Group 4: Non-alienation of Territory

This group consisted of a single article by which China was to engage "not to cede or lease to any other Power any harbour or bay on or any island along the coast of China." This concession would preclude China from making territorial grants to other powers, including the United States.[14]

Group 5: "Wishes" or "Desires"

These "desires" included: (1) that China engage influential Japanese as political, financial, and military advisers; (2) that China grant the right to own land to Japanese hospitals, temples, and schools situated in the interior; (3) that China place her police under joint Sino-Japanese administration in designated regions where Sino-Japanese disputes had occurred; (4) that China obtain from Japan a supply of arms, or that an arsenal be established under Sino-Japanese administration; (5) that Japan be granted a concession to construct certain railways in South China; (6) that Japanese be granted "the right of preaching in China." Only one article of this group, that dealing with Fukien, became a part of the eventual Sino-Japanese treaty settlement in May, 1915; yet as a result of the sweeping objectives revealed by them, it was with these "wishes" or "desires" that world opinion identified Japanese policy, rather than with the more specific demands relating to Shantung and Manchuria. They justified extravagant speculation as to Japan's real purposes, not excluding the possibility that her motive was creation of a Japanese protectorate over China.

[14] In this case Japan had in mind Hay's overtures of 1900 relative to Sam-Sah Inlet.

The Sino-Japanese Negotiations, 1915

In two particulars Japanese diplomacy misjudged the problem it faced in China. In the first place, the Okuma cabinet did not anticipate the violent reaction of the Chinese. In the second place, Japan's method of conducting the negotiations with China from January to May, when the resulting treaties were signed, was calculated to increase the apprehension both of China and of the Western powers. The demands were presented directly to the President, Yüan Shih-k'ai, with insistence upon secrecy. This encouraged China to protect herself by permitting the demands to become known through unofficial channels. Garbled accounts appeared in the Chinese and the foreign press. As these unhappy negotiations dragged on, Japan, finding some of China's counter-proposals unsatisfactory, resorted to an ultimatum on May 7. Two weeks later, on May 25, China and Japan signed a number of treaties and notes embodying many, though by no means all, of the objectives set forth in the original Twenty-one Demands.

The more important treaty commitments gained by Japan included: (1) the German leasehold in Shantung, which was to be returned to China after the close of the war in return for recognition of Shantung as a Japanese sphere; (2) extension of the Kwantung leasehold to 99 years, together with increased railroad and other privileges in South Manchuria; and (3) the right of Japan to be consulted first in case China required foreign capital for railway or harbor construction in Fukien. On paper at least, Japan had won the bases for a commanding position in China.

The United States and the Demands

Since Japan had sought to implement her policy in China at a time when Europe was involved in war, the United States alone was in a position to act in the Far East if she desired to do so. President Wilson had already shown his concern for China. He had been the first to extend formal recognition to the Republic;[15] he had repudiated the Taft-Knox policy in the consortium which in his view infringed China's administrative independence. His policy in the case of the Twenty-one Demands was "to protect China out of sympathy, and American rights out of interest, but to move cautiously lest

[15] Meribeth E. Cameron, "American Recognition Policy Toward the Republic of China, 1912-1913," *Pacific Historical Review,* II (1933), 214-230.

Japan be antagonized against the United States and be more severe with China."[16] The policy of the American government was formulated with restraint in a detailed memorandum from Secretary Bryan to the Japanese Ambassador on March 13. The memorandum raised specific objection to several of Japan's demands. Those concerning Fukien and the purchase of arms were regarded as in violation of the open door; those concerning non-alienation of territory, the employment of Japanese subjects as advisers, and the employment by China of Japanese police officers were described as "clearly derogatory to the political independence and administrative entity" of China. Japan met the American objections by modification or withdrawal of these articles.

Of much greater importance, however, was the position taken by Secretary Bryan on the demands concerning Shantung, South Manchuria, and eastern Inner Mongolia. With respect to these he observed:

> While on principle and under the treaties of 1844, 1858, 1868 and 1903 with China the United States has ground upon which to base objections to the Japanese "demands" relative to Shantung, South Manchuria and East Mongolia, nevertheless, *the United States frankly recognizes that territorial contiguity creates special relations between Japan and these districts.*[17]

Although this voluntary recognition of "special relations" based on geographical contiguity was far from representing Japan's desires, nevertheless, "to get any recognition at all of her special relations to these two areas from the power which had hitherto offered the greatest resistance to such recognition represented a distinct diplomatic gain."[18] The danger lay in the likelihood that Japan would interpret this recognition of her "special relations" in ways not intended or implied by the American government.

The second step in American policy toward the demands was taken on May 11, two days after China had accepted the Japanese ultimatum. In identical notes to China and Japan, Secretary Bryan informed these powers that the United States would not recognize

> . . . any agreement or undertaking which has been entered into or which may be entered into between the governments of Japan and China, impairing the treaty rights of the United States and its citizens in China, the

---

[16] Harley Notter, *The Origins of the Foreign Policy of Woodrow Wilson* (Baltimore, 1937), 233-234, 241-243, 385-386, 410-411.

[17] The italics are mine.

[18] LaFargue, *China and the World War,* 64-65.

political or territorial integrity of the Republic of China, or the international policy relative to China commonly known as the open door policy.[19]

This note was sent after China's acceptance of the ultimatum, but two weeks before the signing of the Sino-Japanese treaties and notes of May 25. The procedure was unusual, and the doctrine that was set forth (that of non-recognition), though it was later to play a most conspicuous part in American policy, had no immediate effect upon Japan. The United States in 1915, although sympathetic to China and concerned for American interests therein, was not prepared to challenge Japan openly. Moreover, the British government indicated that Japan's demands would not be opposed so long as they did not infringe on British rights in the Yangtze Region. France and Russia were not opposed to the principles of Japanese policy, though they were jealous of her growing influence in China. All these considerations suggested that effective opposition to Japan could come only from China herself.

Chinese Politics, 1915-1917

Although the political and diplomatic turmoil stirred up by Japan's Twenty-one Demands aroused unprecedented resentment among the Chinese people, this popular display of an infant nationalism did not produce an effective national government at Peking. The popular anti-Japanese enthusiasm served for the moment to bring a semblance of greater unity among the politicians, but this was short-lived. President Yüan Shih-k'ai was already planning in the spring of 1915 to set up a monarchy with himself as emperor. Factions representative of the old-style politicians promptly contended with one another for power under the new dispensation. However, Yüan's colorful scheme got nowhere. Early in 1915 Russia and France were already hoping to bring China into the European war. They considered striking a bargain by which, if China aligned herself with the Entente, the Allies would continue to give their blessing to Yüan and his proposed monarchy. When this scheme failed because of Japanese opposition, the Allies advised Yüan to defer the monarchy plan. Yüan was indeed forced to hesitate, for the Allies could always threaten to withhold the funds so essential to Peking's bankrupt treasury. Opposition to Yüan's proposed monarchy came also from within China and was perhaps as important a factor as

---

19 United States, *Foreign Relations, 1915,* 146.

foreign pressure. During the early months of 1916, rebellions occurred in many of the southern provinces. These outbreaks were so serious that Peking officially dropped the monarchy plan toward the end of March.

China's political ills, however, were not to be cured by a mere discarding of the monarchy plan. Political disaffection continued to spread through most of the south. At Canton, rebellious provinces organized their own provisional government. Then, in June, death put an end to Yüan Shih-k'ai, and Li Yuan-hung succeeded to the presidency. Again there was a move toward unity, for Li was accepted by most of the rebellious southern provinces. The Provisional Constitution of 1912 was restored, and on August 1, 1916, the parliament which Yüan had disbanded in 1914 met again in Peking. This session, like the former one, was doomed to fail, for the parliament possessed neither mandate from the people nor military power. Five years of nominal republicanism had not served to transfer the politico-military power either to parliament or to the people. Once held by Yüan, it had now passed to provincial military governors whom he had appointed and controlled.

These military governors, or *tuchuns*, as they came to be known, were to monopolize the political stage in China for a decade, 1917-1927. Here it is sufficient to note that these local warlords, former henchmen of Yüan Shih-k'ai, made and broke alliances among themselves, and fought for control of Peking with a nice disregard for fixed principles, loyalty, or sense of responsibility to anyone. And behind the warlords the outside powers wrestled with each other and with the Chinese for position in and control of China. In the midst of this ridiculous uproar China stumbled into and through World War I.

Breaking Diplomatic Relations with Germany

In the midst of her domestic political chaos, China was called upon in February, 1917, to resolve the question of breaking diplomatic relations with Germany. President Wilson, having announced the severance of American relations with Germany, called upon neutral powers to follow the American example. The American Minister at Peking, Paul S. Reinsch, not only conveyed the appeal to Premier Tuan's government, but also proceeded with great zeal to urge its adoption. When Tuan's government showed a disposition to bargain, asking for a $10,000,000 American loan for military purposes and a funding of the American share of the Boxer indemnity, Reinsch, without authority from his government, gave assurances. The result was that although China sent a mild note of protest against Germany's unrestricted submarine warfare, it was made to appear that the American government was attempting to purchase China's support. This was certainly not the case, and the State Department promptly warned its Minister against giving further unauthorized "promises or assurances." Actually the real fear in Peking and Washington was that China's military establishment would fall under Japanese control in the event China severed relations with Germany.

Meanwhile, Japan, having accepted the idea of a diplomatic break between China and Germany, was concerned to secure from her European Allies a pledge of support for her claims in Shantung and the German islands in the North Pacific (the Marianas, Carolines, and Marshalls). In February and March, assurances were received by Japan from Britain, Russia, and France; the French reply stipulated that "Japan give its support to obtain from China the breaking of its diplomatic relations with Germany." Thus the way for a diplomatic break between China and Germany had already been paved when on February 24 the torpedoing by a German submarine of the French ship *Athos* in the Mediterranean resulted in the death of 543 Chinese coolies.

On March 14 China formally severed relations with Germany. The action precipitated another political crisis in Peking, for the new policy was pushed through by Premier Tuan while being opposed vigorously by President Li. Although Tuan's policy had the support of Parliament, it was received with little enthusiasm by the Chinese people in general. Indeed, the break with Germany had been engineered by Tuan and the northern militarists with the primary purpose of reinforcing their own power and with the ultimate view "to getting the upper hand over Parliament and the President."

China Enters the War

Diplomatic relations having been broken, the question of China's entering the war could not be delayed for long, particularly after the American declaration of war on Germany, April 6, 1917. This question, however, raised problems of the gravest import for China. To begin with, the Chinese people, in so far as they understood the war at all, were "distinctly pro-German in their sympathies and remained relatively so up to the signing of the armistice."[20] Moreover, the delicate equilibrium in China's domestic politics was not fashioned to withstand the shocks of war. Certainly there was no popular demand for war, and at best Peking could claim only a very nominal allegiance on the part of many of the southern provinces. In these circumstances, a declaration of war might well prove hazardous. Be this as it may, Tuan's cabinet was prepared to take even this step if a favorable bargain could be struck with the Allied powers and the United States. The difficulty was that the powers were not in agreement on the concessions to be made to China, and they were vexed by China's mild policy toward German residents.

In April, 1917, the question of a Chinese declaration of war became still more deeply involved in the political struggle between Tuan and the Parliament for control of the government. Briefly, Tuan's strategy was to place China in the war in return for Allied loans to maintain himself and his colleagues in power. The *Kuomintang* majority in Parliament was opposed to any such bargain, since it would probably result in enabling Tuan to rule with no parliament at all.

Late in April, many of the provincial military governors assembled in Peking at the invitation of Tuan. These gentlemen, after being socially cultivated by the Allied and the American Ministers, announced that they favored war with Germany. They also made it clear that they were opposed to the new draft constitution then in preparation, since they preferred a government free from parliamentary interference. Then, on May 10, while the legislators were debating a war resolution, a mob of government hirelings surrounded Parliament and by intimidation attempted to frighten the representatives into affirmative action. But Parliament stood its ground, and in response to its demand the entire cabinet save Tuan and one minister resigned. Parliament, not regarding Tuan and one minister as a government, refused to deal with him, whereupon Tuan and his military backers demanded that Parliament disband. At this point President Li stepped into the foreground in aid of Parliament by dismissing Premier Tuan. This inspired the military governors to spring to the support of Tuan by threatening to invade Peking with

[20] LaFargue, *China and the World War,* 101.

their armies unless Li disbanded the Parliament. The hapless President then appealed for mediation to Chang Hsün, an old-line *tuchun,* but Chang Hsün refused to act until Li dissolved Parliament, which he finally did on June 11. Less than three weeks later (June 30), the busy Hsün stole a march on all concerned by restoring the young Manchu emperor, Hsüan Tung, to the throne. This was too much even for the warlords. Under Tuan's leadership, they invaded Peking; Chang Hsün fled; the boy emperor went back into retirement; and *Kuomintang* members of the dissolved Parliament scurried to southern ports, while tired and disheartened President Li, harried by forces which he could not control, resigned. Tuan was now free to re-establish his cabinet. The new government, in which there was no representation of the southern provinces, was dominated by militarists and by pro-Japanese factions. On August 14, the new acting president, Fêng Kuo-chang, declared war on Germany.

The Powers and Their New Ally

China's decision to enter the war was primarily the work of the illegal, unconstitutional, militaristic regime that controlled Peking in August, 1917. Moreover, the war decision was furthered rather than retarded by the policies of the Western powers and the behavior of their Ministers in the Chinese capital. Furthermore, the upsetting of Li's government, the first promising one China had had since 1913, was due directly to the question whether or not China should enter the war. Both Li and Sun Yat-sen, neither of whom was a *tuchun,* were opposed to China's joining the conflict. Tuan, *tuchun* and premier, favored war, and in this was supported in the main by Japan and the Entente Powers. On top of all this, Reinsch, the American Minister, was competing with the Japanese at Peking for influence over China if she did declare war, while the British and the French awaited the opportunity that a Chinese declaration of war would give to liquidate German far eastern assets. American advice to China, given June 4, that her entry "into war with Germany" was "of secondary consideration" to the question of achieving political unity at home carried no weight with the Peking militarists. In approaching China, the United States had proposed that similar advice be given by Britain, France, and Japan. All declined. And finally, it should be noted that when China issued her declaration of war, she did so without definite assurance of concessions, financial or otherwise, from the Allied Powers.

The Lansing-Ishii Notes

In this fashion the powers set about to gain whatever advantages might accrue to them from China's status as a belligerent. Here it should be recalled that China, in her semi-colonial status, was still a major commercial and industrial frontier for capital investment, and by 1917 Japan and the United States were the only powers with funds that might be used in China. Then, too, as the war in Europe drew more deeply on American financial resources, it appeared that Japan, now for the first time a creditor nation, would be free to control Peking through the well-known channels of financial imperialism.

The first round in this diplomatic battle had already ended in a qualified American victory, since the Sino-Japanese Treaties and notes of May 25, 1915, had not given Japan the exclusive control of Peking which she desired. Nevertheless, Japan's gains were substantial enough to bring about a reorientation in official American policy. Whereas in 1913 Wilson had advised the American consortium bankers that they could no longer count on official support, in 1916 the President was urging the American group as well as other American banks to enter the field of Chinese government loans. Two factors explain this change: the first was the steady growth of American business holdings in China; the second was the desire to head off a Japanese financial monopoly at Peking.

Accordingly, the United States did participate in the wearisome negotiations that resulted, but not until 1920, in the creation of a new Four Power Consortium of American, British, French, and Japanese banking groups. The American government also undertook to carry the British and French shares in certain Chinese loans during the war, and in return wrung from the British a qualified declaration condemning the principle of spheres of influence. Meanwhile, Japan, intent on using the European war to strengthen her own position in China, followed closely all evidences of growing American activity there; but it was the activities of the American Minister, Paul S. Reinsch, that precipitated Japanese action.

Minister Reinsch, like Willard Straight, was a zealous if not always a prudent champion of American "rights" in China. His unauthorized diplomatic attacks on Japanese railway pretensions in Manchuria thoroughly aroused the foreign office in Tokyo.

Moreover, in June, 1917, when the United States advised China that her entry into the war was of "secondary consideration," the Japanese government, taking the view that America was following a consciously unfriendly policy, set about to secure from the United States an explicit recognition not only of Japan's "special interests" in Manchuria (the phrase that had been used by Lansing) but rather of her "paramount" interests in China. As a first step to this end, Lansing was asked by the Japanese Ambassador to confirm the Bryan statement of March 13, 1915, on "territorial contiguity" and to reassert "its friendly attitude toward Japan in respect of Chinese problems."

This preliminary move was followed in the summer of 1917 by the arrival in the United States of a special Japanese mission headed by one of Japan's ablest diplomats, Viscount Ishii Kikujiro. The professed purpose of the mission was to bring unity into the combined war efforts of the United States and Japan. Ishii's real purpose was to grapple with the complex problem of American-Japanese rivalry concerning China. More specifically, this meant that he was seeking two objectives: (1) to allay popular American suspicions concerning Japan's motives; (2) to secure from the American government a public admission of Japan's "paramount interests" in China.

In Washington, during the ensuing Lansing-Ishii conversations, Ishii said that Oriental immigration and the China problem were effective weapons in the hands of German propaganda. Lansing countered by saying that Japan's allies and associates feared she was using the war to close the open door and to destroy the integrity of China. Therefore Lansing favored a joint declaration reasserting the open door and at the same time giving public recognition to Japan's "special interests." Accordingly, on November 2, 1917, the conversations were given formal effects in an exchange of notes that acknowledged Japan's "special interests" in China and endorsed once again the already much endorsed open door policy.

The Lansing-Ishii notes were simply a statement of conflicting points of view phrased to hide the disagreement. Wilson seemed to think it was an American diplomatic victory, but it is doubtful that Lansing was deceived.

Publication of the notes did not prove to be an unqualified blessing even as a war measure. Bryan's statement of March 13, 1915, that geographical propinquity creates special relations between countries had not been made public and the American people were unaware of its existence. Therefore Lansing's concession of "special interests" came as a shock to a public imbued with a traditional, if somewhat vague, friendship for China.

In Japan the exchange was received with enthusiasm. Government circles referred to Viscount Ishii's "great diplomatic victory," and in general the Japanese press gave the phrase "special interests" a broad definition. Chinese public opinion interpreted the notes quite generally "as indicating a withdrawal of the American Government, in favor of Japan, from any desire to exercise any influence in Chinese affairs."

China's War Effort

China was neither able nor anxious to contribute much to the war as a belligerent. Not until the latter part of 1918, when the collapse of Germany seemed assured, did Tuan's government bestir itself to adopt a vigorous war policy through more effective control of enemy aliens and through liquidation of enemy property. These tardy steps were a last minute bid for consideration at the forthcoming peace conference. They were also a recognition by the Chinese warlords that Chinese public opinion was becoming more sympathetic to the cause of the Allied and Associated Powers. China, however, was not solely responsible for the shortcomings of her war record. Against the responsibility of her irresponsible *tuchun* government must be weighed the tortuous diplomacy of the European Allies. Britain and France had assisted in pushing China into the war neither for high moral purposes nor in the hope that she would become an effective belligerent, but rather with the specific intent of eliminating German commercial and industrial competition from a post-war China.

For Further Reading

Bailey, T. A., *Woodrow Wilson and the Lost Peace* (New York, 1944).

Birdsall, Paul, *Versailles Twenty Years After* (New York, 1941). An excellent study of the Peace Conference in general with a penetrating chapter on Japanese strategy.

Clinard, O. J., *Japan's Influence on American Naval Power, 1897-1917* (Berkeley, 1947). Contains materials of interest, but its interpretations are often open to serious question.

Curry, Roy Watson, *Woodrow Wilson and Far Eastern Policy, 1913-1921* (New York, 1957). A challenging recent interpretation.

Dutcher, George M., *The Political Awakening of the East* (New York, 1925).

Fifield, Russell H., *Woodrow Wilson and the Far East; the Diplomacy of the Shantung Question* (New York, 1952).

Godshall, W. L., *The International Aspects of the Shantung Question* (Philadelphia, 1923).

Hicks, Charles R., *Japan's Entry into the War, 1914* (Reno, 1944). A short description of British negotiations on the subject.

Idditti, Smimasa, *The Life of Marquis Shigenobu Okuma, A Maker of New Japan* (Tokyo, 1940). An overly sympathetic study.

Jones, Jefferson, *The Fall of Tsingtau* (Boston, 1915).

Li T'ien-i, *Woodrow Wilson's China Policy, 1913-1917* (Kansas City, Mo., 1952). A readable review that emphasizes Wilson's idealism.

MacNair, H. F., *China in Revolution* (Chicago, 1931).

Miller, David Hunter, *The Drafting of the Covenant* (2 vols., New York, 1928).

———, *My Diary at the Conference of Paris* (21 vols., New York, 1924).

Pollard, Robert T., *China's Foreign Relations, 1917-1931* (New York, 1933).

Reinsch, Paul Samuel, *An American Diplomat in China* (New York, 1922).

24

1918–1920

The Legacies of War in the Far East

JUST as World War I had swept away the old balance of power in Europe, so it had also gone far to destroy the balance of power in the Far East. Prior to 1914 Japan had been accorded a nominal status as a so-called great power, a result of her victories over China in 1895 and over Russia in 1905. Actually, however, the great powers of Europe had not considered Japan a full-ranking member of their company. It was the World War that elevated Japan to a new status. Japan, therefore, approached the peace conference conscious of her newly found power. She sought recognition of her status as a great power, and specific recognition of her hegemony in the Far East.

The opposition to Japan's peace conference objectives was to come principally, though not exclusively, from the United States, for the end of World War I witnessed the beginnings of a more intense American-Japanese rivalry concerning China. It was a conflict of Japanese expansion versus the traditional American policy of the open door and the integrity of China, and it was to involve not only the specific issues raised by Japan at the Versailles Conferences, but also others that were to culminate later in the Washington Conference of 1921-1922. The issues in this long-range American-Japanese diplomatic battle were to include: (1) the effort to prevent a Japanese capital investment monopoly in China; (2) the effort to prevent annexation of the Russian Maritime Province by Japan, and to prevent establishment of a Japanese sphere in North Manchuria; (3)

the effort to restore Shantung to China; and (4) the effort to implement the principles of American Far Eastern policy by a treaty structure covering the Pacific and the Far East.

Japan's Demands at Versailles

At the Versailles Conference, Japan presented three demands: (1) she asked for cession of the former German islands in the North Pacific Ocean (the Marianas, the Carolines, and the Marshalls); (2) she asked confirmation of her claims to the former German rights in Shantung province; and (3) she asked for a declaration of racial equality among states as a basic principle of the proposed League of Nations. Unassailable as Japan may have believed these objectives to be, they led nonetheless to widespread and bitter opposition from some of her former allies and associates in arms. The sources of this opposition were many and varied. Japan's claim to the German islands violated the Wilsonian principle of no annexations; her claims to Kiaochow and Shantung ran counter to a young and virile Chinese nationalism; and her demand for a declaration of racial equality raised a storm of protest from some of the British dominions, particularly Australia.

Japan's representatives, Baron Makino Nobuaki and Viscount Chinda Sutemi, approached their task with confidence, for Japan's demands in the case of the German islands and Shantung were supported by powerful legal claims, and, in the case of racial equality, by high moral principles.[1] The German islands and Kiaochow had been captured by Japanese arms and were in Japanese possession. Moreover, in secret agreements (February and March, 1917) England, France, Italy, and Russia had pledged themselves to support the Japanese claims at the peace conference. Likewise, in 1915 Japan had forced China to agree to the transfer of Kiaochow. Whatever moral or legal strength China's resentment against the 1915 treaties may have had, it was weakened seriously in 1918, when China again gave her explicit consent to the transfer of Kiaochow to Japan on the understanding that Japan would in turn restore the leasehold to China but would retain in expanded form Germany's economic rights in the province. So matters stood when the war came to an end. Japan's legal case was strong; and despite the desire of the Allies

---

[1] Japan's ranking delegate was Prince Saionji Kimmochi, ex-Premier and Genro.

and the United States to block her further expansion, they were not prepared to challenge the legal basis of her claims, lest this challenge rebound upon the whole system of unequal treaties pertaining to China.

China Enters the Conference

If the demands on which Japan was to insist were brutally clear, they were also a logical result of the policy on which Japan had embarked in 1914-1915 and to which her preparations had been pointed for many years. In contrast, the role that China might play at the peace table was not so predictable. It is true that by 1918 there was the beginnings of a young Chinese nationalism that was extremely vocal, but neither the warlord government at Peking nor the insurgent government at Canton appeared to represent anything with political substance. Indeed, the program that China did present at Paris was a product of opportunism and of particular personalities in her peace delegation. Although the Peking and Canton governments had not achieved unity at home, they presented a façade of unity at Paris, for the Chinese peace delegation was composed of representatives of both governments, of Canton as well as Peking. In terms of political strategy and showmanship, this Chinese delegation was unsurpassed at Paris, for to the able political strategy of C. T. Wang was added the eloquent English of Wellington Koo. These men fashioned the Chinese program as it was presented at Paris. It was the program of a young, progressive, revolutionary, and idealistic China—a program that must have sounded strange in the ears of Peking's *tuchuns*. Yet these *tuchuns* were the government *de facto* of China; they controlled the administration that was recognized by all the powers; and they were the authority to which the Chinese delegation was responsible. It may be added, too, that no delegation supported with greater eloquence the Wilsonian program. Nevertheless, China's delegation was regarded with suspicion by the European Allies and Japan: first, because in the light of China's internal politics it was questionable whether any delegation could speak for the country; and second, because it was soon evident that Wang and Koo were less concerned with the problem of making peace with Germany than with using the conference to free China from her semi-colonial status. To most of the Allied statesmen this purpose was alarming, for it implied an attack not only on Japan's "special interests" but also upon the larger system of spheres of influence and the "unequal treaties" in general, to which all the victorious great powers were parties. In addition, the mistrust of Japan, England, and France was further aroused because both before and during the Paris Conference, Wang and Koo set out systematically to cultivate the sympathies and enlist the support of the American delegation, which in turn was not loath to give the Chinese the encouragement they desired.

THE DEBATE AT PARIS

Japan's demand for the "unconditional cession" of the German rights in Shantung was made on January 27, 1919. The following day, China's counter-demand that Kiaochow and the German rights be restored directly to China was presented. To President Wilson, the obvious answer to this deadlock between China and Japan was to be found in his own program that promised a new world of international justice under a league of nations. But Wilson could make no progress against the Japanese on this score while Australia, New Zealand, South Africa, France, Italy, and Belgium remained as insistent on annexing the German colonies in their respective regions as were the Japanese in theirs. The best that Wilson could get eventually was the system of mandates which, with the exception of those in Class A, gave to the mandatory power a control which for practical purposes was hardly to be distinguished from annexation. Under this form, a Class C mandate, Japan acquired the former German islands in the North Pacific and the British dominions got those in the South Pacific.

RACIAL EQUALITY: A "HOT POTATO"

Having "compromised" by accepting a mandate instead of annexation in the Pacific islands, Japan turned to her second objective. With the approval and aid of President Wilson and Colonel House, her delegation presented as an amendment to the draft covenant of the League of Nations a resolution affirming the principle of racial equality.

This resolution, which had the approval of Wilson, was a logical if not an essential complement to the whole spirit of the Wilsonian program as well as to the League itself; but, in newsroom parlance, it was also a "hot potato." It aroused the unrelenting opposition of Premier William H. Hughes of Australia, who was supported by the chief British delegates, Arthur Balfour and Robert Cecil. The argument advanced against any provision on racial equality was that it implied the right of the League to interfere in questions concerning immigration and the rights of aliens, which every nation regarded as matters of purely domestic concern. England feared embarrassment in some of the middle eastern colonies. Hughes saw in the resolution a threat to the "white" Australia policy, and he threatened to arouse an outraged public opinion in the British dominions and the United States unless the amendment were dropped. At the same time he stooped to convince the Japanese press that it was the United States and not Australia that was blocking the amendment.

Wilson's dilemma was real. If the racial equality debate were brought into the open, as Hughes threatened to do, what would be the reaction on the American Pacific Coast, especially in California, which had already enacted the discriminatory alien land law of 1913 aimed at the Japanese? But this was not all. American policy at Paris was attempting to hold Japan in check on many fronts. There was Shantung, which Wilson wanted to restore directly to China. There was the prospective Four-Power Consortium, into which he hoped to entice Japan in order to preserve a financial open door in China. There was eastern Siberia, which it was hoped could be rescued from Japan's military expansionists despite its occupation at the time by more than 70,000 Japanese troops. And there was the Island of Yap in the Japanese mandate, where it was hoped the United States might be given submarine cable privileges. Would not American policy have a better chance of achieving these objectives if Japanese racial pride were satisfied by even an emasculated concession to the principle of racial equality. Thus, on grounds of high principle and of practical politics Wilson desired adoption of the amendment.

The vote on Japan's amendment[2] was favorable, eleven to six, but Wilson ruled against adoption of the amendment because the vote was not unanimous. For reasons which to him seemed good, Wilson announced defeat of the measure. The newsmen had been right: racial equality was a "hot potato." Wilson could not risk

[2] It had become merely an "endorsement of the principle of equality of nations and just treatment of their nationals."

the issue in open debate, and he feared that Hughes would force it into the open if it could be defeated in no other way.

SHANTUNG, "OR ELSE"

Two of Japan's objectives at Paris had now been disposed of: in the Pacific islands there had been a "compromise" which the Japanese had accepted but did not like; on racial equality Japan had accepted a defeat particularly galling to Japanese pride, since the race issue was a symbol of discrimination, a label of an inferior people. Japan's government was therefore in no mood to accept further reverses as it approached the debate on its third objective: transfer to Japan, in terms of the peace treaty, of the former German rights in Shantung. Here Japan was determined to accept neither compromise nor defeat. The problem was the more difficult because

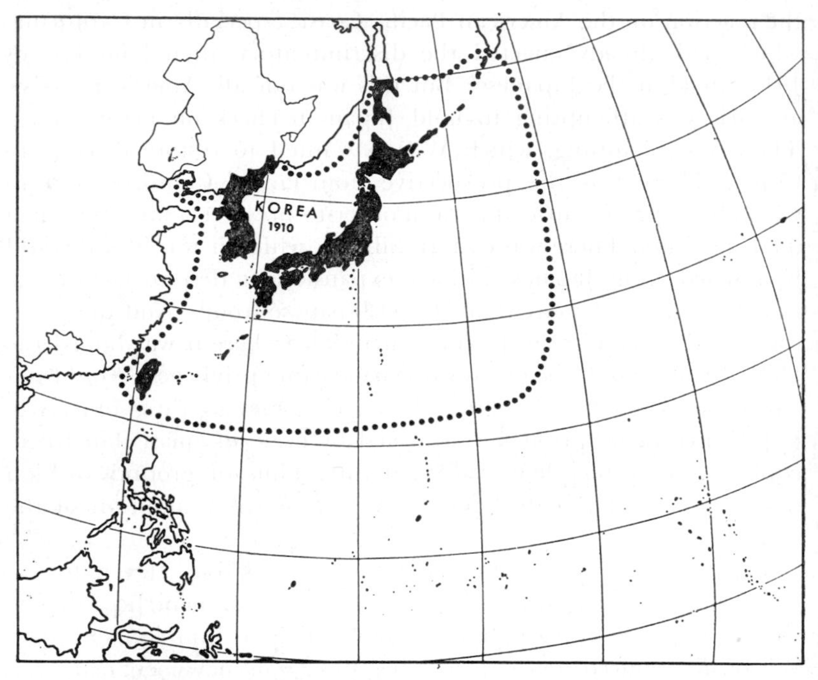

JAPAN, 1910-1919. *Reproduced from* A War Atlas for Americans, *Simon and Schuster, Inc., New York, 1944, by permission from Simon and Schuster, Inc., and from the U. S. Department of State, Division of Map Intelligence and Cartography.*

Wang and Koo had by this time gone far beyond their original and earlier demand for the direct restoration of Kiaochow and the German rights. Their work at Paris had aroused not only the sympathies of Western peoples, but also a new public consciousness within China itself. A new patriotic pride appeared to be taking possession of the Chinese people, expressing itself in a mass movement in support of the Paris delegation. Encouraged by the support of this public opinion, Wang and Koo demanded abrogation of all the 1915 treaties and notes. This was a direct thrust not only at Japan's pretensions in Shantung but also at her "special position" in South Manchuria and eastern Inner Mongolia and at her general ambitions in China as a whole. It was a challenge which the Japanese promptly accepted. They stood firm and demanded Shantung, threatening to withdraw from the Conference if it were denied them.

There seemed to be but one decision that Wilson could make without wrecking the Conference, namely: acceptance of the Japanese demands. In this he differed from some of his close advisers, who felt that the Japanese were bluffing. Wilson, however, was right; his advisers were wrong.[3]

China Learns to Say "No!"

China was now faced with what to her was an unhappy choice. She could accept in the peace treaty a direct cession to Japan of the German rights, or she could accept the obligation to carry out the even larger concessions Japan claimed under the treaties of 1915 and 1918. The Chinese delegation, however, refused to accept either, on the theory (1) that China's declaration of war had cancelled Germany's rights in Shantung, and (2) that the 1915 and 1918 treaties were invalid on grounds of equity. Right here lay the main significance of the whole bitter contest over Shantung. The real issue was the question of the validity of the 1915 and 1918 treaties. A denial of Japan's claims to Shantung would have opened the way for questioning the validity of the entire treaty structure of 1915 and 1918. Not to question that structure implied international approval of Japan's attempts to dominate China. On this issue, the Western powers were as widely separated as were China and Japan. Although

[3] Russell Fifield, "Japanese Policy toward the Shantung Question at the Paris Peace Conference," *Journal of Modern History,* XXIII (1951), 265-272; and *Woodrow Wilson and the Far East* (New York, 1952), 243.

Wilson was careful to refrain from any admission that the 1915 treaties were valid, he was equally careful not to deny positively their validity. There was vagueness and ambiguity in the American position. England and France, on the other hand, did not question either Japan's right to Shantung or the validity of the Sino-Japanese treaties in general.

China's Balance Sheet of War

Although China refused to sign the Treaty of Versailles between the Allied and Associated Powers and Germany, and although her defeat in the Shantung issue was a reverse of great magnitude, her balance sheet of war was not written wholly in red ink. Her appeals to world public opinion had elicited deep sympathy. Within China itself, the stand of Wang and Koo at Paris had produced stirrings of a new national pride. And, more than this, the war had terminated China's old "unequal" treaties with Germany, Austria, and Hungary, thus opening the way for new treaties with these powers negotiated on a basis of equality.[4]

Siberia and the Russian Revolution

If the Versailles Conference was unable to produce a real meeting of minds on so limited and specific an affair as Sino-Japanese contentions in Shantung, it was even less effective in quieting a new turmoil that had arisen in Far Eastern Siberia.

Late in 1917 the Russian Revolutions had created what may best be described as a political vacuum in Siberia and in the zone of the Chinese Eastern Railway in north-central Manchuria. During the years 1918 to 1920 and after, Siberia, North Manchuria, and Outer Mongolia became a confused and cruel battleground for armies, political creeds, and irresponsible brigands, in which all the major powers, England, France, Japan, and the United States, became actively involved. In tracing these various developments in some detail, it will be necessary first to recall some aspects of Russo-Japanese relations in the Far East.

After the Russo-Japanese War, Russia retained her important

---

[4] China did sign the Treaty of St. Germain with Austria, September 10, 1919; the Treaty of Neuilly with Bulgaria; and the Treaty of Trianon with Hungary. China's war with Germany was ended officially September 15, 1919, by proclamation of the Chinese president.

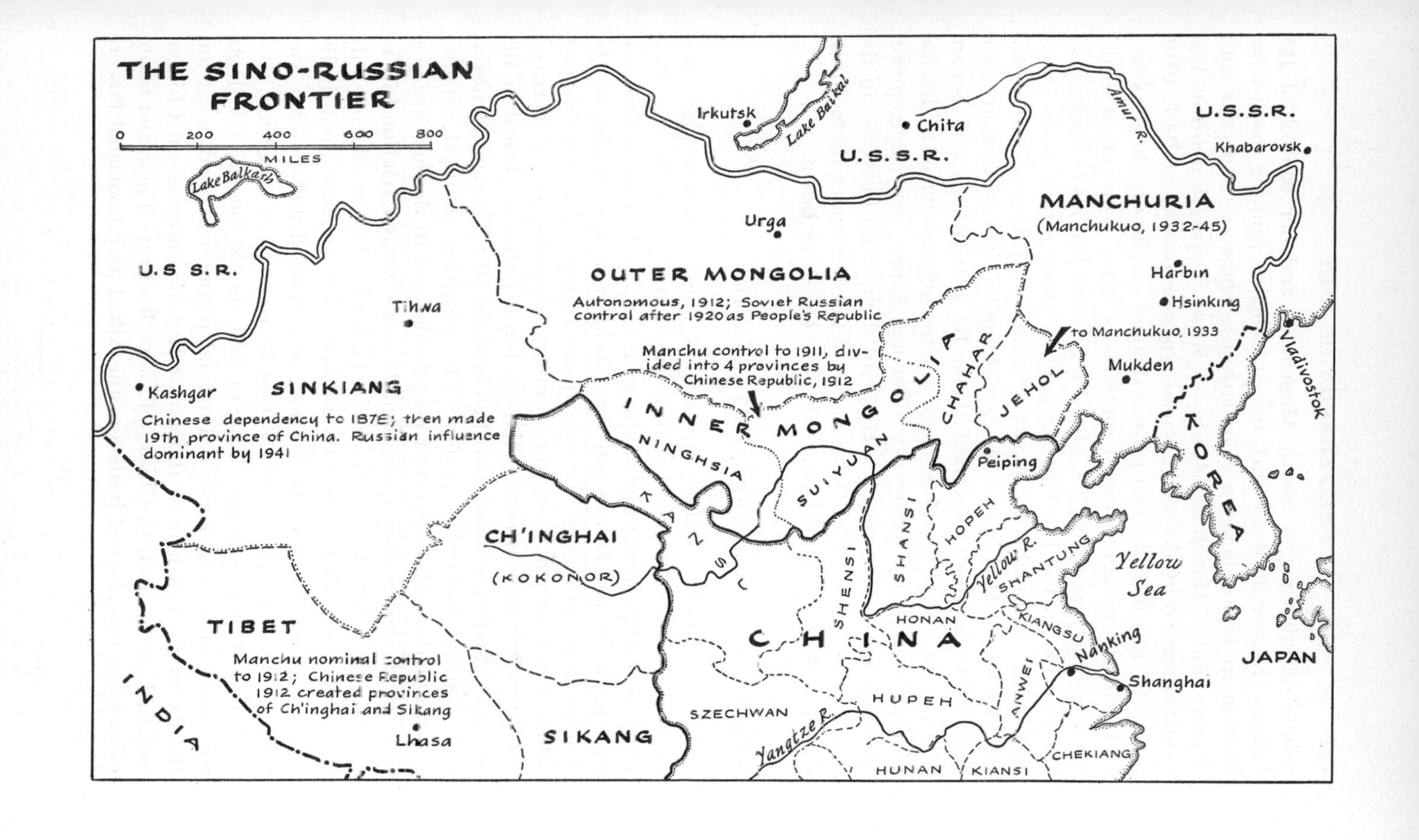
THE SINO-RUSSIAN FRONTIER
0
200
400
600
800
MILES
Lake Balkash
U.S.S.R.
Irkutsk
Lake Baikal
Chita
U.S.S.R.
Amur R.
U.S.S.R.
Khabarovsk
MANCHURIA
(Manchukuo, 1932-45)
Urga
Harbin
Hsinking
OUTER MONGOLIA
Autonomous, 1912; Soviet Russian control after 1920 as People's Republic
Tihwa
to Manchukuo, 1933
Manchu control to 1911, divided into 4 provinces by Chinese Republic, 1912
Mukden
Vladivostok
Kashgar
SINKIANG
Chinese dependency to 1878; then made 19th province of China. Russian influence dominant by 1941
INNER MONGOLIA
CHAHAR
JEHOL
NINGHSIA
SUIYUAN
Peiping
KOREA
KANSU
CH'INGHAI
(KOKONOR)
SHENSI
SHANSI
HOPEH
Yellow R.
SHANTUNG
Yellow Sea
TIBET
Manchu nominal control to 1912; Chinese Republic 1912 created provinces of Ch'inghai and Sikang
HONAN
KIANGSU
CHINA
Nanking
JAPAN
ANWEI
Shanghai
INDIA
HUPEH
SZECHWAN
Lhasa
SIKANG
Yangtze R.
HUNAN
KIANSI
CHEKIANG

sphere of influence in North Manchuria and her control of the Chinese Eastern Railway with the branch line running south from Harbin to Kwan-chengtzu (Changchun), where it connected with Japan's South Manchuria Railway. Russia's special position had been reinforced by the secret Russo-Japanese treaties of 1907, 1910, and 1912, in which the two powers defined specifically their spheres of influence and agreed upon methods of close co-operation in defense of their "special rights." By 1915, Russia had also consolidated her position in the Far East through a "protectorate" over Outer Mongolia. Although the tripartite treaty of 1915 again acknowledged Chinese suzerainty in Outer Mongolia, it was Russian influence *de facto* which prevailed there. By 1916 Russia and Japan, allies in the World War, had come to a further agreement in defense of their contiguous spheres of influence. A new secret convention provided for co-operation in defense of their "vital interests" in the Far East to the end that "China should not fall under the political domination of any third Power hostile to Russia or Japan."

The Russian Revolutions, 1917 and after

The fulfillment of these nicely laid Russo-Japanese plans was precluded shortly by events within Russia itself. The Russian Revolutions of 1917 were to be in the long view as striking in their impact upon the Far East as was the World War. The ousting of the Tsarist Imperial regime, the subsequent collapse of Kerensky's provisional government, and the resulting chaotic warfare between revolutionary and anti-revolutionary forces either weakened or destroyed the political bonds that had held the vast Siberian territorial and political interests together. The resulting political vacuum posed questions of the greatest magnitude, and in the first instance most of these questions concerned Russia's altered relationship to the European war. Could Russia be maintained as an effective ally in the war against Germany? Would not a defeated and a politically helpless Russia become the granary of a revived and possibly victorious Germany? How could Russia be restored as a fighting ally? With what Russians, White, Pink, or Red, should the Allies deal? As the power of the old Russian Imperial regime collapsed, what authority would fall heir to those vast Russian interests on Chinese soil, such as the strategic Chinese Eastern Railway? These and many other questions plagued leaders of the Allied and Associated Powers from 1917 on to the autumn of 1918, while their armies were still locked in a desperate battle on the western front and while the decisive power of the American war effort was yet to be felt.

Political affairs throughout Siberia from late 1917 to 1920 presented a picture of unmeasurable confusion. The collapse of the Imperial government brought first a revival of the late nineteenth-century movement for Siberian autonomy—a movement supported by "socialists of various complexions, liberals, and even moderate conservatives."[5] Opposed to these "regionalists," there was from November, 1917, to the summer of 1918 the rising influence of the local soviets. The defeat of these groups in the summer of 1918 paved the way for the Kolchak White government at Omsk, which "claimed" all power in Siberia from November, 1918, to January, 1920. Although Kolchak's government was accorded a "kind of *de facto* recognition" from the Supreme Council of the Allied and Associated Powers, it was opposed by a nondescript array of Siberian factions great and small. In the end Kolchak's government fell before the rising tide of the Red armies, but meanwhile it was also opposed more or less openly by a variety of self-appointed saviors of Siberia, such as Cossack Captain Grigorii Semenov, who had been commissioned by Kerensky's provisional government to recruit troops in Trans-Baikalia. With the fall of Kerensky, Semenov, seizing the Trans-Siberian Railway in the Chita region, preyed upon the local inhabitants with a nice lack of discrimination.

There was also Baron Ungern von Sternberg, who used Mongolia as a base from which he hoped to set up a Pan-Mongolian empire. There were Social-Revolutionists of divergent shades, some of whom co-operated reluctantly with Kolchak, others with the Bolsheviks. In the Russian railway zone at Harbin there were two principal factions. In July, 1918, Lt. General Dimitrii Leonidovich Horvath, who had been general manager of the Chinese Eastern Railway and administrator of the railroad zone since 1903, proclaimed an all-Russian, anti-Red government. Horvath's regime was opposed at Harbin and later at Vladivostok by a group of political opportunists representing the center-left Social-Revolutionists who formed another "government" headed by Petr Yakovlivich Derber. In addition to these there were many other groups led by Cossack adventurers who were more concerned with opportunities for pillage and

---

5 Elena Varneck and H. H. Fisher, eds., *The Testimony of Kolchak* (Stanford University, 1935), 247.

plunder than with the political future of Russia. Finally, there were almost innumerable bands of peasant "partisans" who had no understanding of the mad political events in which they were enmeshed and impoverished. In the midst of this political turmoil of contending factions, cruelties that tax the imagination were perpetrated by Whites and Reds alike.

The Czechoslovaks in Siberia

Another factor complicated conditions in Siberia. Early in World War I a Czechoslovak detachment was formed in Russia and fought as a part of the Russian army against the Central Powers. During the period of Kerensky's provisional government, this Czech force was increased to some 50,000 men. As the Russian armies disintegrated in the first months of Bolshevik rule, the Czech legions remained intact; they were placed under the Supreme French Command by the Czech National Council in Paris, where the decision was made to transport the force around the world by way of Vladivostok and the Pacific to serve with the French armies on the western front. Permission was granted the Czechs by the Bolsheviks to cross Siberia to Vladivostok en route to France. In the conditions prevailing, clashes soon occurred between Czech and Bolshevik forces. During May and June, 1918, anti-Bolshevik governments appeared at Samara and Omsk sheltered by Czech arms.

The Question of Allied Intervention in Russia

While this checkered pattern of events was developing, the Allied Powers were considering the question of military intervention in Russia to re-establish a new eastern front against Germany. Basically, the object was to keep Russia in the war against the Central Powers; but Allied representatives in Russia were divided as to the means that should be used to this end. While some favored assistance to White elements, others conferred with the Reds. At the close of 1917 opinion among the powers themselves was widely divided. Japan and France favored intervention against the Bolsheviks; Britain favored intervention with Russian consent against the Germans; and the United States was opposed to intervention of any kind. During the early months of 1918, the Allies considered the possibility of Japan acting alone as their mandatory in the occupation of Siberia.

A further stimulus to the case for intervention was given by reports that German and Austro-Hungarian prisoners of war in Siberia were being recruited into the Red armies for defense of the Soviet regime and the expected world revolution. Although in general these reports appear to have been given an exaggerated importance, the tendency in Allied countries was to accept them at face value.

The Decision on Intervention

The break between the Czechs and the Bolsheviks was one of the most decisive factors in the final decision of the Allies to intervene, for the hold of the Czechs on the Siberian Railway and their strategic positions in the Volga region appeared as the first substantial footholds from which a new eastern front might be rebuilt. On June 1, 1918, the Supreme War Council at Versailles decided to reinforce Murmansk in northwestern Russia, already held by British troops since March, and to occupy Archangel also. The United States offered no objection to this move, though it was as yet unwilling to agree to intervention in Siberia. A month later, on July 2, the Allied decision to intervene in Siberia was made final, the basic argument advanced being that the Allies could not win on the western front even in 1919 unless the Germans were forced to divert troops to the East.

Wilson's Decision to Intervene

President Wilson was besieged with appeals to intervene in Siberia. These pressures came from the European Allies, from the Supreme War Council, and from his own diplomatic staff abroad. The only resistance came from Wilson's military advisers. Wilson, to use his own language, was "sweating blood" over what General Tasker H. Bliss later called a "sideshow born of desperation." Wilson's decision for intervention, July 6, 1918, was based on a complex of reasons. His ultimate purpose was to contribute to winning the war in Europe. There must be no quarrel with the Allies. Since the Allies insisted on going into Siberia, the United States would go along with them. By this process the United States would be able to say later: "Now let us come out," instead of, "now you come out." Moreover, if the United States did not go in, so reasoned Wilson, Japan would control the intervention and would have a free hand under the Sino-Japanese military agreements of May, 1918. Therefore, he would invite Japan to join with the United States in an intervention. He did this not because he believed in the intervention but because he thought he could "impose greater restraint on Japan within rather than outside of it." The important thing, he felt, was to maintain the open door in Siberia and North Manchuria against Japanese pretensions.[6]

On July 17, 1918, the United States informed the Allied ambassadors of its decision to intervene, and of its objectives, to which it asked their adherence.

> Military action is admissible in Russia . . . only to help the Czecho-Slovaks consolidate their forces and to get into successful cooperation with their Slavic kinsmen and to steady any efforts at self-government or self-defense in which the Russians themselves may be willing to accept assistance. . . . The only legitimate object for which Americans or Allied troops can be employed . . . is to guard military stores which may subsequently be needed by Russian forces and to render such aid as may be acceptable to the Russians in the organization of their own self-defense.[7]

From August until November, 1918, troops of the Allied Powers, British, Japanese, French, and Americans, were landed at Vladivostok. It was Wilson's intention to curb the Japanese by an agreement limiting the American and Japanese contingents to some 7,000 troops each. In the end the United States sent 9,000 troops; the Japanese something in excess of 72,000.[8]

Theory and Practice in Siberia

Now that the Allied contingents were in Siberia, what were they to do? There was as much disagreement on this question as there had been on the original point of intervention. The policy of the American military forces, commanded by Major General William S. Graves, had been determined by Wilson. It required that the troops refrain from "any interference of any kind with the political sovereignty of Russia" and from "any intervention in her internal affairs." Since these American troops were on Russian soil, these

---

[6] Betty Miller Unterberger, "President Wilson and the Decision to Send American Troops to Siberia," *The Pacific Historical Review,* XXIV (1955), 63-74.

[7] United States, *Foreign Relations, 1918, Russia,* II, 288.

[8] It appears that Japan was careful to reserve the liberty to send additional troops if in her view circumstances demanded it. United States, *Foreign Relations, 1918, Russia,* II, 324-326.

were admittedly difficult instructions to follow. Nevertheless, General Graves attempted to carry them out. Where American troops patrolled the railroads, they did so for all Russians, whether White or Red. Graves' actions in this respect appear to have been proper, but they led to a tense situation, since of all the key personalities in the intervening armies he alone held unswervingly to his instructions and to the announced purposes of the intervention. On the other hand, most of the Allied representatives, including many Americans, disregarded completely the principles of non-interference and neutrality in Russian affairs. The European governments, the Japanese, and some American officials had reached the view that the purpose of the intervention was to fight the Reds. The announced purposes of the intervention were no longer to be the real purposes. Thus England, France, and Japan, with the willing support of certain American consular officials and members of the Department of State, became the *de facto* allies of Semenov. Moreover, the Allies, mainly the British and French, had been responsible for bringing Admiral Aleksandr Vasilevich Kolchak to Siberia where they installed him as head of the White government at Omsk. There this well-meaning but mild and ineffectual sailor was surrounded by discredited Russian Whites, and by the British and French military missions, which appear to have been unaware that Russia could not be pressed back into the political and economic mold of the tsars. From November, 1918, until January, 1920, Kolchak, the Czechs, and their British and French allies fought the Bolsheviks, long after Germany had fallen and the need of an eastern front had disappeared. On the part of the European Allies and Japan, the original stated purposes of the intervention had been sidetracked, without Wilson's consent, in favor of interference in the internal politics of Russia.

The Development of Railway Politics

It was inevitable that the Siberian adventure, regardless of its real or stated purposes, should become involved with the control of the Siberian Railway system and with that integral segment of it, the Chinese Eastern Railway. Whoever controlled these railways controlled Siberia. In March, 1917, after the United States had severed diplomatic relations with Germany but before the declaration of war (April 6), the strategic importance of the Trans-Siberian system had been impressed upon the American government. Shortly after this a special American diplomatic mission, headed by Elihu Root, went to Russia to gain a better understanding of how the United States might co-operate in the solution of Russian war problems. Meanwhile, in May, 1917, a second American mission, known as the Railroad Commission, had entered Russia at Vladivostok. It was headed by John F. Stevens, formerly chief engineer of the Panama Canal. Its task was to find means of rehabilitating the Russian railways, and it began its work by attempting to relieve the congestion in the Vladivostok region. The broad proposals of this commission were accepted by the Russian government in August. These included a program for railway assembly plants to be set up by American technicians with American equipment and under the supervision of American railway engineers. For this purpose a Railway Service Corps of technical experts, headed by Colonel George Emerson, proceeded to the Far East to carry out the recommendations of the Stevens Commission. The work was to be financed by a Russian loan floated in the United States. The entire business was supposed to be a Russian affair. Secretary Lansing had cautioned Stevens that he must in no way create the impression that the Railway Commission either represented or spoke for the American government.

By December, 1917, however, Kerensky's government, with which these plans had been made, had been thrown out by the Bolsheviks, and political conditions were such at Vladivostok that for a time the Railway Service Corps was unable to land.

By April, 1918, Stevens, now in Harbin, was trying to discover what, if anything, could be done to restore traffic on the Chinese Eastern Railway, which was laboring along in a half-hearted way under General Horvath's White government. Emerson meanwhile had been authorized to confer on railway matters with the Reds where this seemed desirable. This situation led Stevens to comment that:

> The new [Horvath] administration of the Chinese Eastern are bitterly anti-Soviet. . . . We are thus placed in impossible situations of trying to help two bitterly opposing [Russian factions] with the usual result facing us [of] antagonizing both.

Nevertheless, Stevens' presence at Harbin seemed necessary if control of the entire transportation system of Manchuria was not to fall into Japanese hands.

Moreover, Japan was legally, as well as strategically, in a position to take advantage of the political uncertainties in Manchuria and Siberia. In May, 1918, she signed two treaties with the *tuchun* government of Peking providing for Sino-Japanese military co-operation if "the general peace and tranquility" of the Far East were menaced. Thus, late in July, when Semenov's forces were hard-pressed by the Reds, Japan invoked these military agreements with China and dispatched troops to the zone of the Chinese Eastern Railway. This made it appear that Japan was already well on the way to make North Manchuria a Japanese sphere. If this was Japan's purpose, it was blocked by the insistence of the United States that inter-Allied, not exclusive Japanese, control be maintained on the Chinese Eastern Railway. Not, however, until January 9, 1919, was an inter-Allied railroad agreement reached. By it, the operation of railroads under Allied military control was to be in the hands of an inter-Allied commission which in turn was to be advised by Stevens and a technical board.

The End of the Inter-Allied Intervention

As the wearied months of 1919 dragged on, evil days settled upon the entire Siberian adventure. The high purposes of military strategy for which it was conceived no longer had any meaning, for Germany had long since collapsed and the war in Europe was over. The ill-concealed desire of the Western powers and Japan to crush Bolshevism in Russia had resulted in dismal failure. By the end of 1919 the remnants of Kolchak's armies were in complete rout before the rising Red tide and the infuriated peasant partisans. The White elements both within and outside Russia had failed to provide any program or any leadership which the Russians would accept. Ambassador Morris in Tokyo went far to explain this when he said:

> The advent of Allied forces [in Siberia] has led to the hope among former [Russian] officials, civil and military, that they will regain the power and influence they had before the revolution. The attitude of these officials indicates that they will be relentless in their endeavor to suppress all liberal or moderate movements. Possibly nothing but their inevitable failure will bring them to reason.[9]

As for the Western Allies, by 1920 they were tired of the whole

[9] United States, *Foreign Relations, 1918, Russia,* II, 414.

business. They therefore withdrew their armies and left Siberia to the Russians—and to the Japanese.

For two years the Japanese remained. The Japanese government and the army regarded the whole eastern Siberian question as being still very decidedly Japan's business. The growth of the revolutionary ferment in Russia and the discrediting of the Whites appeared as the prelude to a possible communist society touching the shores of the Pacific which would be a threat to Japan's position in South Manchuria and even to the social fabric and political structure of her society at home. The massacre of Japanese at Nikolaevsk in 1920 seemed to confirm the wisdom of army expansionists who desired to annex the Maritime Province with Vladivostok. So Japan stayed on, temporarily in control of a great circular area reaching from Vladivostok to Chita, an area traversed by the Chinese Eastern and the Amur Railways. She entertained the hope that a buffer state, friendly to Japan and free of Bolshevik contagion, would yet arise in the Far East. But whatever justification there may ever have been for this hope had already been destroyed by the inter-Allied intervention itself, for in general the Russians appear to have been as happy to see the Allies go as the Allied soldiers themselves were to get out. Writing in 1931, General Graves noted that the participating governments seemed to take "very little pride in this venture. Who can blame them?"[10]

The Four-Power Consortium

Throughout the two years (1918-1920) of international wrangling in Siberia there had been a continuous succession of clashes between American and Japanese Far Eastern policy. One such area of conflict was the broader arena of international finance in China as a whole. It will be recalled that in 1913, President Wilson, disapproving of the control measures employed by the First or Six-Power Consortium as infringements upon the "administrative integrity" of China, informed the American banking group that it would not enjoy official support. In the five years that followed, the basic principles of Wilson's policy toward China—territorial and administrative integrity and the open door—did not change, but his views on the means of achieving and maintaining these principles did change. By November, 1917, the President, though not fully convinced that

10 William S. Graves, *America's Siberian Adventure* (New York, 1931), 356.

independent loans to China were impractical as political weapons, had decided to encourage the organization of a new four-power consortium. The following year, on the initiative of the American government, a new American banking group was formed. The bankers, however, were not of a mind to enter the field of Chinese investments save in concert with British, French, and Japanese banking groups, and with the assured support of the American government. These conditions the American government accepted, and on its part insisted that in turn the prospective consortium must respect the well-established principles of American policy in China—principles which were well known to be at variance with Japan's theory of "special interests" and with the theory of the British and the French on spheres of influence.

The reasons for this complete reversal of method by the Wilson administration are significant. The World War had given Japan a free hand in financing China, and it had also destroyed temporarily any possibility of China's receiving British or French credits. But more was involved than the mere matter of investment. Wilson was forced to recognize that, China's political position being what it was, the political aspects of American policy could no longer be detached with safety from economic considerations. This was made particularly clear during 1918, when as a result of the mysterious maneuverings of Nishihara Kamezo, personal representative in China of Japanese Premier Count Terauchi, the Peking *tuchun* government contracted Japanese loans in the amount of about Yen 120 million. These were not investments in the usual meaning of that word. Rather, they were payments to officials then in power in exchange for certain agreements that would promote Japanese policy, particularly in Manchuria.[11] Japan was thus buying an economic and political stake from a Chinese *tuchun* government that was willing to sell.

Against Sino-Japanese financial politics of this type, doctrinaire slogans of American policy on the open door and the integrity of China were useless unless implemented by more realistic factors. Therefore Wilson sought to revive and apply international co-operative action through a new consortium, his hope being that with British and French support Japan could be held in line and her efforts to gain a financial monopoly at Peking frustrated. Japan, however, was no more prepared to accept the open door in 1919

[11] C. F. Remer, *Foreign Investments in China* (New York, 1933), 539-545.

than she had been in 1915. Indeed, it required two years of dreary negotiation, 1918-1920, before a compromise agreement for the new four-power consortium could be reached. In this compromise the United States, England, and France pledged their "good faith" to "refuse their countenance to any operation [of the consortium] inimical to the vital interests of Japan." These powers also agreed to exclusion from the joint activities of the consortium of the zone of the South Manchuria Railway. It meant that while the powers would now pool all loans, administrative and industrial, in China proper south of the Wall, Japan still retained her "special position" in South Manchuria.

Interpretations of the consortium idea have been many and varied. On the high plane of theory the idea was, in the American view, that the consortium should be regarded not only as an important piece of financial machinery for the industrial development of China, but also as an international pledge of China's integrity and thus of American policy. In this sense the consortium appealed to American public opinion and to traditional concepts of American friendship for China. There were other advantages too, because the idea of a revived consortium had enabled the United States to bring pressure on Britain and France to relinquish in some measure their exclusive options in their respective spheres of influence. In all these ways the consortium was publicized as an instrumentality to preserve China's political and administrative integrity.

Contrary, however, to official and popular expectations, China showed no enthusiasm for the consortium and refused to do business with it. Chinese political leaders in general took the view that the consortium was a "threat of international control of Chinese finance" and "a monopoly or an attempted monopoly" designed to deprive China of a free world market where she could borrow on the best terms available. Again it was evident that the problem of "preserving" China and of serving American interests at the same time was not a simple task.

For Further Reading

Bau, M. J. (Pao Ming-ch'ien), *The Foreign Relations of China* (New York, 1922). Useful for reference but slanted in interpretation.

Birdsall, Paul, *Versailles Twenty Years After* (New York, 1941).

Campbell, Charles S., *Special Business Interests and the Open Door Policy*

(New Haven, 1951). The thesis that business interests were one of the chief factors in the open door policy.

Clyde, Paul H., *Japan's Pacific Mandate* (New York, 1935).

The Consortium (Washington, 1921). Selected correspondence.

Manning, Clarence A., *The Siberian Fiasco* (New York, 1952).

Morley, James W., *The Japanese Thrust into Siberia, 1918* (New York, 1957).

Norton, Henry K., *The Far Eastern Republic of Siberia* (London, 1923).

Tompkins, Pauline, *American-Russian Relations in the Far East* (New York, 1949). A useful survey, marred at times by the author's obsession with the inequities of the balance of power.

Unterberger, Betty Miller, *America's Siberian Expedition 1918-1920* (Durham, 1956). The most definitive account yet written.

White, John A., *The Siberian Intervention* (Princeton, 1950).

25 *Japan: 1889–1918*

The Rule of the *Genro*

IN resuming the story of Japan's political, economic, and social evolution, it will be recalled that on February 11, 1889, the Meiji emperor bestowed a "gift" upon his people—the nation's first modern constitution. The selection of this date was not a matter of accident. February 11 was the anniversary of the day back in the year 660 B.C. when, according to legend, the divinely descended Emperor Jimmu proclaimed his kingdom in Yamato. This "gift" constitution, as the reader already knows, did not create and, indeed, was not intended to create a democratic government. On the contrary, it was a political document, "a fundamental law superbly timed and written" to fit the cause of oligarchy.[1] In a number of ways, such as the grant of representative institutions, the Meiji constitution did make important concessions to Western liberal political theory, but to an even greater degree it perpetuated and strengthened the theory and the myth of the emperor's absolutism. There was thus an apparent contradiction between the constitutional structure and the reforming zeal of the early Meiji era. The constitution was the answer of the Meiji reformers to the growing demands for representative government, yet the document they fashioned was designed to give the appearance of popular government without the substance. Actually, these constitutional craftsmen wrought with consummate skill. For some thirty years, until 1918, they not only monopolized the powers of government without making significant concessions to popular sovereignty, but also achieved their grand purpose, conceived in the early years of Meiji, to create a vigorous, industrialized nation-state, materially modern but spiritually Japa-

[1] Robert A. Scalapino, *Democracy and the Party Movement in Prewar Japan* (Berkeley, 1953), 42. An excellent study to which I am deeply indebted.

nese, that could raise its voice in the company of the great powers. By what processes, then, was this remarkable transformation brought about without sacrificing authoritarian tradition?

Modern constitutional government was born in Japan on July 1, 1890, when the first national election in the nation's history was held. It was in most respects a model performance. Of the 450,000 eligible voters (one out of every hundred persons had the right to vote) all but 27,000 resorted in orderly fashion to the polls and cast their ballots. While this good behavior was in part a sensitive respect for the opinion of foreign governments and peoples, it was also a measure of the serious purpose of the voters and of their faith in the magic of constitutionalism, which, it was supposed, would destroy the arbitrary power of the clan bureaucrats, create a popular and just government, and doubtless reduce taxes. The election results vindicated the faith of the voters and the political parties that their day was at hand. The principal political parties, the *Jiyuto* or Liberal Party, founded in 1881 and dissolved in 1884, and the *Kaishinto* or the Reform or Progressive Party, founded in 1882 and revived on the eve of the election again under the leadership respectively of Itagaki Taisuke and Okuma Shigenobu, won 171 seats in the first Diet of 300 members. Encouraged by this comfortable majority the parties set about the business of controlling the government. They attacked it for its failure to rid Japan of the unequal treaties and they proposed drastic cuts in the government's budget. The will of government was to be bent to the will of the parties.[2]

The Foundations of the Oligarchy

In their endeavor to create a government responsible to the House of Representatives, the political parties had assumed a task that far exceeded their immediate strength or indeed their political maturity. To understand why this was so will require some delving into the institutional structure provided by the Meiji constitution and into the equally important unwritten customary institutions in which the formal constitution operated.

The political forces that were striving to shape Japanese society

[2] A broad survey of the political story, 1890-1918, is given in Chitoshi Yanaga, *Japan since Perry* (New York, 1949), chs. 15, 16, 18, 22, and 26; on the structural aspects of government in this period, see H. S. Quigley, *Japanese Government and Politics* (New York, 1932), chs. 4-13.

in 1890, though highly complex, were polarized around what could be called (a) the Satsuma-Choshu top oligarchs controlling the whole lesser bureaucracy of government, and (b) the political parties apparently dedicated to political theories of Western liberalism and led by such men as Itagaki and Okuma, who, although clan oligarchs themselves, had long since been in opposition to the government. In the parliamentary struggle ushered in by the first Diet of 1890 it was the former oligarchic forces already in control of government long before promulgation of the constitution who held all the aces. The specific ways in which this oligarchy enjoyed decisive advantages of legal position and traditional prestige merit some attention.

In the first instance, although the Meiji constitution was a true reflection of Japanese political society in 1890, it was phrased to preserve the *status quo* rather than to further the evolution of a new political society. The constitution as the personal property of the emperor was subordinate to the throne and "thereby to the oligarchs who controlled the throne." By this simple device, the prestige of the throne was so enhanced that very few men would dare to challenge it. This meant that the oligarchy was in a position, when all other means failed, to use the throne to quiet, if not to crush, parliamentary opposition. These circumstances help to explain why the political parties often played along with the bureaucrats to the neglect of seeking any broad popular understanding and support from the people.[3]

In the second place, the Meiji constitution contained two irreconcilable concepts: absolutism and popular government. This meant that if the constitution was to be honored in operation there would have to be a compromise between these opposing concepts and between the men who represented these concepts. The terms of the constitution itself made it quite clear that the greater concessions would have to be made by the forces of popular government. These same forces faced an even greater disadvantage because they were opposed by the weight of tradition and custom, the unwritten but powerful habits of Japanese political behavior. Whereas under a popular government responsibility for public acts would be fixed and clear, under traditional Japanese politics responsibility was hidden and therefore obscure. Of course this tradition was not wholly without logic. Its function was to subordinate political principles to the machinations of compromise among groups and cliques,

[3] Scalapino, *Democracy and the Party Movement in Prewar Japan,* 146-149.

thus maintaining harmony among the elite ruling class at the top. The most notable example of this customary political behavior was that ultra-select group of oligarchs, the *Genro,* who occupied an unrivalled position in Japanese politics until 1918. Since the *Genro* as an institution was entirely extra-legal, it was not legally responsible for its acts. Nonetheless, it was able to protect the emperor from responsibility for the exercise of his theoretically absolute powers by making decisions in his name and by serving as the actual centralizing agency of the state.

The Oligarchy versus the Parties

The political history of Japan from 1890 until 1918 holds a special interest because it was in these years that the Japanese fashioned the particular structure of political compromise that enabled the constitution, despite its irreconcilable concepts, to function with notable success. There were three stages in the development of this formula in constitutional compromise. The first, from 1890 to 1895, was marked by antagonism and separation between the ruling oligarchy and the "liberal" parties. The second, from 1895 to 1900, involved a series of ententes between the parties and the oligarchy. The third, from 1900 to 1918, was distinguished by oligarchic leadership of "liberal" political parties whose members, with rare exceptions, were commoners.

The period of complete estrangement between the government oligarchy and the popular parties was of great import because in it the Japanese learned that compromise was indispensable if there was to be any constitutional government at all. In this particular instance, however, compromise was not easy. The oligarchy had been entrenching itself in power during all the years that had elapsed since the Restoration of 1867. It was confident of its right and its power. The institution of the cabinet, which continued under the constitution, had been created and had been in operation since 1885, five years in advance of the meeting of the first Diet. The Privy Council, the highest advisory body to the emperor under the constitution, had been created a year before the constitution in order that it might advise the throne on the nature of the document under which it was to be the chief advisory organ. Furthermore, prior to the meeting of the first Diet, Premier Kuroda Kiyotaka and Ito Hirobumi, president of the Privy Council, had proclaimed the government's policy of "transcendental" cabinets, by which they meant that the government under the constitution derived all its power from the throne and was concerned therefore with all the emperor's subjects rather than with the desires of political parties. Such policy was not at variance with the explicit terms of the constitution, but was at variance with the platforms of the *Jiyuto* and the *Kaishinto,* both of which in 1890 made it clear that, given their way, they would use the constitution to subordinate the oligarchy to the rule of party cabinets responsible to the House of Representatives.

So matters stood when in November 1890 a hostile government, headed by the Choshu militarist, Premier and General Yamagata Aritomo, faced equally hostile parties in the first Diet. The spirit of "arrogance and contempt" with which the Premier addressed the House of Representatives was equalled only by the verbal violence with which the parties used the only constitutional weapon they possessed—a limited power to strike at the government's budget. Yamagata was speaking for the oligarchy and its servants the bureaucracy—the vast body of office holders, great and small—when he called on the House for unity with and unqualified trust in the government and its officialdom. In response, as indicated, the parties attacked and clipped the budget. In doing this they were not engaging merely in a general assault designed to reduce taxes or to assert their supremacy. The assault was aimed directly at a more specific target. The principal cuts in the budget proposed by the House involved the personal income of officials: salaries, pensions, residence, and travel allowances. Thus the attack was aimed directly at the lesser civil and military bureaucracy. This bureaucracy was, in the realm of everyday practical politics, the real and the indispensable foundation supporting the oligarchy. In meeting this attack, the government, as was to be expected, was prepared to use all its resources, fair or foul. As a beginning it employed two devices often resorted to in future years: (1) it stood firmly on the constitutional provision prohibiting reduction of expenditures already fixed, and (2) it resorted to intimidation of members of the parties by hired gangsters, or *soshi.* When these methods failed to move the parliamentarians, the government had recourse to bribery of weak-kneed party members. A budget more acceptable to the government was then passed.

The foregoing details are of importance because they revealed at the very beginning of the constitutional period the nature of the basic political conflict between autocratic as against party and responsible government. Among other things it was manifest that the political philosophy of the oligarchy would not go unchallenged, and that the conflict would be fought on the planes of both high constitutional principle and low, unspeakable immorality. Moreover, the impasse in the first Diet suggesting that politicians could be bought marked also the beginnings of a split within the oligarchy on how best to deal with the unruly parties. This internal discord, usually hidden from the public, showed itself, nevertheless, in the rival leadership of Yamagata and Ito, who represented respectively the "military" and the "civil" factions of the oligarchy.

In the light of Yamagata's unhappy experience, no member of the oligarchy welcomed the prospect of becoming the next premier. Yet under the policy of the oligarchy it was inevitable that the post be held by a member of this group, and, as will be seen, until 1918, every prime minister was a *Genro*, a semi-*Genro*, or an agent of the *Genro*. Thus when Yamagata resigned, his Minister of Finance, Matsukata Masayoshi of Satsuma, an able financier but certainly undistinguished as a political leader, accepted the premiership, May 6, 1891. When the second Diet met, it followed precedent by attacking the government's budget, but in this case the reductions were leveled at *new* expenditures such as the naval and shipbuilding programs. To meet this crisis the government dissolved the Diet and ordered a special election for February, 1892, characterized as "the most brutal election in Japanese history." The government had decided to show the parties no quarter and, if possible, to break their hold on the electorate. Voters were intimidated by hired gangsters, some party candidates were arrested arbitrarily while the property of others was burned. Before the election was over at least twenty-five persons were killed and nearly 400 wounded. And yet, the government did not achieve its purpose. In the new Diet, the parties, with 163 seats, maintained a clear majority.

Ito's Solution

It was at this juncture that Ito began to formulate an alternate solution to the strong-arm methods of the Yamagata faction of the oligarchy. Ito's purpose was not to destroy government by the oligarchy but to find a means through which a political party might be created as an administration party and thus provide legislative support for the oligarchy. To this end he even proposed that when a Diet was dissolved, the emperor by imperial rescript should "admonish the people." A rebuke such as this from the throne would undoubtedly quiet the parties and whip them into line, but it would also involve the throne in politics. Ito's plan for the moment was shelved not only because most of the oligarchy was opposed to it but also because of the uncompromising and confident attitude of the parties.

Ito's First Cabinet under the Constitution

When Matsukata resigned, August, 1892, Ito, having received a pledge of unity from all the *Genro,* accepted the premiership and formed a cabinet that included most of the *Genro.* This time the House used the ultimate weapon. It memorialized the throne to impeach the ministry. The emperor's reply, written undoubtedly by the oligarchy, was a major blow to popular government. The House was told that its function was "to aid" the government. Thus matters stood when the outbreak of the Sino-Japanese War, 1894, brought peace to internal Japanese politics. The constitutional question was forgotten as all factions united in prosecution of the war.

The Period of Oligarchic-Party Ententes, 1895-1900

During the brief period from the close of the war until the turn of the century, the oligarchy and the parties experimented with political ententes. The first of these was between the Ito cabinet and the *Jiyuto.* The general pattern set by this and succeeding ententes required party support for the government's program in return for which the party received a post in the cabinet, appointment of party members to office, and, to phrase the matter delicately, contributions to the party's treasury. On the credit side these shaky alliances did provide some stability and enabled a party to get one foot in the door of administrative authority. At the same time this seeming stability was largely fictitious, since neither oligarchy nor party had surrendered their extreme and opposing views as to what government should be. On the debit side of responsible government, the ententes increased factionalism among the parties and destroyed what little chance there was for a united front among the parliamentarians.[4] It was at this time too that Yamagata, the unrelenting opponent of popular government, gave the military services a stranglehold on successive administrations when in May, 1900, he secured an Imperial Ordinance requiring that only generals or lieutenant generals on the active list might hold the post of Minister of War and only admirals or vice admirals on the active list the post of Minister of the Navy.[5]

The Oligarch as Party Leader, 1900-1918

As the new century opened, Japan's constitutional government, now a decade old, had failed to produce a working pattern for the stress and strain of everyday politics. In this respect the record was one of dismal failure. Yet Japan, through the genius of Ito, was about to find a solution that would give some stability to her constitutional structure for two decades. In essence the solution was the fulfillment of ideas with which Ito had long been playing—leadership of the "liberal" parties by oligarchic statesmen.

Actually a faction of the *Kenseito* played into Ito's hands. In 1900, unable to tolerate further its humiliating alliance with Yamagata, this faction asked Ito to become its leader. Ito's terms were severe: (1) the party must be dissolved and a new party more representative of all groups in the State put into its place; (2) party members must accept the orders of the leader. The *Kenseito* accepted these terms. On September 16, 1900, a new party was born, the *Rikken Seiyukai* (Association of Friends of Constitutional Government), with Ito as its president. This development meant that the party men (or at least most of them) had accepted the leadership of one of the most powerful oligarchs without knowing in advance what the policy of its new leader would be. It meant that the *Seiyukai* was willing in some major degree to renounce political principle, if by so doing it might gain access to administrative authority. Yet from the beginning Ito left no doubt as to his purposes. His *Seiyukai* would stand for the "true," that is, the imperial, interpretation of the constitution. In summary, the surrender of the *Seiyukai,* the only strong political party, to oligarchic leadership provided a means by which

[4] During this period there was a brief interlude of the so-called party cabinet of Okuma and Itagaki in 1898. The two leaders had recently formed a new constitutional party, the *Kenseito*.

[5] The ordinance was modified in 1913 enabling reserve officers of these ranks to qualify but reverted to its original form in 1936.

government could be conducted. It did not mean that the struggle for power among political factions was ended.[6]

Katsura and Saionji, 1901-1913

Ito's first ministry, supported by the *Seiyukai* but wracked by internal cabinet discord, survived less than a year. Yamagata, who was the natural successor to Ito in the now well-established process of shuffling premiers among the *Genro,* refused to head the next government. A number of factors influenced this decision: (1) the power of the *Genro* was for the time being secure; (2) Yamagata was of no mind to face the political attacks of Ito and the hostile *Seiyukai* in the Diet; and (3) the time was at hand when younger men were to hold the premiership while the older *Genro* continued their control behind the scenes. Accordingly, it was a military protégé of Yamagata, General Katsura Taro of Choshu, who became premier in June, 1901. Katsura, faced by parliamentary opposition, was forced like others before him to fall back on the budget of the preceding year. Nevertheless, during 1903 the militarists continued to strengthen their position. Ito was made president of the Privy Council and thus removed from party affiliation. His place as president of the *Seiyukai* went to his civilian (Kuge) protégé, Saionji Kimmochi, who was eventually to become a full-ranking *Genro.* At this point too, as in 1894, war came to the aid of the militarists. As the tension with Russia increased, the Diet rallied to the financial support of the army. This fervent patriotism continued unchecked until the signing of the Treaty of Portsmouth. Then political peace promptly gave place to violent attacks on government resulting in declarations of martial law. Unwilling to face the hostile Diet, Katsura resigned, and was succeeded by Saionji as premier.

For two and one-half years (January, 1906-July, 1908) Saionji's government, supported by the *Seiyukai,* maintained itself in office.

---

[6] For conflicting interpretations of the theory of Imperial powers, see Quigley, *Japanese Government and Politics,* 67-68; R. K. Reischauer, *Japan: Government-Politics* (New York, 1939), 167-169; G. E. Uyehara, *The Political Development of Japan 1867-1909* (London, 1910), 19; Tomio Nakano, *The Ordinance Power of the Japanese Emperor* (Baltimore, 1923), 5; H. Sato, *Democracy and the Japanese Government* (New York, 1920), 1; E. W. Clement, "Constitutional Imperialism in Japan," *Proceedings of the Academy of Political Science,* VI (1916), 325; U. Iwasaki, *Working Forces in Japanese Politics* (New York, 1921), ch. ii. The Japanese doctrine postulating the identity of the emperor and the state is known as *kokutai.*

Its fall was due primarily to financial policies that failed to satisfy the military oligarchs. Katsura again succeeded to the premiership, and when in 1909 Ito was assassinated in Harbin, Yamagata, militarist and arch-enemy of all liberal and representative trends, was left as supreme directing head of the *Genro*. Against this newly entrenched position of the oligarchy, the parliamentarians could exert very little pressure, since political discord within the ranks of the *Seiyukai* precluded any vigorous attack upon the government. As a consequence, Katsura was left free to carry through the annexation of Korea. Far from attacking the policy, the House of Representatives urged Katsura to use the "big stick."[7]

The annexation of Korea, another major victory for the militarists, enabled Katsura to retire with glory, while Saionji again headed the government in August, 1911. It was in this administration that the growing inner conflict of principle within Japan's political machinery was exposed. Yamagata and the Army wanted the creation of two divisions for Korea. Saionji, with the civilians of his cabinet, refused to support this policy. Thereupon, the Minister of War resigned, and when Yamagata and the General Staff refused to name a successor, there was nothing for Saionji and his cabinet to do but resign. The army oligarchs had given a practical demonstration of their power to dominate the civilian wing of government.

With doleful regularity, Katsura again became Prime Minister (1912), though by this time he was no longer the disciple but rather the rival of the aging Yamagata. This estrangement and his unpopularity with the parliamentarians led Katsura to form his own political party, the *Rikken Doshikai* (Constitutional Fellow-thinker's Society). However, even with lavish use of funds he was unable to secure a majority in the House. He had failed in his challenge to the power of Yamagata and in his efforts to buy parliamentary support.

Yamamoto and Naval Scandals

The *Genro* then turned to Admiral Count Yamamoto Gombei (Satsuma), but when it was discovered that the Navy was implicated in financial scandals touching battleship construction, the Diet re-

7 Tatsuji Takeuchi, *War and Diplomacy in the Japanese Empire* (Chicago, 1935), 166-167.

fused to pass the budget, and Yamamoto resigned. The next premier was Marquis Okuma Shigenobu (1914), whose command of the Diet during two and a half years was in part due to a new coalition party, the *Kenseikai*. By this time the opposition *Seiyukai* had passed under the able leadership of a commoner, Hara (Kei) Takashi. Although Okuma had been one of the early champions of popular government, his administration from 1914 to 1916 was marked by unprecedented chauvinistic nationalism and thus played into the hands of the military oligarchs. It was significant, however, that the government under Okuma recognized in a measure its responsibility to the Diet.

TERAUCHI AND THE MOB

When Okuma resigned in 1916, the premiership passed with unfailing monotony to one of Yamagata's men, General Terauchi Seiki, a soldier of some reputation but wholly unprepared to meet the political, economic, and social dislocations of a Japan undergoing wartime industrialization. War profiteers had already been the occasion of popular indignation, and, when the government failed to control the price of rice, the authorities were defied, and rioting spread from city to city. These rice riots, as they were called, were symbolic of new forces stirring within Japan—forces with which the military oligarchy lacked the capacity to deal. Accordingly, in May, 1918, Hara Takashi, the first untitled man to hold the office, became premier. Often referred to as Japan's "Great Commoner," Hara was a gifted politician who had achieved leadership of the *Seiyukai* through his ability to command the personal loyalty of his followers. Like many of the military oligarchs who preceded him, Hara was unscrupulous, recognizing only loyalty to party rather than to any abstract program of political ideology. Yet his elevation to the premiership was a significant event. It marked the end of rule by the *Genro* and the clansmen of Satsuma and Choshu. It marked the beginnings of rule by party politicians—men of a new Japan in which the commerce, industry, and finance of a bourgeois society seemed destined to replace the feudal and military traditions perpetuated by the *Genro*.

THE NEW JAPANESE ECONOMY

The clash between oligarchy and parties at the turn of the century to resolve the question of how and by whom Japan should be governed under the constitution was not simply a matter of political theory. The constitutional struggle was never free from the everyday momentum and temper of a revolutionary age. The makers of Meiji Japan, intent on creating a powerful nation-state, were building the new edifice with a strange assortment of materials—some traditional and Japanese, others new and foreign. Nowhere were the new materials more evident than in the new Japan of commerce and industry.

The last decade of the nineteenth century in addition to shaping constitutionalism in operation was also giving form to the new industrial system, the foundations of which had been laid in the earlier years of Meiji. The Japanese had been assimilating machine technology, accumulating banking and industrial capital, and increasing the output of textiles and other consumer goods. The Sino-Japanese and the Russo-Japanese Wars stimulated the growth of transport, banking, and strategic industries. By comparison with the giants of the West, Japan's industrial capitalism in 1914 was still weak, but its character, like that of constitutionalism, had been formed. Before the turn of the century Japan had gained relief from the unequal treaties, a matter of first importance in the economy. The Chinese indemnity of 1895 enabled Japan in 1897 to shift to the gold standard. Total production and real income probably increased from 80 to 100 per cent between 1889 and 1914, the first twenty-five years of the constitutional period. Agriculture and fisheries took care of a 25 per cent increase in population, 1894-1914, with some improvement in dietary standards and with only small imports of foodstuffs.[8]

Japan's industrial revolution, well under way on the eve of World War I in 1914, included three major lines of development: (1) in large-scale industry, (2) in agriculture and traditional industries, and (3) in the textile trades. Large scale industry grew rapidly through government initiative, subsidy, and protection.

More important to the growth in national productivity in the years up to 1914 was the expansion of Japan's basic economy, including agriculture and small-scale traditional industry. With little increase in farm population, food production increased 35 or more per cent, 1894-1914, due to an increase in cultivated areas, improved

[8] W. W. Lockwood, *The Economic Development of Japan* (Princeton, 1954), 18-22.

credit facilities, scientific intensive methods, and double cropping. There was little change in basic organization. Some 5.4 million farm families cultivated holdings averaging 2.6 acres each. High taxes and interest charges continued to weigh heavily on the farmer. By 1910, 39 per cent of farmers owned no land and 45 per cent of farm lands were tenanted. Tenants paid rents in kind amounting to 45 to 60 per cent of the crop on rice land, and the land tax even after the turn of the century was the principal government revenue to meet the rising armament expenditure. In 1908 the farmer was paying a far larger percentage of his income in taxes than was the merchant or industrialist. In a few cases there was an expanding market for traditional handicrafts such as in Japanese paper, pottery, and fine fabrics. The silk industry and cotton textiles were major examples of adaptation and growth of traditional industries responding to foreign demand. In the growth of the cotton textile industry the technical transformation due to Western influence was much greater than in the case of silk. By 1914 the Japanese cotton textile industry supplied not only the home market but was already invading the foreign field with its products. It was in this period that Japan and India displaced Britain in the cotton yarn market in China. Japan was also beginning to capture the Chinese market in piece goods, especially in coarse goods supplied previously by Americans. In a word, the growth of agriculture and of consumer goods industries enabled Japan at the turn of the century to support a growing population and a large national budget for armaments and colonial expansion. But in doing this, government taxes on the low and middle-income classes were increased heavily and there was frequent resort to foreign borrowing. By 1914 Japan was at the edge of financial crisis.[9]

The War Boom of 1914-1919

From this impending crisis Japan was saved by World War I. The war brought to Japan orders for munitions and other manufactures from the Allies; neutral countries of the Far East no longer able to buy in Europe sought their purchases in Japan. As illustrative of what happened, exports of Japanese cotton cloth increased 185 per cent from 1913 to 1918. By 1919 Japan's foreign assets ex-

9 Lockwood, *Economic Development of Japan,* 27-37.

ceeded outstanding debts by 1,300 million yen. Five years earlier Japan had been a debtor in about the same figure. Even when account is taken of fictitious and inflationary prosperity, Japan's gains were substantial. She had become an industrial power of first rank with a major stake in world markets. Moreover she was the first and the only industrialized nation in the Far East.

Education for Industry and Politics

Education was a directing agent in Japan's industrial and political evolution, 1890 to 1918. At an early date the Meiji reformers had discarded the Tokugawa practice of education of the *samurai* only for a national program to destroy illiteracy. By 1900 some five million children were in some 27,000 elementary schools. Above these schools were limited systems of secondary and higher education, the latter available only to the sons of the well-to-do. This system of general and technical education (there were 240 technical schools by 1903) was indispensable to the nation's industrial advance. While technical education rose to increasing standards of excellence, general education, at first strongly influenced by American ideals of freedom, was directed by the oligarchy from 1890 onward toward indoctrination in nationalistic and authoritarian morals. Principles of obedience and subservience to the state, dressed in the garb of Shinto mythology, made education a strong arm of the oligarchy.

Socialism and Labor

Finally, it should be noted that Meiji constitutionalism, subservient as it was to the idea and goal of a centralized, industrial state, was biased in favor of power rather than of the welfare of the common man. This is not to say that the *Meiji* oligarchy took no steps to curb abuses, yet the first factory labor law drafted by the government in 1898 was not submitted to the Diet because of the opposition of the industrialists. When the Japan Social Democratic Party was formed in 1901 by Katayama Sen and Kotoku Denjiro it was ordered dissolved by Home Minister Suematsu Kencho, son-in-law of Premier Ito, within three hours of its founding. During the Russo-Japanese War the socialist movement became more radical, international, and intellectual. In 1907, rioting by miners in protest against outrageous working conditions resulted in millions in property damage and in the arrest of more than 200 miners and labor leaders.

Civil Liberty versus Repression

This policy of repression directed against socialistic parties and associations was merely an extreme aspect of the oligarchy's attitude toward political freedom in general. Although the Constitution made reference to civil liberties, suppression continued after 1890 as it had before. Oftentimes the government, seeking a gradual transition, had a plausible case against the tendency of dissident groups to resort to violence. At first the series of Peace Preservation Laws that were in effect when the Constitution was promulgated were opposed bitterly by the parties in the first Diets, and the most obnoxious of the statutes was repealed in 1898 only to be re-enacted two years later in a form precluding virtually the legal organization and maintenance of labor unions. This law persisted until 1926, though it was not always enforced.

For Further Reading

Allen, G. C., *Modern Japan and Its Problems* (New York, 1928). A study of the effect of Western influences on Japanese civilization.

Araki, Mitsutaro, *Financial System in Japan* (Tokyo, 1933).

Brown, Delmer, *Nationalism in Japan: An Introductory Historical Analysis* (Berkeley, 1955). An able general survey.

Fahs, C. B., *Government in Japan* (New York, 1940).

Fujii Shinichi, *The Essentials of Japanese Constitutional Law* (Tokyo, 1940).

Fujisawa Rikitaro, *The Recent Aims of Political Development of Japan* (New Haven, 1923).

Ito Hirobumi, *Commentaries on the Constitution of the Empire of Japan*, trans. by Miyoji Ito (Tokyo, 1889).

Katayama Sen, *The Labor Movement in Japan* (Chicago, 1918). By one of the early leaders in the movement.

Kawabe Kisaburo, *The Press and Politics in Japan, A Study of the Relation Between the Newspaper and the Political Development of Modern Japan* (Chicago, 1921).

Keenleyside, H. L., and A. F. Thomas, *History of Japanese Education* (Tokyo, 1937). The political philosophy behind the educational system.

Ogawa Gotaro, *The Conscription System in Japan* (New York, 1921).

Takekoshi Yosaburo, *Prince Saionji* (Koyto, 1933).

Wildes, Harry Emerson, *Social Currents in Japan with Special Reference to the Press* (Chicago, 1927).

Young, A. Morgan, *Japan in Recent Times, 1912-26* (New York, 1929). Able and critical journalism.

26

1921–1922

The Washington Conference

As World War I receded into the category of things past, and as mankind welcomed the new years of peace, thoughtful men could evaluate with greater perspective the popular slogans of the war years. It was already becoming clear that decisive victories on the battlefield had not been followed by equally decisive victories at the conference table. There was the suspicion that the world had not been made "safe for democracy." The public mind was troubled with foreboding questions. Had man witnessed the "war to end war"? Had militarism been crushed? Where were "the open covenants openly arrived at"? What of "freedom of the seas," and the removal of economic barriers among the nations? Did the revelations of nationalism at the Paris Peace Conference forecast a better world? Was there to be implementation of the principle of arms reduction? Was the United States, which had deserted its traditional neutrality in 1917, and whose president had given vitality to the concept of a League of Nations, now to return to isolation under cover of "the rhetorical mirage of normalcy"? Indeed, the entire program of Wilsonian principles in which humble men and women had placed their faith seemed, like the war itself, to recede into a past compounded of pleasant but impractical idealism. The new post-war statesmanship would recruit its ranks from the apostles of "normalcy." There were Hardings in every major capital.

By 1920, to this fundamental questioning of the over-all post-war picture had been added new and specific problems, international in character, some created by the war, others magnified by it. These new focal points of friction were by no means limited to particular geographical areas, for they were found in the Old World and the New World alike, but they were particularly acute in the sphere of American-Japanese relations. The co-belligerency of the United States and Japan had not served to harmonize their respective Far Eastern policies. As the reader is aware, the roots of American-Japanese friction had grown lustily since the days of the Russo-Japanese War in 1904-1905. Dollar diplomacy in Manchuria, Oriental immigration in California, and special interests versus the open door in China had already made it quite clear that there was a growing coolness in the traditional nineteenth-century friendship between Japan and the United States. By 1920 there was a widespread popular conviction in the United States and Canada, and to a lesser degree in Great Britain and France, that Japan had shown little interest in the defeat of German militarism and that she had used the war primarily to advance Japanese hegemony in China. This is simply to say that between 1918 and 1920 cordiality in Ameri-

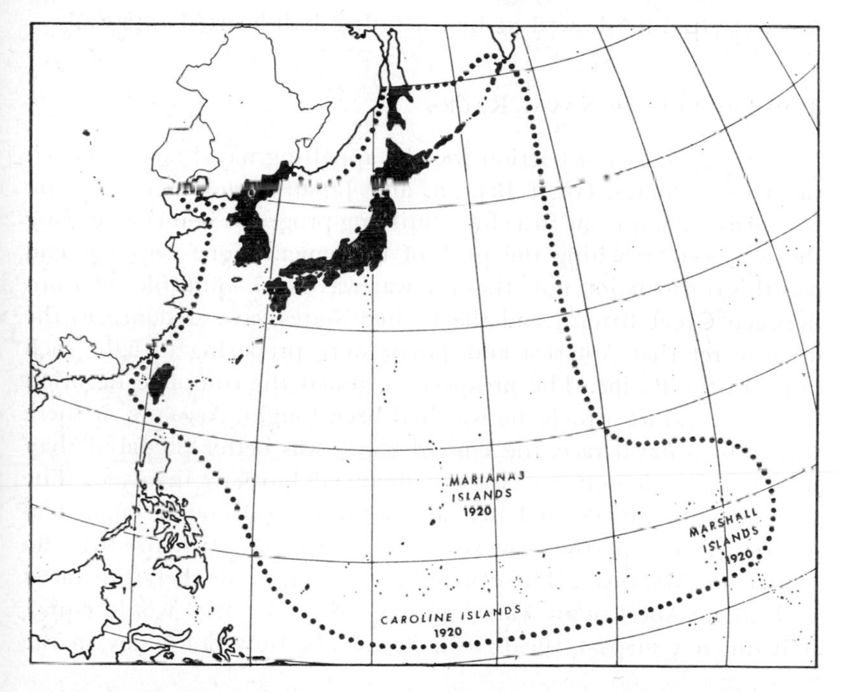

JAPAN, 1920-1930. *Reproduced from* A War Atlas for Americans, *Simon and Schuster, Inc., New York, 1944, by permission from Simon and Schuster, Inc., and from the U. S. Department of State, Division of Map Intelligence and Cartography.*

can-Japanese relations had reached an all-time low. This record was traceable directly and in an immediate sense to the differences that had arisen out of the Twenty-one Demands of 1915, the Lansing-Ishii exchange of 1917, the Japanese program as presented at Paris with respect to Shantung and the German islands in the Pacific, and finally, to Japanese military and railway policies in Siberia and Manchuria during the Inter-Allied Intervention of 1918.

Although there is ample evidence to support the marked deterioration in American-Japanese relations, it should be noted that neither the Senate nor the American public at large can be said to have felt any deep concern over far eastern politics in the early post-war years. It will be recalled that the most impassioned senatorial pleas for the restoration of China's rights in Shantung do not appear to have been prompted by any real concern for the birthplace of Confucius. Even in the case of questions that had a direct and immediate bearing upon real and tangible American interests in the Pacific, the American public showed at best a rather half-hearted interest.[1]

THE TRIANGULAR NAVAL RACE

The largest area of friction was the appalling naval race in which the United States, Great Britain, and Japan found themselves involved as the war came to a close. Building programs launched during the war were reaching the peak of implementation. To what end was this construction now that the war was over? Amicable relations between Great Britain and the United States gave credence to the open secret that America and Japan were preparing to fight each other in the Pacific. The prospect suggested the complete negation of every ideal for which the war had been fought. Actually, if there was to be a naval race, the United States was better prepared than its potential enemies to face the financial burdens involved. The war had seriously affected British resources, and though Japan had grown wealthy in the war years her industrial structure was no match for America's. These maritime powers were therefore faced with the prospect of an American navy which by 1924 would equal, if it did not surpass, the British fleet.[2] The only doubt lay in the

---

1 See Yamato Ichihashi, *The Washington Conference and After* (Stanford University, 1928).

2 R. L. Buell, *The Washington Conference* (New York, 1922), 139-144; H. C. Bywater, *Sea Power in the Pacific* (New York, 1921), 10.

question of whether the American voter would support the naval appropriations called for by the Naval Appropriation Act of 1916. Both Republicans and Democrats hesitated to add to the nation's gigantic war debt. Furthermore, the fact that the United States had repudiated the League of Nations did not mean that the American people had forsaken the ideals of peace for which they believed they had fought. The scrapping of the Versailles Treaty and the election of Harding in 1920 did not mean that the Wilsonian program had been blotted from the American consciousness. Among Harding's advisers and in the Republican Party at large were many leaders such as Charles Evans Hughes, the new Secretary of State, who were committed to the principle of arms reduction among the great powers, and to American leadership to this end.[3]

The Troublesome Anglo-Japanese Alliance

On the international political front no problem of the immediate post-war years was more perplexing than that presented by the Anglo-Japanese Alliance. During nearly two decades this Alliance had remained as the keystone of Anglo-Japanese policy. By 1920, however, when Russia and Germany, the powers against which the Alliance was originally directed, were no longer threatening British or Japanese interests, big navy advocates in the United States, supported by the yellow press and by brochures of more substantial scholarship, had taken the position that the Alliance was aimed at the United States and would eventually involve this country in war against Japan and Great Britain in eastern Asia. The idea was one which the British had sought to allay over a period of years. In 1911, as the Alliance was being renewed for a second time, the British made it clear that the obligation of belligerency would not apply against a power with which either signatory had concluded a treaty of general arbitration. However, the Anglo-American arbitration treaty of August 3, 1911, was not approved by the United States Senate.[4] The subsequent Anglo-American Treaty of 1914 (Bryan Peace Commission Treaty) was not one of general arbitration as interpreted in the Anglo-Japanese Alliance. Finally, Japan's position

---

[3] The Republican platform of 1920, although repudiating the League, had called for "an international association" designed to preserve the peace.

[4] See A. W. Griswold, *Far Eastern Policy of the United States* (New York, 1938), 168.

at Paris relative to Shantung, and her relations with the British in Siberia (1918-1920), led once again to the growing conviction that the Anglo-Japanese Alliance was a bulwark of Japanese policy in Asia. Even British assurances given in 1920 that the Alliance would not be binding in the event of war between the United States and Japan did not dispel these fears.[5] Moreover, official American apprehension was heightened during 1920 by the belief that Anglo-Japanese negotiations leading to further renewal of the Alliance were in progress. Finally, it is to be observed that in Canada the Alliance was regarded with equal apprehension. Like the states of the Pacific Coast, Canada was showing increased concern over Oriental, particularly Japanese, immigration. Canadians readily believed that in an Anglo-American war, Canada would be a principal theater of operations. How strong this Canadian sentiment was may best be judged by the success of Premier Arthur Meighen, who literally forced the London Imperial Conference of June, 1921, to agree that the Alliance must be ended and replaced by a new and broader agreement covering the Pacific.[6]

The Early Bird Catches the Worm

Sufficient has been said to indicate how little had been contributed by World War I to the hopes for peace and tranquility in the Pacific. It is hardly an exaggeration to say that the Pacific rather than the Atlantic had become, temporarily at least, the center of world politics, involving a threatened naval race and increased tension between the United States and Japan. Here, in part, lay the explanation of why a Republican administration that had repudiated Wilson's League now turned to the idea of an international conference on arms reduction. Even before Harding was inaugurated, Senator W. E. Borah of Idaho introduced (February 24, 1921) a resolution for a three-power conference. Despite Harding's opposition, the resolution, widely supported by the press and by public demonstrations throughout the country, was approved by the Senate and House by overwhelming votes (May 25 and June 29). By this time both Britain and the United States were moving rapidly toward the idea of a conference. So far as these two powers were

5 C. N. Spinks, "The Termination of the Anglo-Japanese Alliance," *Pacific Historical Review*, VI (1937), 326.

6 J. B. Brebner, "Canada, the Anglo-Japanese Alliance and the Washington Conference," *Political Science Quarterly*, L (1935), 45.

concerned, it was becoming a question of who should gain the prestige of calling the nations together. But behind this superficial rivalry lay a fundamental political question transcending the more obvious problem of arms reduction. It was the question whether Great Britain under a new Anglo-Japanese Alliance "was to support the special interests of Japan" in the Far East or to align herself more solidly with the traditional American principles of the open door and the integrity of China.[7]

The sequence of events leading to the calling of the Washington Conference may now be briefly told. On March 16, 1921, Lord Lee, First Lord of the British Admiralty, proposed publicly a naval agreement with the United States which would recognize the principle of parity. Shortly thereafter, Adolph Ochs, publisher of *The New York Times,* became the medium of a British proposal to the United States whereby the two states would accept naval "equality," the British navy guarding the Atlantic while the American navy would be concentrated in the Pacific. Thus, Britain, while moving cautiously toward renewal of the Anglo-Japanese Alliance, was also suggesting concentration of American sea power against Japan. Nevertheless, the proposal was welcomed in Washington, where it was becoming clear that Britain was prepared to modify the Japanese alliance to meet the wishes of Canada and the United States. As a consequence, on July 5, Lord Curzon suggested to Ambassador George Harvey

> . . . that the President [Harding] invite [the] powers directly concerned to take part in a conference to be held to consider all essential matters bearing on [the] Far East and [the] Pacific Ocean with a view to arriving at a common understanding designed to assure settlement by peaceful means, the elimination of naval warfare, [and] consequent elimination of arms, etc.[8]

The British also conveyed this proposal to Japan. Harvey's cable to Washington carrying the British suggestion was crossed by one from Secretary Hughes asking whether the British would receive favorably an invitation to a conference called by the United States. Meanwhile, Hughes' concept of the proposed meeting was growing both in point of agenda and membership, and on July 11, 1921, the press

[7] Also, the Republicans called the Washington Conference in part because they had troubled consciences growing out of their failure to find a way into the League.

[8] United States, *Foreign Relations, 1921,* I, 19-21.

of the world announced that President Harding was inviting the powers to an international conference.

The Reluctant Guest

The response to America's informal overtures was for the most part cordial, but there were some discordant notes. The Belgians protested that they had been ignored. Russia, unrecognized at this time by the "respectable" society of nations, asserted her undeniable interest in the Far East and proclaimed her own non-recognition doctrine applicable to "any decision taken" by the proposed conference. Japan, too, as was to be expected, showed her reluctance to rush into a conference that was to discuss questions of the Far East. Japanese opinion, both official and public, was critical. It was impossible to disguise the fact that the conference was designed in considerable measure to apply the brakes to policies which Japan had followed since the Twenty-one Demands of 1915. Moreover, the most influential forces in Japanese politics still favored retention of the Anglo-Japanese Alliance. For various reasons Japan was favorable to the idea of arms reduction, but on the subject of political questions concerning the Far East she suspected that a trap had been set, and she wanted a bill of particulars on the agenda. This, Hughes refused to give, and it was not until July 26 that Japan finally gave her reluctant consent to attend a conference on questions of the Pacific and the Far East as well as on the limitation of armament. In accepting the invitation, the Japanese government gave notice that "problems such as are the sole concern to certain particular powers or such matters that may be regarded [as] accomplished facts should be scrupulously avoided."

Statesmen or Politicians?

The formal invitations went out to the powers on August 11, 1921. Nine powers were on the guest list. The great powers included Great Britain, France, Italy, Japan, and the United States. The lesser powers were Belgium, China, the Netherlands, and Portugal. These were included because of their real or supposed interests in the Pacific. It was not anticipated that they would participate in the arms conference. Since German and Austrian interests in the Far East had been liquidated by the war, these powers were excluded. The absence of Russia from the list of invited guests could be explained, however, only on the basis of a quarantine with which the victorious powers hoped to isolate the Soviet government.[9]

In terms of personalities, the conference was an assemblage of political and diplomatic stars. The American delegation, headed by Secretary of State Charles Evans Hughes, included Elihu Root, long associated with the conduct of American foreign policy; Henry Cabot Lodge, chairman of the Senate Foreign Relations Committee, a politician who more than any other American was responsible for the repudiation of Versailles and the League; and Senator Oscar W. Underwood, Democratic minority leader on the Foreign Relations Committee. Britain's delegation was headed by the Tory aristocrat and scholar-statesman, Arthur Balfour, a former Prime Minister and Foreign Secretary. Japan sent Admiral Baron Kato Tomosaburo, who was to become premier in 1922. Leadership of the French delegation was held first by Aristide Briand, Minister for Foreign Affairs, a diplomat "shrewd and skillful in emergencies," and later, after Briand's departure, by René Viviani, a member of the Chamber, who was eloquent in his appeals to foreign sympathy. Out of this group came the "Big Three"—Hughes, Balfour, and Kato—who in secret negotiations guided the conference and in general determined its decisions.

The Way to Disarm Is to Disarm

It was an illustrious assembly of notables that gathered in Memorial Continental Hall on November 12, 1921, to hear President Harding's exuberant remarks of welcome. He was followed immediately by Secretary Hughes, chairman of the conference, who, avoiding the triteness of diplomacy's language, declared that the nations had come together "not for general resolutions . . . but for action."[10] Thereupon he presented to the startled delegates and the galleries a plan for immediate slashing of naval strength. In brief, the American proposal called for:

(a) a naval holiday for 10 years in capital ship construction;

(b) the scrapping of many ships, including some already in commission and others in process of building;

[9] Russia, of course, as noted, protested against her exclusion, and promised in advance not to be bound by any of the decisions. United States, *Foreign Relations, 1921,* I, 40-43.

[10] *Conference on the Limitation of Armament, Washington, November 12, 1921-February 6, 1922* (Washington, D. C., 1922), 58.

(c) application of the program of scrapping so as to leave the navies of the United States, Great Britain, and Japan in a ratio of 5-5-3; France and Italy, without scrapping, would fit into this ratio as 1.75—1.75;

(d) capital ship replacements would be limited by treaty to 500,-000 tons each for the United States and Great Britain, and to 300,000 tons for Japan;

(e) similar ratios would be applied to aircraft carriers, cruisers, destroyers, and submarines.[11]

The measured words of Secretary Hughes electrified not only the audience that sat before him, but also the far larger audience of press and public opinion. While delegates threw off their complacency and reporters flashed the news to their papers, the galleries burst into wild applause. No diplomatic conference in the world's history had opened in this way. Yet, in reality, the surprise of the delegates lay not so much in the cards that Hughes held as in the boldness of his opening play. No matter how distasteful the idea of naval parity may have been to the British, the fact was that the British government had conceded the principle of parity several months in advance of the conference. Moreover, since the naval ratio proposal could not be detached from political problems of the Far East, Japan's efforts to establish the autonomy of the two conferences was all but defeated from the beginning. In any event, Hughes seems to have been justified in playing most of his cards in the first move instead of holding them in reserve for bargaining purposes. This conclusion seems justified in the light of the final outcome of the conference. But for the moment the future of the Washington Conference would be determined by the measured responses of Britain and Japan to the Hughes proposal. Since Japan was asked to accept an inferior ratio, since her army was "opposed to any reduction," since her government did not believe there could be "any lasting friendship with the United States," the fate of the Hughes proposal was doubtful at best.

The Anglo-Japanese Alliance

Moreover, British acceptance, though likely, could not be taken for granted. Since the question of naval power could not be divorced

[11] United States, Sen. doc. 126, 67th Cong., 2nd sess., *Conference on the Limitation of Armament,* 41-63.

from political policy as represented by the Anglo-Japanese Alliance, Balfour had come to Washington hoping to substitute "a tri-partite agreement with America" for the old two-power alliance. He was convinced that the Japanese would accept this if they could not have the old alliance intact. However, Secretary Hughes would have none of this proposal, for it would have amounted to American recognition of the "special interests" of Japan and Britain in the Far East. Rather, he hoped the alliance could be replaced by an agreement embodying the principles of the Root-Takahira notes of 1908. Opposed at first by both Balfour and Kato, Hughes not only won his case but secured the inclusion of France in the Four-Power Pacific Treaty, signed December 13, 1921. By this ten-year treaty, superseding the Anglo-Japanese Alliance, the signatory powers agreed:

(a) to respect one another's rights in the regions of the Pacific in respect to their "insular possessions and insular dominions";
(b) to meet in joint conference "for consideration and adjustment" of any "controversy arising out of any Pacific question and involving their said rights which is not satisfactorily settled by diplomacy"; and
(c) if the rights of the contracting parties "are threatened by the aggressive action of any other Power" to "communicate with one another fully. . . ."

The early signature of the Four-Power Treaty materially advanced the fortunes of the conference. The inclusion of France was one of the moves designed to win that country to acceptance of the inferior naval ratio (1.75 as against 5-5-3 for the great powers) assigned to it by the Hughes plan. By ending the Anglo-Japanese Alliance and substituting the broader pledge of "consultation," the Treaty went far to remove American and Canadian fears of Anglo-Japanese cooperation in some future war. Furthermore, by combining principles of the Root-Takahira notes of 1908 with those of the Bryan treaties of 1914, the United States had been given a renewed pledge against aggression in the Philippines—a fact of consequence, since Japan, now in possession of the Marshall, Mariana, and Caroline Islands, lay athwart direct American approaches to Manila.

The Status Quo in Pacific Fortifications

Japan's assent to the Four-Power Treaty did not mean that Tokyo was prepared to accept the Hughes program of naval reduction.

Japan regarded the western Pacific as her home waters. Here she proposed to achieve and maintain her own naval supremacy. She found little virtue in the consultative principles of the Four-Power Treaty if these were to function side by side with expanding British and American naval bases at Hongkong, Manila, Guam, and other Pacific islands. Accordingly, Kato, who personified Japanese naval philosophy, suggested that Japan would be more likely to look with favor on the Hughes plan if agreement could be reached on maintenance of the *status quo* in Pacific fortifications and if Japan was permitted to keep the battleship *Mutsu,* which was virtually ready to be launched, and instead scrap the older *Settsu*. On December 15, 1921, the Big Three reached agreement on the non-fortification principle, which later became Article XIX of the Five-Power Naval Treaty (February 5, 1922). The three powers agreed that: "The *status quo* at the time of the signing of the present Treaty, with regard to fortifications and naval bases, shall be maintained" in specific possessions. Specifically, the territories in which new fortifications were prohibited included:

(a) for the United States: the Aleutians, Guam, Pago-Pago, and the Philippines;
(b) for Great Britain: Hongkong and British insular possessions in the Pacific, east of 110 east longitude, excepting islands adjacent to Canada, Australia, and New Zealand;
(c) for Japan: the Kurile Islands, Bonin Islands, Amami-Oshima, the Loochoo (Ryukyu) Islands, Formosa, and the Pescadores.

The Five-Power Naval Treaty

This was the price for Japan's acceptance in principle of the Hughes naval plan. Even then the plan was not wholly acceptable to Britain or Japan. Indeed the plan was whittled down to apply only to capital ships before it could be embodied along with the non-fortification agreement in the Five-Power Naval Treaty noted above. As finally concluded, the Naval Treaty provided for:

(a) a 10-year holiday in capital ship construction;
(b) the scrapping of specified vessels in commission and building (United States, 845,000 tons; Great Britain, 583,000 tons; Japan, 435,000 tons);

(c) limiting the tonnage of capital ships and aircraft carriers to 35,000 and 27,000 respectively, and the caliber of their guns to 16 and 8 inches respectively.

The Treaty was to apply until December 31, 1936, and might be terminated thereafter through two-years' notice by any signatory.

The terms of this epochal treaty are easily stated, but its immediate effect upon the interplay of national policies in the Pacific and the Far East cannot be reduced to simple evaluation. With the exception of Italy, all of the five powers professed their dissatisfaction. Italy's case was unique. Throughout the conference she had been vexingly agreeable, insisting only that she be accorded naval parity with France. France, on the other hand, was piqued not only by this Italian attitude but also by the determined policy of the Big Three to keep France as a third-class naval power. To France, the naval ratio was primarily a matter of national pride, for her policy of security was based on land armaments. Nevertheless, France did not accept the ratio until Hughes had appealed over the heads of the French delegation to Briand in Paris. Likewise, the British, Japanese, and American delegations were far from satisfied. The naval men in particular grumbled that they had given more than they had received.

Granting that the results of the naval conference cannot be measured with mathematical precision, it may nonetheless be conceded that Japan had won tangible and specific advantages. If her sensitive national pride was wounded by the inferior capital ship ratio, her security was greatly increased by the same ratio, by the non-fortification agreement, by her possession of the former German islands in the North Pacific, and by the resulting liberty she enjoyed to pursue her own specific aims in China.

Britain also profited. Although she did forego the right to add to the fortifications of Hongkong and islands in the Central Pacific, she retained full liberty to fortify Singapore, Australia, and New Zealand, which were not likely to be threatened so long as Japan observed the non-fortification clause. In a word, Britain gave up little and received much in return. Her advantage was the more striking because the Far East, although of great importance, was of much less significance in British policy than were the Middle East and Europe.

Did the United States win advantages comparable to those gained by Britain and Japan? Conceding that the conference had made

Japan the naval master of the western Pacific, the arbiter of China's future, and that the United States in terms of naval fortification had agreed to remain east of Pearl Harbor, it would seem that Secretary Hughes had given much in return for a ten-year naval holiday in capital ship construction. But the foregoing discussion by no means gives a complete picture of either the American position in 1922 or of the realities of American public opinion with which Hughes had to deal. As will be seen in subsequent pages, the Five-Power Naval Treaty was not to be regarded as an isolated agreement but as an integral part of a larger settlement embodying the decisions of the concurrent conference on problems of the Pacific and the Far East from which emerged the Nine-Power Open Door Treaty concerning China—a treaty that bound the signatories to respect the traditional principles of American policy in China. Again one must raise the question as to what alternatives Hughes could have proposed to Kato's suggestion for the non-fortification clause. The evidence on this question is reasonably clear. In the first place, it was not Hughes who surrendered the idea of a strong American military and naval base in the Philippines. That surrender had been made in 1905 when Theodore Roosevelt gave his approval to the Taft-Katsura understanding. In the second place, the alternative to the non-fortification clause was an American naval building program that would have blocked any program of naval limitation and thus have made the conference itself unnecessary and futile. Moreover, at the time of the conference, senatorial leaders were convinced that Congress would not vote the appropriations that a large building program would have entailed. This was the view not only of Republicans and Democrats who had favored the League's machinery for peace, but also the "irreconcilables" and the former advocates of the "large policy," including Henry Cabot Lodge. These are the factors that must be weighed in any effort to determine whether Hughes surrendered too much and gained too little.

The Far Eastern Conference

The answer, of course, to the critics who maintained that the United States had not struck a good bargain on naval power in the Pacific was the Nine-Power Open Door Treaty concerning China which emerged from the concurrent conference on Far Eastern questions. This treaty in both its weakness and its strength will be understood best by those who view it as the culmination of nearly a century of American policy in the Far East. That policy had rested essentially on three principles. The first of these was most-favored-nation treatment, to which in 1899 and 1900 had been added the commercial open door and the integrity of China. The resulting composite policy was one of self-interest, not sentiment. Practically, it was vulnerable in the highest degree, because American commercial interests in China were relatively small and because the American people had never shown a willingness to defend by force the open door or the integrity of China. The result was that American policy was never fully implemented. Between 1900 and the end of World War I, the powers had violated the open door and China's integrity whenever they regarded it as advantageous to do so and whenever they were not restrained by their mutual jealousies and fears. American policy had served to retard these encroachments; it did not prevent them.

Traditional Policy Reasserted

In the light of the foregoing historical background, the American delegation had little choice in the course it could pursue. The Conference itself was based on the idea of naval limitation. The Congress and public opinion were opposed to large naval appropriations. Therefore Hughes was limited from the beginning to diplomatic and legal implementation of American principles respecting China. Here, as in the case of the open door notes of 1899, it was the British who made the first positive overtures. Balfour had come to Washington not only with the proposal of a three-power agreement to take the place of the Anglo-Japanese Alliance, but also with a suggested five-power agreement among the United States, Britain, France, Japan, and China. It was designed to insure four principles: (1) the peace of eastern Asia, (2) the independence and territorial integrity of China, (3) equality of commercial opportunity in China, and (4) international co-operation toward China. Using this British suggestion as a starting point, Hughes set about "to give new vigor and reality to the co-ordinated principles of territorial and administrative integrity of China and of the 'open door' or equality of opportunity for all nations in China." He proposed to do this by writing these principles into a multilateral treaty, thus making them for the first time a part of the body of international law. Even here, the obstacles in Hughes' path might well have seemed insurmountable. First, there was Japan's well-publicized claim to a "special position." Second, there was the general confusion in China's domestic politics, in which an "independent" government at Canton under Sun Yat-sen was contesting the claims of the recognized warlord government in Peking. And third, there was the general habit of the powers to give lip service to such ideas as China's integrity while they clung tenaciously to all those special privileges derogatory to China's integrity which they possessed under the so-called unequal treaties. To put it another way, the revolutionary tendencies within China were apt to be as unpopular with the Western powers as they were in official circles in Japan. Adding to Hughes' difficulties was the fact that a chaotic and revolutionary China was represented at Washington by a delegation which, as at Paris in 1919, was demanding a "bill of rights" quashing all the unequal treaties. This would have meant abolition not only of Japan's "special position," but also of the conventional tariff, extraterritoriality, and so forth, enjoyed by all the treaty powers.

The Nine-Power Open Door Treaty

When these obstacles are assessed in their full measure, the extent of America's diplomatic triumph resulting in the Nine-Power Open Door Treaty is more apparent. Here too is revealed the basis for Hughes concessions on Pacific fortifications.

The Nine-Power Treaty was to be so vital to the future of American policy in the Far East that some of its articles must be given in full. The signatory powers (the United States, Great Britain, France, Japan, Italy, Belgium, the Netherlands, Portugal, and China) consented to the following articles:

Article I:

The Contracting Powers, other than China, agree:

(1) To respect the sovereignty, the independence, and the territorial and administrative integrity of China;

(2) To provide the fullest and most unembarrassed opportunity to China to develop and maintain for herself an effective and stable government;

(3) To use their influence for the purpose of effectually establishing and maintaining the principle of equal opportunity for the commerce and industry of all nations throughout the territory of China;

(4) To refrain from taking advantage of conditions in China in order to seek special rights or privileges which would abridge the rights of subjects

or citizens of friendly States, and from countenancing action inimical to the security of such States.

Article II:

Not to enter into any treaty, agreement, arrangement, or understanding either with one another, or, individually or collectively, with any Power or Powers, which would infringe or impair the principles stated in Article I.

Article III:

With a view to applying more effectually the principles of the Open Door or equality of opportunity in China for the trade and industry of all nations, the Contracting Powers, other than China, agree that they will not seek, nor support their respective nationals in seeking:

(a) any arrangement which might purport to establish in favour of their interests any general superiority of rights with respect to commercial or economic development in any designated region of China;

(b) any such monopoly or preference as would deprive the nationals of any other Power of the right of undertaking any legitimate trade or industry in China, or of participating with the Chinese Government, or with any local authority, in any category of public enterprise, or which by reason of its scope, duration or geographical extent is calculated to frustrate the practical application of the principle of equal opportunity.

It is understood that the foregoing stipulations of this Article are not to be so construed as to prohibit the acquisition of such properties or rights as may be necessary to the conduct of a particular commercial, industrial, or financial undertaking or to the encouragement of invention and research.

China undertakes to be guided by the principles stated in the foregoing stipulations of this Article in dealing with applications for economic rights and privileges from Governments and nationals of all foreign countries whether parties to the present Treaty or not.

Other articles bound the signatories: (1) to refrain from supporting their nationals in seeking spheres of influence or "mutually exclusive opportunities in designated parts of Chinese territory"; (2) to respect China's neutrality; (3) to consult fully in circumstances requiring the application of the Treaty. China agreed not to permit discrimination in railroad rates. Powers not signatory to the Treaty were invited to adhere to it.[12]

The Nine-Power Treaty was, beyond any question, a tangible advance over any previous enunciation of American policy in the Far East. By it, historic American principles had been made a part of international law binding upon each of the signatories. However,

[12] Clause 4 of Article I amounted in substance to the secret protocol attached to the Lansing-Ishii notes of 1917.

the Treaty was marked by striking limitations. Far from being a renunciation of "rights" acquired in the past, it was merely a contract limiting future action. Furthermore, the Treaty was wholly lacking in sanctions other than the good faith of the signatory powers. Finally, it was a treaty concerned primarily with principles upon whose definition the powers had more often than not been in disagreement. If, on the basis of these limitations, American policy in 1922 as represented by the Nine-Power Treaty is to stand condemned, the question must still be raised: Was there an alternative policy which the American people would have accepted at that time? To this question, the answer supplied by available evidence is an emphatic "No."

Tariffs, Extraterritoriality, Shantung

Several other major Chinese problems were tackled before the Far Eastern Conference adjourned. The first of these was China's demand for tariff autonomy. To meet this the conference agreed to the Nine-Power Treaty on the Chinese Tariff (February 6, 1922), which, although not granting tariff autonomy, did permit substantial increases in the rates and thus in China's revenue. The basic, though unpublicized, reasons why the conference was not prepared to concede more included a number of considerations: (1) the opposition of foreign commercial interests to increased tariffs, and (2) the conviction that increased revenues would be squandered by numerous warlord factions in fruitless civil wars. However, the Treaty, in setting up a commission for study and reform of the Chinese tariff administration, kept the door open for further concessions if and when China's government showed itself capable of assuming fuller responsibility.

On the vexing question of extraterritoriality, which the Chinese hoped to abolish, the conference resorted to a resolution setting up a commission that was to study the entire complex problem and to prepare the way for abolition in the future. This was far from being what Chinese spokesmen wanted, but it was all that any of the foreign powers at this time were willing to concede. Indeed, for many years after the Washington Conference even the United States remained unwilling to submit its nationals to the mercies of China's system of courts and police. Other resolutions adopted by the conference abolished foreign post offices in China, except those in the leased territories, with, however, the proviso that China must set up a satisfactory postal service. The powers also restricted by resolution foreign-owned and operated radio stations on Chinese soil.

Although the Washington Conference itself did not attempt to deal with the Shantung question, Hughes and Balfour were responsible for bringing the Chinese and Japanese together and for breaking the deadlock which threatened to result. At Washington the Chinese were still demanding, as they had at Paris three years earlier, full and direct restoration of the former German rights. The Japanese were equally emphatic. They were prepared to restore the leasehold, but only under the terms of the 1915 and 1918 treaties and through direct negotiations with China.[13] The good offices of Hughes and Balfour finally resulted in Sino-Japanese discussions extending through thirty-six meetings with British and American "observers." Even then the negotiations were only sustained through persistent and powerful British and American pressure at Peking and Tokyo. By the Sino-Japanese treaty which resulted (February 4, 1922), Kiaochow was returned to China. However, Japan would retain control of the Tsinan-Tsingato Railway for fifteen years, during the life of a loan through which China purchased the road. The settlement was obviously a compromise. Japan retained temporarily a considerable measure of economic and political control while China had won something more than the mere principle of her claim.

China made less headway in her efforts to abrogate the Manchurian clauses of the treaties and notes of May, 1915. None of the great powers at Washington was prepared to concede officially the Chinese claim that these treaties were invalid because they had been forced upon China. Such a concession might well have opened the way for attack on many other treaties. Moreover, invalidation of the Japanese sphere in South Manchuria would have undermined the foundations of the British and French spheres, to say nothing of the Russians in North Manchuria, who were not represented at Washington. Thus China's case against Japan in Manchuria was doomed from the start. Japan, it is true, made a gesture of concessions, but it was largely meaningless, since she had already conceded two of the points mentioned. She opened her railway options to the joint activities of the consortium (this she had already done in 1920 under careful limitations); she withdrew Group V of the Twenty-one Demands,

---

[13] The principle was one on which the Japanese had insisted ever since the Shimonoseki negotiations of 1895.

which she had previously "postponed" because of the unanimous opposition of the powers; and she denied any intention to impose political, military, or financial advisers upon the Chinese government in South Manchuria.

The position of the United States relative to this diplomatic battle between China and the sphere-holding powers was, however, given explicit statement by Secretary Hughes. He stated, first, that under most-favored-nation treatment, the United States would claim from China all benefits enjoyed by Japan under the 1915 treaties; and second, he carefully reserved any American expression as to the validity of those treaties.

Before the conference adjourned, the United States also appeared in what may seem as the curious role of defender of Russia's territorial integrity in eastern Siberia. At this time, it will be recalled, Russia was not recognized by the United States, nor had she been invited to the conference. Nevertheless, repercussions of the Siberian Intervention of 1918 still possessed weight as Hughes won from the Japanese (January 23, 1922) another assurance that their military forces would soon be withdrawn from Siberia and North Sakhalin. It appears, however, that pressure from within Japan rather than the diplomacy of Hughes was responsible for Japan's subsequent withdrawal from Soviet territory.

Finally, but not as a part of the conference, the United States raised again with Japan its claims concerning the island of Yap. These negotiations brought forth an American-Japanese treaty, February 11, 1922, whereby the United States recognized the Japanese mandate over the former German islands in the North Pacific, and Japan in return granted to American citizens residential, cable, and radio rights on Yap.

In Conclusion

When Harding convoked the Washington Conference, much was expected of its labors. When the conference adjourned, much had been accomplished. Outstanding were major steps in the limitation of naval armament and in writing American principles *vis-à-vis* China into the treaty structure of international law. These were positive contributions, but they should be assessed in the light of conditions as they existed at the time of the conference. These conditions, political, economic, and diplomatic, did not suggest that the conference possessed a clear mandate either for disarmament or for the scrapping of historic policies of nationalism and imperialism in Asia or elsewhere. It is true that the conference met at a time when a war-weary world, disillusioned by Versailles, was demanding some tangible evidence that the war had not been fought in vain. On the other hand, there was ill-disguised and world-wide skepticism of the League of Nations as an instrument for peace, particularly after its repudiation by the United States Senate. Harding was not wide of the mark when in 1920 he estimated American opinion by saying:

> America's present need is not for heroics but healing; not nostrums but normalcy; not revolution but restoration; . . . not surgery but serenity.[14]

There was an irresistible, if unseen, pressure to return to ways which men thought of as tried and tested. Men wanted a better world but also, illogically, a world that had returned to "normalcy." Naturally this jumbled post-war philosophy was reflected in the Washington Conference. While the powers were prepared to make limited concessions toward a naval holiday in capital ships, and toward the principle of consultation in future disputes arising in the Pacific and the Far East, at the same time they were not prepared to extend naval limitation to other categories of ships or to land armies, nor were they prepared to surrender in China their special rights resting on nearly a century of unequal treaties. A world that wanted peace still placed its trust in nationalism and special alliances rather than in disarmament and collective security. In China, the conference did little more than freeze the *status quo*.

Finally, it must be concluded that America's policy from Versailles to Washington is a curious commentary on the logic of facts. In 1919-1920 the United States had turned its back on the League of Nations and the principles of collective security. It was thereupon thrown back on its *own* national military and naval power for the implementation of its policies, whether in Europe or in Asia. Then at Washington in 1922 the United States effectively curbed the offensive arm of its navy by capital ship limitation. By making Japan supreme in the western Pacific, the fate of American policy in China was placed in Japanese hands. True, there was the Nine-Power Open Door Treaty, but this was a sad substitute, completely lacking in sanctions, for the system of collective security that might well have emerged had the United States assumed leadership in the League of

---

[14] F. L. Allen, *Only Yesterday* (New York, 1931), 41-42.

Nations. The fact that America had not assumed this leadership cannot be attributed solely to Lodge and the "irreconcilables." Rather it must be explained by the weight of historic traditions. It was natural that policies that in the nineteenth century had served this country well should be surrendered reluctantly as a new world called for new policies.[15]

For Further Reading

Falk, E. A., *Togo and the Rise of Japanese Sea Power* (New York, 1936). By an American naval officer.

———, *From Perry to Pearl Harbor* (New York, 1943).

Kennan, George F., *American Diplomacy, 1900-1950* (Chicago, 1951).

Potter, E. B., ed., *The United States and World Sea Power* (New York, 1955).

[15] As an aftermath to the conference, the Lansing-Ishii Agreement was cancelled on January 2, 1923. For the most incisive study of American politics in the Washington Conference, see John Chalmers Vinson, *The Parchment Peace: the United States Senate and the Washington Conference* (Athens, Ga., 1955). Vinson found that the Senate was not more internationally minded than during the debate on the Versailles Treaty. The Senate approved the Washington treaties because they were constructed with the prejudices of the Senate in mind. The Four-Power Treaty and the Senate reservation thereto are the keys to Senate policy. "The United States," said the reservation, "understands . . . there is no commitment to armed force, no alliance, no obligation to join in any defense." Vinson raises the question: What useful purpose could be served by a document so amended? See also J. Chal Vinson, "The Annulment of the Lansing-Ishii Agreement," *Pacific Historical Review,* XXVII (1958), 57-69.

27

1900–1924

Japanese Immigration

JUST as World War I bequeathed a legacy of international rivalry and suspicion touching every major area of the globe, so also it bequeathed national domestic problems of the most serious import. These problems, though domestic in origin, were international in their immediate and ultimate consequences.

The war that was to have made the world "safe for democracy" created instead an intense nationalism. This new nationalism became a popular hysteria. Responsible American officials warned the public that "ten million people were ready to leave Europe" for America. Bills were proposed to stop immigration entirely since the influx would lower American standards of living and demoralize American character. Moreover, the impression grew that the new immigrant tide would bring to America the contagion of European revolution, in particular the radicalism of the Bolshevist Russian revolutions. Indeed, the immigrant scare assumed a vast variety of forms. Sectarian groups saw in immigration a possible "menace to prohibition and even Protestantism." These were signs of America's post-war and "post-frontier search for a stable and an indigenous civilization." The war had served to emphasize that the era of free land was now past and that the nation's new task was to produce "a civilization peculiar to the American race and suited to a static society."[1] This attitude was a challenge to the historic concept that America was the "asylum for the oppressed." The high peak of the earlier philosophy of free immigration had been reached in the Seward-Burlingame negotiations of 1868. These had imbedded in the solemn words of a treaty the dictum that "man has an inalienable

[1] Rodman W. Paul, *The Abrogation of the Gentlemen's Agreement* (Cambridge, 1936), 3.

right to change his home and his allegiance." But the "march of events" had overtaken and passed Seward and Burlingame and their treaty.

Beginnings of Exclusion

The story of the exclusion of Chinese laborers from the United States and its possessions and of the barring of Chinese nationals from American citizenship has already been told. This principle of Chinese exclusion had seemingly been made final by 1904, when Congress re-enacted the statutes covering Chinese immigration. The occasion was the expiration of the Sino-American treaty of 1894. The result was an outraged Chinese opinion which expressed itself in 1905 in a systematic boycott of American business in China.[2] While the Chinese phase was thus disposed of, the specter of Oriental immigration had raised its head in another quarter.

By 1900 there were 61,111 resident Japanese in the Hawaiian Islands, about 40 per cent of the total population. Most of these had come under the terms of a Hawaiian-Japanese cheap labor convention signed in 1896 at the instigation of Hawaiian sugar growers. The political implications of this fast-growing Japanese population were not lost on those Americans who had now become interested in annexation of the islands. In March, 1897, the revolutionary Hawaiian government, dominated by Americans, created a crisis when it refused entry to 1,174 Japanese immigrants. Japan protested and sent a warship to Honolulu, where its actions were watched by three American warships. Under American mediation, Japan's claims against the Hawaiian government were soon settled, but the importance of the incident was its effect in hastening American annexation of the islands, August 12, 1898.[3]

The Japanese in the United States

The disposal of Chinese immigration by the Congressional enactments of 1904, and the crisis in Japanese-Hawaiian relations in

---

[2] C. F. Remer, *A Study of Chinese Boycotts* (Baltimore, 1933), 29-39.

[3] R. L. Buell, *Japanese Immigration* (Boston, 1924), 286; A. W. Griswold, *Far Eastern Policy of the United States* (New York, 1938), 339-344; T. A. Bailey, "Japan's Protest Against the Annexation of Hawaii," *Journal of Modern History,* III (1931), 46-61. Hilary Conroy, *The Japanese Frontier in Hawaii, 1868-1898* (Berkeley and Los Angeles, 1953), 140-141.

1897-1898, coincided with the rise of a new problem—the Japanese immigrant in the United States. Until 1900 there were virtually no Japanese in the United States. The census reports for 1870 listed 55 Japanese; for 1880, 148; for 1890, 2,039; but for 1900, 24,326. The tendency of Japanese immigration to the United States to show marked increases had been noted as early as 1892, when United States immigration officers protested the wholesale importation of Japanese laborers to the Pacific Coast. As a result of this protest the Japanese government took steps to discourage the movement. Then, in the American-Japanese commercial treaty of 1894, the United States stipulated that while in matters "of residence and travel" Japanese were to enjoy all the privileges of the most favored nation, nevertheless, such rights were in no way to

> . . . affect the laws, ordinances and regulations with regard to trade, the immigration of laborers, police and public security which are in force or which may hereafter be enacted in either of the two countries.[4]

Anti-Japanese agitation first took shape in San Francisco in 1900 when public meetings demanded application to the Japanese of the Chinese exclusion laws. Responsive to this agitation, Japan announced her intention to suspend entirely "for the present" emigration of her laborers to both the United States and Canada. However, Japanese continued to enter the United States from Hawaii. Renewed agitations led by the Japanese and Korean Exclusion League occurred in San Francisco early in 1905. Discriminatory legislation was introduced in Congress and, when these bills failed due to the opposition of the executive, the San Francisco School Board, in October, 1906, ordered by resolution all Japanese children to attend the Oriental school located in Chinatown. Meanwhile, the California legislature had been joined by the legislatures of Nevada, Idaho, and Montana in petitioning Congress to stop Japanese immigration. Japan countered by restricting and then temporarily suspending emigration to Hawaii, but by this time the San Francisco School Board was on record

> . . . for the higher end that our children should not be placed in any position where their youthful impression may be affected by association with pupils of the Mongolian race.[5]

---

[4] W. M. Malloy, *Treaties* (2 vols., Washington, 1910), I, 1030.

[5] T. A. Bailey, *Theodore Roosevelt and the Japanese-American Crises* (Stanford University, 1934), 14.

A California senator urging the exclusion of Asiatics pictured the dangers to American morals and character arising from "criminality, degeneracy, and Orientalism."

As the immigration crisis in California continued to mount, President Roosevelt sought to adjust it to the general picture of American interests in the Pacific and the Far East, where he was fast becoming the key personality in the hoped-for peace conference between Japan and Russia.

> After considerable experimentation he [Roosevelt] rated peace, amicable trade relations, the security of American territory in the Pacific and the effective restriction of oriental immigration all ahead of the territorial integrity of China in the category of American national interest.[6]

In essence, Roosevelt concluded: (1) that Philippine security depended on an understanding with Japan (Taft-Katsura conversations of 1905); (2) that discrimination against a vigorous Oriental state would destroy commercial most-favored-nation treatment for American commerce in the Far East and render illusory the open door in China and the security of the Philippines. These broader aspects of statecraft were, however, receiving little attention in San Francisco and on the Pacific Coast, where the Japanese immigrant had fallen heir to the charges which thirty years earlier had been heaped upon the Chinese immigrant. The Japanese were said to be immoral and vicious, and as children in the schools they were too old to associate with American youth. The charges were either unfounded or deliberately exaggerated.

On October 25, 1906, basing her action on the treaty of 1894, Japan formally protested that the segregation of Japanese children because of nationality was "an act of discrimination carrying with it a stigma and odium which it is impossible to overlook." The President sent Victor H. Metcalf, Secretary of Commerce and Labor, to the Pacific Coast to investigate. The Secretary of the Navy was instructed to submit comparative data on American and Japanese naval strength. The President assured the Japanese Ambassador privately that the question would be placed before Congress; and this was done in the message of December 4, 1906. The message bristled with Rooseveltian vigor. It touched upon the progress and growing power of Japan, upon the historic friendship between the two nations, and upon the School Board resolution as a "wicked absurdity."

---

6 Griswold, *Far Eastern Policy of the United States,* 349.

It ended with a plea that Japanese be admitted to citizenship by naturalization, and threatened use of the army to protect Japanese in their treaty rights. While the message was received with enthusiasm in Japan and with favor in eastern United States, it brought forth fresh bursts of wrath from California, where, after all, a settlement would eventually have to be reached. Accordingly, the President turned to the softer methods of compromise. He tried but failed in securing Japan's assent to a treaty mutually excluding the laborers of both countries. With the San Francisco Board of Education, which he had invited to Washington, he was more successful. In return for Roosevelt's promise to end the immigration of Japanese laborers, the Board agreed to rescind the obnoxious resolution.

The problem before the President was now twofold. The first was to stop the migration of Japanese laborers from Hawaii to the mainland of the United States. This was accomplished by amendment to the immigration law of 1907. The more difficult problem remained —the stoppage of direct labor migration from Japan to continental United States.

The Gentlemen's Agreement, 1907-1908

A solution was found in the proposal of Secretary Elihu Root that Japan herself impose the restrictions desired by the United States. Accordingly, on February 24, 1907, the Japanese government indicated its intention to continue the policy then in force of not issuing passports to the continental United States to any laborers except those

> who, in coming to the Continent, seek to resume a formerly acquired domicile, to join a parent, wife, or children residing there, or to assume active control of an already possessed interest in a farming enterprise in this country.[7]

Details of this Gentlemen's Agreement were not complete until February, 1908, and it was not until the following October that departures of Japanese immigrants exceeded arrivals. Meanwhile, anti-Japanese agitation in California had continued. All in all, it was

---

[7] *Annual Report of the Commissioner-General of Immigration, 1908* (Washington, 1908), 125-126. The Gentlemen's Agreement is not contained in a single document. Its text, on the contrary, consists of correspondence exchanged between the United States and Japan during 1907 and 1908. A résumé is printed in United States, *Foreign Relations, 1924*, II, 339-369. It was published in 1939.

patent that no matter how successful the Gentlemen's Agreement might be in curbing the influx of Japanese, it was not regarded as a wholly acceptable answer to the problem.

The Gentlemen's Agreement, however, was far more than an important executive agreement whereby Japanese immigration was to be controlled. In the mind of the President it was a necessary part of the complex of delicate forces supporting American Far Eastern policy. If there were to be renewed outbursts of anti-Japanese violence on the Pacific Coast, new campaigns for discriminatory legislation, and eventual abrogation of the Agreement, then the whole framework of American Far Eastern policy would again be in jeopardy. There would be no security for the American flag in the Philippines or for the open door in China.

The Pacific Coast Wants Security Too

Vocal elements in Pacific Coast politics did not find the Gentlemen's Agreement to their liking. They continued to find in the pres ence of Japanese communities a threat to American institutions and ways of life. Although the Agreement did provide effective control of the flow of Japanese immigrants, it was found wanting in other respects. From the inception of the Agreement until 1924, total entries of Japanese into the United States were 120,317; departures, 111,636. For the United States and Hawaii, the figures were: arrivals, 171,584; departures, 155,488. This was a net increase of only 16,096, or 7,415 for Hawaii and 8,681 for continental United States. Nevertheless, although immigration was controlled, the Japanese population in the United States multiplied with what was considered alarming rapidity. From 24,326 in 1900, it rose to 72,157 in 1910, and to 111,010 in 1920. Those who viewed with alarm could assert that whereas between 1910 and 1920 the total population of the United States increased 4.9 per cent, that of the Japanese had increased 53.8 per cent. Related figures appeared equally arresting. The excess of Japanese births over deaths in California in 1911 was 523; in 1921 it was 4,379. Actually, these figures taken by themselves were misleading. They represented temporary trends due in part to the fact that virtually all Japanese women in the United States were of child-bearing age.

Renewed troubles were not long in appearing. When the California Commissioner of Labor issued in 1910 a favorable report on the contribution of the Japanese to California agriculture, the document was suppressed as not representing "the wishes of the people of this commonwealth." However, when in 1911 the American-Japanese treaty (1894) of navigation and commerce was renewed, the United States conceded to Japan's wishes by amending the clause that had given the United States the right to legislate the exclusion of Japanese labor. Secretary Knox regarded this as merely an appropriate gesture to Japanese pride, since Congress had the inherent right to control immigration whether or not the right was expressed in treaty provisions.

The Alien Land Laws

California's legislature returned to the anti-Japanese campaign in 1913, when it passed a law prohibiting land ownership by aliens ineligible for citizenship, and limiting leaseholds to three years. Although the Japanese were not mentioned by name, and although the law carefully reserved all rights held by treaty, it was no secret that the legislators had the Japanese in mind. The attack was legally sound, for the American-Japanese treaty of 1911 did not confer on Japanese the right to ownership of land. The Department of State therefore maintained the position that California's act had not violated the treaty. On the other hand, the Department was unable to meet with the same firmness the Japanese charge that the state law was discriminatory. Then, in 1920, California went further by denying to aliens ineligible for citizenship the right to lease land. The passage of both laws was opposed by the government of the United States on grounds of policy, but without success. In general the federal government held to the view that the passage of such laws by the states was "unwise, impolitic and dangerous." Likewise, from Ambassador Roland S. Morris in Japan came a warning to the State Department in January, 1921, that there "can be no reasonable doubt of the deep feeling of resentment which has been aroused among the people of Japan by the California legislation." He added, "Racial discrimination will seriously threaten our country's best interests on the Pacific and in the Far East." To meet the situation, Morris and Baron Shidehara for Japan drafted in 1921 a treaty revising the Gentlemen's Agreement. This would have prevented the immigration of wives, children, or parents of resident Japanese laborers and would have conferred on the United States the power of enforcement through deportation. In return for this effective exclusion the United States was to guarantee resident Japanese from discriminatory treatment. They would enjoy all rights possessed by other foreigners save naturalization. These proposals, however, were swamped by the rising tide of anti-immigration sentiment which followed the World War. The crusade for alien land laws was no longer confined to the Pacific Coast. Fourteen states reaching from Montana to Delaware to Louisiana and Washington enacted legislation on the California model between 1921 and 1925. If there still remained any doubts as to the legality, the constitutionality, of these proceedings, that doubt was removed in 1922 when the United States Supreme Court ruled in the famous Ozawa Case that Japanese were ineligible for citizenship by naturalization. In 1923 the principles of this case were held to apply to all Orientals. Lastly, the constitutionality of the California alien land laws was upheld.

Another factor creating sentiment against the Japanese was the institution known as the "picture brides." The great bulk of Japanese immigrants who entered the United States before 1907 were men. After 1907, however, passports were issued to Japanese women married in Japan by proxy through an exchange of photographs to Japanese men who were already in the United States. The institution was perfectly proper according to Japanese custom, and if the Japanese male population was to remain in the United States it was desirable that this population should acquire wives. The fact that the Chinese in the nineteenth century had not been accompanied by their women had opened the way for charges of immorality against the Chinese. But whatever the merits of the "picture brides" as a social institution may have been, the arrival of these women on the Pacific Coast (legally under the Gentlemen's Agreement) was directly responsible for the rapid increase in the Japanese population between 1900 and 1921.

The Emergence of a National Policy

As World War I came to an end there was a public demand in the United States for more rigid controls on all immigration. The first step was the law of 1921, by which Congress limited the admission of aliens of each nationality to 3 per cent "of the number of foreign-born persons of such nationality resident in the United States" in 1910. This was the Emergency Quota Act of May 19, 1921, renewed in 1922 for two years. In its revised form the Act reduced admissions to 2 per cent based on the foreign-born resident population of each nationality in 1890. The particular years selected for determining the percentage of admissions favored the immigrant quotas from northern and western Europe as against southern and eastern Europe.

In December, 1923, the Congress undertook the drafting of a permanent immigration law to replace these hurried statutes. It was proposed that the new law be based on the quota system of the recent legislation, but, in addition, the new bills in both House and Senate denied entry to aliens who were ineligible for citizenship. The Japanese, although not named, were the obvious target. Secretary Hughes argued with the House Committee on Immigration that although Japanese immigration should be effectively controlled, the method proposed was inadvisable. In his opinion, it was bad policy to offend Japan unnecessarily when, by assigning Japan a quota, not more than 250 would be admitted annually. Furthermore, the proposed legislation would, the Secretary felt, "largely undo the work of the Washington Conference." Nevertheless, in March, 1924, the House Committee recommended legislation excluding all aliens who were ineligible for citizenship. The bill passed the House on April 12, by the overwhelming majority of 326 to 71.

To straighten the case which he proposed to present to the Congress, Hughes had prevailed on Japanese Ambassador Hanihara to give the Secretary a memorandum clarifying Japan's understanding of the Gentlemen's Agreement. This was done in a Japanese note, prepared with the collaboration of the State Department and given to Hughes on April 10. The note reviewed the history of the Agreement, defined Japan's objections to legislation embodying exclusion, and, in conclusion, "truthfully but most ill-advisedly" referred to "the grave consequences which the enactment of the measure [exclusion clause] retaining that particular provision would inevitably bring upon the otherwise happy and mutually advantageous relations between our two countries." Hughes disliked the phrase "grave consequences," for there were few stronger phrases in diplomatic language, but he regarded the Japanese analysis of the Gentlemen's Agreement as excellent, and so sent the note to Congress.

The Senate was considering rather favorably Hughes' suggestion that the Gentlemen's Agreement be recognized and that Japan be omitted from any exclusion clause, when, on April 14, the Hanihara letter was attacked. It was described as "impertinent," as not to be "tolerated" by even a fourth-class power, and as a "veiled threat." The Hughes compromise was voted down, and on April 16 the Senate followed the House by voting 71 to 4 to exclude aliens who were ineligible for citizenship. Last-minute efforts of President Coolidge to delay application to Japan of the exclusion clause in the hope that a new treaty might be negotiated also failed, and on May 15 the immigration bill emerging from conference was passed by House and Senate, the votes being 308 to 62 and 69 to 9. It was to become effective July 1, 1924. The President in signing the bill on May 26 announced that had the exclusion clause not been an integral part of the larger bill, he would have vetoed it on the ground that the method adopted by Congress in securing Japanese exclusion was "unnecessary and deplorable at this time."

With passage of the new immigration bill, including the exclusion clause, into law the United States had entered upon a new phase in its Far Eastern policy. The principle of exclusion, first applied to the Chinese, a weak power, had now been extended to Japan, a proud, sensitive, and powerful state. Only two years previously, at the Washington Conference, American policy had been based on the assumption that this country's interests in the Far East could best be preserved by the limitation of naval armaments and by multilateral treaty commitments (without armed sanctions) to preserve the American open door in China and American sovereignty in the Philippines. It would now remain for the "march of events" to determine whether the new immigration policy adopted by Congress would serve to strengthen or to weaken the foundations of that larger policy.

Immediate reactions to the abrogation of the Gentlemen's Agreement were more pronounced in Japan than in the United States. Japan's official protest was a mild reflection of bitter outbursts in the Japanese press and of deep resentment in the Japanese popular mind. In the United States reactions were varied because the issues involved were more complex. Public opinion throughout the country, though favoring rigid control of Japanese immigration, does not appear to have favored the method used by Congress. Naturally this view was more pronounced in the East than on the Pacific Coast. The Senate, however, was not guided by the general flavor of public opinion, but rather by known public reactions to specific domestic issues. The immigration debate was largely controlled by concurrent domestic reactions that might be expected from "the Southern vote in its relation to the Dyer anti-lynching bill, the issue of Congressional prerogative, the questions of the senatorial investigations and of party loyalty, the need of thinking of the Pacific Coast's presidential vote, to say nothing of the Pacific Coast's racial future." Undoubtedly many Americans believed, as did *The Cincinnati Enquirer,* that "the crux of this matter is that the United States, like Canada and Australia, must be kept a white man's country." An heroic step, so it was thought, had been taken, not in the implemention of race prejudice but in "producing a civilization peculiar to the American race and suited to a static society." After 1924, influential American groups, business and professional, advocated revision which would give Japan and China a quota. The move was halted by the Manchurian crisis, 1931. During World War II, with the intent of protecting the national security, the United States carried out in 1942 the relocation to the interior from the Pacific Coast of all persons of Japanese extraction. Chinese exclusion was repealed in 1943 and Indian exclusion in 1946. A quota of 105 was applied to the Chinese. Japanese exclusion was repealed in 1952. All aliens advocating communism and/or totalitarianism were excluded by the Internal Security Act, 1950.

For Further Reading

Adams, Romanzo, *The Japanese in Hawaii* (New York, 1924). A brief but thorough analysis of the Japanese in Hawaii in 1924.

Lind, Andrew W., *Hawaii's Japanese* (Princeton, 1946). A sociological study of the Japanese in Hawaii.

McKenzie, R. D., *Oriental Exclusion* (Chicago, 1928). Presents an able analysis of the working of the 1924 law.

Mears, E. G., *Resident Orientals on the American Pacific Coast* (Chicago, 1928). Surveys legal and other relationships of the white population and the Orientals.

Shen Tso-chien, *What "Chinese Exclusion" Really Means* (New York, 1942).

Willcox, Walter F., ed., *International Migrations* (2 vols., New York, 1929-1931).

Young, Charles H., Helen R. Y. Reid, and W. A. Carrothers, *The Japanese Canadians* (Toronto, 1938).

28

Japan: 1918–1931

The Failure of Party Government

In the years 1918-1919, as a world war gave place to peace, a new great power had appeared in Eastern Asia. Japan had been moving toward this position of influence for many years, but it was only with the coming of peace that her new status could be appraised and her aspirations more clearly defined. In international affairs Japan's intentions were revealed at the Versailles Conference and at the Washington Conference (see Chapters 24 and 26); but in domestic affairs, particularly in matters of politics and social evolution, Japan's future course was unpredictable. It is true that during the war her alignment with the Allied and Associated Powers had popularized for the Japanese public the Wilsonian democratic program. Furthermore, industrialization had created a new Japanese society foreshadowing a new political leadership which might move toward a more modern, popular, and perhaps democratic government. Japanese literature of the war years had already discarded its sordid naturalism for concepts of idealism. In addition, the *Genro,* the core of the old oligarchy, was all but gone, and no successors of comparable stature had appeared to fill the seats of the mighty. Yamagata, who died in 1922, and Matsukata, who died in 1924, were old men. Saionji, the only remaining *Genro,* was liberally inclined and sympathetic to party government. Consequently, the downfall of the ministry of the militarist Terauchi in 1918 and the selection of Hara, a commoner and president of the *Seiyukai,* to head the government was hailed by progressives as the dawn of a new political era. The stage was seemingly set for the end of rule by oligarchy and for at least the beginnings of a more liberal interpretation of government under the constitution.

Japan's Economy, 1918-1930

What did happen in Japan in the post-war years was influenced most immediately by the extraordinary economic changes which the war had brought about. During World War I Japanese industry and trade experienced an unprecedented boom. Neutral countries of the East turned to Japan for manufactures formerly provided by Europe, and the Japanese merchant marine carried an increasing share of world trade. Between 1913 and 1918 Japanese cotton goods exports, to cite one example, increased 185 per cent from 412 million to 1,174 million linear yards. The Japanese merchant fleet increased from 1,577,000 gross tons in 1914 to 2,840,000 in 1919. By the end of 1919 Japan's foreign assets exceeded her outstanding debts by 1,300 million yen. Six years earlier Japan had been a debtor by approximately the same vast sum. These fantastic gains were accompanied in Japan by expanded bank credit, price inflation, soaring profits, and wild speculation. Allowing for the fictitious nature of much of this prosperity, Japan's productive capacity was increased greatly in the war years but was not accompanied by a corresponding rise in the standard of living. The resulting social unrest due to the rising cost of living expressed itself in the rice riots of 1918.

With the coming of peace, Japan, like other states, met the world-wide economic crisis of 1920 with deflation and readjustment. During the succeeding decade she was involved increasingly in finding economic outlets for her vastly increasing population. Though she held and even extended her industrial gains of the war period, she achieved at best a very meager progress toward the major goal. Indeed, instability was the most general characteristic of Japan's economic history from 1920 to 1930. Agricultural prices (rice and silk) fluctuated widely with eventual major declines while the farmer's operating expenses and his cost of living showed no proportional decline. There were also exchange and recurrent banking disorders associated with inflated capital values and high operating costs. The failure to stabilize prices, costs, and exchange rates and to liquidate wartime values resulted in the great bank panic of 1927. The reduction in the number of banks and industrial concerns which resulted tended to concentrate economic control further in the hands of the *Zaibatsu*. These great family combines grew enormously in size and power during the 1920's. This development of concentrated power in finance and industry was rational in a technical sense, but its social and political implications were equally important. It promoted inequality of income and perpetuated in modern Japanese industry concepts of status and authoritarianism at variance with ideals of political and social democracy. This circumstance was to have a direct bearing on the political trends of the period.[1]

The Era of Party Cabinets

Thus as Japan entered upon the decade of the 1920's she was involved in economic problems and readjustments of the utmost complexity, while at the same time she took the unprecedented step of naming a commoner and party politician to head the government. On the political side Japan was about to experiment with party and semi-party cabinets. Between 1918 and 1932 twelve cabinets guided Japan's destiny. Their average life was little more than one year. Summarized, these cabinets, with the year in which they took office, included:

Year	*Prime Minister*	*Party affiliation*
1918	Hara Takashi	Seiyukai cabinet
1921	Viscount Takahashi Korekiyo	Seiyukai cabinet
1922	Admiral Kato Tomosaburo	non-party cabinet
1923	Admiral Count Yamamoto Gombei	non-party cabinet
1924	Viscount Kiyoura Keigo	non-party Peers cabinet
1924	Viscount Kato Takaakiro	Kenseikai cabinet
1925	Viscount Kato Takaakiro	Kenseikai cabinet
1926	Baron Wakatsuki Reijiro	Kenseikai cabinet
1927	General Baron Tanaka Giichi	Seiyukai cabinet
1929	Hamaguchi Osachi (Yuko)	Minseito cabinet
1931	Baron Wakatsuki Reijiro	Minseito cabinet
1931	Inukai Tsuyoshi	Seiyukai cabinet

This era of party cabinets did not mean a complete break with Japan's past or the unqualified achievement of responsible government. The military service ministries remained beyond party control. In addition, the unstable character of the parties themselves was an ever-present threat to the very principle of party government. For

[1] Japan's economy in these years is treated ably by W. W. Lockwood, *The Economic Development of Japan* (Princeton, 1954), 38-64.

example, the *Seiyukai* encouraged rather than opposed appointment of the Kato non-party ministry of 1922. If the *Seiyukai* could not continue in office itself, the party preferred that power remain with the *Genro* rather than pass to another party. In other words, the *Seiyukai* in 1922 wanted party government only if it was *Seiyukai* government.[2] This lack of dedication by the parties to the principle of automatic party cabinets was an immediate and a continuing obstacle to achievement of free party government and, in the end, was to prove fatal to the parties themselves. At the same time there was in the post-war decade a marked, if temporary, upsurge of political party power due not only to the passing of the *Genro* or to the fact that the parties had long since learned to trim their sails to bureaucratic winds, but also to the appearance in post-war Japan of a popular movement set in motion by the great economic and social changes of the war.

THE HARA GOVERNMENT, 1918-1921

When the surviving *Genro* called Hara Takashi, a commoner, to form Japan's first party government in 1918, there was much to support the claim of the party men and the progressives that a new era had dawned. Hara was one of the ablest politicians Japan has produced.[3] He had entered political life in 1900 under the patronage of Ito. Like Saionji, he had shown an early interest in the liberal movement, had worked in the Foreign Office, had become editor of the great daily, the *Osaka Mainichi,* was a member of the first Saionji cabinet, and became president of the *Seiyukai* in 1913. Nevertheless, Hara's party cabinet of 1918, though described by the press as "popular," was composed mostly of bureaucrats who had been accepted into the party, and included, as Minister of War, General Tanaka Giichi, a protégé of Yamagata. Until Hara's assassination in 1921, this cabinet was a conspicuous administrative success. In matters of policy, however, there was little on which to base the premier's popular title, "the Great Commoner Premier," by which Hara was known. His lasting achievement was that as commoner premier he was able to conciliate the contentious institutional

[2] Robert A. Scalapino, *Democracy and the Party Movement in Prewar Japan* (Berkeley, 1953), 223.

[3] Hara's status as a commoner has been overworked. He was untitled because he had declined to accept a title, but he was from a family of higher social standing than the families of any of the *Genro* except Saionji.

forces of Japanese politics—a rare accomplishment; but he did not advance appreciably the theory or reputation of responsible government. He made few inroads on the power of the bureaucracy and maintained good relations with the militarists through his friendship with Yamagata, but did nothing to build the power or prestige of the House of Representatives, which was allowed to consume its energy in debates on trivia and in interparty violence. He all but ignored his party in policy-making and left the relations between ministry and legislature as unwholesome as he had found them. Though doubtless honest himself, Hara could be blind to the corruption of his party. An extreme conservative, he resisted the embryonic labor movement, social legislation, and all but the most limited extension of the franchise. Yet it is to be remembered that he built the most powerful political party Japan had known. This point was significant because the three transcendental non-party cabinets that followed him, 1922-1924, constituted an interlude demonstrating that the parties, for all their weakness, could not be ignored at this time, and that the reputation of nonparty forces had declined.

The Kato Governments, 1924-1926

The prospect for responsible government had never been so high as it was in 1924, when Kato Takaaki formed the country's first coalition party cabinet from the *Kenseikai,* of which Kato was president, the *Seiyukai,* and the *Kakushin Club.*[4] Kato had a long and distinguished political career. From the presidency of the *Doshikai* in 1913 and later of the *Kenseikai,* he had become foreign minister in the second Okuma cabinet 1914, and had challenged, if unsuccessfully, the *Genro* and the militarists on numerous occasions. By 1924, when he became premier, he was unquestionably Japan's outstanding exponent of responsible government, having long admired British political institutions. Far from being a commoner, he was an aristocrat guided by a philosophy of enlightened conservatism, but he was lacking in qualities of popular magnetism and leadership.

As a reforming government, Kato's coalition made some notable headway. It responded to economic readjustment with reductions in army and navy budgets; it dropped twenty thousand persons from

[4] Excepting, of course, the period of the Okuma-Itagaki cabinet, 1898.

the overcrowded bureaucracy; and it enacted a manhood suffrage law in 1925. Yet it failed to relieve growing economic distress, and, more important in terms of progress toward responsible government, it failed utterly in its program of Peerage reform. This failure was of signal importance. With the passing of the *Genro* the importance of the House of Peers had increased.

When in 1925 Kato formed his second and all-*Kenseikai* ministry, after his coalition had been deserted by the *Seiyukai,* the premier was even less able to advance political or constitutional reform, for he was now more dependent on the bureaucracy and the Peers to maintain his single party government. In these circumstances there was as yet no clear mandate for party government as the custodian of Japan's future. Moreover, the very limited degree of liberalism in the Kato administration was suggested by its passage of a new "Peace Preservation Law," which, though aimed against anarchists and communists, could be used against the press, the universities, and indeed any movement critical of things as they were.

THE TANAKA GOVERNMENT, 1927-1929

The meaning of Kato's failure to deal with reform of the Peerage was soon evident. On Kato's death, January, 1926, Wakatsuki Reijiro, one of his political protégés, succeeded to the premiership and presidency of the *Kenseikai.* The troubles of government mounted as the army attacked the conciliatory policy toward China of the Foreign Minister, Baron Shidehara Kijuro, but it was opposition from the Privy Council, which with the House of Peers was the fortress of the imperial interpretation, that wrecked the Wakatsuki cabinet by the simple expedient of declaring unconstitutional certain emergency measures of the government for dealing with the banking crisis of 1927.

Meanwhile, the *Seiyukai,* thirsting for a return to power and having no leader within its ranks, bestowed its presidency on General Tanaka Giichi. What Tanaka's qualifications were for leadership in a party movement for responsible and representative government would be difficult to say, unless it be that he had been a political colleague of Hara and had thus gained the ill will of many militarists. Tanaka himself was not a military extremist, but as premier his policies of economic nationalism served admirably the cause of irresponsible bureaucracy and militarism. From the beginning Tanaka faced grave problems of political strategy. The first election under the new manhood suffrage law gave the *Seiyukai* 219 seats, the new *Minseito* (*Kenseikai* plus *Seiyuhonto*) 217, the remaining 30 seats being held by independents and representatives of the new labor parties. What followed was legislative scenes of wild uproar. There was the grotesque spectacle of the opposition, presumably the advocates of responsible government, attacking the cabinet for its adherence to the Treaty for the Renunciation of War on the ground that the phrase "in the names of their respective peoples" was an affront to the emperor. With this opposition from the politicians, it was hardly surprising that the Privy Council blocked the treaty until the government gave assurances that this democratic phrase did not apply in the case of Japan.

Even more suggestive of the frail basis of party government was the incident that forced the resignation of the Tanaka cabinet. Tanaka had reversed the Shidehara policy of conciliation toward China for the more positive tactics of Okuma and Hara. This policy, however, backfired. Chinese resentment led to boycotts of Japanese goods. Chang Tso-lin, the Manchurian warlord, whom the Japanese had hoped to use as an ally, found it expedient to abandon his expansive venture into North China and to retreat to Manchuria, where his assassination was plotted and carried out by conspirators of the Japanese Kwantung Army. When, however, Tanaka with the support of his entire cabinet, including the service ministers, sought to punish the conspirators and re-establish discipline in the army, he was blocked by the General Staff and the powerful Military Affairs Bureau. The conspirators were not punished and Tanaka's government resigned. Civilian party government had been forced to retreat before the independent power of the army. Since both government and army favored policies of expansion on the continent, it was evident that the General Staff was more concerned with its power to control the government in Japan rather than with an immediate scheme of conquest abroad.

The *Minseito* Cabinet, 1929-1931

Again the surviving *Genro,* Saionji, recommended a *Menseito* party cabinet with Hamaguchi Yuko, party president, as prime minister. Coming into office with a strong program calling for clean politics, economy, arms reduction, and a moderate China policy, this cabinet failed more tragically than its predecessors. Its plans to reduce the lesser bureaucracy were challenged successfully, and although the government finally won ratification of the London Naval Treaty, October, 1930, it incurred the wrath of the Army and Navy and the Privy Council. In addition, the *Seiyukai,* led by Inukai Tsuyoshi, joined with these bureaucrats in denouncing the government. The real political issue was whether a party cabinet with a majority in the lower House, and with the apparent confidence of the electorate, could challenge successfully the independent and irresponsible power of the militarists and the oligarchs. Hamaguchi maintained that the Navy's approval of the London Treaty was beside the point because the Constitution provided that the emperor on the advice of the cabinet alone exercised his treaty-making powers. The premier was insisting that in foreign policy the military members of the cabinet did not have a veto.

Hamaguchi's victory was short-lived. In spite of the importance of the constitutional issue involved, the opposition *Seiyukai* did everything in its power to embarrass the government. In addition, economic depression coupled with retrenchment policies were creating alarming unemployment. The oligarchs, most of the bureaucracy, the extreme nationalists and expansionists in the military services, and the secret societies were as one in the belief that the Hamaguchi policies of conciliation toward China and of overriding the advice of the Army and Navy were subversive, designed to undercut the power of these special groups. Added support for this view came from politicians, the press, and the public, all of whom were sensitive to any implied weakening of Japan's special position in China. Six weeks after his victory on the London Naval Treaty, Hamaguchi was shot at the Tokyo station by a nationalist patriot. While he lingered for nearly a year, he could no longer be an effective leader. Wakatsuki, who followed as premier, could lead neither the party nor the nation. There was no one to curb the Japanese militarists in Manchuria. On September 18, 1931, these militarists began the seizure of Manchuria. For a brief interlude the *Seiyukai* under Inukai returned to office but not to power. The day of party cabinets was ended, and with it the prospect for civilian responsible government.[5]

[5] Hugh Borton, *Japan's Modern Century* (New York, 1955), 313-316.

Party Government: A Summary

By 1931, Japan for more than a decade had attempted a transition from oligarchic government to responsible government by political parties. In the early years of the period the parties had revealed a new popular power as the potential heirs to the *Genro*-sponsored oligarchs. Long before the end of the period, however, there was a massive evidence that popular support of the parties was uncertain, that the parties themselves were not dedicated to the principles on which alone free representative government could survive, that the politicians were unwilling to seek basic constitutional reform, and that though all the *Genro* save Saionji were gone, the irresponsible principles of Genroism had not been outlived. Political power had not passed from the constitutional bureaucracy and the oligarchs to the representatives of the people. No simple formula can explain this tragic failure in Japanese democracy. The obstacles in its path were formidable. First, the political parties, grounded in personal loyalties to the neglect of political principle, and long accustomed to subservience to oligarchy, were ill equipped to fight for responsible government. Second, the Meiji Constitution itself, and the historic institutions of oligarchy and bureaucracy it was designed to protect, was a redoubtable fortress for the imperial interpretation of government. Third, the nature and the historical development of Japanese capitalism together with the increasing concentration of capital after 1920 was a major hazard to the growth of free economic or political institutions. Fourth, the forces of representative government were frightened into retreat by the labor and radical movements after 1918. The Japanese labor movement, socialist in its origins, grew rapidly during World War I with the organization by Suzuki Bunji of the first trade unions. At the same time Marxism had become a popular doctrine among professors, writers, and university students. The intimate relation between the labor movement and this vocal, proletarian radicalism was as alarming to the political parties as it was to the bureaucrats and oligarchs. To all of these it seemed that political stability was threatened. Both Hara and Kato Takaaki, among the greatest of the liberal party leaders, countered each of their measures toward political freedom with new executive powers by which government could control the people. Fifth, although the army was reduced after the Washington Conference, officers were not retired but were assigned to middle and higher schools and universities to direct the compulsory military training, which in turn increased the military and chauvinistic character of the country. As teachers, many of these young officers, who came from the small rural landowning class close to the depressed peasantry, were exponents of political as well as military science. They opposed the Shidehara policy toward China, condemned the union of government and big business, and equated representative government with the corruption of party politicians. These were some of the obstacles on the road to representative institutions. When these are seen in the perspective of Japan's international position during the 1920's, the fate of Japanese democracy becomes understandable.

Responsible Government and World Politics

The failure of free political institutions to grow within Japan was to have a vital bearing on the methods to be used in Japan's foreign policy. In Japan, as in other lands, the movement toward representative government at home had not precluded a vigorous policy of expansion abroad. "Liberals" such as Saionji, after the Russo-Japanese War, and Okuma, in 1915, had not hesitated to implement Japan's special position in China and Manchuria. After World War I, Japanese "liberals" such as Hara, Kato, Shidehara, and Hamaguchi were no more prepared to forego the nation's privileged status in Manchuria than were the militarists, but they were more sensitive to the implications of direct action and often more disposed to seek solutions through diplomacy rather than force.

World War I not only projected Japan into the company of the great powers, but also increased materially the economic and political power she could bring to bear on Far Eastern politics. Appearing in the wake of World War I were three major issues which successive Japanese governments regarded as of supreme importance. All three of these issues called for fundamental long-range decisions in terms of Japanese foreign policy. The first of these was the question of sea power in the Pacific, a question with which the world's greatest naval powers, Great Britain and the United States, felt an equal concern. The second was the new situation created by the failure of the inter-Allied Siberian Intervention to pave the way for the destruction of Bolshevism in Russia. This meant that Japan as well as China must look to a frontier in northeastern Asia separating a capitalistic from a communistic society. The third was the rapid development of a

Chinese nationalism which, if it prospered, was likely to collide sooner or later with Japan's special position in South Manchuria. To all of these major problems, Japanese statesmen found answers in the decade that followed the Washington Conference, but whether they were good or bad answers is another matter.

In retrospect, the over-all picture of Japanese foreign policy from 1922 to 1931 compares favorably with the record of other great powers. Even her severest critics have attested to this.[6] But a scrupulous regard for treaty commitments was not by itself an answer to the Far Eastern question. The trouble was that the Washington Conference agreements were "primarily a recognition of existing, if brutal, facts, a consolidation of the *status quo*."[7] By themselves alone they could not achieve definitive solutions in a part of the world that was in open revolt against the *status quo*.

The first favorable developments in Japanese policy after the Washington Conference occurred late in 1922 and early in January, 1923, when the government carried out the restoration to China of Kiaochow in accordance with the Shantung treaty signed at Washington. Then on April 14, 1923, the Lansing-Ishii notes of 1917, regarded by public opinion in the United States and China as thoroughly obnoxious, were cancelled by the mutual consent of the two governments. While in the press of America and China this was trumpeted as a great victory for Chinese and American policy, its real significance was limited because the Japanese government accepted the view of Ishii that Japan's "special position was not based upon the discredited agreement but upon concrete realities of history and geography."[8]

Japan and Russia, 1922-1929

A second striking development in the immediate post-Washington Conference period was the formal improvement in Japan's relations

---

[6] W. W. Willoughby, *Japan's Case Examined* (Baltimore, 1940), 8; see also Henry L. Stimson, *The Far Eastern Crisis* (New York, 1936), 36: "The Japanese Government had thus for ten years given an exceptional record of good citizenship in the life of the international world."

[7] A. W. Griswold, *The Far Eastern Policy of the United States* (New York, 1938), 331.

[8] Tatsuji Takeuchi, *War and Diplomacy in the Japanese Empire* (New York, 1935), 203; see also Kikujiro Ishii, *Diplomatic Commentaries* (Baltimore, 1936), 134-135.

with Soviet Russia. At the end of 1922 the last Japanese forces left the mainland of Siberia. Their withdrawal was due to many pressures. In addition to diplomatic pressure exerted on Japan at the Washington Conference, the Japanese public no longer supported a policy that had cost the taxpayer some 700,000,000 yen, had alienated the Russians and aroused the suspicions of the Western powers, and that finally had served to hasten rather than retard the union of eastern Siberia with communistic Moscow. The economic as well as the political interests of both Japan and Russia demanded an end to the chaos created by revolution and intervention. As a consequence of protracted negotiations begun in June, 1923, a treaty was signed, January 20, 1925, restoring relations between the two powers.

The *rapprochement* represented by this treaty was a product of significant and varied forces playing upon Japanese policy. It had become evident even to Japan's chauvinists that military and political intervention had failed utterly to isolate eastern Siberia from the advance of Bolshevism. Furthermore, since there was in Japan an increasing demand for the products of Siberia's mines, forests, and waters, the re-establishment of normal relations in which commerce and industry might develop with some freedom was the natural alternative despite Japan's fear of the infiltration of "dangerous thoughts." Moreover, the success of Russian influence with the Chinese Nationalists at Canton and the conclusion of the Russian treaties with Peking and Mukden in 1924 emphasized Japan's isolation. Indeed, this isolation was now looming much larger in Japanese eyes than it had at the time of the Washington Conference. There was no longer an Anglo-Japanese alliance as a prop to Japanese policy, and "the insensate method" taken by the American Senate in the Quota Immigration Act of May, 1924, to exclude Japanese from the United States was interpreted by the Japanese press, the government, and public opinion as again indicative of an American attitude basically unfriendly to Japan's interests and purposes.

A Period of Sino-Japanese Amity

The period in which normal diplomatic relations were restored between Japan and Soviet Russia also saw the growth of happier prospects in Sino-Japanese affairs. During the greater part of the decade, 1922-1931, Japan's foreign policy was colored by the personality and the philosophy of Baron Shidehara Kijuro, a career diplomat who had married into the Iwasaki family, which controlled the powerful Mitsubishi trust. Shidehara had become the spokesman of those elements that saw the future of Japan's commercial and industrial expansion in terms of membership in the League of Nations, limitation of naval armament, and the development of a policy of conciliation and adjustment to China's new nationalism without renunciation of Japan's "life line" in South Manchuria. From 1924 to 1927 and from 1929 to 1931, while he was Foreign Minister, Shidehara pursued in general what came to be known as the "Shidehara policy." Shidehara summarized the principles of the policy before the Japanese Diet in January, 1927:

(1) To respect the sovereignty and territorial integrity of China.

(2) To promote solidarity and economic *rapprochement* between the two countries.

(3) To entertain sympathetically and helpfully the just aspirations of the Chinese people.

(4) To maintain an attitude of patience and toleration in the present situation in China, and to protect Japan's legitimate and essential rights and interests by all reasonable means at the disposal of the Government.

The crux of the Shidehara policy was the effort to reconcile China's aspirations with Japan's interests.

On two occasions during Shidehara's first term at the Foreign Office Japan did resort to the use of troops "for the protection of Japanese interests in China." In December, 1925, when Kuo Sung-ling, a lesser militarist in Manchuria, revolted against Chang Tso-lin, Japan dispatched some troops to the Mukden area. Again in April, 1927, Japanese marines were used to resist Chinese mobs attacking the Japanese concession at Hankow. But as against these cases, the Japanese naval forces did not join in the Anglo-American bombardment of Nanking in March, 1927, despite the fact that the Japanese consulate had been attacked by the Chinese and several Japanese nationals had been wounded.

Tanaka and the Positive Policy

Shidehara's "weak" policy, which had been pursued in the face of mounting civil war and anti-foreignism in China, aroused bitter opposition among Japanese militarists and bureaucrats and in some business circles. The sentiment was particularly strong in the powerful Privy Council, which, as noted already, forced the resignation of the first Wakatsuki cabinet in April, 1927, at a most critical period in the Chinese Nationalist movement, thus opening the way for stronger policy of Tanaka and the *Seiyukai.* The subsequent failure of Tanaka, a military man, to control the Army has already been told. The nature of his so-called "positive policy" toward China merits some further comment.

The "positive" policy distinguished between the attitude Japan would adopt toward China proper and her attitude toward Manchuria and eastern Mongolia.[9] Tanaka re-emphasized that Japan had "special interests" in these latter areas, "that it was her duty to maintain peace and order there," and that her rights and interests in these areas would be protected if threatened by disturbances incident to the Nationalist movement or other civil strife. In Japan, Tanaka was not alone in the belief that unification of China under the *Kuomintang* would be disastrous to Japan, and that continued Chinese industrialization in Manchuria, particularly the building of Chinese-owned railroads, would threaten Japan's South Manchuria Railroad and therefore her "special position." Moreover, the power of left-wing elements in the *Kuomintang* until 1927 was alarming to the Japanese government and particularly to leaders of the Japanese Kwantung Army in Manchuria, which constantly urged strong meas-

[9] The "positive" policy was given definite form at a conference at the Foreign Office, presided over by Tanaka and attended by representatives of the Finance, Foreign, Navy, and War Departments, the chiefs of the general staffs, the commander of the Kwantung army, the Japanese Minister to China, and three consuls-general in China. (Takeuchi, *War and Diplomacy in the Japanese Empire,* 247-248.) Associated with the decisions of this conference is the history of the so-called "Tanaka Memorial," a document which, purporting to contain the decisions reached at Tanaka's conference, first made its appearance in 1929, and after 1931 was reprinted many times and widely circulated as evidence of Japan's pre-determined policy *vis-à-vis* China in general and Manchuria in particular. Japanese policy in Manchuria and China after 1931 bore a striking resemblance to specific points in the "Memorial." The disputed authenticity of the document is discussed by Willoughby, *Japan's Case Examined,* 146-153. The "Memorial" was a forgery, but the program outlined represented the thinking of some Japanese expansionists. Scalapino, *Democracy and the Party Movement,* 236.

The "weak" versus the "positive" policies of Shidehara and Tanaka respectively involved more than an argument over principles to be applied in foreign policy toward China. In some considerable measure, Shidehara represented the commercialism of Japan's light industries and their quest for expanding export markets. Tanaka was more closely identified with Japan's heavy industries. A strong armament policy enabled the army and navy to place large contracts with Japan's heavy industries, thus in fact subsidizing them, for which reason the heavy industries tended to be willing to go along with the Tanaka policy. But in order to justify armaments and preparedness, Tanaka was forced to adopt a "positive" policy, to maintain that a war-like crisis was perpetually just around the corner on the continent of Asia.

ures. This background led to Tanaka's dispatch of troops to Shantung to check the northern advance of the Chinese Nationalists and thereby prevented the immediate union of Manchuria with the Nationalist cause. It was believed that as a result the Manchurian warload, Chang Tso-lin, would follow more willingly Japanese advice and that Japan's freedom of action in Manchuria would be preserved. Chang, however, was soon acting with marked independence; the Kwantung Army plotted and carried through his murder, which meant that Tanaka and his government had lost control of extremists in the Army. From this time on, as Tanaka resigned in July, 1929, the course of Japanese foreign policy was under the constant and increasing threat of extreme militarists and of a General Staff that was unable or unwilling to restore discipline in its own service or to permit the civilian wing of government to take steps to that end.

Japan and the League of Nations

As the pendulum of Japanese politics swung uneasily between the "weak" and "strong" policies of Shidehara and Tanaka, Japan had continued to play a respectable and in some cases a distinguished role as a member of the League of Nations. A number of Japan's ablest statesmen, jurists, diplomats, and public men served with the League. Until 1926, Nitobe Inazo, one of the best known of Japan's liberals abroad, served as an Under-Secretary-General and as a Director of the International Bureau. He was succeeded by Sugimura Yotaro as Under-Secretary-General and Director of the Political Section.

Japan was also active in the field of arbitration and adjudication of international disputes. She was a signatory of the Convention for the Pacific Settlement of International Disputes, a product of the Hague Peace Congress of 1899 and 1907. When, under the League of Nations, the principle of international adjudication acquired new life, Adachi Mineichiro was named a member of the League committee that drafted the statutes for the new Permanent Court of International Justice, commonly known as the World Court. A Japanese, Oda Yorozu, was one of the original eleven judges of the Court. He in turn was succeeded in 1930 by Adachi Mineichiro, who served also as President of the Court. However, on account of the so-called optional clause in the statutes of the Court imposing compulsory acceptance of its jurisdiction in specified cases, Japan did not accept the Court's full jurisdiction.

Naval Rivalry in the Pacific

The Washington Conference, as will be recalled, had made a beginning toward holding within bounds the race in naval armament among the great powers. However, after 1924, when the United States passed the general immigration act excluding aliens who were ineligible for citizenship, there was noticeable tension in American-Japanese relations and a growing interest in the question of armaments. A naval race was still quite possible, for the Washington Conference ratio, 5-5-3 for the United States, Great Britain, and Japan, was applicable only to capital ships. Indeed, the naval race was already under way, for while the United States failed to maintain its naval strength either in auxiliary categories or in the capital ships to which it was entitled under the Washington agreement, the other powers, Japan and Great Britain, continued to build.[10]

Without adequate preparation, President Coolidge on February 10, 1927, invited the powers to a disarmament conference at Geneva. Although France and Italy declined to attend, Great Britain, the United States, and Japan attempted to extend and supplement the principles adopted at Washington. The United States wanted to apply the 5-5-3 ratio to all categories and to reduce total cruiser tonnage. No agreement, however, was reached, and the conference ended in failure. This was the more lamentable since there was little doubt that public opinion at this time in all three countries favored further limitation. The conference was defeated both by the naval experts and by lobbyists of special groups.

Anglo-American-Japanese relations continued to deteriorate after the Geneva Conference. There appeared to be no solution to the naval problem so long as Great Britain and the United States remained as far apart as they were at Geneva. By late 1929 this doleful picture had been retouched and brightened. Shidehara was back at the Japanese Foreign Office, and President Herbert Hoover and Prime Minister Ramsay MacDonald had talked amicably at the President's fish-

[10] For discussions of the growing armament problem, see B. H. Williams, *The United States and Disarmament* (New York, 1931); J. W. Wheeler-Bennett, *Disarmament and Security since Locarno, 1925-1931* (London, 1932), chs. i and ii; Giovanni Engely, *The Politics of Naval Disarmament*, trans. by H. V. Rhodes (London, 1932), chs. i, ii, iii.

ing camp at Rapidan, Virginia. Evidence of the improved international temper came with a British invitation to the powers, October 7, 1929, to a disarmament conference in London. As at Geneva, this conference was soon mired in the technical details of the experts who again seemed to be "on top" instead of merely "on tap." Yet, on April 22, 1930, the London Naval Treaty was signed by Britain, the United States, and Japan. France, who had demanded a political agreement assuring her of military support, and Italy accepted only parts of the Treaty. Nevertheless, the results of the conference were positive if limited. The three major powers had accepted a maximum upper limit in all categories of vessels. Britain acceded to an over-all principle of parity with the United States. Japan accepted a 10-10-6 ratio in heavy cruisers, was granted a 10-10-7 ratio in light cruisers and other auxiliary ships, and parity with the larger powers in submarines. An escalator clause could release any signatory from its obligations if its position was jeopardized by the naval construction of a non-signatory.

At the London Naval Conference Japan had sought "three fundamental claims": (1) a 70 per cent ratio relative to the United States in 10,000-ton, 8-inch-gun heavy cruisers; (2) a 70 per cent ratio in gross tonnage relative to the United States in all auxiliary craft; and (3) parity with Britain and the United States in submarine tonnage at the then high existing strength of some 78,000 tons. This program of the Japanese naval staff, supported by the press, was designed to give the nation greater relative strength in far eastern waters than was provided by the 5-5-3 capital ship ratio of the Washington Treaty. In Japan it was generally regarded as "adequate for defense in any contingency." As against this the United States proposed for Japan a 60 per cent ratio in total tonnage for auxiliary craft. The ultimate settlement embodied in the treaty was a compromise. Since any compromise that would save the conference from failure would be essentially political in character, Japan's civilian delegates modified "the three fundamental claims" and thereby ignored the advice of the Japanese naval experts. In Tokyo, the Hamaguchi government, which favored acceptance of the compromise, met violent opposition from the naval staff and all ultranationalistic groups. Admiral Kato Kanji, chief of the naval general staff, personified the resolute position of the military services and their supporters. The decision to accept the compromise was therefore a major victory for civilian as opposed to military dominance in the government. Furthermore, it strengthened the constitutional theories of Minobe Tatsukichi, a distinguished jurist, who held that the power to determine the military and naval strength of the state did not belong to the supreme command. In this view, it was the prerogative of the cabinet and not of the military services to advise the emperor.

Japan's adherence to the London Treaty marked the high point in the nation's struggle toward responsible government. But as already noted, the victory was fictitious. There was no united public opinion to support a government that was fighting for democratic and responsible control.

FOR FURTHER READING

Brown, Delmer M., *Nationalism in Japan: An Introductory Historical Analysis* (Berkeley, 1955).

Byas, Hugh, *Government by Assassination* (New York, 1942).

Embree, John F., *The Japanese Nation, A Social Survey* (New York, 1945). A brief survey of pre-war cultural patterns.

———, *Suye Mura, a Japanese Village* (Chicago, 1939). A valuable sociological study.

Grad, Andrew J., *Land and Peasant in Japan, an Introductory Survey* (New York, 1952).

Ishimoto (Baroness) Shidzue, *Facing Two Ways, the Story of My Life* (New York, 1935).

Kawai Tatsuo, *The Goal of Japanese Expansion* (Tokyo, 1938). For the so-called philosophy of *musubi.*

Orchard, John Ewing, *Japan's Economic Position, the Progress of Industrialization,* with the collaboration of Dorothy Johnson Orchard (New York, 1930). Valuable for its analysis of Japanese industry to 1930.

Toynbee, Arnold J., ed., *Survey of International Affairs* (annual volumes, London, 1925-1931).

Utley, Freda, *Lancashire and the Far East* (London, 1931). The growing competition of Japan's cotton industry with that of Britain.

Young, A. Morgan, *Imperial Japan, 1926-1938* (New York, 1938).

29 China: 1916–1931

Warlords, the *Kuomintang,* and Nationalism

THE China that emerged from the catastrophe of World War I was a paradox of indescribable chaos and of magnificent rebirth. From the death of Yuan Shih-k'ai in 1916 until 1931, China survived a plague of internal warlordism, created a new national unity under the revolutionary *Kuomintang,* and took the first major steps in freeing herself from the semi-dependent status to which she had succumbed. As in the case of Japan in this same period, popular opinion in the United States and to a lesser degree in other Western democracies observed China's struggles and her progress with some optimism. It was fashionable in some quarters to assume that in China, as in Japan, responsible democratic government would soon be a fact instead of a hope. These wishful dreams did not become a reality. It should be noted further that the issues to be resolved in Japan and in China in the post-war decade were not identical. It is true that both countries were involved in revolutionary processes of change, but there the likeness ceased. In 1918 Japan was an organized and powerful national state, industrialized, and already expanding politically and economically under able if arbitrary leadership. China was none of these. She emerged from the war in political turmoil. Although she had spoken at Versailles in the language of a new nationalism, this new China was as yet formless, unorganized, non-industrial, and leaderless. Nevertheless, she was about to advance materially the revolution begun in 1911. A very strange assortment of movements and personalities were to play their parts in this perplexing story. There was the phantom warlord government at Peking, which was the only government recognized *de jure* by the foreign powers, 1916-1928. There was the insurgent Canton revolutionary government of Sun Yat-sen which, under the *Kuomintang,* was to formalize China's new nationalism at Nanking after 1927. Between these two political movements and within each there were mad crusades of factionalism, duplicity, civil war, and massacre. And between all of these and the foreign powers there was intrigue and conspiracy in a battle for position, influence, and control in the China that would emerge tomorrow.

The Marvel of Warlordism

When Yuan Shih-k'ai was claimed by death in 1916 and the well-meaning Li Yuan-hung became President of the Republic, there was a momentary swing toward constitutionalism. The original Provisional Constitution of 1912 which Yuan had destroyed was revived, and the old republican parliament he had dispersed was called back to Peking. The premier of this new government was Tuan Ch'i-jui, a northern militarist and head of the so-called Anhwei faction. These happy beginnings were soon ended when parliament failed to resolve the issue of federalism versus centralism in the proposed permanent constitution, and when President Li sought to block Tuan's plan of declaring war on Germany. When Li dismissed the Premier, the latter's *tuchun* colleagues rallied to his support and defied the President. Li in desperation appealed to another militarist, General Chang Hsün, for aid. Chang responded by forcing the dissolution of Parliament, June 12, 1917, and then on July 1, to the amazement of all, restored the abdicated Hsuan-tung emperor to the Manchu throne. This démarche was too much even for Chang's fellow militarists. Mobilized by ex-premier Tuan and aided by General Fêng Kuo-chang and his aids from Chihli, they descended on Peking. The young emperor again descended from his throne; Chang Hsün took to flight, and Tuan, as premier, was again back in power. This time Tuan assembled a parliament of his own choosing. Known as the Anfu Parliament, it survived from 1918 to 1920. Like its predecessors, it dabbled with constitution-making. Meanwhile, the marriage of convenience among the militarists had dissolved as the struggle for power was resumed. From then on until 1928 the government of Peking was a bewildering succession of presidents, premiers, and parliaments bereft of all meaning save ambition for personal advantage. Warfare ravaged the countryside as *tuchun* fought *tuchun* for control of Peking.[1]

Although this Republic of China at Peking was at best a monstrous fraud at home, it maintained an amazing respectability abroad. Its spokesmen at Paris in 1919 and at Washington in 1921 created the fiction of China as a nation sinned against but without sin itself. It maintained an admirable diplomatic service which behaved as though the Republic actually had a government. Its diplomats spoke with deep reverence for international law while at home there was no law save the arbitrary force of *tuchun* armies. Yet beneath this contradiction of domestic brigandage and outward good manners there were real if submerged strivings toward a new order. The disorders of tuchunism were in fact pointing the way to order. After 1917 a return to monarchy was hardly considered. At the same time Peking parliaments, for all the chaos that surrounded them, were concerned repeatedly with the question of legitimacy. What constitution was the legal constitution and under what constitution had a given president been chosen were questions constantly under debate. In a sense these debates were meaningless because the answers were given by armies and not by parliaments, yet even the *tuchuns* liked to be legitimate, and it was significant that only a constitution could confer this virtue upon them. In addition, the experience of the Peking regime illustrated how ill-prepared China was for either presidential or cabinet government. From March, 1912, until December, 1925, Peking produced six constitutions or draft constitutions. There was little difference between them. All were republican in form and democratic in principle. None of them had any relation to a long-range evolutionary process through which the Chinese people might move toward responsible government.

The Revival of Southern Insurgency

The history of south China, 1917 to 1923, bore a striking likeness to the cavalcade of disorder in and about Peking. South China, like the North, had its full quota of provincial governor-warlords who made alliances or fought each other for personal advantage under not the slightest control of the "government" of the Republic in

[1] P. M. A. Linebarger, Djang Chu, Ardath W. Burks, *Far Eastern Governments and Politics* (New York, 1954), 132-135; Ch'ien Tuang-shêng, *The Government and Politics of China* (Cambridge, 1950), 65-69.

Peking. There was, however, one vital difference in the South, a difference that was not immediately apparent, namely, the presence there of Sun Yat-sen and fragments of his revolutionary party, the *Kuomintang*. As late as 1918 Sun and his following at Canton had made little headway. The Party had no organization other than personal bonds of loyalty to Sun. It was filled with factionalism and diverse political creeds and, of course, had no army. In 1920 General Ch'en Ch'iung-ming, a nominal adherent of Sun Yat-sen and head of Kwangtung militarists, having defeated his rivals from Kwangsi, seized Canton, thus enabling Sun to be elected president by refugees from the old Peking Parliament of 1913. This new Canton government was thus declaring itself the "true" government of the Chinese Republic. Then in 1922, after an open break with General Ch'en, Sun fled to Shanghai. Within a year he was back at Canton, this time with the title of Generalissimo. His restoration to power was due this time to the Kwangsi armies that had ousted General Chen, to military aid in Fukien from Tuan Ch'i-jui, no longer in power at Peking, and moral support from a Manchurian warlord, Chang Tso-lin, who was developing ambitions to control Peking, which at the time was held by two other notable *tuchuns,* Ts'ao K'un and Wu P'ei-fu.

The New *Kuomintang*

A new phase of the Chinese revolution had already begun. During 1923-1925 Sun broadened the base of his following, accepted the support of the Russian and Chinese communists, created a new organization and spirit for the *Kuomintang,* and laid the foundations for a military power that by 1928 had brought practically all China within the nationalist movement.[2] There were two basic foundations on which this extraordinary transformation was built. Beginning in 1919, when the Chinese Revolutionary Party was reorganized as the *Kuomintang,* Sun, giving heed to the nation-wide student uprising in protest of the Shantung settlement at Versailles, brought student leaders into the party, thereby bringing to his movement a young intelligentsia, ripe material for revolution. At the same time the Russian revolutions and Moscow's declared purpose to void all tsarist rights in China made a popular appeal to Chinese intellectuals, to

[2] *Kuo* means country, *min* means people, and the combination *kuomin* means nation or as an adjective, nationalist. *Tang* is Chinese for party. Thus *Kuomintang,* the (Chinese) Nationalist Party.

some of whom at least Marxism appeared as China's salvation. Indeed, the Chinese Communist Party was organized in July, 1921. In the following year, Abram Adolf Joffe, who had been sent by Moscow to cultivate both the Peking government and the *Kuomintang,* met Sun Yat-sen, for the moment an exile from Canton, at Shanghai. Sun needed an ally. Not only was he an exile from his own Canton, but his appeals to the Western democracies for aid against the Peking warlords had gone unanswered. In January, 1923, Sun and Joffe reached a common agreement. Sun declared that neither communism nor the soviet system were suitable for China, while Joffe, concurring in this view, assured Sun of Russian sympathy and support in the achievement of China's most pressing needs—national unification and full independence.

In the student movement and the proffered Russian support Sun had discovered a new revolutionary spirit to revitalize his following. Within two years the *Kuomintang* was a totalitarian party in structure and discipline, though its doctrine had not become communist. Much of this radical reorganization was the work of communist advisers from Moscow headed by Michael Borodin, a revolutionary of international repute. Meanwhile the Chinese Communist Party pledged its support to the *Kuomintang,* while communists as individuals were permitted to join it. The First *Kuomintang* Party Congress, January, 1924, brought forth a basic manifesto that set the frame for future party and government relations and, for the immediate future, gave Sun a powerful weapon of propaganda. Simultaneously the military leadership for *Kuomintang* armies was trained at the newly founded Whampoa military academy under the command of a young officer just returned from observing the Red Army at Moscow. His name was Chiang K'ai-shek.

THE *San Min Chu I*

The revolutionary ideology, the political mandate of this reborn *Kuomintang,* was Sun Yat-sen's program for China as it had developed by 1924. Called the *San Min Chu I,* the Three Principles of the People, it had been basic in Sun's thought since 1905, but it was not until 1924 at Canton that he gave the program mature expression as a revolutionary weapon. The three principles were: *Min-tsu, Min-ch'uan,* and *Min-sheng,* meaning literally People's Nationhood, People's Power, and People's Livelihood. The first and second meant Nationalism and Democracy respectively. The third has been rendered variously as Livelihood, or Socialism, or Communism, which could only mean that Sun's term *Min-sheng* is the only satisfactory label to use. In the development of the Three Principles Sun had not succumbed to communism but had succumbed to communist organization and tactics.

Nationalism, *Min-tsu*

Sun's original Nationalism was simply anti-Manchu, a demand that an alien ruler be ousted; but when this was done, in 1912, Nationalism became a new concept of unity embracing Chinese, Manchus, Mongols, Tibetans, and various lesser groups. Here Sun faced a problem of extreme delicacy. The question involved not only patriotism to the state but also the problem of what kind of state. Was it to be a state in which the Chinese, as the overwhelming majority, were to have a corresponding ascendancy over such people as the Mongols? Or was it to be a federated state in which the Mongols and the Tibetans were to have the standing of majorities within their own territories? A number of the Mongol-*Kuomintang* followers of Sun believed that the eventual outcome would be a federated state. The subsequent failure of the *Kuomintang* to create such a state, and the emphasis it gave later to policies that would result in the compulsory conversion of such peoples as the Mongols from a status of "sub-standard Chinese" to a status of "standard Chinese" alienated Mongols and Tibetans and gave their nationalism a trend that was anti-Chinese. For Sun, by 1924, it was extraordinarily difficult to come to grips with this problem. If he had advocated too openly a federated status for the frontier peoples, he would, in view of China's weakness at the time, have exposed them to the danger of annexation or near-annexation by foreign powers. If, however, it was difficult for Sun to resolve the internal character of Nationalism, there was no such problem externally. Against the background of what had happened at Canton, 1919-1924, the First Principle was frankly anti-imperialistic. Here as elsewhere in his program Sun taught a revival of China's ancient morality as a base for the new order in action.

Democracy, *Min-ch'uan*

Sun's ideas on democracy were derived from four principal sources: (1) Western republicanism, (2) the Swiss doctrine of initiative, referendum, election, recall, (3) Soviet democratic centralism, and (4) Chinese ideas of examination and control. Under Nationalism, this Chinese democratic theory would acknowledge the Confucian and traditional inequality of men with first, second, and third class citizens. These would be respectively: (1) the leaders, who could understand the past and thus guide men into the future (a Confucian idea); (2) those who could interpret the leaders to the masses; and (3) the rank and file bereft of understanding but able to say whether they liked what they got. Political powers would be exercised through a fivefold division: executive, legislative, judicial, examination, and control. Training for the exercise of political power would be given to the people by the *Kuomintang* during the period of tutelage that was to follow immediately the military unification.

Min-sheng

Although undoubtedly Sun Yat-sen was deeply concerned for the material welfare of the common man, he did not develop a precise economic theory or program. He proposed to achieve equalization of land tenure in China by having the unearned increment go to the state. Capital would be regulated by state ownership of larger industries. While accepting the idea that "the struggle for a living and not material forces determines history," Sun appears to have been opposed to Marxian materialism and the class struggle. What was important in 1924 was that the Three Principles as revised and enunciated by Sun and the new *Kuomintang* capitalized on the current anti-imperialist frenzy, thus giving the revolution a popular moral power it had never possessed even in 1911 and 1912.

The Passing of Sun Yat-sen

While his new *Kuomintang* and the military government at Canton was acquiring a new power, Sun still hoped for the peaceful unification of China through an acceptable agreement with Peking. Late in 1924 the prospect seemed hopeful. The warlord president at Peking, Ts'ao K'un, had been driven from office and his place taken by Tuan Ch'i-jui as provisional chief executive. Accordingly, Sun went to Peking seeking a basis for settlement. There in March, 1925, he failed and died, calling on his followers to carry on the revolution.

The passing of Sun Yat-sen had disrupting effects, all of which were not apparent immediately upon the nationalist movement and upon the fortunes of the *Kuomintang*. So long as Sun lived, his shortcomings had been obvious not only to many of his immediate followers but also to his enemies. Now that he was gone the failures of the man whom many had regarded as a visionary were forgotten. Sun became the embodiment of all the idealism within the nationalist movement, and the personification of all the revolutionary fervor of the reconstituted *Kuomintang*. As Confucius had become the sage of ancient China, so would Sun Yat-sen inherit the role in twentieth-century China. Confucianism would give place to Sun Yat-senism. On the other hand, no single leader had emerged to take Sun's place. Rivalry among his immediate associates was therefore a natural consequence—a rivalry that tended to rest its case on divergent interpretations of Sun's political and economic philosophy. Here there was ample ground for ideological warfare and party strife because of the vague, general, uncertain terms in which Sun had so frequently expressed his ideas.

For the time being, however, unity as the price of military victory kept factionalism within bounds. The Canton government was declared formally to be the Nationalist government. It was a committee administration with Wang Ching-wei, generally considered to be of the left as a reformer, as chairman. This leftist orientation of the *Kuomintang* was unsuccessfully challenged in November, 1925, when a group of rightist leaders professing to hold a cession of the Central Executive Committee of the Party in the Western Hills at Peking passed resolutions denouncing the leftists and expelling the communists. The place of meeting was where the embalmed body of Sun was resting. At the Second National Congress of the *Kuomintang*, January, 1926, the sacredness of Sun's teachings, the soundness of the Russian orientation, and the purpose to carry the revolution to the people were all affirmed. The Western Hills group was expelled while more communists joined the Party. Meanwhile, *Kuomintang* forces had crushed all military opposition from the Kwangtung and Kwangsi warlords.

With this added security in its southern base, the Nationalist government was ready to move to the military unification of all China. For many reasons the decision was regarded as dubious. Neither the military nor the political position of the Canton regime was strong. The surface unity in the *Kuomintang* did not reflect the factional bitterness beneath. Nevertheless, the military counsel of Chiang

K'ai-shek, commander of the armies, prevailed. Within three months Nationalist armies were on the Yangtze. The Nationalist government was moved, January, 1927, to the sister cities of Hankow, Hanyang, and Wuchang, where it became known as the Wuhan Regime. Here the growing conflict between Nationalists and communists came in view. While Wuhan demonstrators (communists and *Kuomintang* leftists) attacked foreign concessions at central Yangtze cities and demanded a socialist revolution, Chiang K'ai-shek and *Kuomintang* conservatives formed their own National government at Nanking, April, 1927, from which it launched widespread attacks on communists and leftists in the lower Yangtze. Simultaneously there were further disclosures of communist and Russian purposes when Chang Tso-lin, the Manchurian warlord, then heading the Peking government, raided the Soviet offices there. Other disclosures came from the Wuhan Regime, which finally expelled its Russian advisers, dissolved itself, reappeared briefly in Canton, and then was reunited with Nanking. On top of these developments the northern march of the Nationalists continued. Some northern *tuchuns,* Fêng Yü-hsiang, the Christian General, and Yen Hsi-shan, the Model Governor, joined the Nationalist cause. Chang Tso-lin, retreated from Peking to Manchuria, where he was slain by the Kwantung (Japanese) army, but his son Chang Hsüch-liang, the Young Marshal, raised the Nationalist flag at Mukden, December, 1928. No southern *Kuomintang* soldier entered Manchuria, but the Republic of China at Peking was dead. The Nationalists had won the war of unification.

The National Government at Nanking

The National government of China which was taking shape at Nanking in 1927 was to prove by far the most substantial China had known since the time of Yüan Shih-k'ai. Many factors contributed to this stability. The new government played successfully on the name of Sun Yat-sen, the patron saint of the revolution, and his philosophy of the state, *San Min Chu I.* Its armies had already proved their superiority. Its treasury was financed by the Chinese bankers of Shanghai. The foreign powers, since the retreat of the Russians, looked upon the new government with some favor. Its bureaucracy of civil servants had already acquired some experience at Canton and Hankow. Lastly, when in 1928 its armies drove Chang

Tso-lin from Peking, Nanking was accorded diplomatic recognition by the Western powers and Japan.[3]

The Nanking Government was created by and was responsible to the purged *Kuomintang*. Its constitution (1928-1931) was the so-called First Organic Law of the National Government. Under this instrument, power was concentrated at the top and was exercised through five *yüan* (departments or divisions) rather than the three —legislative, executive, and judicial—common to Western government. There was no parliamentary body. Until 1931 the president of the National Government exercised extensive powers controlled by a council of state. The system was altered somewhat in 1931 when the *Kuomintang* promulgated a provisional constitution. Under this the president lost practically all power to the Executive Yüan.

The Fivefold Division of Powers

The fivefold division of powers known as the yüan system was a distinctive feature of Sun Yat-sen's political plan. The Executive Yüan was in a sense the cabinet of the National Government. The Legislative Yüan, a body of eighty-eight members, was neither a parliament nor a legislature as the term is commonly understood in the West. Basically its function was research and the drafting of legislation. The Judicial Yüan comprised the Supreme Court, Administrative Court, the Ministry of Justice, and a Commission for the Disciplinary Punishment of Public Functionaries. It dealt with cases of government personnel in the civil service. The Examination Yüan was concerned with applying a merit system to all government officials, excepting the top political positions. There were two divisions in this yüan: the Examination Commission and the Ministry of Personnel. Merit systems are of course difficult to apply even in the most advanced democracies and it is not surprising that in modern China the work of the Examination Yüan was not outstanding. Merit alone apart from considerations of hewing to the party line, *Kuomintang* or Communist, was not an effective key to public office. The last of the five divisions, the Control Yüan, suggested the Censorate in Old China. Its function, as that of its ancient predecessor, was to denounce (in the modern sense, bring suit) against irresponsible officials.

---

[3] H. F. MacNair, *China in Revolution* (Chicago, 1931); P. M. A. Linebarger, *Government in Republican China* (New York, 1938).

Nanking as a "National" Government

The extraordinary success of the *Kuomintang* armies, the overnight collapse of the Peking regime, and the appearance of a new "national" government at Nanking, as though by the waving of a magician's wand, were not to prove an unmixed blessing. These dramatic events led, perhaps understandably, to extravagant hopes and interpretations, especially in the Western press, of China's new status, as if to say that stability, nationalism, and democracy were the inevitable results of fifteen years of republican tumult. The fact that the Nanking regime was known as the National Government suggested that it was national as Western peoples usually understood that term. Only in a limited sense was this true. As the administration newly recognized by the powers, it was the National Government, but in a geographical sense it was not master of all of China proper within the Wall. Its power was based primarily on the lower Yangtze and diminished as it radiated into more remote areas. The Peking area was controlled by Generals Yen Hsi-shan and Fêng Yü-hsiang, erstwhile northern militarists who had joined the Nationalist cause at the eleventh hour. Nanking's control in Manchuria was nominal and dependent on the good will of Chang Hsüeh-liang, the Young Marshal. In the same way, a number of southern and western provinces gave no more than nominal recognition to Nanking. Yet even with these qualifications Nanking ruled a larger area than any government since the collapse of the Yüan Shih-k'ai military regime. The immediate force making possible this wider but not inclusive territorial control was the power of the Nationalist army under Chiang K'ai-shek. Nationalist soldiers, as a result of indoctrination and training, possessed fighting qualities and a revolutionary spirit completely lacking among the troops of the old-type warlords. It is significant too that their leader, Chiang K'ai-shek, had risen to prominence not as a civilian but as a soldier. At this time there was no conclusive evidence that as generalissimo in the National Government Chiang was more than the most successful general China had produced in a long time. It was not yet clear that Chiang would rise above the mere expression of military power and become the symbol of a united nation. Moreover, there was some tendency to overestimate Nationalist military power. To some degree the Nationalist victories of 1927-1928 were won over a military vacuum, a tactical advantage Chiang had recognized when he insisted on beginning the Northern March in 1926. Finally, in the moment of military victory, when the *Kuomintang* faced the ultimate test of creating and controlling a government to lead China through the period of tutelage to the fulfillment of Sun's revolutionary program, the Party was torn by personal, political, and military strife.

Only the merest outline of these complex lines of cleavage can be suggested here. They included both the traditional and the modern in Chinese politics. Sun's program for modern China involved not only a revolutionary program but also and ultimately a revolution in the traditional Chinese approach to politics: the replacing of government by men with government by law. Until his death Sun was the unchallenged leader of the new *Kuomintang*. With his death leadership passed to a coterie of followers, chief among whom were Wang Ching-wei, Chiang K'ai-shek, and Hu Han-min, representing respectively the left, center, and right wings of the Party. Dissension within the *Kuomintang* on ideological grounds until 1925 had been controlled by Sun's dynamic leadership. When Sun was gone there was no leader with the immediate power to replace him; no one with authority to say what his program meant. The result was a galaxy of interpretations ranging from the Western Hills group on the right to the communists far out beyond the left. After the communists were expelled in 1927-1928 the personal rivalries of the *Kuomintang* triumvirate, often couched in ideological terms, continued until, by 1931, it was clear that no unified government could prevail without Chiang, who controlled the army and had the confidence of the country's financiers. The bitterness of these personal and factional rivalries consumed the energies of the *Kuomintang*. As a result, neither the Party nor its National government could maintain Sun's revolutionary vigor There was no agreement on the implementation of his Three Principles. While the left wing urged rapid movement toward representative government, the right wing demanded that full national power be achieved first.[4]

China's Revolution and the Foreign Powers

The perplexing course of China's internal revolution had been watched with anticipation and with fear by the Western democracies

---

[4] Linebarger, *Far Eastern Governments and Politics,* 206.

and Japan. Would this revolution produce a stable China that would take its place within the international political and legal community of the Western powers? The protestations of Chinese spokesmen at Paris (1919) and Washington (1922) implied that this would be so. Yet there were also dire forebodings of trouble. Would the revolution destroy the whole treaty structure of the Western position in China without suitable guarantees for the future? Would the chaos of revolution open the door to exclusive Japanese control? Would the contagion of Soviet communism subvert Sun Yat-sen's program to its own purposes? A world jostled now by hope, now by skepticism, by clear purpose and by indecision, grappled or drifted with this march of events in China.

The revolutionary program of Sun Yat-sen, in particular the principles of nationalism and democracy, was a direct challenge to the unequal treaty system dating back to 1842, to the concessions and foreign settlements, to the naval leaseholds and spheres of influence, and, in fact, to the entire structure of the foreign position and influence through which China had sunk to a semi-colonial status. This complex framework of foreign rights and interests in China was not the result of an imperialistic conspiracy. On the contrary, it was the labored answer to the problem of adjustment between a traditional, sick civilization in China and the expanding dynamic civilization of the modern, Western world. The unequal treaty system and all that it implied was never the ideal system desired either by China or by the West. From the beginning it was the evolving compromise on which the antagonists could at a given moment agree, even though reluctantly. The system was not challenged effectively prior to World War I. It was challenged during and after the war. This challenge came from multiple and often mutually hostile sources: from the Wilsonian philosophy of the war to end wars and to make the world safe for democracy; from the student movement in China in 1919 protesting not only against Japan and the Twenty-one Demands but also against the democracies that "failed" China at Versailles; from the cumulative effect of Sun Yat-sen's gospel of nationalism; and from Soviet Russia's surrender of tsarist rights in China. It all added up to an aroused public sentiment sufficiently strong to prevent Peking from signing the Treaty of Versailles. Thereafter, Chinese diplomats were eloquent spokesmen in the cause of "national salvation."

The Youth and Student Movement

The spearhead of the newly aroused public sentiment demanding "rights recovery" and nationalism was the student movement. The influence that students exerted at times upon China's nationalist revolution was traceable to the historic position of scholarship and the scholar in Old China. Many Chinese looked to the student for answers in the chaotic revolutionary years after 1911. The students in turn voiced their political opinions with an air of authority. This was particularly true of those who had received a modern education in Japan, in Europe, or in America. After 1911, too, China's modern schools increased with great rapidity, as did also the number of students. In the turmoil of prevailing conditions, many in this increasing body of graduates could not find positions they considered commensurate with their training. These readily became active critics of government. So it was that a growing body of students, inspired by Western learning, became the most active revolutionary agents within China. Many students were fanatical supporters of Sun Yat-sen and members of the *Kuomintang.* Many, too, were ardent supporters of the Russo-communist orientation at Canton, which promised action and results. Yet while many students supported Borodin's program for the new *Kuomintang,* they were less interested in its communist implications than in its immediate promise of a vigorous Chinese nationalism.

Treaty Revision after 1922

This was the China with which the Washington Conference had attempted to deal in 1921-1922. Although in the general area of the Pacific the work of the Conference was largely a freezing of the *status quo,* it had shown sympathy for China and had given some pledges to the future. Some of these were implemented.

The first was a revision of the Chinese tariff to yield an effective 5 per cent as contemplated by the treaties. The new rates provided a measure of financial relief to China by raising the specific duties to the approximate 5 per cent *ad valorem* provided by the old commercial treaties, but they did not meet the Chinese desire voiced at Versailles and Washington that the treaty tariff be abolished because it limited the income of the Chinese government by preventing higher duties for luxuries or for protection.

At Washington the powers had also agreed to relinquish the post offices they had maintained on Chinese soil when there was any adequate Chinese postal service. Before the end of 1922 the British had closed twelve post offices, the Japanese, sixty-six, the French, thirteen, and the United States, one. This last had been maintained at Shanghai. The powers were still permitted to maintain post offices in leased territories "or as otherwise specifically provided by treaty." Under this provision, the Japanese continued to maintain post offices in the zone of the South Manchuria Railway.

In 1922, also, the Japanese fulfilled the pledge given at Washington by withdrawing their troops from Siberia, and the former Allied and Associated Powers terminated their control of the Chinese Eastern Railway, thus bringing to a close the futile intervention undertaken in 1918 and clearing the way for such future settlements China might reach with whatever Russian government eventually emerged in eastern Siberia.

During 1922, the Sino-Japanese agreement concluded at Washington relative to Japan's position in Shantung was carried into effect. Thus the political aspects of Sino-Japanese relations in Shantung had progressed toward a substantial settlement, though Japan's economic influence in the province remained paramount.

These favorable developments in Sino-Japanese relations were balanced, however, by China's unsuccessful efforts in 1923 to reopen the question of termination of the Sino-Japanese treaties and notes of May, 1915. Japan replied that the treaties had been signed by China's recognized government, that they were valid, and were not "susceptible of further modification."[5]

During the Washington Conference, in response to China's demand for retrocession of the leased territories, the British had agreed to surrender Wei-hai-wei as a means of facilitating a Sino-Japanese settlement on Shantung. Intermittent negotiations were conducted by an Anglo-Chinese commission at Wei-hai-wei and Peking during 1923 and 1924, but complete agreement was not reached until April 18, 1930.

Serious obstacles to treaty revision also developed between China and France. After China's entry into World War I, her payments on the Boxer Indemnity had been suspended by agreement with the Allied powers. Payments were to be resumed in 1922, at which time

[5] R. T. Pollard, *China's Foreign Relations, 1917-1931* (New York, 1933), 252-254.

France desired to use the funds due her in paying creditors of the Banque Industrielle de Chine, the recent failure of which had seriously affected French prestige. The balance of payments, if any, were to go to Sino-French educational and charitable foundations. To this China agreed, but trouble appeared when the French government demanded that China pay in "gold" francs at a pre-war rate of exchange. Previous payments, determined by an agreement of 1905, had always been made by China in the currencies of the creditor nations. The franc, however, had now depreciated as a result of the war, and thus France was demanding payment in gold, a demand in which she enjoyed the support of the Boxer Protocol powers. This impasse between Peking and France was far-reaching in its results, for while it continued France refused ratification of the Washington agreement on the conventional tariff, refused to join the commission to investigate extraterritoriality, and refused to consider relinquishment of the Kwangchow leasehold. Finally, in April, 1925, a compromise agreement was reached. Payments were to be made by China in gold dollars and were to be resumed as of December 1, 1924, instead of 1922. With this settlement at last achieved, France gave belated ratification in July, 1925, to the Nine-Power Open Door Treaty and to the Washington Treaty on the Chinese tariff. The treaties thus came into full force on August 5, 1925.[6]

Extraterritoriality

At the Washington Conference China had asked the powers to end the exercise of extraterritorial rights within a limited period, meanwhile adopting a plan of progressive modification. A conference resolution provided a commission to inquire into the practice of extraterritorial jurisdiction in China, into the judicial system and

[6] By 1925 all the powers had agreed to a settlement by which Boxer payments in part at least were to be devoted to educational and philanthropic purposes mutually beneficial. Britain had announced such a policy in 1922, details being worked out by an Anglo-Chinese committee. For its recommendations, see *The China Year Book, 1928,* 631-634. The Japanese government in March, 1923, agreed to devote a small part of the payments due it to cultural purposes; see *The China Yearbook, 1929-1930,* 669-670. The United States by Congressional Act, May 21, 1924, agreed to remit to China for educational purposes the balance of Boxer payments due to this country; see *Treaties and Agreements, 1919-1929,* 132, 147, 156. The Netherlands proposed to devote its share for a survey of flood prevention measures in the Yellow River Valley; see *The China Yearbook, 1928,* 634-635. Portions of the Belgian and the Italian shares were also to be devoted to philanthropic work.

administration of that country, and to make recommendations for improving the system to the end that the several powers might be warranted "in relinquishing, either progressively or otherwise, their respective rights of extraterritoriality." By May, 1923, after the Chinese government had undertaken at the suggestion of the United States to prepare translations of its codes and of other judicial data, the Peking administration notified the powers that it wished the commission on extraterritoriality to meet there on November 1. A number of the powers, however, considered the time ill-chosen, for political chaos within China by the summer of 1923 had exceeded all precedent. To Chinese protests against rumored postponement of the conference, Secretary Hughes informed the Chinese Minister in Washington, Alfred Sze, that it "was idle for China to declaim, as she had at the Washington Conference," about her sovereignty and rights as a nation while she failed to provide herself with a government with national authority or competence to discharge its international obligations. China, the Secretary added, could hardly expect foreign consideration while she exhibited "before the world inability to protect even the lives and safety of foreigners."[7] As a result the first meeting of the extraterritorial commission was not held until January 12, 1926.[8]

The commission's investigations were limited to North China, since the insurgent Canton government, holding that extraterritoriality should be promptly ended without investigation, would not receive it. The commission's report was a qualified tribute to China's efforts in legal reform, but criticized the continued use of military courts. The commission found that China had not entrusted justice to a judiciary effectively protected against interference by the executive or other branches of the government. Nevertheless, the commission agreed to modifications in the consular courts, and indicated that the powers would consider abolition of extraterritoriality when China had made substantial progress on the principal reforms suggested.

The ratification by France in 1925 of the Nine-Power Treaty on the Chinese tariff cleared the way for a tariff conference at Peking in October. China had already demanded complete tariff autonomy.

---

7 United States, *Foreign Relations, 1923,* I, 625-626.

8 The powers represented included: the United States, Belgium, China, Denmark, France, Great Britain, Italy, Japan, the Netherlands, Norway, Portugal, Spain, and Sweden.

The conference recognized "China's right to enjoy tariff autonomy," agreed to remove the tariff restrictions contained in the treaties, and agreed to accept the Chinese National Tariff Law as of January 1, 1929. China on her part agreed to the effective abolition of *likin* as of that date.

From 1925 to 1928, when it fell before the Nationalist onslaught, the Peking government was as aggressive in asserting China's rights and in its demands for abolition of the unequal treaties as the southerners at Canton and Nanking. Its first success was a new treaty of commerce with Austria, October 19, 1925, confirming the wartime ending of Austria's extraterritorial rights. A second treaty between equals was concluded with Finland, October 29, 1926. Encouraged by these minor successes Peking became bolder, asserting its right, when certain clauses of a given treaty were subject to revision, to demand revision of the entire treaty, and failing this, to abrogate the treaty by unilateral action.

This policy was first applied to Belgium. In November, 1926, Peking announced by presidential mandate the abrogation of the Belgian treaty, that country having refused China's demand for complete revision. As a result, in January, 1927, Belgium indicated her willingness to negotiate a new treaty. In August, 1927, Peking, still further emboldened, gave notice that the Franco-Chinese commercial conventions of 1886-1887 and 1895 were no longer in effect. France, too, then agreed to join in negotiations for a new convention on the understanding that the old conventions would remain in force in the interim period. The negotiations continued until Peking fell to the Nationalist armies in 1928.

Peking was also able to initiate negotiations with Japan for revision of the treaty of 1896, and with Spain for the treaty of 1864. Furthermore, during 1927 it applied the Washington surtaxes in areas under its control. When Sir Francis Aglen, British Inspector-General of the Chinese Maritime Customs, refused to collect them, the Chinese dismissed him from office and appointed another Britisher, A. H. F. Edwardes, to succeed him.

Canton, Hankow, and Nanking in Foreign Affairs

The foregoing diplomacy between the Republic of China at Peking and the Powers was in some respects the least significant aspect of China's foreign relations during these years. As the Nationalist movement at Canton gained momentum after 1920, it was Sun Yat-sen and his successors supported by an aroused public opinion rather than the warlords of Peking who determined what China would or would not do to the rights and interests of the Powers and their nationals. Until their regime at Nanking was recognized in 1928, the Nationalists were thorough revolutionaries in diplomacy; thereafter their methods were to be more conservative and conventional. Moreover, until the expulsion of the Russian communist advisers from Wuhan in 1927, the devious methods of Soviet policy not only aided and abetted Chinese nationalism in its more violent forms but also conducted formal relations with the Republic in Peking and with the semi-independent warlords of Manchuria.

Beginnings of Soviet Policy in North China

Soviet Russian policy toward China had begun to unfold in 1918 with declarations that appeared to concede China's political rights in the Chinese Eastern Railway zone while reserving Russia's financial and economic interests. Later, in 1920, the Russians went further, declaring null and void all the treaties concluded with China by former Russian governments. Then in 1922 Adolph Joffe arrived in Peking seeking to re-establish diplomatic relations, to get Peking's approval of the new "independent" People's Revolutionary Government which the Russians had set up in Outer Mongolia in 1920, and to regain a position of influence in the Chinese Eastern Railway. Unsuccessful at Peking, Joffe went on to Shanghai to meet Sun Yat-sen. The result of that meeting was the immediate and remarkable growth of Soviet influence in the new *Kuomintang.* Furthermore, the Soviet position was strengthened by Joffe's subsequent visit to Japan and by the adherence to the Soviet Union (1922) of the Far Eastern Republic of Siberia. Accordingly, the Peking republic was in no position to rebuff further Russian overtures presented by L. M. Karakhan, September, 1923. A treaty concluded by Wellington Koo and Karakhan, May 31, 1924, provided for resumption of formal relations, surrender by Russia of extraterritorial rights and her concessions at Hankow and Tientsin, restoration of Russian legations and consulates and property of the Orthodox Church, Russian recognition of China's suzerainty in Outer Mongolia, and withdrawal of Russian troops. In addition Russia recognized Chinese sovereignty in the Chinese Eastern Railway zone and agreed that China might redeem the line "with Chinese capital," that the fate of the line would be determined by China and Russia to the exclusion of third parties, and that management of the road would be a joint Russo-Chinese concern.

THE RUSSO-MANCHURIAN AGREEMENT, 1924

Since the Chinese Eastern Railway lay in the Manchurian territories of Chang Tso-lin, over which at the time Peking had no control, Karakhan negotiated (September 20, 1924) a separate agreement with the Manchurian dictator. This agreement followed in general the previous Peking settlement. Actually, this agreement did not settle anything. During 1925 and 1926 Sino-Russian relations grew steadily worse. Moreover, by 1926 the Peking government was no longer controlled by the pro-Russian *tuchun,* Fêng Yü-hsiang, but by the anti-Bolshevik Chang Tso-lin of Manchuria. Once in Peking, Chang asked the recall of Karakhan and announced that he would rid North China of Bolshevik influence. Russia could afford to accept this reverse, for at Canton her influence was increasing steadily. It is notable, therefore, that Soviet Russia made treaties with Peking and Manchuria while at the same time her agents worked with Sun in reorganizing the *Kuomintang* at Canton.

THE SHANGHAI AFFAIR, MAY, 1925

Russian diplomacy in North China coincided with new forms of violence at Shanghai, the center of Western influence where the student movement was both anti-imperialistic and anti-Christian. On May 30, 1925, a Chinese mob in the Shanghai International Settlement, aroused by student agitators declaiming against labor conditions in Japanese cotton mills, was fired upon by Sikh and Chinese constables. The order to fire, given by a police inspector of British nationality, resulted in the death of nine Chinese. Chinese anger at this "inexcusable outrage" took the form of a general strike supported by virtually all sections of the populace. Business in Shanghai was at a standstill and remained so during most of the summer.

Repercussions of the incident were not confined to Shanghai. Anti-foreign outbreaks occurred at widely separated points spreading far into the interior, even to Chungking. The most serious disturbances took place at Canton headquarters of the Soviet-dominated

Kuomintang. A few foreigners and more than a hundred Chinese were killed when Chinese demonstrators paraded on the Shakee bund opposite the British and French concessions on the island of Shameen. Canton instituted a successful boycott of all British goods, and a general strike of Chinese workmen paralyzed business in British Hongkong.[9] In the face of these "alarming developments" relations between China and the Washington treaty powers reached a new high point of tension.

The Canton Soviet and the Powers

When, therefore, in 1926 the Nationalists at Canton were preparing for the northern march, they were able to capitalize not only upon the unhappy events just related but also upon a long series of blunders by which the principal powers had shaped their policies toward China. World War I had already done much to destroy the prestige of the white man in the Far East. After the war there was the failure to apply the Wilsonian program of equality and self-determination to Asiatic peoples. Then in 1919 came the failure to restore Kiaochow to China. Lastly, the Washington Conference, while voicing the principle of Chinese sovereignty, perpetuated the unequal treaties under a modest program of prospective revision. The net effect was to drive Sun Yat-sen to make anti-imperialism a clarion call of the Nationalist revolution. Meanwhile the powers knew not what course to pursue, since the end of the unequal treaties was demanded not only by the communists and the left wing of the *Kuomintang* but also by the center, the conservatives and militarists, including Chiang K'ai-shek, and the warlord regime at Peking.

The Anti-British Campaign at Hankow

The drive of revolutionary forces against Britain's position, so successfully begun at Canton, was continued with like success at Hankow in December, 1926. A general strike of industrial labor in the Wuhan cities called in November was followed by mass demonstrations in the anti-British crusade. The agitation was so effective

[9] See the study by Lennox A. Mills, *British Rule in Eastern Asia* (Minneapolis, 1942). It should be noted that popular anti-foreign outbreaks, boycotts, etc., were not entirely spontaneous. There was often much organized intimidation of the populace.

that on December 18, 1926, the British government proposed that the Washington treaty powers: (1) legalize what Canton was already doing by agreeing to immediate collection of the Washington surtaxes; (2) recognize and deal with regional governments; (3) implement a grant of tariff autonomy immediately upon China's promulgation of a national tariff; and (4) seek to develop better relations with China even while no national government existed. Britain's gesture of concession, far from satisfying the Nationalists, spurred them to new outbursts of fury. The British policy was described as a design to weaken China by creating regional governments and by encouraging militarists to seize the ports and to profit by collection of the proposed surtaxes.

Meanwhile, before the powers could reply to the British proposal, the anti-British crusade on the upper Yangtze had been carried still further. During the first week of January, 1927, under the threat of mob violence, the British abandoned their concessions in Hankow and Kiu-kiang. Both concessions were immediately taken over for administrative purposes by the Chinese. Likewise, without waiting for action by the powers, whatever Chinese groups happened to be in control of the treaty ports applied the surtaxes without further ado. In January, this developing situation brought forth hurried assurances from the Japanese and the American governments expressing sympathy with China's "just aspirations" and indicating willingness to aid their attainment in an orderly fashion. In the light of this rising tide of nationalism, Great Britain, already disposed to find a new basis for her relations with China, concluded agreements with the Nationalists during February and March, 1927, handing over the Hankow and Kiu-kiang concessions.

The Nanking Incident, 1927

Almost immediately following these agreements, Britain's policy of conciliation faced new trials at Nanking late in March. No sooner had the old southern capital been captured by the Nationalists than it became the scene of violent and seemingly premeditated attacks by *Kuomintang* troops upon foreign persons and property. American, British, French, Italian, and Japanese nationals were killed, wounded, or subjected to less fatal outrageous treatment. Foreign property was looted. Nor was there an end to these doings of the *Kuomintang* soldiery until British and American gunboats laid a protective barrage about the properties of the Standard Oil Company, where surviving foreigners had taken refuge. The United States, England, France, Italy, and Japan demanded (April 11) an apology, reparations, and guarantees for the future. China's reply was evasive, but despite this the powers did not press for an immediate settlement. To have done so would have strengthened the radical wing of the *Kuomintang*-Soviet leaders at Hankow. Actually, the powers were hoping for the success of a new, conservative, and non-Soviet national regime at Nanking.

Nanking's New Treaty Relations

With the ousting of the old Peking regime, June, 1928, the National Government at Nanking promptly took over the conduct of China's foreign relations. It issued a declaration (June 16) calling for new treaties negotiated with full regard to the sovereignty and equality of states. Then it gave notice that those unequal treaties which had expired were regarded as abrogated. Interim regulations denying extraterritoriality would control the nationals of these countries until new treaties were negotiated. Although these declarations were by no means welcome to the powers, nevertheless they were disposed to negotiate. Indeed, there was no alternative unless they proposed to use force to impose the old treaties. Moreover, China's break with Russia and the new conservative orientation of the *Kuomintang* were pleasing to the foreign business groups and, in the main, to their governments.

The United States was the first power to act. By a treaty concluded at Peking on July 25, 1928, this country conceded tariff autonomy to China, subject of course to most-favored-nation treatment. The agreement was one of the most significant in China's foreign relations, for "it shattered the old international bloc" long opposed to any concessions. On February 1, 1929, the National Government revealed its new-found strength by enforcing a new import tariff, the first since 1843 to be drawn by the Chinese themselves free from foreign interference. The tariff agreement with the United States was followed before the end of 1928 by similar agreements with other powers. Indeed, by January, 1929, Japan was the only power that had not concluded a new tariff agreement. This situation was due to a number of questions outstanding between the two countries. Not until Japanese troops had retired from Shantung and China had agreed to revenue allotments for the security of certain Japanese loans was an agreement reached (May 6, 1930).

The new China tariff treaties with Belgium, Denmark, Italy, Portugal, and Spain contained provisions for abolition of extraterritoriality subject to a similar concession by all the powers. Accordingly, on April 27, 1929, Nanking addressed the United States, Great Britain, and France requesting abolition at the earliest possible date. Similar notes went to Brazil, the Netherlands, and Norway. The replies of Britain, France, and the United States (August 10) were an emphatic denial that China was as yet entitled to full jurisdictional sovereignty. While complimenting China on the progress she had made, they noted that the recommendations of the Commission on Extraterritoriality had not been carried out. In September, 1929, China protested this attitude both directly to the powers and in the Assembly of the League of Nations. In December, Nanking went a step further, announcing the unilateral ending of extraterritoriality as of January 1, 1930, but softening the blow with the assurance that China would negotiate with powers willing to do so.

By the beginning of 1931 there was some reason to believe that China under the Nanking government was finding a new national stability, that the day of the warlord was gone, that the Russian bid for control had failed, that the unequal treaty system would be ended by the orderly processes of diplomacy, and finally that Sun Yat-sen's program for a new China was assured.

For Further Reading

Berkov, Robert, *Strong Man of China* (Boston, 1938).

Borg, Dorothy, *American Policy and the Chinese Revolution, 1925-1928* (New York, 1947).

Chapman, H. Owen, *The Chinese Revolution, 1926-1927* (London, 1928).

Chiang Wên-han, *The Chinese Student Movement* (New York, 1948).

Fishel, Wesley R., *The End of Extraterritoriality in China* (Berkeley, 1952).

Houn, F. W., *Central Government of China, 1912-1928* (Madison, 1957).

Jansen, Marius B., *The Japanese and Sun Yat-sen* (Cambridge, 1954).

Linebarger, Paul M. A., *The China of Chiang K'ai-shek: A Political Study* (Boston, 1941). An able sympathetic study.

Rich, Raymond T., *Extraterritoriality and Tariff Autonomy in China* (Shanghai, 1925). A convenient introductory survey.

Sun Yat-sen, *The International Development of China* (Chungking, 1941).

T'ang Leang-li, *The Inner History of the Chinese Revolution* (London, 1930). A favorable interpretation of the rise of the *Kuomintang* and a justification of both the Soviet orientation and its later repudiation.

———, *Wang Ching-wei, A Political Biography* (Peiping, 1931).

Tayler, J. B., *Farm and Factory in China* (London, 1928). The agricultural and industrial background against which the Nationalist movement developed.

Tong, H. K., *Chiang Kai-shek* (2 vols., Shanghai, 1937).

Tyau, M. T. Z., *China Awakened* (New York, 1922). Good chapters on the intellectual awakening.

Weigh Ken Shen, *Russo-Chinese Diplomacy* (Shanghai, 1928).

Whiting, Allen S., *Soviet Policies in China, 1917-1924* (New York, 1954). A major work of scholarship.

Wilbur, C. Martin, and Julie Lien-Ying How, eds., *Documents of Communism, Nationalism, and Soviet Advisers in China, 1918-1927. Papers Seized in the 1927 Peking Raid* (New York, 1956).

Woodhead, H. G. W., *The Truth about the Chinese Republic* (London, 1925). The contemporary views of a Britisher, long resident in China, editor of *The China Year Book,* who opposed abrogation of the unequal treaties.

30

1929–1937

The Manchurian Crises

MANCHURIA in 1931 was a fertile and strategic land of some 380,000 square miles, as large as the combined area of France and Germany, with an estimated population of 30,000,000 persons, of whom some 28,000,000 were Chinese (including a small percentage of native Manchus), 500,000 or more Mongols, 800,000 Koreans, 150,000 Russians, and some 230,000 Japanese. Until the beginning of the twentieth century Manchuria had played only a minor role in world history. After 1895, Russia, and later Japan, considered Manchuria as the strategic base of Far Eastern politics. After the Chinese Eastern Railway was built, Manchuria assumed importance because of its own natural wealth. In 1928 the total value of Manchuria's agricultural products, including such principal crops as soya beans, kaoliang, wheat, millet, and barley, most of which were exported, was some $650,000,000. There had also been extensive exploitation of the rich timber lands and of such minerals as coal, iron, and gold. This rapid development of a frontier region was made possible by the capital and managerial investments of Russia and Japan and by the toil and industry of millions of Chinese immigrant farmers from Shantung who, after the turn of the century, settled in increasing numbers on the newly opened lands. The Manchu dynasty and the later Republic asserted Chinese sovereignty in Manchuria, but Russia and Japan went on building spheres of influence. Yet while all this was going on, millions of Chinese peasants had taken possession of Manchuria's soil and in this sense had made it irrevocably Chinese. During the years 1905-1928, Manchurian politics, in so far as it was not controlled by Russia or Japan, was run by Chang Tso-lin, an erstwhile bandit who had turned statesman. Chang, like the warlords of any other province, "alternately supported, attacked, or declared his territory independent of the Central Government," but this did not mean that the Manchurians "wished to be separated from China" or that the goal of Chang himself was to set up a separate nation-state. On the contrary, it was a part of the strategy by which one *tuchun* or another hoped to exterminate his rivals and to emerge as head of a unified national China. Although Chang's armies acted at times as though they were allied with the forces of the *Kuomintang*, the Old Marshal was not in general a supporter of the Party's doctrines; yet he favored the unification of China, and, if he had possessed the power to do so, he would have ousted both the Russians and the Japanese from their Manchurian spheres of influence. It was he who prepared the way for the attack on the Chinese Eastern Railway in 1929 and who initiated a policy of Chinese railway construction "which was to cut off the [Japanese] South Manchuria Railway from some of its feeder districts." Although he was long reputed a friend of Japan, he appeared less willing in his last years to permit Japan's "special position" to go unchallenged.[1]

Manchuria under Chang Hsueh-liang, 1928

The Young Marshal, Chang Hsueh-liang, who succeeded as ruler of Manchuria after his father came to a violent end in 1928, was in many respects an ardent Nationalist. He, too, resented the presence of Russia and Japan. In December, 1928, he announced his allegiance to the Nanking Government, accepted the Nationalist flag, and in turn was made commander-in-chief of the North-Eastern Frontier Army and was confirmed as chief of administration of Manchuria, Jehol, and part of Inner Mongolia. So far as the internal administration of Manchuria was involved, the new allegiance to Nanking was nominal rather than real. A Manchurian headquarters of the *Kuomintang* was established, but, in reality, "the old system and its personnel continued to function as before"; the Nanking Government had merely confirmed what the Manchurian authorities were pleased to do.

However, if there was little change in domestic policy, the allegiance of Manchuria to the National Government produced results of great consequence in foreign policy. To the "forward policy" adopted by the Old Marshal before his death was now added a "well-

[1] League of Nations, *Report of the Commission of Inquiry* [The Lytton Commission] (Geneva, 1932), 24-30.

organized and systematic *Kuomintang* propaganda" which dwelt ceaselessly "on the primary importance of the recovery of lost sovereign rights, the abolition of unequal treaties and the wickedness of imperialism." This propaganda was extremely effective in Manchuria, where the presence of the foreigner with his special rights was more obtrusive than in any other part of China except Shanghai. As a result, Russians, both Reds and Whites, and Japanese, including Koreans as Japanese subjects, soon felt the effects of a "systematic persecution" manifesting itself through popular agitation or in specific acts such as the raising of rents or refusals to renew contracts.

In Manchuria, as in other parts of China, there was the tendency for the official *Kuomintang* "line" to focus upon the foreigner and imperialism as the cause of all China's trouble to the exclusion of other contributing factors. Among these contributory factors were the military dictatorship and the administrative bureaucracy through which the Young Marshal ruled the Three Eastern Provinces. Under the system, military expenses consumed about 80 per cent of total expenditure. The Manchurian armies numbered about one-quarter of a million men equipped from an arsenal that cost $200,000,000 (silver). "The treasury was not capable of paying adequate salaries to the officials. As all power rested in the hands of a few military men, office could be owned only through them. Nepotism, corruption, and maladministration continued to be unavoidable consequences of this state of affairs." Taxes were progressively raised, and when even these revenues proved inadequate, there was the handy practice by which the authorities steadily depreciated irredeemable provincial currencies. To a very great extent by 1930, the Manchurian militarists controlled the banks, which in turn bought the harvests with irredeemable and depreciating paper with the idea of forcing the foreign buyers to pay higher prices. The result was to impoverish the Chinese farmer and to infuriate the Japanese. Yet in all this maladministration there were some signs of improvement. The Chinese peasant and Chinese capital were playing under the Changs a greater part than ever before in Manchurian development.

The Russo-Chinese Crisis of 1929

While the National Government at Nanking was regaining tariff autonomy and was seeking to abolish the extraterritorial rights of the great powers, it faced a new crisis in Manchuria with communistic Russia on the recurrent problem of the Chinese Eastern Railway. Since the expulsion of the communists from the *Kuomintang* in 1927, Sino-Russian relations had grown progressively worse. In Manchuria these relations had never been happy even after Chang Tso-lin's agreement with the Soviets in 1924. Chang was bitterly anti-communist. The Soviet was determined to maintain its right in the railway and it used the railroad zone as a base for communist propaganda. The conflict came into the open in 1927 when the Old Marshal, at the time still master of Peking, raided the Soviet headquarters there, charging Russian violation of the no-propaganda clauses of the 1924 Sino-Soviet agreements. Two years later, in May, 1929, the Young Marshal entered Soviet consulates along the Chinese Eastern Railway, arrested communist agents, and seized documentary evidence of Soviet subversion. In July the Manchurians took over the railroad telegraph system and arrested Soviet employees, replacing them with Chinese and White Russians. When China did not respond to an ultimatum addressed to both Nanking and Mukden, the Soviets broke off relations while an informal warfare of raids back and forth broke out on the Siberian-Manchurian border.

Testing the Pact of Paris

These border hostilities were a direct challenge to principles of the recently signed treaty for the Renunciation of War, August, 1928, commonly called the Pact of Paris or the Briand-Kellogg Treaty. Accordingly, the new American Secretary of State, Henry L. Stimson, acting on the theory that the treaty should be "a practical instrument for preserving peace," reminded both Russia and China of their obligations to employ peaceful means of settlement. This appeal, approved by other major signatories, brought assurances from Russia and China that they would resort to force only in self-defense.[2]

Meanwhile, negotiations between the Soviet and local Manchurian officials and between the Russian Ambassador and the Chinese Minister in Berlin were abortive. By November there was open though undeclared warfare on the Manchurian border. A Soviet

[2] In the Pact of Paris the signatories: (1) "condemned recourse to war for the solution of international controversies," (2) renounced war "as an instrument of national policy," and (3) agreed that the settlement of all disputes should be by none but pacific means. All signatories reserved the right of self-defense.

army invaded Manchuria from the west. The forces of Chang Hsueh-liang retreated in confusion. On December 3, Chang agreed to Russia's demands, and Nanking followed suit on December 22.

The brief undeclared war had shown: (1) that in Manchuria, Soviet Russia was as jealous of her interests and as ready to defend them by force as was tsarist Russia before her; (2) that the Briand-Kellogg Treaty was an ineffective preventive of war; and (3) that the National Government at Nanking, involved in suppressing opposition in central and northwest China, was incapable of exerting power in the border provinces of the northeast. These conclusions were not lost on Japan's determined expansionists.

Sino-Japanese Issues in Manchuria

During the quarter of a century before September, 1931, the ties which bound Manchuria to the rest of China were growing stronger and, at the same time, the interests of Japan in Manchuria were increasing. Manchuria was admittedly a part of China, but it was a part in which Japan had acquired or claimed such exceptional rights, so restricting the exercise of China's sovereign rights, that a conflict between the two countries was a natural result.[3]

Manchuria had come to represent, by 1931, a fundamental clash of Sino-Japanese interests. Chinese nationalism regarded it as the "first line of defense"; Japanese governments, as a "life-line." Chinese called it the "granary of China," while the migration of Chinese peasants to it was a sort of safety valve easing the pressure in over-crowded areas such as Shantung. Japanese felt that they had won Liaotung in 1895; that they had saved Manchuria from Russia in 1905; that Japanese capital was principally responsible for the development of the country; and that by reason of patriotism, defense, and exceptional treaty rights they had thus acquired there a "special position."

Principal among specific issues were conflicts arising out of the Sino-Japanese Manchurian treaty and notes of May, 1915. Whereas after 1915 Japan insisted upon the fulfillment of the treaty, the Chinese persistently denied its validity. The issues tended to become more acute after 1928 when the *Kuomintang* was established in Manchuria. After 1927, too, there was a movement among the Chinese to divest the South Manchuria Railway of its political and administrative functions, making of it a purely commercial enterprise. This was

---

[3] *Report of the Commission of Inquiry,* 37.

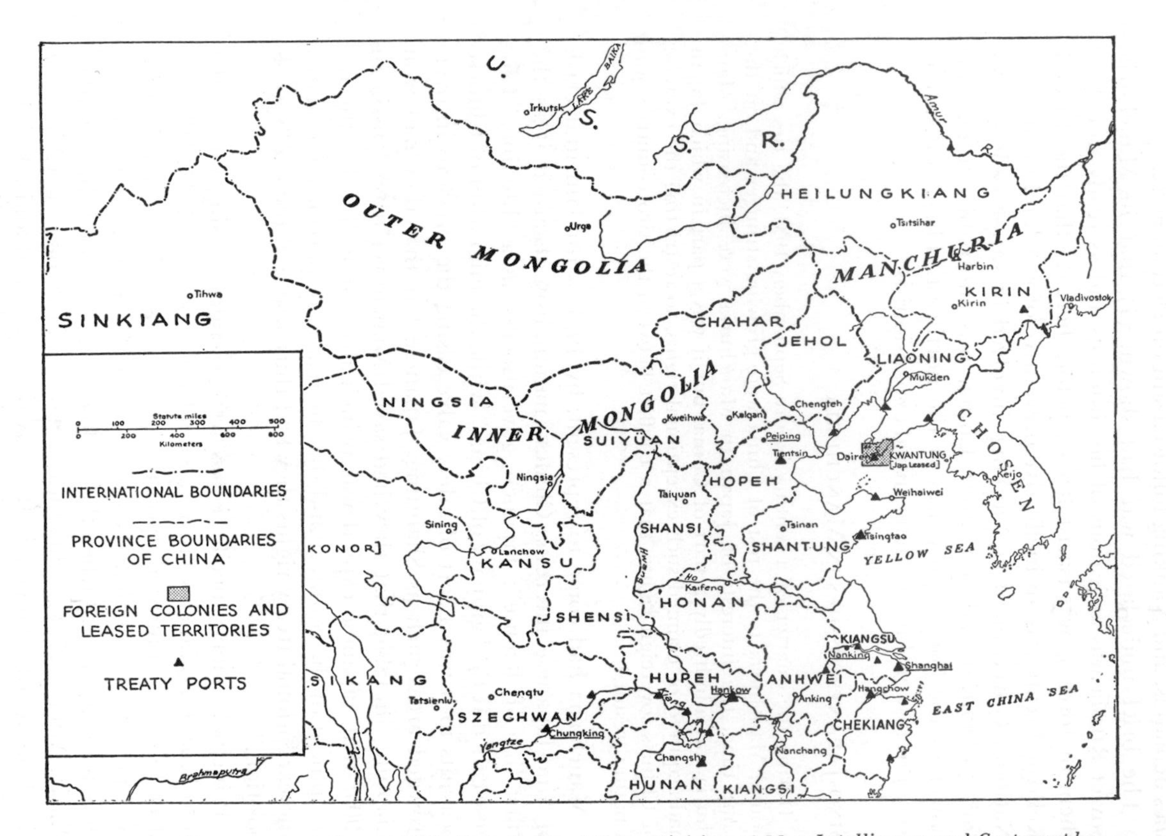

Central and Northeastern China, 1931. *U. S. Dept. of State, Division of Map Intelligence and Cartography.*

a natural nationalistic aspiration, but it struck at the very basis of Japan's position, which in Manchuria was definitely political. Furthermore, although the original Russo-Chinese Railway Agreement of 1896 conferred upon the original Chinese Eastern Railway Com-

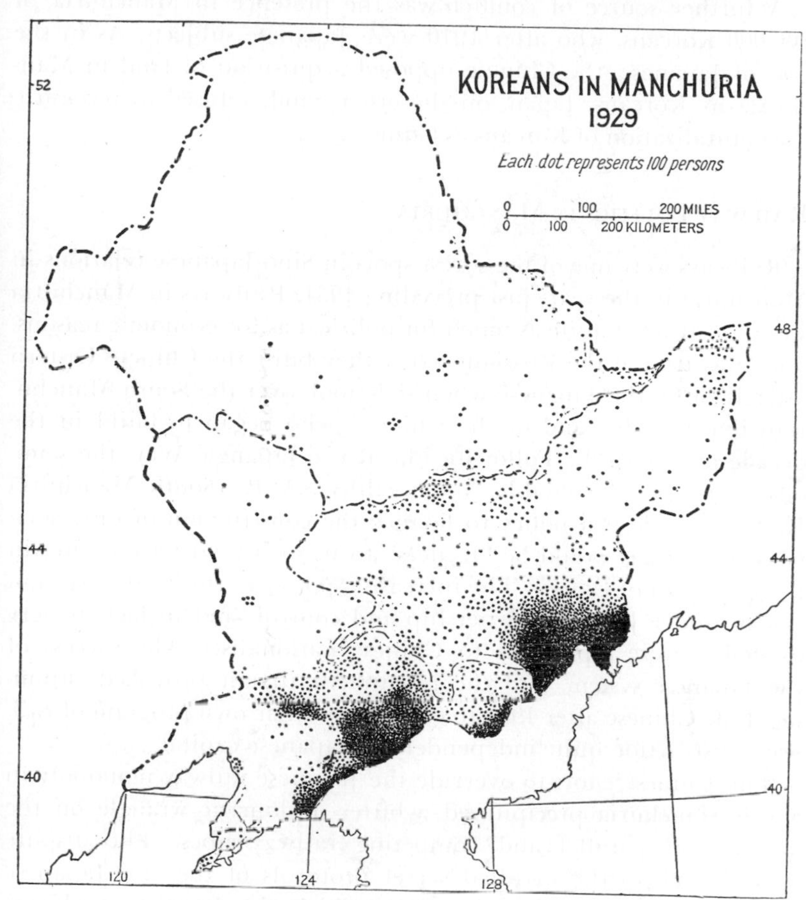

Courtesy of the Geographical Review, *published by the American Geographical Society of New York.*

pany the "absolute and exclusive administration of its [railway] lands," the Chinese government denied on legal grounds that this conferred political control in the railway zone. In addition, the activities of Japanese railway guards, both in and outside the railway zone, and of the Japanese consular police became increasingly irritating as Nationalist sentiment in Manchuria grew. These police were located not only in the railroad areas but also at Japanese consulates in various towns, Harbin, Manchouli, and the Chientao District on the Korean border.

A further source of conflict was the presence in Manchuria of 800,000 Koreans, who after 1910 were Japanese subjects. As in the case of Japanese, the Chinese opposed acquisition of land in Manchuria by Koreans. Japan, on the other hand, refused to recognize the naturalization of Koreans as Chinese.

Railway Politics in Manchuria

Railways were one of the sorest spots in Sino-Japanese relations in Manchuria in the years just preceding 1931. Railways in Manchuria were constructed quite as much for political as for economic reasons. This was true of the Russians when they built the Chinese Eastern after 1896; of the Japanese when they took over the South Manchurian line in 1905; and of the Chinese, who began to build in the decade of the 1920's. Following the Russo-Japanese War, the semi-official, efficient, profitable, and wealthy S.M.R. (South Manchuria Railway) made it a policy to finance the construction of only such Chinese lines as would be "feeders" to its own road terminating in the great port of Dairen. The increasing power of this transportation system under Japanese ownership and control, and in fact its very existence, were repugnant to Chinese nationalists. The success of the Japanese system, and the resentment that it provoked, stimulated the Chinese after 1924 to embark on their own program of railway construction quite independent of Japanese capital.

This Chinese effort to override the Japanese railway monopoly in South Manchuria precipitated a bitter diplomatic wrangle on the question of parallel and competing railway lines. The dispute harked back to the so-called secret protocols of the Sino-Japanese Treaty of Peking, December, 1905, which the Japanese said precluded China from building such lines, and which the Chinese said did not. The legal merits of the argument were never resolved. What did happen was that the Chinese did build railways paralleling and competing with the S.M.R. system and connecting with the Chinese controlled ports of Yingkow and Hulutao, and these lines were quite successful in diverting traffic from the Japanese roads.

Further Sino-Japanese trouble in Manchuria was a result of Japanese financing of certain Chinese Government railways. By 1931, Japanese capital and interest to the value of 150,000,000 yen had been expended in the construction of four major and a number of lesser Chinese lines. Japan complained that China would not pay the loans or appoint Japanese railway advisers as required by the agreements. China countered Japan's arguments with the contention that the loans were primarily strategic and political; that they had been made by the S.M.R. with the idea of monopolizing railroad construction; and that the lines were heavily over-capitalized and could not be put on a paying basis. But here again it was clear that the issues at stake were political. There was in addition a miscellaneous assortment of railway and other disputes involving Sino-Japanese agreements, most of which had political and strategic overtones. One of these, the Wanpaoshan affair (1931) was of little importance in itself, but it led to anti-Chinese riots and bloodshed in Korea, and from there to an anti-Japanese boycott in China. While this furor was at its height, a certain Captain Nakamura, a Japanese intelligence officer, was killed by Chinese troops in Inner Mongolia.

Summary: Manchurian Issues, September, 1931

The Sino-Japanese Manchurian question by mid-September, 1931, had produced a collision of "irreconcilable policies." As the tension increased, both sides made some efforts to find solutions by peaceful means, but by 1931 the more extreme Japanese militarists and the more rabid of the Chinese nationalists had so aroused public opinion as to render negotiation and compromise virtually impossible. Even had the best of intentions prevailed, peaceful settlement would have required restraint and wisdom.

Moreover, for those who in China and Japan favored and planned a policy of force to settle Manchurian issues, September, 1931, was a time well chosen. The full force of a great world-wide depression was being felt by every major power. Everywhere the prospects for Europe's proposed disarmament conference were "as dark as they well could be." In Europe there was economic chaos, which had called forth the Hoover Moratorium. England deserted the gold standard in September, and in both England and the United States there was economic distress with which neither government seemed able to deal. If force were applied in Manchuria, it was unlikely that Europe or America would interfere effectively to stop it.

SEPTEMBER 18, 1931, AND AFTER

On the night of September 18, 1931, the Japanese Kwantung army seized the city of Mukden. The hostilities were precipitated, according to the Japanese, by a Chinese attempt to blow up the tracks of the S.M.R. In these initial military operations, the Japanese also seized Changchun, September 19, and Kirin, September 21. Also on September 21 China appealed to the League of Nations under Article XI, and requested the United States, a champion of the Briand-Kellogg Pact, to aid in preserving Far Eastern peace and the principle of peaceful settlement of international disputes.[4] Following immediate consultation between the League and the American State Department, the Secretary of State, Henry L. Stimson, gave assurance of American "co-operation and frankness," and expressed the opinion that the Japanese military had ignored the Japanese Foreign Office. The American government favored preparations to uphold treaty obligations but felt the Western powers should "avoid action which might excite nationalistic feeling in Japan in support of the military and against Shidehara."[5] From this point on, the United States and the major League powers were in virtually constant but not effective consultation on the Manchurian dispute. On its part, the League, which had just assembled when the outbreak occurred, requested (September 22) both China and Japan to seek a peaceful settlement by withdrawing their troops. At the same time the League considered sending a commission to investigate, and suggested that the United States make similar proposals to the disputants. For the moment, Stimson did not take to this proposal or to the appointment of an American on the commission as proposed by the League, but, independently, he informed the Japanese, September 22, "that the responsibility for determining the course of events with regard to the liquidating of this [Manchurian] situation rests largely upon Japan," and he hinted that both the Kellogg Pact and the Nine-Power Open Door Treaty were at stake. Stimson held that the road to this liquidation lay in "giving Shidehara and the Foreign Office an opportunity, free from anything approaching a threat or even public criticism, to get control of the situation." It was the difficult problem of letting "the Japanese know that we are

---

[4] Detailed treatment is in W. W. Willoughby, *The Sino-Japanese Controversy and the League of Nations* (Baltimore, 1935), ch. iii.

[5] Henry L. Stimson, *The Far Eastern Crisis* (New York, 1936), 41-42.

watching them and at the same time to do it in a way which will help Shidehara."[6]

The Spread of Hostilities in Manchuria

Meanwhile affairs were not progressing smoothly in Manchuria. Japanese troops did not withdraw as a result of the League's discreet request. Indeed, the Kwantung army announced that it no longer recognized the government of Chang Hsueh-liang, and on October 8 the city of Chinchow, near the border of China proper, was bombed by Japanese planes. The purpose was to disperse the remnants of Chang's government and army, but its effect was much broader than this, for it gave clear indication that the Kwantung army was not to be stopped by fine words and that the League hesitated to take any vigorous action. Simultaneously the United States took a more vigorous stand in supporting "independently" the efforts of the League and in suggesting the course to be pursued. The American Consul at Geneva, Prentiss Gilbert, was authorized to participate in meetings of the League Council involving applicants of the Briand-Kellogg Pact.

Back in Manchuria Japanese forces, ignoring a League resolution of October 24 directing Japan to withdraw her army within the railroad zone by November 16, proceeded to extend their conquests into North Manchuria to the town of Tsitsihar beyond the main line of the Russian-controlled Chinese Eastern Railway, and also to move southward toward Chinchow. With these conquests safely achieved, Japan proposed that the League send the often-discussed commission of investigation. On December 10, supported by the Japanese delegate, the League decided to do so. On the following day in Tokyo the Wakatsuki-Shidehara cabinet fell amid a rising tide of popular nationalism. Only a few weeks later the triumph of militarism seemed assured when the Kwantung army, dispersing the last southern remnants of Chang's armies, captured the city of Chinchow, January 2, 1932. The effort to solve the Manchurian conflict by peaceful means had failed. As 1932 advanced Japan completed her military conquest.[7]

---

[6] Stimson, *Far Eastern Crisis,* 34-37.

[7] There were efforts toward "appeasement" made by the Nanking Government which form a part of the general international effort to solve the Manchurian conflict by peaceful means.

AMERICAN NON-RECOGNITION DOCTRINE

The principle, early recognized by Stimson, that the whole fiasco of peace in Manchuria could be solved only by the contestants meant that the function of the League and other interested powers was to find a means of bringing China and Japan together in peaceful negotiation.[8] This seemingly simple goal was never reached. The approaches to it were blocked by the pre-determined purposes of the Japanese army, by the at times unwise diplomacy of China, by the inability of the Western powers to agree on what should and could be done, by the timidity with which governments considered action when the results could not be foreseen, and by the confusion of the public mind both in the United States and abroad as to the real issues and how they should be faced.

From the beginning of the Manchurian conflict in September, the League powers as well as the United States were well aware of the dangers involved. Open conflict between Japan and China was a threat to the Nine-Power Treaty, to the Treaty for the Renunciation of War, to the prestige of the League of Nations itself, and indeed to all governments that regarded their interests as synonymous with the upholding of world peace and the implementation of the principle of collective security. Yet as the closing months of 1931 passed by, and as Japan's military action progressed, neither the League nor the United States applied economic or military sanctions. During 1931, the United States did not propose any policy of sanctions. Indeed, it was the League powers that sounded cautiously the American Secretary as to whether the United States would support a policy of sanctions. Secretary Stimson gave no encouragement to these inquiries; in fact, his expositions of policy and his instructions to American representatives at Geneva, London, and Paris were hostile to sanctions of any kind involving the United States, other than the sanctions of adverse public opinion and official non-recognition of conquests or settlements achieved by other than peaceful means.

The American government attempted to act "independently" of the League, "reserving full independence of judgment as to each step to be taken," while at the same time "endeavoring to support

---

[8] United States, *Foreign Relations, 1931,* III, "The Far East" (Washington, 1946), 411. "We do not care what solution is reached between China and Japan so long as it is done by pacific means." Stimson to Dawes, November 10, 1931

the general objective of the League, namely, the preservation of peace in Manchuria."

Such was the background of the action taken by Stimson on January 7, 1932, when, after informing the British and the French of his intentions but without waiting for their concurrence, he informed China and Japan that the United States

> . . . cannot admit the legality of any situation de facto nor does it intend to recognize any treaty or agreement entered into between those governments, or agents thereof, which may impair the treaty rights of the United States or its citizens in China, including those which relate to the sovereignty, the independence, or the territorial and administrative integrity of the Republic of China, or to the international policy relative to China, commonly known as the open-door policy; and that it does not intend to recognize any situation, treaty, or agreement which may be brought about by means contrary to the covenants and obligations of the Pact of Paris, of August 27, 1928, to which treaty both China and Japan, as well as the United States, are parties.

The United States was moving slowly from a policy of conciliation toward one of diplomatic coercion. The non-recognition doctrine was a reassertion of Secretary Bryan's position of May, 1915, while the note as a whole was a reassertion of traditional American policy since the time of Secretary Hay. As in former cases, the note assumed erroneously that Britain and France would see their far eastern interests as identical with those of the United States.[9] Neither Britain nor France associated itself with this American move.

Hostilities Spread to Shanghai

Toward the end of January, 1932, Sino-Japanese hostilities spread from Manchuria to Shanghai, where a most effective boycott of Japanese goods became the occasion for a naval bombardment of Chinese sections of the city. But, unlike the policy of retreat in Manchuria, at Shanghai a Chinese army (the 19th Route Army) held its position until the arrival early in March of heavy Japanese army reinforcements. Britain, whose interests were now affected seriously, protested Japanese bombings at Shanghai, and concurrently with the United States sent naval and marine reinforcements to the In-

---

[9] See Foster Rhea Dulles, *China and America* (Princeton, 1946), 189-201, for American public reactions.

ternational Settlement. Meanwhile, China invoked Articles X and XV of the Covenant, under which the League was required to assess responsibility and eventually perhaps to apply sanctions. This led to appointment of a League committee at Shanghai consisting of the local consular representatives of the League states to report directly

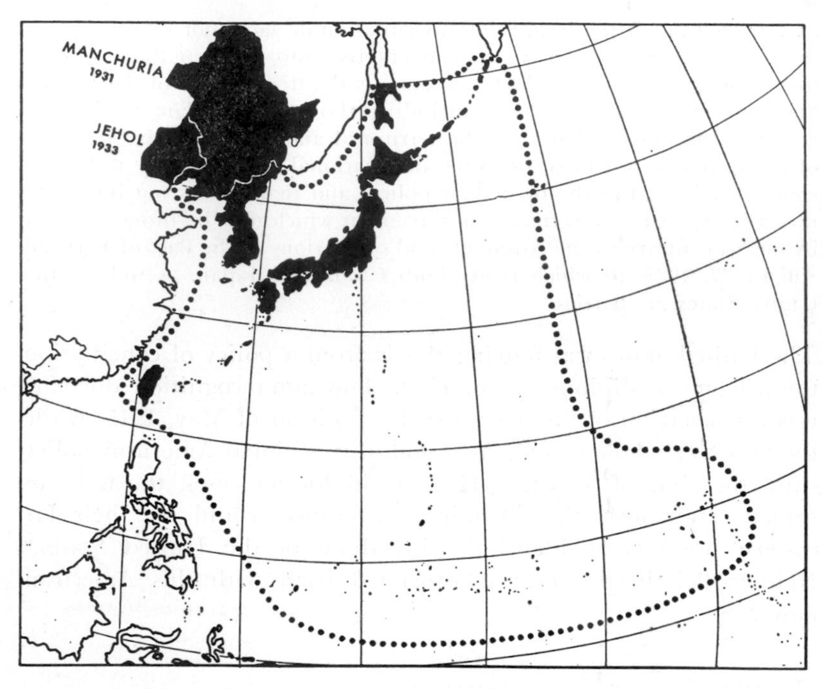

JAPAN, 1931-1933. *Reproduced from* A War Atlas for Americans, *Simon and Schuster, Inc., New York, 1944, by permission from Simon and Schuster, Inc., and from the U. S. Department of State, Division of Map Intelligence and Cartography.*

on conditions there. Meanwhile, in Manchuria the Japanese had consolidated their political as well as their military position. They had encouraged and promoted the organization of local self-governing administrations throughout Manchuria which were gradually combined in a new "State" that declared its independence of China and the *Kuomintang*, February 18, 1932.

On February 24, the developing policy of the United States was revealed in a letter from Secretary Stimson to Senator William E.

Borah, Chairman of the Senate Foreign Relations Committee. It affirmed that a situation had been created in the Far East in violation of the Nine-Power Treaty and the Briand-Kellogg Pact; that the Nine-Power Treaty was merely one of a group of "interrelated and interdependent" treaties; that the willingness of the United States in 1922 to restrict the fortifications of the Philippines and to surrender its freedom in capital ship construction was predicated on the assumption that other powers would accept the self-denying ordinances imposed by the Nine-Power Treaty. Although this letter was a general appeal to the powers to join the United States in the non-recognition doctrine, it had other specific objectives. Stimson hoped to encourage China; to clarify policy to the American public; to influence the coming Assembly of the League of Nations; to remind the Conservative British government of its responsibilities under the Nine-Power Open Door Treaty, which Balfour had helped to write; and, finally, to suggest to Japan that if the Nine-Power Treaty was of no importance to her, other powers might decide that other treaties of great consequence to Japan were of little importance to them.

For a time there was some improvement. The League Assembly, March, 1932, aligned itself with the non-recognition doctrine, and in May, China and Japan made peace at Shanghai on terms worked out by the consular committee of the League. But these improvements were at best temporary. The League's disarmament conference in the spring of 1932 revealed the inability of Europe and America to agree on any formula for arms reduction, let alone present an effective united front against Japan. As a result Japan was accorded a virtual free hand in Manchuria. On March 9, the former and last Manchu emperor of China, now known as Mr. Henry P'u-yi, became regent of the new state of Manchukuo, and on September 15, Japan in a treaty extended formal recognition to this "offspring of aggression." Less than a month later, October 2, the Report of the League's investigating body, the Lytton Commission, made its anti-climactic appearance.

THE REPORT OF THE COMMISSION OF INQUIRY

On the course of immediate events, the Report had no influence at all, but as a clarification of the issues at stake, and as a plan for peaceful settlement (for anyone who wanted a peaceful settlement), its importance could hardly be overestimated.[10] The Report presented Manchuria as a complex product of historical development involving conditions unparalleled elsewhere, and found that neither a restoration of the *status quo ante* nor the continued maintenance of Manchukuo provided a solution.

Japan's reply to the Report, November 21, 1932, insisted that Japan alone was the judge whether her military action was justifiable self-defense.

The League and the Lytton Report

At the League, the report of the Commission was considered by a special Committee of Nineteen, which in February, 1933, recommended: (1) non-recognition of Manchukuo, (2) a Manchurian government compatible with Chinese sovereignty, and (3) an invitation to Japan and China to undertake direct negotiations under the good offices of a League commission. Japan's response was the invasion of Jehol province in January, 1933; a dramatic scene at Geneva where the Japanese delegation, headed by Matsuoka Yosuke, walked out of the Assembly, February 24; and finally, March 27, Japan's announcement of her withdrawal from the League, which under terms of the Covenant would become effective in two years' time. Meanwhile, Japanese armies were completing the conquest of Jehol province. Other forces invaded the Pei-p'ing area south of the Great Wall, where at Tangku a truce was signed, May 31, 1933, creating a broad "demilitarized neutral" zone from which all Chinese military forces were excluded. This invasion of North China pointed directly toward Japanese control of North China by the creation of an autonomous buffer state.[11]

---

[10] Members of the Commission included: H. E. Count Aldrovandi (Italian), Général de Division Henri Claudel (French); the Rt. Hon. the Earl of Lytton (British), chairman; H. E. Dr. Heinrich Schnee (German); and Major-General Frank Ross McCoy (American), who served with the approval of the Department of State but as an official representative of the League and not of the United States. This was a nice distinction, since the United States was not a member of the League, though in the Manchurian dispute the United States, in the opinion of many, had gone a long way toward entering the League by the back door.

[11] George E. Taylor, *The Struggle for North China* (New York, 1940), 17. On Japan's withdrawal from the League, see League of Nations, *Official Journal*, XIV (1933), 657-658.

Manchuria: Interpretations

By the application of force Japan had gained control of nearly half a million square miles of territory by means which the international legal opinion of governments did not regard as war, and which the Japanese termed euphemistically an "incident." It was peaceful war, or war that is not war at all. Nevertheless, the effect was to reshape the Far East more radically than any previous "incident" since the British in 1842 had fashioned the Treaty of Nanking. Japan's creation of Manchukuo was an effort to establish a continental power in Asia as a counterbalance to the maritime power which Western nations had exercised over China through nearly a century.[12]

In a broader sense, the Manchurian "incident" was a second and more disheartening test of collective security as a principle, and of the means of enforcing it. As Russia used direct action in North Manchuria in 1929, so Japan used force in South Manchuria and North China from 1931 to 1933. Although the League of Nations performed a useful task through the investigations of the Lytton Commission, neither France nor Great Britain, the powers which dominated the League, was prepared to apply sanctions against Japan without the active support of the United States. The question of sanctions was settled for all the powers when they received no encouragement from Washington in 1931. Moreover, while the United States co-operated to a limited degree with the League, this country remained outside the world's only permanent machinery dedicated to the principle of collective security, and the American administration was constantly fearful of public reaction should it appear that it was using Manchuria as a back-door entry into the League. In reality, American policy, as the Manchurian affair developed in 1931, remained true to traditional principles of the open door and the integrity of China as embodied in the Washington Treaties, and it called upon Japan to observe these covenants and the Treaty for the Renunciation of War. It prodded the League toward similar action. Whether more could have been expected from a government representative of the same political faith which a decade earlier had repudiated the Wilsonian program of collective security is a matter on which there has been no general agreement. At all events, neither the League nor the United States nor the two together stopped

---

[12] Owen Lattimore, *The Mongols of Manchuria* (New York, 1934), 15.

Japan, and the integrity of China was not preserved by reassertion of the non-recognition doctrine.

It should be noted, too, that the American doctrine of non-recognition revived by Hoover and Stimson in the Manchurian crisis did not mean the same thing to these two statesmen throughout the years 1931-1933. Non-recognition to Hoover was "a substitute for economic pressure or military force, a formula looking toward conciliation and peace and relying on the moral force of public opinion for its effect." Presumably, this was also Stimson's view in the beginning. But, as Japan's aggression spread, the Secretary came to regard non-recognition not as "an alternative, but as a preliminary to economic and military sanctions, a way of drawing sharp the issue between the United States (along with the League of Nations) and Japan, a means of laying down the ideological grounds for war if, as he expected, war eventually should come." It was this later phase of the Stimson interpretation that formed the basis of the still later Roosevelt-Hull diplomacy with Japan.[13]

Finally, the complex causes that led to Japan's seizure of Manchuria will continue to tax the resourcefulness of history. The most widely held and popular interpretation in the years after 1931, especially in the United States, was that Japanese militarism unleashed in Manchuria was simply unprovoked aggression and that these Japanese acts were responsible primarily for the whole later train of events which led to the breakdown of collective security, to the outbreak of war in Europe, and then to Pearl Harbor. The simplicity of this interpretation has been popular in the democracies, but it has been challenged. It was the considered judgment of Joseph C. Grew, American ambassador to Japan from 1932 until Pearl Harbor, that the Lytton *Report,* the primary evidence in Japan's condemnation, was basic but not definitive.[14] Grew emphasized the special importance of the authoritative but unorthodox and unpublicized opinions of John V. A. MacMurray, former United States Minister at Peking and profound student of China, whose unpublished reflections on the Manchurian affair were summarized privately for the Department of State in 1935. In brief it was MacMurray's judgment: (1) that for nearly ten years Japan tried to preserve the letter and spirit of the Washington Treaties in the face of

---

[13] See Richard N. Current, "The Stimson Doctrine and the Hoover Doctrine," *American Historical Review,* LIX (1954), 513-542.

[14] Joseph C. Grew, *The Turbulent Era* (2 vols., Boston, 1952), II, 928-929.

Chinese intransigence; (2) that the Treaty Powers sought in the Far East to advance their selfish interests at the expense of collective security; (3) that when China abrogated unilaterally her treaties with Japan, Japanese forces were bound to act for the protection of

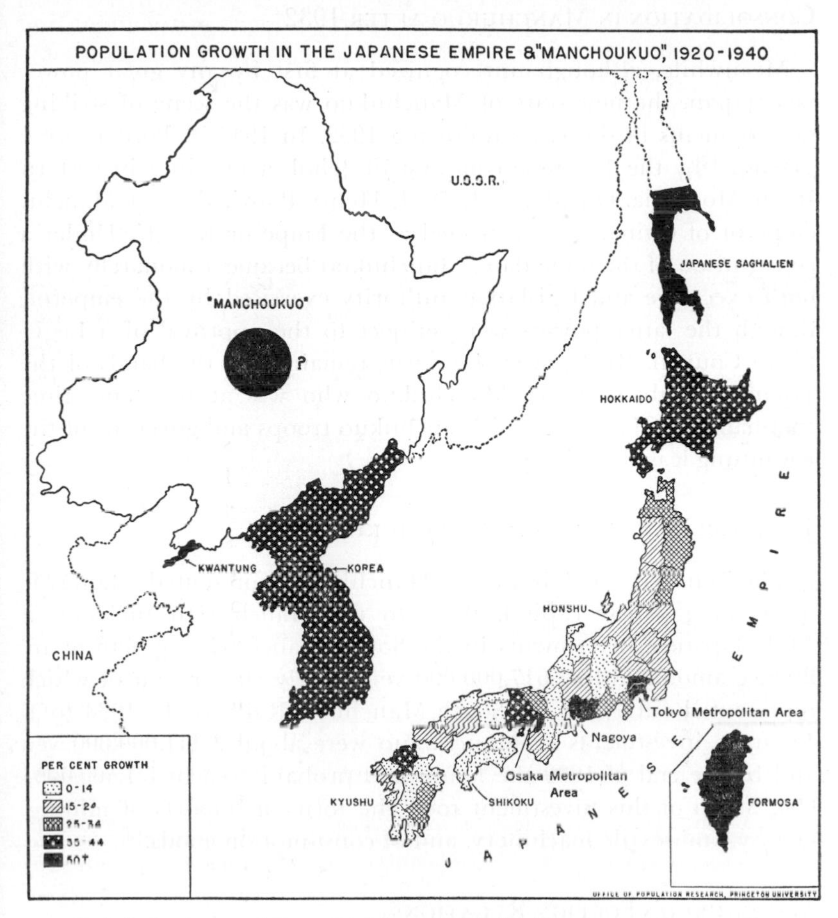

U. S. Department of State, Division of Map Intelligence and Cartography.

life and property; (4) that the effect of American policy was to condone China's behavior and to encourage her to further recalcitrance; (5) that the Chinese were wilful in their scorn of legal obligations, provocative in their methods, and reckless in resort to violence; and (6) that the policy of co-operation which might have averted Japanese action was scorned by the Chinese and ignored by the British and the Americans with the result that Japan was finally persuaded she could depend only on force to defend her legal position in China.[15]

Consolidation in Manchukuo after 1932

Meanwhile, although unrecognized at first by any great power save Japan, the new state of Manchukuo was the scene of striking developments in the years following 1932. In 1933 its borders were extended by the Japanese conquest of Jehol, a province in eastern Inner Mongolia. On March 1, 1934, Henry P'u-yi, the last Manchu emperor of China, was enthroned as the Emperor Kangtê. Under a constitution of the same date, Manchukuo became a monarchy with both executive and legislative authority exercised by the emperor, though the latter powers were subject to the approval of a Legislative Council. Real power, however, remained in the hands of the Japanese Ambassador to Manchukuo who was at the same time commander of Japanese and Manchukuo troops and governor of the Kwantung leased territory.

Japanese Investments in Manchukuo

The industrial exploitation of Manchukuo represented a fantastic influx of Japanese capital. Prior to the Manchurian Incident of 1931, Japanese investments in the South Manchurian sphere of influence amounted to 1,617,000,000 yen, nearly 50 per cent of which represented outlays of the South Manchuria Railway. In 1938 total Japanese investments in Manchukuo were about 3,441,000,000 yen and by the end of 1939 the figure had probably reached 4,500,000,000. Much of this investment took the form of imports of mining, factory, and textile machinery, and of consumption goods.[16]

Manchukuo's Foreign Relations

In line with the American Non-Recognition Doctrine, none of the great powers save Japan at first recognized Manchukuo, and of the small powers, only El Salvador, the Papacy, and the Dominican Republic had extended recognition by 1934. Germany, however,

[15] Grew, *The Turbulent Era,* II, 929-930.

[16] E. B. Schumpeter, ed., *The Industrialization of Japan and Manchukuo, 1930-1940* (New York, 1940), 398.

gave qualified recognition in a trade agreement of the same year, renewed for a second three years in 1937; and in November, 1937, Italy formally recognized the puppet state. Full German recognition came on May 12, 1938, and was soon followed by recognition from

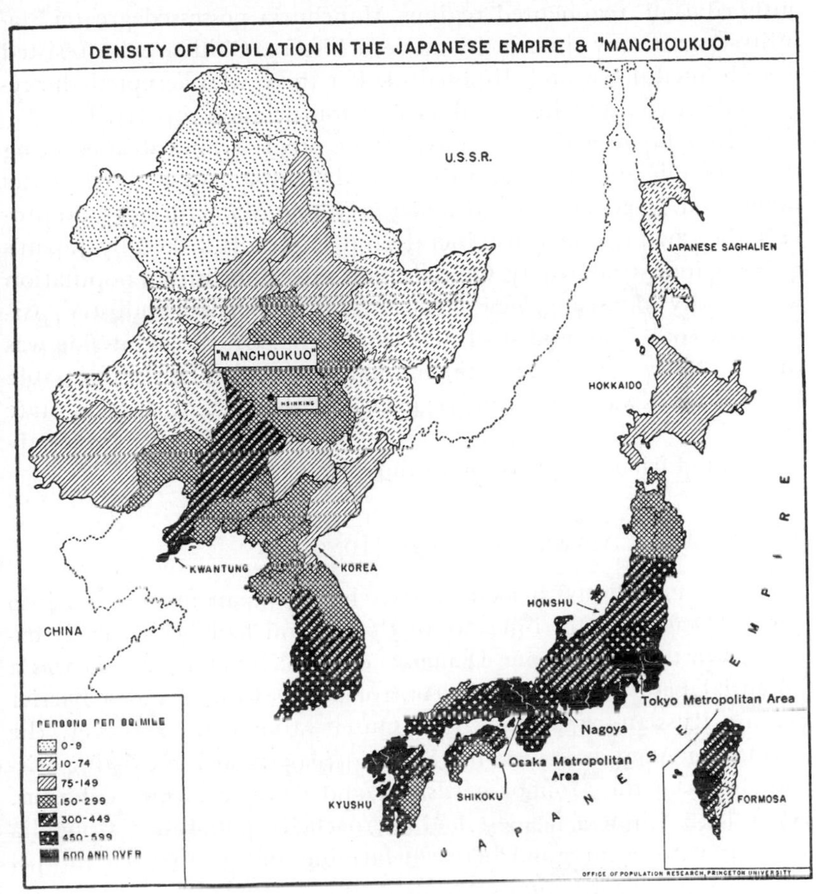

U. S. Department of State, Division of Map Intelligence and Cartography.

Poland and Hungary. On February 24, 1939, Manchukuo became a signatory of the Anti-comintern Pact concluded by Germany and Japan on November 25, 1936. Soviet Russia extended a *de facto* recognition. After two years of negotiations, 1933-1935, Russia sold its rights in the Chinese Eastern Railway to Manchukuo, the payment being guaranteed by Japan.

A Well-ordered Puppet

During the decade of the 1930's the international politics and government of Manchukuo were ordered better than the outside world of non-recognizing powers was prepared to admit. Under an authoritarian, regimented regime, Manchuria possessed greater stability than at any time in its modern history. Chinese who resisted were hunted down and disposed of. For those who accepted the regime, there could be increased security for life and property.[17]

By 1937 Japan had made considerable progress toward integrating the economic and strategic values of Manchukuo with those of the home land. In general, the idea had been that Manchuria would provide the raw materials in minerals and foodstuffs lacked by Japan's growing industrial society. On the credit side Manchurian population was rapidly increasing, new farm lands were opened, industry, particularly coal, iron, and steel, was expanding. On the debit side was the instability of the international picture pervaded by the insatiable fever of the Kwantung Army to insure the borders of the new state by pushing its boundaries into Mongolia and by forcing the establishment of friendly governments in North China.

The Japanese Advance in Inner Mongolia

Having established herself in Manchuria, Japan moved also into Inner Mongolia. Her interests in that region had been clearly expressed in the Twenty-one Demands of 1915. Inner Mongolia was a potential base from which to control North China, and a barrier against Russian expansion from Outer Mongolia. Moreover, the Kwantung Army believed that it could play upon the existing friction between the Mongol herdsmen and Chinese farmer colonists. After 1912, Chinese farmers had encroached upon Inner Mongolia lands that were marginal between farming and grazing. In the period of republican China after 1912, Inner Mongolia had been incorporated as provinces of China—Jehol, Chahar, Suiyuan, and Ning-

---

[17] Although in general this was true, there is also evidence that those who suffered from Japanese rule were not solely those who resisted. See in particular the picture presented by W. I. Ladejinsky, "Manchurian Agriculture under Japanese Control," *Foreign Agriculture,* V (1941), 309-340. Moreover, there was great economic pressure on the people of Manchuria as Japan's war program developed. These factors all served to keep alive a Manchurian resistance movement.

sia. Chinese farmers from heavily populated areas south of the Wall had been encouraged to migrate to these areas.

The first step in Japan's advance was the creation by the Kwantung Army of an autonomous Mongol province in western Manchuria incorporating part of Jehol, which had been added to Manchukuo in 1933. Here, by guaranteeing the Mongols possession of their grazing lands, by insuring and respecting their autonomous government, and by fostering the privileges of the Lama priests, the

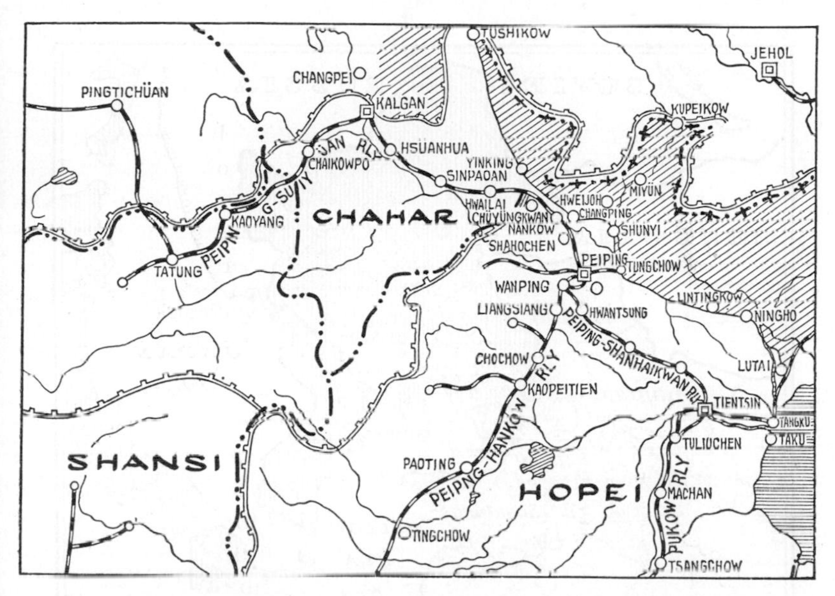

The Demilitarized Zone of the Tangku Truce

Japanese hoped to appeal to the Mongols in general, including those in Outer Mongolia. The scheme was not entirely successful, since the Mongol princes bargained also with the Chinese Nationalists at Nanking.

The Japanese in the Pei-p'ing and Tientsin Area

Just as the Kwantung Army felt it necessary to move westward into Inner Mongolia, so it became even more essential to establish friendly governments in the northeastern sections of China proper, especially in the provinces of Hopei, Shantung, and Shansi. These provinces could be linked, so it was thought, with the Inner Mongolian provinces of Chahar and Suiyuan (yet to be conquered), to give Japan control of all bordering territory to the south and west of Manchukuo. Also, as in the case of Inner Mongolia, Japanese action was declared to be in self-defense. In North China this argument was more plausible, since here the country was controlled after 1932 by Chang Hsueh-liang and his armies, which had retreated from Manchuria. His hopes of regaining his home land and his resistance to the Japanese in Jehol provided the occasion though not the cause

IN 1935, IMPERIALISTIC GROUPS IN JAPAN FAVORED CREATION OF AN AUTONOMOUS NORTH CHINA, FREE FROM THE POLITICAL CONTROL OF NANKING AND UNDER THE TUTELAGE OF MANCHUKUO. *Courtesy of* The New York Times.

for bringing the Kwantung Army south of the Wall into the Pei-p'ing and Tientsin area where, as already noted, in May, 1933, the Tangku truce was signed. This provided for demilitarization of portions of Hopei province but not for removal of Japanese troops maintained between Pei-p'ing and Tientsin under the Boxer Protocol. Chinese police "friendly" to Japan were to maintain order in the demilitarized areas. Confusion was compounded by the fact that the Tangku truce and other agreements subsequently reached were negotiated with local officials whose relationship to the Nanking Government was not always clear. Nevertheless, there was temporary improvement, since in the two years following the truce postal service and rail traffic, passenger and freight, was resumed between Manchukuo and China, though without the latter extending formal recognition. Underlying friction, however, was unabated, and by 1935 the Kwantung Army had exerted enough pressure to force the retirement of more Chinese troops from Hopei and to liquidate the *Kuomintang* in the region. This penetration of North China was all aimed toward the creation of an autonomous North China state to be composed of the five provinces of Chahar, Suiyuan, Shansi, Hopei, and Shantung. The plan was abortive, but it contributed to a general demoralization in North China where the Nanking government sought to preclude exclusive Japanese control by sanctioning local governments that would work with the Japanese.

Simultaneously with the Japanese infiltration into North China came renewed efforts by Japanese diplomacy to reach an understanding with China as a whole. There was always the hope among Japanese statesmen that a workable arrangement could be reached for close political and economic planning among Japan, Manchukuo, and China. Japan's success in Manchukuo and the continued factional strife within China lent some encouragement to the Japanese hope. Indeed, on the surface, Japan appeared to make some progress. There were elements within the *Kuomintang*-National Government which were prepared to adopt a policy of appeasement either from personal conviction on the principle of a Pan-Asiatic policy or because they regarded resistance by China as hopeless. Consequently, during 1935, Nanking made some efforts to stop anti-Japanese boycotts, to prevent publication of inflammatory anti-Japanese articles, and to suppress the student movement. Nanking, however, was not entirely subservient. When in 1934 Japan warned the League powers and the United States to follow a policy of "hands off" China, the

Nanking Government denied the right of Japan to assert a monopoly of political interest in the Far East. It all added up to a situation in North China in which by 1936 there was no Sino-Japanese war but neither was there a Sino-Japanese peace.

For Further Reading

Bassett, R., *Democracy and Foreign Policy: A Case History: The Sino-Japanese Dispute, 1931-33* (New York, 1952). A study of British public opinion with regard to the Manchurian crisis.

Beloff, Max, *Foreign Policy of Soviet Russia, 1929-1941* (2 vols., London, 1947, 1949).

———, *Soviet Policy in the Far East 1944-1951* (London, 1953). Centers on recent Russo-Chinese relations.

Bisson, T. A., *Japan in China* (New York, 1938). A detailed narrative of the invasion of China from 1931 to 1937.

Clyde, Paul H., "The Diplomacy of 'Playing No Favorites': Secretary Stimson and Manchuria, 1931," *Mississippi Valley Historical Review*, XXXV, 1948, 187-202.

Cutlack, F. M., *The Manchurian Arena* (Sydney, 1934).

Grew, Joseph C., *Ten Years in Japan* (New York, 1944).

Hishida, Seiji G., *Japan Among the Great Powers: A Survey of Her International Relations* (New York, 1940).

Jones, F. C., *Manchuria Since 1931* (London, 1949).

Kawakami, K. K., *Manchoukuo: Child of Conflict* (New York, 1933). An able Japanese apology.

Langer, Robert, *Seizure of Territory: the Stimson Doctrine and Related Principles in Legal Theory and Diplomatic Practice* (Princeton, 1947).

Moore, Harriet L., *Soviet Far Eastern Policy, 1931-1945* (Princeton, 1945). A chronicle of what Russia said and did.

Smith, Sara R., *The Manchurian Crisis, 1931-1932* (New York, 1948). Much material on discussions in the League but weak on use of American sources.

Stewart, John R., *Manchuria Since 1931* (New York, 1936).

Tamagna, Frank M., *Italy's Interests and Policies in the Far East* (New York, 1941).

Tanin, O., and E. Yohan, *When Japan Goes to War* (New York, 1936).

31

1931–1941

Politics in Japan and China

THE Manchurian upheaval of 1931 onward was impressive evidence that Japan and China were at war. No matter by what nice terms, legal or political, these events were labelled, the fact was that there had been resort to international hostilities on a large scale, that these hostilities had produced no acceptable solutions for either Japan or China, that the world machinery for collective security had not preserved peace, and that the Far East was becoming more rather than less explosive. There was also impressive evidence that Japan and China were at war each within and against itself, and it is to the nature of these respective internal conflicts that some attention must now be given. After World War I a newly industrialized Japan and a newly national and revolutionary China were achieving a new position in the community of nations and creating new societies at home. Each nation was beset by political, economic, and social instability. In each, men fought with ideas and institutions and guns for political power. In what directions was this turbulence carrying the political adventurers and the peoples of Japan and China? What kinds of societies lay just beyond the political horizon? Were they to be authoritarian or responsible, totalitarian or democratic, capitalistic or socialistic, subservient or free?

JAPAN, 1931: THE POLITICAL ATMOSPHERE

When the Kwantung Army acted on its own authority in Manchuria in 1931 it had behind it in Japan a people prepared to follow any leadership that offered a positive solution for the nation's ills. Japan was deep in the world depression. Population had been increasing at nearly one million annually, overtaxing the country's food supply. The national economy was not absorbing the more than 400,000 new workers annually who were seeking employment. The farmer, already debt-ridden, faced decreasing income. Capital was concentrated in a few great families. Small business was near bank-

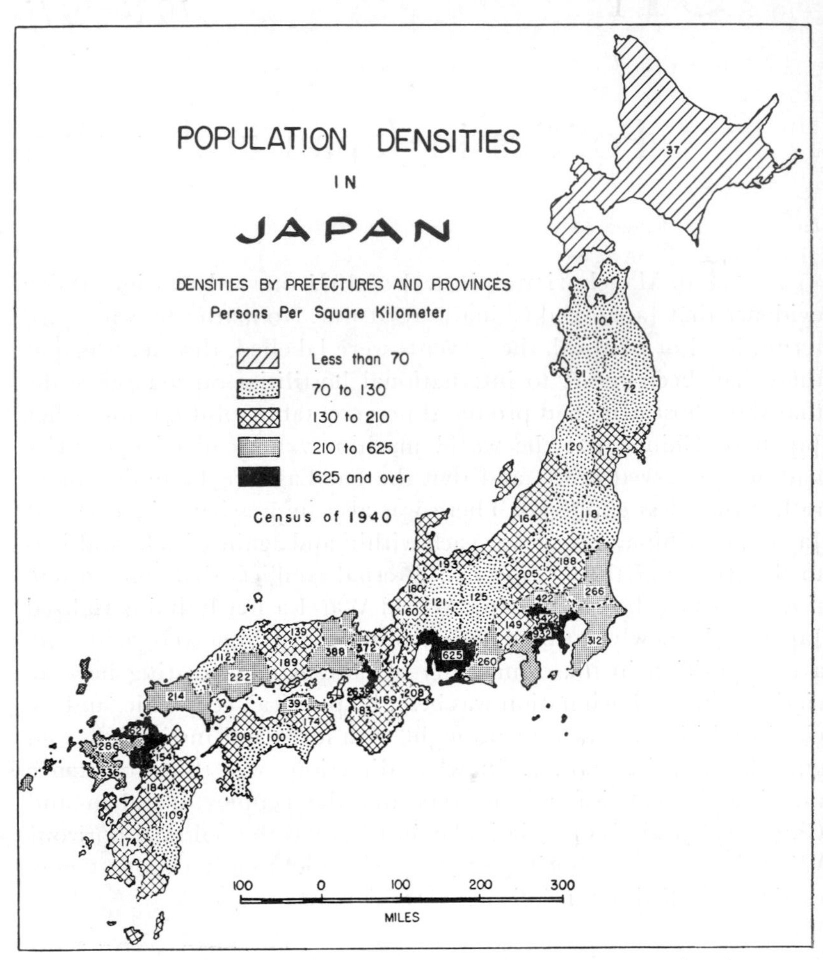

U. S. Department of State, Division of Map Intelligence and Cartography.

ruptcy and without a voice in economic policy. Hamaguchi's theoretically sound policy of retrenchment and return to the gold standard, 1929, cut deeply into Japan's exports of goods and doubled her exports of gold, a dire condition for a nation that lived by foreign trade. The whole economic picture with its social implications was fearful. It set the stage beautifully for those who had long been ready to say that responsible party government was a fraud and that Japan must return to the leadership of her true patriots.[1]

The Rejection of Party Government

In Japan the first victim of the Manchurian incident was responsible representative government. Hamaguchi had died in April 1931. His *Minseito* government was headed by the irresolute Wakatsuki when the army struck in Manchuria. Indeed, the weakness of cabinet leadership was one factor prompting the army to strike at that particular time. It was convinced there would be no effective opposition at home, and the foreign office would have to explain to the world as best it could. As Secretary Stimson said, the Japanese Foreign Office no longer made Japanese foreign policy. To be sure, a semblance of party government lingered on until 1932. When Wakatsuki's *Minseito* cabinet resigned, December, 1931, it was followed by a *Seiyukai* government with Inukai Tsuyoshi, who had become president of the Party in 1929, as premier. The general election of January, 1932, gave the *Seiyukai* with its strong foreign policy program a large majority. Its factions were already seeking informal alliances with the militarists. Inukai himself made some efforts to control the army, but he received neither practical nor moral support from the party politicians. On May 15, 1932, the Prime Minister was dead, murdered by a small group of naval officers and farmers who believed Japan could not be purified until the old politicians and parties were destroyed. Ten days later the *Seiyukai* cabinet resigned. The era of party government that began with Hara in 1918 was ended. The movement toward a Japanese democracy had failed.[2]

The Era of National Cabinets

The fall of the last party cabinet did not mean the immediate adoption of a new theory or structure of government or that the army extremists were in unchallenged control. What did happen was an attempted return to tradition, to government by elder statesmen

[1] W. W. Lockwood, *The Economic Development of Japan* (Princeton, 1954), 55-64; Hugh Borton, *Japan's Modern Century* (New York, 1955), 321-324.

[2] The May 15 incident had been prefaced by a February incident in which Inouye Junnosuke, former Finance Minister and manager of the *Minseito,* was assassinated by a young farmer. Shortly thereafter Dan Takuma, Managing Director of the Mitsui, was murdered.

who could balance opposing political elites, preserve national unity, and prevent revolution or exclusive army control. When Saionji, the only surviving *Genro,* recommended that the Emperor call on Admiral Viscount Saito Makoto to form a national government, he was appealing to Japanese political genius of the late Meiji period. Saito, an admiral, was acceptable to the Army though not its choice. He was acceptable in a society where status still prevailed because of his rank and membership in the aristocracy. The bankrupt political parties could accept him because, though not a party man, he had shown them no violent opposition. The Court circle, the financiers, and indeed reasonable men of independent judgment saw in Saito the hope of moderation. The Saito cabinet included five party men, three from the *Seiyukai,* two from the *Minseito,* two bureaucrats, three militarists, and three members of the House of Peers. It survived until 1934. Thereafter until 1941 nine governments trampled on the heels of their predecessors. The high mortality in these administrations was symptomatic of the turbulent instability of Japanese political society. Saito's immediate successor, Admiral Okada Keisuke, followed the Saito pattern in cabinet personnel. Thereafter cabinets became less "national" and more representative of the growing power of the militarists and the "fascists." Even as early as June, 1932, the new American ambassador in Japan, Joseph Clark Grew, had noted that "one thing is certain and that is that the military are distinctly running the Government and that no step can be taken without their approval."[3]

Military-Fascism Seeks Control

The political history of Japan after 1931 is a history of extreme nationalism nurtured in a strong historical military tradition and

[3] On Saito's position, see Ippei Fukuda, *Sketches of Men and Life* (Tokyo, 1933), 27-35. On the fall of cabinet government, Robert A. Scalapino, *Democracy and the Party Movement in Prewar Japan* (Berkeley, 1953), 370-371. Premiers who headed "national" cabinets, 1931-1941, included: 1932, Admiral Viscount Saito Makoto; 1934, Admiral Okada Keisuke; 1936, Hirota Koki; 1937, General Hayashi Senjuro; 1937, Prince Konoye Fumimaro; 1939, Baron Hiranuma Kiichiro; 1940, Admiral Yonai Mitsumasa; 1940, Prince Konoye Fumimaro; 1941, Prince Konoye Fumimaro; 1941, General Tojo Hideki. From 1939 on, cabinet changes hardly affected national policy. Policy was determined not by cabinets but by a small flexible group of military and civilian oligarchs finding some compromise between factions seeking power. It was the *Genro* idea without any genuine *Genro,* since Saionji's power had declined with age and circumstances. He died in 1940.

directed by a politically-minded, authoritarian military caste. The political manoeuvring in this return to authoritarianism was complex and confused. The resurgence of militarism itself was hardly a revolution because the democratic movement of the 1920's was as much a victim of its own sterility as of attacks by its enemies. After 1936 the Army was unquestionably the most powerful political force, but it was not wholly without competitors for political power. It owed its rapid political resurgence to tradition, to terror, and in part to the collaboration, voluntary or forced, of civilian economic and political elites. Yet conflict at the top level of Japanese leadership was never wholly resolved. As the decade advanced there was faltering opposition to the extremes of militarism from conservative officials of the Court as well as from other sources, but by 1940 the old political parties had dissolved themselves almost without protest to make way for the Imperial Rule Assistance Association, a single, exclusive, and official political party which by 1941 was controlled by the Army. Nevertheless, the military-fascist movement did not create in concept or in reality a *Führer*. Even General Premier Tojo Hideki, the man who carried Japan into total war in 1941, was never a Hitler. Japan's authoritarianism borrowed from the West but did not ape the West. It retained a Japanese pattern shaped by the absence of individualism in Japanese mores. The Japanese people followed the military-fascists because of tradition, because of the psychology of crisis which was constantly kept alive, and because the army alone had a plan, as in Manchuria in 1931, and was willing to act and to promise results.

Military-fascism as a political philosophy or as an administrative structure was not a new idea in the Japan of 1931. Its bases were deeply rooted in Japanese political, social, and national experience. Japanese nationalism in its formative years of the Meiji period was fashioned not primarily by a middle class but rather by military and agrarian leadership which, jealous of the rising power of the commercial urban class, revived the traditional symbols of Shinto, the Emperor as ruler and high-priest, and the union of peasant and soldier. These re-glorified symbols of an earlier military-agrarian society were never replaced by Western middle-class symbols as Japan moved further into industrialization and modernization. As a result her modern nationalism was less an expression of liberal and democratic principles than of traditional authoritarian concepts. The intellectual soil of Japan in 1931 was deeply infected with the potentials of chauvinism. All that was needed was the intrigue, the conspiracy, and the fanaticism of the "true patriots."

The Patriotic Societies

A revival and mushrooming of nationalist patriotic societies had coincided with Hara's victory and the democratic trends of 1918. The social and economic changes of the war years brought forth an assortment of patriotic bands opposed to Western doctrines of liberalism or socialism and communism and dedicated to traditional institutions and to such vaporous tenets as the "Japanese spirit." These groups attracted not only extremists and shallow or fanatical patriots but also substantial conservatives of the aristocracy, the military, the landed, and the business community, all suspicious, if not fearful, of democratic social trends. Organizations such as the *Yuzonsha* (Society to Preserve the National Essence) nurtured national messiahs such as Kita Ikki and Okawa Shumei, whose writings became holy writ especially to the younger military nationalists. The plans of Kita and Okawa were suggestive of the extreme military nationalist movement that swept Japan after 1931. Theirs was a program of so-called reform to be under the Emperor's guidance and under the protection of the military power. They proposed to launch their utopia with a temporary suspension of the Constitution, dissolution of the Diet, and a declaration of martial law. The new administration to be set up, essentially military, was to promote expropriation of private property in excess of given limits, redistribution of land, and policies of expansion abroad. Other reformers were proposing a return to an agrarian-centered economy. Their appeals often rested on the theory of Japanese racial supremacy and on denunciations of city capitalists and Westernization. In addition to these clearly revolutionary groups, there were the conservatives of the oligarchy, the army, the bureaucracy, and business, who, fearing revolution and upholding the imperial interpretation of the Meiji Constitution, were clearly anti-democratic. The most active personalities of this grouping were organized in the *Kokuhonsha* (National Foundation Society) founded in 1924 by Hiranuma Kiichiro. It included a galaxy of Japanese leaders whose views and interests were far from identical, such as, for example, Admiral Saito Makoto and General Araki Sadao. Therefore, when the Kwantung Army struck in Manchuria in

1931, its political base in Japan was already strong and was growing stronger.[4]

The strength of the ultranationalist movement was further buttressed by exceedingly close ties between military men and civilians. This association was not new at high levels. The oligarchy of the Meiji era had always included both civilian and military bureaucrats. Now under the radical nationalist movement the civilian-military alliance became more important, especially as it touched the younger army officers, who were rural in origin themselves, and the rural populace from which came most of the army's recruits. The young officers' movement, encouraged by many senior officers of the stamp of Generals Araki Sadao, Koiso Kuniaki, and Doihara Kenji, expressed the plight of the peasant when it denounced the capitalists, and it expressed the demands of patriotism when it denounced appeasement in foreign policy. By 1933 the *Seiyukai* was parroting the slogans of the young officers, the rabid nationalists, and was appealing to Japanese education and religion (Shinto) to revive the Japanese spirit and the Imperial Way.

Araki and the New Japanism

The tone and temper of rightist ultranationalism, the new Japanism, was best personified by General Araki Sadao, who had risen from humble birth and from labor in a soya bean sauce factory to become Minister of War, 1931-1934. In appearance and temperament a mild and ascetic priest rather than a saber-rattling *samurai,* Araki was a soldier, simple in his personal habits and single-minded in his devotion to *Kodo,* the Imperial Way. It was Araki who became the spiritual leader and the politico-ethical spokesman of a new Japan. As this Japan faced a world hostile toward her because of her continental expansion, Araki rationalized ultranationalism and foreign conquest in terms of the high ethical principles which clothed the traditional Japanese doctrines of *Kodo* and *Kokutai* (National Polity).[5] The implications of *Kodo* and of *Hakko ichiu* (the world under one roof) were reinterpreted as Japan's universal and benign mission designed to bring peace to the world. In the Far East, this mission would spread the beneficent rule of the emperor to

[4] Scalapino, *Democracy and the Party Movement,* 346-361.

[5] *Kokutai* as used by the Japanese is meant to suggest that unity of the state which results from the unqualified loyalty of the people to the Imperial line "unbroken through ages eternal."

those benighted peoples whose rulers had failed them or who had fallen a prey to Western exploitation and the doctrines of capitalism and liberalism. At home *Kodo* would direct Japanese footsteps into the forsaken paths of her own indigenous culture. From these paths she had been enticed, so it was said, by pernicious Western cults—liberalism, capitalism, democracy, individualism, and even communism—and the result had been a Japan where political life was usurped by corrupt political parties, where capitalists grew wealthy while peasants could not eat the rice they grew—a Japan weakened at home and thus denied the right to rescue Asia from European and American exploitation.[6]

The Suppression of "Dangerous Thoughts"

The advocates of ultra-nationalism were ever alert to ferret out the enemies that bored from within. Those Japanese reputed to be friends of Westernism or democracy and responsible government were especially suspect. They were the purveyors of "dangerous thoughts." The most famous case of this sort of attack on intellectual freedom had as its victim Minobe Tatsukichi, a distinguished professor of constitutional law who had long been known for his constitutional theory of the Emperor. His books were widely known and he was a respected member of the Peers. He was not a radical and it would be difficult to know on what grounds he could even be called a liberal. His theory of the Emperor was not exactly a democratic doctrine; in its simplest form it was that the Emperor was an organ of the State and not the State itself. But this proposition was all that was needed by the super-patriots in their search for subversives. The fact that the doctrine had long been taught and accepted by many respectable men was irrelevant. What did matter was that in 1935 the ultranationalists had made of Minobe a traitor to the Imperial Way. Minobe's logical protest that if the Emperor's sovereignty was inherent in his being and personal then the Meiji Constitution was meaningless, fell of course on deaf ears. The clamor of the nationalists and also of the *Seiyukai* politicians forced Minobe's resignation from the Peers and from his professorship. Hardly a voice was raised in his defense.

These irresponsible assaults upon respectable men did not mean that the chauvinists were all of one mind. Within the top echelons of

[6] D. C. Holtom, *Modern Japan and Shinto Nationalism* (rev. ed., Chicago, 1947), 21-23.

the army itself there were violent factional disputes which were carried in some cases to solution by murder. Two army cliques were of particular importance. By 1935, General Araki of the extreme Imperial Way faction had been replaced as Minister of War by General Hayashi Senjuro of the more moderate Control Faction; and General Mazaki Jinzaburo, an idol of the young officers, had been replaced as Inspector General of Military Education by the milder General Nagata. When shortly thereafter Nagata was murdered by a Lieutenant Colonel Aizawa, the latter became a national hero because it was felt his motives were patriotic and pure.

The national election of February 1936, in which the nationalist parties and the *Seiyukai* lost ground to the more moderate and cautious *Minseito*, and in which leftist parties made a surprisingly strong showing, suggested that there was still opposition in Japan to the extremists. The extremists were not slow to accept this challenge. On February 26, four days after the announcement of the election returns, junior officers and a regiment of troops en route to Manchuria attempted by force to overthrow the Okada cabinet. The mutineers murdered Takahashi Korekiyo, the Minister of Finance, Admiral Viscount Saito Makoto, Lord Keeper of the Privy Seal, and General Watanabe Jotaro, Inspector General of Military Education. They attempted to kill Premier Okada but murdered his brother-in-law by mistake. For three days the heart of Tokyo was held by the mutinous troops. Although for the moment the army's prestige was weakened by these outrages, it soon recovered when apologists painted the assassins as young men pure in heart whose sole motive was to restore the "national spirit." Fundamentally the political picture had not been changed, for although the new government formed by Hirota Koki, March 9, 1936, was composed of moderate militarists and civilian bureaucrats, the influence of the army remained high, each minister having been approved by General Count Terauchi Juichi, the Minister of War. Perhaps more important was the way in which the manoeuvrings of the moderates versus the extreme militarists added to the confusion of thought and alignment among civilian groups. Factionalism was already present in the bureaucracy, some of whose members were avowedly fascist, and within the major political parties the *Seiyukai* had long since shown its willingness to support extremes of nationalism. Now there were signs that the great Mitsui house was beginning to look with qualified favor toward extremists at home who could be counted as expansionists abroad. Younger and lesser known capitalists such as Aikawa Yoshisuke, heading army-sponsored industry in Manchukuo, had already accepted army backing as a convenient means of breaking into the industrial monopoly of the established *Zaibatsu* houses. The net result was, as the cross-currents of domestic conflict increased, that the Hirota cabinet moved steadily toward "bureaucratic totalitarianism." The influence of the Diet continued to decline while military and naval budgets reached an all-time high. Further evidence of the army's involvement in politics came in January, 1937. When the Hirota cabinet resigned, the emperor called upon a moderate, General Ugaki Kazushige, to form a government; but Ugaki was blocked when the army refused to appoint a Minister of War. In February, however, the army did accept the elevation to the premiership of General Hayashi Senjuro, who had been Minister of War. In June, after Hayashi had failed to win the nation's unified support, he was succeeded by Prince Konoye Fumimaro, a member of one of Japan's oldest and most aristocratic families. It was the expectation that Konoye's close family relationship with the Imperial Household would lead the nation to unite politically behind his policies.

The unhealthy state of Japan's domestic politics by June, 1937, continued unabated. Political assassins and terrorists were not a new feature of Japanese life, but their reappearance beginning with the attack on Hamaguchi in 1929 bore a special significance. Always garbed in the role of guardians of the emperor, of the Imperial Way, and of the National Spirit, they served as the shock troops for all those who favored ultranationalism, fascism, or military dictatorship. Each time the terrorists struck, the army and its sympathizers won at least a psychological victory, for the very existence of political terrorism was taken as proof of the depths to which the nation had sunk under the rule of "corrupt" industrial capitalists and political parties. Until 1937 the Japanese electorate showed at times a healthy skepticism toward all moves in the direction of fascism or military dictatorship, but their reluctance to give way to the army at home was forever being weakened by the appeal of military conquest abroad, of the expanding empire in China, and of Japan's benevolent mission to insure the peace and tranquility of the Far East. In the case of Japan, as in that of other countries before her, this appeal was too strong for the advocates of liberalism and parliamentary government.

Chinese Politics, 1931-1941

The history of Chinese politics in the 1930's is not easy to capture. Much of the spade work of the historian in this period has yet to be done, but some major aspects of the story are in discernable focus. As a point of departure it may be noted that the Meiji revolution in Japan had produced a modern nation-state which adjusted itself to Westernization through the single-minded leadership of the *Genro,* who knew where they were going and how they proposed to get there. Furthermore, the new Japan achieved an amazing degree of stability by preserving indigenous institutions and symbols surrounding the throne.[7] In contrast, China's modern revolution, coming half a century later, destroyed the moribund Confucian state before there was either a plan or a leadership that could replace it. The vacuum thus created was filled for the moment by the political wreckage of Confucianism and by a local and irresponsible militarism. Sun Yat-sen's task in nation building was thus immeasurably more difficult than that of the Meiji reformers. The old political China was dead. Sun's revolution faced the triple task of devising a theory and plan for the new China, of suppressing militarism and finally of creating a government that could rule while it built the new political edifice. Sun's theory was reasonably precise by 1923. By 1927 his followers appeared to have defeated tuchunism. By the following year a national government was emerging and the *Kuomintang* was faced with the hard fact that it now had to rule China and at the same time find the means whereby the revolutionary program of Sun Yat-sen—nationalism, democracy, and livelihood—could be made the living and working philosophy of more than 400,000,000 people, most of whom had no understanding of these modern doctrines.

From the beginning of the *Kuomintang*-Nationalist era in 1927-1928 the political history of China was therefore a compound of three major ingredients, each amazingly complex in itself. The first was the political character of the *Kuomintang* and of the National Government which it created and controlled. The second was the nature of the opposition to the *Kuomintang* within China. The third was the obstruction of China's revolution from the outside, principally though not exclusively by Japan.

[7] It is true that the *Genro,* particularly Ito and Yamagata, often disagreed violently, but these differences were not permitted to obstruct or becloud fundamental objectives of policy. They were differences of means rather than of ends.

The National Government

The National Government that ruled over much of China from 1928 until 1949 was the first national government China ever had in the sense that it was the first effort to rule China as though it were a Western nation-state. This government was the creation and the agent of the *Kuomintang,* which claimed a monopoly of political power during the period of tutelage, 1928-1948, the second of Sun's three stages of the revolution. In 1928 the Organic Law of the National Government created a presidential and a five-yüan administration. In 1931 a Provisional Constitution, designed to be temporary but which remained in force until 1947, was adopted. Its purpose, so it was said, was to hasten the day of constitutionalism when political power might be returned to a government elected by the people. Until his death in 1943, Lin Sen, scholar and follower of Sun, was President of the National Government and therefore the titular head of the State. Lin Sen did not govern. He was a symbol of respect and a counsel of moderation and dignity in an era of violence. While the Council of State over which he presided was supposedly a policy-forming body, the single party rule of the *Kuomintang* during the period of tutelage meant that policy decisions belonged to the top leaders of the Party, though these same men might at times hold top offices in the government.[8]

The *Kuomintang* as a Ruling Party

When the *Kuomintang* achieved the position of the party in power it did not thereby achieve unity of thought or purpose within itself. While he lived, Sun Yat-sen could command the Party. His mind was its thought; and his decisions, its purpose. After his death there was no single voice that could command at the ideological, intellectual level. During the Northern March, 1925-1927, there was unity of purpose in military conquest. Once the conquest was achieved the unity of the Party was broken. The expulsion of the Communists at Wuhan, 1927, was balm to this wound but did not disguise the presence of right and left wings within the Party. Indeed, the Nanking National Government could hardly have been born but for the conservative backing received by Chiang K'ai-shek and his armies. Thus

[8] For a full description of the National Government, see P. M. A. Linebarger, Djang Chu, Ardath W. Burks, *Far Eastern Governments and Politics* (New York, 1954), 145-183.

a significant result of the Wuhan expulsion was that, although the *Kuomintang* was saved from capture by the Communists, it was no longer the most radical party, and the later development of communist armed revolt meant that the Nationalists were constantly pushed to the right where they were welcomed by every opponent of Sun and his revolution. At the same time the *Kuomintang* was also pulled constantly toward the left by this same revolutionary program which had brought it into being and to power, and by the obvious needs of agrarian and labor reform. Between these pressures of the right and the left were perplexing questions of military power. Although the *Kuomintang* was in substantial control of most of China, some of its power rested on the uncertain loyalty of former warlords and regional commanders. It was foreseen therefore that the military power of *Kuomintang* armies would remain essential to the revolution until nationalism as a popular aspiration became the nationalism of political unity and stability.

Kuomintang Membership and Leadership

In 1930 the *Kuomintang* may have had something in excess of two million members, exclusive of the armed forces. The most active elements were graduates of colleges and middle schools who were employed as party workers, civil servants, teachers, and editors. In time, further important categories of membership included small shopkeepers, factory workers, and postal and railway employees. The interests of the membership were far from identical save in the broad, undefined boundaries of Sun's program. In structure the *Kuomintang* was similar to that of the Russian Communist Party; it operated through four levels of authority from local units at the bottom up through the provincial organization to the central authority at the top composed of the National Congress of the Party with its Central Executive Committee. The Congress met infrequently. The Central Executive Committee was large and cumbersome with the result that continuing authority and control gravitated to its smaller Standing Committee. Even after Sun's death the Party decreed that he should continue to hold the Party title of *Tsung-li,* leader. Consequently it was difficult when Sun was gone for anyone to seek exclusive leadership without doing violence to Sun's memory. This circumstance contributed to the development of rival leaders, Hu Han-min, Chiang K'ai-shek, and Wang Ching-wei, to mention the outstanding ones. It was not until 1938 that a new title of leadership, *Tsung-ts'ai,* was created and given to Chiang K'ai-shek.

The party political dictatorship of the *Kuomintang* was purchased at a high price. In so far as discipline was imposed, revolutionary enthusiasm tended to lag. Militant revolutionists left the Party temporarily or for good. Inside the Party, as was natural in China, men became more important than ends. Intra-Party cliques grew around personalities at the top or at secondary levels in party and government. At the summit the grouping of right, center, and left was associated respectively with Hu, Chiang, and Wang. Lesser factions included the C. C. Clique of Ch'en Li-fu, Minister of Education, and Ch'en Kuo-fu, head of the Central Political Institute, who were masters of political manipulation; the Regenerationists, or Blue Shirts, who mimicked a Fascist pattern; the secret police organization; and the milder Political Science Group, which eschewed violence but was hardly revolutionary. Because of the traditional personal base of Chinese politics, factionalism was to be expected. It was to prove, however, a luxury which the *Kuomintang* could ill afford. It contributed to the Party's tendency, once it had come to power, to lapse into a mood of assurance, to lose its dynamic character. This gradual decline in party zeal was responsible after 1937 for what has been described as the *Kuomintang's* most serious political mistake—"the failure to compete with the Communists for leadership of the guerrillas behind the Japanese lines."[9]

The *Kuomintang* and Military Power

The *Kuomintang* had come to power at Nanking through Sun's revolutionary program, through the Russian inspired reorganization of the Party, and through the might of *Kuomintang* armies. While China's historic tradition of government was civilian, she had acquired in the early years of the twentieth century the beginnings of a military tradition in government typified by Yuan Shih-k'ai. Moreover, Sun Yat-sen and the early *Kuomintang* developed from choice and necessity a leaning toward the institutions of military government. In the period of the Northern March, 1925-1927, the *Kuomintang* denounced the Northern militarists, but it also indulged in the

[9] Paul M. A. Linebarger, "Ideological Dynamics of the Postwar Far East," in F. Morstein Marx, ed., *Foreign Governments* (New York, 1949), 554-555.

dangerous but common Chinese practice of receiving into the revolutionary army miscellaneous local armies that showed a disposition to get on the winning side. The conversion of these armies and their leaders to the revolutionary cause was less a matter of conviction than of expediency and opportunism. After the National Government was in operation at Nanking, an Army Reorganization and Disbandment Conference was held in 1929. This laudable effort

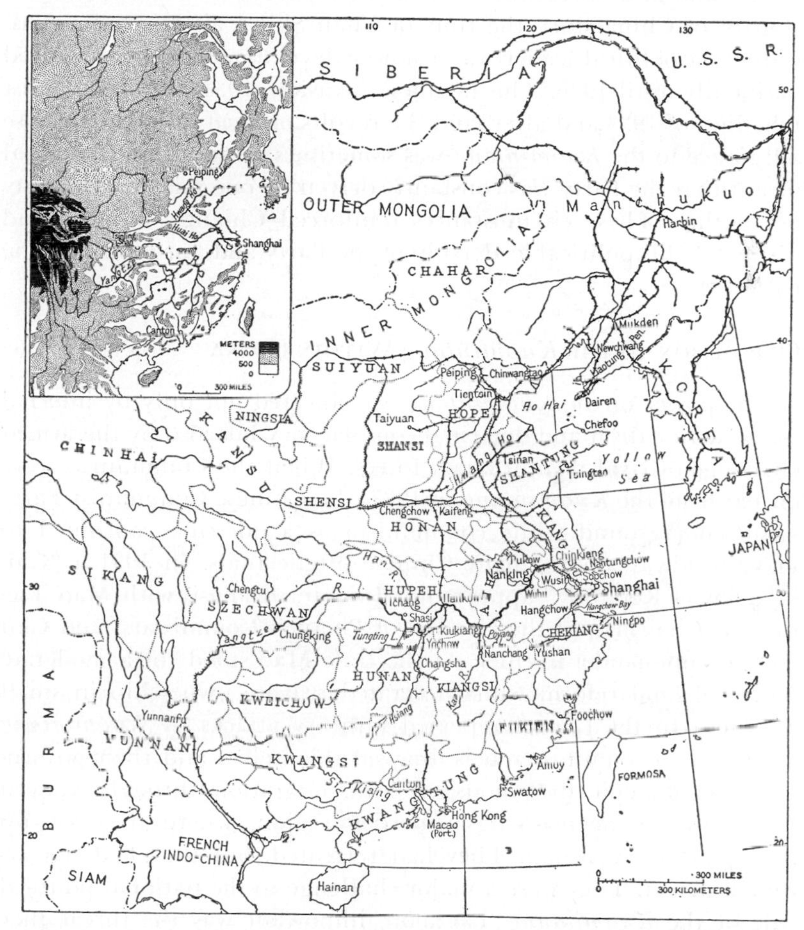

CHINA AND NORTHEASTERN ASIA, 1936. Illustrating the complicated politico-geographical relations of China, Soviet Russia, and Japan (Manchukuo). The inset emphasizes the high mountain and plateau barriers that focus the Yangtze Valley on Shanghai. *Courtesy of John E. Orchard and of the* Geographical Review, *published by the American Geographical Society of New York.*

toward demobilization failed because of economic problems and because political generals were not yet prepared to give up their divisions. Militarism for reasons both good and bad continued to weigh heavily on China and on the *Kuomintang*. In these earlier years of *Kuomintang* government Chiang K'ai-shek had become indispensable to the Party only as a military leader. At first he was regarded not as the inevitable or single heir of Sun Yat-sen but as the newest and most successful of the many warlords who had fought for control of China since the time of Yuan Shih-k'ai. His indispensability as a political leader was a slower development, not recognized nationally until 1936. The Japanese invasion, 1931, the Communist rebellion of 1933 and after, and the revolts of local militarists whose allegiance to the *Kuomintang* was sometimes more formal than real meant that the Party was constantly driven by one military necessity or another. These circumstances reinforced Chiang's military and ultimately his political leadership of the Party and, for a time, of the nation.[10]

Opposition to the *Kuomintang* Within China

The power of the *Kuomintang* was affected not only by internal party factionalism and doctrinal complacency but also by the armed challenge of rival revolutionary forces. When the Communists were ousted from the *Kuomintang* in 1927, the Chinese Communist Party went underground while communism as a doctrine continued to make headway among many Chinese intellectuals. In 1931 a "Chinese Soviet Republic" appeared at Juichin, Kiangsi, with Mao Tse-tung as Chairman of the Council of People's Commissars, and Chu Têh as commander-in-chief. At the time Mao stood for a moderate policy of land reform which tolerated private ownership in small holdings. In the face of repeated military attacks by *Kuomintang* armies, the communist rebels dragged themselves and their government on an epic five thousand mile migration through western China to the Shensi-Ningsia border region, where they set up headquarters at Yenan. They had retreated, but they had not accepted defeat. They were a major challenge to the national political rule of the *Kuomintang*. Far more important was the threat they posed to the *Kuomintang's* ideological leadership of the revolution.

10 P. M. A. Linebarger, *Government in Republican China* (New York, 1938), 57-63; Ch'ien Tuang-shêng, *The Government and Politics of China* (Cambridge, 1950), 177-190.

Since the Communists were an illegal armed camp in rebellion against the State and unencumbered by the responsibilities of national administration, they could be and were uninhibited as fanatical advocates and practitioners of grass-roots agrarian reform and of resistance to the foreign Japanese invader. As such they appealed to an ever-widening and receptive Chinese audience. In the role of radical or progressive reformers they were especially dangerous to a *Kuomintang* no longer dominated by revolutionary zeal.

JAPAN AND THE *Kuomintang*

Meanwhile, the position of the *Kuomintang* and the National Government had been challenged from the outside first by Russia in North Manchuria in 1929 and then by Japan in South Manchuria, 1931 and after. In the case of North Manchuria, Nanking could do no more than bow to the terms Russia imposed on the Manchurian authorities. In the case of South Manchuria, Nanking could and did appeal to the League of Nations, but Manchuria itself passed into Japanese hands while the Young Marshal, Chang Hsueh-liang, reassembled his *Tungpei,* ex-Manchurian army, nominally a part of the Nationalist forces, west of Peking. During 1934-1935, when the Kwantung Army attempted to set up an autonomous state around Peking, the Nationalist Government played a delicate game of appeasement, neither obstructing the Japanese completely nor conceding all they asked. To this point the *Kuomintang* had sought to placate Japan. The policy was to crush internal foes first, then the foreign enemy. Nanking wanted Chang's ex-Manchurian troops to fight the Chinese communists. Chang's commanders and troops, however, were more concerned to fight the Japanese and to regain their homeland. Indeed, there had been fraternization rather than fighting between the Manchurian troops and the communists in the northwest. The situation was a manifestation of the rising popular demand throughout China for a united front against Japan. Already in 1933 Nanking had faced a revolt in Fukien by *Kuomintang* and other elements demanding resistance to the Japanese and democracy for the Chinese. Later, in 1936, Nanking met revolt by southern generals and their political followers in Kwangtung and Kwangsi who professed to represent regional branches of the Central Executive Committee of the *Kuomintang* itself. Again the demand was for resistance to Japan, and again Nanking met the emergency with force, patronage, and assurances that resistance was coming. The culmination of these revolts against the National Government came in December, 1936, when Chiang K'ai-shek was seized and held prisoner by the Young Manchurian Marshal at Sian. Chiang's release, urged even by the Communists, was presumably on the pledge of a united front. Chiang had become indispensable to National resistance.

Disputes on Constitutionalism

Meanwhile, from 1933 to 1936 the inner counsels of the *Kuomintang* had been divided by bitter constitutional strife. The essential issues in debate were: when should tutelage give place to constitutional government, and what kind of constitutional government should it be? The Party controversy that raged about the new Draft Constitution of 1936 centered on two principal problems. The first concerned the powers of the legislature; the second, the argument between the presidential and the cabinet form of government. Since the Draft Constitution that had been prepared appeared to support a continuing authoritarian regime, the *Kuomintang* did not thereby broaden the base of its popular support, especially the popular support that might have been drawn from conservative, non-partisan leaders and groups. For the moment the constitutional question seemed somewhat academic, since before the National Assembly could be called to adopt the Draft Constitution, Japan had attacked at the Marco Polo Bridge near Peking (July, 1937). The long and cruel undeclared Sino-Japanese War had begun. Nanking, the Nationalist capital, was in Japanese hands by December. The National Government retired, first to Hankow and then still farther west to Chungking.

Kuomintang leadership by 1937 was therefore vulnerable. Since 1928 the loose oligarchy that determined policy had been attacked from many quarters both inside and outside the Party: by its own and by allied dissident militarists, by constitutionalists who favored an early end of tutelage, by the opponents of one-party rule, by the enemies of Japanese appeasement, and by the Communists. In particular the decision of the *Kuomintang* military power to fight the Chinese Communists before resisting Japan stimulated eventually popular resentment. Japanese pressure since 1931 in Manchuria and North China and at Shanghai had gone far to subordinate conflicting groups and class interests of Chinese society and to produce a rising popular demand for resistance to Japanese aggression. The popular humiliation before Japanese arms affected all classes, high and low, urban and rural, the *Kuomintang*, the Communists, and the non-partisans. The demand for resistance rested on deep historical foundations. Its origins went back to the beginning of China's protest against the Western impact. These origins involved the composite force of Sun Yat-sen's revolutionary program, especially nationalism and anti-foreignism. The voice of this new China had spoken many times and in many ways: in the Boxer Rebellion of 1900; in the anti-American boycott of 1905; in the Twenty-One Demands of 1915; in the explosive student movement that followed the Versailles settlement of 1919; in the Shanghai affair of 1925; in the attacks on foreign concessions, life, and property at Hankow, Kiukiang, and Nanking in 1926-1927; and in the anti-Japanese boycotts of 1931. These protests were never wholly spontaneous, but neither were they unrelated to a growing vital and popular nationalism. Since the close of World War I there had been in China "a general awakening of national consciousness and a popular demand for political and social reform."[11]

It seemed therefore that the popular demands for nationalism, resistance, and reform had outdistanced *Kuomintang* performance. This is not to say that the *Kuomintang* at this time had failed. It was still regarded by the great majority of Chinese as the party of Sun and of the revolution. In the unspectacular work of economic reconstruction, where deeds were more important than words, the *Kuomintang*, in spite of the multiple handicaps under which it labored, had made some headway. But in the area of political leadership, especially the implementation of constitutional government and democracy, the popular imagination was far in advance of performance by the top men of the *Kuomintang*. The essential political problem of the *Kuomintang* was to find the means of narrowing the gap between this popular revolutionary imagination on the one hand and the need for stable government on the other, between the extravagance of an opposition, often irresponsible, and the at times pedestrian conservatism of the men who held power.

This problem called for a leadership such as Sun Yat-sen might have given. His death had left an unresolved succession that pulled the Party in opposing directions. The rivalry of contending aspirants was sharp in the early years at Nanking between Hu Han-min,

11 Linebarger, *Far Eastern Governments and Politics*, 206.

scholar and conservative, and Wang Ching-wei, the brilliant and opportunistic demagogue. After the expulsion of the Communists at Wuhan, these two had emerged as leaders of, respectively, the so-called right and left wings of the Party. Chiang K'ai-shek's position was more fluid, and anyway he was indispensable as the commander of armies. The point to be noted is that in the first years at Nanking no one of these men achieved a stature that could control the Party and Government. Nor did the *Kuomintang* hierarchy as a whole create a collective leadership of single-minded purpose.

Divided leadership also fostered the irresolution with which China met the Japanese invasion of 1931. Taken together, these complex factors bore heavily on the vitality of the infant Nationalist Government. But more important than this, they indicate that the *Kuomintang* was slipping into a phase of traditional Chinese officialdom and that the *Kuomintang* Party line was becoming "official and sterile." The net result was that under "the Kuomintang the organizational aspect of the revolution developed much more rapidly than the ideological." This was a fact of deep significance, since Chinese civilization had provided one of the best examples of a society that operated by ideological control rather than by organized governmental direction.[12]

Kuomintang Economics, 1928-1937

Finally the *Kuomintang* in this period did not solve the problem posed by economic stagnation in the areas of finance, technology, and institutional change. As indicated earlier, the Nanking period of *Kuomintang* rule cannot be dismissed simply as one of failure. In some respects the National government did set the stage for economic growth. The currency was unified. An end was almost put to the chaos of the old system based on a variable unit, the *tael*. Beginnings were also made in the reform of the fiscal system by centralizing indirect taxation, securing tariff autonomy, and moving toward annual budgets. Transportation and communications were greatly improved and the power industry was expanded. But at the same time the *Kuomintang* was attempting to reshape a Confucian society in which social and economic power followed a traditional course that restricted heavily the capacity of the public to contribute to eco-

---

12 See P. M. A. Linebarger, "Ideological Dynamics of the Postwar Far East," in F. Morstein Marx, ed., *Foreign Governments* (New York, 1949), 549.

nomic progress. Actually, in the years 1932-1936 the gross national product failed to keep pace with increasing population. Political policy encouraged traditional uses of resources and economic output. Distribution of income became more unequal; savings went into hoarding and speculation at the cost of improved technology; Sun Yat-sen's principles were honored in words, but bureaucratic capitalism in fact; the declining role played by foreign investment was not compensated by growth in domestic investment.[13]

For Further Reading

JAPAN

Allen, G. C., *Japan the Hungry Guest* (New York, 1938). On Japan's economic needs resulting from her industrial expansion.

———, *Japanese Industry: Its Recent Development and Present Condition* (New York, 1939). The impact of the Sino-Japanese War, 1937, upon the industrial structure of Japan.

———, and A. G. Donnithorne, *Western Enterprise in Far Eastern Economic Development: China and Japan* (New York, 1954). A survey of Western enterprise in the last 100 years.

Borton, Hugh, *Japan Since 1931—Its Political and Social Developments* (New York, 1940). A standard work on Japan in the 1930's.

Causton, E. E. N., *Militarism and Foreign Policy in Japan* (London, 1936).

Colbert, Evelyn, *The Left Wing in Japanese Politics* (New York, 1952). Traces left-wing developments from the 1918 Proletarian movement through the 1950 purge.

Grad, Andrew, *Land and Peasant in Japan* (New York, 1952). An introductory survey of Japanese rural life.

Hall, Robert King, ed., *Kokutai no hongi. Cardinal Principles of the National Entity of Japan,* trans. by John Owen Gauntlett, with introduction by the editor (Cambridge, 1949). A Japanese text published by the Ministry of Education to further nationalism.

Hindmarsh, A. E., *The Basis of Japanese Foreign Policy* (Cambridge, 1936).

Holtom, Daniel Clarence, *National Faith of Japan: A Study in Modern Shinto* (London, 1938). A standard study of Shintoism.

Ishii Ryoichi, *Population Pressure and Economic Life in Japan* (London, 1937).

Lockwood, William Wirt, *Trade and Trade Rivalry Between the United States and Japan* (New York, 1936). The growth of Japanese trade competition with the U. S. in the 1930's.

---

[13] See Douglas S. Paauw, "The *Kuomintang* and Economic Stagnation, 1928-37," *The Journal of Asian Studies,* XVI (1957), 213-220.

Lory, Hillis, *Japan's Military Masters, the Army in Japanese Life* (New York, 1943).

Mitsubishi Economic Research Bureau, *Japanese Trade and Industry, Present and Future* (London, 1936). On industrial growth in the 1930's.

Schwantes, Robert S., *Japanese and Americans; a Century of Cultural Relations* (New York, 1955).

Tanin, O., and E. Yohan, *Militarism and Fascism in Japan* (New York, 1934). A well-documented study by Soviet writers.

Uyeda Teijiro, *The Small Industries of Japan* (New York, 1938).

Uyehara Shigeru, *The Industry and Trade of Japan* (2nd. rev. ed., London, 1936). A basic study of the subject.

CHINA

Bate, Don, *Wang Ching-wei: Puppet or Patriot* (Chicago, 1941). A biography taken largely from T'ang Leang-li, *The Inner History of the Chinese Revolution* (London, 1930).

Berkov, Robert, *Strong Man of China* (Boston, 1938). A journalistic account of Chiang's rise to power, by a manager of the Shanghai bureau of the United Press.

Bisson, T. A., *Japan in China* (New York, 1938).

Carlson, E. F., *The Chinese Army: Its Organization and Military Efficiency* (New York, 1940).

Chan Wing-Tsit, *Religious Trends in Modern China* (New York, 1953). A study of religious thought and philosophy, especially during the 1920's and 1930's.

Chiang Wên-han, *The Chinese Student Movement* (New York, 1948). A competent study.

De Francis, John, *Nationalism and Language Reform in China* (Princeton, 1950).

Hedin, Sven, *Chiang K'ai-shek* (New York, 1940). A eulogy by the Swedish explorer.

Hinder, Eleanor M., *Life and Labour in Shanghai* (New York, 1944).

Hsiung, S. I., *The Life of Chiang-Kai-shek* (London, 1948).

Hubbard, G. E., *Eastern Industrialization and Its Effect on the West* (London, 1935). Special reference to Anglo-Japanese contacts.

Isaacs, Harold, *The Tragedy of the Chinese Revolution* (rev. ed., Stanford, 1951).

Linebarger, P. M. A., *The China of Chiang K'ai-shek* (Boston, 1941). An able political study sympathetic to the *Kuomintang*.

Ning Lao-T'ai-t'ai, and Ida Pruitt, *A Daughter of Han* (New Haven, 1945). The autobiography of a Chinese working woman, as told to Ida Pruitt.

North, Robert C., *Moscow and the Chinese Communists* (Stanford, Calif., 1953). An account for the period 1921-37.

Purcell, Victor, *Problems of Chinese Education* (London, 1936).

Remer, C. F., *The Foreign Trade of China* (Shanghai, 1926).

Schwartz, Benjamin I., *Chinese Communism and the Rise of Mao* (Cambridge, Mass., 1951). A study of the background of Communism in China, analyzing the conflicts and issues that split the ruling party in China in the 1920's and 1930's.

Shih Kuo-hêng, *China Enters the Machine Age* (Cambridge, 1944).

Snow, Edgar, *Red Star over China* (New York, 1944). A sympathetic description of early communist struggles.

Tong, H. K., *Chiang K'ai-shek: Soldier and Statesman* (2 vols., Shanghai, 1937). An authorized biography by an enthusiastic admirer.

Wagner, Augusta, *Labor Legislation in China* (Peking, 1938).

Wales, Nym (pseudonym of Mrs. Edgar Snow), *The Chinese Labor Movement* (New York, 1945).

32

1937–1941

From the Marco Polo Bridge to Pearl Harbor

THE continental expansion undertaken by Japan's Kwantung Army in September, 1931, was the kind of adventure unlikely to contain itself within the borders of Manchuria. Although important in itself, Manchuria was of even greater significance as the base from which Japanese influence would dominate China and save it from Russian communism. Japan's expansion, however, was forced to deal not only with the new *Kuomintang*-National Government at Nanking, but also with a popular Chinese nationalism, sometimes unorganized, incoherent, even leaderless, yet sufficiently mature and persistent to challenge and to defeat the power of modern armies. From 1932 to 1937 Japan had sought by measures short of war to bend the will of Chinese nationalism to Japanese purposes. The birth of Manchoukuo, the Japanese penetration into Inner Mongolia, and the effort to create an autonomous north China state had all, nevertheless, failed to create a subservient China. Nanking had indulged in appeasement as an immediate tactic, but the will to ultimate resistance had not been broken. Indeed, the Sian affair of 1936 meant that China's nationalism had come of age. The result was the renewal of Sino-Japanese hostilities on a grand scale in the bloody though undeclared war of 1937-1941, and the final merging of this conflict with the world conflagration that began with Pearl Harbor.

The year 1937 was one of acute crises throughout the world. It was a year in which fascism and naziism became bolder in their verbal and diplomatic attacks upon democracy, communism, the territorial *status quo,* and the system of collective security as represented by the League of Nations. In contrast, the democracies were divided at home and unable to unite in opposition to the growing totalitarian group. Russia, rocked by the anti-Stalin conspiracies and purge, remained isolated from both groups. In this atmosphere of crisis occurred the incident that precipitated hostilities anew in China.

Lukouchiao: Hostilities but Not War

Fighting broke out on the night of July 7, 1937, at the town of Wan-p'ing near the Lukouchiao or Marco Polo Bridge not far from Pei-p'ing. The contestants were a Chinese garrison and a Japanese force. The latter was conducting manoeuvres here beyond the localities where foreign troops might be stationed under the Boxer Protocol. The area was important strategically, being crossed by a connecting railway between the Pei-p'ing-Tientsin and the Pei-p'ing-Hankow mainlines. Moreover, without treaty right, the neighboring town of Fengt'ai, through which the short line passed, had been garrisoned for more than a year by Japanese troops. Although in 1913 the Chinese government had authorized foreign commanders to drill their troops in the Lukouchiao district, the magnitude of the Japanese manoeuvres following the long period of tension since the Tangku truce was an invitation to trouble. As on previous occasions, the matter might have been settled as a local incident, but the issue was now manifestly the political control of North China, and both sides believed that "war was inevitable." By the end of July, the Pei-p'ing and Tientsin areas were in Japanese hands. By the beginning of August, Japanese troops had driven further into Inner Mongolia, occupying Kalgan and thus severing China's principal line of overland communication with Soviet Russia. Suiyuan province and its capital Kweihua were overrun and occupied, and this placed the Pei-p'ing-Suiyuan railway in Japanese hands. Other Japanese forces moved south into Shansi to strike at strongholds of the Chinese Communists both there and in bordering Shensi. Here, however, the Japanese met their first significant reverses at the hands of the 8th Route (Communist) Army, so-called since its nominal incorporation with the Nationalist armies in August, 1937. It was here that guerrilla tactics first revealed their power against Japanese forces overwhelmingly superior both in number and weapons. The result was complete frustration of Japan's attempt to drive into Northwest China. "At the end of 1941 the Japanese were no further into Shansi than they had been in 1938."

Hostilities Spread to Shanghai

The new conflict in North China aroused bitter resentment throughout the South and particularly in the Yangtze Valley. Then, while the two powers augmented their forces at Shanghai, came the incident necessary to precipitate hostilities there.[1] The Japanese wished to avoid immediate spread of the conflict to the Shanghai region. On the other hand, the Chinese hoped to relieve the pressure in the north by spreading the conflict to the Yangtze. Here there was greater likelihood of other powers being involved if Japan disregarded the neutrality of the International Settlement. Again, as in 1932, the Chinese at Shanghai were defeated after heroic resistance, and the Japanese moved up the Yangtze to capture Nanking in December, 1937. The National Government had already moved to Hankow and was eventually to retire further westward to Chungking. Chinese resistance had already infuriated the Japanese, and this fury was given free reign at Nanking, where local Japanese commanders permitted wholesale acts of brutality against the local Chinese populace.

Meanwhile, the Japanese, suffering humiliating defeat at Taierchwang, were unable to join their north and central armies until May, 1938, when they had won control of the two north-south railroads: the Pei-p'ing-Hankow and the Tientsin-Pukow lines. It required another five months for the Japanese to reach Hankow on the upper Yangtze, which they took in October, 1938. Less than a week earlier, Canton, the great port of South China, had fallen to the Japanese. The surrender of Canton without effective resistance was not only a blow from which China never recovered, it was also indicative of the failure of the National Government to provide over-all planning in defense, and it lent credence to reports that the city had been "sold." Meanwhile in Central China the war had reached a seeming stalemate. In November, 1939, the Japanese landed at Pakhoi in Kwangtung, invading the neighboring province

[1] When a Japanese sub-lieutenant and seaman attempted to enter the Hungjao aerodrome near Shanghai, and were refused admittance, shooting occurred in which the Japanese and a Chinese sentry were killed.

of Kwangsi to capture the capital at Nanning. But China's over-all strategy was showing improvement. In Hunan province the Japanese were forced to stop in their drive on Changsha, though in June of 1940 they were able to move up the Yangtze to capture Ichang.

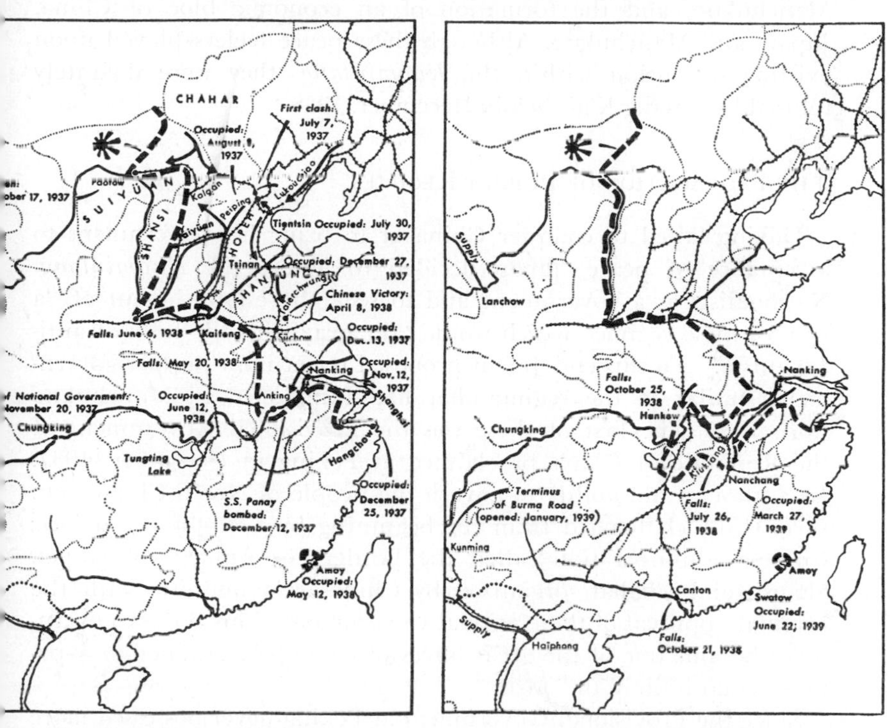

THE FIRST YEAR, 1937-1938.

THE SECOND YEAR, 1938-1939.

Maps appearing on pages 597-601, inclusive, are from A War Atlas for Americans, *Simon and Schuster, Inc., 1944, reproduced by permission from Simon and Schuster, Inc., and from the U. S. Department of State, Division of Map Intelligence and Cartography.*

They had now invaded China on three major fronts, yet China's resistance seemed only to stiffen. To meet this stalemate the Japanese resorted to widespread bombing, much of which was centered on the new temporary capital at Chungking and on key points on the Burma Road. In February, 1939, the Japanese navy seized the island of Hainan off the South China coast, occupied the Spratley

Islands a month later, and continued to maintain a blockade of Chinese shipping at principal Chinese ports.

After the fall of Nanking the Japanese began a series of efforts to sound the Chinese on proposals for peace. All these proposals involved Japanese control of strategic Chinese areas, recognition of Manchukuo, and the formation of an economic bloc of China, Japan, and Manchukuo. Although these peace feelers played upon existing dissension within the *Kuomintang,* they were definitely refused by Chiang K'ai-shek in December, 1938.

The Propagation of Puppet Regimes

Having failed to conquer China or to bring her government to acceptance of peace, Japan decided to ignore the *Kuomintang*-Nationalists as a government and to seek the establishment of "a new Chinese regime" which would "do away with the folly of anti-Japanism." To this end Japan proposed to set up a puppet government similar to the regime that had functioned in Manchukuo since 1932. The first of these was the Provisional Government of the Republic of China proclaimed at Peking in December, 1937. Its authority and ability to govern the people of North China were successfully challenged from the beginning by a new and patriotic Chinese administration called the Border Government of Hopei, Shansi, and Chahar, organized by Chinese Communists with the original approval of the National Government. This border government became one of the great forces of guerrilla resistance to Japanese penetration in the north.[2]

Since the Provisional Government at Peking never possessed more than a wavering local appeal, it was incumbent on Japan to find a Chinese national personality who could head a new puppet regime at Nanking with some prospect of claiming the allegiance of the Chinese people. Their choice settled upon Wang Ching-wei. Wang had a long and distinguished, if erratic, revolutionary record. An intimate of Sun Yat-sen, he had held many of the highest posts in the *Kuomintang* and the National Government. Although originally a leader of the left wing in the *Kuomintang,* he had come to oppose the Communists, had developed a bitter spirit of rivalry toward Chiang K'ai-shek, and was recognized as the leader of appeasement.

---

[2] The techniques of resistance as they developed in North China are portrayed by George E. Taylor, *The Struggle for North China* (New York, 1940).

Moreover, prior to 1941 Wang had convinced himself, probably by political rationalization and personal vanity, that China's future lay in co-operation with Japan. At all events, at Nanking, March 30, 1940, the new National (Puppet) Government, under the leadership of Wang, was proclaimed. Declared to be the true guardian of the principles of Sun Yat-sen, this "returned" and "Reorganized Government" retained the *Kuomintang* ideology and the structure of the National Government as it had previously existed at Nanking. Its personnel was composed in considerable part, though not exclusively, of *Kuomintang* members who had deserted with Wang. Wang's government, soon recognized by Japan, concluded a treaty with Tokyo, November, 1940, providing for joint defense against communism and for co-operation in economic development. Recognition was also accorded to the Wang regime, July, 1941, by Germany, Italy, Spain, Rumania, and other totalitarian governments of Europe.

Fashioning a Co-Prosperity Sphere

Occupied China, measured in terms of the penetration of Japanese arms, constituted a rich block of territory comprising the Yangtze Valley from Shanghai to Hankow in the south to Pei-p'ing and Chahar province in the north. Here Wang's nominal jurisdiction extended over more than a half million square miles of territory with a population of close to 200 million. It included much of the wealthiest and most densely populated areas of China. Japan now turned to economic exploitation that would integrate this area into the co-prosperity framework with Manchukuo and Japan. The groundwork was prepared by intensive campaigns of propaganda to eliminate anti-Japanese sentiment. Against this background the whole economic and commercial structure of central and northeastern China was reorganized. All forms of communication, and all industry, including mining, were to be capitalized and directed by new companies in which Japan held half the stock. Ultimate authority rested with the newly organized China Affairs Board, created in Tokyo on December 16, 1938. The general plan contemplated concentrations of high-precision industry in Japan; heavy, chemical, and electrical industry in Manchukuo; and salt production and light industry in North China.

Resistance in Independent China

Both for China herself and for the world at large the most significant and compelling fact of the four years of undeclared warfare, 1937-1941, was the resistance of independent China, its refusal

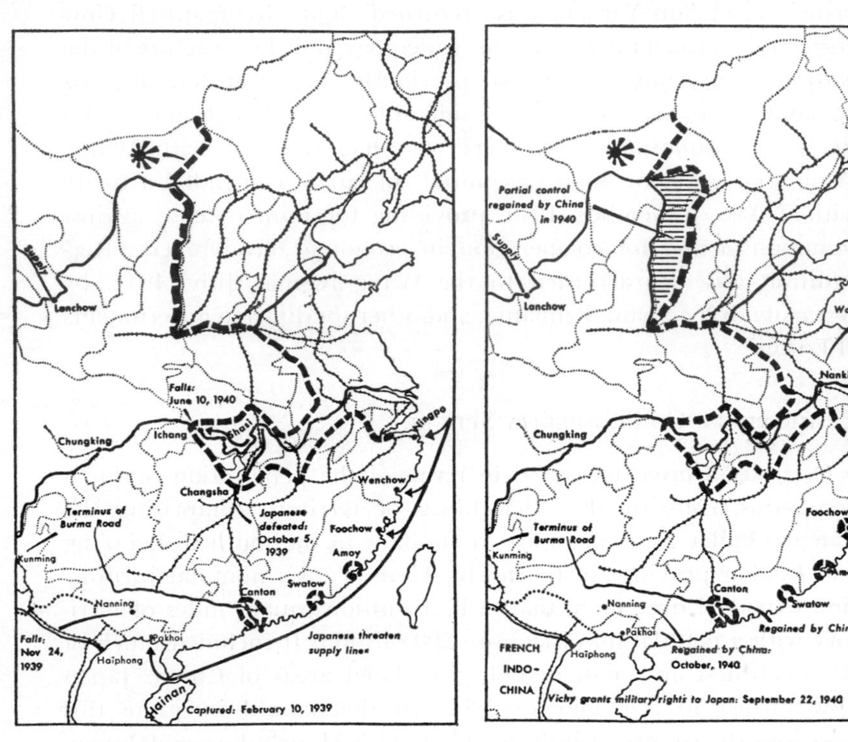

The Third Year, 1939-1940. The Fourth Year, 1940-1941.

to submit. More than half of the territory and population of China proper remained beyond the control of Japanese arms. In terms of economic wealth, it was much the poorer half. Chinese nationalism thus had no alternative but to base its resistance on the great interior hinterland of the west, where political and economic modernization were all but unknown. To this ancient west country, into the provinces of Szechwan, Kweichow, and Yünnan, trekked an astonishing migration of the wealthy, the educated, the politically influential, students, professors, skilled laborers, and some with no other designation than that of patriot. They travelled by boat, by cart, and on foot, carrying what possessions they could. In the old interior, where ancient and feudal traditions were still predominant, they set up the wartime capital at Chungking and reassembled transplanted schools, universities, and factories.[3]

THE UNITY OF COMPULSION

But China's magnificent unity of resistance was clouded by dissensions of the gravest import. The most important of these was the rivalry between the *Kuomintang*-National Government and the Chinese Communists. The latter, by 1937, were the second political power within the nation and their relations with the *Kuomintang*-Nationalists were embittered by ten years of relentless and cruel civil war. The unity which the two groups achieved in 1937 was not a product of basic political settlement but rather of the pressure of the Japanese foe. There were rifts also between the *Kuomintang* and lesser political groups. Although in the spring of 1938 the decision of the *Kuomintang* to create the People's Political Council indicated a wartime trend to more representative government, *Kuomintang* one-party control was not seriously affected. Moreover, after the fall of Hankow in October, 1938, China's desperate military situation, while promoting temporarily closer *Kuomintang*-Communist unity, led eventually to deeper conflicts between the two parties. The Communist strategy of prolonged re-

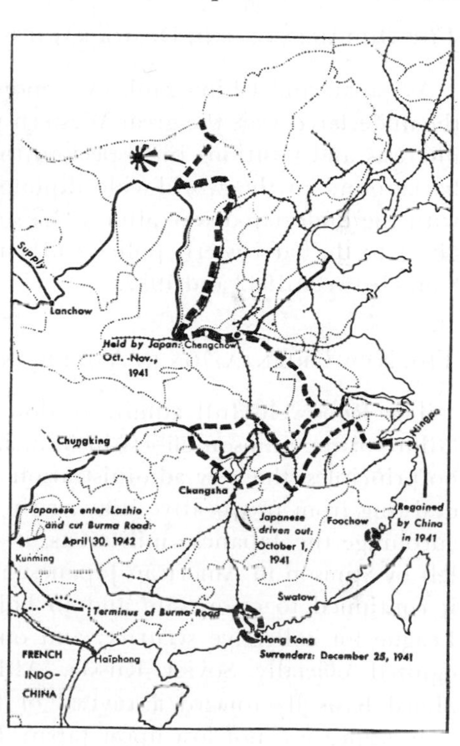

THE FIFTH YEAR, 1941-1942.

[3] On transplanted industry, see the study by Shih Kuo-hêng, *China Enters the Machine Age* (Cambridge, 1944).

sistance through guerrilla warfare, which proved to be one of China's strongest military weapons, was not supported by the *Kuomintang* leadership. After 1938 the success of the Communists in organizing guerrilla resistance in North China behind the Japanese lines, and the refusal of the Communists to submit wholly to the *Kuomintang* dictatorship, widened the breach between the two parties. From then on there were periodic clashes between *Kuomintang* and Communist armies.

The Dilemma of the Democracies

As Japan and China sank ever more deeply into the morass of the undeclared war, the great Western powers sought to define their interests and positions in respect to this unpredictable conflict. As background to the world-wide diplomatic struggle that developed with the undeclared war after 1937, some attention should first be given to the far eastern policies of Great Britain and the United States between 1932 and 1937.

The New Orientation in American Policy

The Roosevelt-Hull administration of 1933 had recognized the failure of the Stimson efforts in Manchuria. Although surrendering no principles, the new administration turned to new tactics. While desisting from provocative note-writing, which had seemed only to encourage the Japanese militarists, it sought to relieve the tension left by Stimson in American-Japanese relations. On the other hand, it continued to co-operate and to bolster the timid efforts of the League for collective security; and on November 16, 1933, it recognized officially Soviet Russia. Although this recognition was aimed basically toward a revival of foreign trade, its diplomatic significance was not lost upon Japan. Beyond these mild efforts the United States was not prepared to go. Like the League, she had found no effective means of opposing Japan short of war. These were years in which the perspective of Americans was circumscribed within domestic efforts to end the depression and in which American political philosophy leaned heavily toward the doctrines of pacifism and isolationism. Indeed, in the six years that followed the invasion of Manchuria there was no serious threat from the outside world to Japan's conquests. No Western government either within or without the League was ready to apply economic sanctions against Japan, much less to make war upon her for the sake of China's integrity.

British Policy in the Far East, 1931-1937

The historic cleavage that had frequently existed between British and American policy in the Far East was not ended with Japan's invasion of Manchuria in 1931. In January, 1932, Great Britain declined to give its formal support when the United States enunciated the so-called Stimson Non-Recognition Doctrine covering Japan's conquests. British policy held that it was not the business of the British government to defend "the 'administrative integrity' of China until that integrity" was "something more than an ideal." Although as the Manchurian affair progressed through the counsels of the League, Great Britain showed greater disposition to support co-operative action, her course from 1931 to 1933 was "on the whole favorable to Japan rather than to China," and she "acted more vigorously and promptly when Shanghai, the center of British interests, was attacked than when Manchuria, in which she had substantial but relatively less important interests, was invaded." Her position was logical since she "could not rely on the United States for more than moral support."[4]

Late in 1935 and in 1936 British diplomacy finally initiated a new policy which, perhaps more than any other single factor, clarified the basic issue of the coming struggle. In June, 1935, the British government announced it was sending its chief economic adviser, Sir Frederick Leith-Ross, to the Far East, and it invited the American, French, and Japanese governments to send similar missions. This request was declined, and in Tokyo the Japanese government rebuffed Sir Frederick's proposals for *joint* financial aid to the Nanking Government. The inspired Japanese press expressed the official view that the time had passed when Japan could co-operate with other powers in China on "an equal footing." This Japanese principle was by no means new in 1935. In April 1934, Amau Eiji, spokesman for the *Gaimusho,* had announced that Japan's position and mission made the peace and order of East Asia Japan's exclusive responsibility. Japan therefore objected to technical aid to China from the League of Nations and to aid or advice of a military or political character tendered China by individual Western powers.

[4] I. S. Friedman, *British Relations with China: 1931-1939* (New York, 1940), 18-42.

Later in 1934 Japan had proposed to the United States her so-called Monroe Doctrine whereby the Pacific would be divided into Japanese and American spheres of responsibility for maintaining the peace. The proposal was declined.

The arrival of the British mission in China coincided with decrees by the National Government nationalizing silver and stabilizing its currency, a program that would probably not have been practical but for "the support given to it by the British government." There was thus emerging a new British policy which recognized "that Britain's position depended on an independent Nanking." British finance would seek to rehabilitate Nationalist China and thus strengthen her against Japan. The Japanese reaction was one of bitter hostility.

Tightening Lines of Cleavage

The new British backing bolstered resistance forces within the *Kuomintang*-Nationalist government at Nanking and indirectly stimulated the movement for a popular front against Japan as manifested in the Sian kidnapping episode of December, 1936. It also stimulated the Japanese to renewed but fruitless efforts to bring China to terms. In October, 1935, the Hirota government suggested a Sino-Japanese settlement based on three principles: China was to abandon the policy of playing one country against another; she must recognize Manchukuo; and she must devise joint measures with Japan for the suppression of communism. To implement diplomatically this program, Japan, in 1936, sent a succession of special ambassadors to Nanking, but without success. By the close of 1936, Japan was also demanding of Nanking recognition of Japan's "special position" in North China, where, as already noted, she had failed to establish an autonomous government. Meanwhile, at Berlin, Japan and Germany on November 25, 1936, signed an Anti-Comintern Pact providing for co-operation in "defense against the disintegrating influence of communism." Secret provisions were directed against the Soviet Union. Finally, it was also in 1936 that Japan withdrew from the London Naval Conference as the Washington and London Naval Treaties expired.

The Collapse of Naval Limitation

The London Naval Conference of 1930 had produced a rather meager victory for the principle of arms limitation. Two years later at the World Disarmament Conference at Geneva, the United States had proposed abolition of all offensive weapons with the alternate proposal that existing armaments be reduced by 33 per cent. Contributing to the failure of these proposals was the situation already prevailing in the Far East, where Japan had invaded Manchuria and was engaged in hostilities at Shanghai. In 1933 the failure of the International Economic Conference at London delivered another blow to the principle of international co-operation and stimulated movements toward economic and political nationalism and their concomitant of big navies. The effects were only partially relieved by the American Trade Agreements Act, June, 1934, designed to give relief from the Smoot-Hawley Tariff Act of the Hoover administration by authorizing the President to raise or lower substantially existing rates in the case of nations prepared to make reciprocal concessions.

Meanwhile, the United States had fallen behind in naval construction, and in March, 1934, Congress passed the Vinson Bill authorizing construction of a treaty-strength navy. In December, 1934, Japan exercised her privilege of giving two years' notice of her intent to denounce the Washington Naval Treaty of 1922. Japan also made it clear that at the next naval conference she would insist on naval parity. Accordingly, when their demand was denied, the Japanese withdrew from the London Conference, which met in 1935-1936. The treaty agreed upon by Britain, the United States, and France, March 25, 1936, without the adherence of Japan and Italy, thus became a sort of death gasp of naval limitation. The whole structure of international naval co-operation so painstakingly erected since 1922 was shattered.

Everyone for Himself, 1937

The background sketched in the preceding pages suggests the impotence of the democracies for effective action when in 1937 Japan undertook the conquest of China. Although the Japanese invasion destroyed the tattered remnants of the Nine-Power Treaty, the democracies did nothing. The United States continued "to make foreign policy out of morality and neutrality alone." Secretary of State, Cordell Hull, said that force should be avoided, that nations should settle their differences by peaceful negotiations, and be faithful to their international agreements. This was what he had been saying with "a uniform of ponderous precision" and what he continued to say "like a litany" until Pearl Harbor. The Japanese replied that American principles were fine but did not fit the facts of the Far East. President Roosevelt did not apply the Neutrality Act—not because there was no war, but because the act would hurt China and help Japan. When at Chicago, October 5, 1937, the President said that "the epidemic of world lawlessness" was spreading and that epidemics had best be quarantined, he soon found that most Americans did not like the idea. They were quite sure the disease would not reach them. To be sure, when the League of Nations Assembly, October 6, 1937, held that Japan's invasion violated the Nine-Power Treaty and the Pact of Paris, the State Department said it agreed, but this act was simply another moral judgment which, as Ambassador Grew had long been warning from Tokyo, would be useless in stopping aggression.[5]

The Brussels Conference

The League Assembly, having marked Japan as a treaty violator, suggested that the signatories of the Nine-Power Treaty find a solution of the Sino-Japanese dispute. Accordingly, at the invitation of Belgium, nineteen powers met at Brussels, November 3-24, 1937. All original and later signatories were invited and, in addition, Germany and the Soviet Union. Japan declined to attend, since she had already been condemned and since she took the position that the dispute concerned herself and China alone. Germany also stayed away. At Brussels the delegates sat and talked and some waited for the United States to propose sanctions. In the end the delegates reaffirmed, Italy dissenting, the applicability of the Nine-Power Treaty and went home. Japan was offered no inducement to make peace, and there was no thought of collective force if she refused. The Brussels effort was dead before it was born. Within a matter of weeks, December 12, the Japanese bombed the U.S.S. *Panay* and the H.M.S. *Ladybird* on the Yangtze. Two Americans were killed. The Japanese government made profuse apologies and promised reparations. The Japanese public made generous gifts to a fund for the victims. The American public seemed anxious to forget the whole affair.

---

[5] Herbert Feis, *The Road to Pearl Harbor* (Princeton, 1950), 8-13; J. C. Grew, *Turbulent Era* (2 vols., Boston, 1952), II, 1167-1168.

THE NEW ORDER IN EAST ASIA

In the autumn of 1938 Japan took stock of its position. It was convinced the democracies would continue to do nothing and that the Soviet frontier was quiet and would remain so. But the Japanese conquests in China, which had reached to Canton and Hankow,

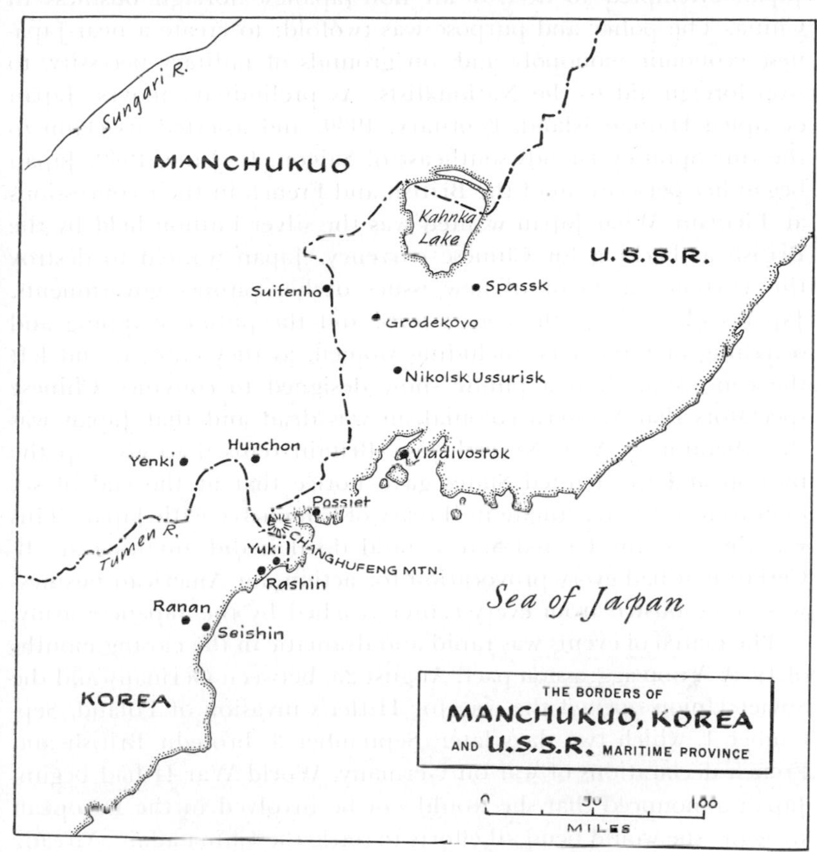

had not broken Chinese resistance. The National Government had retired to Chungking. The Japanese held the railroads and the big cities, but Nationalist forces and guerrillas held the country. Japan had won the battles but she had not won China. The war was a stalemate and seemed likely to remain so indefinitely. Japan therefore sought for a new policy to capitalize on her gains in the conquered territories of eastern China. This policy, announced by

Premier Konoye, November 3, 1938 was "A New Order in East Asia." Its purpose was to bring stability and co-ordination under Japanese leadership between Japan, Manchukuo, and occupied China through creation of an economic bloc of these areas.

The hard-core meaning of the New Order was soon evident as Japan attempted to destroy all non-Japanese foreign business in China. The policy and purpose was twofold: to create a near-Japanese economic monopoly and, on grounds of military necessity, to stop foreign aid to the Nationalists. As preliminary moves, Japan occupied Hainan Island, February, 1939, and asserted its claim to the tiny Spratley Islands southeast of Saigon. In June, 1939, Japan began her persecution of the British and French in their concessions at Tientsin. What Japan wanted was the silver bullion held by the British as backing for Chinese currency. Japan wanted to destroy this currency in favor of new issues of her puppet governments. Japan's blockade of the concessions, and the public stripping and searching of foreigners, including women, as they entered and left the concessions, was a public show designed to convince Chinese spectators that Western colonialism was dead and that Japan was the liberator of Asia. Nevertheless, Britain refused to give up the bullion and the United States gave notice that at the end of six months it would terminate its Treaty of Commerce with Japan. This was the least the United States could do if it did anything at all. Certainly it had every provocation for action, for American business was being ousted from every center reached by the Japanese army.

The march of events was rapid and dramatic in the closing months of 1939. A non-aggression pact, August 23, between Germany and the Soviet Union opened the way for Hitler's invasion of Poland, September 1, which two days later, September 3, brought British and French declarations of war on Germany. World War II had begun. Japan announced that she would not be involved in the European struggle; she would bend all efforts to settle the China affair. Already in August the Kwantung Army had suffered 18,000 casualties in large-scale fighting with Soviet forces at Nomonhan on the Manchukuo-Outer Mongolian border, where again the Japanese finally decided to negotiate rather than push the issues to all-out war. The United States declared its neutrality in the European war, September 5, 1939, but by November 4 the first step had been taken to aid the European democracies. A new neutrality act opened American markets in war goods to buyers on a cash and carry basis.

Japan Starts South, June, 1940

In May and June, 1940, the European war reached the Far East. The fall of Holland, Belgium, and France before German arms gave Japan a new freedom for action in the Far East. In July the British bowed to Japan's demand, agreeing to stop for three months transport of all war materials from Burma and Hongkong to China. The incident came to be known as the closing of the Burma Road. Almost immediately, July 25, 1940, President Roosevelt embargoed the export, without licence, of scrap metal and petroleum, and a few days later of aviation gasoline. The reason given was that all were needed for the armament program at last under way. Japan was already taking two further vital steps. She signed a tripartite treaty of alliance with Germany and Italy, September 27, 1940, and she began her southern march to Indochina and the Netherlands Indies. In French Indochina Japanese pressure closed the border into China, secured the use of certain airfields with the right to station troops, and transit rights for troops attacking southwest China. In the Netherlands Indies, where the Japanese were demanding oil, they met stiffer resistance. A special economic mission, September, 1940, was rebuffed, and later demands for greatly increased quotas of oil, June, 1941, were refused.

Tensions Tighten, 1941

The German-Italian-Japanese alliance, September, 1940, was directed primarily at the United States and was a further step toward world conflict. Its immediate purpose was to discourage the United States from going to war against Germany or Japan. For the Far East it meant that her European partners had given Japan a freer hand. The far eastern possessions of Britain, France, and Holland were almost within Japan's grasp. On the assumption that the Axis Alliance would hold the United States in check, there remained but one and perhaps a fatal weakness in Japan's grand diplomatic strategy. If Japan moved further south, what would the Soviet Union do? The remedy was provided by Foreign Minister Matsuoka Yosuke, the American-educated firebrand of the civilian ultranationalists, of whom Saionji, the last of the *Genro,* had said: "It will improve him if he becomes insane." Matsuoka's plan called for a non-aggression treaty with the Soviet Union. At Moscow, April 3, 1941, he proudly signed his neutrality pact with the Russians. Only one problem remained—to keep the Americans inactive while Japan took over Southeast Asia and liquidated the Chinese Nationalists.

The Arsenal of Democracy

Meanwhile the United States was moving cautiously away from neutrality. As early as November, 1939, Congress had repealed the arms embargo, enabling Britain and France to purchase and ship war goods in and from the American market. By June, 1940, as all Western Europe save the United Kingdom lay prostrate at Hitler's feet, President Roosevelt promised aid to "the opponents of force" and the speedy rearmament of America itself. Congress followed the President's lead with unprecedented appropriations for the armed services and the first peace-time selective service act. Fifty over-age destroyers still useful for submarine patrol and convoy duty were given to the British in September in return for the right to maintain American military bases in British possessions from Newfoundland to Guiana. Since the destroyer deal was a clear departure from neutrality, it indicated how rapidly the United States was moving toward a shooting war. After the President had been elected for a third term he called for making the United States the "arsenal of democracy." Congress implemented the proposal, March 11, 1941, with passage of the Lend-Lease Act, which meant that the United States would lend goods instead of money to the democracies. Lend-lease was a complete denial of neutrality. At the same time British and American military and naval officers were jointly planning the co-ordination of military effort while the United States remained a non-belligerent and for the time when she might enter the conflict. There was particularly close planning for mutual defence between the United States and Canada dating back to August, 1940. By July, 1941, the United States Navy was convoying British lend-lease as far as Iceland. In August, Churchill and Roosevelt issued the Atlantic Charter, proclaiming the goals of the Free World. Thus in early 1941 the United States had moved far along the path to belligerency in the Atlantic while Japanese extremists still gambled with the idea that America would not fight in Asia if she were offered some expendable concessions.

The Hull-Nomura Conversations

Japan's efforts to appease the United States began in 1941 with unofficial feelers and the appointment of Admiral Nomura Kichisaburo as the new Japanese ambassador at Washington. Nomura came with the assurance of his foreign office that he would be backed up in efforts to find a solid Japanese-American understanding. The Nomura-Hull discussions went on from April until the Pearl Harbor attack in December. From beginning to end they were as futile as diplomatic discussions could be. Neither power budged from its fundamental position. The only virtue of the talks was that they gave to both powers a little more time to prepare for what was coming, and the United States needed that time desperately.

The essentials of the American position were four principles which, as Hull had been saying for years, must first be accepted as the basis for agreement on specific issues. The first was respect for the sovereignty and territorial integrity of nations. The second was the principle of non-interference in the internal affairs of other states. The third was support of the principle of equality, including equality of commercial opportunity. The fourth was nondisturbance of the *status quo* in the Pacific except as it might be altered by peaceful means. Two things were quite clear: (1) the American principles were ethically unimpeachable; (2) the Japanese government did not want to debate principles. What Japan did want was an end to embargoes and to American aid to China.

Japan's position was given in her reply to Hull's principles, May 12. The United States was asked to stop aid to Britain in the Atlantic, since the Tripartite alliance was purely defensive. America was further requested to urge the Chinese Nationalists to conclude a friendly peace with Japan on the basis of the independence of Manchukuo, and economic co-operation. The United States and Japan should resume normal commercial relations, and America would assist Japan in securing oil and other products from southeast Asia.[6]

Japan Again Moves South

Germany's invasion of the Soviet Union, June 22, 1941, without previous advice to Japan produced new crises at Tokyo. On July 2 an Imperial Conference agreed to advance in Indochina, to observe the Neutrality Pact with Russia, and to join the European war when the defeat of Russia became imminent. General mobilization was ordered. New bases in Indochina were demanded of the Vichy government. By the end of July new Japanese armies were in the

[6] Feis, *The Road to Pearl Harbor,* 178, 200-201.

French colony. Operational plans were hastened looking to invasion of Malaya, the East Indies, and the Philippines. The navy began practice of an attack on Pearl Harbor, which had been seriously considered as early as January. The Japanese occupation of Indo-china brought swift reaction from Roosevelt. On July 26 the President, "in view of the unlimited national emergency," issued an executive order freezing all Japanese assets in the United States. This meant the virtual end of trade between the two states. It left Japan to choose whether to make terms with or war against the United States. Yet there were some in the Japanese government who believed that some agreement with the United States must be found. Premier Konoye proposed in August a meeting with President Roosevelt somewhere in the Pacific. The meeting was never held, for the President informed Nomura that Japan must first stop the military advances and give a clearer statement of her purposes.

The Last Two Months

With the failure of Konoye's proposal the Japanese High Command led by the Minister of War, General Tojo Hideki and his Manchurian officer clique increased their pressure for a decision on war with America. An Imperial Conference, September 6, concluded that if in a month there was not substantial evidence that the United States would accept Japan's position, war would follow. The substantial evidence was not forthcoming. Nomura had nothing to offer that Hull would accept. American principles and Japanese purposes were as far apart as they had been in May. The time had come when Tojo and his militarists were to have a free hand. They demanded the resignation of Konoye, and on October 18 Tojo became Prime Minister. The Hull-Nomura talks had really ended two weeks earlier, October 2. The distance between them, so Hull thought, was greater at the end than at the beginning.

Tojo Gets His Way

The war plans of the Tojo cabinet were approved by another Imperial Conference, November 5. It was agreed: (1) that a new proposal would be made to the United States which must be accepted by November 25, and (2) that failure would mean war, with simultaneous attacks on Pearl Harbor, Manila, and Singapore. Kurusu Saburo, a special Japanese envoy, reached Washington,

November 17, but had no new instructions. To keep the negotiations going while a Japanese fleet moved toward Pearl Harbor, Japan presented new proposals on November 20. They provided an avenue to new troubles rather than an end to old ones. In reply, Hull gave Nomura, on November 26, a comprehensive basic proposal for a general peaceful settlement. It was not an ultimatum, for it left Japan a choice of four alternatives, but it was a denial of everything Japan had set out to do since 1931. She could choose to reverse her policy; to continue the war in China but refrain from further southern advances; to retreat; or to march on. On December 1, an Imperial Conference made the final decision for war with the United States. The American government had long known that the zero hour was near. The Japanese codes had been broken. Yet it was not known where the Japanese would strike. Would Congress and the American people support the administration in war on Japan if her next attacks were confined to British and Dutch territories in Southeast Asia? The prevailing assumption in Washington was that Japan would attack British and Dutch but not American territory. Moreover, the American Army and Navy were demanding more time for preparation. One final effort—if not for peace, at least for delay—was made. On December 6, the President sent a direct appeal to the Emperor. It reached Grew in Tokyo too late, almost at the moment of the Pearl Harbor attack.

Nomura and Kurusu presented Japan's reply to Hull at 2:20 P.M., December 7. It was a summation of Japan's case against the United States and an announcement that the negotiations were ended. Delays in decoding had prevented its presentation at 1:00 P.M., just in advance of the attack on Pearl Harbor. Thus when the note was presented, Hull knew, but the Japanese envoys did not, that the bombs had fallen. Hull looked at the note (he already knew what was in it), told his callers that it was "crowded with infamous falsehoods," and directed them to leave. Later in the afternoon Japan declared war. The following day Great Britain and the United States declared war on Japan. Germany and Italy declared war on the United States, December 11.

PEARL HARBOR

Japanese planes launched from carriers had crippled the United States Pacific Fleet at Pearl Harbor and destroyed most American aircraft in the Hawaiian Islands. The casualties were as staggering as the damage to the fleet: 2,343 dead, 1,272 wounded, 960 missing, among American service forces. That much of the crippled fleet was back in service within a year was belated compensation for the greatest naval disaster in all American history. Providentially, the Japanese did not follow up their victory with an effort to invade the Hawaiian Islands. Having for the time being paralyzed American naval power in the Pacific, Japan was free to pursue her immediate objective, the conquest of southeastern Asia—Hongkong, Malaya, the Philippines, and the Indies.

Responsibility for the Pearl Harbor disaster presents a complex problem with which historians will wrestle for years to come. By July, 1946, there had already been eight official investigations; yet it seemed that the full story had not been revealed. Although the earliest investigations, made by the then Secretary of the Navy, Frank Knox, and Associate Supreme Court Justice Owen Roberts, laid the major responsibility on the Pearl Harbor commanders, Admiral Husband S. Kimmel and General Walter C. Short, later investigations, including that of a joint Congressional committee, tended to lay less blame on the commanders and more upon departments and personalities in the government at Washington. Whatever the ultimate verdict of history may be, the Pearl Harbor attack was of tremendous importance not merely as a military catastrophe but also in its political implications. If in the American mind there remained on the morning of December 7 any lingering doubts as to the role of the United States in the struggle against totalitarianism, Pearl Harbor removed them.

Americans sought what satisfaction they could by labelling the catastrophe Japan's "sneak attack." At best, this was consolation only to the thoughtless. At worst it was a convenient diversion from the hard and cold fact that it was the business of the government and of the armed services not to be taken by surprise. There were both immediate and long-range reasons suggesting that the attack should have been anticipated. American carriers in war games in 1932 had carried out a successful Sunday morning attack on Pearl Harbor. Grew had warned the State Department, eleven months in advance that if war came Japan might open hostilities with an attack on Pearl Harbor. From September on, intercepted Japanese messages revealed a sharp interest in the location of ships at Pearl Harbor. As the American-Japanese conversations were drawing to a close in

November, Grew and Hull had given repeated warning that the Japanese might depend on surprise and on simultaneous attack at several points. If these immediate reasons were not enough, there was the major and all inclusive fact that American-Japanese relation had been under strain for thirty-five years on the subject of China; that time after time the two powers had tried to hide a basic conflict in policy in the softer phrases of diplomacy and in meaningless assurances on the open door; and that for ten years before Pearl Harbor American-Japanese relations were in perpetual crisis. Yet both the American government and the armed services were taken by surprise.

History has not as yet uncovered the full explanation of Pearl Harbor. Theories and hypotheses have been abundant. Of these the most seductive, especially in times of crisis, involves what may be called the conspirational theory of history. Applied to Pearl Harbor, this theory means that Roosevelt and some of his top advisers planned, plotted, and permitted the disaster as the only sure means of converting the American people to war against Germany and her Axis partners. Although there is evidence of "culpable negligence" at Pearl Harbor and at Washington, the hypothesis of conspiracy in 1941 still remains an hypothesis.[7]

For Further Reading

Biggerstaff, Knight, *China, Revolutionary Changes in an Ancient Civilization* (Ithaca, 1945).

Bisson, T. A., *American Policy in the Far East, 1931-1941* (rev. ed., New York, 1941).

Bloch, Kurt, *German Interests and Policies in the Far East* (New York, 1939).

Carlson, Evans F., *Twin Stars of China* (New York, 1940).

[7] Julius W. Pratt, *A History of United States Foreign Policy* (New York, 1955), 659-662. The conspirational theory is developed in varying degrees in George Morgenstern, *Pearl Harbor: The Story of the Secret War* (New York, 1947); C. A. Beard, *President Roosevelt and the Coming of the War, 1941* (New Haven, 1948); W. H. Chamberlin, *America's Second Crusade* (Chicago, 1950); F. R. Sanborn, *Design for War: A Study of Secret Power Politics, 1937-1941* (New York, 1951); C. C. Tansill, *Back Door to War: The Roosevelt Foreign Policy* (Chicago, 1952); H. E. Barnes, ed., *Perpetual War for Perpetual Peace* (Caldwell, 1953); R. A. Theobald, *The Final Secret of Pearl Harbor: The Washington Contribution to the Japanese Attack* (New York, 1954); H. E. Kimmel, *Admiral Kimmel's Story* (Chicago, 1955).

Cole, Wayne S., "American Entry into World War II: An Historical Appraisal," *Mississippi Valley Historical Review,* XLIII (1957), 595-617.

Colegrove, Kenneth Wallace, *Militarism in Japan* (Boston, 1936).

Dulles, F. R., *China and America* (Princeton, 1946).

Grew, Joseph C., *Ten Years in Japan* (New York, 1944). Compiled from the diary of the American ambassador.

Hishida, Seiji G., *Japan Among the Great Powers: A Survey of Her International Relations* (New York, 1940). An able study in Japanese interpretations.

Holtom, D. C., *Modern Japan and Shinto Nationalism* (2nd ed., Chicago, 1947).

Hull, Cordell, *The Memoirs of Cordell Hull* (2 vols., New York, 1948).

James, David H., *The Rise and Fall of the Japanese Empire* (New York, 1951).

Johnstone, William C., *The United States and Japan's New Order* (New York, 1941). An able account of the effects of Japanese policy on American interests.

Jones, F. C., *Japan's New Order in East Asia, Its Rise and Its Fall, 1937-1945* (London, 1954). A thorough study that views Japanese diplomacy from a global standpoint.

Liu Chih-pu, *A Military History of Modern China: 1924-1949* (Princeton, 1956). The rise and collapse of *Kuomintang* military power.

MacNair, H. F., ed., *Voices from Unoccupied China* (Chicago, 1944).

Maki, John M., *Japanese Militarism—Its Cause and Cure* (New York, 1945).

Mitchell, Kate L., *Industrialization of the Western Pacific* (New York, 1942).

Rauch, Basil, *Roosevelt: from Munich to Pearl Harbor* (New York, 1950).

Rosinger, Lawrence K., *China's Wartime Politics, 1937-1944* (Princeton, 1944).

Stimson, Henry L., and McGeorge Bundy, *On Active Service in Peace and War* (New York, 1948).

33

1913–1941

The Philippines Move Toward Nationhood

BEFORE entering on the narrative of World War II in the Far East it will be useful to recount in some detail the story of American nation-building in the Philippines and also of the birth and growth of European empires in other areas of Southeast Asia. After 1899 the Philippine Islands were the most tangible stake possessed by the American people in the Far East; they constituted the first and the largest responsibility of the American people in that area. The attitudes which Americans adopted from time to time toward their Filipino wards were a measuring stick suggestive of the real and the professed interests of the American public in adjacent areas of the Far East.

During the years that followed Dewey's victory at Manila Bay, the islands and peoples of the Philippines experienced notable development, but in some respects this growth was not an unqualified blessing, since it created new problems with which the American people were not always prepared to deal. First among the notable changes of the twentieth century was the increase of population. In 1903 the Islands (115,600 square miles, slightly larger than the state of Arizona) sheltered a population of something more than 7,000,000; by 1918 the figure was 10,314,310; and by 1939 it had reached 16,000,303. Along with increased population came a rising standard of living resulting from expanded agriculture, exploitation of forest resources, and the sale of these products in the duty-free American market. The principal Philippine exports were sugar, manila hemp (abaca), copra, and tobacco. After 1930 a mining industry produced gold, chrome, copper, iron, and manganese. The possibilities of developing some light industry in the Islands also appeared; but with the absence of coking coal there seemed to be little prospect for heavier industry. Most significant was the phenomenal growth in Philippine-American commerce on the basis of virtually free trade. In 1908, Americans sold some $5,000,000 worth of goods to the Philippines; in 1929, $92,592,000. Philippine exports increased proportionally, and most of these went to the American market. In 1908, total Philippine exports were valued at $32,000,000; in 1929, at $164,446,000. In 1933 American importers were taking 87 per cent of all Philippine exports. The bulk of these exports (about 90 per cent) was made up of sugar, copra, palm oil, tobacco, and abaca. In some years sugar alone made up 60 per cent of the total exports. Thus after some thirty years of American occupation and some twenty years of Philippine-American free trade, the commerce of the Philippine Islands, both export and import, had been channelled almost exclusively to the United States. Trade had indeed followed the flag, and prosperity had been the result, but each year the economic life of the Filipino people became more dependent upon the American market. This condition suggested that the Islands were to continue indefinitely as an "unincorporated" territory of the United States.[1]

Characteristics of Early American Policy

During the years of what may be termed Republican rule (1900-1913), the official American policy concerned itself primarily with the large and basic tasks of cleaning up the pest- and plague-ridden islands, of promoting their economic development, and of providing their peoples with the beginnings of a public educational system. The Americans who pioneered in this work left a record of accomplishment of which their country may well be proud. Successive presidents, McKinley, Roosevelt, and Taft, assumed that these were the primary tasks; that for some years no purpose was to be served by discussions of independence even as a remote possibility. For the present, it was enough, as Taft had said, that the United States was

[1] As an "unincorporated" territory, the legal and political position of the Islands and the civil and political rights of the Filipinos under the American flag were determined by Congress, limited only by those provisions of the Constitution which are prohibitive. See J. R. Hayden, *The Philippines* (New York, 1942), 763-764.

pursuing a policy of "the Philippines for the Filipinos" and was training them in self-government to open an "era of good feeling."

With the triumph of expansionism, imperialism, and empire, signified by the Republican victory of 1900, the interest of the American electorate in the Philippines all but disappeared. On the other hand, the Anti-Imperialist League attempted to sustain interest, and the Democratic Party platforms of 1904, 1908, and 1912 denounced the idea of permanent American sovereignty in the Islands. The corresponding Republican platforms made no commitments for the future.

Some of the early agitation for independence came from Filipino conservatives who had formed the Federal Party in the Islands. By 1907 a number of Filipino political groups, including the nationalist revolutionary leaders of Spanish-American War days, had united in a second and stronger party, the Nationalists, demanding "immediate independence." From 1907 on it was the Nationalists who controlled the Philippine Assembly.[2] In so far as the American public took any interest in this native campaign for independence it appears to have entertained a healthy skepticism. The demand for independence was regarded as an encouraging sign of young nationhood, but it was also recognized that perhaps Filipino Nationalists had their eye on the native ballot box and did not wish to be taken too seriously.

The Democrats Revive Independence

In 1910 the Republicans lost control of the House of Representatives in Washington, and two years later (March, 1912) the Democrats introduced the first Philippine independence bill. This bill, sponsored by Congressman W. A. Jones of Virginia, was reported favorably by the Committee on Insular Affairs but was not acted on by the House. The election of Woodrow Wilson to the presidency was followed shortly by the appointment of Francis B. Harrison as the new governor-general of the Philippines. In his inaugural address at Manila, Harrison expressed the new American policy when

2 To many Nationalist politicians the plank of independence was merely a means of getting votes. "As one Filipino expressed it, 'The peasants remember that they paid heavy taxes under the Spanish regime. They do not pay as much under American rule, and the Nationalist politicians have led them to believe that, when and if independence is achieved, there will be no taxes at all.'" Grayson L. Kirk, *Philippine Independence* (New York, 1936), 42.

he said that every official act would be "taken with a view to the ultimate independence of the Islands and as a preparation for that independence." Independence would be approached as rapidly "as the safety and the permanent interests of the Islands will permit." This policy was soon implemented. A native majority replaced the American majority on the Philippine Commission, the upper house of the native legislature; throughout the government Filipinos were appointed to many posts previously held by Americans. President Wilson in August 1916 approved the Jones Bill, which provided for widening autonomy in the Philippines and pledged the United States "to recognize their independence as soon as stable government can be established therein." Here for the first time the United States went on record in a qualified promise of eventual independence. After the passage of the Jones Bill, it became the practice of Philippine Nationalists to assert that the "stable government" called for by the act had already been achieved, and that independence should therefore be granted. For the time being, however, nothing could be done while the United States was absorbed in World War I.[3]

Immediately following the war, the Philippine government, encouraged by the Wilsonian principle of self-determination, sent a special mission to Washington. From Europe, Wilson informed the mission that independence was "almost in sight," and, in his annual message to a hostile Congress (December, 1920), he reminded the legislators of "our duty to keep our promise to the people of those Islands." No action, however, was taken; and as the Republicans returned to power, it was again taken for granted that independence had once more become a matter of the distant future.

In 1920 President Harding created a commission headed by General Leonard Wood and former governor W. Cameron Forbes to report on conditions in the Islands. The report found that the Harrison administration had proceeded too rapidly in turning the government over to the Filipinos. While General Wood remained in the Islands as governor-general with the unpopular task of imposing stricter American executive authority, the Filipino politicos redoubled their independence propaganda in Washington and throughout the United States. It made little headway.

As the Coolidge administration came to a close, the American people were again content to permit Philippine independence to

[3] See R. W. Curry, "Woodrow Wilson and Philippine Policy," *Mississippi Valley Historical Review*, XLI (1954), 435-452.

wait for the indefinite future. This was not in itself an unwise resolve. Although the Wood-Forbes and later reports were political documents, they were likewise able analyses of unhappy conditions prevailing in the Islands. The real trouble was that the American public in general had long since lost interest in the Philippines. Whether to continue to carry the White Man's Burden there was, as the average American saw it, something that could safely be left to the government to decide. This was a far cry from the popular enthusiasm which some thirty years previously had greeted Dewey's victory at Manila Bay. And if in the meanwhile the United States had, to use Watterson's editorial phrase, become "an imperial republic incomparably greater than Rome," it was not because of any conscious effort or sustained interest on the part of any considerable number of the American people. "Benevolent assimilation" had long since lost its glamour.

The Economics of Benevolent Assimilation

Yet during the very years when Americans in general were showing scant interest in the political, cultural, and educational burdens of empire, the United States was linking the Philippines so closely to the American economic system and market that independence had become an impossibility save at appalling expense to the Islands' political economy.

During the first decade of American rule in the Philippines, there was little change in the Islands' tariff policy; the treaty of peace with Spain had provided that for ten years Spanish ships and merchandise would be admitted to Philippine ports "on the same terms as ships and merchandise of the United States." Then, in 1909, Congress established virtually free trade with the Islands. Full free trade was achieved in 1913 when the quota limitations of the earlier legislation were removed. Under free trade, Philippine-American trade enjoyed unprecedented growth, and the United States acquired almost a monopoly of both the Philippine import and export trade. As a result, too, of free trade, and through stimulation by other factors, such as wartime demands, a number of Filipino agricultural industries experienced a remarkable expansion, thus acquiring a new importance in the export trade and in the financial structure of the Islands. Between 1922 and 1934 sugar, cocoanut, and tobacco exports increased rapidly. It was these developments which enabled the

Islands to buy increasing quantities of American manufactures. Thus at one and the same time the political policy of the United States was to confer a larger measure of autonomy and the hope of ultimate independence on the Filipino, whereas the economic policy was to fashion a Philippine economy dependent upon a free American market—a market that would be seriously curtailed if not closed completely once the Islands had gained their independence.

As early as 1921 some farm groups in the United States had showed an interest in curtailing the importation of Philippine cocoanut products, but it was not until 1928-1929 that the business of putting a stop to the free importation of Philippine agricultural products was undertaken seriously by pressure groups. From 1929 onward, American attitudes toward Philippine independence were shaped by a peculiar mixture of moral responsibility to wards and a desire to be free from the alleged competition of Philippine agricultural products.

Groups other than the farm organizations became interested as it was discovered by patriotic societies and labor that independence was perhaps the speediest and certainly the surest way of putting an end to Philippine immigration. During the decade of the '20's, Filipinos had migrated to the United States at an average annual rate of slightly less than 5,000. There was wide difference of opinion as to how serious this immigration was either as a labor problem or as a general social problem, but its effect was to revive many of the arguments which had been used effectively against the Chinese and the Japanese. The immediate threat, if such it was, from Philippine immigration was not, however, the sole reason for labor's joining the new crusade for independence. For many years the American Federation of Labor had denounced our continued occupation of the Philippines as a policy of imperialism.

Independence and Political Expediency

As the fate of the Philippines was debated in Congress from 1930 on, the question of their independence became less and less a matter of political principle and more and more one of political expediency. In December, 1932, Congress enacted the Hare-Hawes-Cutting Bill. It provided for independence after a transition period of ten years; quota limits were to be applied to Philippine imports; there was to be a gradual application of the American tariff; and finally, the Philippines were to be granted an annual immigrant quota of 50.

The Hoover presidential veto which promptly followed was no surprise, for the firm opposition of the administration to early independence was well known. In one of the ablest state papers of the Hoover regime, the President challenged the statesmanship of virtually every clause of the bill. His over-all denunciation condemned it as a repudiation of the government's moral responsibility to the American people, to the Filipinos, and to the world. As positive alternate proposals the President suggested: (1) a plebiscite to be held in fifteen or twenty years to test Philippine sentiment, (2) immediate restriction of immigration, (3) gradual reduction of free imports, and (4) gradual enlargement of political autonomy. Eventually commercial relationships would be stabilized on the basis of a fixed mutual preference similar to but broader than that between the United States and Cuba. The Hoover veto was immediately overridden by heavy majorities, and the bill became law, though in reality it satisfied no one. As a result, under the leadership of Manuel Quezon, the offer of independence was rejected by the Philippine legislature on October 17, 1933.

Since there was no likelihood that Congress would change the economic provisions of the Law, President Roosevelt suggested the only concession to Philippine sentiment which was likely to win congressional approval. He proposed amendment of the Hare-Hawes-Cutting Act by striking out the provisions for a permanent American military base in the Islands. The question of the American naval establishment was to be left to future negotiations. With this change and some minor revisions of the sugar and cocoanut oil quotas, the old act, now repassed as the Tydings-McDuffie Law, received presidential approval, March 24, 1934. The law was accepted by the Philippine legislature on May 1, the native leaders being convinced that no better terms would be granted. Then, after having thus provided for Philippine independence following a period of economic transition, Congress surrendered completely to the lobbyists through legislation providing for immediate drastic limitations on Philippine sugar and by authorizing a processing tax on all cocoanut oil imports. The conclusion expressed by *The New York Times* was inescapable: "Congress is indifferent to what may truthfully be called the 'plighted word of the United States Government.' "

The Philippines Accept

The Philippines accepted the Tydings-McDuffie Law, May 1, 1934. On July 10 elections for the Constitutional Convention provided for by the Law were held. The Constitution framed by this body was approved by President Roosevelt, and was ratified by the Philippine electorate without opposition. As the Commonwealth of the Philippines was thus inaugurated, Manuel Quezon was elected the first President and Sergio Osmeña Vice-President. An amendment to the Tydings-McDuffie Law, the Philippine Economic Adjustment (the so-called Tydings-Kocialkowski) Act, was approved by President Roosevelt, August 7, 1939, and accepted by the Islands. This was the result of continued efforts to modify the economic clauses of the Independence Law and also of the findings of a Joint Preparatory Committee on Philippine Affairs. A report of this committee showed that even in a period of generally amicable international relations, the abrupt ending of Philippine-American trade preference in 1946 "would endanger the economic and political stability of the independent Philippine state."

Three amendments were also incorporated in the Commonwealth Constitution and approved by the President of the United States, December 2, 1940. The first provided for a return to the bicameral legislature to be known as the Congress of the Philippines. The second reduced the term of the president from six to four years, providing for re-election with the limitation that no president may hold office for more than eight consecutive years. The third set up an independent commission to supervise elections.

After the Japanese invasion of the Philippines, December 8, 1941, the President, the Vice-President, and the United States High Commissioner in the Philippines withdrew to the United States, where in Washington a government in exile was set up. On August 2, 1944, Sergio Osmeña succeeded to the presidency, following the death of Quezon. The new President was installed at Tacloban, the capital of Leyte, October 10, 1944, during the reconquest of the Islands.

The National Development of the Philippines

The forty-three years from the American occupation of the Philippines in 1898 until the Japanese invasion of 1941 have been called the period of national development. They were the years in which the ideal of nationhood, born in the late years of the Spanish regime, was permitted and encouraged to grow to maturity under the inspiration of American political principles and philosophy. There are of course no absolute standards of measurement by which the American political record in the Philippines may be tested. However, the American people did have an over-all policy toward the Filipino, a policy prefaced by the assumption that the Islands were ultimately to be free, and that it was the task of America to prepare them politically for that independence. Although this was the popular purpose, American official policy in the Islands was never quite so simple as this would suggest. The American right hand often pointed the way to political independence while the left held the Islands to economic dependence. This was not a case of sinister design, but rather of what McKinley would have called "the march of events."

The presence of more than forty ethnographic groups, more than eighty languages and dialects, together with the contrasts separating Christian, Mohammedan, and pagan, created serious problems for the young Philippine Commonwealth. Yet these differences were minimized by the fact that the vast majority of the Filipinos are members of one great racial group, the Malays. At the time of the Japanese invasion in 1941, it was as yet too early to evaluate Filipino efforts to win the political allegiance of the culturally heterogeneous "South" and to make it integrally a part of the Philippine nation. It should be remembered, too, that the absence of a common native language remained an obstacle to the development of strong national and democratic institutions. The small educated and wealthy classes had a common language in English or Spanish, but the masses of the people knew only their own local idiom. It is to be remembered, too, that although under the Constitution of the Commonwealth all Filipinos were equal before the law, only the merest beginnings had been made toward social, economic, or political equality.

The Constitution of the Commonwealth

The evolution of Philippine political institutions since the end of the Spanish regime takes account of six basic constitutional documents. The first was the so-called "Malolos Constitution" of the First Philippine Republic of 1899. It was a liberal and democratic document written by Filipino intellectuals voicing their protest against Spanish and American rule.[4] Although somewhat doctrinaire, this constitution revealed broad knowledge of western political institutions and capacity to modify them to meet Philippine conditions. A second document of constitutional importance was the Instructions to the Second Philippine Commisison drawn up by Elihu Root as Secretary of War. These Instructions set forth the principles on which major American policies in and toward the Philippines were to be based. The third and fourth documents were the Organic Act of 1902 and the Organic Act of 1916; both were laws of the United States Congress creating the legal structure within which Philippine government was to be developed. The fifth was the Revised Administrative Code of 1917, an enactment of the Filipino legislature, whereby it created a government taking full advantage of the increased autonomy permitted under the Jones Law. Sixth, and finally, was the Constitution of the Commonwealth of the Philippines of 1935, which, unlike the Constitution of 1899, was drafted by a constitutional convention composed largely of experienced Filipino politicians.[5]

In the Tydings-McDuffie Law, under authority of which the Constitution of the Commonwealth was drafted, the Filipinos were required to provide a constitution, republican in form, containing a bill of rights and providing for complete religious toleration. Since these requirements would have been met regardless of the American mandate, the Islands may be said to have been free to form a government expressive of their own political ideals. The result was a constitution resting on the basic political philosophy of Western democracy and providing for a republican state in which sovereignty was declared to reside with the people. The Filipino bill of rights was more "extended and explicit" than that contained in American constitutions. Reflecting the period in which it was written, the Constitution of the Commonwealth included concepts designed to create "social justice" for all the people. It stressed the duties as well as the rights of citizenship and conferred on the state large powers over persons and property. Indeed, it represented "Rooseveltian rather than Jeffersonian Democracy." In general the Constitution

[4] The Malolos Constitution is in the *Report of the Philippine Commission*, 1900, I, 189.

[5] José M. Aruego, *The Framing of the Philippine Constitution* (2 vols., Manila, 1936), I, 22-23; and Miguel Cauderno, *The Framing of the Constitution of the Philippines* (Manila, 1937), describe the Constitution and the character of the membership of the constitutional convention.

revealed not only American but also Filipino and Spanish influence, and in particular reflected the political philosophy of recent as well as traditional American political thought. Under this Constitution, the Philippine president, elected by the direct vote of the people, was given virtually all the powers possessed by his predecessor, the American governor-general.

The Filipinos wrote into their Constitution the principle of the independence and permanence of the merit system as applied to civil service. More important perhaps were the steps subsequently taken by the Commonwealth government to give immediate effect to the civil service provisions of the Constitution. These steps resulted in substantial improvement; but, as in the United States, so in the Philippines: the legislature at times refused to classify positions which it was politically expedient to preserve as a part of the spoils system. Unfortunately, too, for the merit system, Philippine society, being quasi-feudal in its family and class relationships, encouraged the rapid advancement of young men who had the protection of powerful patrons. Nevertheless, it was the considered judgment of the late Professor J. R. Hayden that "the Philippine Civil Service is one of the most successful products of American-Filipino collaboration in the building of the Philippine state."[6]

Until the establishment of the Commonwealth in 1935, the various legislatures of the Islands, from the first elective Assembly of 1907, were marked by two significant characteristics. In the first instance, they were "colonial" legislatures; in the second, they developed as instruments for the securing of independence rather than as the law-making body in a state whose constitutional structure was already determined. From 1907 until 1935, with the exception of the Harrison period, the position of the American executive in the Philippine government enabled the governor-general to tender advice on legislative policy and indeed to impose decisions with far greater freedom than could have been exercised by a native executive. Although in terms of rules and organization the Philippine legislatures followed the American model, they were nevertheless Filipino in spirit. Moreover, one party, the *Nacionalista,* enjoyed almost unchallenged control and thus wrote the legislative record of the young nation.

The law of the Philippines and the legal institutions created after 1899 derived their form and substance from a number of sources:

[6] Hayden, *The Philippines,* 143.

from Roman law of Spanish days; from English common law as revealed in American practice; from native Filipino customary law; and from the legal code of the Koran as it prevailed among the Mohammedans of Mindanao and Sulu. From the beginning of the American occupation, the substance of the Bill of Rights of the American Constitution was extended to the Islands. With certain specific exceptions, such as trial by jury, it was included in the Organic Acts of 1902 and 1916; and, with additions, it constituted the new bill of rights in the Commonwealth Constitution of 1935.

Under the Commonwealth, the Supreme Court was established by the Constitution; inferior courts were provided for by law. All judges were appointed by the president with the consent of a Commission on Appointments of the Congress. In a number of ways the Constitution sought to guarantee the independence of the courts.[7] The gradual strengthening of the legal system and of the administration of justice was also as notable under the Commonwealth as it was in the days of American rule.

Political Parties in the Philippines

During the period of American rule, Filipinos looked upon their political parties as instruments for political independence. The exception to this generalization was the *Partido Federalista* (Federal Party), which in the days of the insurrection was the party favoring immediate peace with the United States. Since peace could only be had by accepting American sovereignty, this party favored statehood in the American Union as the highest status to which the Philippines could aspire. The Federalists were conservatives of the upper-classes. The Party gave unstinted aid to American authorities in their efforts to end the insurrection. By 1905, however, the Federalists were favoring "ultimate independence."[8]

From 1900 to 1905, sometimes called the "period of suppressed nationalism," a great many political groups appeared which favored immediate or early independence; but it was not until 1907 that these abortive efforts resulted in the union of various groups to form the *Partido Nacionalista*. At the same time the Federalists adopted the name *Partido Nacional Progresista,* and thus became the con-

---

[7] On the Philippine system of law, see in particular Eugene A. Gilmore, "The Development of Law in the Philippines," *Iowa Law Review*, XVI (1931), 465-479.

[8] Dapen Liang, *The Development of Philippine Parties* (Hongkong, 1939).

servative nationalist and independence party. Beginning with the election of the first Philippine Assembly by a semi-popular electorate in 1907, the *Partido Nacionalista* won a majority which it not only held but increased in successive elections. It was this party that succeeded in identifying itself most closely with the cause of independence. It was also this party that took the position that it was responsible to the Filipino voters as well as to the American sovereign power that had created the Assembly in which this majority party now functioned. A third party, the *Partido Democrata Nacional,* making its appearance in 1917, was composed of some members of the discredited *Progresistas* and dissatisfied *Nacionalistas.* It functioned as the opposition party until 1931.

Until 1934-1935, when the Tydings-McDuffie Law was accepted by the Filipino people, the history of political parties in the Islands was affected and controlled primarily by (1) the issue of independence and (2) political rivalries within a small group of able leaders. During the Commonwealth the factor of personalities did not disappear, but in some degree it was subordinated to the major task of constructing a government capable of meeting new problems inseparable from independence. The need for statesmanship was emphasized by the *Sakdalista* rebellion on May 2, 1935. This was an abortive attempt by underprivileged elements to overthrow the government in Manila. The result was to hasten formation of a limited coalition between the dominant leaders, Quezon and Osmeña, and their respective political followings or parties.[9] With Quezon as President and Osmeña as Vice-President, the Commonwealth moved toward the Republic of the Philippines under the same nationalist party and the same leaders who had guided the campaigns for independence since 1907. In the 1941 elections there was no opposition party; to be on the *Nacionalista* list was to be elected.

Education in the Philippines

Since the beginning of the American occupation of the Philippines, Filipino leaders had favored free public education and the separation of church and state. The broad objectives of the American educational program were to abolish illiteracy, to provide every

[9] By this time constant shifts and reunions among political groups had complicated party terminology. Quezon's party was now known as the *Nacionalista-Democrata;* Osmeña's as the *Nacionalista-Democrata Pro-Independencia.*

child with a modern elementary education, to provide a limited secondary and higher education, and to give instruction in the English language for all. In 1925 the accomplishments and failures of the program were revealed by a commission of recognized American educators.[10] In 1939 there were 1,861,861 students in the Philippine public school system, or only 45 per cent of the estimated school population between the ages of 7 and 17. This percentage should be judged in the light of other factors: (1) the inability of the Islands to pay for high-school education for all, and (2) consideration for the social, economic, and political problems which would arise if secondary and higher education were extended to greatly increased numbers under existing conditions.

One of the principal tasks of the Commonwealth was to reorganize its vocational schools and courses, to elevate the prestige of vocational training, and to adjust these courses to the practical needs of the country. Despite these efforts, Filipino students still showed a marked preference for the academic course and the prestige which it carried.

The Philippine Experiment in Perspective

To recapitulate, it may be said that the period of American rule in the Philippines, 1898-1934, and the first years of the Commonwealth that followed, brought great and progressive changes to the life of the Islands. These changes were viewed as substantial foundations for an emerging democratic society. When the Commonwealth came into being in 1934, the new Constitution was received as a logical product of American democratic thought, and as a democratic promise for the future. During the Commonwealth, however, this promise was fulfilled, if at all, to a very limited degree. Filipino democracy in practice showed little in common with its formal description as given in the Constitution. Government possessed the constitutional forms of an American-style democracy. Yet in actual operation it evolved "into a quasi-dictatorship with democratic embellishments."[11] This result might well have been anticipated because, in general, the Filipino had remained by nature a Malay far more than he had become, by indoctrination, an American.

[10] Board of Educational Survey, *A Survey of the Educational System of the Philippine Islands* (Manila, 1925).

[11] Lennox A. Mills, "The Governments of Southeast Asia," *Government and Nationalism in Southeast Asia* (New York, 1942), 65.

It has been said that in the history of the United States and its possessions no chapter can compare in point of "glaring contradictions and inconsistencies" with the chapter on the Philippines. This statement finds its foundation in the fact that while American political policy was directed toward self-government and then toward independence, American economic policy made the Islands dependent on a free American market. Interestingly enough, both policies were implemented by the Democratic party. Moreover, while the Independence Act of 1934 was often described as a pious fulfillment, the motivation behind it was almost wholly the desire of certain American producers to exclude Philippine products. Finally, independence was granted at a time when abler Filipino leaders no longer desired it, and upon terms that were economically disastrous to the Islands. The paradox in all this becomes even more pronounced when it is recognized that the American policy of free trade brought a kind of prosperity to the Philippines and limited economic benefits to the United States itself. Furthermore, the persistent Filipino demand for independence was based on psychological rather than economic factors of national politics. In this demand for independence, Filipino politicos outdid themselves. By 1929 they were admitting privately that they would accept a modified dominion status with continued free trade with the United States. These ideas came too late. In the United States the pressures to be rid of the Islands were already too strong: American producers fancied they needed protection, and Japan's expansion was a warning to get out of Manila or else prepare to defend it.[12]

From 1934 until the Japanese invasion (December, 1941-January, 1942), the Commonwealth of the Philippines was put to the hard test of running its own practical politics. Under the Tydings-McDuffie Law and the new constitution many ultimate powers were still reserved to the United States. The Commonwealth still recognized the supreme authority of the United States. Many acts of the Philippine legislature required approval by the American President before they might become law, such as, for example, acts affecting currency, trade, and immigration. Nevertheless, in the realm of domestic politics a new nation had come into being.

This Commonwealth, measured in terms of political practice, was closer to quasi-dictatorship than to democracy. President Quezon

[12] Julius W. Pratt, *America's Colonial Experiment* (New York, 1950), 291-298.

was the political master of the Islands. He and a few colleagues controlled the patronage. He was adept in influencing all classes, including the little men who liked his program of "social justice." In the election of 1941 Quezon, without effort, was re-elected by 90 per cent of the vote cast. This willingness to accept Quezon and the *Nacionalista* party was partly a tribute from the nation to those who had won independence, but it also signified that there were very few independent political thinkers and that democracy was far from being a reality.[13]

The Social-Economic System

Although American rule had brought to the Philippines a kind of prosperity, it was not of the sort best calculated to reinforce democratic concepts and practices. Surprisingly, little was done to broaden the base of the Islands' internal wealth. The problem was admittedly difficult. The fact was, however, that the United States had not removed the incubus of the old Spanish land grants or dealt effectively with the abuses of landlordism. Thus there was created a paradox in which a humanitarian America built schools, sewer systems, and hospitals while an imperial America tolerated a social-economic system suggestive of the Middle Ages.[14] The well-being of landlords and compradors was not shared proportionately by the peasants. Concentrating on money-crop products such as sugar for the American trade, the Islands had to import rice that might have been grown at home. Out of these economic maladjustments came the report of the Joint Preparatory Committee on Philippine Affairs and the resulting Economic Adjustment (Tydings-Kocialkowski) Act of 1939 extending the period for favored treatment of Philippine products in the American market beyond the date when the Commonwealth was

---

[13] Clause A. Buss, "The Philippines," *The New World of Southeast Asia*, Lennox A. Mills, ed. (Minneapolis, 1949), 38-39. There were, of course, factional quarrels within the *Nacionalista*, but the issues were never permitted to become matters of principle or party program. Men such as Quintin Paredes, José Yulo, Claro Recto, and Manuel Roxas might feign revolt, but in the end they humbly did the bidding of the single party machine. There were a few minority leaders who refused to join the *Nacionalista*, to bow humbly to its dictates, or to be silenced by its machine: Tomas Confesor, who later won added distinction as a guerrilla; Wenceslao Vinsons, a champion of the miners, who was elected to the Assembly though opposed by the *Nacionalista*, and who was later killed by the Japanese; and Pedro Abad Santos, who championed the cause of the peasants of Luzon.

[14] Buss, "The Philippines," *op. cit.*, 40-41.

to give place to the free Republic. By 1941 the Philippine economy was in crisis, and both in the Islands and in the United States there was talk of re-examination and of dominion status.

Social conditions in the Islands were tied closely to and affected by the antiquated economic structure. In 1941, the American high commissioner described the social and political health in alarming terms. He noted that neither a sizeable independent middle class nor an influential public opinion had developed. The bulk of newly-created income had gone to the government, the landlords, to urban areas, and had done little to ameliorate living conditions among the peasantry and tenantry. Maldistribution of population, of land, and of wealth in many forms continued. The gap between the mass population and the small governing class had broadened, and social unrest had reached serious proportions.[15]

President Quezon and the Commonwealth government attempted to meet the growing economic and social crisis. Some new land was opened for settlement, some large estates were purchased for resale to peasants. New laws to protect the underprivileged were passed, a court of industrial relations was established, and better labor standards and conditions were fostered. Nevertheless, the unrest was not curbed. Labor was restive. Farm tenants resorted to riot. Socialist-Communist leaders in central Luzon charged the government with Francoism. These were the conditions prevailing in the Commonwealth when Japan attacked.

For Further Reading

Abelarde, Pedro E., *American Tariff Policy Towards the Philippines, 1898-1946* (New York, 1947). A careful study to 1941, but weak on the post-war period.

Benitez, Conrado, *et al.*, *Philippine Social Life and Progress* (Boston, 1937).

Caballero, Isabelo P., and M. de Gracia, *Quezon: The Story of a Nation and Its Foremost Statesman* (Manila, 1935). An uncritical biography of the first president.

Emerson, Rupert, and others, *America's Pacific Dependencies* (New York, 1949).

Grunder, Garel A., and William E. Livezey, *The Philippines and the United States* (Norman, Okla., 1951). Policy from 1898 to 1946.

---

[15] Fifth annual report of the high commissioner for the fiscal year ending June 30, 1941, quoted by Buss, "The Philippines," *op. cit.*, 42-43.

Kalaw, M. M., *The Development of Philippine Politics, 1872-1920* (Manila, 1926).

Krieger, Herbert W., *Peoples of the Philippines* (Washington, 1942).

Kurihara, Kenneth K., *Labor in the Philippine Economy* (London, 1945). Pre-World War II period.

Laurel, José P., *The Three Powers of Government under the Philippine Constitution* (Manila, 1936).

Malcolm, George A., *The Commonwealth of the Philippines* (New York, 1936).

Osmeña, Sergio, *The Problem of Democratic Government in the Philippines: Its Salient Aspects* (Washington, 1925).

Romulo, Carlos P., *I Saw the Fall of the Philippines* (Garden City, 1942).

34

"Colonial" Southeast Asia

FOUR centuries ago adventurous Western navigators seeking a new and more profitable way to put spices on the dinner tables of Europe founded their first trading posts on the shores of Southeast Asia. From these beginnings there grew in time European empires of great size and wealth comprising the lands known today as Indonesia (formerly Netherlands India), the Philippines, Malaya, Indochina, Thailand, and Burma. With the single exception of Siam (Thailand), these, the principal lands of what is commonly called Southeast Asia, became territorial possessions of great European powers and the United States.[1]

The character of the early Western settlements in Southeast Asia was pre-eminently commercial rather than political. For example, after two centuries of occupation, the Dutch residents in Java still looked upon themselves as merchants staying abroad for purposes of trade. While on occasion they used their constabulary to subdue unruly native peoples in the neighborhood of the commercial settlements, the Dutch trader remained a merchant rather than a colonizer. In general, too, the Portuguese and British settlements in Southeast Asia were for long merely outposts of their Indian settlements. Thus it should be noted that nowhere in Southeast Asia did Europeans go with the conscious or deliberate purpose of building empires, though in the long run that was what they eventually did.

For some three centuries or more—that is, until late in the nineteenth century—the importance of the general area of Southeast Asia

---

[1] The territories were usually referred to as colonies, though in reality they were not colonies because there were no colonists. They resembled colonies because they were not self-governing, but they differed from colonies in being under alien rule and subject to an alien economic system.

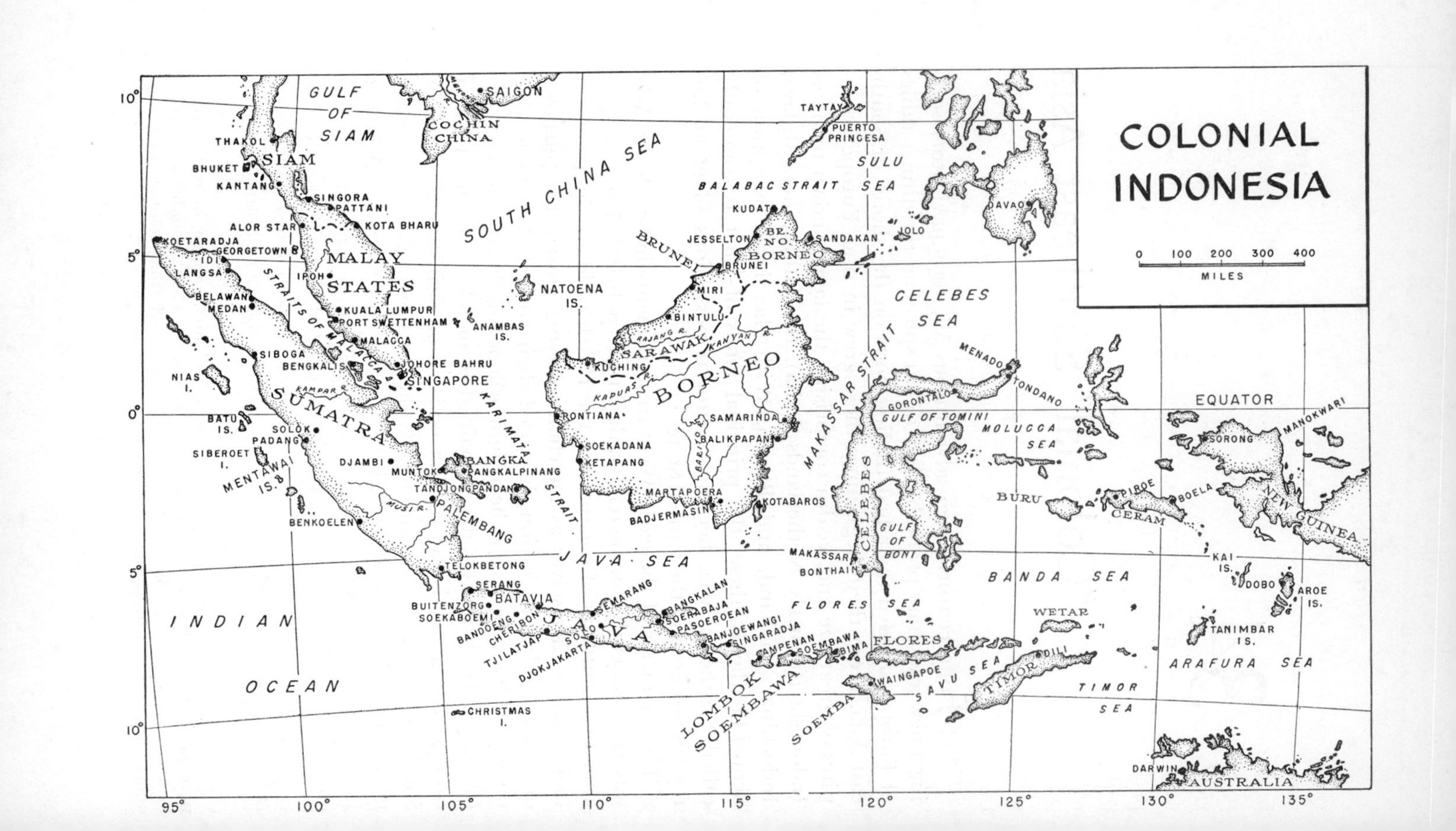
COLONIAL INDONESIA
0 100 200 300 400
MILES
GULF OF SIAM
SAIGON
COCHIN CHINA
SOUTH CHINA SEA
THAKOL
SIAM
BHUKET
KANTANG
SINGORA
PATTANI
ALOR STAR
KOTA BHARU
KOETARADJA
GEORGETOWN
IDI
LANGSA
MALAY STATES
IPOH
STRAITS OF MALACCA
BELAWAN
MEDAN
KUALA LUMPUR
PORT SWETTENHAM
ANAMBAS IS.
MALACCA
SIBOGA
BENGKALIS
JOHORE BAHRU
SINGAPORE
NIAS I.
KAMPAR R.
SUMATRA
BATU IS.
SOLOK
PADANG
SIBEROET I.
MENTAWAI IS.
DJAMBI
MUNTOK
BANGKA
PANGKALPINANG
TANDJONGPANDAN
KARIMATA STRAIT
MUSI R.
PALEMBANG
BENKOELEN
TELOKBETONG
NATOENA IS.
TAYTAY
PUERTO PRINCESA
SULU SEA
BALABAC STRAIT
KUDAT
JESSELTON
BR. NO. BORNEO
SANDAKAN
JOLO
DAVAO
BRUNEI
MIRI
BINTULU
RAJANG R.
SARAWAK
KANYAN R.
KUCHING
KAPUAS R.
BORNEO
RONTIANA
SOEKADANA
KETAPANG
SAMARINDA
BALIKPAPAN
BARITO R.
MARTAPOERA
BADJERMASIN
KOTABAROS
CELEBES SEA
MAKASSAR STRAIT
MENADO
TONDANO
GORONTALO
GULF OF TOMINI
MOLUCCA SEA
CELEBES
GULF OF BONI
MAKASSAR
BONTHAIN
EQUATOR
MANOKWARI
SORONG
BURU
PIROE
CERAM
BOELA
NEW GUINEA
KAI IS.
DOBO
AROE IS.
BANDA SEA
JAVA SEA
SERANG
BATAVIA
BUITENZORG
SOEKABOEMI
BANDOENG
CHERIBON
TJILATJAP
SEMARANG
SOLO
DJOKJAKARTA
JAVA
BANGKALAN
SOERABAJA
PASOEROEAN
BANJOEWANGI
SINGARADJA
FLORES SEA
AMPENAN
SOEMBAWA
BIMA
FLORES
WETAR
DILI
TIMOR
WAINGAPOE
SAVU SEA
LOMBOK
SOEMBAWA
SOEMBA
TIMOR SEA
TANIMBAR IS.
ARAFURA SEA
DARWIN
AUSTRALIA
INDIAN OCEAN
CHRISTMAS I.
10°
5°
0°
5°
10°
95°
100°
105°
110°
115°
120°
125°
130°
135°

rested primarily on the spice trade, on coffee, and on tobacco. In those days, the meat and fish which Europeans ate in winter had been preserved without benefit of refrigeration by salting them away in the fall. When later they were brought to the dinner table, the richly aged taste was softened by heavy doses of spices: pepper, mustard, nutmeg, cinnamon, and cloves. Spices therefore, commanded a price for which men would risk their fortunes and their lives. Control of the spice trade was a major avenue to wealth and power for men and for nations. Since most spices came from the East Indies, as they do even today, Southeast Asia acquired immense political as well as economic importance. In more recent years—that is, since the latter part of the nineteenth century—the spice trade has declined in relative importance, but this has not decreased the significance of Southeast Asia, which in contemporary times has become a source of the world's rubber, tin, oil, sugar, and many other products. This fact in part explains why alien control of Southeast Asia in one form or another was an issue in World War II. One of Japan's chief objectives was to break the political bonds between Europe and America and Southeast Asia, and, under the guise of bringing freedom to this area, to incorporate it into the Japanese sphere known as Greater East Asia. Even before this struggle came to a crisis in World War II, other conflicting forces of great moment were stirring among the native peoples of Southeast Asia. Principal among these was the appearance of nationalistic movements rebelling against foreign control. These movements were further complicated by economic and social problems.

The Nineteenth-Century Empire Pattern

Although the far eastern empires of Spain, Portugal, and the Netherlands dated their beginnings back to the sixteenth and seventeenth centuries, the development of mature patterns of control in Southeast Asia was an achievement of the nineteenth century. These patterns were the work of the Dutch in the East Indies (Netherlands India), of the British in Burma and Malaya, and of the French in Indochina. The British and French systems were closely related to the roles played by these powers in the nineteenth-century opening of China. British policy was also an aspect of Britain's position in India.

NETHERLANDS INDIA

The Portuguese reached the East Indies long before the Dutch, but it was the Dutch who became the first Europeans to rule the islands. Dutch political control did not follow immediately upon the expulsion of the Portuguese, because the Dutch East India Company, which had carried the flag of the Netherlands into the

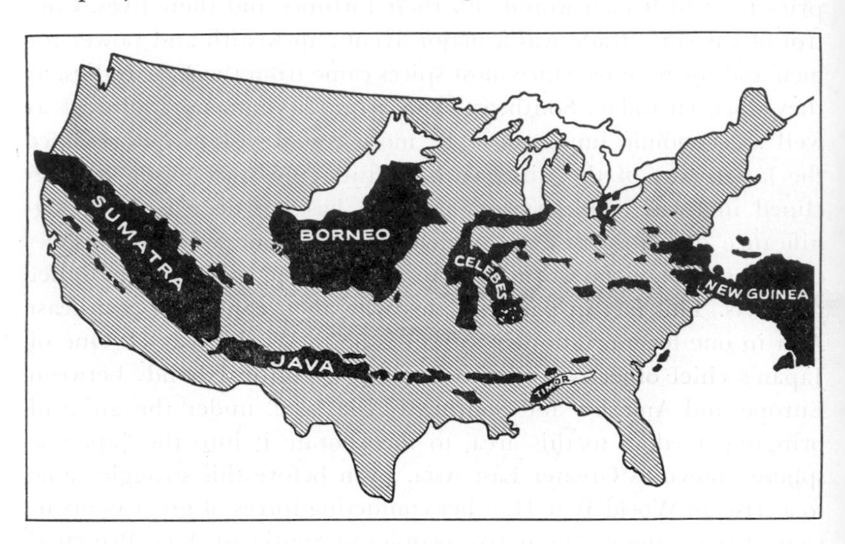

THE AREA OF THE EAST INDIES COMPARED WITH THAT OF THE UNITED STATES. *Netherlands Information Bureau, New York.*

East, was interested in trade and not in government. From 1600 to 1700 the status of the Dutch in the Indies was primarily that of traders. Experience suggested, however, that trade was dependent on government. Consequently, by 1750 the Company had gradually shifted to a territorial and political base. Through agreements with native rulers, the Company from its trading posts acquired indirect control over large areas of the islands. But in the process of doing so, its profits declined, and when in time the Company collapsed, the whole undertaking was assumed in 1800 by the Dutch government.[2]

After the Napoleonic Wars, during which the Indies were held

[2] The best brief account of Indonesia is Amry Vandenbosch, "Indonesia," *The New World of Southeast Asia,* Lennox A. Mills, ed. (Minneapolis, 1949), 79-125. See also the same author's, *The Dutch East Indies* (Berkeley, 1942), and Rupert Emerson, Lennox A. Mills, and Virginia Thompson, *Government and Nationalism in Southeast Asia* (New York, 1942).

briefly by the British, the Dutch, beset in the islands by mounting deficits, adopted a policy called the Culture System. Indonesians under this plan placed part of their land and labor at the disposal of government for the cultivation of export crops. Three principal results came from this system: (1) the Dutch treasury prospered; (2) abuses led to exploitation of the peasantry; and (3) general economic development was retarded, seemingly because of the exclusion of private Western enterprise.

By mid-nineteenth century, demands for reform by Dutch civil servants, along with increased political power at home in the hands of the Dutch middle class, resulted in the abolition of the Culture System (1870), in the entrance into the Indies of private enterprise, and in increased guardianship of the natives by government. This last aspect of policy, the Dutch version of the White Man's Burden, known as the "Ethical Policy," was a major characteristic of Dutch rule by 1900. In addition to the proddings of "moral duty," fear of foreign intervention prompted the Dutch by 1910 to extend their authority throughout the islands. This extension of authority coincided with the beginnings of a native nationalism.

Native nationalism in Netherlands India was in large part a product of the unifying processes of long Dutch rule. The national movement, organized in 1908 by Javanese intellectuals, was at first economic and cultural rather than political, and some wings of the nationalist movement favored the interests of Islam. In 1921, the moderates purged the movement of its radical leadership. Thereupon the extremists resorted to acts of violence, with the result that by 1927 the Dutch turned to a policy of suppressing the nationalists on the theory that the movement was Communist inspired. Already, however, nationalists had established their own schools, which refused government subsidies, and had organized study clubs and political parties, one of which was led by Achmed Sukarno, later to be president of the Republic of Indonesia. Sukarno's party was dissolved by government order in 1929, and thereafter the movement appeared to decline. Its later revival in the mid-1930's was on a more co-operative basis with the Dutch. This more temperate attitude of the nationalists was inspired in some degree by the excesses of totalitarianism in Europe and by Japanese expansion in Asia.

Prior to World War II, the Dutch failed to recognize the potential force of the nationalist movement. Although it was assumed that self-government would eventually be granted, there was no thought of conceding independence. Prior to 1941, plans for an Indonesian partnership in a Dutch confederation were debated, but all revolutionary moves were suppressed; their leaders were arrested and interned. Among these were names later to be heard in the days of the Republic of Indonesia: Sutan Sjahrir and Mohammed Hatta.[3]

Education in the Indies under Dutch rule was the reflection of what has been called a philosophy of empire. It held in general that native peoples were backward. Thus administration became paternalistic, the attitude being one of discovering what could be done for the Javanese rather than of finding what the Javanese could do for themselves.

At any rate, Dutch educational policy was decidedly paternalistic. Whereas in the Philippines American theory held that an ever-expanding system of schools would provide democratic training for the masses, Dutch educational policy was aimed at giving the native greater skill in his traditional calling of agriculture, a Dutch education being reserved for a few potential native leaders and for those entering minor posts in government. The policy, though thoroughly justified in the Dutch view, was not popular because many an Indonesian, like the Burmese and the Filipinos, preferred a literary education leading to the law and government office. The Dutch defended their system by saying that freedom of educational choice would mean economic and social dislocation and the creation of an idle intellectual proletariat. They held, too, that although they did not encourage democratic education, their system was much concerned with improving the native standard of living. Emphasis was placed on the importance of economic literacy for the farmer, whereby he might protect himself from the moneylender, and on the importance of rural credit, health, irrigation, communications, and protection of native land rights.

Economic Status of the Indies Prior to 1941

Under the liberal economic policy adopted in the late nineteenth century, Western enterprise in agriculture and mining prospered. Until 1933, Dutch goods entering the islands paid the same low tariffs as goods from other countries. The world depression of the 1930's was, however, a severe blow; the price of raw materials ex-

3 On the extent of limited self-government in the Indies, 1925-1941, see Vandenbosch, "Indonesia," 85-91. See also the exhaustive study by J. S. Furnivall, *Netherlands India* (New York, 1944).

ported by the Indies fell far more rapidly than the price of finished imports. These conditions forced a departure from the liberal trade policy at a time when Japanese imports of inexpensive manufactured goods were beginning to flood the Indies market. The result was adoption of a quota system resulting in reciprocal trade agreements. As world tensions increased, these agreements became political rather than economic, and were aimed at halting a Japanese economic invasion.

In summary, then, it may be said that on the eve of World War II Dutch control was not considered to be in imminent jeopardy, though in the Indies, as in other subject areas, administrators and home government alike were slow to see what they did not want to see. There was no large and stable native middle class and certainly no understanding by the peasant of democracy. The middle-class petty capitalists of the islands were the Chinese, whose loyalties were often to China rather than to the Indies. The great natural resources, the wealth of the Indies, rubber, oil, etc., were owned and operated by the capital and the technical skill of the West. This is simply to say that Indonesia was a plural society comprising three social orders: the native Indonesians, the Chinese, and the Europeans. These social orders lived side by side, but at the same time they lived separately, "rarely meeting save in the material and economic sphere." Culturally their backgrounds were diverse in the extreme. These facts go far to explain why the developing history of Indonesian nationalism before 1941 was marked by lack of purpose on the part of government and lack of confidence on the part of the people.

Burma

Burma, with an area of 261,000 square miles, about the size of Texas, had an extremely important geographical location between the two great civilizations of Asia, the Indian and the Chinese. On the west, Burma in the nineteenth century was bordered by the Indian province and the Bay of Bengal; on the north, by Tibet; on the east, by southwestern China and Indochina; on the south, by Siam and the Malay peninsula. It was this unique geographical location which explained why Burma, essentially neither Indian nor Chinese, partook of the culture and life of both her more populous neighbors.[4]

[4] John L. Christian, *Modern Burma* (Berkeley, 1942), ch. 1.

The country had two well-defined regions, Upper and Lower Burma. Lower Burma, in the south, comprised the deltas and plains of the Irrawaddy, the Sittang, and the lower Salween, the province of Arakan, and the Tenasserim Peninsula. Here were produced the great crops of rice (prior to World War II Burma was the world's greatest exporter of this grain), tin, and lumber. Upper Burma was

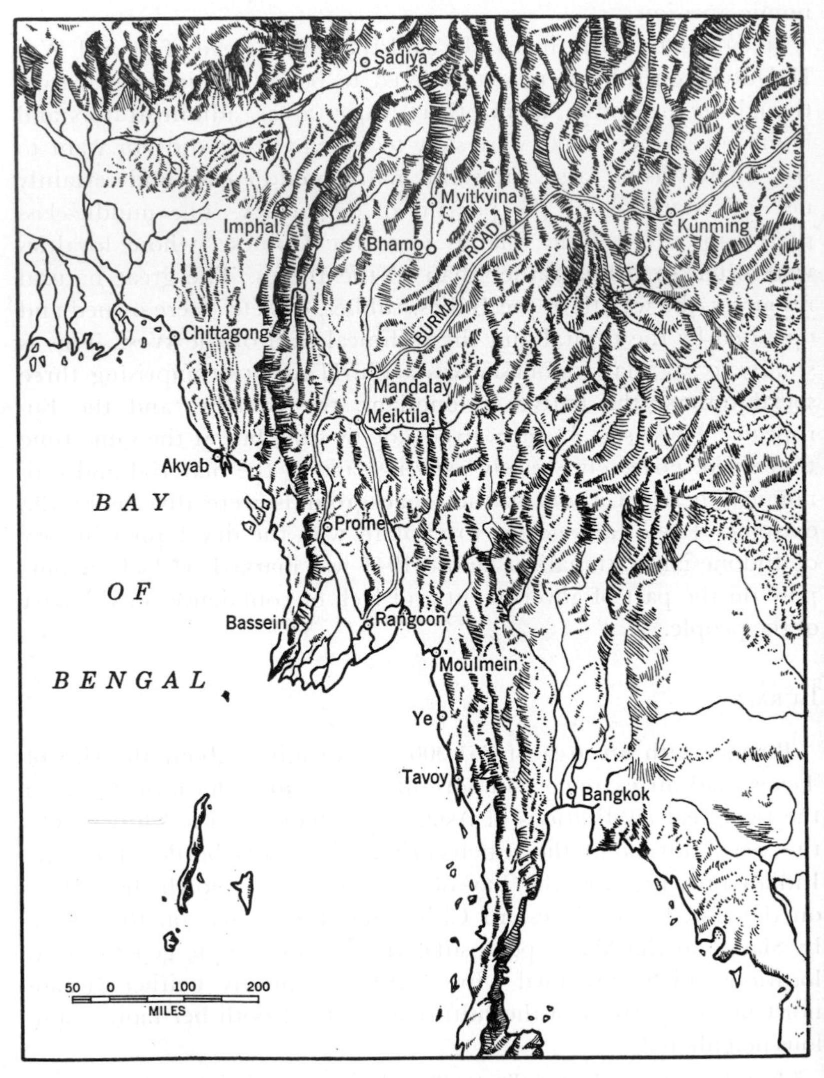

RELIEF OF BURMA

a vastly different country, formed of successive narrow valleys and the towering mountain systems of the north and northwest regions. With the exception of tin and oil, most of Burma's extensive mineral wealth was found in Upper Burma. Only coal was lacking to give Burma the common requisites of an industrial civilization.

Burma's prewar population, 17,000,000, included a number of language groups, of which the outstanding were the Burmese, about 10,000,000; the Karen, 1,350,000; the Tai or Shan, 1,000,000; and more than 1,000,000 who used various Indian languages. The fact that Burmese had not become the universal tongue of the country was due in part to the general hesitancy of the Burmese to enter business.

The long and earlier, as distinct from the short and modern, history of Burma is a story of migrations of peoples who came primarily from eastern Tibet and western China. To this racial tie with China was added in the eleventh century an even stronger cultural bond with India through the conquest of Burma by Hinayana Buddhism. After the thirteenth century, when the Mongols invaded the country, Burmese history was marked by successive periods of political disintegration interspersed with the appearance of aggressive and strong military rulers whose conquests spread at times far beyond the borders of present-day Burma.

Long before the nineteenth century, European traders in the East had a secondary interest in Burmese commerce. As far back as the beginning of the seventeenth century, the English, the French, and the Dutch had exported teakwood from Burma, but the country lay beyond the interests of the spice trade and therefore did not become a major center of European commerce. However, as a prelude to European involvement in Burma's internal affairs, the British and the French, contending for supremacy in India, gave aid respectively to opposing Burmese factions in the decade of 1750. During the next 75 years exaggerated reports reached the outer world of Burma's power and wealth, and eventually frontier incidents provided the occasion for the First Anglo-Burmese War. As a result of three conflicts, the First, the Second, and the Third Anglo-Burmese Wars, 1824, 1852, and 1855, Burma became a British colony; the final steps in annexation (1886) were hastened as a result of French intrigue in Upper Burma.

The new possession was made a province of the British Indian Empire, a status which it retained until 1937, when it was separated from India and became virtually a self-governing dominion. During the twentieth century Burma revealed marked growth toward modernization in her economic and, to a somewhat lesser degree, in her political life. As a measure of this growth, by 1940 no dependent area of Southeast Asia, excepting only the Philippines, enjoyed so wide a measure of political autonomy.

The interest of the Western world in Burma in the nineteenth century was centered primarily on the country's economic development. Whatever may have been the merits or shortcomings of the economic approach, its achievements in Burma under British rule were indeed great.

After World War I, this emphasis on the economic approach met its first serious challenge, and, in keeping with public sentiment of the post-war years, British policy became more responsive to the idea of self-determination and, more specifically, to the idea of self-government. Nevertheless, "the need for economic and political reform in Burma outran the speed of adjustment. Inertia had to be overcome, and it was not easy to decide exactly what to do." Thus many basic economic problems (agricultural credit, farm tenancy, immigration) were not grappled with until after 1937. As a result, prolonged economic maladjustment had already created much popular unrest by the time of the Japanese invasion of 1942. Behind this picture were fundamental evolutionary changes in Burma's economy covering more than a century of British rule.

By the beginning of the twentieth century, a simple, Burmese agricultural society had been invaded by the aggressive, *laissez-faire* commercialism of British, Indian, and Chinese traders and businessmen. The result was a major degree of social dislocation. Instability became typical of native village life; the educational influence of the Buddhist clergy declined; a migrant laboring class appeared and contributed to increasing lawlessness. After the Indian moneylender, the landlord, the tax collector, and the Chinese merchant had each taken his toll or his profit, the peasant had less than enough on which to live until the next crop. The anti-Indian race riots of 1930 and 1938 were the result. The British were also a target for resentment, because British courts gave Indians the protection of the law.

Self-Government, Politics, and Nationalism

Burmese manifestations of nationalism were, in the main, a recent, twentieth-century development. During the nineteenth century

U. S. Department of State, Division of Map Intelligence and Cartography.

most Burmese appeared in general to have welcomed the stability and peace of British control which replaced the factional strife that had existed under native rule. By the later years of the century there was a measure of local self-government.

The central Burmese government acquired a new constitution in 1922 which provided for a legislative council instead of the previous advisory one. More than 17 per cent of the Burmese population enjoyed the suffrage, and more than a majority of the council was elected from Burmese constituencies. The constitution, however, was extremely unpopular, allegedly because it set up a dyarchy dividing executive authority into powers reserved to the governor (defense, foreign affairs, finance, higher education, justice, communications), and those transferred to responsible ministers (agriculture, forests, health, primary education, and local government). Burmese opposition to the constitution was continuous and reached the point where most candidates elected to the council were pledged not to accept posts in the transferred ministries.

By 1930, when economic distress had added its weight to the general political discontent, political groups outside the council had become more noisy than the council itself. A serious rebellion against British authority led by Saya San in 1930 revealed the degree to which popular sentiment was prepared to challenge the established order. Out of the rebellion came the organization of the *Dobama* (We Burmans) Society of young nationalists demanding independence and calling themselves Thakin (Lord) in derision of the earlier custom of addressing Britishers by this term. By 1940, the *Dobama* party had won substantial popular influence, its purposefulness being in marked contrast with the petty and personal rivalry that appeared to control so many Burmese politicians in the legislative council.

The British Imperial Commission of 1929, investigating constitutional reform for the Indian Empire, recommended that Burma be separated from India and that a program of extending representative government be carried out in spite of the fact that in the Commission's view Burma's record with self-government was not encouraging. Accordingly, the new Burmese constitution of 1935 gave to Burma a qualified dominion status. Ministerial responsibility to an elected legislature was still limited by extensive powers reserved by the governor. The new constitution went into effect in 1937 with the active support of the Burmese electorate. Thus on the eve of World War II Burma had achieved a remarkable degree of responsible government and a vital national consciousness.

Malaya

Prior to World War II, Great Britain held a large and wealthy empire cutting across the tropics of Southeast Asia, composed of Burma, British Malaya, and portions of the great island of Borneo (Sarawak, Brunei, and British North Borneo). In this empire, the most important area in economic terms was a group of small settlements and protectorates known as British Malaya. Like many another region remote from the Western world, British Malaya was thrust upon public attention by the early military disasters of World War II. Previously this tropical empire was largely taken for granted even by Britishers, and about all the average man knew was that it produced tin and rubber and had a strong naval base.

In 1819, Singapore, a small island that lies off the southern tip of the Malay Peninsula, was chosen by Thomas Stamford Raffles, a young English East India Company agent "insatiable in ambition," as the site for a factory of the Company. A century later, Singapore had become a city of almost half a million inhabitants and one of the greatest commercial crossroads of the world.

The Malay Peninsula, with an area of 53,000 square miles, approximately the size of the state of Florida, and with a population of about 5,000,000 in 1940, was a region characterized by a central mountain chain with altitudes ranging from 4,000 to 8,000 feet, below which were the rolling foothill country and the coastal plains that in some places are extremely narrow while in others they broaden out to as much as thirty miles in width. It was here on the western shore in the coastal plains, and in the undulating terrain of the lower foothills, that the rubber-growing lands of Malaya were found. Here, too, in the valleys of the lowlands, were the deposits of tin washed down from the high granite ranges.

In modern times, agriculture in Malaya has consisted of two principal kinds: (1) the small plots of the natives (Malays), where, in many cases, rubber is grown together with rice and tropical vegetables, and (2) the large-scale plantations of Europeans and Chinese, where, prior to World War II, about 45 per cent of the world supply of rubber was produced. Here it may be noted also that in the

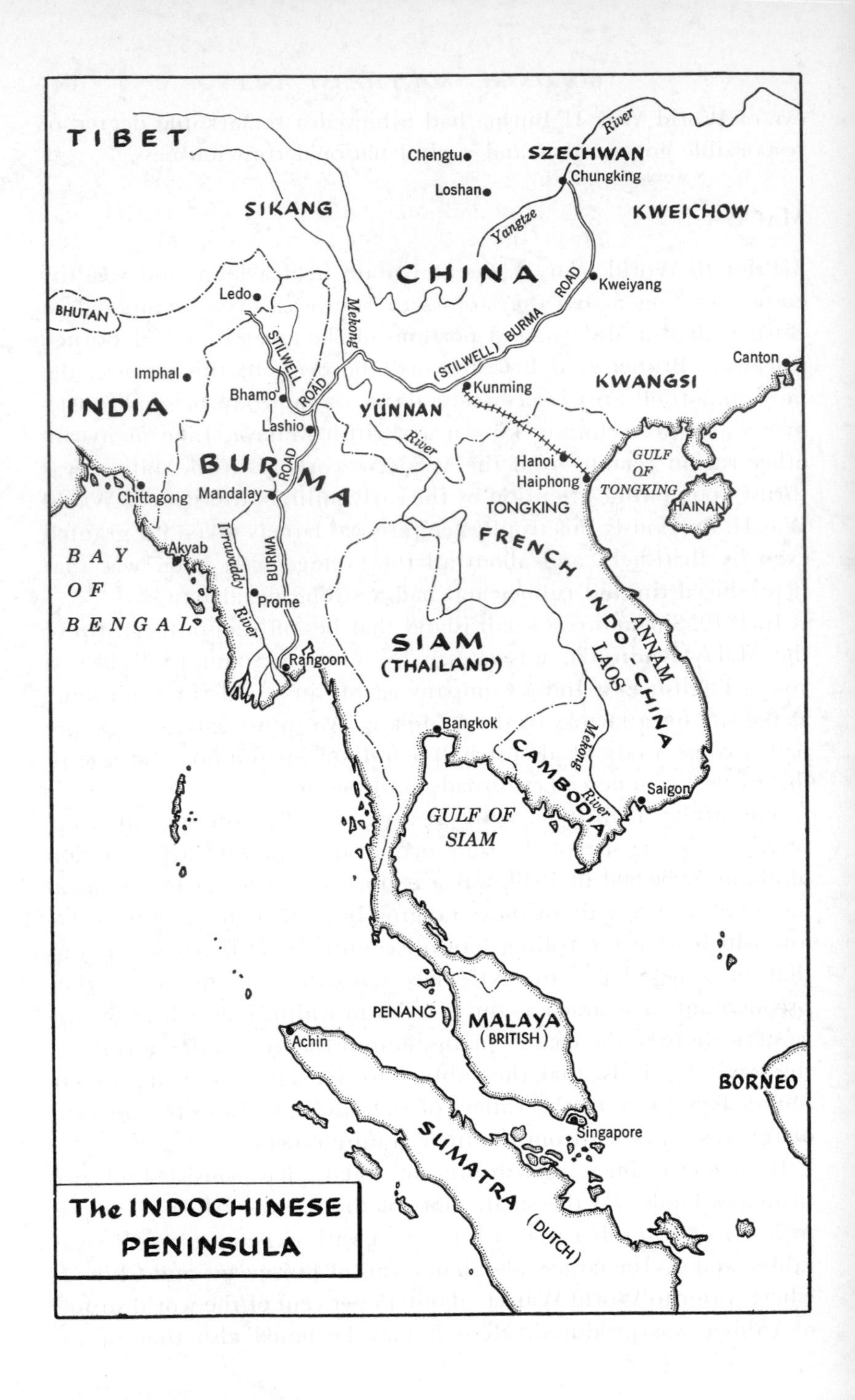

The INDOCHINESE PENINSULA

decade of the 1930's Malaya held first place in the world's production of tin, with 28 per cent of the total output.

The native of the peninsula was the Malay, a descendant of the Proto-Malay with a considerable mixture of Arab, Indian, and Chinese blood. In 1947, the total population of 5,808,000 included: Malays, 2,512,000, 43 per cent; Chinese, 2,608,000, 44 per cent; Indians, 605,000, 10 per cent; Europeans, principally British, 18,000. Most of the Malays were British subjects or British-protected persons, whereas in the case of the Chinese the majority were foreign residents: 1,000,000 out of a total Chinese population of 1,709,000 in 1931.[5] But although the Chinese formed the overwhelming foreign group in Malaya in the twentieth century, it was Indian rather than Chinese culture that influenced the historic patterns of Malayan life. Indian commerce, Indian Buddhism, and Hinduism reached Malaya by sea in the early centuries of the Christian Era. Out of these early contacts arose a number of rival empires which for many centuries struggled for control of the Straits and the wealth that passed through them.

The Europeans Reach Malaya

The Portuguese, the first Europeans to reach China by the all-sea routes, seized Malacca in 1511, some four years before they reached Canton. Under Portuguese control, Malacca soon became the great entrepôt of Lisbon's commerce in the East. Here were handled the nutmegs, mace, pepper, camphor, gold, and silk which for a century made Portugal master of the Eastern trade. A little more than a century later, in 1641, Malacca was captured by the Dutch, who were already strongly entrenched at Batavia. Malacca remained in Dutch hands until the period of the French Revolution when, the Dutch and French Republics having formed an alliance, Malacca was seized and held by the British until 1818, and then returned to Holland, only to be finally ceded to Britain in 1824. By the beginning of the twentieth century, therefore, Malacca had been continuously a European possession for four centuries.

Meanwhile, the British had acquired the island of Penang in 1786, and a strip of land on the opposite mainland, known as Province Wellesley, in 1800. In 1819 Thomas Stamford Raffles made the first agreements with the Sultan of Johore whereby land was granted for

5 Sir Richard Winstedt, *Britain and Malaya, 1786-1941* (London, 1944), 6.

factories on the Island of Singapore in return for a small annual allowance. In 1824 Singapore was ceded to Britain in perpetuity. Thus, by that year the English East India Company held in Malaya in the name of Britain the island of Penang and Province Wellesley, Malacca, and the island of Singapore, all of which came to be known collectively as the Straits Settlements.

Status of Malaya, 1786-1867

The further history of Great Britain in Malaya from 1786, when Penang was occupied, until 1858 was a further chapter in the history

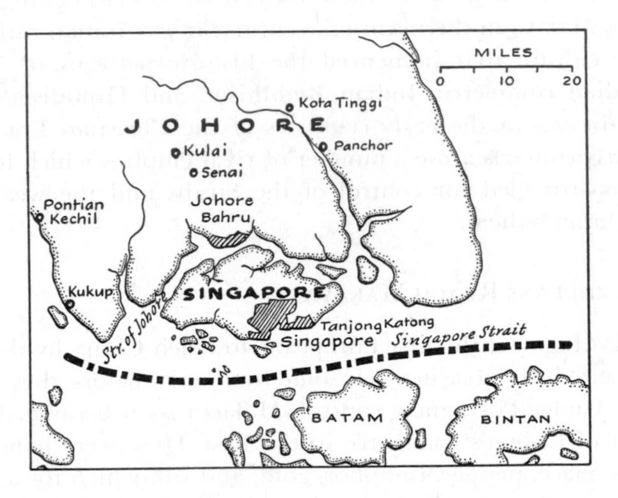

of the English East India Company. When the Company was abolished in 1858, the Straits Settlements passed for nine years under the control of the India Office without any significant change being effected in the structure of their administration. This was an interlude of stagnation. It was abruptly terminated in 1867, when the decision was made to divorce the Straits Settlements from India and give them a separate existence as a crown colony.

After 1867 the Straits Settlements, constituting a crown colony, were administered by a governor who in time was assisted by an executive council composed of the commandant of the British garrison, leading officials of the administration, and three appointed members supposedly representative of the public. Whereas final legislative authority in the crown colony remained with the British Parliament, this authority was exercised only in emergency. Customarily, local legislation was passed by a local legislative council. In the Settlements this council consisted of the governor, thirteen officials of his administration, and thirteen non-officials (British subjects), representatives of the public and appointed by the governor. These latter representatives usually included Chinese, British Indians, and Eurasian elements of the population. The governor plus the official members of the council constituted a majority and thus had the controlling voice in all legislation.

Prior to the last quarter of the nineteenth century, Britain's control in Malaya was limited, as noted, to the Straits Settlements. However, much earlier in the century, officials of the East India Company, acting in the interest of peace among the native states, had arbitrated in boundary disputes, had used force to repel invasions by Siamese forces, had offered protection to certain states in case of attack, and had sometimes determined the succession to native thrones. After 1857, and despite almost constant war among the native states of the peninsula, the British government did not encourage a policy of interference in native affairs. But in 1873 a new policy was adopted whereby the governor of the Straits Settlements placed British advisers in the native states of Perak, Selangor, and Negri Sembilan; and a few years later, in 1887, Pahang also received a British adviser. Thus was initiated the process by which the native states were to become eventually British protectorates.

The Federated Malay States

Each of the States of Perak, Selangor, Negri Sembilan, and Pahang became a British protectorate as a result of treaties signed with their respective rulers between 1874 and 1880. These treaties provided: (1) that each native ruler accept a British resident whose advice was mandatory in all matters "other than those touching Malay religion and customs"; and (2) that revenues be collected and all appointments made in the name of the respective state sultans. Each of these states had a state council combining legislative and executive functions, but there was as yet no over-all interstate control, with the result that there were in fact wide variations in law, in taxation, and in administration of land in the various states, despite the presence of a British adviser in each.

To achieve greater uniformity and more effective administration, the four states were federated in 1895 under a common civil service controlled by a resident-general. A federal durbar was also formed with advisory but no legislative powers. In 1909 a federal council was created which, with the purpose of protecting the vested inter-

ests of the tin and rubber industries, curtailed further the autonomy of the states. These various moves toward centralization soon led to abuse and eventually to criticism of the entire administration. As a result, in 1935 reforms looking to decentralization were effected.

Five states, Johore, Kedah, Perlis, Kelantan, and Trengganu, remained outside the Federation. Although the international status (protectorates) of these states was fixed by treaties similar to those between Britain and the federated states, the administrative tie was not so close.

The Problem of Twentieth-Century Malaya

Thus, British Malaya entered the twentieth century as ten separate governments under three different varieties of administration. The practical difference between the Straits Settlements, a crown colony of the traditional type, and the protected states was not very great, for in both areas the actual administration adhered closely to the crown colony pattern. This complexity of governmental organization arose as an evolutionary process, in most respects a result of a growing mixture of races. The advent of British control in Malaya had been followed by a large immigration of Chinese and Indians until, in 1937, the number of Chinese almost equalled the Malay population. The process was one in which rubber and tin (developed by Western capitalists, Chinese traders, and laborers) suddenly transformed medieval Malaya into modern Malaya. In this process the Malays, one of the least politically minded of peoples, were destined to be submerged unless their political and economic interests received special protection. Thus the fundamental problem of government in Malaya was how "to discharge this obligation," and at the same time give legitimate weight to the interests created by Chinese and Indian immigrants and British owners of tin mines and rubber plantations.

Unlike many other areas of Southeast Asia, British Malaya prior to 1941 was untouched by native demands for democratic government or by any assertive movements of nationalism. This circumstance was due to the fact that the Malay States were not the unwilling victims of European conquest but rather "sought the protection of European powers against the encroachments of foreign Asiatics." As a result there was in general an absence of resentment toward the British overlord.

Siam or Thailand

Siam in modern times has been a political curiosity in Southeast Asia—a small independent state wedged between and hedged about by the possessions of Europe and the United States. On the west and northwest, Siam bordered on Burma; on the east and northeast, on Indochina; on the south, it was open to the Gulf of Siam, beyond which was Britain's Malay Peninsula, the South China Seas, the Indies, and the Philippines. This legal, and in some respects actual, independence, however, was not a result of the military prowess of Siam or the wisdom of its rulers, but rather of agreement between European rivals—England in Burma and Malaya, and France in Indochina—to preserve this small kingdom as a buffer state.

Siam, with an area of some 200,000 square miles, slightly smaller than Texas, had a natural border of mountains on the west, north, and northwest. In general, the country has three geographical areas. The southwestern delta and plain in the vicinity of Bangkok, the capital, is the region of rice culture; the north is mountainous with steep valleys running north and south; the remainder of the country, chiefly the northeast, is an area of rolling hills. Siam is a land of the monsoon, featured by two rather distinct seasons: the rainy season of the southwest monsoon, May through October; and the dry season of winter, November through February, followed by the early spring heat.

Siam's population in 1950 was 18 million, some 3 million of whom were Chinese whose loyalties have usually been to China. There were also other foreign groups including: 700,000 Moslem Malays, 50,000 Vietnamese, and 50,000 Indians. Most of the people are rice farmers; the Chinese are merchants. Life in Siam has depended almost exclusively on rice culture. Some 95 per cent of the crop land produces rice and, prior to 1940, about one-third of the crop was exported. In the earlier years of the century this export trade went primarily to Europe. After World War I it was diverted to China and India.

Although Thailand had been peopled in the long course by successive immigrant waves of Mongol extraction from the north, the principal stock was the Thai, who spoke a language of the same name. The Thai were among the more recent comers and probably entered the peninsula from Yunnan.

Just as in the seventeenth century it was Siam's almost incessant military involvement with her neighbors that prompted her to seek aid from Europeans, so it was in the early nineteenth century when she again began to exchange native products for firearms secured at first from the Portuguese. Her first major commercial treaties were made with Great Britain in 1822 and 1826, and with the United States in 1833. This last was the first treaty concluded by the United States with a nation of the Far East. In 1855-1856, Britain, France, and the United States concluded further treaties with Siam containing rights of extraterritoriality and a conventional tariff. On this occasion Townsend Harris was the American envoy.

During most of the nineteenth century, despite these commercial accords, the fate of Siam as a nation hung in the uneasy balance of Anglo-French rivalry in Southeast Asia. Britain's successive annexations in Burma made her a territorial neighbor of Siam on the west and north; the advent of France in Cochin China, Cambodia, and Annam brought her to Siam's border on the north, east, and southeast. Indeed, the French protectorate in Cambodia was achieved by breaking the control of Siam over that state. Much later in the century (1893), Siam, in a treaty with France, renounced her claims to territory east of the Mekong (Laos). This territory was ceded technically to Annam, already a French protectorate, and then organized by France as the separate protectorate of Laos. In 1896 growing friction between the European rivals on the borders of Siam was abated by an Anglo-French treaty which created British and French spheres in western and eastern Siam respectively. In 1904 France secured at Siam's expense further cessions of territory to Cambodia and Laos. After these transfers the Anglo-French rivals agreed to annex no further territory in their respective zones of influence. Nevertheless, in 1907 some 7,000 square miles were added to Cambodia, although France restored some territory previously acquired, and agreed that Siamese courts should exercise jurisdiction over French Asiatic subjects and protected persons on Siamese soil. Two years later, in 1909, Britain added territory to her protected Malay states of Trengganu, Kelantan, and Kedah. In return Siam regained jurisdiction over British subjects in her territory. Later treaties, following World War I, provided for the complete relinquishment of extraterritoriality when Siam's new and modernized codes should go into effect. As against these gains, Siam gave up her claims to some 90,000 square miles of territory on the east, and some 15,000 on the southwest.

Twentieth-century Siam has been confronted with three major political problems: (1) the movement from autocracy to some form of representative government; (2) the effort to create national unification; and (3) the task of maintaining the country's independence, so frequently threatened in the nineteenth and twentieth centuries, at first by the missionary, the mercantile, and the political interests of the Western powers, and then by the expansion of Japan.

A program of modernization in the late nineteenth century effected many changes in Siam. Slavery was abolished. Many Siamese studied abroad and returned with new technical skills and new viewpoints toward politics, thus preparing the way for the downfall of absolutism. The gradual creation of a new and more widely selected body of civil servants provided the beginning of a new political group and ultimately a revolutionary party. When in the depression years of the late 1920's the dynasty applied a policy of retrenchment, the "Promoters," as the revolutionary group called itself, including a number of army officers, took over the government in June, 1932, and imposed a constitution upon the king, who himself favored constitutionalism but who had been restrained by members of the royal house. The revolution was entirely peaceful, because both the royal and the revolutionary parties hoped to avoid giving any pretext for foreign intervention. Among the revolutionary leaders were Luang Pradit Manudharm, a civilian, and Luang Pibun Songgram, a militarist.

The new constitution, which excluded the royal family from political power, placed the new Assembly in the hands of the Promoters. The power of the latter, so long as they remained united, became as absolute as had been the king's. The new government promoted education as an ultimate test for the franchise, sought to implement a program of a national economic policy to provide remunerative work for all, and attempted to stimulate a political consciousness that would eventually express itself through political parties. Meanwhile, however, factionalism had appeared between the civilian and the military wings of the Promoters' party. For five years, 1932-1937, Phya Bahol, as Prime Minister, held the two groups in unsteady balance. When he was succeeded by Luang Pibun Songgram, Siam entered upon a program of extreme nationalism implemented by the methods of the dictator.

INDOCHINA

Indochina in the late nineteenth and early twentieth centuries included five political and administrative divisions: the French possession of Cochin China, and the French protectorates of Tonkin,

Annam, Laos, and Cambodia. The total area, 286,000 square miles, was approximately the combined area of Texas and West Virginia. The population in 1941 was some 24,000,000, including nearly 500,-000 Chinese, and 42,000 Europeans, almost all of whom were French. The concentrations of population were in the Mekong Delta

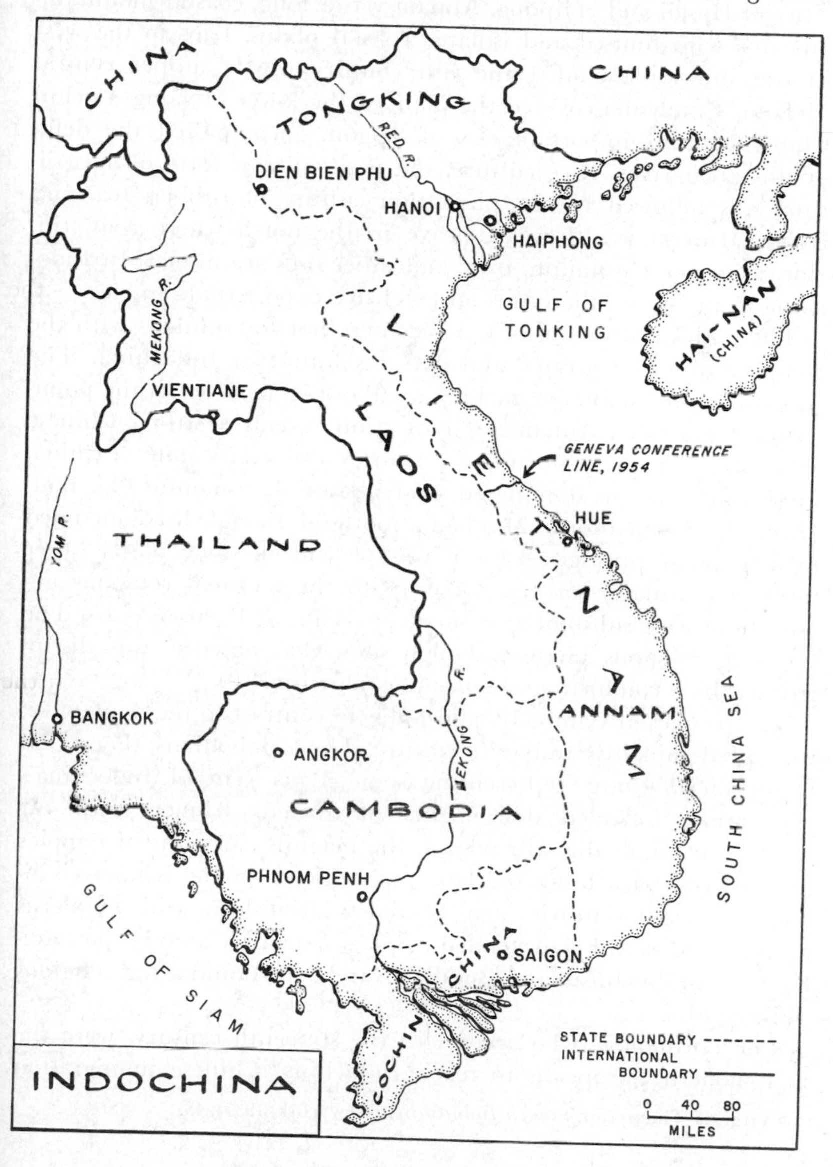

and valleys of the south and the Red River Valley in the north. The central mountainous area had scattered settlements along the seacoast and in the Mekong Valley of the interior. Each of the five states had its own peculiar geographical setting. Life in Tonkin, the northern state, centered in the valley of the Red River and in the cities of Hanoi and Haipong. Annam was a long, coastal mountainous area with limited and isolated coastal plains. Laos to the west in the interior included the hill country of the upper central Mekong. Cambodia covered the plain of the lower Mekong. Cochin China, with its important city of Saigon, encompassed the delta of this great river. Rice culture, the predominant form of agriculture, was followed by the plantation culture of rubber, tea, and coffee. Mineral wealth is extensive in the north where coal, tin, zinc, tungsten, chromium, iron, and other ores are mined. In Indochina as in Burma there was an extensive export trade in rice.

The political divisions of the area were not coterminous with the complex of racial groups and cultures found in Indochina. The Annamese predominated, making up about 70 per cent of the population. Culturally, Annamese civilization reveals a strong Chinese influence; Annam was for many centuries a tributary state of China. Confucian concepts dominated most phases of Annamite life. Buddhism in modified forms also had a foothold, though it commanded little popular prestige. Taoism was present in some of its lower forms, particularly sorcery. Mixed with these formal religious importations were substantial remnants of many indigenous cults. The resulting religious picture, though somewhat obscure, was distinguished by a comforting absence of fanaticism.[6]

The peoples of Cambodia and Laos, in contrast to the Annamese, were predominantly Indian in culture. The Cambodians, the second major racial group, representing some 6 per cent of Indochina's population, included descendants of ancient Khmer stock. At Angkor in Cambodia still remain the magnificent ruins of temples and palaces, built by forced labor, as evidence of the Khmer civilization of eight centuries ago. Feudal relationships, with emphasis on powerful ties of clan, tended to persist strongly among the Cambodians. Brahmanism and Buddhism were the dominating religious philosophies.

The Portuguese, who arrived in the sixteenth century, were the first modern Europeans to reach Indochina. Chinese immigration

6 Virginia Thompson, *French Indo-China* (New York, 1937), 43.

here as in Malaya, the Philippines, and Indonesia long antedated the arrival of Europeans, but in some respects was similar to it. The early Chinese immigrants were controlled by the seasons, which prevented merchant vessels from crossing the seas in the months of the typhoons. Hence "factories," or trading posts, were established and grew into Chinese communities. In general they were not militant, and they were unsupported by the home government. Thus in time they disappeared. The Europeans, in contrast, were armed, able to fight off pirates, able to pit local princes against each other, and thereby able to establish permanent posts. Portuguese objectives here, as in China, were trade and the establishment of Jesuit missions. French missionaries and traders appeared in the seventeenth century, but the real foundations of French political power in Indochina were laid in the years from 1747 to 1858. In the earlier years of this period, 1747-1774, France made diplomatic contact with Annam in the hope of opening trade and using the region as a base for attacks on Dutch and British commerce. In 1787 the first treaty between France and Cochin China was signed. This was the work of Pigneau de Behaine, Bishop of Adran, ecclesiastic, diplomat, and soldier of fortune, who aided the king of Cochin China against rebels in the hope of furthering French territorial expansion and the spread of Catholic missions. The early nineteenth century, however, was marked by violent anti-Christian movements and the refusal of native rulers to receive French diplomatic and naval missions. Later, Napoleon III, failing in 1855 to secure a treaty with Annam that would put an end to the executions of French and Spanish ecclesiastics, in co-operation with Spain dispatched a naval expedition, 1858, at the time of the *Arrow* War in China. Successful campaigns were conducted against Tourane and Saigon. In 1862, France wrested a treaty from Annam which guaranteed religious toleration, opened three ports to French and Spanish trade, and provided that Annam pay an indemnity of $4,000,000 and cede portions of Cochin China to France. The following year Cambodia was made a French protectorate, and soon the remaining provinces of Cochin China were annexed.

From this time until the beginning of the present century, France moved steadily forward to complete the conquest of Indochina, each move seemingly timed nicely by intervals of a decade as though there were some peculiar magic in this regularity. After the French had applied military pressure in 1874, France formally recognized the independence of Annam, and in return Annam opened the Red River in Tonkin to French trade, designated a number of ports open to French commerce, and granted extraterritoriality to Europeans. By the close of another decade, 1884, Annam was forced to become a protectorate of France. Since Annam had been, at least formally, a tributary state of China, this development precipitated Franco-Chinese hostilities, ending in Chinese defeat. In still another decade, 1893, France demanded of Siam, in the name of Annam, certain inland territories to the east of the Mekong which were organized as the new French protectorate of Laos. Again in a decade, 1904, further territory held by Siam was ceded to both Cambodia and Laos, and an additional grant to Cambodia at Siam's expense was made in 1907. Thus, by the beginning of the twentieth century, France by military force had become the master of an empire in Indochina.

Government in French Indochina

Government in French Indochina was designed to attain objectives quite different from those sought in neighboring British territories of Southeast Asia. Whereas in the latter, autonomy within the Empire became the goal during the twentieth century, with self-government being introduced by progressive stages, in the former "the intention has been that the dependency should be drawn progessively closer to France as an integral part of a closely knit empire dominated by the mother country."[7] In practice this meant that the governor-general had little local independence; that most natives did not acquire French citizenship but remained subjects; that legislative councils had little authority; and that the very limited representation of the colony (Cochin China) in the French Chamber of Deputies was chosen by and spoke for the French and not the native community.

While Cochin China was administered directly by French officials, the other four provinces of Indochina, technically protectorates, maintained their native administrations, operating under close French supervision and control. Although the native mandarins in the protectorates were not simple figureheads, the power of the French officials was hardly less than it was in the colony of Cochin China, where direct rule prevailed.

7 Mills, "The Governments of Southeast Asia," in *Government and Nationalism in Southeast Asia* (New York, 1942), 108.

Beginnings of Nationalism

It is hardly possible to generalize on the origins of nationalism in French Indochina. Divergence of race and culture, a product of the many migrations that peopled Indochina, meant that nationalism struggled in an extricable tangle of minorities of race, language, and religion.

The roots of Annamese nationalism in varying forms may be traced to the distant past when Annam was under the political as well as the cultural sway of China. In modern times, Annamese nationalism sprang from the influence of the French conquest. Although French administrators never consciously promoted nationalism, "French institutions were so impregnated with the liberal ideas of 1789 that they unconsciously fostered patriotism and a love of political liberty in subject peoples."[8] Moreover, French rule was the result of a long and bitter conquest in which native resistance was compounded of diverse elements: patriotism, brigandage, and piracy.

Unrest, political and economic in its base, was typical of Indochina in the decade prior to World War I. Stimulation came from Japan's victory in the Russo-Japanese War, but more particularly from a new interest among Annamese intellectuals in the eighteenth-century French political philosophy of Rousseau and Montesquieu. Many native intellectuals, however, were disillusioned in 1908, when, as the result of a conservative reaction among the French in Indochina, Hanoi University was closed. This reactionary trend in French policy was further emphasized a few years later when France used forced Indochinese labor in Europe during World War I. During and after that war, the more rapid economic development of Indochina created additional cause of native resentment.

As in other parts of Southeast Asia, the Chinese in French Indochina were a focal point of native attack. An outstanding case was the anti-Chinese boycott of 1919. The Chinese in Indochina had shown little interest in politics, but they controlled the native rice and fish trade and the sources of native credit. In general the Annamite attitude toward the Chinese was one of admiration of Chinese control of native commercial economy. At the same time Annamite nationalists were as much opposed to Chinese economic as to French political control. An additional factor closely linked with the na-

[8] Virginia Thompson, "Nationalism and Nationalistic Movements in Southeast Asia," in *Government and Nationalism in Southeast Asia,* 198; and the same author's larger study, *French Indo-China,* 475-494.

tionalist agitations of the 1920's was the rapid development of the communist movement.

Prior to World War II, however, the native nationalist movement itself was not basically constructive. In the first place, it possessed distinct racial limitations, since it was confined to the Annamese, who continued to regard Cambodians and Laotians as fit only to be subject peoples. Moreover, Annamese nationalists were divided among themselves by mutual jealousies and by the lack of a constructive national program, and they were unsupported by any vital public spirit. Moreover, French policy in the pre-war years was rigid and cruel in its suppression of nationalist and communist groups.

The philosophy behind French rule in Indochina from the middle nineteenth century until World War II was to have tremendous repercussions on the history of this area in the post-war years. From its beginnings in the nineteenth century, French imperialism in the Far East was motivated primarily by national pride. In general the considerations behind French policy were political rather than economic—the determination not to be outdone by the British. Toward the close of the nineteenth century the policy was fully matured and expressed itself in a persistent urge to enhance French national prestige and cultural superiority. The reality and substantial character of French motives was attested by the scholarly achievements of the École Francaise d'Extreme Orient, which opened at Hanoi in 1898. French imperialists could conceive of no higher goal than the making of brown-skinned Frenchmen out of Annamese in an ever more perfect union with France. Of all Westerners in Southeast Asia the French were outstanding for their lack of racial prejudice and for their willingness to treat Asiatics as equals when in fact they were equals in education, refinement, or attainment. There was indeed no antagonism to Indochinese nationalists of French education so long as they abstained from political propaganda among the peasantry. What led to persecution was that the Indochinese nationalists, French in almost everything but appearance, learned principally from China that their own political futility would end the moment they became leaders of mass movements. Thus France in southeast Asia was trapped by her own logic. She could not admit the possibility of political or cultural equality with herself. Prior to 1941 France had succeeded in indoctrinating native intellectuals with French culture, but by her failure to embody the concepts of this culture in native political institutions, she had failed to win native loyalty.[9]

For Further Reading

GENERAL

Adloff, Richard, and Virginia Thompson, *Cultural Institutions and Educational Policy in South East Asia* (New York, 1948).

Callis, Helmut G., *Foreign Capital in Southeast Asia* (New York, 1942).

Dobby, E. H. G., *Southeast Asia* (New York, 1951).

Furnivall, J. S., *Educational Progress in Southeast Asia* (New York, 1943). A valuable comparative summary of pre-World War II educational policies.

———, *Progress and Welfare in Southeast Asia* (New York, 1941).

Hall, D. G. E., *A History of South-East Asia* (New York, 1955).

Lasker, Bruno, *Peoples of Southeast Asia* (New York, 1944).

LeMay, Reginald, *The Culture of South-East Asia* (London, 1954). Studies India's contributions to the culture of Siam and, to a lesser extent, other nations in Southeast Asia.

Pelzer, Karl, *Pioneer Settlement in the Asiatic Tropics* (New York, 1945).

Purcell, Victor, *The Colonial Period in Southeast Asia: An Historical Sketch* (New York, 1953).

Thompson, Virginia, *Labor Problems in Southeast Asia* (New Haven, 1947).

BURMA

Andrus, J. Russell, *Burmese Economic Life* (Stanford, 1947).

Donnison, F. S. V., *Public Administration in Burma: A Study of Development During the British Connexion* (London, 1953).

Furnivall, J. S., *Colonial Policy and Practice: A Comparative Study of Burma and Netherlands India* (Cambridge, 1948).

Harvey, G. E., *British Rule in Burma, 1824-1942* (London, 1946).

INDOCHINA

Ennis, Thomas E., *French Policy and Developments in Indo-China* (Chicago, 1936). Treats at some length of economic and social problems.

Janse, Olov R. T., *The Peoples of French Indo-China* (Washington, 1944).

Levy, Roger, Guy Lacam, and Andrew Roth, *French Interests and Policies in the Far East* (New York, 1941).

[9] The definitive study is John F. Cady, *The Roots of French Imperialism in Eastern Asia* (Ithaca, 1954), 294-296.

INDONESIA

De Klerck, Eduard Servaas, *History of the Netherlands East Indies* (2 vols., Rotterdam, 1938).

Emerson, Rupert, *Malaysia: A Study in Direct and Indirect Rule* (New York, 1937). A comprehensive and scholarly study of Dutch colonial administration.

Furnivall, J. S., *Netherlands India: A Study of Plural Economy* (New York, 1944). A fine and exhaustive study.

Kennedy, Raymond, *The Ageless Indies* (New York, 1942). A basic introduction to the history of the area.

MALAYA

Broek, Jan O. M., *Economic Development of the Netherlands Indies* (New York, 1942). A short survey of the Dutch East Indies economy at the start of World War II.

Clodd, H. P., *Malay's First British Pioneer: the Life of Francis Light* (London, 1948). A biography of one of Britain's foremost colonial administrators in Malaya.

Coupland, Sir Reginald, *Raffles, 1781-1826* (Oxford, 1926). The best general sketch of the founder of Singapore.

Dobby, E. H. G., *Malaya and the Malayans* (London, 1947).

Kaberry, Phyllis, *British Colonial Policy in Southeast Asia and the Development of Self-Government in Malaya* (London, 1944).

Mills, Lennox A., *British Malaya, 1824-1867* (Oxford, 1926). A sound, critical study.

———, *British Rule in Eastern Asia* (London, 1942). The most comprehensive and scholarly survey of economic, political, and social conditions yet made of Hongkong, the Straits Settlements, and the Malay States.

Purcell, Victor, *Malaya: Outline of a Colony* (London, 1946). A defense of British colonial policy.

Winstedt, Sir Richard, *A History of Malaya* (London, 1935).

———, *The Malays: A Cultural History* (rev. ed., London, 1950). An introduction to Malay society and culture.

THAILAND

Ingram, James C., *Economic Change in Thailand Since 1850* (Stanford, 1955). Emphasizes changes brought about by world trade since the Bowring treaty first opened the country.

Landon, Kenneth P., *The Chinese in Thailand* (London, 1941).

———, *Siam in Transition: A Brief Survey of Cultural Trends in the Five Years Since the Revolution of 1932* (Shanghai, 1939).

Landon, Margaret, *Anna and the King of Siam* (New York, 1944). A delightful story based on Anna H. Leonowens' books picturing Siam in the 1860's.

Smith, Malcolm, *A Physician at the Court of Siam* (London, 1947). By a court physician giving observations on Siamese society and court life.

Thompson, Virginia, *Thailand: The New Siam* (New York, 1941). A convenient general survey.

35

1941–1945

The Far East in World War II

EVEN as the democracies had been on the defensive ideologically and diplomatically since 1937 and earlier, so for many uncertain months after Pearl Harbor they were to remain militarily on the defensive. The Axis Powers fought with many advantages. They had planned and prepared for war. Their armies were mobilized, and many of their troops had already been tested in battle. Finally, they possessed interior lines of supply contrasting with the far-flung ocean routes on which the anti-Axis group depended. The weakness of the Axis lay in its two territorial spheres, the German-Italian in Europe and the Japanese in the Far East; but this disadvantage was for the time being more than overcome by the momentum of the Axis attack. Since the democracies were on the defensive, the Anglo-American chiefs of staff determined early in 1942 to concentrate first to defeat Hitler while simply holding Japan. Time was to prove the wisdom of this decision, though at the moment it was an anathema to the Chinese and others threatened by Japanese invasion.

BEGINNINGS OF THE UNITED NATIONS

Within a month of Pearl Harbor the anti-Axis nations sought to give political as well as military purpose and cohesion to their belated preparations for war. On January 1, 1942, in response to an American proposal, twenty-six governments at war with the Axis pledged their united action in prosecuting the conflict, agreeing to conclude no separate peace. By this means the principles of the Atlantic Charter became a basic manifesto of these United Nations and the preliminary blueprint for war and eventual peace in Asia as well as in Europe. The immediate problem, however, was to hold the Axis offensive within limits until the productive power of America as the "arsenal of democracy" should enable the United States to assume the offensive first in Europe and then in the Pacific and Asia. To this end Anglo-American unity of military action was assured through a joint strategic command exercised by the Combined Chiefs of Staff dating from February 6, 1942. Liaison with Russia and China was maintained through military missions in Moscow and Chungking.

JAPAN'S OFFENSIVE, 1941-1942

Japan's attack immediately following Pearl Harbor spread like a great fan southward and westward to encompass southeastern Asia and the island empires that lay off its shores—the East Indies and the Philippines. Co-ordinated attacks were launched not only from the Caroline Islands and Formosa but also from naval bases and airfields which the Vichy French had permitted Japan to acquire in French Indochina, and from bases in Thailand acquired after December 8. Japan moved swiftly to the conquest of the peoples and the great natural wealth of Southeast Asia, her immediate objectives being Midway, Wake, and Guam, Hongkong, the Philippines, Thailand, and Malaya.

The attack on Hongkong came at almost the identical hour of the attack on Pearl Harbor. The island fortress and one of the great commercial ports of the world surrendered to the Japanese on December 25, 1941. It had been a British possession for a century.[1]

Far more sensational than the fall of Hongkong, which had been anticipated, was Japan's conquest of the Malay peninsula and Singapore. Japanese troops trained for tropical and jungle warfare entered Malaya in the north from Thailand and Indochina and moved south in three lines to converge just north of Singapore. Already on December 10, British naval power had been crippled when Japanese planes sank the *Prince of Wales* and the *Repulse*. This made Singa-

1 For the techniques of the Japanese occupation, military, political, and economic, see Robert S. Ward, *Asia for the Asiatics* (Chicago, 1945).

pore a naval base without a navy. On the peninsula, retreating British ground forces fought bravely but hopelessly. On February 15, 1942, the city which Stamford Raffles had founded in 1819 surrendered. Japan's road to Burma and India was open. Simultaneously with the campaign in Malaya, Japan had invaded Burma, occupied lower Burma, taken Rangoon, cut the Burma Road, and by June, 1942, was in possession of the entire country. Save for the air route, "the Hump," over the Himalayas, no communications line remained between the Anglo-American front and China.

The Conquest of the Philippines

Japan's first attack on the Philippines came within a few hours of the assault on Pearl Harbor. Here as in Malaya, despite the bravery of Americans and Filipinos, it was a story of "too little and too late." There were less than 20,000 American troops in the Islands under General Douglas MacArthur. Manila was occupied January 2 as American and Filipino forces (covered by the guns of Corregidor) retired to the Bataan peninsula. There a heroic defense was maintained by Lt. General Jonathan M. Wainwright until the inevitable surrender, April 9. Bataan was a costly sacrifice to unpreparedness. Meanwhile General MacArthur had been ordered to Australia, which became the base for the later counter-offensive. Corregidor, reinforced by remnants that crossed the channel from Bataan, held out for some weeks, but was finally taken on May 6. Japan's conquest of the remaining islands was soon completed.

With speed unabated, Japan moved on to the conquest of the rich Netherlands Indies. Allied naval forces and aircraft again fought delaying actions. Simultaneously the Japanese moved south and east of the Philippines with the ultimate objective of invading Australia. Only after the invaders had occupied the Bismarck and Solomon Islands and parts of New Guinea was their progress checked. Meanwhile the American Navy had executed tactical thrusts at Japanese outposts in the Marshall and Gilbert Islands, culminating in the famous air raid on Tokyo, April 18, 1942, by bombers commanded by Colonel James H. Doolittle. Later on May 7 and 8, in a naval air battle over the Coral Sea, American naval planes broke up a Japanese attempt to cut the Australian supply lines across the southwestern Pacific to Honolulu and the American Pacific Coast.

THE BATTLE OF MIDWAY AND AFTER

The first major Japanese reverse of the war was the naval air battle of Midway, June 3-6, 1942, which inflicted heavy losses on the enemy fleet and prevented the occupation of Midway and possibly of the Hawaiian Islands. After Midway, save for their invasion of

MANILA BAY

the Aleutians, the Japanese were no longer a menace in the central or eastern Pacific. This impotence in turn added greater security to the 8,000-mile supply line from the United States to the new military bases in Australia. However, these bases remained under constant threat from the Japanese in the Solomons and New Guinea. To meet this danger American forces struck first at the Solomons. The largest of the Solomons, Guadalcanal, was won after fierce air, naval, and ground campaigns lasting from August 7, 1942, to February, 1943. At the same time, Australian and American troops turned back the Japanese in Papua (southeastern New Guinea), thus halting the Japanese advance in the Southwest Pacific. Far to the west, British, American, and Chinese forces were striving to hold and strengthen bases in India and China, the area which came to be known as the CBI (China-Burma-India) Theater. After Japan's conquest of Burma, all supplies reaching China went by air over the Hump. After great effort extending over many months, the battle of supply was won. By January, 1944, air-borne supplies to China exceeded peak capacities carried over the Burma Road, and American air forces were operating from fields in India and in China. At the far eastern extremity, too, of the Asiatic and Pacific battlefront in the Aleutian Islands American forces took the offensive in May, 1943, and by August had retaken the entire archipelago. Later, these islands provided bases for bombing raids on northern Japan.

The year 1943 marked the end of Japan's march to conquest and the beginnings of her ultimate defeat. In the Pacific and in Asia, as in Europe, this defeat could not come until the United Nations had achieved a realistic unity in over-all policy and strategy, had won the battle of production, and had brought this newly created power to bear on far-flung battlefronts on the land, the sea, and in the air. In the battle against Japan, the contributions of China, Australia, and New Zealand are not to be minimized; yet for reasons that are clear, the major responsibility fell to the United States. Until May, 1942, these Pacific allies waged a desperate defensive struggle. The victory at Midway in the summer of 1942 restored something of a balance in naval power. The campaigns of the succeeding year until August, 1943, halted Japan in the Southwest Pacific. The line of battle was thus being stabilized against the day of counter-offensive.

The Diplomatic Background of Victory

From the beginning of the war in Europe and the Far East, it had been the ill-concealed boast of the totalitarian powers that their opponents were incapable of uniting in resistance. Nevertheless, in a series of momentous conferences the principal powers of the United Nations did achieve a common policy aimed at winning a speedy military victory and providing the bases of a durable peace.

At Quebec, Canada, August 11-24, 1943, Roosevelt, Churchill, and T. V. Soong approved policies designed: (1) to strike at Japan through greater aid to China, (2) to achieve closer collaboration with Russia, and (3) to speed the invasion of Italy. The Moscow Conference of Foreign Ministers was a logical sequel. There, October 19-30, 1943, Britain, the Soviet Union, and the United States proclaimed the principles of the coming peace. Fascism was to be destroyed and war criminals brought to justice. China also joined in declarations demanding "unconditional surrender" by the Axis and promising a post-war international organization based on the sovereign equality of states to maintain peace and security.

Since Russia was not at war with Japan, the Moscow Conference of Foreign Ministers had not dealt specifically with war plans in the Far East. Such plans were the subject of the meeting of Roosevelt, Churchill, and Chiang K'ai-shek at Cairo, November 22-26, 1943. The war was to be prosecuted until Japan accepted "unconditional surrender." Japan was to be deprived of all the lands which she had seized since 1894. Korea was "in due course" to be free and independent. Following immediately on Cairo came the first meeting of Stalin with Roosevelt and Churchill at Teheran, November 26-December 2, which gave final shape to plans for destruction of Hitler's Germany, and produced Russia's first promise to enter the war against Japan.

Meanwhile, at Dumbarton Oaks in Washington, D. C., representatives of the United States, Great Britain, Russia, and China drafted preliminary proposals for an international organization to replace the League of Nations. It was later to materialize as the United Nations Organization. Subsequently, at Yalta in the Crimea, February, 1945, Roosevelt, Churchill, and Stalin again met and, among other things, announced a coming international conference at San Francisco to create a charter for the permanent organization of the United Nations.

Military Offensive of the United Nations, 1943-1944

Even before the achievement of a complete diplomatic and military coalition, the United Nations were winning their first campaigns. In the Pacific, these included, as already noted, the Battle of Midway and the campaigns at Guadalcanal and in the Aleutians.

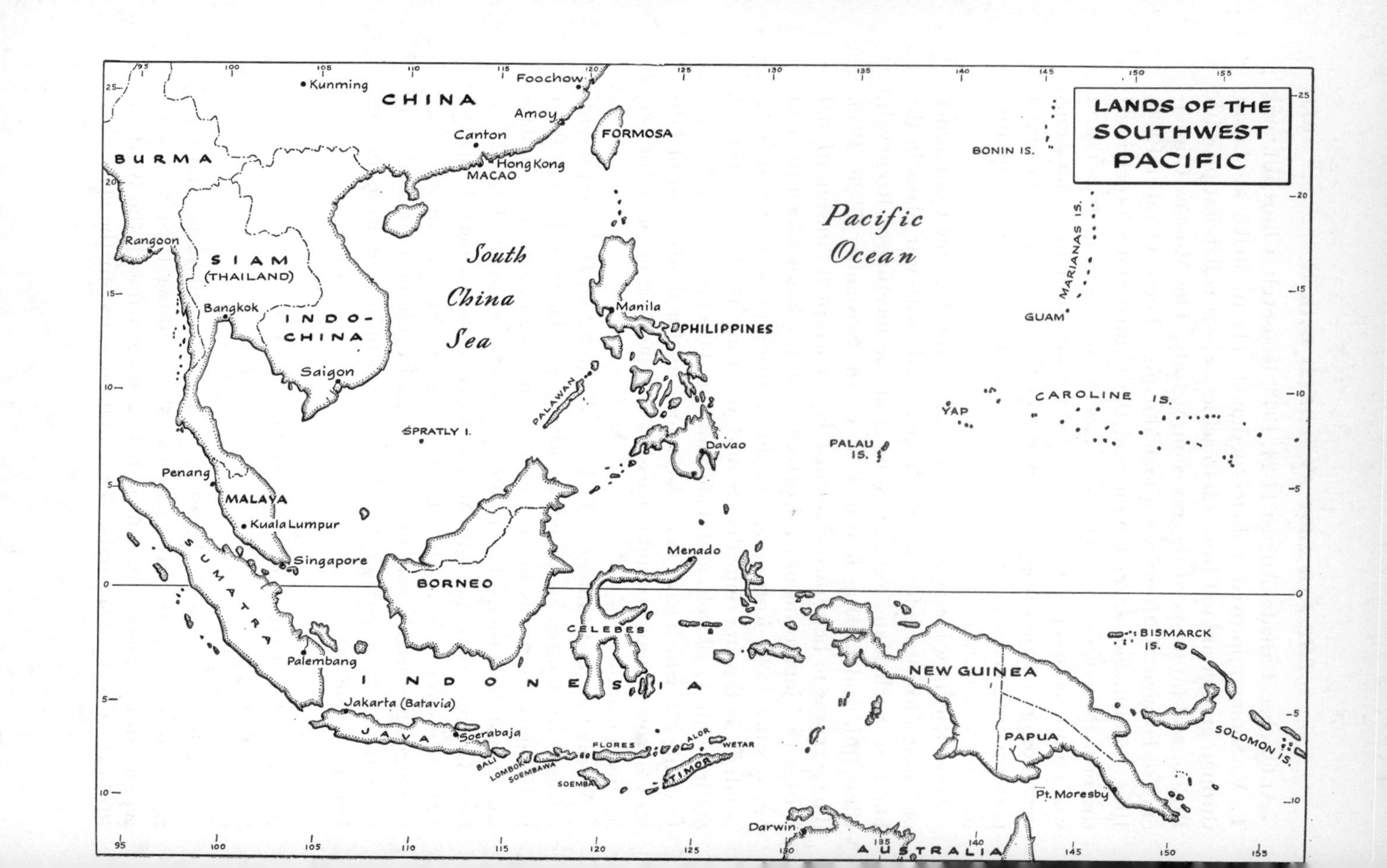

LANDS OF THE SOUTHWEST PACIFIC
CHINA
Kunming
Foochow
Amoy
Canton
Hong Kong
MACAO
FORMOSA
BURMA
Rangoon
SIAM (THAILAND)
Bangkok
INDO-CHINA
Saigon
South China Sea
Pacific Ocean
BONIN IS.
MARIANAS IS.
GUAM
Manila
PHILIPPINES
PALAWAN
SPRATLY I.
Davao
CAROLINE IS.
YAP
PALAU IS.
Penang
MALAYA
Kuala Lumpur
Singapore
SUMATRA
BORNEO
Menado
CELEBES
Palembang
INDONESIA
Jakarta (Batavia)
JAVA
Soerabaja
BALI
LOMBOK
SOEMBAWA
SOEMBA
FLORES
ALOR
WETAR
TIMOR
NEW GUINEA
PAPUA
Pt. Moresby
BISMARCK IS.
SOLOMON IS.
Darwin
AUSTRALIA

Simultaneously, British and American forces broke the German and Italian armies in North Africa (May, 1943). Soviet armies had stopped the German advance at Stalingrad (September-November, 1942), and in 1943 were engaged in the first great Soviet counter-offensive. In September, 1943, came the unconditional surrender of Italy. By the spring of 1944 the Germans had been driven from all of southern Russia.

In the summer of 1943, American forces, military and naval, were prepared to advance from the toe-holds at Guadalcanal and in New Guinea. Through some of the cruelest campaigns of the war, fought in New Georgia, Bougainville, and New Guinea, American and Australian armies neutralized Rabaul, Japan's principal military and naval base in the Southwest Pacific. The American Navy took Makin and Tarawa Islands in the Gilberts (November, 1943), and Kwajalein in the Marshalls (February, 1944). Far to the west its bombers struck the Japanese bases on Truk in the Carolines and Saipan in the Marianas in a drive destined to cut Japan's communications with her empire in Southeast Asia.

For the first two years of the war, the Japanese were in almost undisputed control of the China-Burma-India front. The impenetrable jungle, devastating heat and disease, lack of transportation, paucity of supplies and troops, all conspired to delay the day of counter-offensive. In the winter and spring of 1943-1944, air-borne invasions of the northern Burma jungle were launched by Wingate's British Raiders and Merrill's American Marauders. Bitter campaigns were fought by the British on the Manipur-Imphal front, but most successful for the United Nations was the work of American and Chinese forces in northern Burma (1944) covering construction of the Ledo Road, the new supply route from India to China.

American occupation of the Gilbert and Marshall Islands was the prelude to a great naval offensive that developed in the summer of 1944. Striking westward toward the China coast, American forces moved to the conquest of the major islands of the Mariana group (Saipan, July 9, and Tinian, July 23) and to the reconquest of Guam, August 3. All were taken after bitter fighting and great loss of life, both American and Japanese. Also in the spring and early summer, American and Australian land and air forces, with naval support, had broken Japan's New Guinea armies into isolated and powerless groups, thus opening the way for the invasion and reconquest of the Philippines.

Other pressures, too, were reducing Japan's power to resist. By the summer of 1944, American submarines had sunk a total of nearly 700 Japanese vessels. These losses contributed to the eventual collapse of Japanese war production at home. To this latter task the United States brought the world's mightiest airplane, the B-29 bomber, which flew from secret airfields deep in independent China. The first raid by these flying superfortresses against southern Japan was made on June 15, 1944. Later raids struck at the eastern part of North China and Manchuria. Subsequently, Saipan became the principal base for superfortress raids.

The Reconquest of the Philippines

As a prelude to the reconquest of the Philippines, American forces had battled their way into Palau of the western Carolines and the Halmahera group off northern New Guinea in September, 1944. After air operations had neutralized Japan's air force in the Philippines, American forces invaded Leyte, October 21. A series of fierce naval battles which followed ended Japan's naval efforts to prevent a full-scale invasion. Long and costly military campaigns followed in Leyte and Mindoro, leading finally to the invasion of Luzon and the siege of Manila, February 8-24, 1945. Not until July had American and Filipino forces destroyed the last effective Japanese resistance in northern Luzon. In the liberation of the Philippines, some twenty-three Japanese divisions were annihilated. By July, also, Australian and Dutch forces had completed the reconquest of the rich oil lands of Borneo.

As the reconquest of the Philippines became merely a matter of time, American land, sea, and air forces pressed the attack closer to Japan itself. On March 16, 1945, the capture of desolate Iwo Jima, the most costly operation in the history of the United States Marine Corps, removed at least one danger from the path of the increasing raids of B-29 bombers based on Saipan. Almost simultaneously the Americans landed on Okinawa in the Liu-ch'iu (Ryukyus). Possession of Okinawa enabled the American air forces to bring the weight of their full striking power to bear on Japan's home islands.

The Sea and Air Assault on Japan

As the weight of American military and naval power moved closer to Japan Proper in 1945, the devastating effect of the B-29 superfortress raids over Tokyo was brought home to the Japanese populace. The new bases on Iwo Jima and Okinawa made it possible, by the summer of 1945, to co-ordinate the attack of "land-based medium and heavy bombers with B-29's, and with carrier and land-based fighters." As the great air assault developed, Japan's defenders were struck not only in Japan itself but also on the farther edges of her conquered and now crumbling empire—in Bangkok, Formosa, Saigon, Singapore, Rangoon, Penang, and Kuala Lumpur. In the early months of 1945 the attacks on Japan itself were concentrated on industrial centers: Tokyo, Nagoya, Osaka, Kobe, and others; and on the destruction of Japanese airfields, principally in Kyushu. Although American losses in all these attacks were heavy, they could not be compared with the frightful destruction wrought in Japan. By June 1, 1945, more than fifty square miles of Tokyo had been reduced to rubble and ashes. In July, 1945, British carrier planes joined the attack. By the same month, more than 2,000 American planes were sometimes over Japan in a single day. The land-based attacks were supported by naval carrier-plane attacks and by naval bombardment of Japan's coastal cities. The combined Anglo-American Third Fleet in the final two and one-half months of the war destroyed or damaged nearly 3,000 Japanese planes and sank or damaged some 1,600 enemy naval and merchant vessels, thus completing the destruction by August 1, 1945, of Japan's power on the sea and in the air.

Thus by the summer of 1945, Japan's military position was hopeless. In Europe, Germany had already collapsed (May 7-8, 1945). It was now possible to warn the Japanese people that particular cities would be destroyed. The resulting raids carrying out these threats made it increasingly clear to the Japanese populace that their own defenders were powerless. Yet as late as June 9, Premier Suzuki Kantaro, who had succeeded General Koiso Kuniaki in April, 1945, replying to President Truman's warning that Japan would be destroyed unless she surrendered, declared that Japan would fight on. Then, on July 26, during the Potsdam Conference, the United States, Britain, and China delivered a final ultimatum to Japan demanding immediate unconditional surrender.[2] Japan replied (July 30) that she would ignore the demands of the Potsdam Declaration.

---

[2] Text in *Occupation of Japan* (Washington, D.C., 1946), 53-55.

The Atomic Bomb

While the ultranationalist Japanese fanatics declared they would fight on, other events conspired to end hostilities without an invasion. On August 6 the Japanese city of Hiroshima and its army base were destroyed in the space of minutes by the first atomic bomb used in warfare. Nearly a month earlier (July 13), the Japanese government had asked Russia to intervene with Britain and the United States to bring about peace. Russia's reply, not delivered until August 8, announced immediate severance of her diplomatic relations with Japan and that "from August 9 the Soviet Government will consider itself to be at war with Japan." Within hours of Russia's severance of relations, a second atomic bomb destroyed the city of Nagasaki and its naval base (August 9). On the same day Russian armies invaded Manchuria, seized the Korean ports of Rashin and Yuki (August 12) and advanced in the southern or Japanese half of Sakhalin Island. On August 10, the Japanese government announced its willingness to accept the Potsdam terms (to which Russia had now subscribed), provided they comprised no "demand which prejudices the prerogatives of His Majesty [the Emperor] as a sovereign ruler." The reply of the United States (August 11) stated that "the authority of the Emperor and the Japanese Government to rule the State shall be subject to the Supreme Commander of the Allied Powers." Japan accepted these terms August 14, and the surrender was effected on board the U. S. battleship *Missouri* in Tokyo Bay, September 2, 1945.

The Japanese decision to surrender was not produced by the atomic bomb or the Soviet Union's declaration of war. These factors, however, intensified an existing crisis, and gave to the Japanese Emperor an extraordinary role in a decision that had long been in the making. It was a case in which the personal opinion of the Emperor became an imperial decision and therefore the will of the state. The crisis of July and August gave to the men who had long known that Japan must surrender the chance to stop the fanatics and to allow the historic influence of the Throne to end the carnage.[3]

Japan During the War

The people of Japan were faced in the years 1941-1945 with two of the great crises of their history. In the first, they were called upon

[3] Robert J. C. Butow, *Japan's Decision to Surrender* (Stanford, 1954), 228-233.

to wage total war for the achievement of Japan's divine mission: establishment of the "New National Structure" at home and the "New Order in Greater East Asia" abroad. The latter of these objectives has already been discussed in previous pages. It will remain here to note some of the final steps taken in the years after 1937 to complete the "New National Structure." In the second crisis, a proud and sensitive people, having met complete military defeat in 1945, was called upon to face a future compounded of social confusion in its homeland and of uncertainty in its relations with the outside world of conquerors.

The political philosophy and the structure of government which had developed in Japan by 1941 and which were to persist throughout the war were in many respects logical developments of earlier steps taken after 1931 toward totalitarian control. Yet neither before 1941 nor after that date did Japan become a corporate state in the manner of Germany or Italy. She produced no all-powerful Nazi or Fascist party, and no single political leader capable of emerging as a dictator. Likewise, in matters of economics and production, she failed to create the full corporate state in the manner of her European allies. What happened in Japan both before and during the war was, of course, influenced by these European pace-setters; but Japanese conditions, problems, and the methods of dealing with them remained essentially Japanese.

When by her attack on Pearl Harbor Japan engulfed the Pacific area in World War II, she was operating under a governmental structure that had been altered vastly since the invasion of Manchuria a decade earlier in September, 1931. The movement toward parliamentary government, from which so much had been expected in the decade 1920 to 1930, had been extinguished. The Imperial Diet had declined in political importance, though its entire influence had not been destroyed. The traditional political parties, the *Seiyukai* and the *Minseito,* had abolished themselves under the pressure of extremists in 1940, and the country had returned to non-party ministries. The armed services had secured increasing control over the civil administration but had been unable to gain a monopoly of political power. There was, however, an increasing concentration of political power in the cabinet and especially in the office of the prime minister. The functions of government had been increased greatly, in part by cabinet-inspired legislation in the Diet and by a much greater use of Imperial ordinances, ministerial orders, and departmental regulations. When she attacked Pearl Harbor, Japan seemed to be not far from the goal of the corporate state. While this was in part true, the corporate state that was appearing was peculiarly Japanese in character. It was not simply an imitation of a European counterpart. The most important results of the governmental changes from 1931 to 1941 were to increase the number and the power of bureaucratic agencies, to enhance the prestige and the political influence of the bureaucracy as a whole, and thus to create in wartime Japan what may best be called "a dictatorship of the bureaucracy."[4]

Peculiarities of the Japanese Bureaucracy

The growth of bureaucratic agencies and of bureaucratic power in Japan after 1931 was not unique. There were similar tendencies in the Western world and particularly in the United States under the New Deal. Nevertheless, bureaucracy in Japan possessed indigenous qualities that did give it a degree of uniqueness. Throughout the history of modern Japan bureaucracy had a greater political force, a broader and more complex mechanism, than in other countries. During the entire constitutional period the ministers of state (the cabinet) were linked more intimately with bureaucratic elements than with the Diet. In addition some factions of the bureaucracy, the army and the navy, enjoyed a position of political independence and power guaranteed by constitutional organization. Again, Japan's bureaucrats enjoyed a unique political strength because of the influence they had wielded in the formulation as well as in the execution of policies. Ministers of state in Japan's bureaucratic cabinets long recognized that government's fortunes depended less on the adoption of important national policies than on giving appropriate political recognition to each major bureaucratic group and maintaining a balance among these groups. Membership in the bureaucracy was equivalent to membership in a privileged class. The Japanese bureaucracy, however, was not a unit but a collection of rival factions. As the bureaucratic agencies of government increased in size and number after 1931 and as the political parties lost influence and

[4] Charles Nelson Spinks, "Bureaucratic Japan," *Far Eastern Survey,* X (1941), 219-225. The term "bureaucracy" as applied to government in Japan is used in a much broader sense than is common in Western usage. It includes not only the civil servants but also the agents of the military services, and at times of the political parties and the *Zaibatsu.*

finally disappeared, it became the function of the prime minister to act as a mediating officer between these factions of permanent office-holders. As a result, no individual was able to dominate the entire bureaucracy sufficiently to create a unified political machine or to create a one-man dictatorship. Even had a supremely capable leader appeared, his path to one-man dictatorship would have been obstructed, perhaps effectively, by the unique position of the emperor.

The absence of commanding political leadership in pre-war and wartime Japan was as notable as the power of the bureaucracy. There were efforts, indeed, to perpetuate the *Genro* system. In a limited way it did live on in a loose organization made up of the Lord Keeper of the Privy Seal, former prime ministers, and high representatives of the army and navy. Its influence, however, never equalled or even rivalled that of the *Meiji Genro*. Outstanding among the so-called new *Genro* was Prince Konoye Fumimaro, who headed three cabinets on the eve of the war. Konoye was chosen not because of his ability to lead but because of the aristocratic prestige of his family and his capacity, despite nebulous political thinking, to keep on reasonably good terms with all factions.

As the power of the bureaucracy increased, successive governments after 1932 sought to provide the prime minister with agencies through which he might exercise more effective leadership. A five-minister conference or inner cabinet had become fully established by 1940. In the spring of 1941, Premier Konoye turned to a second expedient, the creation of an unofficial but informally recognized "Big Three of the Cabinet," including the premier, the vice-premier, and the minister of finance. Although more flexible than the five-minister conference, this device also failed. A third device designed to increase the efficiency of Japan's top bureaucratic leadership was the *Taisei Yokusan Kai,* or Imperial Rule Assistance Association, which made its appearance on the demise of the traditional political parties in 1940. The idea of a single national party had been inspired by the European fascist model. Konoye was prevailed upon to lead the movement. The new association emerged as an agency of "spiritual mobilization," and was soon controlled by the army. Early in the war, the political impotence of the IRAA led to the creation of a new and closely related organization, the Imperial Rule Assistance Political Society. This body, at first associated with the efforts of the government to pack the Diet with "approved candidates," enjoyed only a very limited success. As the war progressed, the

IRAPS tended to become a species of Diet members' club dominated by conservative, but not extremist, party leaders.

The New, Expanded Bureaucracy

The new, enlarged bureaucracy, which created its own dictatorship, included: (1) an expansion of ministerial agencies and the creation of extraministerial boards under the jurisdiction of the Cabinet, and (2) the so-called national policy companies. There was also the addition of new ministries: the Ministry of Welfare, 1938, the Ministry of Greater East Asia, 1942, and the Munitions Ministry, 1943.

Some of the more important extraministerial agencies created in the immediate pre-war years included: the Manchurian Affairs Board, entrusted with the co-ordination of policy between Japan and Manchukuo; the Cabinet Planning Board, a species of politico-economic general staff; the China Affairs Board, responsible for furthering the New Order in occupied China; and the Cabinet Advisory Council, an effort to recognize the modern would-be *Genro* and through them to find a means of reconciling rival bureaucratic factions.

The national policy companies, the number of which was multiplied on the eve of World War II, were the instruments of Japan's expansion at first in Manchuria and then in occupied China. The idea involved in this form of financial organization was not new. It had been employed early in the Meiji era in such cases as the Hokkaido Development Company and the Yawata Iron Works. As an instrument of national expansion abroad, the system was first fully matured in the South Manchuria Railway Company, founded in 1906, in whose hands Japan's exploitation of the South Manchurian sphere remained a practical monopoly until 1932. The pattern of organization for which the S. M. R. provided the model was that of an official corporation in which the government held a controlling number of shares. In the later national policy companies, particularly those that operated in occupied China, the companies were holding concerns controlling subsidiary companies which conducted the business enterprises involved.

Although political power in pre-war Japan had gravitated toward this cumbersome and leaderless bureaucracy, and although there was increasing state intervention in economic life, the nation was still far from possessing a planned economy. As late as 1941, most of the nation's business was financed and operated by private enterprise with only limited government interference. From the autumn of 1940, however, the need for national control of industry became more pressing, but there was no agreement as to the degree of control desirable or as to who should exercise this control. Extremists in

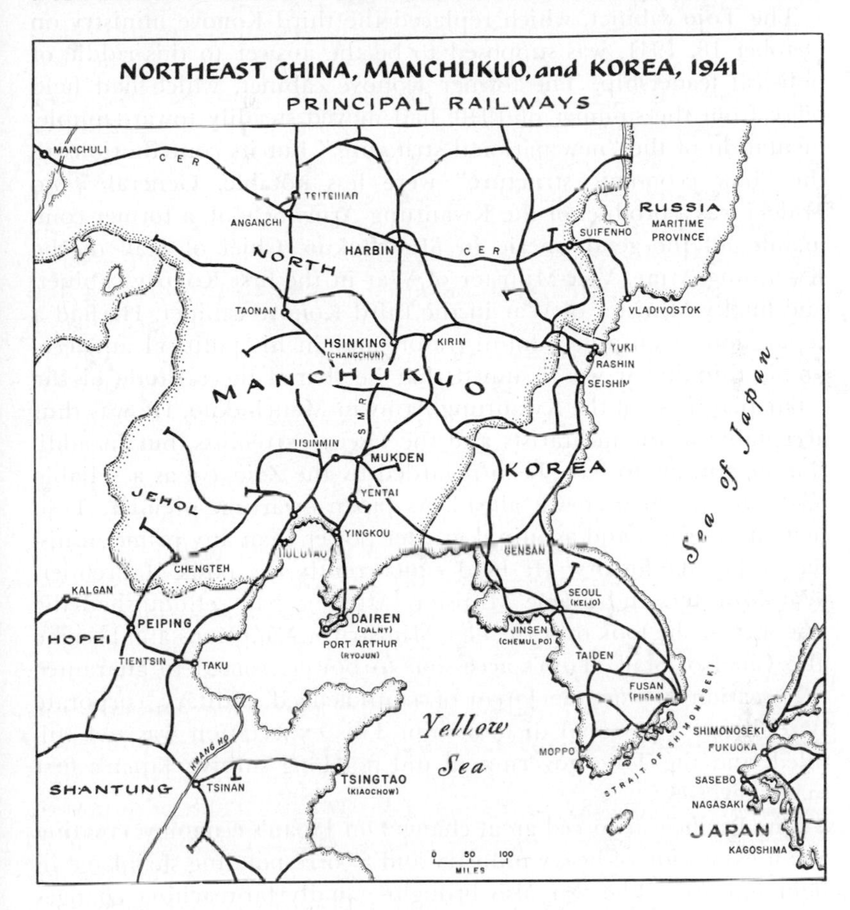

the army, the navy, and some factions of the bureaucracy clamored for total control in which the state would simply take over all industry. The business interests, particularly the *Zaibatsu,* were opposed to this program and remained so throughout the war. They were not hostile to greater wartime integration of industry enforced by the state—in fact, they perceived some advantages to themselves in such a system—but they were determined that their ownership and their prerogatives of management should be safeguarded and preserved.

The Tojo Cabinet

The Tojo cabinet, which replaced the third Konoye ministry on October 18, 1941, was supposed to be the answer to this riddle of political leadership. The former Konoye cabinet, which had held office from the summer of 1940, had moved steadily toward implementation of the "new national structure," but its contributions to the "new economic structure" were less notable. General Tojo Hideki was a product of the Kwantung Army School, a former commander of the gendarmerie in Manchukuo, Chief of Staff of the Kwantung Army, Vice-Minister of War in the first Konoye cabinet, and finally Minister of War in the third Konoye cabinet. He had a reputation as an able administrator, and in his political and economic thinking it was assumed that he shared the attitude of the "state planners" of the Kwantung Army in Manchukuo. He was thus acceptable to the militarists and the fascist extremists, but in addition he appears to have been regarded by the *Zaibatsu* as a reliable leader for the greater war ahead. As Japan's wartime premier, Tojo held more offices and acquired greater power than any prime minister in Japan's history. He held concurrently the posts of Premier, War Minister, and Home Minister. After he had relinquished the last of these, he took over the new Ministry of Munitions and became also Chief of Staff. Tojo's accession to power seemed to guarantee the creation in wartime Japan of a full-fledged, military, corporate state, if not a personal dictatorship. This expectation was not fulfilled, and the Tojo government did not long survive Japan's first major reverses.

The Pacific war forced great changes on Japan's economy, creating a vast expansion of heavy industry and a corresponding shrinkage in light industry. The war also brought equally far-reaching changes in the administrative control of industry. Until the war, the general industrial monopolies of the *Zaibatsu* operated in general as semi-autonomous units "linked neither with each other nor with the government through any effectively coercive administrative authority." Before the close of the war the major enterprises were under the control of the newly created Ministry of Munitions. This centralized control and relatively efficient management of war production was secured, however, only after two war years of chaotic administration which Tojo had been unable to overcome. This early failure on Japan's home-production front contributed to her first military and naval reverses. The new centralization of administrative power over production which the government finally acquired in January, 1944, was not a political victory for the militarists and the extreme "state planners," but rather an acceptance by the government of control measures proposed by and acceptable to the industrialists, the *Zaibatsu.*

THE RETURN TO TRADITIONALISM IN POLITICS

Although the war thus forced a greater concentration of administrative power than Japan had known previously, the failure of these belated measures to achieve victory, together with the rising specter of defeat, encouraged a return to traditional politics under more conservative guidance of the so-called new *Genro*. When the Tojo cabinet fell, the new ministry that succeeded was still essentially a military cabinet headed by a Kwantung Army extremist, General Koiso Kuniaki, but was tempered by the presence of Admiral Yonai Mitsumasa as Deputy Prime Minister and Navy Minister. Koiso's cabinet survived less than a year in the face of mounting military reverses. On April 7, 1945, it was succeeded by a ministry headed by Admiral Baron Suzuki Kantaro. Suzuki was a former Lord Chamberlain who had been attacked by the extremist assassins in 1936. This cabinet represented a careful balancing of conservative bureaucrats, the military services, and the business interests, and a conscious effort by the Elder Statesmen to defeat all extreme forms of political control. It was the Suzuki cabinet that tendered Japan's surrender in August and then gave place, September 16, 1945, to a new ministry under a prince of the Imperial Household, Higashikuni Naruhiko, a cousin of Emperor Hirohito. The selection of an Imperial prince as Premier was an effort to stabilize public opinion as the Japanese people witnessed the occupation of their homeland by a foreign army. Once the first phase of the occupation and demobilization was complete, Higashikuni resigned, October 5. He was succeeded the following day by one of Japan's few surviving "liberals," a man whom the nation had repudiated in 1931, Baron Shidehara Kijuro, who remained in office until April 22, 1946. It was Shidehara who faced the first problems of a defeated and broken

Japan—the problems of food, of housing, of inflation in a nation without leadership and without purpose. These crises were beyond the grasp of the aged Shidehara, and in May the premiership passed to Shigeru Yoshida.[5]

Although Japan's unconditional surrender was brought about by the overwhelming powers of American armament, the time and the manner of the surrender were conditioned by the political, economic, and bureaucratic character of the Japanese state. Indeed, Japan's surrender would probably have come earlier had the political structure of the nation permitted a more rapid and decisive determination of national policies or if the allies had been content with something short of unconditional surrender. As early as mid-1944 those Japanese leaders who possessed the basic information foresaw the economic collapse which was already underway and which assured the coming military disaster. By August, 1945, even without direct air attack, the level of Japan's production would have declined below the peak of 1944 by 40 to 50 per cent solely as a result of the interdiction of overseas imports. As it was, the damage from air attacks approximated that which was suffered by Germany. Something like 30 per cent of the urban population of Japan lost its homes and much of its possessions. With this appalling physical disaster came declining morale. Japan's civilian casualties numbered about 806,000, of which 333,000 were deaths. A declining belief in the power to win was accompanied by loss of confidence in both the military and the civilian leaders. Although a few of Japan's statesmen foresaw the ultimate defeat as early as February, 1944, it was not until May, 1945, that the Supreme War Direction Council, a creation of the Koiso cabinet, considered seriously means to end the war.

China During the War

For China, the global scale that hostilities assumed by the close of 1941 appeared as a limited blessing. It seemed to foreshadow the ultimate defeat of Japan by Anglo-American arms, the triumph of China's Nationalist revolution, and the elevation of China to the envied position of a great power. These, however, were hopes for the future. Against these hopes, the realities of early 1942 were foreboding. There was no certainty when the democracies would win, or

[5] Shidehara died in 1951. See Hugh Borton, *Japan's Modern Century* (New York, 1955), 375-396.

indeed, that they would win at all. Moreover, within China, the revolution that began on the Yangtze in 1911 had neither completed its course nor remained united in its objectives. The conditions that created the revolution had not been removed, and Sun Yat-sen's program, which gave the revolution life and purpose, had not been realized. The failure to reach Sun's goal was understandable, for China's revolution had travelled a very rough road. Two road-blocks frequently obstructed its progress. The first was the weight of Chinese tradition itself. Old habits were tenacious. It was difficult for the Chinese to decide what of the old should be retained and what of the new might be adopted. The second obstacle was raised by the great foreign powers, which, though they had in part created the revolution, were often afraid of it and sought to interfere with it by directing it into this or that particular channel. Yet, in spite of all these hazards, China appeared to be pushing forward into a new future. During the four and one-half years of the undeclared war the will of the Chinese to resist had not faltered. In so far as resistance to Japan was concerned, the Chinese had preserved a notable unity; but this unity did not mean that China was at peace with herself. There were dissensions and open conflicts within the revolution itself which the leadership of the *Kuomintang* had not resolved.

In December, 1941, China, for the second time in the era of the republican revolution, became engulfed in a world conflict. She followed the American and British declarations by herself declaring war on Japan. Her own long conflict with Japan thus became merged with the world-wide struggle against the Axis powers. As in 1917, China was ill-equipped in the material weapons with which modern nations fight. Her moral strength was symbolized by her ready adherence to the Declaration of the United Nations on January 1, 1942. The darker side of the picture was that China's new allies, the United States and Britain, were unable to give her immediate aid. Independent China remained locked in the great western interior, governed from the fugitive capital at Chungking. China's plight grew progressively worse. Isolation from her allies became almost complete as all of Southeast Asia fell to Japan. For many months after the tide of battle in the Pacific had turned, there could be only limited relief in munitions, guns, or planes for China.

Yet within limitations the United States did go to China's aid. At first this aid was little more than verbal assurance that the war would be fought until Japan was defeated. There followed financial aid, a

$500,000,000 loan in 1942.[6] There was also implementation of long-range planning to reopen communications with Chungking. The chief of the American military mission to China, General Joseph Stilwell, became chief-of-staff to Generalissimo Chiang K'ai-shek and commander of ground forces in the CBI (China-Burma-India) theater. After the retreat from Burma, it was Stilwell's task to train Chinese troops for the reconquest, to open air transport from India over the Hump of the Himalayas to Chungking, and to construct the Ledo Road (later known as the Stilwell Road) from Assam through northern Burma to link with the upper Burma Road. One of the heroic stories of the war was written by the Americans who, beginning with scanty equipment, flew lend-lease supplies across the roof of the world to Chungking.[7] There was also aid to China from the American Volunteer Group. Under Colonel, later General, Claire L. Chennault, these American "Flying Tigers" had operated prior to Pearl Harbor under contracts with the Chinese government to protect the Burma Road. Later they continued to operate in China as the Fourteenth Air Force of the United States Army Air Forces.

On the political and diplomatic front, the United States also moved to bolster Chinese confidence by discarding the last remnants of the unequal treaty system. Tariff autonomy had already been conceded to China more than a decade earlier. Now, on January 11, 1943, both the United States and Great Britain concluded treaties with China providing for immediate relinquishment of their extraterritorial rights and for the settlement of related questions. This act and similar relinquishment of special rights by all the remaining "treaty powers" completed the long process of restoring and recognizing the full sovereignty of China. At the same time, impelled by the pressures of war, Congress ended Chinese exclusion on December 17, 1943. Under the new law, a presidential proclamation fixed an annual quota of Chinese immigrants at 105.

The fuller significance of the ending of extraterritoriality and the exclusion laws was given at the Cairo Conference, November 22-26, 1943, where Roosevelt and Churchill met with Chiang K'ai-shek to consider problems of war and peace in the Far East. The implication was that China was now accepted as one of the great powers; that the National Government had the full support of Britain and America;

---

[6] Previous loans had been made in the pre-war years.

[7] See Charles F. Romanus and Riley Sunderland, *Stilwell's Mission to China* (Washington, 1953), for an authoritative account of American military aid.

and that the post-war Far East would be built around a fully sovereign, independent, and strong China. Indeed, the year 1943 revealed new heights in America's traditional and sentimental admiration for China. This newly aroused enthusiasm was associated with Madame Chiang K'ai-shek, who had come to the United States early in 1943 to win American support for the National Government and to criticize the strategy of merely holding the front against Japan until the defeat of Hitler had been achieved. Her eloquence and charm appeared to personify the heroism of a China that had refused to be beaten. "Chinese unity and Chinese democracy were accepted uncritically under the spell of her magnetic personality."[8] Madame Chiang spoke of the high lights; she avoided the shadows. Neither she nor other spokesmen of the National Government were in a position to say what all knew—that China's prosecution of the war had reached its lowest point since Japan struck at Lukouchiao in July, 1937.

Factors in China's Deteriorating War Effort

Basic in China's declining war effort by 1943 was the fact that the Chinese people had been worn down and disillusioned by six years of war. Millions had lost their homes and all their worldly possessions. The early hopes that aid from America and Britain would soon be at hand were shattered. The news of early Axis victories dispelled what hope was left. Economic crisis, immeasurably aggravated though not wholly created by the war, was basic to China's declining morale. Even in times of peace, China's economy provided no surplus. In years of war, as productivity declined prices rose in an inflation which was soon beyond control; profiteering became rampant not only in business circles but among high officials in the National Government. "National goals were dissipated in making money and protecting special privilege."[9] As inflation increased, the new Chinese middle class, which had been the backbone of *Kuomintang* liberalism, was progressively beggarized. In this situation the extreme right wing in the *Kuomintang* exercised increasing power and authority. There was a steady deterioration in economic life and a growing paralysis within the governmental administrative hierarchy.

---

[8] Foster Rhea Dulles, *China and America* (Princeton, 1946), 240.
[9] Dulles, *China and America,* 241.

In addition, the administration of the land tax in kind was estimated to cost two-fifths of the value of the grain collected. No phase of China's war economy escaped the effects of these disastrous conditions. Where famine was added to the shortages of war, the peasantry took to arms to disarm their own soldiers. Chinese who dared to protest against the official policies that appeared to condone these conditions felt the heavy hand of the secret police. Chinese reactions were human reactions: they blamed the government.

The character of China's revolutionary National Government, the stress and strain to which it had been subjected before 1941, have already been touched upon in some detail (see Chapter 31). After 1941 the pressures of prolonged warfare multiplied the problems of the National Government and of the source of its authority, the *Kuomintang*. Party and Government still faced the herculean task of providing leadership in prosecution of the war and in preserving and furthering the nationalist revolution of Sun Yat-sen. In the context of government under one-party political tutelage a staggering responsibility continued to rest on the *Kuomintang* hierarchy. The problem of maintaining its political power on a broad base of popular consent was peculiarly difficult in the atmosphere of wartime China not only because Chinese politics was traditionally a very personal thing but also because constitutionalism did not yet exist in fact. Those who were beyond the Party and many of the rank and file of the Party, having no effective means of influencing policy, became something less than ardent adherents of *Kuomintang* leadership.[10] To be sure, this leadership was able to support a large, though ill-equipped and low-morale army, but it did not produce the patriot-fanatics prepared to pay any price for victory.[11] This lack of revolutionary politico-military heroes plus the earlier trend on the political front for the *Kuomintang* revolutionary party line to become "official and sterile" meant that *Kuomintang* wartime leadership labored under serious disabilities. This problem of leadership was the more serious because, in addition to the challenge from the Communists, the *Kuomintang* was confronted by a whole group of minor political parties, jealous of *Kuomintang* power, who thought they knew what ought to be done.

---

10 On the structure of the National Government as affected by the Japanese invasion, see Lin Nai-chen, "The Framework of Government in Unoccupied China," *Voices from Unoccupied China,* H. F. MacNair, ed. (Chicago, 1944), 1-15.

11 P. M. A. Linebarger, "Ideological Dynamics of the Postwar Far East," *Foreign Governments,* F. Morstein Marx, ed. (New York, 1949), 555.

MINOR POLITICAL PARTIES

These minor political parties at best were a symptom of China's political awakening. At worst they were evidence of personal factionalism. A motley array of political ideas and programs were represented by these parties. The Young China Party (sometimes called the Chinese Youth Party) had been organized in Paris, 1923. It called itself democratic and filled its platform with vague aspirations, extreme nationalism, and anti-communism. The National Socialist Party, dominated at the outset by university professors, had been formed in 1931 by Carsun Chang among intellectuals who had been followers of Liang Ch'i-ch'ao. The party was largely an attempt to restore traditional values modified by Western thought. The National Salvation Association was organized by intellectuals at Shanghai, 1936, to promote armed resistance against Japan. Its thinking was leftist, and for this many of its members were imprisoned, though in reality its objective was unity of the country above all party considerations. During the war the *Kuomintang* continued a policy of suppressing this movement. Two additional minor groups, the National Association for Vocational Education and the Rural Reconstruction Group, favored popularizing vocational education and implementing rural reform respectively. These groups were less important as political parties than as symbols of political needs. Finally, the Democratic League, founded in 1941 by progressives of the People's Political Council, had a more valid claim to the label "democratic" than any other political group. In the *Kuomintang*-Communist conflict during and after the war the League was divided between those inclined toward close co-operation with the Communists and those aspiring to be neutral mediators.

During the early war years beginning in 1937, although the minor parties were allowed no share in the *Kuomintang's* monopoly of political power or in responsibility for the conduct of war, they did seek to co-operate with the government even when their status as independent parties was not fully recognized in law. After 1941, however, when the *Kuomintang*-Communist united front failed, the National Government revived a policy of repression which in turn alienated popular support at the very moment it was most needed.[12]

---

[12] Ch'ien Tuan-shêng, *The Government and Politics of China* (Cambridge, 1950), 371-375.

Revival of the Constitutional Movement

When the undeclared war broke out in 1937 the *Kuomintang* set up a National Defense Advisory Council which included members of opposition parties and independents. Demands for enlargement of this small Council led the *Kuomintang* to strengthen the war effort by establishing in 1938 a People's Political Council, an advisory body averaging some three hundred members. Although wartime would hardly seem the most opportune moment to begin constitutionalism in a land where constitutionalism in fact had never been known, nevertheless constitutionalism was one of the first issues discussed by the People's Political Council. Chiang K'ai-shek accordingly appointed a Constitutionalism Promotion Committee representing divergent views within the Council to stimulate discussion of constitutional issues. Meanwhile the *Kuomintang* leadership decided to call the National Congress late in 1940. For reasons of both war and politics this meeting was not held; but in 1943, when Chiang again emphasized the importance of constitutionalism, the *Kuomintang* Central Executive Committee decided to call the Congress within a year of the end of war to adopt a constitution. These were indeed signs of progress, but they did not mean that solution had yet been reached on fundamental issues or indeed that any considerable number of China's people understood the relation of constitutionalism to government. As China's eight years of war came to an end, the Communists and the independent Left continued to hold as in earlier years "an enormous leverage in popular interest." They had ignored class lines, illiteracy, and had drawn the common people into "a real share in government and social reconstruction." The *Kuomintang* leadership had not capitalized in the same measure on this opportunity.[13]

Wartime *Kuomintang*-Communist Strife

A major factor in China's lapsing war effort was the disintegration of the *Kuomintang*-Communist united front. Its maintenance from the beginning in 1937 had been exceedingly difficult not only because the united front had been imposed from without by Japan's aggression, but also because of the bitter memories of the *Kuomintang*-Communist warfare from 1927 to 1937. Although a marked

[13] P. M. A. Linebarger, *China of Chiang K'ai-shek* (Boston, 1941), 156-157.

unity appeared to be forecast by the first meeting of the People's Political Council, 1938, the unification movement was gripped from that time onward by a creeping paralysis. Both the National Government and the Communists continued to fight Japan, but the united front became merely a name, and eventually, by 1944, not even that. The total effect was to cripple China's limited powers to resist Japan and to pave the way for a renewal of civil war.

This deterioration in *Kuomintang*-Communist relations dated back specifically to the latter half of 1938. Late in that year Communist-sponsored mass organizations in the Hankow-Wuchang area were outlawed when it appeared they were gaining influence inimical to the National government. After the fall of Hankow in October, 1938, *Kuomintang*-Communist relations worsened steadily. The Communists failed to yield control of their area in Shensi province to the Nationalists or to permit the latter to exercise direct command over Communist armies. As time went on the charges and countercharges of failure to abide by the promises of 1937 became violent, often leading to local clashes between Chinese National and Communist forces. The one policy common to both parties was resistance against the Japanese invasion, and even this was often neglected amid the jockeying for advantage between the two parties. Nevertheless, hostilities on a large scale were avoided. During 1939 the National government at Chungking, convinced that the Communists were seeking complete control, began to enforce a military blockade of the Communist areas to prevent Communist infiltration into Nationalist China. Moreover, the expansion of Communist military forces into areas outside the regional defense zones assigned them by the National government led to repeated "incidents." The arguments and actual clashes over demarcation of military zones culminated in the New Fourth Army incident of January, 1941, the most serious wartime clash between Nationalist and Communist armies, and the beginning of real civil war.

Nevertheless, in spite of frequent incidents and continual friction, the stated policy of the Nationalist government remained that of seeking a political settlement with the Communists. At meetings of the People's Political Council, some minor parties attempted mediation with the object of preserving *Kuomintang*-Communist co-operation. On a number of occasions, too, there were direct negotiations between Nationalist and Communist officials in which suggestions for a "coalition government" were brought forth for the first time. Although no settlement was reached, it did appear that from May to September, 1944, the National government and the Chinese Communist party were at least going through the forms of seeking a peaceful settlement. But behind these manoeuvres was the government's fear of offending elements within the *Kuomintang* if "radical measures of reform" were passed, and the government's well-justified conviction that the Communists would extend their power at the first opportunity.[14]

Wartime Role of Chiang K'ai-shek

The wartime and, as will be seen later, the post-war role of Chiang K'ai-shek was to become one of the most bitter, controversial subjects of recent history. As noted (Chapter 31), Chiang was one of the heirs of Sun Yat-sen. His gradual emergence between 1927 and 1937 as the indispensable leader of the Nationalist revolution and of the resistance movement against Japan was an event of great import. In this earlier period his rise was due principally though not exclusively to his stature as a soldier. Chiang, the military man, had won a new degree of unity within China by defeating the warlords. His military problem in resisting Japan, 1937-1945, was difficult not only because of Japan's military power but also because the Chinese army "was a coalition army rather than a unified national force." Most divisions were lightly armed and poorly trained. Soldiers were tough and often courageous but their allegiance tended to be to their local commanders. Sometimes cheated of part of their small pay, living on irregular rations, widely dispersed in a vast country (sometimes because it was feared they would desert if moved), the army was no match for Japan's divisions, and a doubtful domestic political asset. Out of some three-hundred-odd divisions in 1942, some thirty were directly under the National Government. The result was a political problem of military control and reorganization with which Chiang was unable to deal effectively.[15]

As the popular movement for resistance to Japan grew after 1937, the role which devolved upon Chiang became extremely complex and demanding. In a land where nationalism was still a vibrant, popular aspiration rather than a realized system of administration, he was called upon to give military leadership, to maintain the

---

[14] Herbert Feis, *The China Tangle* (Princeton, 1953), 75.
[15] Feis, *The China Tangle,* 45-46.

ideological inspiration of Sun's revolution, and to move rapidly toward the implementation of that program through political, economic, and social reform. Moreover, these demands for leadership came at a time when nearly half of China's territory was in the hands of the invader, when factionalism within the *Kuomintang* was increasing rather than decreasing, and finally when Chiang's position was constantly under challenge by the Communists and by non-Communists both inside and outside the *Kuomintang*. In 1937 and 1938 Chiang appeared to be rising to the crisis that called him. In response to popular demand he made peace with the Communists and moved in the direction of constitutionalism. He showed some qualities of political as well as military leadership and of ethical stature; but unlike Sun Yat-sen he was not a "political philosopher and utopist" who could stir the loyalty of men by his power of expression, nor was he a saint like Gandhi who could convince a world of his selfless devotion.[16]

Chiang's Political Creed

Chiang's political creed was revealed not only by what he did but also by his book, *China's Destiny,* first published at Chungking in Chinese in 1943.[17] It is a textbook on Chinese nationalism in which Chiang appears as a disciple of nineteenth-century nationalism similar to the models provided by Germany, Italy, and Japan. Chiang's program, as presented, was in close parallel to the reform philosophy of *Meiji* Japan. Emphasis was on "an emotional race and national consciousness with the Yellow Emperor presented as the common ancestor of Chinese, Manchus, Mongols, Tibetans, and Mohammedans, just as Amaterasu, the Sun Goddess, became the ancestress of the Japanese emperor and the Japanese race." Chiang reviewed the decline and fall of the Manchus, the story of Western imperi-

16 P. M. A. Linebarger, "Government in China," *Foreign Governments,* F. Morstein Marx, ed. (New York, 1949), 597.

17 Editions in English include: (1) Chiang K'ai-shek, *China's Destiny* (authorized translation by Wang Chung-hui, with an introduction by Lin Yutang, New York, 1947); (2) Chiang K'ai-shek, *China's Destiny and Chinese Economic Theory* (with notes and commentary by Philip Jaffe, New York, 1947). Although there was much controversy as to the relative merits of the two English editions, as a matter of fact "as translations they are about equally faithful to the author's original," despite "the servile acceptance of Lin Yutang" and "the bitterly hostile presentation of Mr. Jaffe." See the evaluation on this point by Earl Swisher in *The Far Eastern Quarterly,* X (November, 1950), 89-95.

alism (the unequal treaties), the subversion of the 1911 revolution by Yuan Shih-k'ai and the warlords, the reorganization and triumph of the *Kuomintang,* its record of national reconstruction from 1928 to 1937, and, finally, China's achievement of new nationhood signified by termination of the unequal treaties with Great Britain and the United States in 1943. China's revolution, therefore, could be held together no longer by anti-imperialism. It required a new positive nationalism that Chiang proposed to base on Confucian morality, which he believed could still inspire the nation. The weakness of his position lay in the fact that his plea for loyalty to the state was backed by no sound political theory relevant to the war-time China of 1937-1945.[18]

Whatever may be said of *China's Destiny* as a sincere revelation of Chiang's mind and soul, as a political manifesto it was a lamentable miscarriage. It opposed the intellectual trends of the pre-war years by berating those Chinese who had sought inspiration from the West. It scolded Chinese businessmen of the Treaty Ports for their Western free enterprise while it advocated restriction of private capital and a government-planned economy. It alienated the youth of China by offering it nothing more than an exhortation to obedience and frugality. It sought political and social stability by appeals to tradition which had no meaning in the ferment of modern China and which served only to alienate potential allies in the struggle against Communism.

Efforts to Bolster China

Although there had been warning rumors in 1943, it was not until early in 1944 that an alarming picture of China's deteriorating war effort and morale broke through the Chungking censorship to reach the American public. In the shock of this disclosure, American public opinion swung from emotional admiration to almost un-

[18] "The weakness and confusion of his [Chiang's] thesis lie in the fact that Confucian morality has been outmoded for several generations of students and political leaders who regard it as old-fashioned, and the additional fact that Confucius' political philosophy is moralistic, nonlegal, and antistate and thus ill-suited to modern nationalism, even of the conventional sort. The fact that Chiang tries to append an argument for a government of law over a government of men only serves to confuse his dominant and basically untenable thesis. . . . No attempt is made to reselect from China's rich tradition those elements that would support a new and modern state; no search is made for the democratic elements in China's history and philosophy." Swisher, *The Far Eastern Quarterly,* X (November, 1950), 93.

qualified denunciation. President Roosevelt was afraid that China would not hold together to the end of the war. Vice-President Henry A. Wallace was sent to Chungking to encourage Chiang and to get the Nationalist and Communist armies to stop fighting each other. The American government wanted Chiang to form a combined war council to co-ordinate all Chinese forces against Japan, and under Chiang's authority to place General Joseph W. Stilwell in command. In August, 1944, General Patrick J. Hurley went to Chungking as the President's personal representative to Chiang to sweeten the already bitter relations between Chiang and Stilwell, to keep China in the war, the Chinese army in the field, and to unify all Chinese military forces against Japan. Hurley soon came to the view that relations between Chiang and Stilwell over the question of China's war effort and the means of promoting it had deteriorated beyond repair. Accordingly, following Hurley's recommendation, Stilwell was recalled and Major General Albert C. Wedemeyer was designated to replace him as Chiang's chief-of-staff, October, 1944. Coincident with these events, Clarence E. Gauss, ambassador to China, resigned November 1, 1944, and was replaced by General Hurley who continued as ambassador until November 26, 1945. Hurley's activities included: (1) efforts at mediation between the Nationalists and Communists, and (2) efforts to clarify relations between China and the Soviet Union. By this time, however, the American offensive against Japan through the Philippines and the Mandated Islands was reducing the China theater to lesser importance in American military planning. As a result there was less effort to deal with the problem of Nationalist military and political power. General Hurley was instrumental in a resumption of negotiations between the Nationalists and the Communists, but the basic question of powers between the two groups remained unresolved. Thus matters stood as, with Japan's sudden surrender, hostilities in the Pacific came to an end.

For Further Reading

MILITARY AND NAVAL AFFAIRS

Baldwin, Hanson W., *Great Mistakes of the War* (New York, 1950).

Cannon, M. Hamlin, *United States Army in World War II. The War in the Pacific. Leyte: The Return to the Philippines* (Washington, D.C., 1954).

Considine, Robert, ed., *General Wainwright's Story* (Garden City, 1946). The general's account of four years of defeat, surrender, and captivity.

Craven, Wesley Frank, and James Lea Cate, eds., *The Army Air Forces in World War II* (5 vols., Chicago, 1948-53). See vols. I, IV, and V for the Pacific story.

Crowl, Philip A., and Edmund G. Love, *United States Army in World War II: Seizure of the Gilberts and Marshalls* (Washington, 1955).

Eichelberger, Robert L., *Our Jungle Road to Tokyo* (New York, 1950).

Field, James A., *The Japanese at Leyte Gulf* (Princeton, 1947). Based on interviews with high-ranking Japanese commanders who took part in the battle.

Hachiya Michihiko, *Hiroshima Diary; Journal of a Japanese Physician, August 6–Sept. 30, 1945.* Trans. and ed. by Warner Wells (Chapel Hill, 1955).

Halsey, William F., and J. Bryan, III, *Admiral Halsey's Story* (New York, 1947). A personal narrative by the commander of the South Pacific and the Third Fleet.

Hashimoto Mochitsura, *Sunk: The Story of the Japanese Submarine Fleet, 1941-1945,* trans. by E. H. M. Colegrove (New York, 1954). By a junior Japanese naval officer.

Haugland, Vern, *The AAF Against Japan* (New York, 1948). A good treatment of a broad topic.

Hersey, John, *Hiroshima* (New York, 1946). A graphic story of atomic destruction.

Hough, Frank O., *The Island War* (Philadelphia, 1947). A part played by U. S. Marine Corps in the Pacific war.

Isely, Jeter A., and Philip A. Crowl, *The U. S. Marines and Amphibious War: Its Theory and Practice in the Pacific* (Princeton, 1951).

Karig, Walter, Welbourn Kelly, Eric Purdon, Russell L. Harris, and Frank A. Manson, *Battle Report* (6 vols., New York, 1944-1952). A nontechnical narrative of the Navy's war prepared from official sources, paralleling and complementing Morison's account. Volumes I, III, IV, and V cover the Pacific war.

Kenney, George C., *The MacArthur I Know* (New York, 1951). An appraisal by the air force general who worked with MacArthur in World War II.

Kimmel, Husband E., *Admiral Kimmel's Story* (Chicago, 1955). The Commander-in-Chief of the U. S. Pacific Fleet in 1941 gives his side of the Pearl Harbor disaster.

King, Ernest J., and Walter M. Whitehill, *Fleet Admiral King, A Naval Record* (New York, 1952).

McKelvie, Roy, *The War in Burma* (London, 1948). A balanced account of British and American forces.

Morison, Samuel Eliot, *History of United States Naval Operations in World War II* (11 vols. to date, Boston, 1947–). The most detailed operational history of American naval warfare in World War II. To be completed in 13 volumes.

Morton, Louis, *United States Army in World War II: The War in the Pacific: The Fall of the Philippines* (Washington, D.C., 1953). A comprehensive study.

Seagrave, G. S., *Burma Surgeon* (New York, 1943). The story of a doctor in the retreat from Burma.

T'an Pei-ying, *The Building of the Burma Road* (New York, 1945).

DIPLOMACY AND COLLECTIVE SECURITY

Angus, H. F., *Canada and the Far East, 1940-1953* (Toronto, 1953).

Becker, Carl, *How New Will the Better World Be?* (New York, 1944). An historical background for realistic peace planning.

Dulles, Foster Rhea, *The Road to Teheran* (Princeton, 1944). A readable survey of American-Russian relations, 1781-1943.

Graebner, Norman A., *Empire on the Pacific. A Study in American Continental Expansion* (New York, 1955).

Johnson, Walter, ed., *Roosevelt and the Russians: the Yalta Conference* (Garden City, 1949).

Kase Toshikazu, *Journey to the "Missouri"* (New Haven, 1950). A Japanese account of Japan on the eve of and during World War II by a former member of the Japanese Foreign Office.

Riggs, Fred W., *Pressures on Congress: A Study of the Repeal of Chinese Exclusion* (New York, 1950).

Snell, John L., ed., *The Meaning of Yalta,* with foreword by Paul H. Clyde (Baton Rouge, 1956). An historical analysis.

Stilwell, General Joseph W., *The Stilwell Papers* (New York, 1948). Selections from the journal of the controversial American commander of the CBI theater.

Togo Shigenori, *The Cause of Japan* (New York, 1956). A wartime Japanese foreign minister gives a careful review of the policies of the government.

POLITICS AND ECONOMICS OF WAR

Bisson, Thomas Arthur, *Japan's War Economy* (New York, 1945). An analysis of the changes in Japan's wartime economy, stressing the role of the *Zaibatsu.*

Chiang Monlin, *Tides from the West* (New Haven, 1947).

Cohen, Jerome B., *Japan's Economy in War and Reconstruction,* with foreword by Sir George Sansom (Minneapolis, 1949). The best economic study.

Haring, Douglas G., ed., *Japan's Prospect* (Cambridge, 1946). A composite work by scholars who trained personnel for military government in Japan.

Johnston, B. F., *Japanese Food Management in World War II* (Stanford, 1953). A voluminous reference work describing the impact of the war on food supplies and the policies and measures adopted by the government to cope with the problems created by wartime conditions.

Maki, John McGilvrey, *Japanese Militarism* (New York, 1945). Portrays the causes and prescribes a cure for Japan's military spirit.

McWilliams, Carey, *Prejudice; Japanese-Americans: Symbol of Racial Intolerance* (Boston, 1944). A study of the treatment of the nisei during World War II.

Smith, Nicol, and Blake Clark, *Into Siam: Underground Kingdom* (New York, 1946). An account of the OSS in Siam.

36

1945–1952 and after

The Occupation of Japan

V-J Day, August 14, 1945, which ended the hostilities of World War II in the Pacific and the Far East, did not bring peace to Eastern Asia. To be sure, victory in war freed the Orient of the incubus of Japanese militarism, and imperialistic expansion; but the war had not and could not of itself rid Asia of all the ills from which it suffered. In many areas of the Far East men were still prepared to fight, and they continued to fight to achieve the things they desired. Many of their goals were old and revived aspirations not traceable exclusively to the recent policies and behavior of Japan. Rather, they were the recurring manifestations of an Asia stirred by political and social revolution, and it was this revolution, in process before World War II, that remained as the most characteristic feature of the post-war Far East. Throughout the entire area there was not a single country or a single people unaffected by dynamic forces of change. The processes of Westernization and modernization, present before the war, were in many respects accelerated by the conflict, and they continued to operate with even greater force after hostilities had ceased. Thus Japan's surrender was but the first step toward meeting a vast array of perplexing questions which war had not solved, and which in some cases were the creation of the war.

Basic in Asia's post-war turmoil was its traditional "low" standard of living made even lower by the ravages of war: the destruction of life savings and property, the interruption of trade, the displacement of large segments of population, and the general dislocation resulting from extreme shortages and uncontrolled inflation. Some areas of Eastern Asia were affected more adversely and radically by the war than others. Yet in general the words of Manuel Roxas, a Filipino leader, that war and the Japanese had brought "physical ruin" to the Philippines could as well be applied to large areas of the Far East. This was not to say of course that the economic problems of the Far East were insuperable. It was to say that they were proving to be exceedingly difficult. The relative poverty of Eastern Asia in resources for an industrial society, its historic problems of population, the sub-subsistence income of the peasant masses, the lack of industrial capital—all these and many other factors suggested that Asia's economic recovery was to be a long-range process. Moreover, the rate of economic recovery in the Far East was conditioned by traditional historic social habits which had by no means adjusted themselves fully to a Western and modern world.

The Political Turmoil

Politics no less than economics presented an Eastern Asia shaken by war. Traditional views of Asia's political status became untenable. Japan, the one "great power" of the Far East was reduced to the status of a third- or fourth-class power. China, for one hundred years a quasi-dependent area, regained her full sovereignty and was dignified with nominal inclusion among the great states. The Philippines became an independent republic. Other native republics, semi-independent in fact, were born in French Indochina and the Netherlands Indies, and independence "in due course" had been promised to Korea. The Mongolian People's Republic acquired nationhood under Soviet patronage. Burma and India entered upon a new and independent political future. These signs of vital political consciousness were partly a result of what may loosely be called nationalism, of a refusal to be governed longer by alien powers, but they were also symptoms of a much broader social unrest. Westernization and modernization brought Eastern Asia out of her seclusion, affected her intellectual as well as her material life, created the stirrings of a new social consciousness, and supplied her with a new intellectual and social leadership, whether in the person of a Sun Yat-sen, a Chiang K'ai-shek, or a Mao Tse-tung in China, a Roxas or a Taruc in the Philippines, a Sukarno in Indonesia, a Ho Chi-minh in Indochina, a Syngman Rhee or a Yo Unhyong in Korea. The principle common to all these leaders was the concept of Asia's inherent right to political independence. Their disagreements, at times violent, concerned the political, economic, and social structure in which independence was to function.

THE AMERICAN CONCEPT OF OCCUPATION

Originally the American plan for the occupation and military government of Japan was fashioned out of experience gained in Germany, Italy, and the Pacific Islands. The assumption was that the invasion of Japan would be accompanied by great loss of life, physical destruction, and the complete disorganization of the Japanese government. Japan's sudden surrender and the resulting peaceful occupation by American forces altered the problem completely. Accordingly the decision was made not to administer Japan directly through a corps of American military government officers, but to exercise authority through the Emperor's government. "The Japanese Cabinet would operate subject to directions from General [of the Army Douglas] MacArthur's headquarters."

Under this concept of the problem there was to be no large military government establishment, but rather a much smaller organization of staff sections created as a part of General MacArthur's headquarters to plan the execution of Occupation policy in respect to political, economic, and social problems involved in the remaking of Japan. Under this plan, the Occupation authority acted not directly upon the Japanese populace but through the constituted Japanese government. The private Japanese citizen acted on the instructions of his own government.

Although many of the day-to-day steps in the occupation of Japan were determined by events in Japan and by personalities commanding the occupation forces, the American government regarded the occupation forces as "the instruments of policy and not the determinants of policy." The ultimate objectives were to insure that Japan would cease to be a threat to peace and security, and to encourage the development of responsible government supported by the freely expressed will of the Japanese people. Implementation of these objectives was to be secured by limiting Japan's sovereignty to her main islands and a few outlying minor ones, by complete demilitarization, by elimination of the militarists and encouragement of democratic associations, and by affording opportunity for the building of an economy adequate for peacetime requirements.

The relationship between the Supreme Commander of the Allied Nations and the Japanese government was to be one of employing the already constituted agencies, including the Emperor, to the extent that this method furthered satisfactorily the objectives of the

United States. The policy, however, was not to prevent evolutionary change. In theory at least the policy was to use the existing Japanese government, not to support it.

The more notable objectives of the Occupation were: (1) destruction of the economic base of Japan's military strength; (2) reduction of heavy industry to the minimum requirements of an economy for peace; (3) encouragement of "the development of organizations in labor, industry, and agriculture, organized on a democratic basis"; (4) encouragement of policies "which permit a wide distribution of income and of the ownership of the means of production and trade"; and (5) dissolution of the great family combines that controlled Japanese industry and trade.

From the moment of Japan's defeat it was clear that the United States would assume a predominant position in the Occupation. Although America gave assurance that it would consider the wishes of the principal Allied powers, it was emphatic that "in the event of any differences of opinion among them, the policies of the United States will govern." This idea of a completely free hand for the United States in fashioning the new Japan did not meet with international favor. Since the control of Japan would have a direct bearing on larger questions concerning the Far East, it was to be expected that China, Russia, Australia, Great Britain, and France would seek a voice in policies applied in Tokyo. Anticipating such demands, the United States seized the initiative by inviting participation, but the original American proposal for a purely advisory committee representing the chief Allied powers was not received favorably. The problem was eventually resolved in December, 1945, when the foreign ministers of Great Britain, Russia, and the United States, after consultation with China, agreed upon the creation of a Far Eastern Commission and an Allied Council for Japan. The functions of the Commission, located in Washington, were to formulate policies, to review on the request of any member any directive issued to the Supreme Commander, and to consider other matters referred to it by agreement among the participating powers. Military operations and territorial adjustments were beyond the Commission's powers. After establishment of the Commission, it still remained the task of the United States to issue directives to the Supreme Commander in accordance with the policy decisions of the Commission. In theory at least, the Commission was a severe limitation on the freedom of the United States to formulate policies, but this did not mean that the

United States had lost its predominant position. American directives to General MacArthur continued to be issued in accord with American interpretation of policy decisions, and the Supreme Commander continued to apply the directives according to his own interpretation of them. The Allied Council in Tokyo was designed to be a consultative and advisory body without power to act.

Japan as a Victim of War

The Japan that had embarked on arrogant conquest was vastly different from the Japan that bowed before the victors in 1945—a picture of physical destruction, economic collapse, and social and spiritual emptiness; yet withal a Japan that responded with habitual discipline to the Emperor's bidding to surrender. The catalogue of the nation's losses included nearly two million lives and some 40 per cent of the aggregate urban area including 2.5 million buildings. Nearly 700,000 buildings were destroyed in Tokyo alone where, during the war, population in the terror of bombing attacks shrank from more than 6.5 million to less than 3 million.

Frightful as the physical destruction was, its consequences were by no means so damaging as the breakdown of the economy at war's end. The extraordinary gains of the pre-war decade (1930-1940), during which industrial output doubled, were wiped out by defeat, leaving the nation in 1946 with less than a third of its 1930 production. The only immediately useful vestige of Japan's wealth was the paddy field. The peasant became an important person as desperate city dwellers sought food through the illicit channels of the black market. Prized family possessions were traded for rice; vegetables were grown where houses had stood; inflation consumed the meager savings that millions of little people had gathered through long hard years.

Possibly most damaging of all to a disciplined people was the enforced departure from discipline. Men defied authority, or they perished. It was no longer possible to live within the law. The price was paid in morale and in character. Petty lawlessness and juvenile delinquency flourished, while gangsterism and protection rackets terrorized whole communities.[1]

[1] A graphic picture of Japan in defeat is given by Edwin O. Reischauer, *The United States and Japan* (Cambridge, Mass., 1950), 205-223. For a critical appraisal of the Occupation, see Robert B. Textor, *Failure in Japan: with Keystones for a Positive Policy* (New York, 1951).

At the same time, the picture of Japan, as the victors found it, was not hopeless. Millions of Japanese accepted surrender and humiliation with dignity. They met the cruel reality of defeat, surrender, and hunger, and, with little effort to shift the blame to others, accepted it as their own responsibility as well as that of their leaders. Whatever later successes the Occupation enjoyed were attributable in a major degree to this attitude that enabled the Japanese people to co-operate with the inevitable. Troops of the Occupation were received without visible animosity: a strange and friendly reception for Americans who had been taught, or had learned in battle, to hate the Japanese.[2]

MacArthur, His Staff, and the Japanese

Americans in 1945 were ready to agree that Japan should cease to be a military menace, and to hope that she could be guided into democratic ways. But by what human agency were such extraordinary changes to be brought about in Japanese character and behavior? This function of supreme importance was given by the United States with the consent of other powers to General Douglas MacArthur, the Supreme Commander of the Allied Powers (SCAP), who thus came to combine with his military authority in the Occupation the executive authority to direct policy toward the political, economic, and social objectives of the Occupation.

The implementation of the Occupation was directed by MacArthur's staff of military officers in key posts and by civilians, some of whom were at relatively high levels. This rather small group undertook the amazing task of renovating politically, economically, and socially a nation of more than 80 million people. Many members of the Occupation staff were persons with wide or specialized knowledge of Japan; others, although not conversant with Japan, had brilliant records in government, business, or the professions in the United States. To their staggering tasks in Japan they brought not only expert knowledge but also, and perhaps as important, a crusading zeal to create a new and, by contrast with the past, a revolutionary though peaceful and democratic Japan. As the Occupation continued, however, it became increasingly difficult to procure and hold

---

[2] The operation of military government at the local level is discussed by Ralph J. D. Braibanti, "Administration of Military Government in Japan at the Prefectural Level," *American Political Science Review*, XLIII (1949), 250-274.

staff personnel of high competence. In addition, the Occupation by its very nature tended to pervert its own members who enjoyed standards of living no Japanese could afford, whose judgments were always right while the Japanese were always wrong. Nevertheless, it should be added that the "corruption of conquest" would have been

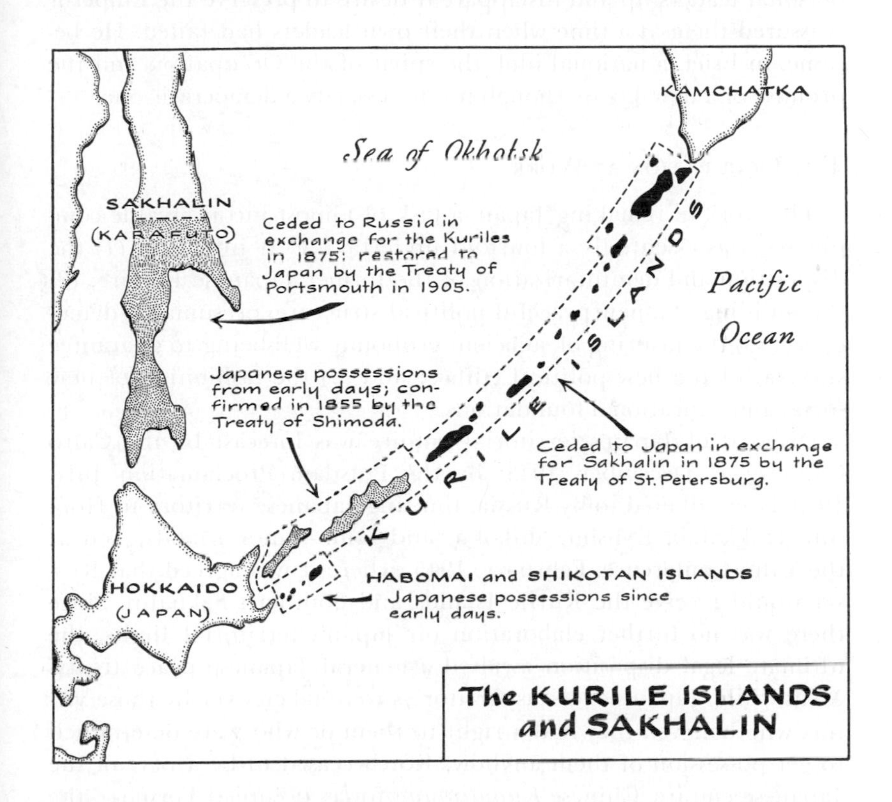
KAMCHATKA
Sea of Okhotsk
SAKHALIN
(KARAFUTO)
Ceded to Russia in exchange for the Kuriles in 1875: restored to Japan by the Treaty of Portsmouth in 1905.
Pacific Ocean
KURILE ISLANDS
Japanese possessions from early days; confirmed in 1855 by the Treaty of Shimoda.
Ceded to Japan in exchange for Sakhalin in 1875 by the Treaty of St. Petersburg.
HABOMAI and SHIKOTAN ISLANDS
Japanese possessions since early days.
HOKKAIDO
(JAPAN)
The KURILE ISLANDS and SAKHALIN

far greater had not the majority of Occupation personnel retained their perspective and their honesty of purpose.

Throughout the Occupation, both the staff of SCAP and the Japanese government upon which it operated felt the unique personal influence of MacArthur. To Japanese as well as to Americans, his name was synonymous with military tradition. Entering Japan as conqueror, he came, as it were, with the Emperor's approval to assume the role of super-Emperor. Autocratic, austere, decisive, always the dramatist, yet benevolent, MacArthur personified qualities which, although respected and admired by the traditional Japanese mind, were not wholly representative of the American democracy which was about to re-educate Japan in peaceful and democratic ways. Certainly, MacArthur was a stabilizing influence on the war-shaken Japanese. They understood his insistence on personal loyalty. His personal leadership and his apparent desire to preserve the Emperor reassured them at a time when their own leaders had failed. He became, in brief, a national idol, the spirit of the Occupation and the promise of a new Japan, though not necessarily a democratic one.

The Occupation at Work

The work of remaking Japan, a task of almost inconceivable complexity, was essentially a fourfold undertaking. It involved: (1) the disposition and demilitarization of the former Japanese Empire; (2) the building of a new peaceful political structure, presumably democratic; (3) the insuring of sufficient economic well-being to guarantee survival of the new political edifice; and (4) the fashioning of new social and educational foundations.[3]

Disposal of Japan's territorial empire was forecast by the Cairo Conference, December, 1943; by the Potsdam Proclamation July, 1945, later adhered to by Russia, limiting Japanese territory to Honshu, Hokkaido, Kyushu, Shikoku, and some minor islands; and at the Yalta Conference, February, 1945, where it was agreed that Russia would receive the Kurile Islands and Southern Sakhalin. Since there was no further elaboration on Japan's territorial limits, the ultimate legal disposition awaited a general Japanese peace treaty. Meanwhile, Japan's overseas territories were taken over by those victors who believed they had a right to them or who were determined to get possession of them anyhow. Korea ceased to be a part of the Japanese empire. Chinese *Kuomintang* forces occupied Formosa, the Pescadores, and part of Manchuria. United States forces remained in the Caroline, Marshall, and Mariana Islands, the Bonin Islands, and the Ryukyu Islands. Russia took *de facto* possession of Southern Sakhalin and the Kuriles.

[3] Basic documents and commentary on the Occupation to the end of 1947 are in Edwin M. Martin, *The Allied Occupation of Japan* (Stanford University, 1948). The period 1948-1950 is covered in Robert A. Fearey, *Occupation of Japan: Second Phase, 1948-1950* (New York, 1950). Two major official accounts are of interest: (1) *Summation of Non-Military Activities in Japan,* published by SCAP in 35 volumes; and (2) *Political Reorientation of Japan,* 2 volumes published by SCAP, 1949. Both cover the period to 1948.

DEMILITARIZATION OF THE JAPANESE HOMELAND

Demilitarization in the Japanese homeland involved the effort to destroy both the physical machinery of war and the intellectual or spiritual sources of war. It was easy to cope with the former. Those parts of the industrial machine that fed directly the military services were closed, naval bases were destroyed, and the army and navy were disbanded. There remained, however, the second objective, to destroy the authority and influence of those who had led Japan into world conquest.

The most spectacular phase of this effort in political fumigation was the Tokyo trial of twenty-five Japanese leaders in which the prosecution attempted to show that these men were personally responsible for Japan's misdeeds and were therefore guilty of crimes against humanity. The Tokyo trial was instituted pursuant to the Potsdam Declaration of July 20, 1945, and the Instrument of Surrender of September 2, 1945, and was conducted under the terms of the Charter of the International Military Tribunal for the Far East, approved by the Supreme Commander of the Allied Powers on January 19, 1946, with amendments of April 26. In the indictment, Japan's "major war criminals" were charged with: (1) crimes against peace, (2) murder, and (3) conventional war crimes and crimes against humanity. The specific purpose of the trials, as expressed by Joseph B. Keenan, Chief of Counsel, was to confirm the already recognized rule that such individuals of a nation who, either in official positions or otherwise, plan aggressive warfare, especially in contravention of sound treaties, assurances, and agreements of their nations, are common felons and deserve and will receive the punishment of ages meted out in every land to murderers, brigands, pirates, and plunderers.[4]

[4] Documents, including the opening statement of the prosecution, the Charter of the International Military Tribunal, and the indictment, are in *Trial of Japanese War Criminals* (Washington, D.C., 1946, Department of State Publications 2613, Far Eastern Series 12). See also, *Judgment of the International Military Tribunal for the Far East* (10 vols., Washington, 1948).

The case for the natural law school of international law as manifested in the trials in Germany and Japan is J. B. Keenan and Brendan Brown, *Crimes Against International Law* (Washington, 1950). The juridical basis of the Tokyo War Crimes Trial and of the corresponding earlier trial in Nurnberg was also given by Henry L. Stimson, "The Nuremberg Trial: Landmark in Law," *Foreign Affairs,* XXV (1947), 179-189.

For an able attack on the theory of the trials, see Nathan April, "An Inquiry into the Juridical Basis for the Nuremberg War Crimes Trial," *Minnesota Law Review,* XXX (1946), 313-331.

The decision the Military Tribunal handed down in December, 1948, condemned seven defendants to be hanged and consigned the remainder, with the exception of two, to life imprisonment. If the trial and the punishments were designed to convince the Japanese people that the real culprits had been brought to justice, it must be concluded that the effort failed. The Japanese public did not appear to be convinced that the magic of the judicial process had solved the question of war guilt.[5] With the trials there was also the dissolution of some 1300 Japanese chauvinistic societies and organizations, and the disbarment of nearly 200,000 persons from public office.

The effort to destroy Japan's war potential was carried into even broader fields than those already mentioned. The aircraft, synthetic oil, and synthetic rubber industries were liquidated. Atomic research was proscribed. Steel, chemical, and machine tool industries were limited. These measures, too, were related of course to the whole problem of reparations. Although plans were made for the removal of Japanese plants, there was little actual transfer of these materials, not only because the cost was prohibitive, but also because the Allies could not agree on who was to get how much. In addition, by 1949 American policy itself underwent a profound change from the concept of stripping Japan to one that contemplated building her up as an ally in Eastern Asia against the forces of Communism in Russia and China.

The New Political Structure

The political policy of the United States for post-war Japan involved some inherent contradictions. The policy was to foster "a peaceful and responsible government" and to see that this government conformed in general "to principles of democratic self-government," while at the same time it assured the Japanese that no form of government would be imposed on them that "was not supported by the freely expressed will of the people." How were these objectives to be brought about with a people who were not democratic, and by means that would not prostitute the essence of democracy itself?

---

[5] See Reischauer, *The United States and Japan*, 244-245. In the Philippines, in 1946, a number of Japanese military leaders were tried for alleged war crimes, were sentenced to death, and were executed. Among these were Generals Yamashita Tomoyuki and Homma Masaharu. Other trials were held in Shanghai. See the able and critical study by A. Frank Reel, *The Case of General Yamashita* (Chicago, 1949).

The demilitarization program was the first major, though negative, step toward a democratic political structure. By demilitarization it was hoped to liquidate both the leaders and many of the agencies of totalitarianism. As this ground-clearing proceeded, the Occupa-

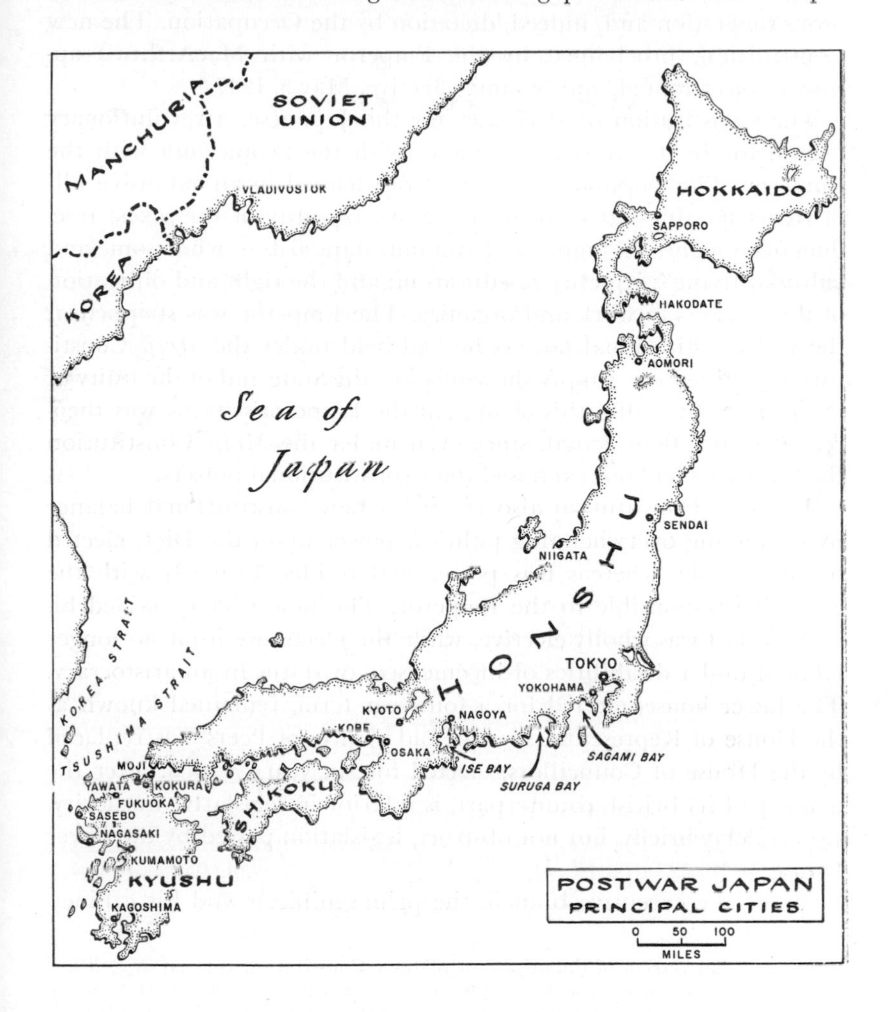

tion also undertook its positive program to remodel the old political and legal edifice which had been built since the early days of *Meiji*. The result was the complete revision of the *Meiji* Constitution, amounting really to the writing of a new constitution, though this was done by procedures well-established under the *Meiji* Constitution: namely, amendments initiated by Imperial Ordinance and later approved by the Diet. The task of revising the old constitution was undertaken at the bidding of SCAP late in 1945, but the results were meager, and a satisfactory draft constitution emerged only after vigorous suggestion and, indeed, dictation by the Occupation. The new Constitution, proclaimed by the Emperor with MacArthur's approval, was adopted, and became effective, May 3, 1947.[6]

The Constitution of 1947 was, for the Japanese, a revolutionary document. In it, sovereignty reposes with the people, not with the Emperor. This popular sovereignty was defined in an extensive bill of rights spelling out such principles as: equality of the sexes; freedom of thought; the right to "minimum standards of wholesome and cultured living"; equality of education; and the right and obligation of the workers to work and organize. The Emperor was stripped of the vast constitutional powers he had held under the *Meiji* Constitution, and became simply the symbol of the State and of the unity of the people. In reality this change in the Emperor's status was theoretical rather than actual, since even under the *Meiji* Constitution the Emperors had not exercised their constitutional powers.

The new Constitution also created a new constitutional balance by conferring overwhelming political power upon the Diet, elected by the people, whereas this power had resided formerly with the executive responsible to the Emperor. The new Diet remained bicameral but was wholly elective, while the electorate itself no longer labored under disabilities of income, sex, or status in an aristocracy. The lower house, elected for a four-year term, remained known as the House of Representatives; the old House of Peers was replaced by the House of Councillors, elected for six years, which, after the manner of its British counterpart, is inferior in legislative authority. It may delay briefly, but not obstruct, legislation passed by the lower House.

As for the executive branch, the prime minister and his cabinet,

---

[6] The official version of the origins of thc new Constitution is given in *Political Reorientation of Japan,* vol. I, 82-118; the various drafts are in vol. II, 625-655, 671-677. A useful analysis and a comparison is Harold S. Quigley, "Japan's Constitutions: 1890 and 1947," *American Political Science Review,* XLI (1947), 865-874. Observe Quigley's comment, regarding the emperor system, that "there is small likelihood that a Japanese Emperor will seek to govern. The opponent of democracy is not autocracy but bureaucracy." The problem of bureaucracy itself is treated by John M. Maki, "The Role of the Bureaucracy in Japan," *Pacific Affairs,* XX (1947), 391-406.

the new Constitution made it directly responsible to the Diet. The prime minister is selected by the Diet, and a majority of his cabinet must be Diet members. Thus the Diet through its control of the cabinet and the budget was given the constitutional power to direct the formerly all-powerful bureaucracy. The first step taken by the Diet in this direction was enactment of a new civil service code.[7]

While Diet and Executive suggested the British model, the new Japanese judiciary was patterned after American ideas. Recognition was given to the principle of an independent judiciary, beginning with a Supreme Court, that passes on all questions of constitutionality. The Court also nominates for judgeships in the lower courts, although the actual appointment of the judges is done by the Cabinet. Members of the Supreme Court are also appointed by the Cabinet, but such appointments are subject to review by the people at the next general election.

Local government, formerly a mere agent of the central power, was strengthened in the new Constitution by provision for the popular election of the chief local officials, the abolition of compulsory neighborhood associations, the elimination of the centrally controlled police, and the giving of larger powers to local legislative bodies.

Finally, in the Constitution of 1947, Japan renounced war and the right of belligerency forever. As the expression of a moral principle and human aspirations for a more decent world, this constitutional declaration was not without value. In a sense, however, it was reminiscent of the pious hopes embalmed in the Kellogg-Briand Treaty for the Renunciation of War, 1928. It also appeared paradoxical that militaristic Japan should be the first to ban war. Nevertheless, the renunciation appealed to many Japanese as further evidence of Japan's unique character and mission.

Practically all activities of the Occupation were undertaken with the object of bringing about in Japan a reformation by education. The wiser counsels of the Occupation recognized that no paper reforms such as new constitutions, codes, etc., could possibly outlive the Occupation itself unless the Japanese people themselves acquired a sense of democratic values and some experience with democratic ways. Therefore, Japan would be taught the values of democracy.

---

[7] On the broad subject of Japanese law, see Thomas L. Blakemore, "Postwar Developments in Japanese Law," *Wisconsin Law Review* (July, 1947), 632-653.

The method seemed well-fitted to the Japanese, a literate nation of tireless readers. Moreover, the moment also seemed opportune because the Japanese, stunned by defeat, appeared to retain little confidence in their own traditional ways. Intellectually, they sought feverishly for new horizons, much as they had done toward the end of the nineteenth century.[8]

In the first years of the Occupation, therefore, the broad educational reform program enjoyed a wide popularity and a measure of success. To the vast majority of the Japanese, democracy (however vague their concept of it might be) appeared as a happy substitute for their own way of life which had led them to war, and disaster. At the same time, the business of teaching democracy, always a difficult affair, became even more so by reason of acts of the Occupation itself. Reminiscent of the days of Japan's warlords was the rigid censorship applied on imported printed matter lest "dangerous thoughts" enter Japan. Criticism of the Occupation and of Allied countries was banned. American Occupation personnel, civilian and military, were themselves subject in word and deed to military controls. They were the agents of a policy, and, of course, it is doubtful whether any policy can be promoted in an occupied country if that policy is not followed at all levels. In occupied Japan the censorship was aimed quite specifically at communist propaganda. Nevertheless, Occupation personnel, not being free themselves to voice independent judgments, were handicapped from the start in attempting to behave as democrats. In a word, the Occupation found it difficult to pose as a model of democracy in action.

Specific educational reforms effected by the Occupation were aimed at creating a more intelligent and critical public mind and at training the younger generations for responsible citizenship. The period of compulsory education was extended from six to nine years. Beyond this elementary level, the old Japanese system was replaced by creating a three-year compulsory junior high school, a three-year senior high school, and a four-year college course. The effort was made to equalize the quality of education at all levels, but the program suffered from lack of democratically trained teachers, and from the serious question of how a penurious Japan was to pay for this major expansion in schools and curriculum. In the curriculum itself, the traditional emphasis on ethics (a synonym for supernationalism)

---

[8] The basic treatment on educational reform is Robert King Hall, *Education for a New Japan* (New Haven, 1949).

gave way to concern for social studies. Efforts were also made to re-write the textbooks, to introduce modern methods of instruction, and to break the stifling centralized control of the old Ministry of Education.

The New Social Pattern

Having set out to remodel Japan's government and its schools, the Occupation, partly by desire, partly by compulsion, found it necessary to go further into the tangled areas of what may be called social reform. A first step was to strike at the traditional form and behavior of the Japanese family. Equality, a strange principle to Oriental ears, was applied to the sexes by the new Constitution. Japanese women acquired equal legal rights with men in politics and education. Furthermore, this principle of equality, and the new educational program in general, tended to weaken the control formerly exercised by family heads over the youth and even over other adult members of the family. Tendencies toward individualism which had appeared in Japan long before World War II were encouraged by the Occupation. This shifting from the family to the individual as the basic unit of society was among the most vital effects of the Western impact on the Far East.[9]

Dissolution of the Combines

The Occupation went far beyond the status of family and of women. It attempted to strike at the high concentration of wealth held by a few families—the *Zaibatsu*—to break up these combines and to encourage a wide distribution of income and the ownership of the means of production. *Zaibatsu* leaders were barred from business and politics; the great central holding companies were dissolved; assets were taken over by the government for later sale; and capital levies, heavy income taxes, and inflation all but wiped out the great family fortunes. The attack was then directed against the larger corporations capable of exercising monopoly power in restraint of trade. This latter program, however, was abandoned in 1949, for a variety of reasons: Japan's failure to achieve economic recovery, and the appearance of communist control in China.

---

[9] Kazuya Matsumiya, "Family Organization in Present Day Japan," *American Journal of Sociology,* LIII (1947), 105-110.

The Right of Collective Bargaining

On the opposite side of the industrial picture, the Occupation paved the way for Japan's first free development of a labor movement in terms of labor unions, whose membership by 1950 had mushroomed to some seven million. Japanese labor, which lacked tested organization, experience, and leadership, found itself suddenly possessed of a new freedom and power just at the moment when the nation itself was prostrate from defeat and economic collapse. There were efforts by some unions through strikes to take over policy control of an industry. High-pressure methods, rather than the slower electoral process, were exerted on government. Labor disputes diminished the already disastrously low national industrial output. Sabotage under communist instigation became the policy of some unions. This kind of behavior was not tolerated by the Occupation. Occupation authorities, concerned by labor's growing pains, tended to join forces with Japan's conservatives who had shown little sympathy with a responsible role for labor in either industry or politics.[10]

Land for the Peasant

Among the most striking of all Occupation reforms was the redistribution of agricultural land. Essentially this reform entailed: (1) enforced sale to the government of all land held by absentee landlords; (2) resale of these lands to former tenants who had cultivated them; (3) permission for farmer-landlords to retain the land cultivated by their families and in addition some 2½ acres of tenant-cultivated land. The program of purchase and resale was effected at pre-war values, making it a possible transaction for the tenants but virtual confiscation for the former owners. The extent of this reform was suggested by the fact that by 1952 more than five million acres of land had been purchased from landlords and sold to working farmers. This meant that about 90 per cent of all cultivated land had been acquired by those who worked it, as compared with less than 50 per cent in 1945. Moreover, legislation reduced land rents by about 50 per cent, and provided further protection by means of rent ceilings. Although this land reform implied social consequences of

---

[10] Miriam S. Farley, *Aspects of Japan's Labor Problems* (New York, 1950), and "Labor Policy in Occupied Japan," *Pacific Affairs,* XX (1947), 131-140.

the utmost importance, it was in no sense a magic formula. Japan's basic agricultural problem—how to feed too many people from too little land—was still unsolved.

Credits versus Debits of the Occupation

In evaluating the Occupation of Japan a multitude of complex factors have perplexed the historian. Democratization of an alien civilization by military occupation was a unique experiment for Americans as well as the Japanese. Moreover, democratization in the case of Japan was undertaken by the victor toward the vanquished in the immediate wake of a prolonged and bloody war during which the opposing sides had been indoctrinated with mutual hatred. Thus, by the very nature of these circumstances, democratization was applied by fiat, sometimes direct, sometimes implied.

Recognizing these serious limitations in any occupation looking to democratic political, economic, and social reform, and recognizing that the case of Japan is much too close for historical judgments to be definitive, it can nevertheless be noted in the short view that the Occupation: (1) gave the Japanese a dynamic, if brief, schooling in American concepts of government, politics, economic structure, and social organization; (2) demonstrated, for all its shortcomings, a profound American faith in the efficacy of the democratic process and a general sense of integrity in the personnel who were agents of American policy; and (3) stirred in the Japanese mind a vigorous interest in the American way, and searching inquiry on its application to things and affairs Japanese.

Politics During the Occupation

The effect of the Occupation in action upon Japanese government and politics was profound from the beginning. In October, 1945, when the Occupation directed implementation of a "Bill of Rights" guaranteeing basic human freedoms, the release of political prisoners, and curbing the Ministry of Home Affairs and its powerful centralized police, the surrender cabinet of Prime Minister Higashikuni resigned on the ground it could not maintain order. The new premier was Shidehara Kijuro, heading a conservative ministry amenable in most things to Occupation bidding. Nevertheless, it was this ministry that failed to produce a new draft constitution acceptable to the Occupation, a failure that resulted in the "MacArthur Constitution."[11]

At the same time the Occupation directed that a general election be held in April, 1946. New election laws were passed by the Diet extending the franchise to women and lowering the voting age to 20 years. To create an atmosphere free from terroristic pressures, the old extremist societies were abolished while ultranationalist leaders were purged and excluded from running for public office. New political parties had also appeared as a result of the "Bill of Rights" directive. Communists were released from prison or returned from foreign exile and for the first time were permitted to organize a party legally. Nozaka Sanzo returned from abroad to head the new party and to become one of the ablest of the post-war political manipulators.[12] The Social Democrats, refusing a united front with the Communists, formed their own party, which drew its strength from the intellectuals and the labor movement. More conservative elements were grouped in the Liberal and the Progressive parties, the former led by Ashida Hitoshi and Yoshida Shigeru, the latter by Shidehara. Most members had belonged to the old *Seiyukai* or *Minseito*.

The April, 1946, elections gave the Liberals the strongest representation, and Yoshida replaced Shidehara as premier in May. It was during this administration that the new constitution was accepted, to become effective, May 3, 1947. Meanwhile Yoshida's popularity had declined under attack by the Social Democrats and by the insistence of the Occupation on carrying the purge of undesirable persons into the areas of local politics. Yoshida also had to face the political results of economic collapse. Labor in the big cities demanded minimum wage legislation, demonstrated 150,000 strong before the Imperial Palace, and called a general strike for February, 1947. It was prevented by the Occupation, which called for a new election in April, 1947. The result gave the Social Democrats, not a majority, but the largest bloc of seats, 143, in the House of Representatives. They had profited by the purge, by their refusal to support the Communist plan for a general strife, and by their demands for control of industry pending nationalization. The new cabinet formed by Katayama Tetsu, President of the Social Democrats, depended on the uncertain support of two conservative parties, The Democrats and

---

[11] Hugh Borton, *Japan's Modern Century* (New York, 1955), 401-403, 423-424.

[12] On Communists in Japan, see Rodger Swearingen and Paul Langer, *Red Flag in Japan . . . 1919-1951* (Cambridge, 1952).

the Co-operatives. Katayama himself was a true political democrat and a Christian, but he was limited by the frail coalition that supported his cabinet. His government lasted until February, 1948, by which time a wider separation had developed between the right and left wings of Japanese political thought and organization.

Katayama was followed, February 1948, by Ashida Hitoshi as premier in a conservative Democratic party cabinet. In October, Yoshida was again back in power with a Liberal party government, which he was to lead for the next six years. The period was marked by increasing centralized control and the undoing of many of the Occupation reforms. The march of Communism in Asia was reflected in Japan in a rebirth of conservatism and a reappraisal of Occupation policies. Yoshida's Liberal party won an easy majority in the general election of January, 1949. In mid-1949 MacArthur indicated that the close control of Japanese domestic affairs by the Occupation was no longer necessary. By 1950, too, there was a marked falling off of Communist strength.

Economic Rebuilding, 1948-1950

From the beginning of 1948 the Japanese government and the Occupation gave less attention to reform and more attention to the historic economic problem of increasing the export of manufactures to pay for imports needed for a population that had increased by nearly 8 millions, 1945-1948. American aid had not met the problem and in any case was a temporary measure. There could be no political stability in a land where prices were completely out of control and bore no recognizable relationship to wages. Belatedly the Occupation moved in 1948 to meet this crisis through an all-inclusive program of stabilization to balance the budget, limit credit, renovate the tax structure, and deal with tax evasion. At the same time the United States took the lead toward an eventual dropping of demands for further reparations from Japan. By 1950 there was marked improvement in Japan's economic and financial status, but the improvement was more apparent than real. Japan's improved industrial production and export trade were not unrelated to American aid, a matter of 1¾ billion in goods, 1945-1950. Finally, the Korean war of June, 1950, brought temporary relief to the Japanese economy.

The Japanese Peace Treaty

The outbreak of war in Korea emphasized the need, as the United States saw it, of ending the Occupation by concluding a peace treaty with Japan and thereby bringing her into the company of the Free World and against the Communist powers. Earlier efforts toward a treaty had broken down in 1948. On American initiative, conversations among the former allies were resumed in September, 1950, which were to result a year later in the San Francisco peace conference and a treaty of peace with Japan. By July, 1951, there was sufficient agreement for the United States and the United Kingdom to issue a joint invitation to the fifty-five powers at war with Japan to a peace conference at San Francisco, September 4, 1951. Suggested revisions of the draft treaty inclosed with the invitations were to be submitted promptly so that the final text might be circulated by August 13. The treaty would thus be completed before the conference assembled.

The Treaty of Peace with Japan

Accordingly, at San Francisco, September 8, 1951, a peace treaty was signed by Japan and forty-eight nations at war with her. Japan agreed to seek membership in the United Nations and to respect the civil rights of her own new constitution, to accept the territorial clauses of the Potsdam Declaration, to recognize the independence of Korea, to forgo her claims to Formosa, the Pescadores, the Kuriles and Karafuto (southern Sakhalin), and to agree to a United Nation trusteeship in the Ryukyu and Bonin Islands. The treaty recognized Japan's right of self-defense. Within three months after the treaty was in force, occupation armies would leave, though limited foreign forces might continue to be stationed there under special agreements.[13] The Occupation came to an end April 28, 1952, the day the treaty became effective. The Soviet powers had refused to sign the treaty.

Also on September 8, 1951, Japan and the United States concluded a security agreement permitting American forces to remain in Japan for an indefinite period, which meant that the United States was assuming responsibility for Japan's defense for an indefinite future.

---

[13] Such an agreement was concluded by the United States and Japan, September 8, 1951, as a result of which American forces remained in Japan. Occupation troops became security troops.

The peace treaty with Japan was a necessary step toward ending the war, but it was not a solution of Japanese problems. Rather, it was merely the formal beginning of Japan's efforts as a sovereign state to chart her course at home and abroad in the post-war world. In so far as the reforms of the Occupation, including the Constitution of 1947, could be taken at face value, Japan was a democracy, but she had had as yet no free experience in making democracy work, her peoples were not of one mind as to what democracy meant, she did not have a stable and prosperous economy that could afford policies of drift, and in world affairs she was on the explosive Asiatic frontier between Communism and the free world. From 1952 onward, therefore, Japan's political, economic, and social history was a reflection of her efforts to find a new life in the ominous turmoil of these pressures.

Until December, 1954, Japanese politics remained under the control of Premier Yoshida and his so-called Liberal party. The party won major elections in 1952 and 1953 and as a result of labor and Communist inspired demonstrations and riots in May, 1952, enacted an anti-subversive activity law in July so loosely worded as to be a threat to some basic reforms of the Occupation if administered by an arbitrary government. Yoshida also sought re-establishment of centralized control of the police. Meanwhile his policy on the rearmament of Japan was under heavy attack. The Constitution of 1947, on MacArthur's insistence, had outlawed war and precluded the maintenance of land, sea, and air forces. Then came the shift in American policy toward the rebuilding of an industrial Japan and the need for Japanese industry in the Korean war of 1950. When American soldiers were transferred from Japan to Korean battlefields, the first step was taken in Japanese rearmament by creating a police reserve of 75,000 men. Japan was encouraged by the United States to create an internal security force. However, these simple steps were not an adequate measure of general Japanese reactions to the rearmament question. The Occupation had only recently disarmed Japan physically. The new constitution with its renunciation of war had disarmed the Japanese people in spirit. Many of them were ready to assume that war and the burdens of war had been cast aside and should not be reassumed lightly. A spirit of neutralism was being born. Parliament debated hotly the question of revision of the constitution. Yoshida took the astute political position that there was no real issue since the police reserve, renamed a National Security

Force, and later the National Defense Force, was entirely defensive. At the same time, to protect Japan from possible attack by Russia, he continued to seek protective arrangements with the United States. In this latter respect he met determined opposition from Communists, left wing Socialists, and many intellectuals, including students and Christians who were opposed to rearmament and to rigid alliance with the United States. This opposition, while including the Communists, was not simply a blind following of the Communist line. In Japan's plight, the attitude was a basic objection to being *used* by the United States as its instrument against Communist China. Japanese resentment mounted as official American policy continued to urge Japanese rearmament. The result was an American-Japanese Mutual Defense Assistance Agreement, March, 1954. It provided for United States military assistance to Japan, for the exchange of information on defense, for restrictions on trade with Red China, and for Japanese contributions to her own defense structure.

These politico-military problems and manoeuvres were not a basic solution of the economic problem, which in its simplest terms was how to increase exports to pay for imports. The Korean war had given only temporary relief. In 1955 Japan was importing increasing amounts of food to feed a population of about 88 millions living in an area smaller than the state of California. For this problem Yoshida and his Liberal party had found no solution. When he finally succeeded in passing laws creating a national police and implementing Japan's obligations under the Mutual Defense Agreement to the accompaniment of riots in the House of Representatives, the opposition finally triumphed. He was succeeded as premier by Hatoyama Ichiro, who had previously been President of the Liberal Party and who promised a broader policy of closer relations with China and Russia as well as with the United States.[14]

For Further Reading

GENERAL ACCOUNTS

Ball, W. MacMahon, *Nationalism and Communism in East Asia* (New York, 1952). A critical evaluation of the way Western nations have been trying to meet the Asian revolution.

---

[14] For a detailed survey of Japan since World War II, see Hugh Borton, *Japan's Modern Century* (New York, 1955), 399-467.

———, *Japan: Enemy or Ally* (rev. ed., New York, 1949). Critical of American occupation policy.

Bisson, T. A., *Prospects for Democracy in Japan* (New York, 1949). Questions the success of the American occupation policies.

Clifton, Allen S., *Time of Fallen Blossoms* (New York, 1951). A description of the simple dignity of the country people of Japan in the early post-war years.

Dangerfield, Royden J., *The New Japan* (New York, 1953).

Gibney, Frank, *Five Gentlemen of Japan. The Portrait of a Nation's Character* (New York, 1953). An attempt to portray the nation's character through the Emperor, a farmer, an admiral, a newspaperman, and a steel worker.

Reischauer, Edwin, and others, *Japan and America Today* (Stanford, 1953). By both American and Japanese contributors.

Schwantes, Robert S., *Japanese and Americans: A Century of Cultural Relations* (New York, 1955). Deserves careful reading.

Wildes, Harry Emerson, *Typhoon in Tokyo, The Occupation and Its Aftermath* (New York, 1954). An entertaining and informative account marred by questionable interpretations.

Yanaga Chitoshi, *Japanese People and Politics* (New York, 1956). Emphasis is on the forces of politics rather than the structure of government.

GOVERNMENT, POLITICS, AND PARTIES

Colbert, Evelyn S., *The Left Wing in Japanese Politics* (New York, 1952). The role of the Socialist and Communist parties, principally in post-war Japan.

Coughlin, William J., *Conquered Press: The MacArthur Era in Japanese Journalism* (Palo Alto, 1952). The nature of the press in Japan after the tight wartime controls were lifted.

Quigley, Harold S., and John E. Turner, *The New Japan—Government and Politics* (Minneapolis, 1956).

ECONOMIC STRUCTURE

Ackerman, Edward A., *Japan's Natural Resources and their Relation to Japan's Economic Future* (Chicago, 1953). An effort to explain Japan's problems of supporting her expanding population on her meager resources.

Bisson, T. A., *Zaibatsu Dissolution in Japan* (Berkeley, 1954). Studies the American occupation policy of dissolving the *Zaibatsu,* its results and its implications for future American policy.

Cohen, Jerome B., *Economic Problems of Free Japan* (Princeton, 1952). A statistical analysis of Japan's post-war economic problems.

Fine, Sherwood M., *Japan's Postwar Industrial Recovery* (Tokyo, 1953).

EDUCATION, PHILOSOPHY AND RELIGION

Baker, Richard T., *Darkness of the Sun: The Story of Christianity in the Japanese Empire* (Nashville, 1947). A post-war survey of the religious situation in Japan, with an estimate of the difficulties of the Christian church before and during the war.

Stoetzel, Jean, *Without the Chrysanthemum and the Sword: A Study of the Attitudes of Youth in Postwar Japan* (New York, 1955).

Vining, Elizabeth Gray, *Windows for the Crown Prince* (Philadelphia, 1952). A valuable record by the American woman employed as a tutor for the Crown Prince after the war.

Yanaihara Tadao, *Religion and Democracy in Modern Japan* (New York, 1948). By a Japanese Christian and liberal scholar.

37

1945 and after

From *Kuomintang* into Communist China

THE year 1949 had a uniqueness without parallel in the history of Chinese civilization. When the Chinese Communist armies drove the *Kuomintang* Nationalists from continental China they were merely repeating in one sense what had happened many times in China's long past—the destruction of a government that had apparently failed and the substitution of another professing to have the Mandate of Heaven. It suggested the old cyclical theory of Chinese history by which dynasties rose in virtue and fell in decay. According to that historic theory, there was never a new play, simply a new set of actors. It was a convenient rationalization of how dynasties had come and gone. After 1911, however, this theory was no longer quite so satisfying. The Republican revolution of that year did propose a new play as well as new actors. What it sought was a composite vehicle resting on foundations that were both new and old, on values that were new and Western mingled with others that were old and Chinese. The successes and the failures of the Republican era, 1912-1949, were a reflection of how the *Kuomintang* met or failed to meet this theory of what the new China should be. Then in 1949 a power professing a vastly different theory seized the Mandate of Heaven. The communist conquest rested on assumptions of total revolution uninhibited, for the moment at least, by the traditions or values of China's great history. Here lay the uniqueness of 1949.

The story of what has happened in China since 1945 is an aspect of contemporary history, and therefore its telling will not be free of imperfections. Yet even allowing for these imperfections, the broad outlines of this story are no longer in serious question. In the United States, this clarification should be of supreme importance, because in 1949 to the overwhelming majority of Americans the communist conquest of China was simply unbelievable. It would be difficult to exaggerate the historical implications of the conquest or of American incredulity.[1]

The reader has already been introduced in previous chapters to much of the background of the expanding revolution that engulfed China between 1923 and 1949, such as, for example, the credits and debits of the early Republican and Nationalist revolutions, the opposition, external and internal, that opposed the National government, the conflict between Japanese expansion and Chinese nationalism, the devastations of a war that for China lasted from 1937 to 1945. Here it will be of advantage to add some details by way of further background on the history of the Chinese Communist Party prior to 1945, on the doctrines and practices which enabled it with the assistance of its most implacable enemies to do what so many had regarded as impossible.[2]

The Chinese Communist Party: Beginnings

The origins of a communist movement in China go back to 1918 to a nucleus of Marxist study groups among intellectuals at Peking University at the end of World War I. Three years later, 1921, the Chinese Communist Party was organized at Shanghai. Twelve delegates attended this first National Congress. From the outset the CCP was affiliated with the Communist International (the Comintern) and was under the influence of the Russian Communist Party during the two decades that separated the First from the Second World War. In the beginning the CCP displayed a notable flexibility in tactics. Recognizing the power of Chinese nationalist sentiment in the early 1920's, the Party encouraged its members to join the *Kuomintang* as individuals. The subsequent Sun-Joffe understanding, 1923, opened wide the door for Communist infiltration of Sun Yat-sen's Nationalist Party and for the reorganization and sovietizing of that Party. This arrangement came to an end in 1927 when the

[1] See H. Arthur Steiner, "The United States and China: the Prospect before Us," *The Yale Review*, XLIV (December, 1954), 161-179.

[2] For detailed accounts of the communist period, see Harold M. Vinacke, *Far Eastern Politics in the Postwar Period* (New York, 1956), 115-152.

Communists were expelled from the *Kuomintang* as a result of their effort to control the Hankow government and through it the *Kuomintang* itself. They had hoped to capitalize on the gulf between the conservative and the radical wings of the *Kuomintang* and thereby to direct the revolution toward extreme economic and social purposes. The immediate effect of the Hankow purge was the liquidation of many Communists and the strengthening but by no means the full consolidation of the position of Chiang K'ai-shek. Badly shaken by the 1927 break, the CCP for a number of years barely managed to exist. Its official policy, guided by the Comintern, continued to rest on the idea of an urban, proletarian revolution set forth by Li Li-san, the leader of the Chinese Communist Party at that time. Eventually this policy had to be abandoned, since it was clear after 1927 that the Communists could neither take nor hold urban positions of strength.[3]

In contrast to those Chinese Communists who insisted on following the direction of the Comintern and the Li Li-san line were those who, like Mao Tse-tung, had been in closer association with the Chinese peasantry during the early years and who, after the 1927 purge, worked to set up Soviet governments among the non-urban peasantry of Kiangsi province. In time the heresy on which Mao acted separated the CCP from its urban base and established the theory that a Communist Party might function on a base of peasant and army support. It was this shift in the theory and framework of CCP operations which made it possible for the Party to emphasize a program of agrarian reform.

The shift in Communist operations from an urban to a peasant base involved an element of genius, whether conscious or unconscious. To understand how this was so it should be recalled that when the Ch'ing empire fell in 1911-1912, the stabilizing influence

---

[3] In following the history of the Chinese Communist Party the reader will find it helpful to bear in mind four fundamental theses of Marxian doctrine. Stated briefly, these are: (1) Marxism is primarily a revolutionary doctrine; (2) its objective to effect revolutionary change in the structure of society from the so-called bourgeois to the so-called proletarian pattern can be attained only through the forcible destruction of existing governments as a prelude to seizing power; (3) the Communist revolution cannot be regarded as complete or secure until the revolution has been carried out in all countries; (4) that while the Communist revolution is to be regarded as the *inevitable* result of capitalism in its final imperialistic form, nevertheless, this inevitable result can and should be hastened by human effort, that is, by the efforts of Communist parties and States. Whatever Communists might be saying at a given moment, these theses remain as fundamental doctrine.

of the scholar-gentry class came to an end. The enormous influence which this class had exercised over the common people, whether in the performance of legal and political functions left to the gentry by the officials or in the exercise of social responsibilities to the community, was destroyed. What remained was the economic power of the landlords now no longer tempered by the social restraints which the gentry could exercise. The result was calamitous. During the Republican era after 1912, farm tenancy increased, landlords acquired greater power, and local taxation became more oppressive on the peasantry. Although these conditions were not equally true in all parts of the country, it can be said that the "livelihood" of the peasantry, the third of Sun Yat-sen's Three Principles, became "the most obvious and pressing internal problem."[4] It was a problem with which the *Kuomintang* and the National Government failed to deal effectively. Mao and his associates saw in the peasant problem a means of winning popular mass support through the simple process of expropriating the land of the landlord in the interest of a landless or nearly landless peasantry. Later, when the Communists moved by the long march to the Northwest, the policy of expropriation was modified, in line with the United Front policy, to one of reform of interest rates, rents, and taxes. These things the Communists could do without alienating anyone in the countryside save the landlords and the rich peasants who were already opposed to them. Then, too, the broad peasant base thus created made it possible for the CCP to present its gospel as a national and unifying force in contrast to a class struggle, while its demands for the United Front against Japan, made in 1936, appealed to the new national patriotism. In addition, the Communists after the shift to the Northwest Border Region were much less concerned with the organization of a centralized soviet government. They operated instead through local governments in which non-party personnel was permitted and encouraged to participate. Although this practice did not deprive the Communists of control, it gave them a telling advantage in popular support. Up to 1945 the *Kuomintang* had failed to develop popular participation in government at the local and provincial level. The Communists in contrast were able to assert that theirs was the Party with truly democratic objectives, however fictitious these claims may have been.

---

[4] Harold M. Vinacke, *Far Eastern Politics in the Postwar Period* (New York, 1956), 121.

The Approach of Mao Tse-tung

Mao Tse-tung, who by 1935 had become the ablest exponent of Communist strategy and tactics in China, was born in Hunan province in 1893 in a prosperous peasant family. As a student at Peking University at the end of World War I he was a close observer of the intellectual agitations of the time; he became a student of Marxism and one of the first members of the CCP. After organizing peasant associations in Hunan in 1926, Mao saw and described the indispensable role he believed the peasant would play in the revolution. At this particular time the CCP was condemning the violence of the peasants in order not to alienate the left wing of the *Kuomintang*. But with the purge at Hankow in 1927, Mao was sent again to Hunan to incite peasant disorder. The failure of the peasants to rise resulted in Mao's dismissal from the Party Politburo. Under this reverse, Mao with a band of armed peasants and deserters from *Kuomintang* armies retired to the Chingkan mountains that divide Hunan and Kiangsi. In the following year, as his control of rural areas was extended, Mao was joined by Chu Têh, who had studied at Yunnan Military Institute and later at Berlin. This was the beginning of a personal partnership in which Mao was the political leader and Chu Têh the military leader. Even in these early years rivals for political power were liquidated by the Mao-Chu Têh alliance.

Communist Military Tactics

The military tactics which the Communists were later to use so effectively against Japan were first employed at this early rural and military base in Kiangsi. When Nationalist armies moved in columns against this countryside they were met not with frontal attacks but with guerrilla warfare. With the aid of a peasantry organized for intelligence, the Communists could strike where the Nationalists were weak, cut lines of communication, and retreat before the enemy could recover and strike back. What forced the Communists in 1934 into the long march from Kiangsi to the Northwest Border was not the striking power of Nationalist armies but the effectiveness of a blockade by which the Nationalists surrounded the entire Communist area, cutting it off from indispensable supplies such as salt. The long march itself, 6,000 miles through western China to northwestern Shensi, was an epic in Chinese Communist history, though its immediate cost was devastating. Of more than ninety thousand who undertook the march only some twenty thousand men reached Shensi and the new headquarters at Yenan. What the Communists had lost in strength the National Government appeared to have gained with the added prospect that these Communist remnants could soon be driven into Outer Mongolia and thus eliminated as a practical military and political problem. At this point it was a change in Comintern strategy to the tactic of the United Front that had much to do with saving the Chinese Communists. This change, occurring in 1935, brought Russia into the League of Nations seeking protection against Nazi Germany, and enabled the weakened Chinese Communists to shift from a policy of civil war against the National Government to advocacy of a Chinese United Front against the Japanese invader. This policy was to pay untold dividends, since it enabled the Communists to appeal to the nation, to pose in the role of national patriots, and thus to capitalize on the emotional and intellectual potential of China's revolution, which was crying for vigorous leadership. The United Front line had an enormous appeal to Chinese in general, for in 1935 Japanese armies from their Manchurian base were invading Inner Mongolia. The fact that Chiang K'ai-shek and the National Government did not accept these Communist proposals for a United Front until after the crisis of the Sian incident weakened further the prestige of the Nationalists and strengthened that of the Communists, since the National Government had been compelled by a combination of provincial troops (Chang Hsueh-liang's Manchurian army) and Communists to alter its policy from one of civil war to one of a United Front.

Communist Advantages in War, 1937-1945

In its basic purpose, which was to seize power from the *Kuomintang* Nationalist Government, the Chinese Communist Party enjoyed advantages derived directly from the Japanese invasion of 1937 and from previous *Kuomintang* failures in political strategy. The depth of Japan's military invasion of eastern and coastal China with the resulting retreat of the National Government to far western Chungking meant that effective Chinese resistance would rest in a major degree on the organized co-operation of the rural, peasant population. The Communists already had a large measure of practical experience in working with the peasantry. The National Government, in contrast, had received its principal financial backing from the coast cities and treaty ports. Deprived by the Japanese invasion of this support and of the revenue of the Maritime Customs, the government was thrown back on the salt and land taxes. Fearful of offending the landowners, on whom it was now financially dependent, the government was inhibited from grappling with the problem of land reform despite the fact, previously noted, that the livelihood of the peasantry was "the most obvious and pressing internal problem." In other words, the failure of the *Kuomintang* and the National Government before 1937 to devise new rural institutions that would have given the government a peasant as well as an urban base became ominous and eventually fatal to *Kuomintang* power on the continent. The irony in the situation was that the Communist land reform program under the United Front was lifted from an early *Kuomintang* blueprint for land reform which the *Kuomintang* had failed to carry out. As a result, the Communists won the allegiance of the rural population in the areas they controlled and in the sectors where they conducted guerrilla warfare. After the United Front failed, Nationalist-Communist relations, 1939-1945, became nothing more than an uneasy truce, while the position of the National Government grew weaker and that of the Communists stronger.

The New Democracy of Mao Tse-tung

Meanwhile Mao Tse-tung at Yenan was interpreting Stalinist doctrine for application in China. *On the New Democracy,* which appeared in 1940, confirmed Mao as the authority on Russian Communist doctrine for China and made him master of the Chinese Communist Party. As theory, *On the New Democracy* gave the Communists justification for their claim to leadership in the Chinese revolution. In Mao's reasoning, although China was classed in Communist theory as a feudal society, the capitalist and the socialist stages of the revolution could be fused. Thus there would be a joint dictatorship in China of revolutionary classes (proletariat, peasantry, intelligentsia, and petty bourgeoisie) who would accept the leadership of the Communist Party. Mao maintained that his program was a reinterpretation of Sun Yat-sen's Three Principles of the People. In this manner many Chinese, including some *Kuomintang* members, were convinced that co-operation with the Communists was not merely expedient but fundamentally sound. Mao gradually emerged therefore as master of doctrine and as dictator of the Party, a dictatorship that was solidified by purging those who deviated and by rigorous indoctrination of new converts, who expanded the Party membership from some 40,000 in 1937 to perhaps 1,200,000 in 1945. Therefore, when World War II terminated with Japan's surrender there was in China a powerful Communist Party composed of highly trained revolutionists who were thoroughly disciplined under Mao's dictatorship, which had an army of more than half a million men, and which claimed mastery of an area populated by nearly 100 million people.

Conflict Within China, 1945-1949

At the time of the Japanese surrender, Chiang K'ai-shek as Allied Commander-in-Chief in the China theater and as head of the National (and recognized) Government was to receive the Japanese surrender in China and in northern Indochina. Three major tasks confronted the Nationalists: (1) to take over the occupied territory from the Japanese armies and restore the administration of the National Government in these areas; (2) to reach a settlement of the Communist problem; and (3) to revive China's war-torn economy.

For the task of accepting the Japanese surrender, Nationalist forces could hardly have been in a less advantageous position. These forces had been driven by the Japanese invasion into southwestern China. Nevertheless, with substantial American air transport and other assistance, Nationalist armies were flown to the east and northeast, where they took over the cities and lines of communication the Japanese had held. But this did not solve the problem for the Nationalists. Prior to the end of the war, the Communists had carried their guerrilla warfare into areas occupied by the Japanese in northeastern China. They not only harried the Japanese but won the support of the villages and the peasantry by implementing their program of agrarian reform and organizing the villages both for local government and for resistance to the Japanese. In this way the Communists in the areas they controlled became the champions of the peasantry against the local gentry, who had often collaborated with the Japanese, and the national and patriotic leaders against the Japanese foreign invader. Thus it was that the Communists had extended their control far beyond the Northwest Border Region eastward to the North China coast. When the Nationalists took over the cities of northeast China, the villages and countryside were unwilling to accept Nationalist authority unless the reformed local governments instituted by the Communists were also accepted. As a consequence the National Government found itself opposed in the countryside by both the Communists and the peasantry.

The National Government and Economics

The return of the National Government to Nanking and its re-occupation of the coast cities took place amid scenes of general re-joicing over the long-awaited victory. The reputation of Chiang K'ai-shek, which had suffered in the later war years, seemed to be re-established. To be sure, although the war had brought indescrib-able suffering to millions of Chinese and had disrupted the nation's economy, the productive potential of agriculture and industry were by no means hopeless. The major economic problem was less one of reconstruction of productive equipment than of organization of production and distribution through facilities already available. This is not to suggest that the tasks were small but rather that the real and potential assets could provide a solution if used effectively. Although the currency was wildly inflated, the revenue of the rich eastern areas was again available to the government, and here the level of production in most areas was as high as before the war. Dur-ing the war the Japanese had organized and encouraged production in the occupied areas and, when fighting ceased, foreign financial and technical assistance was available. To meet pressing needs for immediate relief the United Nations Relief and Rehabilitation Ad ministration (UNRRA) supplied food and repaired power lines and lines of communication to an amount of some $650,000,000, of which the United States contributed $474,000,000. But these reasonably bright prospects for recovery were not translated into reality. The failure was due to the growing power and opposition of the Com-munists and to the shortcomings of the National Government and the party that controlled it, the *Kuomintang*.

In terms of broad strategy the National Government wanted natu-rally to control North China and Manchuria, the latter being the most highly industrialized area of all China. Government objectives in these respects were dictated by considerations of economics and political prestige. The difficulty was that Communist control of the countryside in North China cut directly across Nationalist lines of communication between the lower Yangtze, which they controlled, and Manchuria, which they hoped to control. If the Nationalists moved into Manchuria they would at the same time endanger their lines of communication unless the Communists could be driven from North China. Faced with this perilous choice the Nationalists decided to occupy Manchuria against the counsel of both Generals George C. Marshall and Albert C. Wedemeyer. The decision was a fateful one for the National Government and the *Kuomintang.*

Efforts At Political Settlement

These military developments in the stage setting of Nationalist-Communist conflict had not precluded efforts toward a peaceful political settlement. Chiang K'ai-shek had given repeated assurance that the settlement would be "by political means," and negotiations to this end had been undertaken, it will be recalled, in 1944 at a time when the United States was concerned that the Chinese civil conflict would destroy China's war effort. At that time there was a clear distinction between the solutions acceptable to the Nationalists on the one hand and the Communists on the other. The Communists wanted a coalition government of all major political parties, and they professed willingness to place their military forces under the control of a coalition government. The Nationalists proposed that the Communists be taken into the existing National Government and be accorded membership in the National Military Council. There being no compromise between these positions, Chiang K'ai-shek stated that solution must be found in a nation-wide convention that would establish a democratic constitution. As a preliminary step he proposed a Political Consultative Conference (PCC) of party and non-party representatives to lay the groundwork for military unification and constitutional government. In August, 1945, the Communists agreed to the calling of the PCC, which met in January, 1946, and reached three agreements forecasting a settlement. These agreements included: (1) a military truce, (2) a political and constitutional agreement, and (3) an agreement on the reorganization and control of military forces.

Under the truce agreement military advances were to be halted while local outbreaks were to be settled by truce teams composed of a Nationalist, a Communist, and an American officer. For a time this plan operated with some success. The second or political agreement confirmed the Nationalists or the Communists in control of the territory each held and provided for a State Council in the National Government in which all political groups would have representation. Unlike the old State Council this new body was to determine policy. Moreover, the political agreement provided for a parliamentary system when constitutionalism was achieved. The third or military agreement, to which General Marshall contributed in the discussions, provided an arrangement whereby the Communist army was to become a part of a Chinese national army. All three of these basic and encouraging agreements were interdependent. A failure of one meant a failure of all. The reasons that were soon to bring this failure were many and complex. They involved disputes over means of control in local and provincial areas and Communist demands for greater representation in the State Council, but the most serious clash concerned the mastery of Manchuria. At the time of Japan's surrender Manchuria was in the hands of the Russian army. The PCC military agreement had set up quotas of Nationalist and Communist troops for Manchuria. The Communists arrived first in greater numbers than had been agreed upon and proceeded to recruit local forces. The Nationalist forces, denied the use of Dairen by the Russians, fought their way into Manchuria. The Russians then turned over the main cities and railroads to the Nationalists as had been agreed, but, at the same time, allowed large quantities of arms surrendered by the Japanese to fall into Communist hands. The Communists were thus fully prepared to challenge the Nationalist bid to control of Manchuria. Then, too, while the Communists were violating the military agreement in Manchuria, the right wing of the *Kuomintang* forced the National Government to disavow the PCC agreements. Each side could accuse the other of bad faith. By the beginning of 1947 all pretense of keeping the agreements had vanished from both sides. To this failure civil war was the answer.

The Appeal to Constitutionalism

Faced by the prospect of a desperate civil war and recognizing the need to gain popular support, the National Government sought to save itself by a belated appeal to constitutionalism. A National convention open to all parties, but which was attended only by the *Kuomintang* and some of the minor groups, adopted a constitution generally in line with the principles of the PCC agreements. Providing for a parliamentary system, it became effective in December, 1947, but during the emergency of civil war large special powers were to be retained by Chiang as President.[5]

A Case of Crumbling Foundations

The efforts toward constitutionalism and parliamentary government in 1947 were doomed from the beginning. They were made at a time when the National Government was not only beset by civil war but also when it had already lost the revived prestige it had enjoyed briefly when Japan surrendered in 1945. At that time there was still hope that the government's economic and financial assets, including foreign aid, if used wisely, could provide a sound economic structure, a base for intelligent political reform demanded alike by the business, professional, and intellectual classes. But neither the *Kuomintang* nor the National Government found or effected the means of using its assets wisely. The government, having embarked on the questionable policy of reoccupying Manchuria, opened itself to violent attacks by the Communists on its lines of communication. These attacks forced the government into larger and larger military expenditures that could only be met by printing more money. In mid-1947 the Chinese national currency rate to the U. S. dollar was 45,000 to 1, and the top had not yet been reached. The foreign financial reserves which the government held in 1945 had already been spent to no effect.

But even if it had not been forced by military needs to increase the currency, the fiscal policy of the government would have promoted inflation. There was no budget in fact. Expenditures, particularly by the military, were wasteful, and in any event no one could tell what proportion of the taxes collected reached the treasury, due to the flagrant dishonesty of tax collectors. Moreover, at a time when, if ever, the government needed all the productive capacity Chinese business could provide, it did the very thing best

[5] The new constitution and the parliamentary system was due largely to the efforts of Carsun Chang, head of the Social Democratic Party, who had striven to overcome party dictatorship and militarism through adoption of the parliamentary principle. His plan was so modified by the National convention as to subvert largely the representative principle. Thus when the new government under the constitution was formed many of the minor parties, united in the Democratic League, refused to co-operate and allied themselves with the Communists. See Chang Chia-sên (Carsun Chang), *The Third Force in China* (New York, 1952).

designed to alienate Chinese private enterprise. It took over the industrial enterprises that had been operated by the Japanese and operated them as state concerns. Chinese industrialists resented this practice on two grounds. First, they regarded it as providing unfair competition, and second, some of the properties taken over by the government had previously been privately owned. Finally, Chinese business in the former Treaty Ports no longer enjoyed any protection from whatever pressures the National Government sought to place upon it. Foreign relief funds to China, including direct American aid, were handled by a Chinese National Relief and Rehabilitation Administration, which was in effect the National Government. This meant that the government could direct relief materials to undertakings that were government owned or controlled. Foreign aid therefore helped the government to compete with Chinese private industry and thus helped to alienate private business from the *Kuomintang*, which it had previously supported.

It would appear, however, that the worst effects of inflation were neither economic nor military but moral. The unending spiral of worthless paper corrupted every man who was forced to use it. For those dependent on salaries and wages the problem was not one of iniquity but of survival. Soldiers, lesser officials, and the intellectuals suffered most. These last, who could have contributed so much to the *Kuomintang*, were at best ignored; at worst they were persecuted or liquidated. These were the men who had recognized that in China ideology was important. They were the carriers of the Chinese revolution that had begun in the nineteenth century. Most of them were not Communists. Perhaps a majority of them were opposed to the civil war and favored compromise with the Communists and the establishment of a truly representative government. When the PCC agreements failed and the full civil war was resumed in 1947, many of these intellectuals were dismissed from their positions or arrested, and some were slain. This type of repression was another example of the forces that had undermined from within the National Government and the *Kuomintang* at the very moment when this Government and Party were to meet in full battle all the power which the Chinese Communists could bring against them.

The Communist Military Victory

The civil war that followed the failure of the Nationalists and the Communists to effect a political solution was of brief duration, 1947 to 1949, and resulted in the complete defeat of the Nationalist armies. The first defeat of Nationalist forces took place in Manchuria, to which Chiang had sent his best troops. By 1948 the Communists in the Manchurian countryside were strong enough to cut the railroad lines and thus to make the Nationalist armies in the cities dependent on supplies brought in by air. By the end of 1948 the Nationalist garrisons had been forced to evacuate the major Manchurian cities, and in the process most of the troops and their American equipment were taken by the Communists. The whole Manchurian fiasco was a disaster from which the Nationalist armies never recovered. The responsibility for this military disaster was attributed by American military observers to incompetent army administration and supply, high officers who lacked ability, unimaginative strategy and tactics, which could not see beyond the holding of major cities, and finally the lack of a sound economic program in support of military action.

In North China, the Nationalist forces, denied adequate support, surrendered Peking to the Communists. In December, 1948, the Communists destroyed the main Nationalist armies in central and eastern China. Again Communist strategy won over the superior armament of the Nationalists. At this point Chiang K'ai-shek could no longer ignore demands for negotiation. He resigned the presidency. Li Tsung-jên became acting president and opened negotiations with the Communists. In essence, the Communist demands were for unconditional surrender. In April the Communists renewed the attack, penetrating south to Canton and west to Chungking. With the remnants of the Nationalist armies Chiang K'ai-shek escaped to Formosa, where, in March, 1950, he resumed the presidency of all that was left of Nationalist China.

Who Was to Blame?

Many explanations have been offered for the collapse and defeat of the National Government and its armies in 1948-1949. Some of these explanations, such as, for example, the charge that United States policy was primarily responsible (a charge that for a time was widely believed in America), were obviously absurd. Nevertheless, the hard fact was that the general ignorance of the American people on what China was like and on what had been going on in the Chinese mind for the past century made it possible and even natural for Americans to be misguided by fantastic and even subversive charges presented in the guise of patriotic revelations.[6] To those who have followed this history of China's journey into the modern world, it will be apparent that there is no single or simple interpretation of the fall of the National Government and of its armies, and, since this catastrophe is a matter of recent history, historians are not in complete agreement on its meaning. Yet for the most part their differences of interpretation are in emphasis rather than in substance. For example, one interpretation is that "the victory of the Chinese Communists was a victory of military organization and strategy."[7] Another interpretation maintains "that Chinese politics have been primarily a reflex of ideological dynamics, with armies, economics, and governments playing secondary and tertiary roles."[8]

In the immediate sense the Communist victory was due to superior military organization and strategy. But this interpretation by itself does not explain why it was that the Communists were able to build an effective military machine and a basis of popular support in the areas they controlled while the National Government, even with American military supplies, was unable to compete in military organization and strategy or in popular support from the people it was supposed to represent. It is of course quite true that the National Government was not overthrown by a spontaneous and popular rising of the Chinese people. Revolutions have not happened and presumably do not happen that way. In the case of China a vast revolution affecting every aspect of Chinese life had long been under way, as the reader of these pages knows well. Ever since the fall of the Ch'ing dynasty in 1911-1912, there had been an unremitting search for an acceptable ideology for the New China and for the leadership and the organizational power that could translate the principles of the ideological program into living and working institutions for the everyday use of the nation. The result of this quest was the program of Sun Yat-sen and the leadership and organizational power of the *Kuomintang* and the National Government,

---

[6] See H. Arthur Steiner, "The United States and China: The Prospect Before Us," *Yale Review,* XLIV (1954), 161-179.

[7] Franz H. Michael and George E. Taylor, *The Far East in the Modern World* (New York, 1956), 447.

[8] Paul M. A. Linebarger, Djang Chu, and Ardath W. Burks, *Far Eastern Governments and Politics* (New York, 1954), 252.

which in 1937 "was at the height of its influence and power."[9] After 1937 the ideological goals of the revolution remained unchanged in theory (they were still the Three Principles of Sun Yat-sen), but there was no leadership that could say with sufficient authority what these principles meant or how rapidly they should be applied in order to hold the allegiance of a Chinese populace that was no longer controlled by the Confucian system. In this sense the fall of the National Government was not primarily a military collapse but rather a failure in ideology and its application to practical and revolutionary politics.[10]

Communist China: The People's Republic

As the Chinese Communists moved toward military victory, they also prepared to set up a national government. Prior to 1948-1949, in the areas they controlled they had limited their own membership in all representative and administrative organs of government to one-third of the total membership, the other two-thirds being made up of non-Communist personnel sympathetic with the Communists. The procedure produced the appearance of democratic, multi-party government while enabling the Communists to retain decisive power by reason of their influence, their close party discipline, and their military resources. This same "representative" principle, somewhat modified, was carried into the organization of the People's Republic of China, which came into being at Peking in 1949, once the military victory was achieved. Thus the new government could be advertised to the Chinese and to the world as a coalition government under the leadership of the Communist Party.

The new regime was said to be based on the principle of the "People's Democratic Dictatorship," a principle supplementary to Mao's earlier "new Democracy." This new concept expounded a joint revolution of workers, peasants, petty bourgeoisie, and the new national capitalists—namely, those capitalists in sympathy with the

---

[9] Michael and Taylor, *The Far East in the Modern World,* 433.

[10] The *Kuomintang* not only failed to create a peasant base of support, it also alienated important bases which it traditionally held among the intellectuals, students, professional classes, businessmen, and even officials who assumed an attitude of neutralism. Michael and Taylor, *The Far East in the Modern World,* 446-447. It should not be assumed that the Communists once in power remained true to the programs they used to attain power. "The problem of winning power was different from that of use of power when secured." Vinacke, *Far Eastern Politics in the Postwar Period,* 132.

socialistic objectives of the revolution. By associating with themselves these non-Communist reform groups and classes, the Communists were profiting by their own early errors and by a basic mistake of the *Kuomintang* hierarchy, which had tried to run China all by itself.[11]

In a formal sense the new Communist government of China grew out of the actions of the Chinese People's Political Consultative Conference, which met at Peking in September, 1949. This body emerged from a Communist suggestion in April, 1948, for the calling of a conference of all democratic parties and groups, excluding all groups the Communists regarded as "reactionaries." The resulting meeting in 1949 produced: (1) the Organic Law of the CPPCC, (2) the Organic Law of the Central People's Government, and (3) the Common Program of the CPPCC. The CPPCC was to exercise the powers and functions of a supreme legislative body until an All-China People's Congress should be elected.

The *Organic Law of the Central People's Government,* a kind of provisional constitution of the People's Republic of China, established a Central People's Government Council as the highest policy-making body, composed of a president (Mao Tse-tung), four vice-presidents, and fifty-eight members. Responsible to this Government Council was an Administrative Council of twenty members, each heading a ministry or committee. This Administrative Council, which might be described as a cabinet, was headed by Chou En-lai. Chou En-lai thus became the executive or administrative head of the new government and served also as foreign minister. He had been with the Communist movement since its beginning, having joined Mao in Kiangsi days, 1931, and by 1949 was the ablest administrator and diplomat in the CCP and government. Coming from a gentry family, some of whose members had been officials under the Manchus, Chou had enjoyed all the advantages education could give. Finally, there was the People's Revolutionary Military Council, with Mao as chairman, which was given direct authority over the army.

The *Common Program* adopted by the CPPCC was an important political manifesto announcing the basic principles of state power, military organization, economic, cultural, and educational policy, and foreign policy. From the Communist point of view it was a mini-

---

[11] Linebarger, Djang, and Burks, *Far Eastern Governments and Politics,* 217-222.

mum program, a plan of action for the immediate future, not to be confused with the ultimate purposes of the Chinese Communist Party.

The three documentary products of the 1949 meeting of the CPPCC revealed some basic principles on the political system in the People's Democratic Dictatorship. Individual rights were guaranteed within a rigid system of thought control. For example, the press was free to report only "true" news that was "beneficial to the people." Moreover, even these popular rights were denied to "reactionary elements, feudal landlords, bureaucratic capitalists." Democratic centralism, already the principle of operation in the Chinese Communist Party, was adapted to the government of the People's Democratic Dictatorship. In time the principle of representation was to be given expression through an elaborate system of "people's congresses" responsible to the "people" and electing government councils responsible to the congresses; but always the councils at lower levels were to be confirmed by councils at higher levels and were to obey the central government that eventually was to be elected by the All-China People's Congress. In a word, the emphasis was on centralism, not on democracy. Emerging, too, from democratic centralism was the principle of unitary government assuring to the central government complete control of policies at all local levels. To these principles was added the inseparability of powers. This denial of the separation of powers was a rejection of both the Western concept and of the fivefold division of powers devised by Sun Yat-sen. It was clear also that the state would be involved actively in controlling the development of the entire social economy, since the People's Republic was not to be regarded as static but as in a transitional phase of its development to maximum communism.[12]

THE CONSTITUTION OF 1954

Communist China entered the "constitutional stage" of its history with the adoption by the first National People's Congress, September 20, 1954, of the Constitution of the People's Republic. The pre-constitutional measures of 1949 were now to be regarded as merely the prelude to the emerging Communist state. Beginning in 1953 with the election of local "People's Congresses," which chose provincial

---

12 A more detailed treatment is in H. Arthur Steiner, "The People's Democratic Dictatorship in China," *The Western Political Quarterly,* III (1950), 38-51.

congresses, there appeared in 1954 the first National Congress, which accepted without dissent or amendment a draft constitution, the work of a drafting committee (chaired by Mao) of the Central Executive Committee of the CCP. This constitution did introduce some changes that distinguished the new governmental system from that established in 1949, but these changes were in matters of structure which did not involve constitutional principle.[13] In a word, the Constitution represented a tightening of centralized control by Mao and his immediate trusted lieutenants. The looseness of control in some areas which had developed during the rapid conquest was considered a potential danger to Mao's dictatorship. Manchuria provided the best example of a growing regional autonomy under the administration of Kao Kang, whom Mao regarded as heading a rival Communist faction. By 1955 Kao and some of his associates had been expelled from the CCP.

Remaking a Civilization

With the military and the politico-administrative victory secured, the Communist masters of China, unlike previous successful rebels in China's history, set about to secure their power not by reviving the past but by creating the future. They proposed to make a new China, Communist in design and substance, for the perpetuation of their control and for the glorification of Communist philosophy. In attempting this revolution they employed all the weapons of the Communist arsenal—ideological attack, mass propaganda, brainwashing—to prepare the way and develop the momentum for the new order of life in economic affairs and social relations. Military warfare against the National Government became intellectual warfare against Chinese traditions and mores. In this battle the price of survival for the individual was conformity.

The Communists applied themselves from the beginning to problems of economic recovery. They were particularly concerned with the repair of railroads, the building of new lines, and administration of barge traffic on the rivers still so important to Chinese transportation. Agriculture responded to a succession of good crop seasons. Light industry revived more rapidly than heavy industry. Most important, however, were the measures to control the inflation. The

---

[13] A convenient summary of these changes is in H. Arthur Steiner, "Constitutionalism in Communist China," *The American Political Science Review*, XLIX (1955), 1-21.

improvement achieved here was due to rigid restrictions on credit and to government control over the release of major commodities exercised by state trading companies to maintain greater stability in prices. These measures were bolstered by a firm national budget and a system of national taxation enforced relentlessly. Additional government revenue accrued from fines upon businessmen or confisca-

tion of their property. When these levies could not be met the government extended loans to the victimized private enterprise in question and thereby gained control over it. By 1952, trade, industry, and bank loans and deposits were substantially in the hands of government agencies and enterprises. Meanwhile the Agrarian Reform Act of 1950 to effect a redistribution of land was carried out with a thoroughly heartless intensity. Landlords lost their land and often their lives. The purpose here was to exterminate the "exploiting" landlord class and in its place to create in the countryside and villages a ruling class of men who owed their new status of authority directly to the Communist regime.

The foregoing first steps encouraged the government in 1952 to announce that the First Five Year Plan would begin in 1953. Its purpose was to speed industrialization as rapidly as possible. To this end substantial aid in technical personnel and equipment was promised by the Soviet Union, but most of the investment came from China herself in the form of forced labor and grain deliveries at fixed prices. At the same time the government moved cautiously toward collective agriculture. The movement toward the collective farm was, it was said, to be voluntary, but the peasant would be guided and assisted in the right direction by the organization of "mutual aid" teams whereby peasants would learn to co-operate with each other, and through the organization of co-operatives, which in their "highest" form would not be unlike the collective farm itself. By 1957 the government had not achieved the rapid success in the collectivization of agriculture for which it had hoped.

The Social Revolution

Again it is useful to recall that Communist efforts to remake China politically and economically formed only a part of the Communist program which in its ultimate goal was aimed at a complete social revolution. In the case of China a revolutionary process had been under way for a century, and especially since 1900, and had been effecting, as the reader will remember, political, economic, and social changes of great magnitude. These changes, many of which preceded the Communist conquest, need to be kept in perspective. What the Communists tried to do and in some ways did was to speed the whole revolutionary process and to channel it directly toward Communist ends. Their military victory gave them political power. Political power opened the way for building the Communist economic structure. More basic, however, than these programs was the unremitting campaign to capture and subjugate the Chinese mind. This warfare involved every aspect of Chinese life, from details of dress to revelation of dreams. The Communists capitalized on conditions of a social vacuum to which they had contributed but of which they were not the sole creators. For example, the traditional Chinese family system with its personal loyalties and mutual responsibilities, the most stabilizing of all institutions in the Old China, was decayed beyond repair before the Communist conquest. Unhappily it was left to the Communists to determine by fiat and force what the new institutions should be and were to be. With power in their hands and with no scruples about using it, the Communists were able to confront opposition groups with the simple choice between intellectual regimentation or extermination. Even this choice was not open to all because legislation in 1950 provided imprisonment or death for "war criminals, traitors, bureaucratic capitalists, and counter-revolutionaries" and because it was the Communists themselves who determined who belonged to these groups. There was no independent judiciary. The revolutionary edicts were applied in a veritable uproar of propaganda in which every useful enemy of the Communist regime was castigated. The vehicles of this planned vituperation were many and varied. For example, the "Three Anti Movement" denouncing "corruption," "waste," and "bureaucracy," was designed to eliminate weak Communist Party officials and former *Kuomintang* officials whom the Communists had used but needed no longer. The "Five Anti Movement" of 1951-1952 against "tax evasion, bribery, cheating in government contracts, theft of economic intelligence, and stealing of national property" was directed against the urban businessman. This movement was not a case of judicial procedure. The campaign itself and the "trials" that followed were "a state-organized political persecution of a social class." Other campaigns to whip up mass hysteria in which "the people would demand that enemies of the state be purged" included drives against "feudalism," "American imperialism," "running dogs of capitalism" etc.[14] The public trials and public executions and the general persecutions that punctuated this constant furor accounted for many millions of lives.

Personnel for Intellectual and Mass Control

The power of the Chinese Communist Party to effect wide social and intellectual control was due mainly to its trained staff workers, the *kan pu* or cadres. These were young party or sympathetic workers educated for leadership in government and party activities. Their chief qualifications were capacity to develop "loyalty, obedience, initiative, and ability in organizing the masses." The Communists had begun the formal training of cadres back in the days at Yenan.

---

14 Michael and Taylor, *The Far East in the Modern World,* 458.

This training consisted of both classroom learning and of field work whereby the student acquired a mastery of doctrine and technique and also an intimate knowledge of how the common people lived and thought. The cadres were indispensable at the time of the conquest, when the CCP itself was still relatively small.[15] They made possible whatever progress was made in the social and intellectual revolution. Moreover, this vast army of trained staff workers was kept "pure" in thought and deed by periodic requirements of self-examination known as "rectification movements." Any cadre member could be called upon to identify his own faults and to demonstrate his doctrinal capacity to correct his errors.

The New Intellectuals

In seeking to effect a social and intellectual revolution, the Chinese Communists did not rely solely or even primarily upon naked force. They were equally concerned with applying the techniques of persuasion. They saw their own ultimate salvation in the rapid conversion of the intellectuals—teachers, scholars, students, writers, artists—to the "true" faith as revealed by the modern sages, Marx, Lenin, Stalin, and Mao. Many of the intellectuals were in fact "neutralists" who had accepted the Communist regime because they were disillusioned with the *Kuomintang* and not because they believed in Communism. Their conversion was encouraged in two principal ways. The first, known as "brain-washing," required public repudiation of ideas previously held and public condemnation of the sources from which these ideas came, whether from the church, the liberal state, or even fathers or relatives who had taught these ideas.[16] Thus "brain-washing" served many purposes. It made public property of the convert's confession, placed a stigma of responsibility on liberal Westernization, particularly American, since many intellectuals had been educated in the United States, and finally it weakened the bonds of the old family system. The second method of stimulating conversion, applied to lesser intellectuals, was the public meeting or

---

[15] CCP membership in 1937 was some 40,000; by 1945 it was about 1,200,000; by 1952, about 5,000,000; by 1954, about 6,000,000. Linebarger, Djang, and Burks, *Far Eastern Governments and Politics,* 236.

[16] Vinacke, *Far Eastern Politics in the Postwar Period,* 141-142. Nice examples of the denunciation of fathers by sons were given by the sons of the brilliant modern leaders, Hu Shih and Liang Ch'i-ch'ao.

forum. At these gatherings public confession of past error, together with penitent resolves for the future, enabled the convert to emerge with a washed and clean mind.

The intellectual revolution was not a mere denunciation of the past. It embodied positive study by the intellectuals of the new "classics." Confucius was overtaken and passed by Marx, Lenin, Stalin, and Mao.[17] The new gospel was not only for the elite. It was to be carried by the cadres and the intellectuals to the people through the schools, through adult education, the press, and a vast variety of cultural forums and institutes. The media for effecting the new intellectual outlook included all the vehicles of art and literature. Plays and the theater, fiction and the periodical press, folk dances and songs with the new message were all employed to the end of political and social uniformity. Art and literature stood or fell according as they served or failed to serve the political and social aims of the state and its master the CCP. It was not enough for the individual, particularly the intellectual, to try to believe. Constant evidence of actual belief was demanded. Hu Shih, in exile in the United States, captured the real spirit of the Communist regime when he said it not only denied freedom of speech but also freedom of silence.[18]

For Further Reading

HISTORY

Brandt, Conrad, Benjamin Schwartz, and John King Fairbank, *A Documentary History of Chinese Communism* (Cambridge, 1952). Translations of Chinese Communist documents.

Fairbank, John K., *The United States and China* (Cambridge, 1948). An analysis of the growth and character of modern Chinese civilization.

---

[17] The Communist attack on the Old Classics and their authors included "re-evaluation" of the Ancients because not everything that was old was thereby bad according to Communist standards. In the early stages of this "re-evaluation" Confucius was rescued from oblivion because, although he was "over-conservative, over-cautious, and not radical," he had "exercised a certain function according to his determined historical stage." Mencius did not fare quite so well because he was an "idealist," believed in God, and safeguarded the reactionaries. Nevertheless he did lean toward the people rather than toward the rulers, and his writings had "a dialectical revolutionary drive." See Michael and Taylor, *The Far East in the Modern World,* 470.

[18] Vinacke, *Far Eastern Politics in the Postwar Period,* 143-145.

Fitzgerald, C. P., *Revolution in China* (London, 1952). A study of the indigenous forces underlying the Chinese revolution.

Isaacs, Harold, *The Tragedy of the Chinese Revolution* (rev. ed., Stanford, 1951).

Mao Tse-tung, *Selected Works of Mao Tse-tung* (4 vols. of a projected 5 vols., London, 1954).

North, Robert C., *Moscow and Chinese Communists* (Stanford, 1953). A good introduction to the subject.

———, and Ithiel De Sola Pool, *Kuomintang and Chinese Communist Elites* (Stanford, 1952). An effort to correlate the social origins and experiences of the leadership cadres with the general political lines of the parties, bringing statistical methods to bear upon data compiled from biographical studies.

Schwartz, Benjamin I., *Chinese Communism and the Rise of Mao* (Cambridge, 1951). An excellent examination of the ideological side of Chinese Communism from 1918 to 1932.

Tang, Peter S. H., *Communist China Today: Domestic and Foreign Policies* (New York, 1957). A comprehensive survey of domestic and foreign policies from the beginnings of the CCP in 1921.

Wales, Nym (pseudonym of Mrs. Edgar Snow), *Red Dust, Autobiographies of Chinese Communists* (Stanford, 1952).

Walker, Richard L., *China under Communism: The First Five Years* (New Haven, 1955).

GOVERNMENT AND POLITICS

Ch'ien Tuan-sheng, *The Government and Politics of China* (Cambridge, 1950). Note in particular explanations for the failure of the *Kuomintang.*

Mao Tse-tung, and others, *Mao's China: Party Reform Documents, 1942-1944*, Boyd Compton, ed. and trans. (Seattle, 1952).

Thomas, S. B., *Government and Administration in Communist China* (New York, 1953). A technical description of the machinery and techniques employed by Chinese Communists to govern China.

FOREIGN RELATIONS

Beloff, Max, *Soviet Policy in the Far East, 1944-1951* (New York, 1953).

Feis, Herbert, *The China Tangle* (Princeton, 1953). A dispassionate, able survey of the American effort in China 1941-1946, with emphasis on the objectives of American policy.

Mandel, William, comp., *Soviet Source Materials on USSR Relations with East Asia, 1945-1950* (New York, 1950).

Thomas, S. B., *Communist China and her Neighbors* (Toronto, 1955).

Wu Ai-ch'en, *China and the Soviet Union* (New York, 1950). A survey of Sino-Russian relations since 1618.

CONTEMPORARY ACCOUNTS

Band, Claire and William, *Two Years with the Chinese Communists* (New Haven, 1948). Experiences of two war-time years in Communist guerrilla areas.

Bodde, Derk, *Peking Diary: A Year of Revolution* (New York, 1950). The Communist occupation of Peking and a careful analysis of what this event meant to its inhabitants.

Kuo Ping-Chia, *China: New Age and New Outlook* (New York, 1956).

Liu Shao-t'ang, *Out of Red China* (New York, 1953). A student's picture of life under the Communist regime.

Low, Sir Francis, *Struggle for Asia* (New York, 1956). A semi-popular and useful account of the forces struggling to capture the Asian mind.

Moraes, Francis, *Report on Mao's China* (New York, 1953). A perceptive report by the editor of *The Times of India,* who travelled briefly but widely in China in 1952.

Sun K'o, *China Looks Forward* (New York, 1944). The son of the "Father of the Chinese Revolution" gives his estimate of *Kuomintang* accomplishments and failures.

SPECIAL STUDIES

De Francis, John, *Nationalism and Language Reform in China* (Princeton, 1950).

Elegant, Robert S., *China's Red Masters: Political Biographies of Chinese Communist Leaders* (New York, 1951). Treats the history of Chinese Communism through a series of biographical sketches of uneven quality.

Hsia, Ronald, Foreword by A. Doak Barnett, *Economic Planning in Communist China* (New York, 1955).

______, *Price Control in Communist China* (New York, 1953).

Lattimore, Owen, *Nationalism and Revolution in Mongolia.* With a translation of Sh. Nachukdorji's *Life of Sukebatur* by Owen Lattimore and Urgungge Onon (New York, 1955). A portrayal of Mongolia as the first Russian satellite.

Li Tieh-tseng, *The Historical Status of Tibet* (New York, 1956). A history of Sino-Tibetan relations.

Lieu, D. K., *China's Economic Stabilization and Reconstruction* (New York, 1948). A balanced study providing much factual material.

Mao Tse-tung, *China's New Democracy* (New York, 1944).

Outerbridge, Leonard M., *The Lost Churches of China* (Philadelphia, 1952).

Payne, Robert, *Mao Tse-tung: Ruler of Red China* (New York, 1950). A subjective treatment, to be used with caution.

Rigg, Robert B., *Red China's Fighting Hordes* (Harrisburg, 1952). A study of the Nationalist defeat.

Riggs, Fred Warren, *The Economics of Red China* (New York, 1954).

Rostow, W. W., and others, *The Prospects for Communist China* (Cambridge, 1954).

Steiner, H. Arthur, ed., *Maoism, A Sourcebook: Selections from the Writings of Mao Tse-tung* (Los Angeles, 1952).

Thomas, S. B., *Recent Political and Economic Developments in China* (New York, 1950).

Wu Yuan-Li, *An Economic Survey of Communist China* (New York, 1956).

38

1941 and after

The New Southeast Asia

THE history of Southeast Asia since 1945 has often been described very neatly but not very accurately by saying that World War II brought an end to colonialism and opened the way to a new era of nationalism. There is a limited degree of truth in this statement, but it is also misleading. It is quite true that many states in Southeast Asia acquired their freedom and political independence: the Philippines and the Associated States of Vietnam, Cambodia, and Laos in 1946; the Union of Burma in 1948; and Indonesia in 1949. Malaya won independence in the Commonwealth in 1957. There could, in fact, be no doubt that the territorial and political empires of the United States, France, Great Britain, and Holland in Southeast Asia were rapidly disappearing, but this is not just another way of saying that *colonialism* was being replaced by nationalism, unless by colonialism is meant something very different from the actual meaning of the word. These lands of Southeast Asia were not colonies, though in a loose way they have usually been designated by this term. Politically, they were territorial possessions. Colonies must have colonists. Neither the British, the French, nor the Americans were ever colonists in Southeast Asia, and although the Portuguese, the Spaniards, and the Dutch made some feeble efforts toward colonization, they certainly did not succeed. The Europeans or Americans who went to Southeast Asia to make a fortune and then retire at home were not settlers or colonists. There were colonies of Indian and Chinese settlers in Southeast Asia, but the real Western colonists, if such they may be called, were not men but business firms.

These business firms were among the great carriers of the Western impact upon Southeast Asia, and their principal contribution was the introduction of capitalism as an economic system. The basic character of this system was to direct production on rational lines with a view to achieving the maximum surplus or profit for the economic energy expended, together with the habit of employing this surplus for the further increase of production. In Southeast Asia, as in the West, there was much to be said for capitalism as an economic system. It did, however, have its limitations: its tendency to become "capitalism as a social system" and its aptitude for turning "the social order into a business concern." These tendencies had been resisted in the Western world by social forces for much more than a century, but the same tendencies of capitalism in Southeast Asia were not resisted by the alien or, as they were called, the colonial rulers. Therefore, in dealing with the recent history of Southeast Asia the student will need to distinguish, if he may, between what is often called the aftermath of colonialism when in reality he may be dealing with the aftermath of capitalism as an economic system directed by alien rulers and uncontrolled by limiting social forces.[1]

Southeast Asia in 1941

The advance of Japan southward to and into Southeast Asia in 1940 and 1941 highlighted for the free world of the West the economic and the strategic importance of this vast area. The economic factor was represented by a foreign investment of some $4,370,-000,000; the strategic factor was symbolized by the great British naval base at Singapore. More meaningful was the fact that the area produced about 90 per cent of the world's rubber, 65 per cent of its tin, most of its quinine, and large portions of its sugar, coconut oil, and hemp. The area was also a vital element in the equation of American foreign trade. Just before the war the United States sold annually to Europe goods whose value was about $500,000,000 in excess of what it bought from Europe. At the same time the United States brought from Southeast Asia far more than it sold there. These surplus dollars enabled Southeast Asia to buy from Europe more than it sold to Europe, and Europe in turn used these surplus funds to help pay its annual debt for United States goods.[2]

These economic and strategic stakes and the prestige of empire held by the free Western world in Southeast Asia were swept away

---

[1] J. S. Furnivall's "Commentary," in Philip W. Thayer, ed., *Nationalism and Progress in Free Asia* (Baltimore, 1956), 66-70.

[2] Lennox A. Mills, and associates, *The New World of Southeast Asia* (Minneapolis, 1949), 1-5.

by the Japanese invasion of 1941-1942. To be sure, the Japanese conquest was short-lived. At the close of the war Southeast Asia was reoccupied by its former rulers, but these rulers in most cases returned to lands and peoples that were no longer willing to receive them. Everywhere the returning European was opposed by revolutionary nationalism in a great variety of forms. This nationalism, as the reader knows, in its demands for self-government and political independence was not a creation of World War II. Most of these movements had their origins in the period of World War I or even earlier. Their growing vitality in the interwar period was derived from the declining prestige of European civilization in Asia, from the Western doctrine of self-determination, from resentment against economically powerful minorities (such as the Chinese who controlled the retail trade and credit), from the ambitions of the small Western-educated native classes that aspired to political power, and from the beginnings of Communist parties that sought to use the new nationalism for their own revolutionary purposes. What World War II did do was to open the way for the already existing nationalism of Southeast Asia to assert itself.

Southeast Asian Politics, 1941 and After

The political evolution of Southeast Asia after 1941, often described under the simple label of nationalism, was in fact a movement far more complex than this term is apt to suggest to Western students. Moreover, although this evolution was in general democratic it was not patterned wholly in the images of Western parliamentary or presidential government. When the political control of Europe and then of Japan was destroyed by World War II, Southeast Asia faced the practical problem of finding the political principles and institutions upon which its new-found freedom would be built and insured. Some political opportunists and obscurantist elements sought a solution in the revival of indigenous institutions such as divine kingship. Although traditionalism did not lose all its power, it seemed evident that in the area of political standards it was deteriorating rapidly, whether in Buddhistic Burma, Islamic Indonesia, or Confucianist Indochina. In contrast there were positive political trends in the revolutionary movements in Southeast Asia after 1945. The first of these was a belligerent and vocal nationalism; the second was a strong leaning among most young nationalist politicians for free constitutional government and broad individual liberty; the third was a predilection for a state-planned economy, touching particularly industrial development and foreign trade; and the fourth was an insistent emphasis on central unitary control within each country. It should not be forgotten, however, that the history of Southeast Asia during and since World War II is a history of revolution and that this revolution is still in process. Conflicts and contradictions are the essence of this story in which Southeast Asians who acquired their political independence had the uncomfortable feeling that they were still not free and that their former alien masters or new alien masters were plotting to resubjugate them.[3]

1. *The Philippines*

It will be remembered that on the eve of World War II the Philippine Commonwealth was moving rapidly toward independent nationhood (see Chapter 33). The movement was a product not only of the long incessant clamor of Filipino politicians but also of the so-called Philippine "menace" as exploited by American special interests in particular and isolationists in general. The Commonwealth of the Philippines had come into being in 1934 and full independence was to follow in 1946. Whether the Philippines would be ready for independence at that time was a question to which there was no one answer, but it was certainly clear that the Commonwealth faced staggering problems. If American policy had prepared the Islands for political independence, it had not prepared them for economic independence. The state of agriculture, plagued by abuses of landlordism, was economically unhealthy for nationhood and socially unsuited to democratic citizenship.

The Japanese conquest of the Philippines. In 1941, the United States, which was still responsible for the defense of the Philippines, was not adequately prepared to defend them. A small Philippine army was in the making after 1937, but on December 8, 1941, a few hours after Pearl Harbor, the United States air forces in the Islands were destroyed. Japanese armies landed at Lingayen Gulf on December 22; American troops on Bataan were forced to surrender on April 9; Corregidor was given up a month later, May 6. Japan was master of the Islands.

Philippine political leaders were then called upon to make difficult

[3] John F. Cady, "Evolving Political Institutions in Southeast Asia," in Philip W. Thayer, ed., *Nationalism and Progress in Free Asia* (Baltimore, 1956), 113-127.

decisions affecting their personal fortunes and reputations and their official leadership of a young nation. President Manuel Quezon and Vice-President Sergio Osmeña escaped to the United States, where they maintained a Philippine government in exile. Most political leaders did not and could not leave the Islands. They could co-operate with the Japanese conquerors or they could fight the Japanese from the jungle, jeopardizing their families and fortunes. Most of them co-operated, perhaps with varying motives. The Philippine Republic, which the Japanese set up in 1943, was headed by José Laurel, a former justice of the Supreme Court. Manuel Roxas, who was to play an important political role after the reconquest of the Islands, helped to draft the constitution of the puppet Republic and held office in the government. He had originally fought the Japanese, but when captured he agreed to collaborate. Nevertheless there was increasing hostility and resistance to the Japanese, particularly among tenant farmers and agricultural laborers who were literally enslaved to meet Japanese demands for deliveries of rice. The guerrillas who fought both the Japanese and their Philippine allies came in the main from the countryside, where anti-Japanese sentiment was strong and where opportunities for resistance were greatest.

The Commonwealth was gradually restored in 1945 with the American reconquest of the Islands. Quezon had died in the United States and Osmeña had succeeded to the presidency. The restored government was completely dependent on the American army for all supplies and services needed for immediate rehabilitation and the implementation of its authority, and in the longer run upon the United States for the restoration of the national economy. Most Filipino politicians regarded the rehabilitation of the Islands as an American duty and obligation, since in their view the devastation of the war was a direct result of Filipino loyalty to the United States. This problem in psychology was closely related to the whole question of the future economic relations between the Islands and the United States after July 1946 when the Commonwealth would become the independent Republic, a question that would ultimately be resolved by the United States Congress.

Meanwhile, Philippine independence was achieved by presidential proclamation in Washington, July 4, 1946. A Rehabilitation Act, 1946, provided $400,000,000 for war-damage claims and for subsequent larger appropriations. The United States continued to assume responsibility for the protection of the Islands under terms of a military alliance authorizing American bases. The Philippine Trade Act, 1946, known as the Bell Act, attempted to provide a workable transition for the Philippine economy from its protected position in the American market to the day when it would no longer have this protection. Under this agreement the full American tariff was to apply by 1974. The Bell Act required an unwelcome amendment of the Philippine Constitution, enabling Americans to enjoy equal rights with Filipinos in industrial exploitation.[4]

Collaboration in morals and politics. Filipino politics in the first post-war years was deeply infected with the ugly malady of collaboration. President Franklin Roosevelt had taken the position, June, 1944, that Filipino collaborators, all of whom had indulged in action against the United States as well as against the Commonwealth, were to be denied any authority in the future political or economic life of the country. During the reconquest, however, General Douglas MacArthur "liberated" Manuel Roxas, who was serving with Laurel's puppet government, making it possible for him to re-enter politics and government as President of the Senate when the old pre-war Commonwealth legislature was reconvened. The term of this legislature had expired but it seemed expedient to recall it rather than hold new elections in the devastation and confusion prevailing at war's end. The rub was that most members of House and Senate had worked with the Japanese and thus by definition were collaborators. President Osmeña was therefore placed between the demands of a Washington that was pressing for action against collaborators and the temper of a legislature that was not likely to provide legislation designed to punish a majority of its own members. Thus the moral and legal issue of collaboration became involved with a very earthy level of politics both Filipino and American.

The first general election in the Commonwealth, April, 1946, on the eve of the proclamation of the Republic, was dominated by the collaboration issue. It resulted in the defeat of President Osmeña and the election of Manuel Roxas, who was regarded as the collaborators' candidate. Elpiaio Quirino became vice-president. The decision in this election involved the moral and psychological effects of the Japanese occupation upon the Filipinos as individuals and as a people. Japanese propaganda had played effectively on the theme of "American exploitation" and "Asia for the Asiatics," a campaign that

[4] Harold M. Vinacke, *Far Eastern Politics in the Postwar Period* (New York, 1956), 382-385.

was partly neutralized by the harshness of the Japanese military administration. While the Japanese did all in their power to de-Americanize and to Japanize the Filipino, the Japanese economic program drove thousands of Filipinos to starvation, despair, sabotage, and into the ranks of the guerrillas. Resentment against Japan grew steadily among the mass of the people. For those elements of the population who had fortunes to lose (the landed aristocracy, industrialists, compradors) the temptation to collaborate was strong, and the majority succumbed in varying degrees and with mixed and varying motives. Many lesser officials carried on in their jobs to earn a living and to maintain morale in the community. Others actively helped the Japanese set up the puppet government, perhaps because they were forced to do so, or because they hoped for personal reward, or because as Filipino patriots they believed Japan would speed independence, or because by collaboration they might hide their anti-Japanese purposes. In the over-all picture there seemed to be some ground, perhaps superficial, for the conclusion that those who had profited most from American rule were the first to betray it, while those who had profited least were the first to fight for their homes and for America. For the collaborators the rationalization was that America had failed to protect them and that collaboration was the only alternative to complete Japanese rule.[5]

As a matter of practical politics in the post-war Philippines the issue of collaboration lingered and then died. The Osmeña government, urged on by Washington, set up some machinery, such as the People's Courts, to try collaborators who were in custody. But since no one had resolved as a legal concept just what the categories of collaboration were, and since Roxas had been rehabilitated politically by the American military high command presumably on the assumption that he was a "good" collaborator, it was difficult to push collaboration as a legal or a political issue. The conclusion seemed to be that the issue could only have been dealt with by United States authorities immediately after the reconquest. This was not done. Instead the matter was thrown into the lap of the restored government of the Commonwealth.[6]

Politics and the Hukbalahap. Mixed with the issue of collaboration was the task of dealing with the "Huks" (Hukbalahap, or Peo-

---

[5] Claude A. Buss, "The Philippines," in *The New World of Southeast Asia,* 44-49.

[6] Vinacke, *Far Eastern Politics,* 385-387.

ple's Army against the Japanese), a well-organized guerrilla force in central Luzon.

The Huks were the fighting guerrilla arm of a conglomerate resistance movement against Japan, a movement that in the beginning included elements from practically every corner of society: laborers, peasants, middle class, intellectuals, religious organizations, the Chinese colony, and the Socialist and the Communist parties. The Huks, organized in 1942 in a rich agricultural area of Luzon where the economic tensions between landlord and tenant were a scandal, fought the Japanese, kept them from getting the rice of central Luzon, took over the estates of collaborator landlords, and set up the machinery of democratic local self-government to replace the semi-feudal and dictatorial patterns of pre-war days. It was a new experience for the peasant, who gained a glimpse of freedom and enjoyed relief from the absurdly heavy land rents. But in the process landlords were sometimes killed because, according to the Huks, the landlords were collaborators, or, according to the landlords and the government, because the Huks at best were bandits and at worst Communists. Both explanations contained a measure of truth but not the whole truth. Certainly land reforms were long past due; some of the Huks were avowed Communists; and some of the landlords were not only collaborators but were also incapable of leadership in terms of social responsibility to the nation. During and after the liberation the attitude of the United States military command and of the government of the Philippine Republic appeared to be unsympathetic to the whole reform movement represented by the Huks. As a consequence the door was opened even wider for Communists to dominate the Huks. By 1949, when Quirino succeeded Roxas as president, the movement was clearly controlled by a subversive leadership enjoying a vicarious prestige derived from the Communist victory in China. The later suppression of the Huks was due in large measure to the policies of Ramon Magsaysay as Defense Secretary. Magsaysay used both force and conciliation. He employed the regular Philippine army instead of the irresponsible constabulary, and took concrete steps in reform to re-establish peasant confidence in the government.

The economic and social ills affecting the peasantry were, however, only one phase of a national economic and social decline. The temporary economic revival after the liberation was due to American aid rather than to sound planning and administration by the Republic. It was soon apparent that much American relief was simply being poured down the drain, that politics, especially as revealed in the election of 1949, was a colossal travesty on democracy, and that further American aid would be based on guarantees of better behavior. The Bell Mission sent by Washington in 1950 recommended further American loans to the Republic but stipulated careful supervision of their disbursement. The distressing state of Philippine politics was in part a product of old habits, which clung to personalities rather than principles, and in part to new factors emerging from the war.

The death of Quezon broke the unity of the old *Nacionalista* one-party machine that had controlled politics for forty years. Schism was created when Roxas created the Liberal Party, leaving Osmeña in command of what was left of the *Nacionalista*. This creation of a two-party system did not result, however, in any major differences between the parties on questions of public policy. What was involved was not principle but personal politics. Nevertheless, there was some improvement in the administration of elections by 1953. In the election of that year Magsaysay won the presidency on a coalition ticket (*Nacionalista* and a new and third Democratic party), which made corruption in government the principal issue. This election, though a personal victory for Magsaysay, gave evidence of increasing political maturity in the Filipino people. Magsaysay's death in an airplane crash, March 17, 1957, was a major loss to the Philippines and to the United States.

2. *Indonesia*

The Dutch empire in the East Indies was destroyed in 1941-1942 not by the power of native nationalism but by a Japanese naval and military invasion. The early native nationalist reaction was that the expulsion of the Dutch by the Japanese should be welcome as a first major step to the liberation of Indonesia from foreign rule. This optimism was short-lived. The Japanese drained the islands of whatever produce they needed, impoverished the populace, and maintained an oppressive military government until the eve of their defeat. Indeed, Japanese behavior encouraged the Dutch government in exile at London to believe not only that Dutch rule would be restored at war's end but also that the Dutch could choose their own time in effecting political reforms toward Indonesian self-government.

The Dutch as post-war prophets. The first indication of Dutch plans for the post-war Indies was given in December, 1942, in a vague blueprint for the future suggesting a prospective commonwealth in which all parts of the Dutch realm, including Indonesia, would enjoy "complete self-reliance and freedom of conduct" in internal affairs "but with readiness to render mutual assistance." Had this declaration been made and acted upon prior to the Japanese attack it might have been the basis of an evolutionary political development. The war, however, created new conditions which the Dutch did not foresee, just as they had failed before the war to judge correctly the potential of early Indonesian nationalism. Although the Japanese had not encouraged an independence movement, they did use Indonesian nationalists as advisers in their administration in the later years of war. Other nationalists engaged in anti-Japanese activities. Just before the Japanese surrender the collaborating nationalists were permitted by the Japanese to declare the country's independence, August 17, 1945, with Sukarno as President and Hatta as Vice-President. Local militia, which had been organized with Japanese consent, became the military wing of the new Republic. Batavia on Java, renamed Jakarta, became the capital.

When the war ended the Dutch had no troops available for immediate occupation of the Indies, and the Allies had assigned to the British responsibility for accepting the Japanese surrender in the Indies. The British arrived some six weeks after the close of the war, disarmed the Japanese occupation army of some 300,000 troops, and, in refusing to undertake for the Dutch a reconquest of Java, really extended *de facto* recognition to the Indonesian Republic. Dutch policy on the arrival of their troops was to take over the islands first and then consider Indonesian demands. Indonesian policy was to demand recognition of the independent Republic first before negotiating on the future relation of the islands to the Netherlands. At first the Dutch refused to negotiate at all with Sukarno because he had collaborated. This difficulty was surmounted when Sutan Sjahrir, a non-collaborator, became Premier of the Republic. Negotiations dragged on until the conclusion of the Linggadjati Agreement, March 25, 1947, establishing principles that were to determine the basis of settlement. In it, the Republic was recognized as the *de facto* authority in Java, Madura, and Sumatra. Dutch and Allied forces were to leave these islands by January 1, 1949. The Indies as a whole were to be organized as three united states: Indonesia,

Borneo, and the Great East. This federal state was then to be joined with the Netherlands and the Dutch West Indies to form the Netherlands-Indonesian Union. The Republic also agreed to recognize the rights and claims of non-Indonesians for restitution of property. The agreement was a partial victory and partial defeat for both sides. Recognition of the Republic was a substantial gain for the Indonesians, but the Dutch had managed to relegate the Republic to a local status first in the United States of Indonesia and then in the Netherlands-Indonesian Union.

It may be doubted whether either side had the intention to set the stage for fulfillment of the Linggadjati Agreement. On their part the Dutch made efforts without success to set up rival governments on Java and Sumatra and imposed an economic blockade on the Republic. The Indonesians tried to secure recognition from India and countries of the Middle East. When the Dutch demanded immediate establishment of an interim federal government, the Indonesians refused to co-operate until the Dutch lifted the economic blockade. At that point, July, 1947, the Dutch resorted to "police measures," which was simply an effort to re-establish their authority by force. With superior armament they drove the Republican forces into the hills of central Java. The Republic then appealed to the United Nations. Six months of mediation by a U. N. committee finally produced the Renville truce, so named because it was signed on the U. S. Navy Transport *Renville*. The agreement established a truce line between Dutch and Indonesian forces, left the Dutch in possession of the territory they had conquered, and provided for elections on Java and Sumatra in which the people would decide their political future. Like its predecessor, this agreement also failed. Extremists among Indonesian nationalists demanded direct action, while in December, 1948, Indonesian Communists led by Muso attempted but failed to take over the Republican government. Dutch extremists in Holland were determined to force Indonesian submission. By mid-December, 1948, the Dutch had again resorted to military action. Meanwhile the Dutch were setting up beyond the Republic states and governments resting on Dutch military power. As the military campaign proceeded, Jakarta was occupied and the Republican leaders imprisoned. The Dutch announced that the Republic was destroyed, but in reality they had destroyed neither the spirit of the Republic nor its guerrilla forces in the hills.

This time the Dutch had misjudged not only Indonesian resistance but also Western opinion. As a result they found it expedient to release Sukarno and others and to agree to a conference at The Hague, October, 1949. Out of this conference came agreement for a United States of Indonesia (the Republic and eighteen states created by the Dutch). This in turn would be a part of the Dutch-Indonesian Union, whose main power was to deal with foreign relations. No settlement was reached concerning Dutch New Guinea (West Irian), claimed by both the Dutch and the Indonesians. It remained under Dutch administration. The Dutch hoped, of course, that the states they had set up would be an effective curb on the Republic. In this they were again wrong. No sooner had The Hague Agreement been effected, December, 1949, than the new Dutch-sponsored states voted under its terms for union with the Republic. By August of 1950 the United States of Indonesia had been replaced by a united and unitary Republic of Indonesia. Four years later, in 1954, the Dutch-Indonesian Union itself passed into history. Political independence had become a reality.

Government in the Republic. The Republic of Indonesia, with an area of some 750,000 square miles (almost three times the size of Texas), a vast archipelago stretching more than 3,000 miles along the equator, and with a population of 80 millions began its life with a simple governmental structure and an impressive burden of demanding problems for government to solve. The central government included a one-house legislature, a President selected by the parliament, a Vice-President named by the President but recommended by the legislature, and a cabinet responsible to Parliament. Because no single party commanded a majority in practice, the first cabinets were interparty selections. The political parties, though springing from pre-war groupings, were in the main creations of the post-1945 period. The *Partai Nasional Indonesia* (PNI), having concentrated on the issue of independence under Sukarno's leadership, found itself after independence playing the difficult role of trying to be all things to all men. The largest Islamic party was the *Masjumi,* in which leading Moslems were attempting to adjust traditional religious doctrine to contemporary political problems. A more militant Islamic group, violently national, was the *Darul Islam,* which was opposed both to the Republic and to Communism. Rebellions of this party against the government occurred principally in Western Sumatra. By 1953 the working alliance between the PNI and the *Masjumi* which had controlled politics was weakened by dissensions over the question of character and control of the armed forces. A government crisis resulted in a new cabinet under Ali Sastroamidjojo which for a time maintained itself against *Masjumi* opposition through Communist support in Parliament. The *Parti Komunis Indonesia* was thus able to regain prestige lost at the time of its attempt to seize the government in 1948. Its later tactic was to play heavily on the popular themes of nationalism and reform. In 1955 a new cabinet under Burhanuddin Harahap, of the *Masjumi,* held the first general elections, which revealed the strength of the four major political parties at the time. The most powerful were the PNI and the *Masjumi,* whose lesser but significant rivals were the Moslem Teachers party (*Nahdlatul Ulama*) and the Communists.[7]

Politics and economics. The Republic of Indonesia from the beginning was beset by a multitude of hazards. The infant state set out to practice parliamentary democracy in a land where about 50 per cent of the population was illiterate; where there had been no experience with democracy, a foreign importation; where deeply rooted tradition was authoritarian; and where the number of available trained civil servants was wholly inadequate. Yet the new government, once hostilities with the Dutch ceased, was called upon not only to maintain order but also to re-establish and improve the productive capacities of the economy.

In the re-shaping of its economic life, Indonesia, like most new states in Southeast Asia, reacted strongly against unfettered private capitalism. Private capitalism was intimately associated in the Indonesian mind with foreign rule. Prior to the war the foreign investor had often been the most outspoken opponent of self-government and independence. Thus the achievement of political independence carried with it the drive to end foreign economic control through economic nationalism operating as state capitalism. This meant the development of a state-planned economy to meet national ends.[8] Complicating the problem of state planning, however, was a rapidly increasing population (a medieval birth rate with a modern death rate), which in itself was proving in this underdeveloped area to be a hindrance rather than an aid to economic development. Domestic capital formation in Indonesia under the Republic was

---

[7] For a detailed treatment, see Vinacke, *Far Eastern Politics,* 342-374.

[8] Cady, "Evolving Political Institutions," in Philip W. Thayer, ed., *Nationalism and Progress in Free Asia* (Baltimore, 1956), 118-120.

negligible, and there was reluctance on the part of the government to give foreign investors the security they desired.[9]

3. *Burma*

In Burma, it will be recalled, the British had made substantial concessions in the direction of self-government before World War II. These concessions had not satisfied Burmese nationalism. The economic structure was still geared to the advantage of the European investor and the Indian moneylender. The Burmese laborer was still being replaced by the lower-paid Indian laborer. Nor had the system of British education prepared the Burmans to be masters of their own house. There were practically no Burmese engineers or doctors, scientists or economists, and only a handful who had received special training in England for government service under British rule. There were no political parties other than personal groupings at the time the British made their constitutional reforms in the 1930's, so that the first Burmese legislature of 1936 with 132 members was also "said to contain 132 parties." Therefore, in 1941 it appeared that there was a very great difference between the aspirations of the Burmese nationalists for independence and their preparation to operate an independent modern state.

The Japanese overran Burma in the first five months of 1942. At first they were welcomed and assisted by the Burmans, particularly by the extremists of the Thakin Party who had been clamoring for independence. In August, 1942, the Japanese military administration recognized Burmese independence under a puppet government headed by Ba Maw, a former premier with a pronounced anti-British record. Ba Maw's government soon lost its initial popular support. Its subservience to the Japanese was clear, while the behavior of the Japanese themselves contradicted their own propaganda that they were the saviors of Asia. The result was that many Burmans who had first assisted the Japanese joined the growing resistance movement organized as the Anti-Fascist Peoples Freedom League (AFPFL). As finally constituted in 1944, the League was a union of many revolutionary, independence, and Communist groups under the leadership of General Aung San, who only a few years earlier had helped the Japanese conquer Burma. The uniqueness of the

[9] B. W. Hodder, "Demographic Influences on Economic Development in Southeast Asia," *Nationalism and Progress in Free Asia,* 214-215.

AFPFL was that by the time the British returned at the end of the war it was able to confront them with its own effective army.

The Burma to which the British returned in 1945 was a picture of desolation and destruction. Twice invaded, it had twice been subject to a scorched earth policy. Plantations, oil fields, and mines had been wrecked. Rice, formerly the great export crop, was so worthless it was fed to pigs. The productive capacity of the country had been cut by two-thirds. The immediate British plan for Burma was to restore the pre-war political structure. Burmese parties would then be encouraged to propose and agree on a new constitution, after which there would be negotiations looking to Dominion status. In economic affairs, normal competitive business was to be restored as rapidly as possible. All this must have appeared very sensible to the British, but in reality it showed that they did not understand what had happened in Burma during their absence. The rapid Japanese conquest had destroyed British military and, in a degree, political prestige, while the war experience itself had produced in Burma her own military and political leaders possessed of a limited experience and a boundless determination. The welcome extended to the returning British and the "official" Burmans who three years before had fled the country with them was not unfriendly until it became evident that for an indefinite period the British Governor was to exercise all power to the exclusion of the AFPFL, which had fought for liberation of the country. The League, however, was so strong in popular support that within three months the Governor had created an Executive Council of eleven members, six of whom represented the League. In December, 1946, the British Government affirmed that Commonwealth status or independence, according to Burma's desire, would be granted "by the quickest and most convenient way possible." A subsequent conference at London, in which the Burmese delegation was headed by Aung San, president of the AFPFL, reached a settlement in January, 1947. It provided for an elected constituent Burmese assembly to frame a new independent Burmese government. Provision was also made for a transitional government consisting of a legislative council, a Governor's Executive Council, and a High Commissioner for Burma at London. The British Government was to support Burma's application for membership in the United Nations, and to invite other governments to establish diplomatic relations with Burma. Though this settlement was opposed by Communist and other extreme groups it was accepted by Aung San, the AFPFL, and the country at large. The new constitution was accepted, September, 1947, and Burma's independence dated from an Anglo-Burmese treaty, January, 1948.

Government structure in the Republic of the Union of Burma consisted of a President elected by a bicameral legislature; a cabinet responsible to the lower house, the upper house being representative of nationalities; and an independent judiciary. Within Burma the transition to this new independent Republic was not achieved without violence and bloodshed. In July, 1947, Aung San and six associates in the interim Executive Council were assassinated by U Saw and extremists attempting to take over the government. Although the attempt failed, it did deprive the country of some of its best and most experienced leaders.

Once independence was realized the new government encountered determined internal opposition from both the right and the left. The former represented elements opposed to the government's socialistic program. The latter were led by the Communists who had already split into two factions. There was also opposition from the lesser nationalities, especially the Karens, who had approved federation but were reluctant to practice it. To secure their ends these various groups resorted to intermittent violence, and it was not until 1954 that the government could be said to be reasonably secure. Meanwhile the administration had proceeded with its policy of limited socialism with British financial assistance.[10]

4. *Malaya*

In Southeast Asia at the beginning of World War II Western power and prestige were symbolized by the much-publicized British naval base at Singapore, an immense bastion of security completed in 1938 at a cost of £20,000,000. Singapore was the guarantor of the vital trade routes of the British Empire in the Far East and indeed of all international trade between Eastern Asia and Europe. World War II was less than three months old when this island of security surrendered to the Japanese. This catastrophe, sealing the wartime fate of all Southeast Asia, was a blow from which British prestige and power never fully recovered. When the British reoccupied Malaya in September, 1945, they found, as they had in Burma, a land where war had destroyed much of the wealth but where it had

[10] See Vinacke, *Far Eastern Politics,* 311-321.

also created a native nationalism that previously had been all but non-existent. This native nationalism in the short view was first a resistance against the Japanese and later a response to Japanese concessions to self-government.

Recognizing the need for a new form of administration, the British government set out to create a Malayan Union of all Malay states and the Straits Settlements of Penang and Malacca, but excluding Singapore, which was to continue as a crown colony. As a preliminary step the Malay sultans had been required to transfer their authority to the crown, and under the Union were to exercise only limited religious authority over their Moslem peoples. The essence of the Union plan, unlike the pre-war British policy that had given the Malays a preferred position over Chinese and Indians and had not encouraged self-government, was now to hasten democratic government and to grant equal rights of citizenship to all three races—Malays, Chinese, and Indians. These reforms, which were seemingly adopted without consulting anyone in Malaya, were designed admirably to give the Chinese populace decisive control in Malayan politics, since citizenship was to be enjoyed by all who were born in Malaya, to immigrants who had been there for ten years, and to future immigrants after five years residence. The result, therefore, of the Union proposal was a violent protest from the Malays.

Malay opposition was organized in the United Malays National Organization, led by Western-educated Malays, among whom were officials of the native states who exercised a wide influence with the peasantry. Their reaction against the Union plan was understandable, for at the time it was proposed the population of Malaya was 5,808,000, of whom 43.3 per cent were Malays, 44.9 per cent Chinese, and 10.4 per cent Indian. In Singapore itself, 77.4 per cent of the population was Chinese and only 12.1 per cent Malay. Under the influence of the new nationalism, the Malays, thinking of themselves as the only true people of the country, regarded the Chinese and Indians as interlopers who came "after the British made it safe for them to do so." As Moslems they looked upon the Chinese with intense religious aversion—an aversion magnified by the capacity of the Chinese businessman to corner the profits as retail traders, as buyers of native produce, and as moneylenders. Racial, religious, and economic animosities had not been softened by intermarriage, since religious barriers proscribed intermarriage. At war's end then there was no longer among the Malays an unquestioning acceptance of British rule, nor was there a united Malayan nationalism common to the three Asiatic races, but rather a triangular communal nationalism that was particularly bitter between the Malays and the Chinese.[11]

Under the protests of the Malay nationalists that the Union plan would violate Malay sovereignty and be subversive to the Malay race itself, the British government revised its policy. A new plan evolved in co-operation with the UMNO retained the essential structure of the native states in a federal constitution. It conferred citizenship on Malays, Chinese, and Indians born in Malaya. Permanent immigrants might acquire citizenship after fifteen years residence. This plan, which excluded Singapore, became effective in February, 1948. The central government of the new federation included a British High Commissioner with an executive and legislative council. The executive council was to aid and advise the Commissioner. The legislative council, which eventually was to be elected, was to give a distribution of racial representation, with the Malays having the largest single group. In the government of the states the sultans were to exercise the same authority they had prior to the Japanese invasion. The British government retained complete control of defense and foreign affairs.

Communist Rebellion. As the new policy and government went into operation Malaya was shaken by a violent and prolonged Communist-led rebellion. As early as 1939, when war broke out in Europe, Chinese Communists in Malaya fomented trouble for the British among the dock workers at Singapore. The same Communists supported the British after Germany attacked Russia, and when the Japanese took Malaya the Communists continued to direct an active underground anti-Japanese resistance. The movement did not oppose the British when they reoccupied Malaya in 1945. From this time on, however, the Malayan (Chinese) Communists sought to control the labor unions, and, in 1948, resorted to armed force. The strategy, which for a time was very successful, was to terrorize the populace by the murder of officials, plantation owners, businessmen, and supporters of the *Kuomintang* in Malaya. The Communists drew their supplies and recruits from Chinese who, several hundred thousand strong, had moved from the cities into the countryside during the Japanese occupation. From these bases

---

11 Lennox A. Mills, "Malaya To-Day," *World Affairs,* Jan., 1951, 26-36.

the Communists organized (sometimes by force) their Malayan National Liberation Army, whose professed purpose was to set up an independent Malayan People's Democratic Republic with equality for all races. Failing to deal effectively with the crisis by use of their superior military force, the British turned to more fundamental measures designed to starve out the Communist jungle strongholds by the resettlement of Chinese peasants in government-controlled villages. By 1955, Communist guerrilla strength had not been destroyed, but it had been so reduced as to be no longer a critical threat to the economy. Some orderly implementation of the new government of the Federated Malay States was now possible, and in the first elections of 1955 the elements favoring early independence won an easy victory. Meanwhile the Communists attempted to disrupt the political scene at Singapore. They instigated strikes of Chinese students which closed the schools and formed a left-wing Political Action party dedicated to independence for the Crown Colony.[12]

In 1957 the Federation of Malaya became an independent member of the (British) Commonwealth of Nations. The island of Singapore remained outside the new state as a British possession.

5. *Indochina*

Nationalism in Indochina, though repressed rigidly by French authority, was potentially an explosive force when World War II reached the Far East. The French by their political and cultural policy had failed completely to win the loyalty of the Annamese, and the economic status of the native had deteriorated rapidly in the pre-war decade as a result of increasing population. The profits of the rubber plantations and the coal mines went to French investors; those of the rice trade to the Chinese. There were two organizational bases of Annamese nationalism: (1) the Vietnam Nationalist party, which held its first congress on foreign soil at Canton in 1914, and (2) the Vietnamese Communist party, organized at Hongkong in 1930 by Ho Chi Minh.[13] During the 1930's the

[12] See the detailed treatment by Vinacke, *Far Eastern Politics,* 322-341.

[13] The latter party's origins went back to 1917 when Nguyen Ai Quoc (Ho Chi Minh) drew together a group of Vietnamese Communists at Paris, where Ho was a student. He later had Communist schooling at Moscow; and was at Canton with Borodin in 1925, where he formed a Vietnamese Revolutionary Youth party and secured appointment of young Vietnamese cadets for training at the Whampoa Military Academy. Later these men emerged as commanders of the Vietminh army. For further details, see Franz H. Michael and George E. Taylor, *The Far East in the Modern World* (New York, 1956), 584-586.

French administration in Indochina destroyed the Nationalist movement by putting its leaders to death, but it did not deal so successfully with the Communist leadership, a circumstance that was to have profound results later, especially in an area where "virtually no steps had been taken to introduce liberal governmental institutions which could have provided a pattern and a training agency for self-government."[14]

Indochina and the war, 1941-1945. The fall of France to German arms in 1940 gave Japan an open road to the control of Indochina. By treaty in that year the Japanese occupied Tongking. The following year they extended their occupation throughout Indochina and permitted Thailand to regain territory in Laos and Cambodia which France had annexed to these states many years earlier. During the greater part of the war the Japanese maintained in Indochina a false front of French administration. The willingness of French administrators to serve as Japanese puppets destroyed what little prestige they still had with the natives and enabled Vietnamese nationalism as an underground revolutionary force to strike at both the Japanese invader and the French ruler. Moreover, since the French had already disposed of the ablest nationalist leaders, the direction of the resistance movement devolved on the only organized group, the Communists. It was as though France were determined to destroy the last vestige of native loyalty to an overlord.

The Communists seized upon the opportunity. They organized the Vietnam Independence League (Vietminh), headed by Ho Chi Minh, in the form of a united front of diverse patriots, but in which the dominant leadership was Communist. Its program as announced was an invitation to all "true" patriots to unite to destroy imperialism and to achieve independence and democracy. These objectives were so phrased as to appeal to a broad base of nationalism comprehending the woes of the hard-pressed peasant, the fears of native business, and the political ambitions of the Western-educated native intellectuals. Toward the close of the war a guerrilla army of the Vietminh was master of most rural areas of Tongking.

In these same closing months of the war the Japanese themselves took over the administration of Indochina, declared the end of alien rule, and "restored" native governments and their kings in Annam, Cambodia, and Laos. Then in August, 1945, when the Japanese surrendered, a Democratic Republic of Vietnam was

[14] Cady, "Evolving Political Institutions," *Nationalism and Progress in Free Asia,* 118.

formed by the Vietminh, and it declared its independence on September 2, 1945. This government, soon in control of most of Annam, replaced the Japanese puppet regime under Emperor Bao Dai.

The new Republic, which was intended to include Cochin China, Annam, and Tongking, found that France was not prepared to concede independence. French policy, in principle at least, was willing to accept an autonomous Indochinese federation inside a French federal union, and in March, 1946, the Republic was recognized by France as the Free State of Vietnam within an Indochinese Federation and within the French Union. The Vietnamese nationalists regarded this plan as conceding neither full independence nor autonomy. In the south at Saigon the French had re-established their control by December, 1945, due to the fact that the British who accepted the Japanese surrender there released and rearmed the interned French troops. In the north in Tongking, where Chinese Nationalist troops had received the Japanese surrender, the French found it expedient to negotiate with the Republic, which in reality meant that France recognized the Free State before French troops entered Hanoi. It remained for France and Vietnam to agree on what the French scheme of federation was to mean. On this point no agreement was ever reached. To the nationalists of the Vietminh, federation of the three states meant limited economic co-ordination. To the French it meant close co-ordination under a French High Commissioner who would represent France and the French Union and at the same time be President of the Indochinese Federation. Furthermore, France separated Cochin China from the Free State under a separate puppet administration. Since this government never had any local standing, and since the French saw their only hope in subservient native regimes such as they already had in Cambodia and Laos, they decided to set up an alternative regime to the Republic in Vietnam. Meanwhile, armed clashes were occurring between French and Vietnam forces.

In their search for an alternate regime to the Republic of Vietnam, a regime that might attract non-Communist nationalists, the French hit upon the former Annamese emperor Bao Dai, who was still nominally an adviser to the Republic. While apparently willing to serve the French, Bao Dai was also playing the game of nationalism. When in 1949 he consented finally to head a French-sponsored Vietnam government (called the Provisional Government of Vietnam) in opposition to Ho's Republic, it was on condition that: (1)

the state have independent military forces, (2) that it have direct relations with foreign states, and (3) that Cochin China be included in the new state. From its beginning the Provisional Government rested on foundations of sand. It had no substantial support in either the cities or the countryside. It was operated by a clique of Bao Dai's friends, while the former emperor himself basked in the Mediterranean sunshine of southern France. Its only strength lay in its opposition to the Communist leadership of Ho Chi Minh's Republic, but it did not succeed in unifying special groups who were also opposed to Communism, such as the native Catholics of Tongking who followed the political leadership of their own bishops, or the indigenous religious sects of the south, such as the Caodaists and the Hoa Hao.[15]

While the Provisional Government was failing to gain either popular native support or any real autonomy from French control and was subsisting on what it was against rather than on what it was for, Ho Chi Minh's Republic was casting aside the veil of the United Front, was replacing moderate nationalists with Communists, and accepting publicly the People's Republic of China as its model. Indeed, the Communist victory in China, 1949, was a tremendous boost to the Republic, which was recognized by Peking and Moscow in 1950 and was soon receiving technical military assistance from these sources. As against these gains for Ho in the north, the position of France in the whole of Indochina was weakening. Bao Dai's government together with those of Cambodia and Laos were now demanding full independence, which the French now felt it expedient to grant at least formally. At the same time French military prestige suffered a fatal blow when the French garrison at Dien Bien Phu to the West of Hanoi surrendered to Ho's troops.

With both the political and the military tide running strongly against them in all Indochina, the French agreed to seek a settlement with the now clearly Communist Republic. At a conference at Geneva, beginning in May, 1954, as Dien Bien Phu was falling, Vietnam was about equally divided at a line just north of Hué near the 17th parallel, the north assigned to Ho's Republic, the south to Bao Dai's French-supported regime. Each government withdrew its troops from the other's territory. Civilians might move from the

[15] The latter was a militant Buddhist secret society. The former professed a mixture of Buddhist and Christian teachings.

Communist north if they desired to do so. Communist guerrillas were to be withdrawn from Cambodia and Laos. After two years elections were to choose a government for the entire country. France affirmed the full independence of Cambodia, Laos, and Bao Dai's Vietnam, though all were to remain within the French Union. Following this settlement Vietnam pursued a more vigorous policy under the premiership of Ngo Dinh Diem, who with American aid achieved some internal improvement by crushing the internal opposition of the religious and racketeering sects. When the first elections of 1955 confirmed Ngo Dinh Diem's government, the authority of Bao Dai was repudiated while Diem was declared chief of state.[16]

6. *Thailand*

On the eve of World War II, Thailand, which had been permitted by Britain and France to maintain a precarious independence, was moving into the orbit of growing Japanese influence. A commercial treaty of 1938 gave Japanese businessmen a favored position and appealed to the Thai as a means of curbing the Chinese. A new Japan-Thailand treaty of friendship concluded in 1940 coincided with Japan's benevolent mediation when Thailand seized the lost Cambodian provinces at the expense of France. Therefore, when Japan in December, 1941, demanded the right of military transit to attack the British in Malaya, the government of Luang Pibul Songgram after a token resistance consented, allied itself with Japan, and declared war on the United States and Britain. From the beginning, however, a civilian faction led by Pridi Phanomyong (Luang Pradit Manudharm), who as a member of Pibul's government had opposed the Japanese demands and the declaration of war, formed a resistance movement that served the Western Allies. At the close of the war the British after accepting the Japanese surrender in Thailand proposed to impose a settlement that would have made Thailand a British protectorate. This plan was opposed by the Thai and by the United States, which had not recognized the Thai declaration of war. As a result, the peace settlement of January, 1946, deprived Thailand of territories she had taken after December 7, 1941, and compensated British subjects for war losses. Thailand's admission to the United Nations, December, 1946, was achieved after some difficult adjustments in her relations with *Kuomintang* China, the establishment of diplomatic relations with

[16] A detailed narrative is given in Vinacke, *Far Eastern Politics,* 264-294.

the Soviet Union, and the return to France of the territories taken in 1941. From this point on Thailand's foreign policy tended to follow closely the lead of the United States and Great Britain.

The most notable characteristic of Thailand's post-war internal politics was the recurrent outbreaks by which administrations were threatened or overthrown. These so-called revolutions had little if anything to do with nationalism, or Communism, or even good government. They were in reality a more recent version of the factional struggle for power that had colored the Thai political stage in the 1930's. By 1948, Pibul Songgram, temporarily discredited because of his collaboration with Japan, was back in power with his military faction and the blessing of the United States and Great Britain. His predecessor Pridi, who had worked with the Allies during the war in the resistance movement and whose following, at least in theory, favored a more democratic government, had not made democracy work. There had been plenty of corruption in high places, economic problems had not been faced, and the government had appeared to be implicated in the unexplained death of the young king. These conditions had opened the way for the return of Pibul to power. And since Thailand was entering a period of prosperity in her export trade (rice, rubber, and tin), it was a poor field for Communist agitation. Pibul was thus able to maintain himself in power due to favorable circumstances which he himself had not brought about, due to his ruthless suppression of any opposition and due to his pronounced nationalism and anti-Communism.[17]

For Further Reading

Southeast Asia: General

Bailey, Sydney D., *Parliamentary Government in Southern Asia* (New York, 1952). An essay on parliamentary democracy in Burma, Ceylon, India, and Pakistan.

Cady, John F., Patricia G. Barnett, and Shirley Jenkins, *The Development of Self-Rule and Independence in Burma, Malaya, and the Philippines* (New York, 1948).

Crane, Robert I., and Burton Stein, *Aspects of Economic Development in South Asia* (New York, 1954). A critical analysis of Western assistance programs.

Dobby, E. H. G., *Southeast Asia* (New York, 1951). A survey of economic and social structures.

[17] See Vinacke, *Far Eastern Politics,* 295-309.

DuBois, Cora, *Social Forces in Southeast Asia* (Minneapolis, 1949).

Elsbree, Willard H., *Japan's Role in Southeast Asian Nationalist Movements 1940-45* (Cambridge, Mass., 1953). Japan's difficulties in dealing with the nationalist movement in Burma and Indonesia.

Emerson, Rupert, *Representative Government in Southeast Asia* (Cambridge, Mass., 1955). Discusses the prospect for the development of democratic government.

Hall, D. G. E., *A History of South-East Asia* (New York, 1955).

Holland, William L., ed., *Asian Nationalism and the West: A Symposium Based on Documents and Reports of the Eleventh Conference of the Institute of Pacific Relations* (New York, 1953).

Jacoby, Erich H., *Agrarian Unrest in South East Asia* (New York, 1949). Stresses the political implications of the revolt against landlordism.

Kahin, George, *The Asian-African Conference* (Ithaca, 1956). A summary of the Bandung conference.

Landon, Kenneth Perry, *Southeast Asia: Crossroad of Religions* (Chicago, 1949). A description of the survival of simple indigenous beliefs despite the arrival of Hindu, Moslem, Chinese, and Christian religions.

Lasker, Bruno, *Human Bondage in Southeast Asia* (Chapel Hill, 1950). Aspects of economic conditions in Southeast Asia.

Mende, Tibor, *South-East Asia Between Two Worlds* (New York, 1955). The influence of Chinese and Indian nationalism on the area.

Purcell, Victor, *The Chinese in Southeast Asia* (New York, 1951). The basic work on the subject.

Rosinger, Lawrence K., and associates, *The State of Asia* (New York, 1951). A survey consisting of independent analyses by leading specialists on particular countries.

Thayer, Philip W., ed., *Southeast Asia in the Coming World* (Baltimore, 1953).

Thompson, Virginia, and Richard Adloff, *The Left Wing in Southeast Asia* (New York, 1950). Particularly good on the techniques employed by Communists in their attempt to capture nationalist movements.

———, *Minority Problems in Southeast Asia* (Stanford, 1955).

———, *Cultural Institutions and Educational Policy in Southeast Asia* (New York, 1948).

BURMA

Andrus, J. R., *Burmese Economic Life* (Stanford, 1947). A well-documented study.

Donnison, F. S. V., *Public Administration in Burma* (London, 1953).

Hall, D. G. E., *Burma* (New York, 1950). A short introduction.

U Nu, *Burma under the Japanese,* ed. and trans. by J. S. Furnivall (London, 1954).

INDOCHINA

Devillers, Philippe, *Vietnam and France* (New York, 1950).

Hammer, Ellen, *The Emergence of Vietnam* (New York, 1947).

———, *The Struggle for Indochina* (Stanford, 1954). A detailed history of the relations between Indochina, the Vietminh, France, and the outside world since World War II.

INDONESIA

Kahin, G. M., *Nationalism and Revolution in Indonesia* (Ithaca, 1952). A scholarly account of the Indonesian Nationalist Movement.

Kattenburg, Paul, *A Central Javanese Village in 1950* (Ithaca, 1951). An examination of social change since 1945.

Sjahrir, Soetan, *Out of Exile,* trans. and with an introduction by Charles Wolf, Jr. (New York, 1949). The experiences and ideas of one of Indonesia's foremost intellectuals and first prime minister of the Republic.

Wolf, Charles, Jr., *The Indonesian Story: The Birth, Growth, and Structure of the Indonesian Republic* (New York, 1948). Particularly good for the Dutch-Indonesian negotiations.

MALAYA

Hanrahan, Gene Z., *The Communist Struggle in Malaya* (New York, 1954). The organization and methods of the party in the years 1924-1953. Well documented.

Purcell, Victor, *The Chinese in Malaya* (New York, 1948).

———, *Malaya: Communist or Free* (Stanford University, 1954). A criticism of British policy since World War II.

Winstedt, Sir Richard, *Malaya and Its History* (London, 1948).

THE PHILIPPINES

Abaya, Hernando J., *Betrayal in the Philippines* (New York, 1946). Critical of American policy on the ground that it resulted in the return of collaborators to office.

Castillo, Andres V., *Philippine Economics* (Manila, 1949).

Jenkins, Shirley, *American Economic Policy Toward the Philippines* (Stanford, 1954).

Pratt, J. W., *America's Colonial Experiment* (New York, 1950).

Romulo, Carlos P., *I See the Philippines Rise* (Garden City, 1946).

Scaff, Alvin H., *The Philippine Answer to Communism* (Stanford, 1955).

Seeman, Bernard, and Laurence Salisbury, *Cross Currents in the Philippines* (New York, 1946). A discussion of tensions in the post-war Philippines.

Spencer, J. E., *Land and People in the Philippines: Geographic Problems in Rural Economy* (Berkeley, 1952).

Taruc, Luis, *Born of the People: An Autobiography* (New York, 1953).

THAILAND (SIAM)

Crosby, Sir Josiah, *Siam: The Cross Roads* (London, 1945).

Reeve, W. D., *Public Administration in Siam* (New York, 1951).

deYoung, John E., *Village Life in Modern Thailand* (Berkeley, 1955). A study based on observation of a group of villages in the northern part of the country.

39

1945 onward

The Interminable Cold War

In the years that have passed since the end of World War II in 1945, eastern and southern Asia have lived through the most revolutionary period of their entire history. This revolution, or rather complex of revolutions, which is still gathering momentum, is the direct and tangible product of the story of the impact of Western modernism on the venerable traditionalism of Asia. Viewed in a broad focus, Asia's contemporary revolution has been operating in the immediate past in two distinct but intimately related ways. The first of these, recounted in chapters 36, 37, and 38, is the story of domestic upheaval in which every country of eastern and south Asia has been reconstructing for good or ill its political foundations, its economic structure, and its social framework. In the second sphere of operation, Asia's contemporary revolutions have been and they remain a part of the vast maze of world politics. In the nineteenth and the early twentieth centuries the voices of Asia carried little weight in the councils of the great powers, but since World War II these voices have often been a determining factor in decisions of world-wide import. The old pattern in which the West made decisions for Asia has been giving place to a new pattern in which Asia decides for itself and somtimes for the West as well. This new international behavior of Asia is the essence of what has been called since 1945 the Cold War in the Far East. Some suggestions of what has been happening in this war is therefore the substance of this chapter.[1]

The Cold War in the Far East, which began as World War II came to an end, was not a creation of 1945 but of the whole preced-

[1] The ablest extensive study of this subject is Harold M. Vinacke, *Far Eastern Politics in the Postwar Period* (New York, 1956).

ing century. The forces of which it was made were the immediate product of great movements of historical evolution which, taken together, tend to defy explicit definition. It has been said, and this is certainly true, that the Cold War in Asia resulted from the struggle of Asian nationalism to destroy and replace the rule of imperialism. This attempt at definition, however, only acquires meaning if the varied natures of imperialism and of nationalism as historical developments in Asia have been examined and are understood. For example, it may be recalled that the American theory and practice of imperialism in the Philippines was not the same as the Japanese theory and practice in Korea. Likewise, nationalism in the Far East, although arising from the common desire for freedom from alien rule or control, was shaped and colored in many ways by the diverse cultural settings in which it arose.

The Cold War began in 1945 not because World War II came to an end but because it was in that year that the Japanese Empire collapsed. In the preceding century Japan had grown from an insignificant feudal state to the stature of a great power. Prior to the rise of this Japanese power, international politics in the Far East was mainly a reflection of the balance of power in Europe. In eastern Asia this balance of power was maintained through a competitive rivalry among the great Western states for political and economic control of their spheres of influence, principally in the decadent Manchu Empire. Japan's rise was therefore a movement affecting world politics rather than far eastern politics because the extent and the timing of Japanese territorial expansion in Formosa (1895), Korea (1910), Manchuria (1905 and 1931), and China (1937) were determined by the capacity of the imperial powers of Europe (and later of the United States) to resist her, and not by the capacity of China to defend herself. Japan's expansion, beginning as a strategic and defensive policy, became in time a drive for a political and economic empire clothed in the slogan of "Asia for the Asiatics." The economic as opposed to the political side of Japan's imperialism was suggested by her efforts to create a "Greater East Asia Co-Prosperity Sphere" through which the far eastern economy, focused toward Japan as the industrial center, was to be separated from the world economy. Thus Japan's rise and her emerging objectives added up to a frontal assault on the possessions and interests of Europe and the United States in the Far East. After 1930, Western resistance to Japan was ineffectual. Unable or unwilling to risk blocking the extension of Japanese political control in China and elsewhere, the powers tried simply to safeguard their interests within those areas now under Japanese control. This formula did not halt the expansion of Japanese power. On the contrary, it made clear the point that China must preserve herself as an independent state if she were to be preserved at all. Actually, between 1938 and the end of the Japanese threat in 1945, China's power tended to decline rather than increase, for she was not one but three Chinas: (1) Nationalist China, (2) Communist China, and (3) Japanese-occupied China. Again the significance of Western power in the Far East was made clear in 1940, when the Japanese shifted their drive from north to south China and later to Indochina and to the conquest of Southeast Asia. The Japanese made these moves only when the British, the French, and the Dutch, completely involved in the European war, could offer only local resistance in their far eastern empires. In all these advances the Japanese enjoyed at first a psychological advantage. They posed as the political and cultural liberators of Asia from Western imperialism and professed to be fighting for the independence of Asian peoples.

In Southeast Asia this Japanese strategy did two things of importance to this narrative: (1) it encouraged Asian independence movements, and (2) it embarrassed the British, French, and Dutch, who were not yet prepared to dissolve their empires. During the war years, 1941-1945, these powers did pledge the liberation of their subject peoples in Southeast Asia from Japanese rule, and they hinted cautiously at future moves in the direction of self-government, but there was no renunciation of so-called colonialism in favor of independence. These hesitant gestures in no way met the realities in Southeast Asia by war's end in 1945. By that time there was strong native resistance to Japan taking the form of vigorous and armed nationalist movements demanding independence not only from Japan but also from the former rulers—British, French, and Dutch. Thus the war had disposed of only one large problem in the Far East. It had settled the question of Japanese power by bringing about its destruction, but it had resolved no other international problem of Eastern Asia. Indeed, the destruction of Japanese power meant that for the moment the Far East was a political vacuum in terms of effective power. This vacuum could be filled only from two sources: (1) the internal force of Asia's contemporary revolution, namely, its infant but eruptive nationalism, and (2) power from outside the Far East, polarized after 1945 in the Communist world of Soviet Russia and in the democratic world of the United States and its free allies.

What happened, therefore, at war's end was neither mysterious nor historically unpredictable. Nationalist and revolutionary forces within Asia attempted to seize power so far as they could. Where there were rival revolutions, as in China, Nationalists and Communists, though sometimes talking of peace, fought each other for control of the state. In the former empires of Europe, such as, for example, Netherlands India, a newly born independent republic resisted the returning Dutch. Again, as she had done in 1898 and 1900, Russia occupied Manchuria and half of Korea, the most strategic of all bases for the control of China, while the United States in occupying south Korea and a fallen Japan bolstered Nationalist China against the Communists in its efforts to accept the Japanese surrender and to reoccupy its own territory. The war therefore had not solved the problem of imperialism in Southeast Asia. It had opened the way for the return of Russia to the Far East, this time a Communist Russia, as a contender for power in Manchuria, Korea, and China. It had given the United States, the chief belligerent in the Pacific and Asian theater, an unprecedented position of responsibility in the Far East. These were the primary stage settings as the curtain rose on what was to be called the Cold War.

The Power to Make Decisions

Since in the pre-war Far East power exerted from outside the area was often a stronger determinant than internal pressures in ordering political affairs, and since the Far East was therefore subject to the currents of world politics as much, if not more, than to local and domestic tensions, it is essential to observe who held the reins of power in the Far East when the war ended. From 1931 to 1941 the predominant power of decision was held by Japan, but by 1945 this power had shifted to and was dispersed among the United States, the Soviet Union, and, to a lesser degree, the British Commonwealth. This new location and division of power had resulted from Japan's defeat and from a varying wartime co-operation among the great powers opposed to her. Between the United States and the British nations there was intimate joint planning and allocation of resources for the war. Both the American and the British government also gave great material aid to the Soviet Union, but Russia did not encourage full co-operation and, in fact, as a Communist revolutionary state, continued throughout the war to look upon its Western allies in arms with deep suspicion. The severe and obvious limitations that Russia placed on her co-operation, and her continuing attitude of distrust certainly did not suggest that the making of peace in Europe or in the Far East would be a simple task once Germany and Japan were defeated. Nevertheless, the powers appeared to entertain the assumption that wartime co-operation would increase and that it would be continued in some degree in the post-war period, since it was thought to be the only principle on which world order might be restored and maintained. This ideal of continued co-operation among the victors was the basis of the formula whereby the five so-called great powers (the United States, Britain, France, Russia, and Nationalist China), who were the permanent members of the Security Council of the United Nations, could take action for the maintenance of peace only when all of them were in agreement. This assumption that there would be continued co-operation between Russia and her wartime allies soon proved to rest on an unstable foundation.

The failure of the principle of co-operation created for a time the misconception that there was a dual contest for power, one in Europe and a second in the Far East. In reality the two were not separate. The capacity of western Europe (Britain, France, and the Netherlands) to recover from the war and to establish a balance against Russia in Europe was affected directly by the conditions of disorder, failing production, and nationalist revolts in their empires in the Far East. Not one of the revolting or newly created independent states of South or Southeast Asia possessed the resources for rapid rehabilitation or for the creation of stable independent governments without assistance from Europe or the United States. This interdependence received a very tardy recognition in the United States only as the importance of the Southeast Asian economy to European recovery became obvious, and as it was realized that conditions of economic and political disorder in the Far East were opening the door there to Communist agitation.

This interdependence between the European and the Far Eastern theaters in the problem of making peace was emphasized in 1945 by the positions of power held by Russia and the United States in Eastern Asia. At the end of the war Russia reassumed a position of great strength in Northeastern Asia. She entered the war against Japan by invading Manchuria, August 9, 1945, and concluded a Sino-Soviet Treaty of Friendship, August 14, 1945, with the Nationalist Government of China. The practical effect was to give Russia immediate control of Manchuria, to restore old historic rights in the Manchurian railways and the Kwantung leased territory, and to guarantee the "independence" of Outer Mongolia under a government controlled by Moscow. In return for these Manchurian and Mongolian concessions Russia was pledged to give moral support and material aid only to the National Government as *the* government of China, to respect China's sovereignty in Manchuria, and to refrain from interference in the internal affairs of Sinkiang. These conditions were acceptable to the Chinese National Government because they appeared to deny to the Chinese Communists any support from Russia. The fact, too, that Russian military operations in Manchuria and Korea continued long after the Japanese surrender gave to Russia a position of power beyond anything granted in the Yalta Agreement or the Sino-Soviet Treaty. Within a few weeks and with the expenditure of a minimum of effort Russia acquired a stronger position in the limited but key area of Northeast Asia than she had ever held before.

Against this focal area of revived Russian power was the perhaps even greater though more widely dispersed power of the United States in the Far East. This predominant American position was a creation of the military campaigns of the war and not of the longer development of historical American policy. Immediately following Japan's surrender, the United States: (1) was master of the Philippines and the entire western Pacific, (2) was in a position to set the terms on which the Dutch, French, and British might reoccupy their empires in Southeast Asia, (3) was indispensable to the National Government of China as a source of military transport for purposes of the Japanese surrender, (4) was the only external power other than Russia capable of exerting strong pressure on the National Government, (5) was the unqualified military and political master of Japan, and (6) was in occupation of Korea south of the 38th parallel. This extraordinary position of power did not mean, however, that the United States could dispose of Far Eastern problems of peace by simple mandate or in complete disregard of forces of opposition which it did not and in all probability could not control. In the Philippines and in Japan the United States was at greater liberty than in other areas to pursue its own purposes, but even in these areas its power was subject to various restraints imposed by local conditions or by the traditions of its own institutions and historic policies. In Southeast Asia the United States was limited by a conventional policy which postulated that the Dutch, French, and British would of right determine policy in the empires they were reoccupying there. For the time being, therefore, American influence on nationalist and independence movements tended to be either negative or favorable to the imperial powers. Finally, with respect to China, the power of the United States to make decisions designed to influence or determine the future of that State was limited: (1) by the force of traditional American policy there, (2) by the re-occupation of Northeast China by Russia, and (3) by the division of Chinese power itself between Nationalists and Communists.

China and World Politics, 1945 and After

The end of hostilities altered decisively the long-standing conflict within China between the Nationalists and the Communists, and also the bearing of this internal struggle on international affairs. The most immediate change—the removal of Japanese military power by surrender—opened the way for a violent competitive scramble between Nationalists and Communists to take over Japanese-occupied China, which included Manchuria (already seized by Russia) and the whole area of central and eastern-seaboard China. In the closing months of the war, American policy, recognizing that the *Kuomintang* had ceased to be an effective unifying and progressive force, and that the Chinese Communists were capitalizing on the resulting demoralization, sought to strengthen the National Government by urging it to effect: (1) economic, administrative, and democratic reform, and (2) a coalition with other parties, including the Communists, to achieve internal strength and peace. It was this policy which General Patrick Hurley tried to implement between September, 1944, and November, 1945. The coalition scheme failed because the Communists were determined to have a guaranteed position of strength in the National Government before giving up control of their armies, while the *Kuomintang* government, although willing to give political promises to the future, was equally determined to have military integration first under its own control. Such were the conditions when Japan surrendered and when General Albert C. Wedemeyer, who had succeeded General Joseph Stilwell as American commander in China, was required to assist in disarming Japanese troops without becoming involved in the *Kuomintang*-Communist conflict. Wedemeyer's task was the more difficult because American policy as applied during the Hurley period was undergoing subtle but significant modifications. As the hope for a coalition between the National Government and the Communists became more remote, Hurley became more sympathetic to the position taken by the *Kuomintang* and exerted less pressure on the National Government to reform its administration. Some members of Hurley's staff disagreed with this shift in emphasis. They took the position that it was hopeless for the United States to pose as a mediator unless its purposes were regarded as impartial. The reputation of impartiality, they said, could not be maintained if mediation could be approached only on terms set by the *Kuomintang*.

The Marshall Mission

In an effort to revive the mediation policy, President Truman sent General George C. Marshall to China late in 1945 to seek "the unification of China by peaceful, democratic methods." This effort was based on specific premises: (1) that American assistance would not be extended indefinitely to a China that could achieve no unity within itself, (2) that a united and democratic China was essential to world stability and the proper functioning of the United Nations. In January, 1946, Marshall brought the National Government and the Communists to agreement on a cease fire. For a time the truce enjoyed a measure of success save in Manchuria, but a like success did not attend current *Kuomintang*-Communist negotiations on plans for political reorganization, the Communists refusing ultimately to join in the preliminary steps toward constitutional reorganization. In the main, Marshall's failure was due to the military situation that developed in Manchuria. Marshall and his successor as Ambassador to China, J. Leighton Stuart, attempted the impartial role of mediators, a role that was perhaps impossible, since in fact they were accredited to the National Government. Marshall himself attributed the failure of his mediation mission to: (1) "the complete, almost overwhelming suspicion" between the *Kuomintang* and the Communists, (2) the conflict between the clearly acknowledged Marxian purposes of the Communists and the non-Marxian philosophy of the men who controlled the National Government, and (3) the presence in the *Kuomintang* of "a dominant group of reactionaries" and, among the Communists, of extremists willing and able to resort to any extreme measures. American policy had failed to achieve its purpose under Hurley, and it failed for a second time under Marshall.

U. S. Policy: North China and Manchuria, 1947-1948

From the moment of the Japanese surrender the National Government had been intent on the reoccupation of Manchuria for obvious economic and political reasons. Its efforts to do so were pursued against the counsel of the United States Military Mission in China. The disastrous effects of the *Kuomintang* military effort and failure were expressed by General Wedemeyer, September, 1947, when he reported to Washington that: (1) Manchuria was on the verge of becoming a Soviet satellite, (2) the Chinese Communists were close to control there and to the setting up of a government, and (3) the result would be agreements between Manchuria, Outer Mongolia, and Russia of the utmost danger to China, the United States, and the United Nations since it could lead ultimately to a Communist-dominated China. Wedemeyer therefore suggested that China ask the United States to end Manchurian hostilities and then place Manchuria under a trusteeship composed of China, Russia, the United States, Britain, and France. The Wedemeyer proposal could not be considered practical politics unless: (1) the National Government was willing to admit that Manchuria was not China, and that it was unable to deal with its own Communists or with Russia, (2) the United States was willing to pledge military forces in a situation in China which in terms of reality could only be described as civil war. Neither Nationalist China nor the United States was prepared to take these steps, and, in consequence Chiang was advised by Washington to concentrate on strengthening his position in North China. Again, by pursuing the Manchurian conquest, Chiang disregarded the advice, with the result that he lost Manchuria and the armies sent there, and ultimately North China as well.

By 1947-1948 it was even more manifest than in 1944-1945 that the United States, within the limitations within which its China policy operated, was exerting less rather than greater influence on the course of events in China. American aid had given the Nationalists an immediate military superiority, but American mediation efforts had failed, and the resulting Nationalist demands for further American aid suggested clearly that the *Kuomintang* was dependent on foreign support. These circumstances opened the way for the Communist propaganda attack affirming that: (1) the *Kuomintang* no longer represented Chinese nationalism, and (2) the Americans were interventionists and imperialists.

Recognition of the People's Republic of China

The Communist military victory and the establishment, October 1, 1949, of a central government at Pei-p'ing of the People's Republic of China was followed immediately, October 2, by Russian recognition of the new regime. The action was designed to bolster the Pei-p'ing government, to enable both governments to repudiate the 1945 Soviet-Nationalist treaty, and to permit Russia to join with Pei-p'ing in attacking the policy of the United States as one of intervention and imperialism. By January of 1950 Mao's government had also been recognized by Russia's satellites, by India, Burma, Britain, Finland, Sweden, Israel, and Denmark, and soon thereafter recognition was extended by Ceylon, Pakistan, Afghanistan, Indonesia, the Netherlands, and Switzerland. All acts of recognition prior to January, and this included Britain and India, were premature and therefore like Russia's were acts of intervention. In all cases recognition was extended or withheld as an instrument of national policy. Britain's early recognition was extended in the hope of protecting her territorial and commercial interests, and of counter-balancing the preponderant Russian influence. The Indian position as expressed by Prime Minister Jawaharlal Nehru was that power had passed to the Chinese Communists, that they rather than the *Kuomintang* had popular support, and that the people of Asia must be allowed to decide their political future without foreign interference.

The U. S. Withholds Recognition

The United States did not recognize the new Communist government at Pei-p'ing. At first the presumption was, though this was not stated explicitly as policy, that the United States would follow its traditional practice of extending recognition when: (1) the military outcome was decisive, (2) the stability of the new regime was beyond reasonable doubt, and (3) the new government gave evidence that it could and would be internationally responsible. Actually in the months and even years that followed October, 1949, when the Chinese Communists proclaimed their government, it was never possible for any American administration to approach the subject of extending or withholding recognition on the basis of this foregoing sound and tested formula of American policy. To the overwhelming mass of the American people the news of the collapse of the *Kuomintang* and the easy Communist conquest was simply unbelievable. To an American public that for a century had been encouraged to believe that historic Chinese policy was the expression of a unique Chinese attachment to the United States and its institutions, it was clear that American policy had met disaster and that it was imperative to fix responsibility for this colossal and unexplained tragedy. Beginning then in 1950, this search for those responsible became for a time one of the primary functions of domestic American politics.

The movement was spearheaded by American partisans of the *Kuomintang* both in and outside the Congress, who advanced the theory that the collapse of the National Government was due not to its own weakness and revolutionary vacuity but to the failure of the American Government to give it adequate support. The theory, if true, meant that the Democratic Administration of President Harry Truman had indirectly helped the Chinese Communists to power. From this position the *Kuomintang* partisans argued that the conclusions were inescapable. Either the Administration had so miscalculated affairs in China as to bring upon the American people a disastrous defeat in the Cold War to "contain" Communism, or it had knowingly pursued a course that was manifestly easy on communism if not sympathetic with it. These charges came to be accepted so widely by an American public less concerned with examining their validity than with fixing responsibility that the American government was precluded from dealing with the question of recognition or non-recognition in the light of established policy or of national interest. The prominence given by anti-Administration and pro-*Kuomintang* politicians to the general issue of communism befogged the whole picture. In reality, there was small reason at best for the United States to recognize the People's Government. Nevertheless, the fact that the real issues never became the substance of American public debates created in Asia a conviction that the United States would not deal with governments whose institutions and programs were repugnant to American ideas. This obscuring of issues tended also to prolong the hope that nationalism rather than international communism would predominate in the People's Government and that a Chinese Titoism would be the result. Such a result would have been welcome to American opinion. As it was, American support for the fugitive National Government on Formosa, and the involvement of China in the later Korean conflict stimulated the "Hate America" campaign, drew China closer to Russia, and aided the communists in their efforts to put the imperialist tag on America. On February 14, 1950, Russia and Communist China concluded a treaty of alliance and mutual assistance. This alliance directed in terms against a disarmed and an American-occupied Japan was in reality aimed at the United States. The treaty aligned China in international affairs with the Soviet bloc of states, precluded economic assistance from the United States to Communist China, and drew closer the economic and cultural ties between Mao's government and the Soviet Union. With the backing of this treaty the Chinese Communists were able to continue the groundless charges that America's China policy was one of imperialism. At the same time Mao, if he did not welcome it, was willing to tolerate Soviet imperialism in Manchuria, Mongolia, and Sinkiang.

The Korean Question

One of the less obvious but vital results of the outbreak of World War II was a revival of Korean nationalism. After the abortive uprising of 1919 Korean nationalists had agitated their cause in both China and the United States. A Korean Provisional Government, unrecognized but nevertheless aided by China, existed first in the International Settlement at Shanghai and later at Nanking and Chungking. In the United States a second group of exiles, headed by Syngman Rhee, but including several factions, sought unsuccessfully for American recognition. At the end of World War II in 1945, two years after the Cairo Declaration of November, 1943, had pledged an independent Korea "in due course," there was still no agreed policy among the allies on Korea's future other than the principle of independence, and there was no agreed understanding among rival Korean factions in exile concerning their proposed return to Korea and their assumption of authority there when Japan surrendered. Thus when the war ended there were no agreed plans for Korea's future. The exiles had no experience in the exercise of political authority; they were divided among themselves, and there was no leadership on the Korean question, either single or united, among the great powers. It was not even known whether the Korean people who had lived under Japanese rule were prepared to accept the leadership of the factions in exile. The only positive step of the powers was the understanding reached at Yalta between Roosevelt and Stalin that for a time Korea might be made a trusteeship. So matters were when the war ended and Korea, for purposes only of accepting the Japanese surrender, was divided into two zones at the 38th parallel, the Russians to accept the surrender in the north, the Americans in the south.

The collapse of Japanese power in Korea was accompanied not only by Russian and American military occupation but also by revolutionary efforts on the part of Korean factions to seize political power. In the north these groups, heavily weighted with Korean Communist Party leaders returned from exile, were encouraged and given authority by the Russians. In the south, revolutionary groups that had formed a People's Republic at Seoul were not accepted by the American occupation forces as a *de facto* government. Indeed for a time the Americans retained Japanese in administrative posts and then set up an American military government employing Koreans where qualified. The net result was that in the south the government was American in appearance and power, while in the north the government seemed to be Korean though the actual control was Russian.

Against this background the American and the Soviet commands in Korea were unable to reach any agreement on ordinary matters of relations between the two zones. Korea in fact had become two hostile camps dominated by the Soviet Union and the United States and thus a battleground of the Cold War. The respective commands failed, in addition, to agree on how to form a provisional government for all Korea or on what Korean parties were to be consulted and allowed to participate toward this end. In consequence the United States took the Korean problem to the United Nations in

August, 1947, while Russia proposed that both powers withdraw their military forces. Both the United States and the United Nations General Assembly rejected this proposal for reasons that were quite clear, namely, the Russian success in creating in north Korea a government which it felt could be counted on to do Moscow's bidding and extend Communist control to the south once American troops had left. The northern government, composed of approved parties acting as a coalition and led by the Labor (Communist formed) Party, was so organized as to insure Communist control, but it had the appearance of being Korean and of being based on a broad elective system.

In the southern zone progress toward some kind of self-government was much slower than in the north. The United States wanted Korea to build a truly democratic system and government, but it did not wish to turn over authority to a Korean democracy that might be hostile to American policy. Here the dilemma was very real and the ultimate solution not very satisfactory. While the American military government tolerated the agitation of all factions, it tended to support the moderate and conservative elements, and as American-Russian relations became more bitter the American tendency to bolster the extreme Korean conservatives grew. The result was that the American-supervised elections for an interim legislative assembly were regarded as fraudulent even by middle-of-the-road Korean leaders. At the same time the continuing efforts of north Koreans to escape to the south suggested that there were many who preferred to rely on ultimate American purposes rather than on the imposed regime of the Communists.

Aggravating these questions of internal politics operating under the pressure of external power was the economic plight of Korea. Its industry and mining were concentrated in the north, its best agriculture was in the south, and its foreign trade had all been developed by Japanese owners, managers, and technicians for the Japanese market. Apart from the question of training Korean personnel to replace Japanese, there was the artificial obstacle to recovery provided by the political division at the 38th parallel, which meant that the industrial north and the agricultural south were unable to perform their complementary functions. In these circumstances only large importations of food and fertilizer from abroad by the American military government saved the far larger southern population from starvation. Eventually the problem was relieved further by land reform which allotted Japanese-held land to Korean tenants. There could be, however, no fundamental solution to economic problems while the political situation was deadlocked. This deadlock continued, and a U.N. Temporary Commission sent late in 1947 to see that freely elected representatives of the Korean people were permitted to determine the form of government for all Korea was refused admittance to the Russian zone. Elections held in the south in 1948 under the Commission's supervision (with seats reserved for the north) brought into being the first assembly of the Republic of Korea. A constitution having been adopted, July, 1948, the assembly elected Syngman Rhee the first president. Authority of the American military government was transferred to the new regime, which was approved by the U.N. General Assembly as a lawful government, and was soon recognized by most countries other than the Soviet bloc. North Korea's reply to these developments was elections in the north for a supreme People's Assembly for all Korea. This assembly set up a rival constitution and government in the north as Russia's answer to the American effort to solve the Korean question through the United Nations.

Withdrawal of American troops from south Korea was completed in June, 1949, while the Russians had announced that their withdrawal would be complete by the beginning of the year. The resulting balance of power in the peninsula was uneven. In the north what amounted to a single-party Communist regime with south Korean representation in the government and backing by Russia was single-minded in the purpose to consolidate its power. In the south the government of Rhee, purportedly a free administration, was attacked from many quarters on the ground that it had gained power by unscrupulous methods, that the cabinet was chosen unwisely, that no north Koreans were included, and that the president and the ministry were intent on achieving personal power rather than a democratic national government. The American government was thus in a position where it might be forced to exert strong pressure on Rhee or find itself committed to an anti-Communist government that had no other virtue and was so lacking in popular support as to deny it any claim as a democratic government. This American dilemma was the more telling at this particular time, 1949, because of the fate that had overtaken the *Kuomintang*-National Government in China. There followed therefore a cut-back in American economic aid to Korea on the theory that American assistance must be used for political and economic rehabilitation and not to advance the political ambitions of individuals or factions. In principle the American position was unassailable; in practice it was an invitation to the north Korean regime to strike south Korea at its most vulnerable spot—its questionable leadership.

War in Korea

North Korean armies, well equipped and reportedly led by Russian officers, struck across the 38th parallel in a surprise attack on June 25, 1950. The attack was presumably based on two theories: (1) that the United States, having already excluded Korea from the American security zone, would not intervene with military force, and (2) that a Soviet veto would prevent effective action by the United Nations, or that the U.N. could not act in the absence of one of the great powers, since Russia at the time was absenting herself from the Security Council. However, the Security Council passed a cross-fire resolution calling on the north Koreans to withdraw, and the United States authorized additional military supplies to the defenders. On June 27 U.S. air and sea forces were ordered to cover and support south Korean troops, and when on June 30 it was clear that south Korean forces were facing complete defeat American ground forces were ordered to Korea. These American actions were in support of the resolution of the Security Council, and in terms of American policy were to halt Communism in its attack upon a free nation. In implementation of policy the United States, by presidential mandate, proclaimed the neutralization of Formosa debarring hostilities between the Nationalist and Communist Chinese through the policing operations of the Seventh (U.S.) Fleet in the Formosan Straits. On July 8 President Truman named General of the Army Douglas MacArthur as commander of United Nations forces in Korea. Russia, on August 1, resumed her seat on the Security Council, taking the position that the conflict in Korea had been precipitated by a south Korean attack and that the resolutions of the Security Council were illegal. By October, with reversal in the tide of battle, south Korean troops were invading the north, MacArthur had called upon the north to surrender, and had been authorized by the U.N. General Assembly to exercise civil authority on its behalf in the territory north of the 38th parallel.

An entirely new situation had been created by the end of October when, as U.N. forces moved across the 38th parallel and as Republic of Korea troops in advance of them neared the Yalu river boundary against Manchuria, Communist Chinese armies, termed "volunteers," joined the north Korean forces. By January, 1951, the Chinese Communists had entered the war in overwhelming force, had driven U.N. forces back to the 38th parallel, and had the power to drive into south Korea. This offensive was contained by April, 1951, when U.N. forces were again north of the parallel. Meanwhile negotiations for a political settlement had again failed. The United States was prepared to discuss such proposals once a cease-fire had been achieved. Russia and Communist China would discuss nothing until there was prior acceptance of their terms of a general far eastern settlement. These terms included: (1) evacuation of all foreign troops from Korea, (2) admission of Communist China to the United Nations, (3) termination of American "intervention" supporting the Chinese Nationalists on Formosa, and (4) a general far eastern conference to seek a comprehensive settlement and a peace treaty with Japan meeting the wishes of Moscow and Pei-p'ing. In the face of these demands the United States appealed to the U.N. General Assembly, which on February 1, 1951, found Mao's government guilty of aggression.

The impasse in Korea in the spring of 1951 revealed the widest implications of the Cold War. The problem of finding a unified policy for the Korean question was relatively simple for Russia and Communist China. Such was not the case with the leadership of the United States and other powers, European and Asiatic, which in general had supported the United States through the United Nations. Many of these governments differed with the United States on principles of policy or on solutions for particular problems. In western Europe there was fear that if the United States became too deeply involved in Asia it would be unable to join in the defense of Europe against Russia. This view was shared by the U.S. Joint Chiefs-of-Staff and expressed by General Omar Bradley when he said participation in a general far eastern conflict with Red China would involve the United States "in the wrong war, at the wrong place, at the wrong time and with the wrong enemy." The problem of American policy was also complicated by the so-called neutralism of India and other newly created Asian states. Led by India, these "neutrals" were intent to retain their independence of judgment and not to commit themselves in advance to follow in far eastern matters the leadership of the United States, a non-Asiatic state.

The problem of discovering what the United States should and could do to achieve victory in Korea in line with principles enunciated by the United Nations was brought to a head by the position taken by the U.N. Commander, General MacArthur. MacArthur had been advocating: (1) a broad blockade of China, (2) permission for air reconnaissance over Manchuria and the China coast, and (3) authority for the Nationalists on Formosa to operate against the mainland. These proposals were not considered favorably in Washington. The blockade was not regarded as a weapon that could be immediately effective against the Chinese economy, and the right of reconnaissance was regarded as a first step toward the bombing of Manchurian bases, which in turn might well bring Russia into the armed conflict. MacArthur did not accept the continuing efforts of the U.N. to negotiate a cease fire as satisfactory, since even if successful the result would be a division at the 38th parallel, which line could only be held by forces so strong that they could advance to the Yalu. On this line of reasoning MacArthur asked for more troops and for authority to bomb Manchurian bases. Publication of a letter from MacArthur to Congressman Joseph Martin critical of existing policy brought in Washington the conclusion that the military command was interfering with political decisions. Accordingly, on April 11 President Truman removed MacArthur from command. Renewed efforts to a cease fire and armistice were undertaken in July, 1951, and continued unsuccessfully for two years while limited hostilities continued along the 38th parallel. Meanwhile, within the Republic of Korea, President Rhee, opposed by the assembly because of his dictatorial methods, maintained himself in power by martial law, by censorship of the press, and by coercion of the Assembly.

The Formosan Problem

Formosa (Taiwan), in accordance with the Cairo Declaration, was to be restored to China at the end of World War II. Following the end of hostilities a provincial government set up by the Nationalists was distinguished chiefly for its record of maladministration.[2] In 1949 the defeated Nationalist Government and the remnants of its

---

[2] For a detailed discussion, see P. M. A. Linebarger, Djang Chu, and A. W. Burks, *Far Eastern Governments and Politics* (New York, 1954), 184-205.

armies retreated to Formosa, where a provisional government was maintained. Although at this time there had been no peace treaty determining the disposition of enemy territory, both the Chinese Nationalists and the Chinese Communists took the position that Formosa had again become a part of China. The Communists were preparing to attack the island; the Nationalists were proposing to

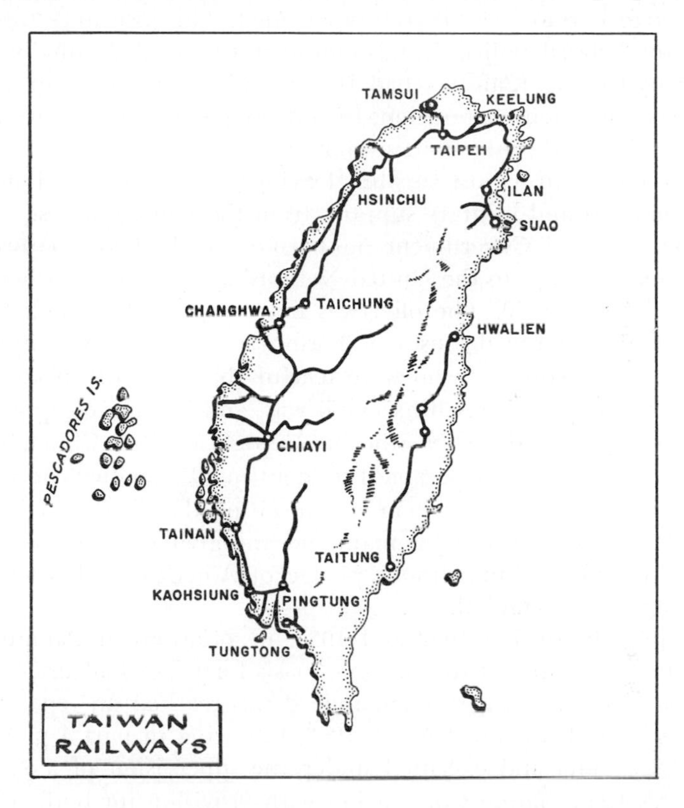

use it as a base for reconquering the mainland. From the Chinese point of view, therefore, Formosa was simply a stake in a domestic Chinese struggle for power. From the American viewpoint the matter was not so simple. It was evident that Formosa could not defend itself without American aid and that some military opinion regarded the island, in friendly hands, as essential to American security. Yet early in 1950 American political policy regarded Formosa as an issue in China's civil war. Thus the American government would not take military action to repel an invasion by the

Communists. This policy changed when war broke in Korea in June, 1950, and Formosa was "neutralized" by American presidential fiat backed by U.S. naval power. By this change and acceptance of a part of the MacArthur thesis the United States was assuming the task of aiding the Nationalists on Formosa and of opposing any attempt by the Communists to invade the island. American military assistance to Formosa was therefore resumed. This assistance together with the belated political and administrative reforms finally instituted by Chiang K'ai-shek had by 1953 placed Formosa in a relatively strong defensive position. In addition, economic reforms made it possible for the island to support more than a million refugees and to create an export surplus, leaving out of account, however, economic aid and military supplies from the United States.

The National Government on Formosa had offered a force of some 30,000 troops to the United Nations' army in Korea when war broke there in 1950. The offer was not accepted because it would have weakened the defenses of Formosa, because it was opposed by the south Koreans, who were fearful that it would make their land a battleground of China's civil war, and because of opposition from members of the U.N. who had recognized Red China. When Dwight D. Eisenhower became President in 1953, policy concerning Formosa altered to the extent of cancelling the American ban on Nationalist raids against the mainland and giving the nod to a Nationalist invasion but without pledge of American aid if such an invasion were attempted.

Meanwhile, during 1952 and 1953, negotiations at Panmunjom near the 38th parallel to find some basis for peace had dragged on without success. No agreement indeed was reached on repatriation of prisoners of war until April, 1953, following in part a plan proposed by India and executed under the supervision of a Neutral Nation's Repatriation Commission with provision for both sides to "persuade" unwilling prisoners to return home. The plan was threatened when south Korea simply released north Korean prisoners it was holding without requiring their return north, thereby opening the way for the Communist charge of bad faith on the part of the Republic of Korea and of inability of the U.N. Command to speak for and to control the Republic. This incident spotlighted the fact that the objectives of Rhee on the one hand and of the United Nations on the other were not the same. In brief, Rhee wanted an armistice that would in no way preclude unification of the country under Rhee's government. The U.N. was primarily concerned with stopping aggression, and President Eisenhower wanted to stop hostilities without further extension of Communist control. With grave uncertainty as to what Rhee's government might do, and without its formal approval, an armistice was signed July 27, 1953, providing for a demilitarized zone near the 38th parallel, and for a conference to negotiate withdrawal of troops and a peaceful settlement. Because of the recalcitrant attitude of south Korea toward the armistice, the United States felt it necessary to reassure the Republic through a Mutual Security Treaty. It was not, however, until February 18, 1954, that a conference was agreed upon to be held at Geneva to deal with Korea and Indochina. It was in this interim period that the Communist powers had conducted their most violent campaigns in psychological warfare, charging the United States among other things with waging germ warfare in Korea. The United States invited impartial investigation, but opportunity to investigate was always denied by the Communists.

The Geneva Conference of 1954, sponsored by the United States, Britain, France, and Russia, attempted to meet the Korean question by finding a means to unite the country under a single independent government. Rhee's south Korean government held that all that was necessary was to hold supervised elections in the north for the seats that had been reserved in 1947 under the original U.N. plan of elections. The Communists wanted new elections supervised by the two Korean governments. A compromise supported by the United States proposed new elections supervised by the U.N. This the Communists refused to accept. Geneva, too, had failed to produce a Korean settlement.

Indochina and the Cold War

The Geneva Conference was of greater importance in the affairs of Indochina. The continuing efforts of France to re-establish and hold her Indochinese empire, efforts thoroughly repugnant to Asian nationalism, had created larger problems for American diplomacy. Until the Communist victory in China and the outbreak of the Korean war, the United States was opposed to the French use of American aid to maintain an empire against native nationalism. This policy was altered, however, when in the light of the Korean war, the struggle in Indochina aided by the Chinese Communists could be regarded as another front in the general struggle against Communist aggression. As a result the United States provided aid to France and the Associated States of Indochina to preclude successful Chinese intervention. But even with increased American economic and military aid France was unable to contain or defeat the Vietminh regime, which now had increased support from China. The French task was admittedly difficult if not impossible. Ultimate French purposes were suspect among all Indochinese nationalists. Even if the French had intended to move toward Indochinese autonomy, they had chosen a hopeless vehicle in the Bao Dai government. Accordingly, as the political and military position deteriorated, France sought an armistice at the Geneva Conference. This agreement drew a demarcation line near the 17th parallel, the Vietminh of Ho Chi Minh holding the north, the south going to the French-sponsored Vietnam regime. Laos and Cambodia were to be neutralized. In addition, elections to determine the future government were to be held within two years, supervised by the armistice committee. The Geneva settlement, for the time at least, was a Communist victory. For the Western powers, especially the United States, it meant that the geographical line against Communism in Southeast Asia had been forced to withdraw further. Subsequently, American aid to South Vietnam went, not through France, but direct to the government of Premier Ngo Dinh Diem. By 1955 the power of the French empire in Indochina was a thing of the past, but the country itself remained divided between a totalitarian Communist Vietminh in the north, and a troubled south torn by factionalism, where the future of the democratic process was far from secure.

The New Far East

World War II and the decade that followed created an Eastern Asia which on the surface at least looked very unlike the Far East of pre-war times. The power of Japan was broken. The United States and Soviet Russia became dominant powers in the Far East. China's nationalist revolution was captured and exploited by the Chinese Communists, and the Western empires of south and southeast Asia were destroyed and replaced by independent national states such as the Philippines, Indonesia, Burma, Ceylon, Pakistan and, most significant of all, India. These extraordinary upheavals, as noted in the opening lines of this chapter, belonged not only to Asia's internal revolution but also to world politics—the global struggle for power. As a result, Asia's aspirations were not wholly free to chart their own course or to choose their own times. Many of Asia's post-war goals had been acquired from a turbulent and divided West, and Asia's struggle toward them was promoted or hampered by pressures of Western power, whether from the free world led by America or the Communist world led by Russia. This power struggle, the essence of the Cold War, laid bare the emerging structure of the new Far East.

First in importance in the new Far East was the re-creation of the Chinese empire. The Chinese Communists, having made themselves masters of China proper, reasserted Chinese authority in the old dependencies—Manchuria, Sinkiang, and Tibet; pushed their influence into the old tributary states of Korea and Vietnam; allied themselves in ideology and politics with Russia; and by these means made of China a greater power in world politics than at any time in her modern history. Just as in her great past she controlled her neighbors by Confucianizing them, so after 1949 she pushed out her cultural boundaries to control her neighbors by Communizing them. In both cases she used military power, but her main weapon now as then was ideological penetration and control.

Second only in importance to the rebirth of Chinese power with its historical implications centering about the concept of the old Middle Kingdom was the passing of the nineteenth-century empires of Europe and America in South and Southeast Asia—the end of at least one historic phase of what was often called Western capitalistic colonialism and imperialism. The occasion for the ending of these empires was the chaos of World War II and the violent assertions of native Asian nationalism, but these things were not the basic cause. Independence and nationhood in South and Southeast Asia were the end product of Western political philosophy itself. If Europe and America had carried politico-economic imperialism to the Far East, they had also taken to Asia the doctrines of nationalism, liberty, equality, and the dignity of the individual. In so far as the West believed and preached these doctrines in Asia it renounced the right of ruling subject peoples and, indeed, invited them to declare their independence. In the case of the Americans in the Philippines and the British in India and Burma the renunciation was voluntary. In the case of the Dutch and the French there was a determined predisposition to resist the logic of history and philosophy, and to retire only when faced with overwhelming opposition from Asian nationalism and Western democratic opinion. Independence meant self-government in South and Southeast Asia but not necessarily better government. No country of the entire area possessed the means of meeting its aspirations for quick modernization without foreign aid, which in the main could come only from the United States. Yet the new states were often inhibited from seeking or accepting such aid lest their new political freedom be restricted by economic dependence.

A third compelling factor in the new post-war Far East was the influence of American and Russian policy upon the course of events in Asia and upon the character of far eastern nationalism. There was a pronounced and perhaps natural tendency in the years after 1945 for Americans to see events in the Far East wholly in terms of a struggle between the Communist and the non-Communist world. The world-struggle aspect was not to be ignored, since it involved a new balance of power, but as an exclusive interpretation of what was happening in Asia the world-struggle theory was historically untenable. Indeed, the preponderance of evidence made it clear that the march of events in Asia after 1945 was also distinctly a product of internal forces and thus a further development of a distinctly Asian revolution that had its beginnings far back in the nineteenth century when there were no Communists in Asia and very few anywhere else. The Chinese revolution, for example, possessed a reality and an identity of its own distinct from the question of what particular party might rule in China or what foreign influences played upon China. That is, the Chinese revolution had been busy for the better part of a century evolving a character to meet conditions within China. Furthermore, the Western democracies (which in 1918 supposedly included Russia) had been amazingly slow to recognize this essentially Chinese character of China's revolution. As a result, not only in the years since 1945 but more significantly in the years since 1898, they lost much of the influence which they could have exerted and which they had many opportunities to exert upon revolutionary China. The consequences of this fact can hardly be exaggerated because, in many respects, China's modern revolution was precipitated in the first instance by the expansion of nineteenth-century Western liberal democracy. However, the democracies in general: (1) did not comprehend that the Western impact destroyed the society of old China; (2) did not understand the revolutionary aspects of the emerging new China; (3) were too often unsympathetic toward Chinese aspirations; and (4) did not recognize that the political, economic, or social philosophy of Western Europe and America in the early twentieth century might not be considered by the Chinese as acceptable or adequate for twentieth-century China. At the same time during and after World War II the international relations of the Far East and South Asia were often shaped and controlled more by external power than by Asia's capacity to direct her own course. Post-war politics throughout Eastern Asia was affected constantly by the Cold War and its principal opponents, the United States and Soviet Russia. These outside forces often operated in ways which American opinion did not foresee or understand. It was easy for Americans to see that the Chinese Communists were assisted to power by Russia's behavior in Manchuria beginning in 1945. It was not so easy for Americans to foresee that American aid to a *Kuomintang* government which no longer had the confidence of the people might be of even greater assistance to China's Communists than the direct aid that came from Russia. It enabled Mao and his government to secure their hold on the nationalist revolution by pinning the tag of imperialism on the United States and thus obscuring the actual imperialism of Soviet Russia.[3] Moreover, because the Chinese Communists set their course so irrevocably against America, they could not accept American economic aid. At the same time the violent reactions of American public opinion toward Communism precluded any American offer of assistance to China through which the latter's dependence on Russia could be lessened. Such an offer might not have succeeded, but if it had been made and refused it would have enabled the United States to place the guilt where it clearly belonged, namely, on the Communist governments of China and the Soviet Union.[4]

The exercise of influence by the great Western states took new forms after 1945 but was not a new factor in far eastern politics. What was new was the emergence of India as a great independent state ambitious to form and assume leadership of a group of independent Asian states expressing and implementing the aspirations of Asian nationalism and following a course of neutralism in the Cold War. India's neutralism often appeared to be more benevolent

[3] Vinacke, *Far Eastern Politics,* 457.
[4] Vinacke, *Far Eastern Politics,* 457-458.

toward the Soviet bloc than toward the Western democracies, who, as the erstwhile "colonial" powers, were still looked upon with distrust. In general the policies of the new Asian states involved planned economics and varying degrees of socialism and the welfare state. The new governments were particularly sensitive on the point of "the equality of states," and ever fearful that American aid would involve economic dependence or be used as a lever to influence or control their foreign policies.

The Bandung Conference, 1955

A tangible expression of the reality of an Asian bloc was the conference at Bandung, Indonesia, April, 1955, attended by twenty-nine Asian and African countries, which gave some form to their own inter-state relations and their attitudes to the world beyond Asia. Although the common denominators of agreement were largely in the realm of abstractions, the conference as seen by its sponsors restrained China's aggressiveness, decreased the possibilities of Sino-American hostilities, and gave non-Communist Asia a forum in which to express itself with confidence.[5]

Long before the Bandung Conference the problem of United States influence in Asia had become less a matter of steeling itself to meet Chinese military expansion and more a matter of dealing with China's most powerful weapon—her capacity to infiltrate new states in Southeast Asia through native Communist parties taking their orders from Peking, supplied by Peking, and bent on creating subversion and chaos. Steps toward security had been taken earlier by the conclusion of American security treaties with Japan, the Philippines, Australia, New Zealand, and finally South Korea. Faced by the reverses of the Geneva Conference the United States extended the system in the Southeast Asia Treaty Organization (SEATO). It included the U.S., Britain, France, Australia, New Zealand, and only three Asiatic countries—the Philippines, Thailand, and Pakistan. Its stated purposes were to provide strength against aggression and internal subversion, and in essence this meant economic aid that would give stability to young governments.

Meanwhile a key problem of American policy in the Far East was unresolved. The United States had continued to recognize the fugitive Nationalist regime on Formosa as the government of China.

---

[5] George McT. Kahin, *The Asian-African Conference* (Ithaca, 1956), 1-2, 36-38.

This policy had led to friction among the Western allies, who believed it implied a commitment by the U.S. to support the Nationalists in war against the mainland. This uncertainty as to American policy was removed partially in a U.S.-Formosa defense treaty providing for American defense of Formosa and the Pescadores, but not to the support of the National government as a general principle. The related question of the off-shore islands held by the Nationalists—the Tachens, Quemoy, and Matsu—remained as a delicate phase of American relations with Communist and non-Communist China.

By 1958 the modern Western impact on eastern Asia had taken its place as one of the most revolutionary movements of all history. Directly and indirectly in the first instance it bent eastern Asia to its will, but it also gave to Asia the will and sometimes the means to assert and find a new independence. Whether this independence would be free or confined remained for the future to say.

For Further Reading

GENERAL STUDIES AND SURVEYS

Latourette, Kenneth S., *The American Record in the Far East* (New York, 1952). An outline of recent American far eastern foreign policy.

Zinkin, Maurice, *Asia and the West* (London, 1951).

AMERICAN POLICY AND DIPLOMACY

Byrnes, James F., *Speaking Frankly* (New York, 1947). An account of the author's record as Secretary of State.

Dulles, Foster Rhea, *America's Rise to World Power 1898-1954* (New York, 1955). Stresses isolationism versus internationalism in development of U.S. policies.

Fairbank, John King, *The United States and China* (Cambridge, 1948).

Fisher, Harold H., *America and Russia in the World Community* (Claremont, California, 1946). Discusses the bases for co-existence.

Morgenthau, Hans J., *In Defense of the National Interest: A Critical Examination of American Foreign Policy* (New York, 1951).

Pomeroy, Earl S., *Pacific Outpost; American Strategy in Guam and Micronesia* (Stanford, 1951).

Reischauer, Edwin O., *Wanted: An Asian Policy* (New York, 1955).

Snell, John L., Forrest C. Pogue, Charles F. Delzell, and George A. Lensen, with a Foreword by Paul H. Clyde, *The Meaning of Yalta* (Baton Rouge, 1956). A non-partisan summary of the personal diplomacy of the Big Three in planning for peace in World War II.

Tompkins, Pauline, *American-Russian Relations in the Far East* (New York, 1949). A useful survey, marred at times by the author's obsession with the iniquities of the balance of power.

Vinacke, Harold M., *The United States and the Far East, 1945-1951* (Stanford University, 1952). A brief but thoughtful review of post-war U.S. policy in the Far East.

Westerfield, H. Bradford, *Foreign Policy and Party Politics: Pearl Harbor to Korea* (New Haven, 1955).

Williams, William A., *American-Russian Relations 1781-1947* (New York, 1952).

KOREA

Goodrich, Leland M., *Korea: Collective Measures Against Aggression* (New York, 1953).

Joy, Admiral C. Turner, *How Communists Negotiate* (New York, 1955). The author's story of the Korean negotiations, in which he participated as the U.N. command's senior delegate.

Kennedy, Edgar S., *Mission to Korea* (London, 1952). By the United Nations' relief administrator.

McCune, George M., *Korea Today* (Cambridge, Mass., 1950). A comprehensive account of political and economic developments in Korea after World War II.

——, and John A. Harrison, eds., *Korean-American Relations: Documents Pertaining to the Far Eastern Diplomacy of the United States* (3 vols., Berkeley, 1951-). Vol. I: The Initial Period, 1883-1886 (1951).

Meade, E. Grant, *American Military Government in Korea* (New York, 1951).

Tewksbury, Donald G., *Source Materials on Korean Politics and Ideologies*, vol. 2 of the series, *Source Book on Far Eastern Political Ideologies* (New York, 1950).

Wint, Guy, *What Happened in Korea* (London, 1954). By the Far East editor for the *Manchester Guardian*.

SOVIET RUSSIA

Bailey, Thomas A., *America Faces Russia: Russian-American Relations from Early Times to Our Day* (Ithaca, 1950). A lucid and well-documented survey.

Beloff, Max, *Soviet Policy in the Far East, 1944-1951* (New York, 1953). Deals mainly with Russo-Chinese relations.

Dallin, David J., *The New Soviet Empire* (New Haven, 1951).

——, *Soviet Russia and the Far East* (New Haven, 1948).

Dean, Vera Micheles, *The United States and Russia* (Cambridge, Mass., 1948).

Haines, C. Grove, ed., *The Threat of Soviet Imperialism* (Baltimore, 1954).

Wu Ai-ch'ên, *China and the Soviet Union* (New York, 1950). A useful general summary, but lacking in fundamental interpretation.

CHINA AND FORMOSA

Ballantine, Joseph W., *Formosa: A Problem for United States Foreign Policy* (Washington, 1953). An analysis of the factors that have influenced American policy in the post-World War II years.

Ch'ien Tuan-shêng, *The Government and Politics of China* (Cambridge, Mass., 1950).

Ginsburg, Norton Sydney, *The Economic Resources and Development of Formosa* (New York, 1953).

Riggs, Fred W., *Formosa Under Chinese Nationalist Rule* (New York, 1952).

Wiens, Harold J., *China's March Toward the Tropics* (Hamden, Conn., 1954). A history of China's southward penetration.

INDONESIA

Collins, J. Foster, *The United Nations and Indonesia* (New York, 1950).

INDOCHINA

Farley, Miriam S., *United States Relations with Southeast Asia, 1950-55* (New York, 1955).

Hammer, Ellen J., *The Struggle for Indochina* (Stanford, Calif., 1954).

MONGOLIA

Friters, Gerard M., *Outer Mongolia and Its International Position* (Baltimore, 1949). Concerned primarily with Russian-Mongolian relations.

Index

D

T

C